LANDSCAPE AND PC
EARLY CHIN.

MW00785208

The ascendancy of the Western Zhou in Bronze Age China, 1045–771 BC, was a critical period in the development of Chinese civilization and culture. This book addresses the complex relationship between geography and political power in the context of the crisis and fall of the Western Zhou state. Drawing on the latest archaeological discoveries, the book shows how inscribed bronze vessels can be used to reveal changes in the political space of the period, and explores literary and geographical evidence to produce a coherent understanding of the Bronze Age past. By taking an interdisciplinary approach which embraces archaeology, history, and geography, the book thoroughly reinterprets late Western Zhou history and probes the causes of its gradual decline and eventual fall. Supported throughout by maps created from the most current GIS datasets and by numerous on-site photographs, *Landscape and Power in Early China* gives significant new insights into this important Bronze Age society.

LI FENG is Assistant Professor of Early Chinese Cultural History at the Department of East Asian Languages and Cultures, Columbia University. He has undertaken extensive fieldwork on Bronze Age sites and is the author of numerous research articles on the Western Zhou Period.

LANDSCAPE AND POWER IN EARLY CHINA

The Crisis and Fall of the Western Zhou, 1045–771 BC

LI FENG

Columbia University

CAMBRIDGE
UNIVERSITY PRESS

CAMBRIDGE UNIVERSITY PRESS
Cambridge, New York, Melbourne, Madrid, Cape Town, Singapore, São Paulo, Delhi

Cambridge University Press
The Edinburgh Building, Cambridge CB2 8RU, UK

Published in the United States of America by Cambridge University Press, New York

www.cambridge.org
Information on this title: www.cambridge.org/9780521108119

First published 2006
Reprinted 2008
This digitally printed version 2009

A catalogue record for this publication is available from the British Library

ISBN 978-0-521-85272-2 hardback
ISBN 978-0-521-10811-9 paperback

In Memory of
Professor Chen Gongrou
A respected teacher and a man of great intellectual depth
who passed away on
October 13, 2004

Contents

Figures

Maps

Acknowledgments

The plan for this book was conceived in the late 1990s, but the research it presents goes back far beyond that time. Over many years, I have come to owe accumulated debts of gratitude to a long list of people who have guided, supported, and assisted the project. But my deepest gratitude must go first to the three mentors of my life whose training gave me the foundation of this book and influenced the way it is – my Chinese teacher, Professor Zhang Changshou, who trained me as a field archaeologist back in the years when I was a young graduate and then research fellow in the Institute of Archaeology, CASS; my Japanese teacher, Professor Matsumaru Michio, who exposed me to the various fascinating aspects of bronze studies; and my American teacher, Professor Edward L. Shaughnessy, who taught me the conventions of Western scholarship and the essence of modern historiography, and under whose guidance the plan for this study was developed and first put in practice. I also want to express my thanks to Professor Barry B. Blakeley and the late Professor Gilbert L. Mattos for their advice, when I moved in 1992 to continue my pursuit of scholarship in the United States.

I owe special thanks to my colleagues at Columbia University, Professors Shang Wei, Madeleine Zelin, Robert Hymes, David Wang, and Henry Smith, who have supported the project in various capacities and have made helpful suggestions in numerous ways. I thank also the anonymous reviewers for Cambridge University Press for their support and valuable comments, but my special debt of gratitude must be paid to the one who wrote for me, over and above the official report for the Press, a chapter-long document full of highly constructive and inspiring recommendations with accurate understanding of the mission of the book. My thanks go further to many colleagues who have read portions or the entirety of the manuscript in different stages and have made helpful comments for its improvement. Among them are Nicola Di Cosmo, Sarah Allan, Lothar von Falkenhausen, Anne Underhill, Wu Hung, Richard Saller, Jonathan Spence, Ann-ping Chin, and David Branner. On particular issues covered by the book I have also benefited from conversations with other colleagues whose names are too many to be mentioned here. I thank Han-Peng Ho, our graduate student at Columbia, for his assistance.

Quite a large part of the research presented in the book was done in the field, centering on my three trips between 1997 and 2003 to the regions discussed in this study during which I was honored with assistance from many fellow archaeologists in China. I would like to acknowledge in particular the following individuals: Zhang Long of Gansu Provincial Bureau of Cultural Relics, Luo Feng of Ningxia Institute of Archaeology (formerly the Guyuan Museum), Jiao Nanfeng of Shaanxi Institute of Archaeology, Hu Zhisheng of Baoji Museum, Jiang Tao of Henan Institute of Cultural Relics and Archaeology, Lin Xianting of Yantai Management Committee on Cultural Relics; and back in Beijing, my former colleagues who helped arrange my trips outside of the capital: Liang Zhonghe, Fu Xianguo, and Zheng Ruokui of the Institute of Archaeology, and Song Xinchao of the State Bureau of Cultural Relics. In this connection, I would also like to thank David Sena for his company on the long and dangerous trip we took together to northern Shaanxi in summer 1998, reaching as far as Yulin, and my brother Li Gang who took me on another difficult trip to the upper Wei River valley in summer 2003, reaching as far as Lixian.

I am grateful to Simon Whitmore, Commissioning Editor at Cambridge University Press, for his generous support and always timely advice, without which the book could never have appeared. In the completion of the book, I would also like to thank Jeremiah Trinidad, our GIS librarian at Columbia University, for providing me with the base-maps that are used to present the historical and political geography. My thanks are due further to the following for their kind permission to reproduce images in this book: Institute of Archaeology, CASS (Figs. 8, 10, 14, 27, 28, 29, 35, 42); Cultural Relics Publishing House (Figs. 15, 31, 33, 43, 44); Zhonghua Books Co. (Beijing) (Figs. 18, 19, 30, 32, 40); Shaanxi People's Fine Arts Publishing House (Figs. 17, 23, 31); Shanghai People's Fine Arts Publishing House (Figs. 22, 30); Shandong University Press (Fig. 39); the journals of *Kaogu yu wenwu* (Fig. 25); *Jianghan kaogu* (Fig. 41); *Shanghai bowuguan jikan* (Fig. 37); J. J. Lally & Co. (Fig. 37); Mr. Wang Longzheng (Fig. 13). Every effort has been made to contact rights holders to obtain permission to use the copyright material in this book. The author and publisher apologize for any errors or omissions and would welcome these being brought to their attention.

In many ways, the book marks a conclusion of my scholarly pursuits in the last twenty years as well as a milestone in my personal life. I would not have come to this point without the continual support of my wife Min and my son Richard, who have exempted me from almost all domestic duties in the last four years to concentrate on writing. I owe to them special thanks and appreciation that were orally expressed only very rarely.

Scholarly conventions

In general, the conventions established in Loewe and Shaughnessy, *Cambridge History of Ancient China: From the Origins of Civilization to 221 BC* (Cambridge: Cambridge University Press, 1999), pp. xxiv–xxv, are followed in this book. These conventions are reiterated below with minor modifications and additional new standards introduced to meet the special purpose of this study.

REFERENCES

For convenience, references to the "Thirteen Classics" are commonly made to the *Shisanjing zhushu* 十三經註疏, 2 vols. (Beijing: Zhonghua, 1979). For philosophical texts, references are to the *Ershier zi* 二十二子 (Shanghai: Shanghai guji, 1986). For the twenty-four dynastic histories beginning with the *Shiji* 史記, the modern punctuated editions published by the Zhonghua shuju (from 1959) are used. For the Chinese texts included in these publications for which English translations are available, page numbers in both the Chinese texts and their English translations are provided. For the widely read *Analects* and *Mencius*, the English texts alone are referred to. For bronze inscriptions used in the book, references are commonly made to the *Yin Zhou jinwen jicheng* 殷周金文集成, 18 vols. (Beijing: Zhonghua, 1984–94) (hereafter, JC) and *Jinchu Yin Zhou jinwen jilu* 近出殷周金文集錄, 6 vols. (Beijing: Zhonghua, 2002) (hereafter, JL). Those that are not included in the two works, usually the very recent ones, are separately noted. References to archaeological reports and secondary studies in the monthly or bimonthly Chinese journals are given with year followed by the number of the issue, and by page numbers (e.g. 1996.9, 20–35). Archaeological reports, monographs, and catalogues are listed by their titles alone without the usually lengthy institutional authorial names in Chinese.

TRANSLATIONS

Except for the well-established English titles such as the *Book of Poetry* and the *Bamboo Annals*, the Chinese titles of most texts are directly used with English translations provided only at their first appearance. Quotations from ancient texts are presented in both Chinese and English translation. For the *Book of Poetry*, I use the poetic translation by Waley in the *Book of Song* (New York: Grove Press, 1996). Translations of other texts and bronze inscriptions are all mine.

CHINESE CHARACTERS AND ROMANIZATION

For smooth reading, Chinese characters are kept at the necessary minimum and are provided only for the *Pinyin* Romanization of personal names, place-names, and bronze inscriptions at their first appearance in the text and the notes. Alterations of the conventional rule of *Pinyin* are made to differentiate the following frequently seen homophones: Han 漢 and Hann 韓, Wei 魏 and Wey 衛, King Yi 夷王 and King Yih 懿王, Shanxi 山西 and Shaanxi 陝西. For the homophones that appear, though infrequently, in close context, Chinese characters are provided as needed to differentiate them.

PLACE-NAMES

Place-names that represent ancient administrative units are rendered with the *Pinyin* Romanization followed by an English term describing their bureaucratic levels such as Mi County 密縣 and Yewang County 野王縣, or Anding Commandery 安定郡 and Henei Commandery 河内郡 (based on Han system). The term "Circuit" is used for *dao* 道, "Prefecture" for *zhou* 州, and "Superior-Prefecture" for *fu* 府 (based on Tang system). Modern place-names, where well known, are given without noting their bureaucratic levels, except for cases where the same name existed at different levels such as Baoji City 寶鷄市 and Baoji County 寶鷄縣. Terms that designate villages and other small areas are rendered in accordance with Romanization, for example Qijiacun 齊家村 and Mawangzhen 馬王鎮. For land features, I use their conventional Chinese names combined with English terms that explain their natures.

POLITICAL AND ARISTOCRATIC TITLES

Translations of the aristocratic titles such as *hou* 侯, *bo* 伯, *zi* 子, and *nan* 男 with medieval European titles are avoided, but the well-established translation of *gong* 公 as "Duke" is maintained along with "King" for *wang* 王. In the same way, medieval "feudo-vassalic" terms such as "fief," "enfeofment," and "investiture" are abandoned to avoid the misplaced comparison of Western Zhou China with medieval Europe.

SYSTEM OF DATES

For convenience, the dates of Western Zhou kings proposed by Shaughnessy in the *Sources of Western Zhou History* (Berkeley: University of California

Press, 1991), p. xix, are systematically used in this book. While trusting that these dates reflect better the condition of our current evidence, it is to be noted that other systems of dating, e.g. the dates recently proposed by the "Xia–Shang–Zhou Chronology Project," also exist (see *Xia Shang Zhou duandai gongcheng: 1996–2000 nian jieduan chengguo baogao* [Beijing: Shijie tushu, 2000], p. 88), and that conclusions on most of the dates still have to wait for further evidence. It should also be noted that Shaughnessy's system of dating accepts the theory advanced by Nivison in 1983 that each king had two "First Years," that in which he started his new reign, and that which came after the completion of the mourning period for his father. Therefore, in the Nivison–Shaughnessy system, two first years are provided for the majority of the kings.

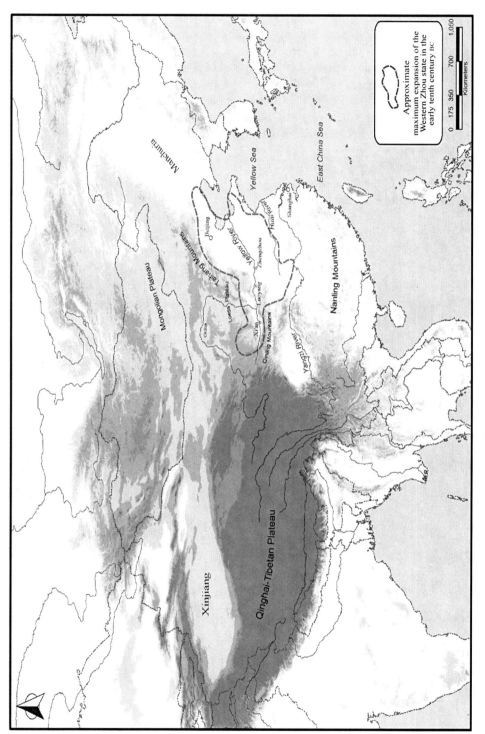

Topographical map of China

Chronology of Western Zhou kings

King Wen	1099/56–1050 BC[a]	
King Wu	1049/45–1043	EARLY
Duke of Zhou	1042–1036	WESTERN
King Cheng	1042/35–1006	ZHOU[b]
King Kang	1005/3–978	
King Zhao	977/75–957	
King Mu	956–918	
King Gong	917/15–900	MIDDLE
King Yih	899/97–873	WESTERN
King Xiao	872?–866	ZHOU
King Yi	865–858	
King Li	857/53–842/28	LATE
Gong He	841–828	WESTERN
King Xuan	827/25–782	ZHOU
King You	781–771	

[a] Absolute dates for Western Zhou kings proposed by Edward Shaughnessy; see Shaughnessy, *Sources of Western Zhou History* (Berkeley: University of California Press, 1991), p. xix.
[b] Periodization follows the widely accepted system proposed by Chen Mengjia; see Chen, *Xi Zhou niandai kao* (Shanghai: Shangwu, 1945), p. 55; "Xi Zhou tongqi duandai 1," *Kaogu xuebao* 9 (1955), 138–39.

The sixty-day circle
(Ganzhi 干支)

Jiayin 甲寅 51	*Jiachen* 甲辰 41	*Jiawu* 甲午 31	*Jiashen* 甲申 21	*Jiaxu* 甲戌 11	*Jiazi* 甲子 1
Yimao 乙卯 52	*Yisi* 乙巳 42	*Yiwei* 乙未 32	*Yiyou* 乙酉 22	*Yihai* 乙亥 12	*Yichou* 乙丑 2
Bingchen 丙辰 53	*Bingwu* 丙午 43	*Bingshen* 丙申 33	*Bingxu* 丙戌 23	*Bingzi* 丙子 13	*Bingyin* 丙寅 3
Dingsi 丁巳 54	*Dingwei* 丁未 44	*Dingyou* 丁酉 34	*Dinghai* 丁亥 24	*Dingchou* 丁丑 14	*Dingmao* 丁卯 4
Wuwu 戊午 55	*Wushen* 戊申 45	*Wuxu* 戊戌 35	*Wuzi* 戊子 25	*Wuyin* 戊寅 15	*Wuchen* 戊辰 5
Jiwei 己未 56	*Jiyou* 己酉 46	*Yihai* 己亥 36	*Yichou* 己丑 26	*Yimao* 己卯 16	*Jisi* 己巳 6
Gengshen 庚申 57	*Gengxu* 庚戌 47	*Gengzi* 庚子 37	*Gengyin* 庚寅 27	*Gengchen* 庚辰 17	*Gengwu* 庚午 7
Xinyou 辛酉 58	*Xinhai* 辛亥 48	*Xinchou* 辛丑 38	*Xinmao* 辛卯 28	*Xinsi* 辛巳 18	*Xinwei* 辛未 8
Renxu 壬戌 59	*Renzi* 壬子 49	*Renyin* 壬寅 39	*Renchen* 壬辰 29	*Renwu* 壬戌 19	*Renshen* 壬申 9
Guihai 癸亥 60	*Guichou* 癸丑 50	*Guimao* 癸卯 40	*Guisi* 癸巳 30	*Guiwei* 癸未 20	*Guiyou* 癸酉 10

Introduction

In the long Chinese tradition, the Western Zhou dynasty has been held in high esteem as the paradigm of political perfection and social harmony. More than once Confucius (551–479 BC) praised the Zhou institutions, and their founders King Wen, King Wu, and especially the Duke of Zhou,[1] and it is no exaggeration that the entire Confucian tradition was centered on the core texts that were passed down from the Western Zhou period. There was, perhaps, a practical reason for Confucius' love for the Western Zhou dynasty: by his time the reported Xia dynasty, and even the Shang dynasty from which Confucius actually claimed his own ancestry, had already become largely unknowable owing, in the Master's own words, to a lack of historical documents.[2] It was only about the Western Zhou dynasty that Confucius was apparently confident in recounting some historical details. True enough still today, the Western Zhou is the earliest time for which we can construct informed analyses of the political and social systems characterizing the early Chinese states,[3] particularly because of the widely available written evidence from the period including both the transmitted texts and, to an even higher degree, the inscribed texts on bronze vessels.[4] It is also the first dynasty whose historical development can be firmly and systematically linked to geographical settings on the basis of both written and archaeological records. The Western Zhou was certainly the time during which the fundamental concepts and institutions of the Chinese civilization were constructed, and our understanding of this critical period will inevitably shape the way in which we view pre-imperial China.

---

[1] See, for instance, *The Analects of Confucius*, trans. Arthur Waley (New York: Vintage Books, 1938), pp. 93, 97, 123, 135, 222.

[2] See *The Analects of Confucius*, pp. 96–97.

[3] By "early Chinese states" I mean pre-imperial states that existed within the geographical confines of modern China and were apparent cultural predecessors to the Qin and Han empires.

[4] Written evidence exists for the preceding Shang dynasty in the form of oracle-bone inscriptions. However, these inscriptions provide only a limited scope, emerging exclusively as the records of Shang royal divination. Compared with the long texts on Western Zhou bronzes, the oracle-bone inscriptions are often fragmentary and difficult to contextualize. For the value of the Shang oracle-bone inscriptions as historical sources, see David Keightley, *Sources of Shang History: The Oracle-Bone Inscriptions of Bronze Age China* (Berkeley: University of California Press, 1978), pp. 134–56.

OUTLINE OF HISTORY

In the first month of 1045 BC, the Zhou and their allies decisively defeated the mighty Shang armies in a battle near the Shang capital in northern Henan, and the once great Shang dynasty went to its fate. From their main base in the Wei River valley in central Shaanxi, the Zhou swiftly moved on to gain control over most of the middle and lower Yellow River regions and a part of the Yangzi River region – from the Yanshan Mountains in the north to the Huai and middle Yangzi Rivers in the south, and from the Liupan Mountains in the west to the Shandong peninsula in the east – the largest geopolitical unity ever achieved by a single power until the time of the First Emperor of Qin (259–210 BC). In this politically configured space, the Zhou capital was not located in its geographical center but was close to its western limit, and therefore the dynasty was referred to by later historians as the "Western Zhou." At the core of the Western Zhou state there lay the concept of the Mandate of Heaven which gave the Zhou king, literally called the "Son of Heaven" (*tianzi* 天子), a sacred character to preside over the Zhou realm. There were twelve such "Sons of Heaven," starting with King Wen (r. 1099–1050 BC) and King Wu (r. 1049/45–1043 BC) who actually achieved the conquest, and the royal succession, the central institution of the Western Zhou state, was thoroughly regulated, and normative rules determining the succession of father by son met relatively little challenge. Unlike the Shang who basically left the local groups to rule themselves under presumed Shang jurisdiction, as a result of which the Shang state was an aggregation of self-governing communities,[5] the Zhou were determined to manage their conquered space by themselves. This was achieved through the extension of the royal lineage over areas of Zhou political dominance where a large number of Zhou royal descendents and close relatives were established as local rulers. These numerous regional states, bound to the Zhou royal court through a unified ancestral cult and by their need of royal support to survive in the new environment, formed the macro-geopolitical structure of the Western Zhou state.[6]

---

[5] In Keightley's view, the Shang were only the most eminent among the numerous local groups; see David Keightley, "The Late Shang State: When, Where, and What?" in *The Origins of Chinese Civilization* (Berkeley: University of California Press, 1983), pp. 527–28. See also Keightley, *The Ancestral Landscape: Time, Space, and Community in Late Shang China (ca. 1200–1045 BC)* (Berkeley: Institute of East Asian Studies, 2000), pp. 56–57. Earlier, Matsumaru suggested that the various groups may have existed in a "hypothetical kin-relationship" with the Shang, in which the local leaders worshiped the Shang ancestors *as their own* ancestors, but no actual kinship can be confirmed between them. See Matsumaru Michio, "In Shū kokka no kōzō," in *Iwanami kōza: Sekai rekishi* (Tokyo: Iwanami shoten, 1970), pp. 72–79.

[6] In the present book, the term "state" is used in two ways: the "Western Zhou state" refers to the entirety of political unity of the Western Zhou centered on the Zhou king, while the "regional Zhou states" refers to regional polities such as Qi, Lu, Jin, and Qin. The translation of these polities as "states," while following the common practice in Sinology, reflects also the fact that, as will be shown later, they performed the same set of functions performed by the Western Zhou state, though at a much smaller scale, and enjoyed the combined rights over both civil and military affairs in their given territories and rights to determine their own domestic and external policies. In other words, they were replicas of the Western Zhou state at the regional level.

The founding of the regional states was itself a process of further expansion that very much marked the political development throughout the early Western Zhou, particularly in the time of King Cheng (r. 1042/35–1006 BC) and King Kang (r. 1005/3–978 BC). However, when the Zhou turned their focus from the east to the south, they met strong resistance in the middle Yangzi region, and in a major campaign led by the next king, Zhao (r. 977/75–957 BC), nearly half of the Zhou royal armies vanished in the Han River. This disaster served to end the great early Western Zhou expansion, and the loss of military advantage on the borders led subsequently, starting in the reign of King Mu (r. 956–918 BC) and continuing through the mid-Western Zhou, to readjustments in both the internal affairs of the Zhou state and its foreign policy. One of these readjustments apparently took direction in the bureaucratization of the Zhou government when many new offices were created and old ones had become divided and further stratified. But soon Western Zhou society was to see a transition that had its impact on almost every aspect of Zhou culture, from the style of inscriptions to the design of pottery, and from court ritual to burial practice. Outside, while continuing the use of both military force and diplomacy, the Zhou seem to have preferred to reach their political goals through militarily less costly actions. After a major foreign invasion that happened in an early decade of King Mu, striking deeply into the Zhou territory from the Huai River region, the priority for the Western Zhou state was no longer how to expand its space for better security, but how to hold what it had in the face of immediate foreign threat.

As external circumstances changed, internal rifts began to emerge in the infrastructure of the Western Zhou state, threatening the power of the Zhou king. In the first century of the dynasty, royal rule proved effective in keeping the regional states in line with the common goals of the Zhou state. However, during the mid-Western Zhou, disputes between the central court and the localized Zhou elite began to appear, amounting even to the use of royal forces against some of the regional states such as Qi 齊 in Shandong; the very state was attacked by order of King Yi (r. 865–858 BC), a weak king who was once himself denied the right to royal power upon the death of his father King Yih (r. 899/97–873 BC). Internal disorders, whether at the royal court or among the regional states, had their external consequences, and a rebellion led by a former Zhou subject, the Ruler of E (Ehou 噩侯), almost brought the Zhou regime to the verge of collapse. The regime survived this external blow, but the internal conflicts then had to find relief in an uprising that stormed the royal capital and forced the controversial Zhou king, Li (r. 857/53–842 BC), into exile from which he never returned.

The geographical situation also played an important part in accelerating the process of Zhou's weakening. The crisis can be seen first of all as a process of spatial dissolution in which the constituting blocks of the Western Zhou state gradually drifted away from the center. Facing such a situation, the location of the Zhou capitals in the Wei River valley, near the western border and separated by mountain ranges from the east, could not help but slow down the royal effort to restore order once a problem broke out. But more significant was that, being isolated from the regional states in the east, the royal forces alone had to fight enemies in the west. It so happened that the fatal and constant threat to the Western Zhou state was from the west, cast by a people known from the bronze inscriptions as the Xianyun 獫狁. From the middle through the late Western Zhou, the Xianyun tribes launched repeated invasions penetrating the Zhou defense, directly threatening the Zhou capital. Thus, the Zhou found themselves striving hopelessly between two strategic goals: the integration of the Zhou state that depended on continuous royal engagement in affairs of the east, and the survival of the dynasty on condition of security of the west. The Zhou could not do both.

A temporary relief to the tension came with the accession of King Xuan (r. 827/25–782 BC), whose government evidently gave the second goal priority. As soon as the threat in the west was held back after a series of campaigns, royal authority was restored for a time in the east. However, the victory of royal power in the first two decades of King Xuan could not reverse the course of the dynastic decline, and even before the death of the king the royal forces had already suffered a number of major defeats in regions not far from the royal domain. Finally, in 771 BC, the eleventh year of King You (r. 781–771 BC), the Quanrong 犬戎, most likely an ethnic group related to the Xianyun, broke into the Zhou capital and killed the last king at the foot of Lishan 驪山 Mountain. The Western Zhou dynasty came to an end. When the royal court was restored by King Ping (r. 770–720 BC), the Zhou capital was relocated in Luoyi 洛邑 (present-day Luoyang) in the east, therefore beginning the Eastern Zhou period.

PURPOSE OF THE BOOK

There have been many ways in history in which a dynasty could reach its end; for instance, foreign invasion, power usurpation, revolution, and peasant rebellion as more often in later Chinese history, are all forces that could terminate a dynasty. The fall of the Western Zhou took the typical form of a foreign invasion that struck down the Zhou center and had as its consequences the disintegration of the geopolitical unity once constructed by the Zhou. The fall was related as closely to the internal politics of the Western Zhou state as to the prolonged cultural and military confrontation between the Zhou and the northwestern peoples through the difficult terrain of northwestern China. It was the result of a long and complex interplay between politics and geography that should be understood as both a historical and a geographical process.

Since the 1980s, our knowledge of the Western Zhou period has been significantly altered by archaeological excavations. These excavations, most notably of half a dozen cemeteries belonging to the regional Zhou states Jin 晉, Guo 虢, Ying 應, Yan 燕, Xing 邢, and Qin 秦, have redirected Western Zhou studies in two prominent ways. First, scholarly research, previously concentrated on the major capital cities in the core areas of Shaanxi and Henan, has shifted its focus to the periphery of the Zhou world. That has raised questions regarding the relationship between the Zhou court and the regional Zhou states and with this the question of the general geopolitical structure of the Western Zhou state. Second, these excavations have yielded outstanding new materials, especially inscribed bronze vessels from the second half of the Western Zhou, reminding us of the importance of this problematic period, during which there was a gradual move from central control to regional competition. The convergence of these two issues calls for a systematic investigation into the rationales and dynamics of late Western Zhou history.

The purpose of this book is to examine the complex relationship between geography and its political configuration in the particular case of the crisis and fall of the Western Zhou state as a continuous historical and geographical process. With special attention to the natural condition of the western half of the Zhou realm, the study will not only demonstrate how but also explain why the Zhou political system could not stand the passage of time, but led eventually to the dissolution of the Western Zhou state and the collapse of the royal domain. It is intended not to be a general history of the Western Zhou period, or even a general history of the late Western Zhou, but rather to construct a consistent historical interpretation of a particular problem on the basis of solid evidential research into issues surrounding the historical fall of the Western Zhou. Within this general purpose, there are five specific and interrelated objectives.

As the foundation for this study, I hope first to reveal the geographical dimensions of the Western Zhou state and to construct a geographical framework in which sociopolitical changes can be measured by the extension of their spatial relations. This will be done in a dual process: on the one hand, the study demonstrates how the shape of land, the *landscape*, influenced and guided the development of the Western Zhou state, and on the other, it shows how the Western Zhou state built its agencies into, and hence they became participants in, the region's landscape (see below for discussion on the meaning of landscape). The discovery of bronze inscriptions throughout the Zhou world, very often bearing the names of their casters in the regional Zhou states, provides us with a real chance actually to delimit the spatial presence of the Western Zhou state. The study further shows how, under changing circumstances, the Western Zhou state responded to external pressures and internal tensions through the reconfiguration of its geographical space. To this end, I offer a realistic construction of the

Zhou–Xianyun war, situating it in the actual terrain of western Shaanxi and eastern Gansu, and show the extent to which the war constituted a major threat to the Zhou royal domain.

The second objective of this study is to rediscover the complex political circumstances surrounding the fall of the Western Zhou capital in 771 BC. In this regard, traditional historiography has failed to present a consistent account of this critical period in Chinese history: not only are many aspects of the historical fall obscured by legends and illusions, but even a general outline of the period is derogated from by various discrepancies and contradictions in the received sources. The present study aims at a clear understanding of the political dynamics at the court of King You, and at an interpretation of the immediate causes of the historical fall. Underlying this interpretation, the study will show how the court politics in the Zhou center was related to the geopolitics of the northwestern frontier in a reciprocal relationship, and how the landscape, as the visible aspect of the region's geography, played an important role in the fall.

Third, outside crisis had inside reasons. Under this assumption, the study investigates the origins of political and social disorders that had served to undermine the Zhou's capability to sustain their early spatial presence. The study looks into the basic structural characteristics of the Western Zhou state and the principles of its government for the causes of its gradual weakening. Although this is not a study to address systematically the various aspects of the Zhou political system, it will discuss problems in that system. Through the study, I hope to reveal a logical link between the "sudden" fall of the Western Zhou dynasty and the much longer historical process of its gradual decline. Although a "fall" did not have to be the inescapable outcome of a "decline," in this particular case the long-term disorder in the Western Zhou state and the outside pressure evidently worked together to prepare the ground for its eventual fall. I hope too, through this study, to gain a concrete understanding of the fundamental problems and challenges facing the early Chinese states and their possible responses.

Fourth, the study aims at an explanation of the origins of the interstate warfare that marked the Eastern Zhou period and of the preconditions for the rise of empire in China. To this end, I conduct a systematic reexamination of the geopolitical transition by looking into the actual process of the relocation of the Zhou center in Luoyi as well as the migration of a number of important Zhou polities to the eastern plain. Through this examination, I hope to explore the far-reaching impact that the fall of the royal domain in the west had on the geopolitics of the east.

Finally, with this book, I review some of the most important archaeological discoveries that have been made since the 1980s and discuss their implications for the study of Western Zhou history. There have only been two general histories and one sourcebook, in addition to a handful of sporadically published articles, on this critical period in Chinese history in the English language.[7] Apart from a recent introduction to Western Zhou archaeology,[8] a fuller coverage of the archaeological findings of the Western Zhou period, especially recent ones, not only is needed, but has long been overdue. In this regard, I hope the present book will serve as a useful tool for future researches using archaeological materials from the Western Zhou period. However, it must also be noted that although the book reviews archaeological findings of the period, its main theme is historical and is designed to answer historical questions; therefore, it should not be measured as purely an archaeological work.

SOURCES

The sources for this study are of three types: archaeological, inscriptional, and textual. In the following, I will discuss their nature and meaning for the study of Western Zhou history.

The archaeological materials provide us with a direct link between our time and the Western Zhou, and a concrete experience of the distant past. According to the conventional classification in archaeology, the material from the Western Zhou period can be largely divided between portable artifacts and non-portable remains, apart from the organic and environmental evidence of the time.[9] As the Western Zhou was in the heyday of China's Bronze Age, there seems little need to emphasize the importance of the bronze articles, especially bronze vessels, to understanding Western Zhou culture, religion, and social conditions. But, from the standpoint of the present study, it is especially worth noting that, with the high social and economic values placed on them as the end-products of a long process of material transportation and distribution in a political structure, they are evidence of elite activities. As such, they are particularly significant as indications of social and political focuses in a given landscape of which they are an integral part. However, bronzes are not the only type of artifact excavated from the elite sites, which also contain items such as pottery, jades, and lacquerware; quite often, though not always, the elite burials are also accompanied by burials of horse-drawn war-chariots, the most complex industrial products of the time. Pottery wares are extremely important in Western Zhou studies because, reasonably locally manufactured, they were

---

[7] Herrlee Creel, *The Origins of Statecraft in China, vol. 1: The Western Chou Empire* (Chicago: University of Chicago Press, 1970); Cho-yun Hsu and Katheryn Linduff, *Western Chou Civilization* (New Haven: Yale University Press, 1988); Edward Shaughnessy, *Sources of Western Zhou History: Inscribed Bronze Vessels* (Berkeley: University of California Press, 1991).

[8] See Jessica Rawson, "Western Zhou Archaeology," in *The Cambridge History of Ancient China: From the Origins of Civilization to 221 BC*, ed. Michael Loewe and Edward L. Shaughnessy (Cambridge: Cambridge University Press, 1999), pp. 352–449. A brief and much earlier introduction to Western Zhou archaeology is found in Kwang-chih Chang, *The Archaeology of Ancient China*, 4th edition (New Haven: Yale University Press, 1986), pp. 339–67.

[9] See Colin Renfrew and Paul Bahn, *Archaeology: Theories, Methods, and Practice* (New York: Thames and Hudson, 1991), pp. 41–42.

tied closely to the diverse local traditions, showing regional characteristics of the Western Zhou culture that cannot be learned from the bronzes. Moreover, because they display more rapid stylistic changes and shorter duration, pottery wares are sometimes, at least in the intensively researched areas, better indicators of the date of sites than the bronzes are.

The non-portable remains include features that we can only see in the field, including man-made structures such as palace foundations, houses, pits, trenches, workshops, and the various burials. These are the indicators of residential life of the Western Zhou and depositories of information about past cultural and religious practice. However, the importance of these structural remains lies not only in the information they contain, but also, more critical to the present study, in the fact that they are the locus of the various meaningful artifacts. They provide a direct link between culture and space, and only through such links are the artifacts meaningful as archaeological evidence. Moreover, in the conjunction of the two types of evidence there lies a special type of archaeological evidence: the way in which the various artifacts were arranged and grouped. Such information is very important for the study of the cultural and religious thought of the Western Zhou.

However, the importance of archaeological materials does not lead to the conclusion that they are perfect evidence for the Western Zhou past; perhaps they are far from being perfect. Their disadvantage lies first of all in the fact that they do not themselves constitute a systematic arrangement of information, but are highly fragmentary and even accidental, as many archaeological discoveries are the result of chance and not of planned excavation, which is becoming more and more difficult in China today. Despite the increasing volume of materials we have, they are but a fragment of the Western Zhou past. More significantly, the archaeological materials are not exactly "fresh" from the condition of their creation; they have come to most of us, especially to scholars in the West, in the form of published "records" that inevitably carry with them the imprints and reflect the views of the archaeologists who produced them. Such records can sometimes be highly selective and the choice of what is to be included in a report and what is not can be very subjective.

Inscribed bronzes constitute a unique type of material because they are, when known from archaeological contexts, simultaneously archaeological materials and historical texts for our study. Inscribed bronzes of the Western Zhou period were known to scholars as early as the Han dynasty (206 BC–AD 220) and an enormous number have now been accumulated.[10]

[10] See Shaughnessy, *Sources of Western Zhou History*, pp. 5–13. The *Yin Zhou jinwen jicheng*, the most comprehensive collection of rubbings and hand-drawings of inscriptions in eighteen volumes (based on careful evaluations), registers 12,113 inscribed bronzes: see *Yin Zhou jinwen jicheng* (Beijing: Zhonghua, 1984–94). This work is accompanied by transcriptions in five volumes: *Yin Zhou jinwen jicheng shiwen* (Hong Kong: Chinese University of Hong Kong Press, 2001). Another 1,258 recently

As archaeological evidence, the inscribed bronzes became widely available only during the Western Zhou, and declined in significance after the end of the period. Some inscriptions are remarkably long and informative regarding contemporary events at the Zhou royal court or in the regional states. In fact many, especially the "Appointment Inscriptions," contain portions that were evidently copied from the official "appointment letters" on the wooden or bamboo strips that the casters of the bronzes received directly from the Zhou king.[11] Excavated inscriptions from a particular area that mention events and personnel associated with the Zhou court from a demonstrably Zhou cultural context best testify to the political relations between the Western Zhou state and that area. Even in the case of short inscriptions, of which an essential part is the name of the caster (often given along with the name of the local state), they too are helpful in identifying the political affiliation of the sites from which they were excavated. Certainly, as historical documents, the inscribed bronzes are much more important than just a mere geographical indicator. For the very fact that their casting was motivated on various occasions by a variety of reasons – the commemoration of administrative and military merits, facilitation of marriage relationships, religious prayer to ancestral spirits, recording family history, preservation of important treaties or deals of territorial or material exchange, marking their owning families or origins of manufacture (as often on weapons and tools), and so on – the inscriptions are our primary evidence of almost every aspect of political and social life during the Western Zhou.

Scholars have long recognized the high historical value of the bronze inscriptions as primary sources for Western Zhou history.[12] However, in their strength also lies their weakness. As contemporaneous historical sources, the bronze inscriptions only allow us to access Western Zhou reality through the eyes of their composers, whose vision was inevitably conditioned by the social context in which they lived. As such, even if the inscriptions are truthful records of their composers' views, the views could be biased. This can be seen in the plain fact that the only facts-recording inscriptions are those that record honors and accomplishments of their

---

discovered inscribed bronzes are collected in *Jinchu Yin Zhou jinwen jilu* (Beijing: Zhonghua shuju, 2002), edited by Liu Yu and Lu Yan. The majority of these inscriptions are short; however, according to a conservative calculation by the author, the number of inscriptions that have more than fifty characters exceeds 350 pieces.

[11] For the definition of "Appointment Inscriptions," see Li Feng, "'Offices' in Bronze Inscriptions and Western Zhou Government Administration," *Early China* 26–27 (2001–2), 14–18. See especially note 143 on p. 50 for the use of written documents in the court ritual of appointment. For transmission of documents from wooden or bamboo media onto the bronzes, see also Lothar von Falkenhausen, "Issues in Western Zhou Studies: A Review Article," *Early China* 18 (1993), 146, 167; Li Feng, "Ancient Reproductions and Calligraphic Variations: Studies of Western Zhou Bronzes with Identical Inscriptions," *Early China* 22 (1997), 40–41.

[12] For the historical value of the bronze inscriptions, see as early as Herrlee G. Creel, "Bronze Inscriptions of the Western Chou Dynasty as Historical Documents," *Journal of the American Oriental Society* 56 (1936), 335–49. This position was reconfirmed by Shaughnessy, who took careful note of their subjectivity and partiality; see Shaughnessy, *Sources of Western Zhou History*, pp. 175–82.

owners, and not their disgrace and failures.[13] This aspect is highly relevant to and indeed disappointing for our study of the fall of the Western Zhou because we can never expect to find an inscription that will tell us in great detail about how the Zhou capital was ravaged and the Zhou king was killed by the foreign enemies; such a topic would simply not have been of serious interest to the owners of inscribed bronzes. This example may be extreme, but it shows that there are certain aspects of Western Zhou history that the inscriptions will, by their very nature, never tell us. Therefore, we must always be aware of the partiality and subjectivity of the inscriptions while using them as primary historical sources. Certainly, the limits of the bronze inscriptions can still be explored in other contexts, such as their regional differences, cultural and ethnic background, process of manufacture, and ritual, especially religious ritual, uses. The last point was stressed by Lothar von Falkenhausen, who argued that since they were cast on "ritual" bronzes that were used in religious contexts to communicate with ancestral spirits, "the bronze inscriptions must be understood as essentially religious documents."[14] But, in order to understand the full complexity of this particular issue, one should also not overlook the appealing point made more recently by Wu Hung that it was the life events of the caster, but not the need to dedicate them to the ancestors, that provided the reason for making bronzes with commemorative inscriptions.[15] While the issue needs to be examined more closely in a separate study, it is my conviction that the bronze inscriptions in huge number constitute such a complex body of documents that no single theory has the merit to explain the creation of all of them. In short, while being aware of their limits and bias, the present study draws heavily on the bronze inscriptions as primary sources of Western Zhou history.

The third category of sources, the textual records, involves a more complicated situation and hence needs discussion in more detail. The Western

[13] In this regard, it is probably justified for Shaughnessy to note that "their Zhou composers never intended them to provide a complete or objective historical record or to describe, in the words of Leopold von Ranke (1796–1886), 'how it really was'"; see Shaughnessy, *Sources of Western Zhou History*, p. 176. The only exception that speaks directly about the dark side of Western Zhou society is the inscription on the Mu *gui* 牧簋 (JC: 4343), but such a statement was recorded to form the background of the caster's new government appointment. On this unique inscription, see Li Feng, "Textual Criticism and Western Zhou Bronze Inscriptions: The Example of the Mu *Gui*," in *Essays in Honor of An Zhimin*, ed. Tang Chung and Chen Xingcan (Hong Kong: Chinese University of Hong Kong, 2004), pp. 291–93.

[14] See Falkenhausen, "Issues in Western Zhou Studies," pp. 145–52; quote from p. 146. It should be noted that, on the other hand, Falkenhausen also admits that the bronze inscriptions "encode concrete bits of information of undeniable historical validity." See *ibid.*, p. 167.

[15] In other words, if the recorded events had not taken place, the inscriptions would not have been cast. Therefore, Wu Hung argues that the meaning of a Western Zhou bronze had already changed from that of Shang: "it was no longer an instrument in a ritual communication with deities, but a proof of glory and achievement in this life." See Wu Hung, *Monumentality in Early Chinese Art and Architecture* (Stanford, CA: Stanford University Press, 1995), p. 63.

Zhou is the earliest time from which written records have been passed down to us through the long textual tradition. These contemporaneous or nearly contemporaneous written records can be seen first of all in the chapters included in the *Shangshu* 尚書 (Book of Documents). It is generally agreed that the five "Announcement" chapters are authentic Western Zhou documents and are most likely to have been works of the early part of the Western Zhou, all having something to do with the Duke of Zhou.[16] Scholars have long noted the close parallels between the archaic language of these chapters and that of the Shang oracle bones and Western Zhou bronze inscriptions, which evidences their earliness compared with other chapters in the book.[17] Another group of about seven chapters that purport to speak about the early Western Zhou, though probably after the event, are most probably also Western Zhou chapters.[18] While these chapters are critical sources of early Western Zhou history, providing us with the basic outline of the period, there is, unfortunately, only one chapter, the "Lüxing" 呂刑, in the entire *Shangshu* that purports to speak about the middle–late Western Zhou period, particularly about the reign of King Mu. But even this chapter is probably a later composition created during the Spring and Autumn period.[19]

However, information on the middle–late Western Zhou is found in another classical text, the *Shijing* 詩經 (Book of Poetry), a collection of 305 poems, particularly in the "Minor Odes" and "Major Odes" sections of the text. There are more than twenty poems in the two sections relevant to the present study, that can be divided under three historical subjects. The first group of poems is found in the "Minor Odes" and provides important information on Zhou's war with the Xianyun.[20] The second cluster of poems, mainly found in the "Major Odes," speaks consistently about the political events and Zhou's military campaigns in the eastern and southern regions during the long reign of King Xuan.[21] The third group of poems, scattered in both the "Minor" and "Major" sections, speaks

[16] These five chapters are: "Kanggao" 康誥, "Jiugao" 酒誥, "Shaogao" 召誥, "Luogao" 洛誥, and "Dagao" 大誥. See Michael Loewe (ed.), *Early Chinese Texts: A Bibliographical Guide* (Berkeley: Society for the Study of Early China, 1993), pp. 379–80.

[17] See Michael Nylan, *The Five Confucian Classics* (New Haven: Yale University Press, 2001), pp. 133–35.

[18] These chapters are: "Zicai" 梓材, "Duoshi" 多士, "Wuyi" 無逸, "Junshi" 君奭, "Duofang" 多方, "Lizheng" 立政, and "Guming" 顧命.

[19] See Loewe, *Early Chinese Texts*, p. 380.

[20] This group includes four main poems: "Caiwei" 采薇 (no. 167), "Chuche" 出車 (no. 168), "Liuyue" 六月 (no. 177), and "Caiqi" 采芑 (no. 178). The numbers of the poems and section divisions follow Arthur Waley (trans.), *The Book of Songs: The Ancient Chinese Classics of Poetry*, ed. Joseph R. Allen (New York: Grove Press, 1996). This system of numbers is based on the arrangement of the poems in the received Mao tradition of the book. For the arrangement of the poems, see Nylan, *The Five Confucian Classics*, pp. 77–78.

[21] Included in this group are: "Yunhan" 雲漢 (no. 259), "Hanyi" 韓奕 (no. 261), "Jianghan" 江漢 (no. 261), and "Changwu" 常武 (no. 263), etc.

about the eventful reign of King You and the subsequent transition to the Eastern Zhou.[22] These poems with apparently political-historical orientations, put together, provide the earliest textual layer of information on the late Western Zhou period. It is impossible to date precisely every single poem in the *Book of Poetry* as their authorship is obscure, as with most early Chinese texts,[23] and in general there is a great deal of uncertainty regarding the circumstances in which these poems were composed and subsequently recited. However, since Confucius had apparently systematically commented on these poems, as evident in the text "Confucius on Poetry" among the bamboo strips recently published by the Shanghai Museum,[24] an anthology of poetry similar to the text we have today must already have been in circulation by the middle of the sixth century BC. This well reflects the dates of 1000–600 BC that most modern scholars would assign to the composition of most of the poems.[25] Since most people place the two "Odes" sections before the "Airs of the States," probably the latest part of the book,[26] this reasonably suggests that the poems relevant to the present study were mostly composed in a period stretching from the late Western Zhou to the first century of the Spring and Autumn period, thus not far removed from the fall of the Western Zhou. Indeed, based on their close parallel with the contemporaneous bronze inscriptions with regard to many personnel and geographical specificities as will be subsequently demonstrated in this book, I tend to think that at least some of the politically historically oriented poems were composed within the limits of the Western Zhou.

However, the real challenge to using the *Book of Poetry* in historical studies is how we can retrieve valid information from the highly rhetorical and often exaggerated poetic expressions. But since they are not the only sources we have, there are ways by which we can differentiate the historical facts they mention from what is probably the poets' art. In this regard, comparison of the poems with the bronze inscriptions (see chapter 3), both emerging from the same historical contexts such as the warfare between the Zhou and the Xianyun, can probably offer a basis for evaluating the historical value of the

[22] Those found in the "Major Odes" include: "Sangrou" 桑柔 (no. 257), "Zhanyang" 瞻仰 (no. 264), and "Shaomin" 召旻 (no. 265); those found in the "Minor Odes" include: "Jie nanshan" 節南山 (no. 191), "Zhengyue" 正月 (no. 192), "Yu wuzheng" 雨無正 (no. 194), and "Shiyue zhi jiao" 十月之交 (no. 193). Whether the events and individuals mentioned in the "Shiyue zhi jiao" should be dated to King You or King Li has long been a subject of controversy, but I believe that after the discovery of the Han Huangfu *ding* 函皇父鼎 (JC: 2548), Tang Lan has demonstrated convincingly that they must be from the reign of King You. See Tang Lan, *Tang Lan xiansheng jinwen lunji* (Beijing: Zijincheng, 1995), pp. 107–08.
[23] This aspect of early Chinese texts has been recently noted in contrast to the Western historiographical tradition, starting in works by Herodotus and Thucydides. See David Schaberg, *A Patterned Past: Form and Thought in Early Chinese Historiography* (Boston: Harvard Asia Center, 2001), pp. 258–59.
[24] See Ma Chengyuan (ed.), *Shanghai bowuguan cang Zhanguo Chu zhushu*, vol. 1 (Shanghai: Shanghai guji, 2001), pp. 119–68; Qiu Xigui, "Guanyu Kongzi shilun," *International Research on Bamboo and Silk Documents* (Newsletter) 2.3 (2002), 1–2.
[25] See Loewe, *Early Chinese Texts*, p. 415.   [26] See Nylan, *The Five Confucian Classics*, pp. 87–89.

poems. The close parallel between the two types of sources suggests that
there was an underlying primary account of such historical events, whether
in written or oral form, that gave rise to these sources of very different
natures, and the task of the historian is to recover such a primary account
or accounts of history through examining the various sources. Therefore,
despite the literary nature of these poems, interpreting them in a historical
context that is also shared by other types of evidence can potentially reveal
their true historical meaning.

In addition to the above two texts that contain contemporaneous or
nearly contemporaneous parts from the Western Zhou period,[27] two Warring States sources are very important to the present study. The first source
is the *Zhushu jinian* 竹書紀年 (Bamboo Annals), the final composition of
which is dated to 299 BC when the text was buried in a tomb in present-day
Jixian 汲縣 in northern Henan.[28] The chronicle of the Warring States period
in the book was clearly based on archival records preserved at the court of
the state of Wei 魏 where the book was composed, but it also contains
chronicles for the preceding Spring and Autumn period and the Western
Zhou period, probably based on records transmitted from the state of Jin,
the predecessor of Wei. In any event, as there seem to have been different
versions of transcriptions of the bamboo text from the tomb immediately
after its excavation in AD 281, there are also different traditions of the text
available today: the *Current Bamboo Annals* that was passed down, and the
Ancient Bamboo Annals that was recomposed by extracting early quotations
of the book in other medieval texts. The *Current* version was judged by
the scholars who produced the *Siku quanshu* 四庫全書 (Complete Collection of Books in Four Stores) in the eighteenth century as a later forgery
after the text from the tomb disappeared. However, new studies have sufficiently shown the merit of using records in the *Current Bamboo Annals* to
reconstruct the dates of the Western Zhou period, especially the date of the
Zhou conquest of Shang verifiable from the inscriptional and astronomical
evidence, although some systematic errors also exist in the text.[29] Some of
the errors may have been caused by the dislocation of some bamboo strips
in the text by the post-excavation editors, a possibility that itself testifies

---

[27] The third source that contains records passed down from the Western Zhou period is the *Zhouyi*
  周易 (Book of Changes), but except for a few lines the book is largely uninformative for our study.
[28] For the date of composition of the *Bamboo Annals*, see Loewe, *Early Chinese Texts*, pp. 42–43.
[29] For studies that explore the historical value of the chronological records in the *Current Bamboo
  Annals*, see David Nivison, "The Dates of Western Chou," *Harvard Journal of Asiatic Studies* 43.2
  (1983), 481–580; Edward Shaughnessy, "The 'Current' *Bamboo Annals* and the Date of the Zhou
  Conquest of Shang," *Early China* 11–12 (1985–87), 33–60; "On the Authenticity of the *Bamboo
  Annals*," *Harvard Journal of Asiatic Studies* 46.1 (1986), 149–80; David Pankenier, "Astronomical
  Dates in Shang and Western Zhou," *Early China* 7 (1981–82), 1–37; "The *Bamboo Annals* Revisited:
  Problems of Method in Using the Chronicles as a Source for the Chronology of Early Zhou, Part
  1," *Bulletin of the School of Oriental and African Studies* 55.2 (1992), 272–97; "Part 2: The Congruent
  Mandate Chronology in *Yi Zhou shu*," *Bulletin of the School of Oriental and African Studies* 55.3
  (1992), 498–510. On this issue, see also Loewe, *Early Chinese Texts*, pp. 42–510.

to the *Current* version's authenticity.[30] But what is more important is that, as Shaughnessy has demonstrated, some of the historical figures and dates recorded in the text are mentioned nowhere else in the received textual tradition but are confirmed only by the Western Zhou bronze inscriptions.[31] These studies strongly suggest that the entries in the *Bamboo Annals*, both *Current* and *Ancient*, contain genuine historical information passed down from the early period and therefore their implications for the study of Western Zhou history should be fully explored.

Quite different from the brief entries in the *Bamboo Annals*, somewhat lengthy narratives of the period of Western–Eastern Zhou transition are found in another received text, the *Guoyu* 國語 (Speeches of the States), which came into being some time between the late fifth and the fourth centuries BC.[32] The work contains about a dozen essays developed around speeches that are introduced by a historical frame pointing to the middle to late Western Zhou, including three highly relevant to its fall. The first two essays are by nature political analyses of the reign of King You, while the third one is a critique of the politics in the court of the state of Jin during the early Spring and Autumn period, in which the fall of the Western Zhou is used as very much a metaphor. It has been argued recently by David Schaberg that the speeches contained in these narratives, like many others in the *Zuozhuan* 左傳 (Zuo Commentary), are generated according to a general structure that includes three main parts: judgment, principle (often including citations from an early text, or historical precedents), and application. Therefore, Schaberg is in general suspicious about the reliability of the speeches as historical sources.[33] While such a structural approach to historical narratives in the early texts is generally valid, structural analysis does not itself provide a basis for judging whether the historical knowledge

---

[30] See Shaughnessy, "On the Authenticity of the *Bamboo Annals*," pp. 165–75. Pankenier, on the other hand, demonstrated that the two planetary conjunctions are rendered correctly 517 years apart in the text, one for the Mandate of Heaven to Shang in 1576 BC and the other for the Mandate to Zhou in 1059 BC; the value given in modern astronomy to such planetary conjunction is 516.33 years. Based on this, Pankenier decided that the Shang dynasty was founded in 1554, a date that Keightley now accepts as the first year of Cheng Tang, the founder of the Shang dynasty; see Pankenier, "Astronomical Dates," pp. 17–20. See also David Keightley, "The Shang: China's First Historical Dynasty," in *The Cambridge History of Ancient China: From the Origins of Civilization to 221 BC*, ed. Michael Loewe and Edward L. Shaughnessy (Cambridge: Cambridge University Press, 1999), p. 248.

[31] See Shaughnessy, "On the Authenticity of the *Bamboo Annals*," pp. 152–55.

[32] For the date of composition of the *Guoyu*, see Loewe, *Early Chinese Texts*, pp. 263–64. For an extended discussion of the various attempts to date the *Guoyu* in relation with the *Zuozhuan*, see also Schaberg, *A Patterned Past*, pp. 315–17, and note 13 on p. 436.

[33] See Schaberg, *A Patterned Past*, pp. 42–46. For a criticism of Schaberg's position on the validity of such speeches for the intellectual history of the Spring and Autumn period, see Yuri Pines' new book, *Foundations of Confucian Thought* (Honolulu: University of Hawaii Press, 2002), pp. 35–39. Pines, on the other hand, has argued that the *Zuozhuan* speeches could have been based on existing archival sources passed down from earlier times; therefore, they can be used as sources for intellectual thought of the Spring and Autumn period. See Yuri Pines, "Intellectual Change in the Chunqiu Period: The Reliability of the Speeches in the *Zuozhuan* as Sources of Chunqiu Intellectual History," *Early China* 22 (1997), 86–95.

they present is either right or wrong, for the very simple reason that both true and false historical knowledge can be encoded in a text according to certain patterns of presentation.[34] Moreover, one should also be aware of the dramatic degree to which these speeches vary, especially in the *Guoyu*, both in the way they progress and in terms of the historical particularities they convey. Some of the speeches are extremely long, containing in themselves historical narratives that in turn contain shorter speeches. The value of the historical particularities contained in such speeches has to be evaluated in the broad historical context with relation to other texts, as Schaberg himself argued about the general chronological frameworks of and some detailed historical facts in the speeches, "whose accuracy we have little reason to doubt."[35]

The disadvantage of these relatively later sources is apparent: in the interval between the historical events they record and the time of their composition, important pieces of information could have got lost and the primary account of the events could have undergone literary reworking and even revisions that, as Schaberg argued for the speeches in the *Zuozhuan*, may reflect the views of later times.[36] Even the contemporaneous textual sources are not free of problems because in the long process of textual transmission they were subject to copy errors and inferior editing. However, the reason for including such post-Western Zhou sources in the scope of the present study is also very clear: as the chronological studies using the *Bamboo Annals* show, they contain concrete historical information passed down from the Western Zhou period. This point has been illustrated repeatedly by archaeological discoveries in the past and is again now by another excellent example: the very recently discovered Lai *pan* 逨盤 that records eleven Western Zhou kings from King Wen to King Li in a narrative sequence.[37] Among the received texts, the complete genealogy of the Western Zhou kings is found only in the *Bamboo Annals* and another even later source, the *Shiji* 史記 (The Grand Scribe's Records; compiled in the first century BC),[38] that is now proven accurate on this point. We would have made a big mistake had we rejected this received king list just because we knew it only from later sources before the discovery of the Lai *pan*. There are numerous such examples. Clearly, true historical knowledge could be passed down to later times. If we think also about how much of what we know about Alexander the Great is dependent on Plutarch and Arrian, sources

---

[34] For instance, one can easily detect such patterned presentations by comparing just a number of essays in the corresponding sections of the highly stylistic official dynastic histories, or even essays in the same section of a single history.

[35] See Schaberg, *A Patterned Past*, pp. 26, 319.   [36] See *ibid.*, pp. 26–27.

[37] The bronze was found in a cache in Meixian 眉縣, Shaanxi, on January 19, 2003, together with another twenty-six inscribed bronzes. See *Shengshi jijin: Shaanxi Baoji Meixian qingtongqi jiaocang* (Beijing: Beijing chubanshe, 2003), pp. 7–14, 30–35. See also, *Wenwu* 2003.6, 4–42; *Kaogu yu wenwu* 2003.3, 3–12.

[38] This new English title for the *Shiji* follows William H. Nienhauser (ed.), *The Grand Scribe's Records, vol. 1: The Basic Annals of Pre-Han China* (Bloomington: Indiana University Press, 1994).

produced four centuries later in Roman times, and that even the earliest surviving account of the hero was written 200 years after his death, we can probably all agree that "later" sources have a historical value.[39] Perhaps the very unfortunate fact is that almost all historical records were produced at a slightly later time; even the most "contemporaneous" sources are not exactly concomitant with the events they describe. Historical study cannot achieve its goals without drawing on such relatively later sources.

To take an extremist's view, one may even say that the date of texts is irrelevant because, as pointed out above, even a contemporaneous text could be edited by later hands and a later text could contain genuine information passed down from the earlier time. What is important is the core information deposited in the texts. For this very reason, our current textual scholarship has evolved with much stimulation from the newly discovered texts in a direction that considers a text not as a whole, but as an accumulation of layers produced in different periods. The importance of the textual records does not rest in the traditional authority of the texts that had already been rightly undermined by the *Gushibian* 古史辨 (Discriminations on Ancient History) scholars;[40] for the problems pointed out above, even the contemporaneous bronze inscriptions and the archaeological records are not naturally qualified to assume such authority. The importance of the textual sources lies in the way in which they correlate with each other in revealing an underlying coherent account of events in a historical context shared also by other types of evidence in which the independent sources can be interpreted to make the best sense of history. Put in a simple way, if two or three independent sources (with no demonstrable textual derivation from one another) agree on a certain historical development, we then must seriously consider the possibility that they were based on an early or possibly primary account, whether in written form or as orally transmitted cultural memory, of that history, unless one can demonstrate that a single hand had forged all of these independent records. In the particular case of Western Zhou history, we certainly do have a number of independent sources. For instance, the *Bamboo Annals* was derived from the state of Jin and its successor Wei, different from the poems in "Odes" sections of the *Book*

---

[39] On this point, one can consult the most recent treatment of historical sources on Alexander the Great by Heckel and Yardley; see Waldemar Heckel and J. C. Yardley, *Alexander the Great: Historical Texts in Translation* (Malden, MA: Blackwell, 2004), pp. xx–xxix.

[40] The *Gushibian* was a scholarly movement led by Gu Jiegang and centered on the journal *Gushibian* that was published in seven issues between 1926 and 1941, including as many as 350 essays. The movement aimed at the destruction of traditional beliefs in China's antiquity that were viewed by Gu as the accumulation of layered fabrications throughout the long Chinese textual tradition. The movement, while contributing significantly to undermining the methodological basis of traditional historiography and the unguaranteed authority of the texts on which it was based, as serious scholarship, was itself hindered by many logical and methodological deficiencies. On the origin of the *Gushibian* movement, see Laurence Schneider, *Ku Chieh-kang and China's New History: Nationalism and the Quest for Alternative Traditions* (Berkeley: University of California Press, 1971), pp. 1–52, 218–57. For a recent reflection on this issue, see Tian Xudong, *Ershi shiji Zhongguo gushi yanjiu zhuyao sichao gailun* (Beijing: Zhonghua, 2003), pp. 111–76.

of Poetry that were probably derived from the Zhou court, and probably also from the *Zuozhuan* and *Guoyu* that were traditionally associated with the Shandong region. In fact, the *Bamboo Annals* was completely unknown to any historians and philosophers until its excavation in AD 281. In a more fundamental way, these relatively late textual sources will not be used alone in the present study, but in relation to inscriptional sources and early textual sources in a historical context that is sometimes also supported by the archaeological evidence, when available. Certainly, there are also inconsistencies and contradictions in the later sources, but I think the problem can be at least partly solved by textual criticism. By demonstrating what is wrong, we will be in a better position to say what is probably right. But the problems can never be solved by excluding them from the study.

Having said all this, I should also note that the textual sources used in this study are generally limited to pre-Qin dates. This is based on the consideration that the Han dynasty was an important period of literary re-creation, and much new knowledge may have been introduced to the texts at this time. The *Shiji*, though presenting a concise narrative of the Western Zhou period, is used only as a secondary source showing a Han opinion on Western Zhou history when it is the sole source on a subject. However, for the history of early Qin, it is the primary and in many cases earliest source because the two chapters on Qin are evidently based on an earlier text named *Qinji* 秦紀 (Records of Qin), now lost.[41] For ancient geographical records, the coverage of the present book goes down to the medieval period. But since they form a different category of sources of unique nature, I will discuss them in a different context below.

APPROACH AND METHOD

The present book is grounded in three different fields of knowledge: geography, archaeology, and history (including both epigraphic and textual studies). The study of geography means much more than just putting things on a map; by putting things on a map we actually suggest a relationship between them, and the interpretation of any one of the agents concerned must take into account its relationships with the others. At the same time, we suggest a relationship between the historical process and its geographical setting, especially the *landscape* as the collective existence of the physical features on the surface of the earth in a human-conceived space. According to Jackson, who traces the word's origin in Old English, its first component, *land*, was used not as a generic term referring to the natural surface of the earth, but rather as meaning a unit of area clearly defined by boundaries. The second syllable, *scape*, on the other hand, meant essentially the same

---

[41] On this point, see Takigawa Kametarō, *Shiki kaichū kōshō* (Tokyo: Shiki kaichū kōshō kōho kankōkai, 1956), p. 104; Loewe, *Early Chinese Texts*, pp. 406–07.

as *shape*.[42] Thus, the *landscape*, as the main matrix in which the present study constructs the relationship between history and geography, is quite different from the popular art historical use of the term in its scenery sense referring only to the earth's visual quality.[43] Instead, it is a system of arrangement, a structure, or a system of human management of the land's features such as mountains, valleys, and rivers, created by natural forces, together with features such as settlements, roads, and defenses created by human forces. It entails a reciprocal relationship between human society and its environment that mutually influence each other.

China is predominantly a mountainous country, especially in its western part where ranges of mountains and numerous valleys on the Loess Plateau formed a complex landscape in which the heartland of the Western Zhou state was situated. Such geographical conditions clearly had a significant influence on history, for the Western Zhou state had to act in accordance with the difficult landscape, and had to turn the geographical disadvantages into advantages. However, the impact of geography on history has to be understood in a dialectical way. A mountain can be an obstacle to a people, or it can protect them from enemies; but if the enemies take control over the mountain, it then becomes an advantage for the enemies. On the other hand, human societies not only use geography in their best interest, but also create elements such as settlements, roads, canals, and defenses that become integral parts of the landscape, and can overcome geographical limits to achieve great success.[44]

However, the possibility of clarifying the complex relationship between history and geography in a context far back in the past depends on our ability to recover the historical geography of the given time. In his study of the geography of the Shang state, David Keightley proposed the following working principle:[45]

If, for example, a cache of oracle-bone inscriptions referring to Shang settlements in X or Y has not yet been found, then we are not able to refer to such sites, even though they have been excavated, as part of the state. Similarly, if sites have not been excavated in areas where the inscriptions suggest they should be found, we cannot yet claim with assurance that the state embraced these areas.

Keightley here sees the possibility of recovering Shang geography in the combination of history and archaeology on two conditions: reference in

---

[42] Thus, Jackson defines *landscape* as "a composition of man-made or man-modified spaces to serve as infrastructure or background for our collective existence." See John Brinckerhoff Jackson, *Discovering the Vernacular Landscape* (New Haven: Yale University Press, 1984), pp. 6–10.

[43] Jackson also noted the different uses of the term in America and in England: while the Americans tend to think that landscape can mean natural scenery only, in England a landscape almost always contains a human element. See Jackson, *Discovering the Vernacular Landscape*, p. 5.

[44] For a discussion on this complex relationship between history and geography, see W. Gordon East, *Geography behind History* (New York: W. W. Norton, 1965), pp. 1–14.

[45] See David Keightley, "The Late Shang State," p. 526.

the oracle-bone inscriptions to Shang settlements in that area; and presence of sites with Shang-style cultural contents. The two conditions must be simultaneously satisfied in order to claim an area to be politically Shang. In practice, however, this methodology meets major obstacles in Shang studies. The Shang inscriptions certainly do not suggest correlations between place-names they record and the present-day geography. Since such connections have to be made through later geographical records, and in view of the great gap in time between Shang and the geographically well-documented imperial period, the accuracy of pinpointing place-names in Shang inscriptions on the ground can always be questioned. The problem has long hindered the study of the geography of the Shang state, which has made very little progress since the 1970s.[46] Moreover, the use of archaeological material involves more problems and it is always a good question to ask what the Shang culture is or is not.

However, with the Western Zhou state we can be more optimistic, and such optimism is based on a simple fact: while the Shang oracle-bone inscriptions have been found almost exclusively at the Shang capital, Anyang,[47] the Western Zhou bronze inscriptions, mentioning the names and activities of historically documented regional Zhou states, have often been excavated in areas where these states were once located. In addition to the "first-hand" information that we gain from the bronze inscriptions, the study of Western Zhou geography can also be better grounded in traditional geographical records. Since most Western Zhou states continued to exist into the Eastern Zhou period, and many are actually mentioned frequently in Warring States texts, associated with which there is a continuous and valuable Han–Jin geographical tradition, we can be much more confident about their locations than for the place-names appearing in Shang oracle-bone inscriptions. In short, only with the Western Zhou period will the historical and cultural contexts allow us a real opportunity to recover the geographical space of the political Zhou state.

Theorists of historical geography identify four approaches to the relationship between history and geography: The first, "geographical history," studies the natural geography of the past based on historical records and changes in geographical conditions. The second, "history of geography," studies changes in human perception and presentation of geographical environment. The third studies changes in geographical conditions caused not by natural forces but by human activities, while the fourth, "historical geography" in the narrow sense, studies the spatial distribution of human

---

[46] In his most recent work, Keightley points out that "the political geography of these relationships [between the royal lineage and the various local communities] cannot yet be determined with precision." See Keightley, *The Ancestral Landscape*, p. 57.

[47] The only exception is the recent discovery of oracle-bone inscriptions from Daxinzhuang 大辛莊 in Jinan, Shandong, but the implications of this discovery for Shang geography are still not clear. See the brief report, "China Unearthed Shang Oracle Bones Again, 104 Years after the First Discovery," *People's Daily Online* (http://english.peopledaily.com.cn), April 9, 2003.

activities and the spatial relationships between different parts of human society at a given time.[48] All of these approaches have important bearings on the present study of geography and its political configuration in the Western Zhou state. To demonstrate such historical geography, we must first rely on the extensive land survey recently undertaken by geographers in China.[49] We need to know not only the precise locations of mountains and rivers, but also the distribution of cities and the transportation systems that link them. In other words, we need a comprehensive knowledge of China's present geography as a background to studying its past geography. Second, we should always keep up with new developments in the field of geographical history, the first approach mentioned above. Two aspects of such study are most important: changes in climate and in river courses. These changes had significant impact on the political and military conduct of the Western Zhou state. Third, we must pay close attention to the ancient routes of transportation, "the essential instruments by which people and ideas were diffused, and the activities of commerce, travel, and war were conducted."[50] Routes reveal the potential as well as the limitations of a region's topographic features, and such features remained basically unchanged during the historical period. In this regard, the historical-geographical study of the better-documented routes of transportation and war of later dynasties can provide us with an important foundation for understanding communications during the Western Zhou. Finally, we must also consider the ways in which the Zhou perceived their own landscape because such perceptions could have strongly influenced policies of the Western Zhou state.

From the Han dynasty on, geographical records have been systematically produced in China as a means of imperial administrative control; therefore, there is no major difficulty in tracing the administrative divisions through the next two millennia.[51] This means that if we could pinpoint an ancient state on a map of the Han dynasty, for which the critical Han work, the "Dili zhi" 地理志 (Geographical Records) chapter of the *Hanshu* 漢書 (History of the Han Dynasty), provides valuable links, we would certainly be able to determine its approximate present-day location. Some of the geographical records were produced when the ancient sites were still standing

---

[48] For a discussion of the various studies involving both geography and history, see articles by H. C. Darby and C. T. Smith in D. Brooks Green (ed.), *Historical Geography: A Methodological Portrayal* (Savage, MD: Rowman and Littlefield, 1991), pp. 59–103.

[49] In recent decades, geographers in China have conducted extensive surveys throughout China proper. The results of these surveys are best summarized in the multivolume work under the general title *Natural Geography of China*, published by the Chinese Academy of Sciences between 1979 and 1985. See *Zhongguo ziran dili*, 12 vols. (Beijing: Kexue, 1979–85). For related information on this project, see also Zhao Songqiao, *Physical Geography of China* (Beijing: Science Press, 1986), pp. 1–3.

[50] See East, *Geography behind History*, p. 56.

[51] One can simply check in the fundamental work directed by Tan Qixiang; see Tan Qixiang, *Zhongguo lishi ditu ji*, 8 vols. (Beijing: Zhongguo ditu, 1982). One can also consult some electronic datasets based on Tan's work, such as the Hartwell dataset provided through the "Harvard China Historical GIS," or the "Chinese Civilization in Time and Space," provided by the Academia Sinica.

above ground, known to the local peoples and observed by the scholars of the time. Certainly, traditional geographical records also have problems with regard to the locations of some historical sites. It is possible that a monument could be constructed on a likely site of an ancient state based on uncertain historical-geographical knowledge, or even on misinformed beliefs. In the next period, that monument would then be registered as proof of the location of the ancient state. This process could be repeated many times, generating endless discrepancies. Of course, accurate information was also passed down through such an information reproduction process. An excellent example is the very recent discovery of twenty-two high-ranking tombs along with Western Zhou oracle bones inscribed the "Duke of Zhou" from a site near the Zhougongmiao 周公廟, the popular temple for the "Duke of Zhou" in Shaanxi whose history goes back only to the Tang dynasty (AD 618–907). But the Tang dynasty temple stood right on this walled cemetery site where the important archaeological discovery was made.[52] In order to extract the valuable information from the traditional geographical records, we must always be concerned with their historical sequence and origin, and the circumstances in which they were produced. In general, as the archaeological excavations since the 1970s have repeatedly shown, records of Han dynasty works on the locations of the Western Zhou states are largely accurate and particularly informative.

Archaeology provides the natural link between geography and history because every artifact that comes from a controlled archaeological excavation bears two contexts: a historical context by which the particular artifact can be integrated into a specific cultural tradition of a particular time, and a geographical context within which it occupies a specific spatial location. Because of the interweaving of these two contexts as the result of archaeological excavation, historical events can be firmly related to their geographical settings. On this crucial point, modern archaeology can contribute a great deal to the study of history. In the context of Western Zhou studies, as indicated above, this point is reinforced by the discovery of bronze inscriptions which provides a situation where the historical texts can be firmly connected to spatial locations. However, material remains do not themselves make claims; such claims must be made when they are examined in a theoretical framework constructed on the basis of a set of carefully defined questions. There are different fields of study, such as history, anthropology, art history, and sociology, in which the archaeological materials can be put to use and fully examined through their distinctive methodologies to answer a whole range of legitimate questions about social stratification, kinship structure, artifact production and distribution, daily life and subsistence, customs and religious practices, and so on. Certainly, the present

---

[52] See "Zhougongmiao yizhi kaogu fajue zhunbei gongzuo jiben jiuxu," *Cultural Relics of China Information Online* (http://www.ccrnews.com.cn), accessed September 23, 2004.

study does not and cannot claim to do all of these, since they largely lie beyond its scope; however, as a study designed to address the relationship between the historical process and geography, especially landscape, it does explore deeply the potential of using archaeological materials to answer a set of historical questions with geographical dimensions.

The close relationship between history and archaeology is recognized by many historians as well as archaeologists, especially those with an Old World background.[53] Archaeologists who conduct their research in ignorance of the rich historical records are as partial as historians who neglect ongoing archaeological excavations. Since the publication of the *Cambridge History of Ancient China* in 1999, a number of scholars have expressed dissatisfaction over the inconsistencies in the monumental work's presentation along two parallel and sometimes conflicting tracks, one on history and the other on archaeology, for each period it covers.[54] The division certainly reflects the unfortunate chasm separating the two disciplines in both China and the West that has been increasingly widened, for good and bad reasons, during the last half century. If we are dissatisfied with the way that history has been separated from archaeology, we should probably try to blend the two disciplines in the hope of producing a more coherent reading of our evidence for at least a relatively short period of Early China. With such a hope, the present study values both historical and archaeological evidence and integrates archaeological analysis with historical study to demonstrate the weakening and fall of the Western Zhou. This does not entail a simple combination of conclusions already drawn by historians and archaeologists, but requires fundamental reexamination of problems in both fields. It is the basic premise of this study that when we bring history and archaeology together we see a much better and less fragmentary picture of the past.

[53] Just to give a few examples, in a widely used standard textbook of archaeology in the English language, Colin Renfrew and Paul Bahn describe archaeology as both an aspect of anthropology and a part of history; see Renfrew and Bahn, *Archaeology: Theories, Methods, and Practice*, p. 11. David Clarke highly valued the importance of written records for archaeology, suggesting that the tribal units and confederations discussed by classical European historians can usefully be sought in the archaeological records. See David Clarke, *Analytical Archaeology* (London: Methuen, 1968), pp. 388–98. Daphne Nash, on the other hand, stresses the importance of textual accounts for recovering the social and political system of a past society on which the archaeological evidence remains largely silent; using Celtic archaeology as an example, Nash indicates how the two types of evidence can be used together to study social and political changes. See Daphne Nash, "Historical Archaeology," in *The Cambridge Encyclopedia of Archaeology*, ed. Andrew Sherratt (New York: Crown Publishers Inc., 1980), pp. 43–45. Among the historians of the classical West, for instance, M. I. Finley outlined in particular how archaeology can contribute to the study of history. He even expressed the idea that the contribution of archaeology to history becomes greater as the volume and reliability of non-archaeological evidence increase. See M. I. Finley "Archaeology and History," *Daedalus* 100.1 (1971), 172–83. For recent contributions to methodologies of integrating historical and archaeological studies, see David B. Small (ed.), *Methods in the Mediterranean: Historical and Archaeological Views on Texts and Archaeology* (Leiden: E. J. Brill, 1995).

[54] See for instance Sarah Allan, "Review: The Cambridge History of Ancient China: From the Origins of Civilization to 221 BC," *American Historical Review* 106.1 (2001), 144–45; David Schaberg, "Texts and Artifacts: A Review of the *Cambridge History of Ancient China*," *Monumenta Serica* 49 (2001), 464–65.

Why is archaeology particularly important for the study of Western Zhou history? Perhaps the most important contribution can be found in the spatial reconstruction of the Western Zhou state as a political organization. By correlating the distribution of archaeological remains in a region with the underlying historical process evident in both the bronze inscriptions and the textual records with regard to that region, we can suggest whether the region is likely to have come under the political dominance of the Western Zhou state. With help from a crucial kind of evidence – locally excavated inscribed bronzes – we can delimit the space of Zhou control with a considerable degree of assurance. However, when written records concerning a region are lacking, there is a general problem in making historical claims based solely on archaeological evidence. The problem arises from the possible discrepancy between the spheres of material culture and of human societies, a widely recognized problem in archaeology.[55] The present study also provides evidence that different cultural traditions coexisted in the same region that may or may not have been controlled by the Zhou. This indicates further the danger in the simplistic use of isolated archaeological finds to define political spheres. Nevertheless, most archaeologists admit that material culture and human society do overlap, and therefore it is possible, as long as exceptions are assumed, to study the layout of human societies through analyzing archaeological cultures.[56] In view of such potential and the risks in doing so, the present study adopts the model that assumes different "layers of space," including at least a cultural layer that suggests the spatial influence of the Zhou culture, and a political layer that suggests the sphere of Zhou political dominance.

Furthermore, archaeology presents us with a complex picture of Western Zhou society, many aspects of which simply cannot be learned from the historical record. Two points stand out as most significant to the present study. First, it is generally valid to draw a distinction between the elite culture, which is represented in archaeology, though not exclusively, by bronze vessels and bronze inscriptions, and the non-elite culture, which is represented by pottery wares. It is also evident that the elite and non-elite cultures sometimes show different trends or different paces of development. Thus, there are different layers of culture, and this point is highly relevant to the present study of the ways in which political power was constructed in a given landscape. In order to recover such information from archaeological materials, the present study emphasizes the analysis of pottery wares as a way to define local traditions that existed within the Zhou

---

[55] This problem in archaeology has been fully discussed in Ian Hodder, "Simple Correlation between Material Culture and Society: A Review," in *The Spatial Organization of Culture* (Pittsburgh: University of Pittsburgh Press, 1978), pp. 3–24.

[56] For instance, David Clarke demonstrated this possibility with ethnographic examples that suggest linkages between tribe and culture and tribal group and cultural group. He showed that the elements of a culture diminish as one moves from the center to the periphery of the tribe. See Clarke, *Analytical Archaeology*, pp. 365–88, 398; especially pp. 367–77.

elite cultural space. Second, archaeology presents a complex picture of the frontier of the Western Zhou state as a transitional zone with a high degree of cultural sharing on both sides, but not a line dividing the "civilized" and the "barbarians" as the written records would suggest. Both of these points will be discussed with actual examples in this book.

ORGANIZATION OF THE BOOK

This book is composed of six chapters and three appendixes that can be largely grouped under four themes: chapter 1 and appendix 1 provide a comprehensive survey of the spatial presence of the Western Zhou state based on archaeological, inscriptional, and textual evidence. They show how the Western Zhou state was constructed with respect to the difficult terrains of North China and what strategy was developed to stabilize its new geographic perimeter. Chapters 2 and 3, together with appendix 2, explore the crisis of the Western Zhou state and its possible causes. They show how internal structural problems and external pressures had worked together to set the Western Zhou on a long track of gradual decline. Chapter 4 and appendix 3 present in-depth research into the various historical and geographical problems surrounding the fall of the Western Zhou. Chapters 5 and 6 examine the aftermath of the fall and the transition to the Eastern Zhou. They show how the Zhou world survived the collapse of the political Zhou state and what impact the political Zhou state had had on China and the Chinese civilization.

Chapter 1 deals with the central area of the Western Zhou state from the Wei River valley in the west to the Central Plain in the east. It explains the foundation of the Western Zhou state and also reveals the administrative framework built into the region's landscape. The chapter begins with the Wei River valley, examining the basic structure of the Zhou royal domain. It also examines the highland crescent stretching from northern Shaanxi to the upper Wei River valley in southeastern Gansu, forming the northwestern frontier of the Western Zhou state. Then, the chapter studies the deployment of the regional Zhou states in the Central Plain as the result of the Zhou conquest of Shang, addressing the basic structural characteristics of the Western Zhou state in relation to geographic reality. The peripheral regions are explored in the same manner in appendix 1.

Chapter 2 examines the long process of weakening of the Western Zhou, starting by identifying signs of political and social disorder. In doing so, it provides an overview of the middle and late Western Zhou periods, highlighting the most important sociopolitical developments prior to the accession of King You. The chapter looks into the ruling structure of the Western Zhou state and proposes a new explanation of Zhou's decline. Inside, the Zhou state adopted a "suicide method" of government by granting officials estates instead of salaries. This system in the long run contributed to the growing wealth and power of the aristocratic families and at the same time the impoverishment of the Zhou royal house. Outside the royal domain, the regional states established during the early Western Zhou under the "Fengjian" system gradually developed into a centrifugal force, splitting the Western Zhou state. Under attack by these two forces, the weakening of Zhou royal power would seem to have been inevitable, and so was the gradual dissolution of the Western Zhou state. The chapter further discusses archaeological evidence for the weakening of the Western Zhou state.

Chapter 3 examines outside pressures faced by the Western Zhou. However, it is not intended to be a general study of Zhou's foreign relations. Instead, it focuses on Zhou's war with the Xianyun, a northwestern people who had repeatedly attacked the Zhou royal domain during the middle and late Western Zhou. The chapter examines in detail the history of the Zhou–Xianyun war, using bronze inscriptions as well as textual records to reconstruct a number of important battles. It presents a geographical reconfiguration of this prolonged warfare between the Zhou and the Xianyun, locating it in the upper Jing River valley in the immediately adjacent areas of the Zhou capital. The analysis shows how the landscape in the upper Jing River valley influenced the progression of the war and why the Zhou–Xianyun war was so critical to the survival of the Western Zhou dynasty. Furthermore, the chapter puts the war in a broader cultural context, demonstrating the cultural complexity of the northwestern frontier of the Western Zhou state.

Chapter 4 focuses on court politics during the last eleven years of the Western Zhou dynasty under King You. It suggests that the fall of the Western Zhou in 771 BC was the direct result of factional struggles between the king's party and the elder generation of officials led by Huangfu 皇父 (August Father). These struggles eventually led to the military showdown between the Zhou royal army and the allied forces of the states of Shen 申 and Zeng 缯, and the Quanrong, who jointly defeated the Zhou and captured the Zhou capital. The geographical analysis of the locations of the relevant states in this open military confrontation with the royal court reveals that the battles again took place along the Jing River valley, as did the many battles between the Zhou and the Xianyun. The chapter clarifies many previous misconceptions about the fall of the Western Zhou and thoroughly reinterprets the historical process of this troubled period.

Chapter 5 examines the political transition to the Eastern Zhou, focusing on the eastward migration of the Zhou court and the Zhou aristocratic lineages. The process can be seen as the geopolitical reconfiguration of the Western Zhou state. The chapter first studies the relocation of the Zhou court in Luoyi in the context of its struggle with the rival court remaining in the Wei River valley. Then it studies the history and migrations of two aristocratic lineages – Zheng 鄭 and Western Guo 西虢 – which exemplify a general move of population from the west to the east as a result of Zhou's fall. The relocation of these lineages to the Central Plain having the status of new regional states triggered fierce struggles between them and the native states, thus driving the interstate warfare that marked the next 500 years. The last section of the chapter demonstrates how the evacuation of the Zhou court from the Wei River valley opened a way for the development of the state of Qin 秦, the creator of China's future empire.

Chapter 6 discusses the role played by the Western Zhou state in the formation of the cultural and political basis of the Qin–Han empires. It suggests that the Western Zhou state presented an important political lesson – an approach to political unity through the organization of kinship – that was reinstituted and incorporated into the political culture of imperial China. More importantly, the Western Zhou was a period in which the people in North China acquired a common cultural identity that was fully recognized only after the fall of the dynasty when China was under new pressures from the outside world during the Spring and Autumn period. The chapter concludes that the foundation of China's empire must be sought in the political and cultural practice of the Western Zhou state.

Appendix 1 continues to explore the periphery of the Western Zhou state in three regions: the far east, the south, and the north. By studying the archaeological evidence together with inscriptional and textual records relevant to each region, it provides an informed delimitation of the geographical extent of the Western Zhou state. It also shows how continuous expansion and the presence of Zhou power were conditioned by the geographical reality of these regions. Appendix 1 further takes a cultural approach to the periphery, analyzing both bronzes and pottery assemblages to demonstrate how Zhou cultural elements gradually merged with the various local traditions. This analysis answers the question of the origin of the regional Zhou cultures that became fully recognizable during the Eastern Zhou period. Appendix 2 examines the historical relationship between the Xianyun and the Quanrong, while appendix 3 examines the historiographical development of the legend of Bao Si.

CHAPTER I

Foundation of the Western Zhou state: constructing the political space

In the first month of 1045 BC,[1] the Zhou troops and their western allies, after a long march east from the Zhou base in the Wei 渭 River valley, smashed the Shang army at a place called Muye 牧野 and subsequently occupied the Shang capital in present-day Anyang 安陽.[2] The once great Shang dynasty went to its fate. The conflict, though political and military in nature, can well be considered as a contest between the eastern plain, where the Shang state and its numerous subject communities were located, and the mountainous west, dominated by the rising power of Zhou. The historical invasion had brought the Zhou to confront a challenge that soon proved to be more formidable than the defeat of the Shang army in battle – the consolidation of Zhou rule in the distant and vast eastern plain and its peripheral regions. In the decades following the conquest, the

[1] There have been two traditional dates for the Zhou conquest of Shang. The first, 1122 BC, is based on Liu Xin's 劉歆 (46 BC–AD 23) "Santongli" 三統曆, incorporated into Ban Gu's *Hanshu*. The second, 1027 BC, is based on an entry in the *Ancient Bamboo Annals* (quoted in Pei Yin's 裴駰 fifth-century AD commentary on the *Shiji*) that states that the interval between the Zhou conquest and King You was 257 years. While 1027 BC was accepted by many modern scholars, more than a dozen "new" dates have been proposed by others. In recent years, the range has been significantly narrowed down to 1045 BC, as proposed by David Nivison (before) and Edward Shaughnessy, or 1046 BC, as proposed by David Pankenier and the "Xia–Shang–Zhou Chronology Project." See David Nivison, "Western Chou History Reconstructed from Bronze Inscriptions," in *The Great Bronze Age of China: A Symposium*, ed. George Kuwayama (Los Angeles: County Museum of Art, 1983), pp. 46–7; "The Dates of Western Zhou," p. 517; Shaughnessy, "The 'Current' *Bamboo Annals*," pp. 52–53; *Sources of Western Zhou History*, pp. 217–36; Pankenier, "Astronomical Dates," pp. 14–15; "The *Bamboo Annals* Revisited," p. 285; *Xia–Shang–Zhou duandai gongcheng: 1996–2000 nian jieduan chengguo baogao* (Beijing: Shijie tushu, 2000), pp. 48–49. Nivison later proposed 1040 BC as the date of the Zhou conquest; see David Nivison, "An Interpretation of the 'Shao Gao'," *Early China* 20 (1995), 192–93; for more details, see also David Nivison, "The Key to the Chronology of the Three Dynasties: The 'Modern Text' *Bamboo Annals*," *Sino-Platonic Papers* 93 (1999), 1–24. The "Xia–Shang–Zhou Chronology Project" is a state-sponsored program to determine the dates of the early dynasties in China, inaugurated in 1996 and concluded in 2000. While the Project's date is based on the calendrical records in the "Wucheng" 武成 chapter of the *Shangshu* (surviving as the "Shifu" chapter in the *Yi zhoushu* 逸周書 "Remainder of Zhou Documents"; compiled before 299 BC) and in the *Guoyu*, Pankenier based his date mainly on fixing the date of the planetary conjunction and the pre-conquest chronology in the *Current Bamboo Annals*. Shaughnessy, on the other hand, considered a wide range of texts and inscriptions and arrived at 1045 BC as the year of the Zhou conquest that is followed here.

[2] In an attempt to reconstruct the conquest campaign, Shaughnessy suggested that the operation began in the middle of the eleventh month, 1046 BC, and was concluded on the morning of the fifteenth day of the first month, 1045 BC; See Edward Shaughnessy, "'New' Evidence on the Zhou Conquest," *Early China* 6 (1981–82), 66–67.

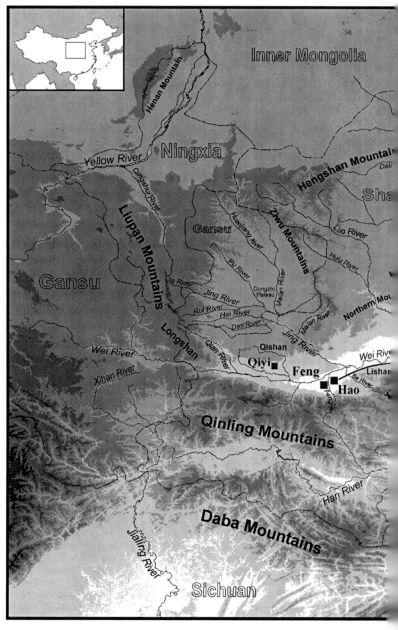

Map 1 Topography of the Zhou central area: Wei River valley–eastern plain (topographical layers derived from "ESRI Data & Maps: 2004"; river course based on "Harvard China Historical GIS Dataset, Version 2.0: August 2003")

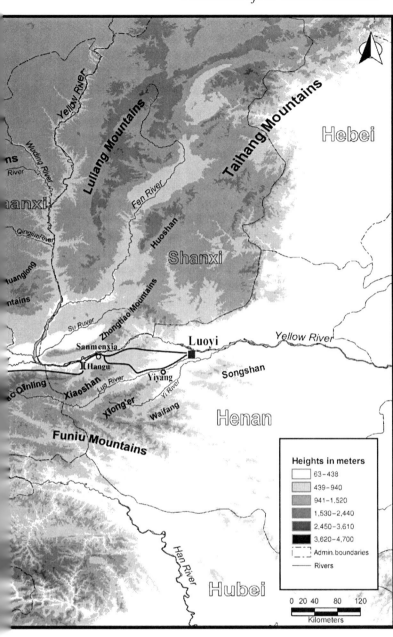

Zhou had fought hard to expand the fruits of the conquest, and by the end of the reign of King Kang (r. 1042/35–1006 BC) the foundation of the Western Zhou state was firmly consolidated. Thus, a new geopolitical unity, which was substantially wider than the Shang state, integrating the two main geographical zones in North China, emerged on the horizon of East Asia.

The axis of Zhou power was the transportation route that connected the Wei River plain, where the Zhou capitals Feng 豐 and Hao 鎬 were located, and the Luo River valley, where the eastern capital Luoyi 洛邑 (or Chengzhou 成周) was situated, through the difficult and often dangerous mountains in western Henan (Map 1). Located off but not far removed from this axis are other geographic units of political and military importance such the upper Jing 涇 River valley and upper Wei River valley in eastern Gansu and the Fen 汾 River valley in southern Shanxi. These areas, located together in the center and western half of the Western Zhou state, were directly affected by the rise and demise of Zhou royal power and were theaters of late Western Zhou history. In this first chapter, I will study the formation of this geopolitical axis and examine how Zhou power was constructed in the diverse areas, and how, as the result of such construction, the different geographical units were integrated with each other. I argue that such political power construction was at the same time a historical process and a geographically guided enterprise. The analysis presented here will demonstrate the real foundation of the Western Zhou state and will provide a necessary background for understanding its crisis and eventual fall, to be analyzed in later chapters.

THE ZHOU HOMELAND AND ITS IMMEDIATE ADJACENT AREAS

The heart of the Western Zhou state lay in the Wei River valley in central Shaanxi, which was the Zhou homeland before their conquest of Shang and continued to serve as their political center throughout the Western Zhou period. More importantly, this was the area managed directly by Zhou royal administration and defended solely by the Zhou royal forces;[3] it was the model of the so-called "royal domain" (*wangji* 土畿) described in the Confucian ritual texts.[4] This is also the area where we have the highest concentration of archaeological finds.

Landscape and environment

Although today the region is locked deep in inner China, far from the fast-developing coastal east, 3,000 years ago the Zhou started a tradition that was to last for the next two millennia during which the Wei River valley

---

[3] On this division of Zhou administration, see Li Feng, "'Offices' in Bronze Inscriptions," pp. 14–29.
[4] See *Zhouli*, 33, p. 863. For a study of the concept of "royal domain," see Lü Wenyu, "Zhou dai wangji kaoshu," *Renwen zazhi* 1992.2, 92–101.

Fig. 1 The Wei River valley at present-day Baoji (photograph by the author)

almost constantly served as the heartland of China. Certainly its fertile soil
and abundant water resources in a wide valley defended on its edges by
mountains are among the factors that contributed to its suitability as royal
or imperial capital.

This wide and rather flat valley follows a huge fault, created by massive
land movement during the Tertiary period of the Cenozoic era.[5] On its
southern edge the peaks of the Qinling Mountains rise abruptly, many of
them to as much as 3,000 meters above sea level, cutting the valley off from
southern Shaanxi (Fig. 1). The northern edge of the valley is marked by
a series of calcareous mountains, including the famous Qishan 岐山, the
symbol of the Western Zhou state, generally referred to as the Northern
Mountain system. The valley is narrower in the west and opens up to
the east, and the frequently migrating river course has created a lowland
extending 360 kilometers and some 50 kilometers wide in its middle and
eastern sections. Another impressive aspect of the landscape is the widely
and thickly distributed loess that constitutes a part of the Loess Plateau of
North China. This loess step extends uninterruptedly from the foot of the
Northern Mountain system to the bank of the Wei River, forming a steep
and high ridge in the west section of the valley. The top of this loess step is
remarkably flat, but in the last 5,000 years water has carved out many deep
gullies, dividing it into a number of large pieces.[6] On the south side, the
present bed of the Wei River leaves only a short section of loess step east

---

[5] See Nie Shuren, *Shaanxi ziran dili* (Xi'an: Shaanxi renmin, 1981), pp. 8–9.
[6] Shi Nianhai has estimated that in the last 3,000 years these gullies in the central section of the step
had cut down on average about 50 meters. See Shi Nianhai, "Zhouyuan de lishi dili yu Zhouyuan
kaogu," *Xibei daxue xuebao* 1978.2, 82–83.

of Xi'an, at the foot of Lishan Mountain which forces the river to move slightly north.

The prominent tributaries of the Wei River include, on the north side, the Qian 汧 River, Jing River, and Luo 洛 River (not to be confused with the Luo River in the east, written with the same character). To the south, there are shorter rivers and streams such as the Feng 灃 River and the Ba 灞 River, originating in the Qinling Mountains. These secondary river valleys provided access to the outlying areas, leading to the renowned five passes that defended the Wei River valley through much of history and gave the land the nickname "Land within the Passes" (*Guanzhong* 關中).[7] Today the region enjoys moderate winters but sometimes hot summers, with an annual average temperature above 13 degrees centigrade and an annual precipitation of about 600 millimeters; it also enjoys abundant groundwater flowing out under the loess steps in the north and from the high Qinling Mountains in the south that freed the Wei River plain from most serious droughts in history. It should also be noted that the thick vegetation on the slopes of the Qinling Mountains has provided the people of the region with a variety of natural resources, including, most importantly, the timber that was used to construct palaces and temples in the valley.

Beyond the Wei River valley, the region that was historically most intimately related to it was the upper Jing River valley that, as will be demonstrated in later chapters, occupied a key position in the fall of the Western Zhou. The region is a highland dustpan-shaped basin in the western part of the Loess Plateau. Although not as naturally fertile as the Wei River plain, it is, with an annual temperature of 7–10 degrees centigrade and precipitation varying from 400 to 700 millimeters, the richest agricultural area of the northwestern province of Gansu. The Liupan 六盤 Mountains (1,400–2,800 meters in elevation) separate the area from the upper Wei River valley and anyone who travels through the long tunnel under the Liupan will be impressed by the difference in vegetation on the mountain's two slopes (Fig. 2). To the east the area is edged by the Ziwu 子午 Mountain ranges (1,500–1,800 meters), and to the south the Loess Plateau gradually gives way to the Northern Mountain system.[8]

However, the bottom of the upper Jing basin is by no means flat but has been sliced into numerous fragments by the Jing River and its branches such as the Malian 馬連, Pu 蒲, Hei 黑, and Daxi 達溪 rivers. Only in its northern half are there some large plateau areas such as the Dongzhi Plateau 董志原 around present-day Qingyang 慶陽 (see Map 3 for modern county names). Owing to the fragmented nature of the basin, the river courses provide the main sites for human habitation and communication routes.

---

[7] These five passes are the Hangu Pass 函谷關 in the east, the Long Pass 隴關 and San Pass 散關 in the west, the Wu Pass 武關 in the south, and the Xiao Pass 蕭關 in the north; see Shi Nianhai, *Heshanji*, vol. 4 (Xi'an: Shaanxi shifan daxue, 1991), pp. 145–46.

[8] See Sun Yongqing and Zheng Baoxi, *Gansu sheng dili* (Lanzhou: Gansu jiaoyu, 1990), pp. 290–91.

Fig. 2 The Liupan Mountains from the east (photograph by the author)

This is particularly true of the Jing River, originating at the foot of the Liupan Mountains in Ningxia and flowing north along their eastern edge.[9] From Pingliang 平涼 eastward the river bed is straight and wide, providing an ideal superhighway running for about 100 kilometers until it reaches the vicinity of Changwu 長武 county where sandstone rocks underneath the loess have forced the river to run though a very narrow and tortuous gully (Fig. 3).[10] Descending from Changwu, one arrives in the Binxian 彬縣 area where the river again occupies a wider valley, before eventually being confined to a narrow gorge at a place called "Cutting off the Jing River" (Duanjing 斷涇) to the southeast of Binxian, where the river enters the calcareous rocks of the Northern Mountain system before entering the Wei River plain (Fig. 4).[11]

To the west, across the high Liupan Mountains, the upper Wei River valley centers on the modern city of Tianshui 天水. At the region's western-most point, the Wei River originates in Niaoshu 鳥鼠 Mountain at the edge of the Qinghai–Tibetan Plateau and flows east through the valley.

---

[9] In ancient times the Jie 頡 River originating in Jitou 笄頭 (雞頭) Mountain in Ningxia was often regarded as the main stream of the Jing River. On the history of the Jing River, see the fundamental work by the Qing historical geographer Gu Zuyu (AD 1624–80), *Dushi fangyu jiyao* (Taipei: Lotian, 1973), p. 2,540; see also Lu Renyong, Wu Zhongli *et al.*, *Ningxia lishi dili kao* (Yinchuan: Ningxia renmin, 1993), pp. 355–57.

[10] Virtually all county towns, except Changwu and the modern Xifeng City 西峰市, are located in the valleys of the Jing River and its tributaries. The reason that the town of Changwu is located on the top of Qianshui Plateau 淺水原 is because the Jing River in this section becomes very narrow, forcing the main transportation route up onto the plateau. This route has not changed since antiquity.

[11] See Nie Shuren, *Shaanxi sheng dili*, pp. 168–69.

Fig. 3 The upper Jing River valley at Pingliang (photograph by the author)

Fig. 4 The Jing River at present-day Binxian, descending from the Qianshui Plateau
(photograph by the author)

The upper Wei River valley is relatively wide, having an environment very similar to that of the lower valley in Shaanxi. It receives more abundant rainfall than does the upper Jing River valley and was the cradle of several Neolithic and early Bronze Age cultures of northwestern China.[12] The valley itself provides a dividing line in the landscape of southern Gansu: to the north the boundless sea of loess hills extends all the way to the desert of southern Inner Mongolia. The area is very dry, with an annual precipitation around 300 millimeters, and in the springtime of bad years local residents have to depend on outside water sources for daily life. But to the south of the valley, the loess hills gradually give way to low, thickly vegetated hills and deeply cut streams.

East of the Ziwu Mountains is the heartland of the Loess Plateau of northern Shaanxi. Most of the region is not in fact a plateau at all; surface water has long since transformed it into a large area of loess hills above layered sandstone and sedimentary rocks (Fig. 5).[13] Such topography allows only limited agriculture, but provides the possibility for pastoralism on the hill-slopes. The region is cool, with an annual temperature around 9 degrees centigrade, and relatively dry, with precipitation below 500 millimeters. The Luo River and its numerous tributaries form the primary water supply and transportation routes through the region. But many of the deep valleys are dangerous and landslides are a regular hazard owing to the unstable condition of the base rocks. At Ganquan 甘泉 and Fuxian 富縣 the valley becomes more level and increases in width to some 400 meters, but from Fuxian southward it narrows again to about 100 meters, passing tortuously through the Northern Mountain system very much like the lower Jing River.[14]

Route and accessibility

Looking at a simple map, one might expect that the Wei River had served as a main path of transportation between the Wei River plain and China's northwest. But this was not the case, for on its way east the Liupan (the southern section of which is called Longshan 隴山) and Qinling Mountains make a formidable natural obstacle between Gansu and Shaanxi. In most parts, the river cuts the granite rocks as deeply as 400 meters to form an extremely narrow and barely passable channel until it enters the fertile plain of central Shaanxi at Baoji 寶雞. This made it almost impossible to move a

---

[12] For instance, the pre-Yangshao culture found in Dadiwan 大地灣, and the Majiayao 馬家窯, Qijia 齊家, and Xindian 辛店 cultures. In the Western Zhou period, the area was the homeland of the Siwa 寺洼 culture, which was evidently in communication with the Zhou culture. For the distribution of these cultures and their possible relationship to the Zhou culture, see Li Feng, "Xian Zhou wenhua de neihan jiqi yuanyuan tantao," *Kaogu xuebao* 1991.3, 265–84. See also Chang, *The Archaeology of Ancient China*, pp. 89–90, 142–43, 281–85, 376–85.

[13] For a brief geological history of the Loess Plateau of northern Shaanxi, see Ji Naijun, *Yan'an shihua* (Beijing: Jiaoyu kexue, 1988), pp. 1–2.

[14] See Nie Shuren, *Shaanxi ziran dili*, pp. 166–67.

Fig. 5 The Loess Plateau of northern Shaanxi in the area of Ansai (photograph by the author)

Fig. 6 The Wei River valley between Baoji and Tianshui (photograph by the author)

large army or body of people along the riverside until the construction of the modern railroad during the 1950s (Fig. 6).[15] It was not much easier to climb the Longshan Mountains by way of the so-called Long Pass, located to the west of Longxian 隴縣; the road was infamous from the Han dynasty for its great difficulty.[16]

From the earliest historical times until the present, the most important, if not sole, route entering the Wei River plain from China's northwest has been the upper Jing River valley (Map 2). This was called the "Road to Xiao Pass" because the Xiao Pass in present-day Guyuan 固原 controlled the road during the Han dynasty. The road starts from the foothills of the Helan 賀蘭 Mountains and goes south through the Qingshui 清水 River valley to the foot of the Liupan Mountains, where it enters the Jie River valley and thereafter the Jing River valley leading to Pingliang.[17] Because the sources of the two rivers, both on the east side of Liupan, are separated by a few

---

[15] Only recently was a road constructed along the Wei River linking Baoji and Tianshui. But because of the difficult terrain it runs through, the condition of the road is bad and a falling rock can block the traffic for four or five hours. However, the difficult conditions did not prevent communication between adjacent cultures through the narrow valley in ancient times, as indicated by similarities between two local types of the Xindian culture: the Jijiachuan 姬家川 type located in the upper Wei River valley and the Chaoyu 晁峪–Shizuitou 石嘴頭 type located in the Baoji region. For details on this point, see Li Feng, "Xian Zhou wenhua de neihan," pp. 274–78.

[16] The "Road through Long Pass" linked Tianshui and Longxian, and hence the upper Wei River valley and central Shaanxi. See Shi Nianhai, *Heshanji*, 4, pp. 157–58, 200.

[17] See Shi Nianhai, *Heshanji*, 4, p. 110. Today's interprovincial highway no. 312 which connects Lanzhou and Xi'an, the two provincial capitals in western China, comes down directly from the Liupan and merges with the ancient "Road to Xiao Pass" in the upper Jie River valley. But in ancient times, the main transportation line had to go north, exactly following the "Road to Xiao Pass," and then turned west leading to Lanzhou from the north of Guyuan.

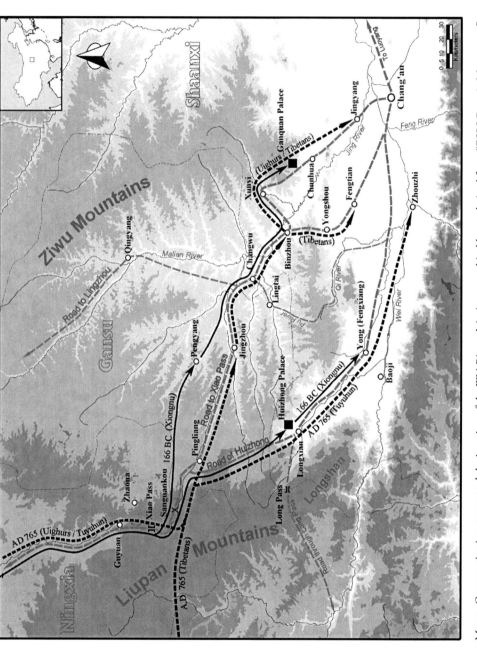

Map 2 Communication routes and the invasion of the Wei River plain (topographical layers derived from "ESRI Data & Maps: 2004"; river course based on "Harvard China Historical GIS Dataset, Version 2.0: August 2003")

loess ridges in only a few miles, there is no great difficulty on the road. This is also precisely the route taken by people who traversed the world-famous "Silk Road" during the early centuries of the first millennium, and also precisely the route of the newly constructed railway connecting the Ningxia region on the edge of the northern steppe and the Wei River valley in central Shaanxi.

Having entered the very narrow pass between the rock cliffs traditionally called Sanguankou 三關口 (the most frequent battleground between the Song Empire and the Western Xia Empire during the eleventh century) to the west of Pingliang, the road splits. The northern road goes by the "superhighway" of the Jing River valley to the Changwu–Binxian area. From there, because of the difficulties of traversing the narrow lower Jing valley through the Northern Mountain system, it goes either east to Xunyi 旬邑 and then turns south over the hills, entering the Wei River plain on the east side of the Jing River, or south by way of Yongshou 永壽, entering the Wei River valley on the west side of the Jing River. According to Shi Nianhai, the eastern road was used most often before the Han dynasty and the western road was taken more often thereafter.[18] The southern road, which is now roughly followed by the new railroad, goes along the eastern edge of the Liupan Mountains all the way down to Longxian in the upper Qian River valley and then the Wei River valley; this particular section was also called the "Road of Huizhong 回中" owing to the location of the Huizhong Palace in the Longxian area during the Han dynasty.[19]

Our historical records inform us of the military value of these roads. In 166 BC, the Xiongnu from the northern steppe overran the Xiao Pass with a force of 140,000 horsemen and rode east from there, sending vanguard units as far as present-day Chunhua 淳化 on the northern edge of the Wei River valley; at the same time, the Xiongnu rode down the "Road of Huizhong" and, after burning the palace, reached as far as the present-day Fengxiang area.[20] Nine centuries later, in AD 765, the allied forces of Tibetans, Uighurs, and Tuyuhun again took the two roads, marching as far as the district of the Tang capital Chang'an.[21] Between the lower Jing River in the east and the Qian River in the west, there was a third possible path, though more difficult, through the Pu 蒲 River valley and the Qi 漆 River valley from Lingtai 靈台 to the Wei River plain.[22]

---

[18] Shi Nianhai, *Heshanji*, 4, p. 157. The eastern road took the same route as today's interprovincial highway no. 211, and the western road interprovincial highway no. 312. The conditions of the two roads are similar.

[19] See Shi Nianhai, *Heshanji*, 4, pp. 110, 158. In my own experience, the present road connecting Pingliang and Longxian is a difficult one. In many sections, the road has to run tortuously along the extremely narrow ridge of the mountains.

[20] See *Hanshu*, 64, p. 3,761. This was the deepest invasion by the Xiongnu into the heartland of the Han Empire. Another direction of the Xiongnu's invasion was the Wuding 無定 River valley, east of the Hengshan Mountains, but the Xiongnu never succeeded in reaching Yan'an.

[21] See Shi Nianhai, *Heshanji*, 4, p. 215.

[22] See Gao Jingming, "Sichou zhi lu Chang'an – Longzhou dao," *Wenbo* 1988.6, 46–50.

In the middle of the upper Jing River basin, the extraordinarily long valley of the Malian River provided another channel for military invasion and transportation from the north, especially from the Ordos region. In the south, the road merges with the "Road to Xiao Pass" at Changwu. The Tibetans of the seventh and eighth centuries and the Western Xia of the eleventh century, while focusing on the "Road to Xiao Pass," both took this road to attack the upper Jing River valley.[23] But since the northern section of this road (about 190 kilometers) runs between desert hills with no water or vegetation, moving a large body of troops through this area was very difficult.[24]

At the center of the Loess Plateau of northern Shaanxi, Yan'an, the Communist capital during World War II, with its archaic name Gaolu 高廬, was from ancient times a key fort controlling transportation and military movement. All major ancient roads through the valleys or along the eastern edge of the Hengshan Mountains eventually meet at Yan'an, and then go down the Luo River valley; therefore the road was called "Road by Yanzhou 延州."[25] One of these roads goes through the Dali 大理 River valley and then turns into the Yan River valley; on this road one can still observe the beacon-fire towers of the Han dynasty every 7 or 8 kilometers. In my own experience, all of these roads are extremely difficult. Because of the difficulties of the lower Luo valley, the road goes over the loess hills on either sides of the Luo River, leading to the ancient capital Chang'an. In the later fifth century, troops of the Xiongnu kingdom of Xia based on the northern fringes of the Hengshan Mountains marched along this route all the way to Chang'an. Later, the "Road by Yanzhou" became an important route of Turkish and Mongol invasion.[26] However, as Shi Nianhai noted, because of the difficulty of providing logistics along this extremely long road and the risk of falling into ambush in the complex valley system, it was always the northern invaders' choice to take the "Road to Xiao Pass" or the "Road to Lingzhou" instead of this.[27]

Locating the heartland of the Western Zhou state

From the earliest time that can be fully confirmed in archaeology, the Wei River valley had been the homeland of the Zhou people and it continued to serve as the base of Zhou royal power after the conquest, although the location of the pre-dynastic Zhou community is still an issue of

[23] This road bore the name of "Road to Lingzhou 靈州" during the Tang dynasty. Owing to the discovery of a Han site along the road, some consider that it was already in use during the Han dynasty. See "Sui Tang Song shiqi Qingyang diqu daolu de fazhan," *Xibei shidi* 1988.4, 83–90.
[24] See Gu Zuyu, *Dushi fangyu jiyao*, p. 2,520; Shi Nianhai, *Heshanji*, 4, pp. 109–10.
[25] See Shi Nianhai, *Heshanji*, 4, pp. 76–79, 84.   [26] See *ibid.*, p. 109.
[27] See *ibid.*, pp. 108–9. The defeat of the Chinese Nationalist troops in the area by the Communist forces in 1946 during the civil war best exemplifies the strategic advantage given to the defenders over the invaders.

controversy.[28] As it is impossible to review all archaeological discoveries here, I choose to highlight only some of the most important finds that can reveal the basic macro-geopolitical structure of the Wei River plain as the heartland of the Western Zhou state (Map 3).

There have been a number of major concentrations of archaeological finds in this area. One of these concentrations is located on both banks of the Feng River (Fig. 7), about 12 kilometers to the southwest of the modern city of Xi'an, where excavations have been undertaken for more than half a century. Rich archaeological remains have been found in an area of 6 square kilometers around the modern villages of Mawangcun 馬王村, Keshengzhuang 客省莊, Zhangjiapo 張家坡, Dayuancun 大原村, and Xinwangcun 新旺村 (Map 4).[29] These include most importantly the excavation in the 1980s of a huge palace complex composed of the foundations of six buildings to the north of Mawangcun. Around the same time, as many as 1,500 Western Zhou tombs on the high land south of Zhangjiapo were confirmed, of which nearly 400 had been excavated by the end of 1986.[30] The excavations, together with surveys of the distribution of the various sites in the area, have not uncovered the overall layout of the large city, but show quite sufficiently the high status of the sites, appropriate to a political

[28] There have developed two schools among both historians and archaeologists on the location of the pre-dynastic Zhou: the "Western School" looks to the Shaanxi region, in either the Wei River or the Jing River valley, for the origin of the Zhou culture and its historical connections, while the "Eastern School," starting with the rather radical article by Qian Mu, locates the original base of Zhou in the Fen River valley in Shanxi and suggests a Zhou migration from the east into the Wei River valley. Each school has a long list of literature that cannot be given in full here, but the following represent the two positions. For the western origin of Zhou, see Qi Sihe, "Xi Zhou dili kao," *Yanjing xuebao* 30 (1946), 63–106; Liang Xinpeng, "Xian Zhou wenhua shangque," *Kaogu yu wenwu* 1982.4, 86–91; Hu Qianying, "Shitan Xian Zhou wenhua jiqi xiangguan wenti," in *Hu Qianying Zhou wenhua kaogu yanjiu xuanji* (Chengdu: Sichuan daxue, 2000), pp. 124–38; "Nanbin Nianzipo Xian Zhou wenhua juzhuzhi he muzang fajue de xueshu yiyi," in *Zhou Qin wenhua yanjiu* (Xi'an: Shaanxi renmin, 1998), pp. 153–62; Li Feng, "Xian Zhou wenhua de neihan," 1991.3, 265–84; Liu Junshe, *Xian Zhou wenhua yanjiu* (Xi'an: Shanqin, 2003). For the eastern origin of Zhou, see Qian Mu, "Zhou chu dili kao," *Yanjing xuebao* 10 (1931), 1,955–2,008; Zou Heng, "Lun Xian Zhou wenhua," in *Xia Shang Zhou kaoguxue lunwen ji* (Beijing: Wenwu, 1980), pp. 295–355; Xia Hanyi, "Zaoqi Shang Zhou guanxi jiqi dui Wu Ding yihou Yin Shang wangshi shili fanwei de yiyi," *Jiuzhou xuekan* 2.1 (1987), 20–32. For a recent summary of the various arguments, see Zong Li and Liu Dong, "Xian Zhou wenhua yanjiu liushi nian," in *Zhou Qin wenhua yanjiu* (Xi'an: Shaanxi renmin, 1998), 268–85. It should also be noted that, in the *Cambridge History of Ancient China*, while Shaughnessy adopts the position of the "Eastern School," Rawson, carefully noting links through pottery typology to the local Shaanxi area, leaves the issue largely open. See Shaughnessy, "Western Zhou History," pp. 303–7; Rawson, "Western Zhou Archaeology," pp. 378–82. Although this issue cannot be dealt with fully here, I believe that as far as our archaeological evidence shows, and if we move beyond the Wei River valley, there is a much closer link between the Wei River valley and the upper Jing River valley, where a more archaic Zhou pottery assemblage was found in Nianzipo 碾子破, than any connection that can be established with the Fen River valley, where almost nothing of the contemporaneous time has been discovered. On the last point, see also Li Liu and Xingcan Chen, *State Formation in Early China* (London: Duckworth, 2003), p. 24.
[29] For an overview of excavations in this area, see *Xin Zhongguo de kaogu faxian he yanjiu* (Beijing: Wenwu, 1984), pp. 253–57; Hu Qianying, "Feng Hao kaogu gongzuo sanshi nian (1951–1981) de huigu," *Wenwu* 1982.10, 57–67.
[30] See *Kaogu* 1987.8, 692–700; *Zhangjiapo Xi Zhou mudi* (Beijing: Zhongguo da baike quanshu, 1999), pp. 2–4.

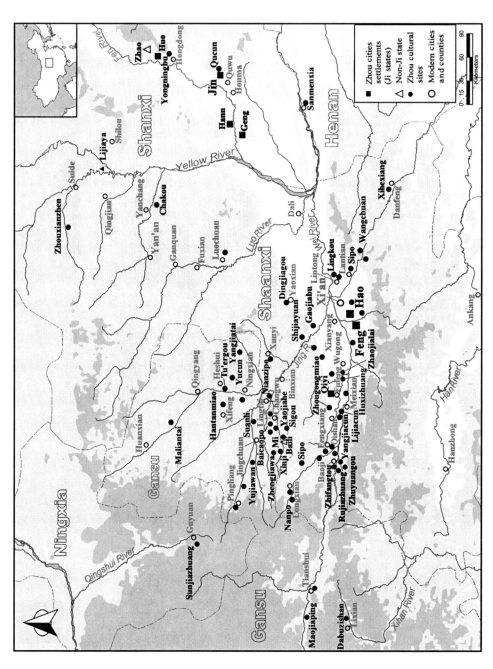

Map 3 Political map of the Wei River plain and its adjacent geographical units (topographical layers derived from "ESRI Data & Maps: 2004"; river course based on "Harvard China Historical GIS Dataset, Version 2.0: August 2003")

Fig. 7 The Feng River running between the capitals Feng and Hao
(photograph by the author)

center. This is certainly evidenced also by the discovery of a large number of
inscribed bronzes from the site during the last fifty years, including most significantly the fifty-three bronzes excavated together from a cache to the west
of Mawangcun in 1965.[31] Between 1984 and 1986, a section of a cemetery
composed of high-status tombs was excavated to the south of Zhangjiapo,
identified by the bronzes from them with the Jingshu 井叔 family which
was active in the mid-Western Zhou according to both inscriptional and
textual evidence (Fig. 8).[32] In addition to these significant discoveries, the
material sequence and standard for periodization established on the basis
of the local pottery assemblage has served as the foundation of Western
Zhou archaeology.[33]

Across the Feng River, Western Zhou sites are widely distributed in an
area of 4 square kilometers between Doumenzhen 斗門鎮 and Fenghaocun
豊鎬村. Because of constructions during the Han dynasty, especially the
excavation of the Kunming Lake 昆明池 during the reign of Emperor Wu
(r. 140–87 BC) for the training of the Han navy, the area was badly damaged.
However, rich cultural deposits were preserved in areas to the north of
the lake. A large earth foundation was excavated in 1986 to the north of

---

[31] See *Chang'an Zhangjiapo Xi Zhou tongqi jiaocang* (Beijing: Wenwu, 1965), pp. 1–24.
[32] See *Kaogu* 1986.1, 22–27; 1987.1, 15–31; 1990.6, 504–10; *Zhangjiapo Xi Zhou mudi*, pp. 16–35.
[33] This sequence was proposed in two major reports: *Fengxi fajue baogao* (Beijing: Wenwu, 1962),
pp. 129–30; *Kaogu xuebao* 1980.4, 481–87. A compatible but much more refined periodization of 390
tombs excavated in 1983–86 has recently been published; see *Zhangjiapo Xi Zhou mudi*, pp. 339–73.

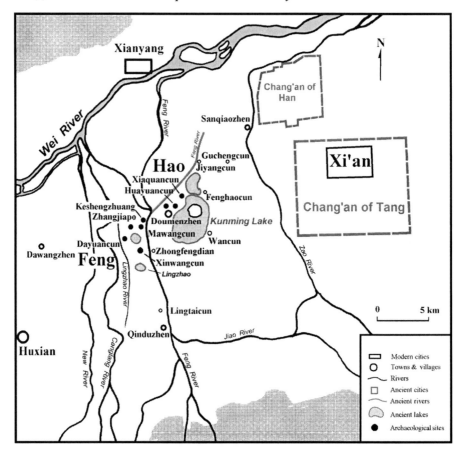

Map 4 The capitals Feng and Hao on the two banks of the Feng River

Doumenzhen.[34] Western Zhou tombs are widely distributed in the area, and the bronze Duoyou *ding* 多友鼎 (JC: 2835), one of the most important inscriptions for the study of the war with the Xianyun, was discovered in Xiaquancun 下泉村 in 1980.[35]

From surveys conducted during the 1950s, these two areas have been identified with the capital Feng (west bank) and the capital Hao (east bank), and the identifications are unanimously accepted by scholars.[36] According to historical tradition, the capital Feng was constructed in the time of King Wen and is said to have demonstrated the king's ambition in the east, while the capital Hao was constructed by King Wu. Thereafter, the twin cities

---

[34] See *Wenbo* 1992.4, 76–80.

[35] See Tian Xingnong and Luo Zhongru, "Duoyou ding de faxian jiqi mingwen shishi," *Renwen zazhi* 1981.4, 115–18.

[36] For the identification of the capitals Feng and Hao, see Wang Shimin, "Zhou du Feng Hao weizhi shangque," *Lishi Yanjiu* 1958.2, 63–70.

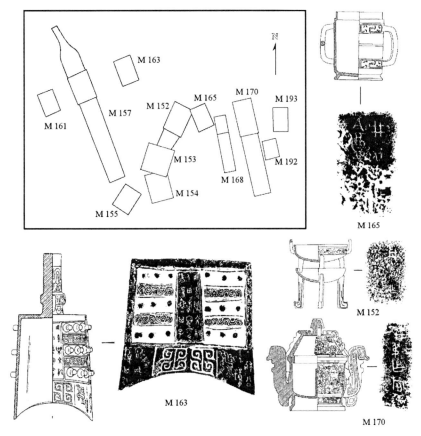

Fig. 8 The recently excavated Jingshu cemetery and Jingshu bronzes from Zhangjiapo (from *Kaogu* 1990.6, 504: *Zhangjiapo Xi Zhou mudi*, pp. 138, fig. 103.5; 143, fig. 106; 155, fig. 115.2, 5; 160, fig. 119; 161, fig. 120; 165, fig. 124.1; 166, fig. 125)

at the center of the Wei River plain served as the pivot of the political and administrative system of the Western Zhou state.[37] The names Feng and Hao certainly appear in the contemporaneous bronze inscriptions that fully testify to their importance in Zhou political and social life. The capital Feng appears in four inscriptions, the Xiaochen Zhai *gui* 小臣宅簋 (JC: 4201), Zuoce Hu *you* 作冊魖卣 (JC: 5432), Qiu Wei *he* 裘衛盉 (JC: 9456), and Xing *ding* 瘭鼎 (JC: 2742), as the place where the Zhou king met with his officials and assigned them duties. The capital Hao, more often called

---

[37] The construction of the capitals Feng and Hao is the subject of the poem "Wen Wang yousheng" 文王有聲 (no. 244) in the *Book of Poetry*; see *Shijing*, 16.5, pp. 526–27 (Waley, *The Book of Songs*, pp. 241–42). For a discussion on the locations of the two capitals based on textual evidence, see Qi Sihe, "Xi Zhou dili kao," pp. 87–89; Wang Shimin, "Zhou du Feng Hao weizhi shangque," pp. 63–70. For a recent analysis of archaeological evidence for the two capitals, see Lu Liancheng, "Xi Zhou Feng Hao liangjing kao," unpublished paper presented at the conference for the 30th anniversary of the Shaanxi Provincial Institute of Archaeology and the Banpo Museum (Xi'an, 1988), pp. 1–56.

Zongzhou 宗周,[38] is mentioned in more than twenty inscriptions such as the Xianhou *ding* 獻侯鼎 (JC: 2626), Yanhou Zhi *ding* 燕侯旨鼎 (JC: 2628), Da Yu *ding* 大盂鼎 (JC: 2837), Shi Song *gui* 史頌簋 (JC: 4229), and Da Ke *ding* 大克鼎 (JC: 2836) that demonstrate its paramount importance as the Zhou political center where the state ritual and receptions for the regional rulers were frequently held, quite in contrast to the poor condition of preservation of the site today.

Another concentration of archaeological remains is located on the top of the loess step north of the Wei River, in the area conventionally referred to as the "Plain of Zhou" (Zhouyuan 周原), straddling the border between present-day Fufeng 扶風 and Qishan 岐山 (Map 1; as Qiyi). The area had been known for yielding inscribed bronzes since the Han dynasty, and the archaeological works conducted in the 1970s confirmed that it is doubtless the richest Western Zhou site ever found. While pre-dynastic Zhou tombs were found in Hejiacun 賀家村, the excavations have fully demonstrated the prosperity and prominence of the site during the entire Western Zhou.[39] Besides the two famous groups of building foundations at Shaochen 召陳 and Fengchu 鳳雛,[40] the "Plain of Zhou" is also well known for caches yielding a large number of inscribed bronzes. Among them, the most important are the thirty-seven bronzes from Dongjiacun 董家村, the thirty-nine bronzes from Qijiacun 齊家村, and the 103 bronzes from Zhuangbai 莊白, including one, the famous Shiqiang *pan* 史墙盤 (JC: 10175), the inscription on which directly calls the local site "Zhou" 周.[41] While many eminent Western Zhou families are represented by these bronzes that indicate the locations of their residences on the site, royal activities are fully evident in oracle-bone inscriptions preserved in one of the pits dug into the building foundations excavated at Fengchu, and in the discovery of the Hu *gui* 趞簋 (JC: 4317) at Qijiacun in 1978, one of the very few bronzes known to have been cast by a Zhou king.[42] Many of the bronzes found in Zhouyuan actually carry "Appointment Inscriptions" based on administrative records used in the Zhou central court. It is no exaggeration that, had these inscribed bronzes not been found, the field of Western Zhou studies would have been very different from what it is today.

[38] It should be noted that Chen Mengjia once identified "Zongzhou" with Qiyi 岐邑 located far to the west (see below); Chen Mengjia, "Xi Zhou tongqi duandai: 1–6," *Kaogu xuebao* 9–10 (1955), 1956.1–4, 2.139–40. However, most scholars think that it should be identified with the capital Hao. See Tang Lan, *Tang Lan xiansheng jinwen lunji*, p. 268; Li Xueqin, *Xinchu qingtongqi yanjiu* (Beijing: Wenwu, 1990), pp. 228–29; Lu Liancheng, "Xi Zhou Feng Hao liangjing kao," pp. 31–35.

[39] See *Kaogu yu wenwu* 1980.1, 7–12. For an overview of the excavations in Zhouyuan, see Chen Quanfang, *Zhouyuan yu Zhou wenhua* (Shanghai: Renmin, 1988), pp. 21–36.

[40] See *Wenwu* 1979.10, 27–34; 1981.3, 10–22; Chen Quanfang, *Zhouyuan yu Zhou wenhua*, pp. 37–67.

[41] See *Wenwu* 1978.3, 1–18; 1976.5, 26–44; *Fufeng Qijiacun qingtongqi qun* (Beijing: Wenwu, 1963), pp. 7–10.

[42] See Xu Xitai, *Zhouyuan jiaguwen zongshu* (Xi'an: Sanqin, 1987), pp. 3–10. For an introduction to these oracle-bone inscriptions, see also Edward Shaughnessy, "Zhouyuan Oracle-Bone Inscriptions: Entering the Research Stage?" *Early China* 11–12 (1985–87), 146–63. On the discovery of the Hu *gui*, see *Wenwu* 1979.4, 89.

Fig. 9 Qishan Mountain to the north of Qiyi (Zhouyuan)
(photograph by the author)

In the received textual tradition, as the term "Zhou" is used as the dynastic name, the site is more often called the "Settlement of Qi" (Qiyi 岐邑) owing to its location at the foot of Qishan Mountain (Fig. 9).[43] The poem "Mian" 绵 (no. 237) in the *Book of Poetry* mentions that it was the Ancient Duke, Danfu 亶父, grandfather to King Wen, who led the Zhou people to settle at the site, a move that would have happened sometime during the late twelfth century BC.[44] This event may have been an important turning point in Zhou history; after only two generations the Zhou developed into a political and military power, strongly challenging the security of the western border of Shang. Current archaeology, despite the finding of late pre-dynastic tombs on the site, cannot verify this date as the beginning of the settlement's history. But it has made perfectly clear that the site continued to be an important base of royal power and aristocratic activities, paralleling the capitals Feng and Hao. The study of the bronze inscriptions shows further that all of the royal temples after King Kang were located in Zhou, suggesting that the site was probably a religious center for the Zhou people as well as a base of royal administration.[45] It is above all astonishing that in May 2004 a group of twenty-two high-ranking

[43] On the identification of Qiyi with Zhou, see Li Xueqin, *Xinchu qingtongqi yanjiu*, pp. 229–30; Lu Liancheng, "Xi Zhou Feng Hao liangjing kao," p. 31.

[44] See *Shijing*, 16.2, pp. 509–11 (Waley, *The Book of Songs*, p. 232). Based on the *Book of Poetry*, Sima Qian retells the story of a migration of the Zhou people from an early site named Bin to Qiyi. See *Shiji*, 4, p. 114 (Nienhauser, *The Grand Scribe's Records*, 1, pp. 56–57).

[45] In the Appointment Inscriptions, the royal temples such as Kang Gong 康宫, Kang Shao Gong 康卲宫, and Kang Mu Gong 康穆宫 are constantly said to have been located in Zhou. See Li Feng, "'Offices' in Bronze Inscriptions," pp. 12–13.

tombs, including probably the burials of the Zhou kings or that of the Duke of Zhou, within a walled enclosure, a situation never seen before, was discovered at Zhougongmiao 周公廟, 18 kilometers to the west of Zhouyuan (Map 3).[46] While waiting for more information to be brought to light, one can surely expect that further excavations will bring very significant changes to the field of Western Zhou archaeology.

Another important site of royal activity was probably located in present-day Meixian 眉縣 on the north bank of the Wei River and not far to the southwest of Qiyi. In 1955, five bronzes cast by Li 盠 were found in Majiazhen 馬家鎮 (Lijiacun 李家村) near the train station of Meixian, providing us with one of the earliest documents on the court ritual of appointment.[47] In 1972, a huge bronze *ding* was found at the same location.[48] Again, in 1985, a group of sixteen bronze bells was found 100 meters from the location where the large *ding* was found.[49] About 30 kilometers to the east of Majiazhen, a bronze *ding* cast by an early Western Zhou king for a royal consort was found in 1981, providing us with one of the few examples of bronzes cast by the Zhou king.[50] Most recently, in January 2003, twenty-seven inscribed bronzes were excavated, at Yangjiacun 楊家村, close to the west of Lijiacun, including the crucial Lai *pan* 逨盤 that carries the most complete genealogy of the Zhou kings.[51]

Beyond these central sites where royal activity was evident, Western Zhou bronzes have also been found in virtually every county on the Wei River plain, both from tombs and from caches, and most of them were cast by members of the various aristocratic lineages. For instance, in the eastern section of the Wei River valley, five bronze vessels, including a *he* cast by a Zhou king for his consort Feng Ren 豐妊 and a *gui* cast by the Ruler of Chen 陳 as dowry for another royal consort, were found in a cache in Lintong 臨潼 in 1976. Remarkably, included in this group is the famous Li *gui* 利簋 (JC: 4231), the single most important inscription recording the Zhou conquest of Shang.[52] A year earlier, a mid-Western Zhou tomb containing thirteen bronzes was excavated 200 meters to the north of the cache that contained the Li *gui*.[53] To the south, in the valley of the Ba River, the Yong *yu* 永盂 (JC: 10332), which describes the process of a land transaction, was discovered in Lantian 藍田 in 1979.[54] In the same county, numerous bronzes cast by members of the Mi 弭 family were found in the late 1950s.[55] In the western section of the Wei River valley, the Baoji area has another concentration of Western Zhou bronzes, related to a number of important lineages such

[46] See "Zhougongmiao yizhi kaogu fajue zhunbei gongzuo jiben jiuxu," *Cultural Relics of China Information Online* (http://www.ccrnews.com.cn), accessed September 23, 2004.

[47] See *Wenwu cankao ziliao* 1957.4, 5–9.   [48] See *Wenwu* 1972.7, 3–4.   [49] See *Wenbo* 1987.2, 17–26.

[50] See *Kaogu yu wenwu* 1982.2, 6.   [51] See *Zhongguo wenwubao* 2003.1.29, 2.

[52] See *Wenwu* 1977.8, 1–7.   [53] See *Wenwu* 1982.1, 87–89.   [54] See *Wenwu* 1972.1, 58–62.

[55] A group of sixteen bronzes including the Mishu *gui* 弭叔簋 (JC: 4253) and the Xun *gui* 詢簋 (JC: 4321) was found in Sipo 寺坡 near the town of Lantian in 1959; *Wenwu* 1960.2, 5–10. Earlier, a bronze *gui* cast by Mibo 弭伯 (JC: 4257) was found upstream at Wangchuan 輞川. *Wenwu* 1966.1, 4–6.

as Jing 井, Guo 虢, Yu 強, San 散, and Ze 夨. As will be discussed later, the ruling lineage of Yu probably had a foreign origin and had relocated itself in Baoji on the edge of the royal domain. In 1974, two large Western Zhou tombs with ramp-ways were excavated at Rujiazhuang 茹家莊, to the south of the Wei River. Inscriptions from the tombs indicate that they were burials of Yubo 強伯 and his wife Jing Ji 井姬, who was probably from the same lineage as the Jingshu family whose cemetery has been found in the capital Feng.[56] Subsequently, twenty-two tombs have been excavated in Zhuyuangou 竹園溝 and another in Zhifangtou 紙房頭, producing a great number of fascinating Western Zhou bronzes, all belonging to the Yu lineage.[57] Besides these sizeable excavations, Western Zhou tombs have also been excavated in Longxian 隴縣 and Fengxiang 鳳翔,[58] while Western Zhou bronzes have been found in many other locations in the western half of the Wei River valley.[59]

In general, the discovery of inscribed bronzes beyond the royal centers indicates properties or burials of the aristocratic lineages in various socioeconomic relationships with the royal centers. However, none of these secondary settlements has been seriously investigated except for some cemeteries that are associated with them. But, as we know from the inscriptions, there seems little doubt that these properties were local centers, surrounding which were located numerous small settlements or hamlets that belonged to and supported the lineages that lived in the secondary centers. In fact, two such small settlements were excavated in Wugong 武功.[60] Despite the fact that previous archaeological works were concentrated on a few central sites in the region, and settlement deposits of the lineages were rarely made the target of archaeological excavation, the available evidence enables us to see quite typically a settlement hierarchy incorporated into the geopolitical power structure that was built into the landscape of the Wei River plain, contemporary with the Western Zhou period.

On the fringes

Archaeological discoveries along the upper Jing River reflect a gradual cultural expansion into the region from the Wei River valley in the south. They show that during the early Western Zhou dominance by a culture found in the Zhou central sites was firmly established at both the elite and non-elite levels. In view of the distribution of the early and mid-Western

---

[56] See *Wenwu* 1976.4, 34–46.

[57] See Lu Liancheng and Hu Zhisheng, *Baoji Yu guo mudi* (Beijing: Wenwu, 1988), pp. 17–269.

[58] For the excavation of Western Zhou tombs at Nanpo 南坡, Longxian, see *Wenwu* 1982.2, 48–57. For the excavation at Xicun 西村, Fengxiang, see *Kaogu yu wenwu* 1982.4, 15–38.

[59] For some of these discoveries, see *Kaogu yu wenwu* 1981.1, 8–11; 1984.1, 53–65; *Wenwu* 1983.7, 93.

[60] These two sites are Huxizhuang 滸西莊 and Zhaojialai 趙家來, reported in *Wugong fajue baogao* (Beijing: Wenwu, 1988), pp. 75–82, 144–47.

Zhou sites in the entire upper Jing River region, the Lingtai area appears
to have held a major concentration of Western Zhou settlements. In the
narrow area between the Hei and Daxi rivers, Western Zhou tombs have
been found at eight locales.[61] The central position of this area is also indicated by the large size of tombs and the large number of bronzes buried in
them.[62] Inscriptions from tombs no. 1 and no. 2 at Baicaopo 白草坡 suggest
that the occupants of the two tombs were Heibo 潶伯 and Yuanbo 夐伯;
such titles normally designate the head of an aristocratic lineage.[63] In this
case, the unusually large number of bronze weapons from these tombs may
indicate that these were military commanders stationed in the region. To
the west, in Xinji 新集 and still in the same valley, another large tomb containing a bronze *yan* cast by Bingbo 幷伯 was found.[64] The concentration
of tombs of high-ranking Zhou elite in this small area seems to suggest its
central position in Zhou administration as well as Zhou military defense
of the upper Jing region. Lingtai is at the entrance to the Pu River valley,
the third path connecting the upper Jing River region and the Wei River
plain mentioned above (Map 2), and is only 25 kilometers from Changwu,
where all traffic from the west and north can be effectively controlled. However, some findings in the upper Jing River region evidently pre-date the
Western Zhou period by the standards of dating established on the basis of
the pre-dynastic Zhou pottery found in the Wei River valley. For instance,
such pottery types were excavated from a number of tombs in the Yujiawan
于家灣 cemetery that evidently straddled the Zhou conquest of Shang.[65]
Bronze vessels of probably pre-dynastic date were also discovered at Suanli
蒜李 and Zhengjiawa 鄭家洼, both in the southern part of the basin.[66]
These findings, though scattered, suggest a cultural expansion from the
Wei River valley into the region prior to the founding of the Western Zhou
dynasty.

   The presence of pre-dynastic Zhou cultural remains in the upper Jing
River valley can be well explained by the historical circumstances under
which the region entered into contact with the Zhou, who were at this
time based on the Wei River plain. There has been a strong historiographical tradition that, before the Zhou conquest of the east, military actions
were first launched into the upper Jing River valley. This tradition is present
in a number of ways, but first of all in the poem "Huangyi" 皇矣 (no. 242)
in the *Book of Poetry*. The poem speaks about an invasion by a polity named

---

[61] See *Kaogu* 1976.1, 39–43; *Kaogu xuebao* 1977.2, 128; *Kaogu* 1981.6, 557–58.

[62] This becomes clear when we compare the size of the tombs at Baicaopo with those found in the
Yujiawan 于家灣 cemetery near the main channel of the Jing River. Of the nine tombs found at
Baicaopo, seven are more then 3 meters and two are 2.7 meters in length. In contrast, all sixteen
tombs at Yujiawan are between 1.90 and 2.65 meters. See *Kaogu xuebao* 1977.2, 101; *Kaogu yu wenwu*
1986.1, 6.

[63] See *Kaogu xuebao* 1977.2, 99–129.   [64] See *Kaogu yu wenwu* 1987.5, 100–1.

[65] Among the sixteen tombs already published, at least five, nos. 5, 6, 7, 9, and 10, can be surely dated
to the pre-dynastic period. See *Kaogu yu wenwu* 1986.1, 1–7.

[66] See *Wenwu* 1977.9, 92; *Kaogu* 1981.6, 558.

Mi 密 against two of its neighbors – Gong 共 and Ruan 阮 – and the action was seen as the declaration of war against the bigger state of Zhou. The Zhou subsequently marched on Mi and destroyed the polity.[67] The ancient geographical works consistently locate Mi in the upper Jing region, about 25 kilometers to the west of Lingtai at the west end of the narrow Daxi River valley; in fact, the Tang geographers were still able to identify Mi with a walled enclosure that evidently stood above ground into the early twentieth century.[68] Although we should not take the poem at face value, there seems no ground to doubt that the campaign had ever taken place. On the contrary, while the description of the campaign in the poem seems to collaborate well with a record in the *Zuozhuan* that mentions a drum captured from Mixu 密須,[69] this geographical configuration agrees also with that of another important event remembered in early Zhou history. It is frequently mentioned in the Zhou tradition that King Wen had once mediated in a serious border dispute between two small polities, Yu 虞 and Rui 芮, that in the end came to peaceful terms. The event is celebrated in the poem "Mian" 綿 (no. 237) in the *Book of Poetry* as the hallmark of King Wen's hegemony in the west.[70] While no doubt the two states were later moved to the east and relocated themselves in southern Shanxi, geographical works of the Han and Northern Wei (AD 386–534) periods suggest quite convincingly that, as many scholars have already argued, they were originally located to the northwest of Zhou, in the area between the Qian River and the Rui River, and thus not far from Mi.[71] The correspondence in political geography between these two incidents conveys a deep sense of pre-dynastic Zhou involvement with the upper Jing River valley that would suitably explain the dates of the archaeological materials from the region. Moreover, this historical development fits reasonably into the pre-conquest context: in order to deal with the mighty Shang in the east, it would obviously be important

[67] See *Shijing*, 16.4, p. 521 (Waley, *The Book of Songs*, pp. 236–39).

[68] The "Geographical Records" chapter of the *Hanshu* says that the Mi County 密縣 in Anding Commandery 安定郡 of the Han dynasty (25 kilometers to the west of present-day Lingtai) was the site of the ancient state Mi mentioned in the *Book of Poetry*; see *Hanshu*, 28, p. 1,615. The Tang dynasty geographical survey *Yuanhe junxian tuzhi* says that Mi is related to the town of the Lingtai County of Tang. In a local gazetteer composed in 1935, Wang Zhaojun notes that the ancient city wall of Mi was still visible in the west part of Bailizhen 百里鎮, the site of the Lingtai County of Tang. See *Yuanhe junxian tuzhi*, pp. 56–57; Wang Zhaojun, *Chongxiu Lingtai xian zhi* (1935), 1, p. 59. However, no systematic archaeological work is being conducted on this site at present.

[69] See *Zuozhuan*, 47, p. 2,078; 54, p. 2,135.

[70] See *Shijing*, 16.2, p. 512 (Waley, *The Book of Songs*, pp. 232–33). In the *Shiji*'s reconstruction of pre-conquest chronology, Sima Qian dates the event to the same year as King Wen's receipt of Heaven's mandate; see *Shiji*, 4, p. 119 (Nienhauser, *The Grand Scribe's Records*, 1, p. 58).

[71] Many ancient polities derived their names from landmarks such as mountains and rivers. In this case, Rui is most likely to have been related to the Rui River, while Yu is close to Yushan 虞山 (or Wushan 吳山) Mountain located in the upper Qian River valley. The geographical closeness of the two landmarks suggests that Rui and Yu were probably neighbors. For the location of the Yushan, see *Hanshu*, 8.1, p. 1,547; *Shuijing zhu*, 17, p. 582. For studies of the locations of the two states in the west, see Qi Sihe, "Xi Zhou dili kao," p. 84; Liu Qiyi, "Xi Zhou Ze guo tongqi de xinfaxian yu youguan de lishi dili wenti," *Kaogu yu wenwu* 1982.2, 44; Liang Xiaojing and Ma Sanhong, "Lun Yu Ze liangguo de zushu yu Taibo ben Wu," *Zhongyuan wenwu* 1998.3, 44–45.

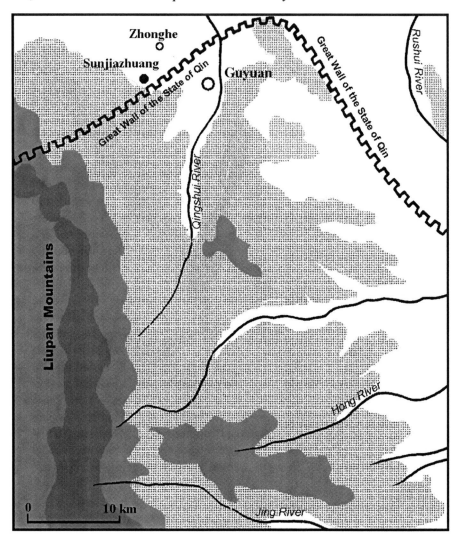

Map 5 The upper Jing River–Guyuan area

for the Zhou to consolidate their hold on the west, and the most likely
direction of threat to the security of the Wei River plain was the upper Jing
region.

Of particular importance is the discovery of a Zhou tomb and an
accompanying chariot-burial at Sunjiazhuang 孫家莊, Guyuan 固原, in
the Qingshui 清水 River valley in southern Ningxia, on the edge of the
northern steppe (Map 5). Two bronze vessels and several chariot-fitting
parts as well as a pottery *li* were found in these two pits, all identical to
bronzes and pottery types found in Zhou central sites (Fig. 10).[72] Given their

[72] See *Kaogu* 1983.11, 982–83.

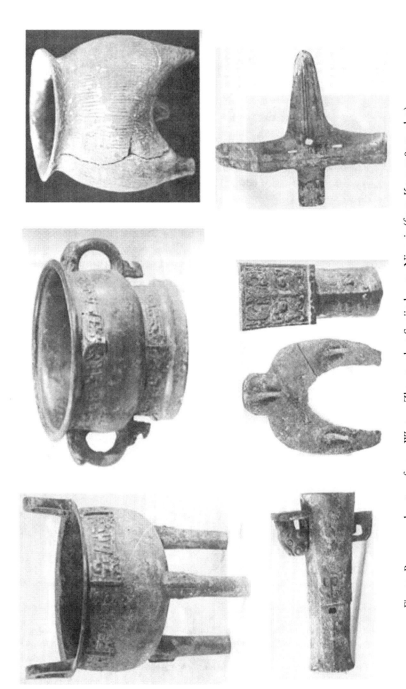

Fig. 10 Bronzes and pottery from a Western Zhou tomb at Sunjiazhuang, Ningxia (from *Kaogu* 1983.11, pl. 2)

unmistakable Zhou cultural identity and their distant position from the
upper Jing valley, the discovery fully suggests that during the early Western
Zhou expansion the Zhou troops or communities had advanced beyond the
confines of the upper Jing valley and attempted operations in the northern steppe region. Beyond the Liupan Mountains to the west, a bronze
gui-vessel was discovered in Tianshui in 1924.[73] Sixty years later, controlled
archaeological excavations at Maojiaping 毛家坪 revealed a large group of
pottery vessels from both the tombs and the settlement deposit (Map 3).
Although twenty-two of the thirty-three tombs excavated at Maojiaping are
characterized by flexed burial of human bodies, different from the stretched,
supine burial characteristic of Zhou tombs in Shaanxi, their pottery assemblage is very similar to that of central Shaanxi.[74] These discoveries indicate
that the Zhou extended their cultural and possibly also political influence
over regions to the west of the high Liupan Mountains, into the upper Wei
River valley. This certainly laid a foundation for the rise of the state of Qin
in the region during the late mid-Western Zhou.

Compared to the upper Jing River region, we have very little information
about Zhou's connection to the heartland of the Loess Plateau in northern
Shaanxi. The only linking thread concerns two military campaigns against a
society called Guifang 鬼方 during the reign of King Kang (r. 1005–978 BC),
recorded in the inscription of the famous Xiao Yu *ding* 小盂鼎 (JC: 2839).
In the first campaign the Zhou killed 4,812 enemies, and captured another
13,081. Guifang was once at war with the Shang for three years and this is
mentioned both in the Shang oracle-bone inscriptions from Anyang and in
the Zhou text, the *Book of Changes*.[75] From the study of the Shang oracle-
bone inscriptions, some scholars have proposed that Guifang was located
in northern Shanxi, in the area from present-day Taiyuan in the east to
the banks of the Yellow River in the west.[76] The area of possible Guifang
activity coincides well with the independent bronze culture of the lower
Ordos region contemporary with the late Shang, represented by the bronze
vessels and weapons from locations in Suide 綏德, Qingjian 清澗, Shilou
石樓, and Liulin 柳林, and by the pottery inventory found at Lijiaya 李家崖
in Qingjian.[77] Therefore, a link between them is strongly advocated.[78] If

[73] See *Wenwu cankao ziliao* 1955.6, 117–18.   [74] See *Kaogu xuebao* 1987.3, 359–96.

[75] See *Zhouyi*, 6, p. 73 (Edward Shaughnessy, *I Ching: The Classic of Changes* [New York: Ballantine
Books, 1996], p. 145).

[76] See Shima Kunio, *Inkyo bokuji kenkyū* (Hirosaki: Hirosaki daigaku Chūgokugaku kenkyūkai, 1958),
pp. 416–17.

[77] On this independent bronze culture, see Zhang Changshou, "Yin Shang shidai de qingtong rongqi,"
Kaogu xuebao 1979.3, 289–91; Li Feng, "Shilun Shaanxi chutu Shang dai tongqi de fenqi yu fenqu,"
Kaogu yu wenwu 1986.3, 60.

[78] See Luo Kun, "Gaozong fa Guifang shiji kaobian," in *Jiaguwen yu Yinshang shi*, ed. Hu Houxuan
(Shanghai: Guji, 1983), pp. 108–15; Lü Zhirong, "Shilun Shan Jin beibu Huanghe liang'an diqu
chutu de Shang dai qingtongqi ji youguan wenti," in *Zhongguo kaoguxue yanjiu lunji – Jinian Xia
Nai xiansheng kaogu wushi zhounian*, ed. Shi Xingbang (Xi'an: Sanqin, 1987), pp. 221–24; "Guifang
wenhua ji xiangguan wenti chutan," *Wenbo* 1990.1, 32–37.

Guifang was indeed located in the northern region, the two campaigns recorded by the Xiao Yu *ding* would be more likely to have been carried out through the Luo River valley leading to the north. However, current archaeology provides some, but not very strong, support to this hypothesis: a tomb containing a bronze *ding* and a pottery *li* of typical early Western Zhou styles was excavated in Luochuan 洛川 county in 1997; and a middle Western Zhou style pottery *li* was found in Zhouxianzhen 周嶮鎮, Zizhou 子洲 county, in 1981.[79] They seem to suggest that the region had received some intermittent Zhou influence, though permanent control over the region does not seem to have been achieved by the Zhou. But perhaps it is a reasonable supposition that the destructive campaigns recorded in the Xiao Yu *ding* may have been in some way responsible for the demise of the local bronze culture during the early Western Zhou.

Curiously, in recent years, two bronzes bearing important inscriptions were discovered in southern Shaanxi. The Shi Mi *gui* 史密簋 from Ankang 安康 in the Han River valley records a southern campaign by the royal army with assistance from the eastern state – Qi.[80] The Hu *gui* 虎簋 (JL: 491) found at Xihexiang 西河鄉 in Danfeng 丹鳳 in the Dan River valley records an appointment ceremony in which Hu was given a military post by the Zhou king.[81] Since we have no reliable information about the local pottery assemblage with which these bronzes were associated, and given the great difficulty of transportation through the high Qinling Mountains, the bronzes do not provide us with a firm basis for determining any constant Zhou political relations with regions south of the Qinling Mountains.

The macro-geopolitical structure

The above analysis of archaeological findings in relation with their historical background that can be established on the basis of bronze inscriptions and early textual tradition reveals the basic geopolitical framework of the Zhou royal domain and its adjacent regions. It seems likely that this framework was quite different from that which once underlay the power of the late Shang state. During the late Shang, Anyang was the only identifiable site of permanent royal residence, called on the oracle bones "Great Settlement Shang" (Dayi Shang 大邑商) or "Middle Shang" (Zhong Shang 中商), the focal point of the entire Shang world, although the Shang king did frequently go out on hunting trips.[82] The Zhou royal power, in contrast,

---

[79] The information given here is based on travel notes from my trip to northern Shaanxi in 1998. Since these materials have not yet been published, further discussion about them is not appropriate.

[80] See *Kaogu yu wenwu* 1989.3, 7–9.   [81] See *Kaogu yu wenwu* 1997.3, 78–80.

[82] Keightley now thinks that the various oracle-bone place-names such as Dayi Shang 大邑商, Zhong Shang 中商, Qiu Shang 丘商, and Zi Shang 茲商 all refer to the Xiaotun site in Anyang, that "symbolized the legitimating concentration of political-religious energy that the peripatetic Shang kings needed to preside over their relatively undifferentiated emerging state structure." See Keightley, *The Ancestral Landscape*, pp. 57–58; quote from p. 58.

seems to have rested on a network, but not a point, that connected a number of major royal cities of comparable size and structural complexity through which the Zhou king regularly traveled. In addition to Feng, Hao, Qiyi (Zhou), and probably also the Meixian site, whose status has been revealed by archaeology, the bronze inscriptions also mention two other cities as sites of the Zhou king's ritual and administrative conduct: Zheng 鄭 and the capital Pang 菶; the latter city is literarily mentioned as *jing* 京, "capital." It seems probable that Zheng was located in the area of present-day Fengxiang to the west of Qiyi,[83] while the capital Pang, according to new inscriptional evidence, is most likely to have been located very close southeast of the capital Hao at the center of the Wei River valley.[84]

Certainly, the Western Zhou state was formed on different principles from the "incipient" Shang state, as Keightley once called it,[85] and was managed through a formally constructed administrative structure according to routine administrative procedures that extended to these major royal centers. Indeed, the bronze inscriptions show the clear notion of "Five Cities" (*wuyi* 五邑), most probably referring to the royal centers mentioned above, for which specialized administrative responsibilities were often collectively assigned to the Zhou officials.[86] These cities were clearly the hubs of royal administration, though they had probably also accommodated multiple social functions, including serving as aristocratic residences and centers of industrial and craft production.[87] They manifest a macro-geopolitical structure as well as a system of social integration built into the special landscape of the Wei River valley, along the major rivers and crossing the flat highland tops. Back in the Western Zhou, they were themselves the most important features of the landscape of the Wei River plain and probably commanded a unique sense among the people that they did not necessarily live *around* a royal center, but lived *among* the royal centers that together

---

[83] On the location of Zheng, see Lu Liancheng, "Zhou du Yu Zheng kao," in *Guwenzi lunji* (Monograph of *Kaogu yu wenwu* 2; Xi'an, 1983), p. 10; Wang Hui, "Zhou jinei diming xiaoji," *Kaogu yu wenwu* 1985.3, 26–27. For a discussion of the Zheng-related inscriptions, see also Matsui Yoshinori, "Sei Shū ki Tei no kōsatsu," *Shirin* 69.4 (1986), 1–40.

[84] In the past, some considered Pang to be the same as the capital Feng, while others identified it with the capital Hao. But scholars agreed that Pangjing was somewhere at the center of the Wei River plain. See Guo Moruo, *Liang Zhou jinwen ci daxi tulu kaoshi*, 8 vols. (Beijing: Kexue, 1958), pp. 32, 42; Shirakawa Shizuka, "Kinbun tsūshaku," *Hakutsuru bijutsukanshi*, 56 vols. (Kobe: 1966–83), 7.30:343–44; 11.60:632; Chen Mengjia, "Xi Zhou tongqi duandai," 2, p. 141. The Mai *zun* 麥尊 (JC: 6015) and the Chenchen *he* 辰臣盉 (JC: 9454) indicate that it must have been near the capital Hao. New evidence from the Wuhu *ding* 吳虎鼎 suggests that Pang may have been somewhere to the southeast of the capital Hao and northwest of Bi 畢. The inscription mentions Pang as the western limit of the land granted to Wuhu, the caster of the bronze, which was found in Chang'an in 1992. For the Wuhu *ding*, see *Kaogu yu wenwu* 1998.3, 69–71.

[85] See Keightley, "The Late Shang State," pp. 551–58.

[86] On the administration of the "Five Cities," see Li Feng, "'Offices' in Bronze Inscriptions," pp. 25, 56.

[87] One certainly should not forget the city of Luoyi in the east, where government branches were installed and more than half of the royal military forces were stationed, as the extension of Zhou administration from the Wei River plain.

had tremendous influence on their lives. Surrounding these royal centers, as the discovery of the inscribed bronzes shows above, were located the secondary local centers that were properties of the aristocratic lineages, side by side with the royally possessed and managed rural estates. In fact, the archaeological evidence shows that many of these lineages, while located at a distance from the royal centers, simultaneously held portions of residence in the royal centers, and some may even have been buried in the vicinities of the royal centers. Surrounding these lineage centers, as the bronze inscriptions suggest, were numerous small settlements or hamlets that defined the units of agricultural production and rural communities. These settlements, together with the peasants who lived in them, not only supported the lineage centers, but, as the inscriptions show, often became items of exchange between them. While this situation will need detailed treatment in a separate study, there seems little doubt that on the basis of our current evidence such was the basic settlement hierarchy in the Wei River valley and the way of integration of the Wei River society that formed the foundation of the Western Zhou dynasty.

The upper Jing River region was a natural extension of the Zhou royal domain from the Wei River valley into the northwestern highlands. This was in part due to the difficulty of expansion to the south or straight west, blocked by the high Qinling Mountains. Culturally, the region was thoroughly integrated with the Zhou central area, but it formed a part of the northwestern frontier of the Western Zhou state and, given its direct access to the Zhou heartland, was critical to the security of the Zhou capitals. The archaeological discoveries show that the region clearly had a center of political power, located near the entrance to the main roads leading to the Wei River valley. A notable fact is that the locally excavated bronze inscriptions indicate that the leaders of the local communities were the heads of the various aristocratic lineages, referred to normally as *bo* 伯, the first-born of the family, different from the rulers of the Zhou regional states, referred as *hou* 侯 and located mainly in the eastern regions.[88] This suggests that the communities in the upper Jing River region were managed through a political system that is similar to that of the Wei River plain. There seems little doubt that during at least the early Western Zhou the upper Jing River region constituted a part of the royally administered territory and was fully integrated with the royal domain in the Wei River valley. However, the situation in the upper Wei River valley and northern Shaanxi was probably different from that of the upper Jing region. Although the two regions were undoubtedly under Zhou cultural influence, and intermittent adventures into the regions either by the royal army or by Zhou settlers were likely to have taken place, it is not likely, because of the difficulty imposed by the

---

[88] On the meaning of these aristocratic titles, see Li Feng, "Transmitting Antiquity: On the Origin and Paradigmization of the 'Five Ranks'," in *Perceptions of Antiquity in China's Civilization*, ed. Dieter Kohn (Monograph of *Monumenta Serica*), forthcoming.

regions' geographical character, that Zhou royal power had ever established firm hold over them.

Despite the pivotal importance of the Wei River plain as the heartland of the Western Zhou state, it was not its geographical center. The real geographical center, the place that was in a roughly equal distance from its frontier in all directions, lay instead in the Luo River valley of Western Henan. Although the valley itself is narrower than the Wei River valley in the west, its easy access to the vast plain lying east of it provided great possibilities for the rising power of Zhou.

Mountains and plains

The Luoyang plain, the locus of Zhou royal power in the east, was created by the sediment of the Luo River and its tributary Yi River, both originating in the high mountains in the southwest. To the east, the Luoyang plain is separated by Songshan 嵩山 Mountain from the alluvial plain of the east. To the west, the Qinling extends into the region and splits into four major Palaeozoic mountain ranges – Xiaoqinling 小秦嶺, Xiaoshan 崤山, Xiong'er 熊耳, and Waifang 外方 – running in parallel to the northeast. Especially the Xiaoshan Mountains, the main peaks of which are 1,500–1,900 meters high, constitute the major geographical obstacle in the region (Map 1).[89] In general, the northern part of the region is lower and is extensively covered by Quaternary loess, the landscape changing gradually from high mountains to lower foothills and to loess steps, with shallow valleys and basins fairly suitable for ancient agriculture.

The alluvial plain in the east, referred to more often historically as the "Central Plain," was created by the sediment of the Yellow River which in the historical period alone, from 602 BC to the present day, has changed its course twenty-six times.[90] While the Yellow River now goes east from Zhengzhou to Lijin 利津 near the coast,[91] during the Shang and Western Zhou periods the river turned north along the Taihang Mountains and entered the sea near Tianjin (Map 6).[92] This presents the most dramatic

---

[89] See *Henan sheng zhi: Quyu jianzhi zhi, dimao shanhe zhi* (Zhengzhou: Henan renmin, 1994), pp. 52–54, 68–78.

[90] The Yellow River has broken its banks 1,573 times in history; see Zhao Songqiao, *Physical Geography of China*, p. 115.

[91] In 1855, the Yellow River entered the Bohai Sea at Lijin, but today the river mouth is 80 kilometers east from Lijin, protruding into the sea. See Zeng Zhaoxuan, *Zhongguo de dixing* (Taibei: Shuqing, 1995), p. 281.

[92] See Wu Chen and He Naihua, "Liangwan nian lai Huabei pingyuan zhuyao heliu de hedao bianqian," in *Huabei pingyuan gu hedao yanjiu lunwenji*, ed. Wu Chen (Beijing: Zhongguo kexue jishu, 1991), pp. 137–38.

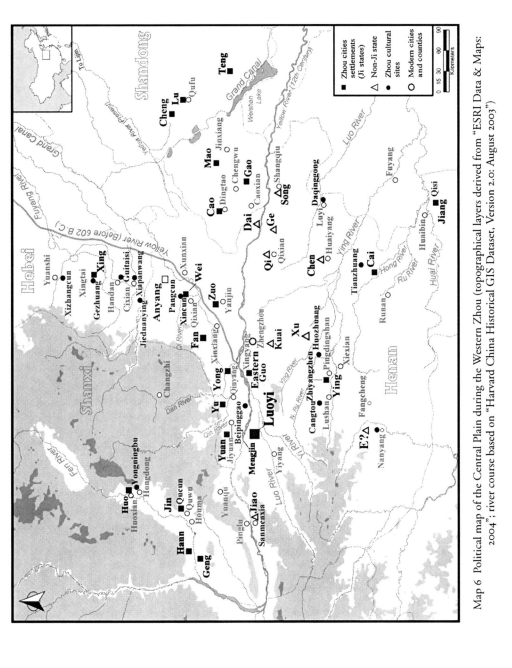

Map 6 Political map of the Central Plain during the Western Zhou (topographical layers derived from "ESRI Data & Maps: 2004"; river course based on "Harvard China Historical GIS Dataset, Version 2.0: August 2003")

difference in the ancient landscape of the eastern plain from what it is now.
The natural condition of the plain is by no means the same as the American
Midwest, for the ancient river beds have become parallel sand ridges as high
as 5–10 meters and as long as 40 kilometers. In eastern Henan, sand was
often carried away by the wind and accumulated in numerous sand hills
as high as 10–20 meters, and salinization has been a serious environmental
problem throughout history.[93] In addition to these features, the shift of the
Yellow River created another special feature in the landscape: the numerous
marshes on the alluvial plain. According to a study, about forty marshes
are mentioned in ancient texts by the end of Former Han, and the actual
number may have been close to 180.[94] It is imaginable that during the
Shang and the Western Zhou times the alluvial plain was much marshier,[95]
and recent archaeological and geoarchaeological research in eastern Henan
suggests that in ancient times human habitation was basically limited to
the hilltops.[96]

Route of communication

Owing to the mountainous topography of western Henan, the road that
connected the Wei River valley and the Luoyang plain, the power axis of
the Western Zhou state, was extremely difficult. The major ancient road,
which has not changed in the last 2,000 years, goes from Luoyang over the
lower loess hills south of the Yellow River, and then pierces the Xiaoshan
and Xiaoqinling ranges, entering the Wei River valley by way of present-day
Sanmenxia 三門峽 City (Fig. 11).[97] According to some studies, there was
another road going southwest to Yiyang 宜陽, and then passing through
the deep valleys in the south section of the Xiaoshan and merging with
the northern road at Shanxian 陝縣. Compared to the northern road, this
southern road is longer and more tortuous.[98] In Lingbao 靈寶 County the
road goes through a long and deep rift, the so-called "Container Valley"

[93] See *Henan sheng zhi: Quyu jianzhi zhi*, pp. 15–18, 35–38.

[94] Most of these marshes, e.g. the famous Dalu Marsh 大陸澤 in southern Hebei and the Juye Marsh
巨野澤 in western Shandong, gradually dried up after the Song dynasty. See Zou Yilin, "Lishi shiqi
Huabei dapingyuan huzhao bianqian shulue," *Lishi dili* 5 (1987), 25–39.

[95] It is agreed by climatologists that the Shang–early Western Zhou period was one of the warm episodes
in the past. Zhu Kezhen suggested that the annual average temperature in North China was 2 degrees
(centigrade) higher than today. See Zhu Kezhen, "Zhongguo jin wuqian nian lai qihou bianqian
de chubu yanjiu," *Kaogu xuebao* 1972.1, 15–38; Kenneth J. Hsu, "Did the Xinjiang Indo-Europeans
Leave Their Home because of Global Cooling?" in *The Bronze Age and Early Iron Age Peoples of
Eastern Central Asia*, vol. 2, ed. Victor Mair (Washington, DC: The Institute for the Study of Man,
1998), pp. 686–90.

[96] See *Yudong Qixian fajue baogao* (Beijing: Kexue, 2000), pp. 2–6; Jing Zhichun, "Geoarchaeological
Reconstruction of the Bronze Age Landscape of the Shangqiu Area, China," unpublished PhD
thesis, University of Minnesota (1994), pp. 57–66.

[97] See Lu Yun, "Zhanguo shiqi zhuyao lulu jiaotong chutan," in *Lishi dili yanjiu*, 1 (Shanghai: Fudan
daxue, 1986), pp. 37–40; Shi Nianhai, *Heshanji*, 4, pp. 165–68.

[98] See Wang Wenchu, "Xi'an Luoyang jian lulu jiaotong de lishi fazhan," in *Lishi dili yanjiu*, 1 (Shanghai:
Fudan daxue, 1986), pp. 12–16, 18–19.

Fig. 11 Road through the Xiaoshan Mountains in western Henan
(photograph by the author)

(Hangu 函谷), from which travelers could barely see the sky.[99] It is very
probable that this was also the major communication road during the
Western Zhou, and we have a number of accounts in Western Zhou bronze
inscriptions and texts that a trip between Luoyang and the two capitals Feng
and Hao would take a long time (see below, note 113 on p. 65). This suggests
that the political center of the Western Zhou state was virtually locked off
from the eastern plain, a major issue that the Zhou had to deal with.

In the east, communication between the Luoyang area and the eastern
plain was through the openings on each side of the Songshan Mountain:
in the north, it goes along the south bank of the Yellow River by way of
Xingyang 滎陽 which was historically a key point; in the south, it goes
through the flat valley of the Ying 潁 River and arrives at Pingdingshan
平頂山. The inscriptions suggest that both roads were in use during the
Western Zhou period. However, in the Shang–Western Zhou transition,
the most important road leading out of the Luoyang plain was probably that
which connected with the Shang capital, and this point is illustrated by the
geography of two pre-conquest campaigns recorded in the Zhou tradition.
The first was an attack led by King Wen on the state of Li 黎, located near
present-day Changzhi 長治, upstream in the valley of the Dan 丹 River, a
branch of the Qin 沁 River.[100] The second was an attack one year later on the

[99] This is the location of the "Container Valley" in the Warring States period. See Shi Nianhai,
   Heshanji, 4, pp. 165–66.
[100] This campaign is the subject of the "Xibo kan Li" 西伯戡黎 chapter of the *Shangshu*; see *Shangshu*,
   10, pp. 176–77 (James Legge, *The Chinese Classics, vol. 3: The Shoo King, or The Book of Historical*

state of Yu 邘, located near Qinyang 沁陽 in the lower Qin River region
(the site of the Zhou state Yu; see below, p. 72).[101] Both states were not far
from the Shang capital Anyang, and indeed Yu was located in the southern section of the long and narrow transitional belt between the Taihang
Mountains and the Yellow River. This location also corresponds well with
the route of the conquest campaign during which the Zhou troops evidently crossed the Yellow River at a place called Mengjin 盟津, located to the
north of Luoyang.[102] Thus, it is very likely that the three campaigns had traversed the same road that goes north from Luoyang and arrives at the Shang
capital through the southern section of the Taihang–Yellow River belt. This
was probably the most important transportation line through the most
populated area in East China during Shang and Western Zhou times.

Luoyi: the eastern administrative center

Although past archaeological discoveries of inscribed bronzes had long ago
confirmed the political importance of the present-day Luoyang area as the
site of the eastern administrative center Luoyi 洛邑 (and/or Chengzhou
成周), the specific location of the city remains one of the most opinion-
dividing problems in Western Zhou archaeology. Before 1949, three groups
of Western Zhou bronzes were discovered in Luoyang, fully testifying to
the high status of the site.[103] In the early 1950s, archaeologists discovered

---

Documents [Hong Kong: Hong Kong University Press, 1960], pp. 268–70). The lost Tang dynasty
(AD 618–907) geographical survey *Kuodi zhi* (quoted in the "Zhengyi" commentary to the *Shiji*
where the state is written as Qiguo 耆國) says that Li was located to the northwest of Licheng
County 黎城縣 of Tang, to the north of present-day Changzhi. See *Shiji*, 4, p. 118 (Nienhauser,
The Grand Scribe's Records, 1, p. 58).

[101] See *Shiji*, 4, p. 118 (Nienhauser, *The Grand Scribe's Records*, 1, p. 58). The *Shiji* account of the
campaign is supported by the Shang oracle bones that record Yu as one of the hunting grounds of
the Shang king, located to the west of the Shang capital. See Chen Mengjia, *Yinxu buci zongshu*
(Beijing: Kexue, 1956), pp. 260–62; Edward Shaughnessy, "Historical Geography and the Extent
of the Early Chinese Kingdoms," *Asia Major* 2.2 (1989), 10–12. Keightley used to follow Shima
Kunio to locate Yu to the northeast of Anyang, but recently has accepted the Qin River region as
the central area of the allied Shang groups including Yu. See Keightley, "The Late Shang State,"
pp. 538–44; *The Ancestral Landscape*, p. 57. The Han dynasty dictionary *Shuowen jiezi* indicates that
Yu was in Yewang County 野王縣 (present-day Qinyang) of Henei Commandery 河内郡; the Jin
dynasty (AD 265–316) writer Xu Guang (quoted in the "Jijie" commentary to the *Shiji*) says that it
was to the northwest of the county town. See *Shuowen jiezi*, 6b, p. 133; *Shiji*, 4, p. 118. The local
archaeologists identified Yu with an ancient walled site 15 kilometers to the northwest of Qinyang,
but no excavation was carried out to prove it. See *Henan sheng zhi: wenwu zhi* (Zhengzhou: Henan
renmin, 1994), p. 119.

[102] See *Shiji*, 4, p. 121 (Nienhauser, *The Grand Scribe's Records*, 1, p. 59). For an analysis of this conquest
campaign, see Shaughnessy, "'New' Evidence of the Zhou Conquest," pp. 66–67; "Western Zhou
History," pp. 307–8. The name of the ferry may be a later term that does not appear in the bronze
inscriptions, but it is quite logical for an army from the west to cross the river at this point where
the banks are relatively low and the river is narrow. In fact, the inscription of the He *zun* 何尊 (JC:
6014) mentions King Wu's presence in the Luoyang area on his way back from the Shang capital,
supporting a conquest trip that came across Mengjin.

[103] These include the famous Ling 令 vessels reportedly discovered in Mapo 馬坡 in 1929; the Chenchen
臣辰 vessels discovered in Mapo in the same year; the Jing 竸 bronzes reportedly from Miaogou 廟溝.

the walled enclosure of the "Royal City" (Wangcheng 王城) of the Eastern Zhou period, located on the banks of the Jian 澗 and Luo rivers (Map 7).[104] In the center of the walled city, about ten Western Zhou tombs were excavated.[105] However, later excavations indicate that the greatest concentration of Western Zhou remains is to the east, on the two banks of the Chan 滻 River. These include the excavation of as many as 348 tombs, together with another eighty-seven confirmed but not excavated at Beiyao 北窯, beside a deep gully that is called Pangjiagou 龐家溝 on the west side of the Chan River.[106] Close by to the south, in an area of more than 100,000 square meters, a major site of bronze workshops was located, not far from the east train station of Luoyang.[107] To the south of these two sites, at the center of the old town of Luoyang, four well-preserved chariot-burials were recently excavated.[108] On the east bank of the Chan River, in 1952, more than twenty Western Zhou tombs were excavated in four different locations.[109] In the most recently excavated tomb C5M906 at Yangwen 楊文 two bronzes cast by Shaobo Hu 召伯虎, a well-known minister at the late Western Zhou court, were found together with four other bronzes.[110]

The construction of Luoyi is documented in two chapters of the *Shangshu* and the records are supported by other textual sources and the inscription of the He *zun* 珂尊 (JC: 6014).[111] However, the rationale behind the construction is found in the historical circumstances of the post-conquest period.

Of these bronzes, the long text on the Ling *fangyi* 令方彝 (JC: 9901) is the most important. The inscription describes the mission of Mingbao 明保, a son of the Duke of Zhou, to the eastern capital, where he was greeted by a large number of officials as well as rulers from the numerous regional states. This inscription fully demonstrates the importance of the site as the eastern administrative and military center of the Western Zhou state. For a list of bronzes discovered in the Luoyang region before 1940, see *Jinwen fenyu bian* (1940), 3, pp. 15–16.

104 See *Kaogu xuebao* 1959.2, 13–36.

105 See *Luoyang Zhongzhoulu (Xi gongduan)* (Beijing: Kexue, 1959), p. 4.

106 See *Wenwu* 1972.10, 20–28; 1981.7, 52–64. The formal archaeological report on the excavation at Beiyao has been published recently; see *Luoyang Beiyao Xi Zhou mu* (Beijing: Wenwu, 1999).

107 See *Kaogu* 1983.5, 430–41.   108 See *Kaogu* 1988.1, 15–23.

109 These tombs were divided by the authors of the original report into two groups: "Burials of the Shang people" and "Burials of the Zhou people." See *Kaogu xuebao* 9 (1955), 91–116. By today's standards, the so-called "Burials of the Shang people" are actually early (some middle) Western Zhou tombs, while the "Burials of the Zhou people" are, judging from the published chariot fittings, late Western Zhou tombs.

110 See *Kaogu* 1995.9, 788–91. For an overview of the Luoyang sites, see also Mochii Yasutaka, "Sei Shū jidai no Seishū chūdō kōbō ni tsuite," in *Sei Shū seidōki to sono kokka*, ed. Matsumaru Michio (Tokyo: Tōkyō daigaku, 1980), pp. 185–99.

111 See "Shaogao" 召誥 and "Luogao" 洛誥 in *Shangshu*, 15, pp. 211–17. In the *Current Bamboo Annals*, the construction of Luoyi began in the fifth year of the Duke of Zhou's regency. The He *zun* records that King Cheng established his residence in Chengzhou in his fifth year; most scholars consider that this was the fifth year after the Duke of Zhou handed over the government. See *Zhushu jinian*, 2, p. 4 (James Legge, *The Chinese Classics, vol. 3: The Shoo King, or The Book of Historical Documents* [1865; reprinted Hong Kong: Hong Kong University Press, 1960], Prolegomena, p. 145). For the inscription of the He *zun*, see Tang Lan, "He *zun* mingwen jieshi," *Wenwu* 1976.1, 60–61. On the construction of Luoyi, see Chen Gongrou, "Xi Zhou jinwen zhong de Xinyi Chengzhou yu Wangcheng," in *Qingzhu Su Binqi xiansheng kaogu wushiwu nian lunwenji* (Beijing: Wenwu, 1989), pp. 386–87.

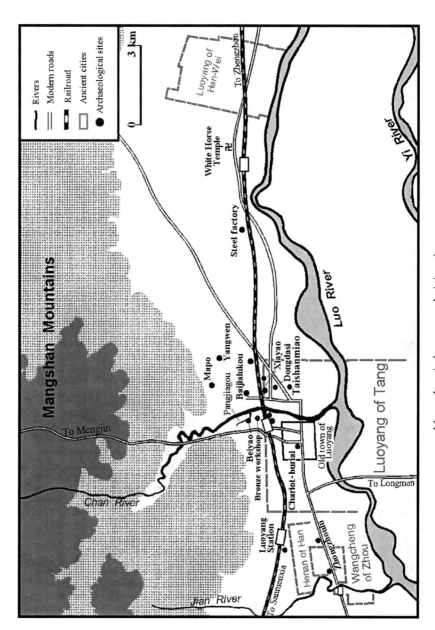

Map 7 Luoyi: the eastern administrative center

After the capture of the Shang capital, King Wu returned to the west, leaving his brothers, Guanshu 管叔, Caishu 蔡叔, and probably also Huoshu 霍叔, stationed near the Shang capital to watch over the Shang people who were left to the rule of Wu Geng 武庚, a son of the last Shang king. These were called the "Three Overseers" (*sanjian* 三監) by later historians.[112] However, this occupation policy proved to be a complete failure when, after the death of King Wu, Guanshu and Caishu joined Wu Geng and rebelled against the Zhou court in the hands of the Duke of Zhou, who took up the actual role of regent overshadowing the young King Cheng (r. 1042/35–1006 BC). It took the Zhou some three years to put down this rebellion, and the rebels were either killed or captured. Despite the eventual victory of the "Second Conquest," it had been proven crystal clear to the Zhou that it was virtually impossible to maintain their superiority in the eastern plain from their base in the Wei River valley without a major political and administrative establishment in the east. The trouble that they had just come through was partly a problem of miscommunication and therefore mistrust between the Zhou commanders stationed on the eastern plain and the new leadership in the capital. We have reliable information that such communication in the Western Zhou period would take forty to sixty days to traverse the difficult mountain roads in western Henan.[113] And when rebellions broke out, it might take nearly two months for the Zhou to move their forces out of the Wei River valley and deploy them on the eastern plain before the situation went out of control. Thus, the construction of an eastern administrative center seemed inevitable if they were to maintain their rule in the east.

While the construction of Luoyi is fully explainable from the grand strategy of the Western Zhou state, the controversial point is whether one city or two cities were built. Most historians believe that there were two cities: Luoyi (also called Wangcheng) located between the Jian and Chan

---

[112] The institution of the "Three Overseers" involves a traditional debate. While some scholars think that there were three brothers left to watch over the Shang heartland, others maintain that there were only two: Guanshu and Caishu. For the first view, see for instance Sun Xingyan, *Shangshu jinguwen zhushu*, 2 vols. (Beijing: Zhonghua, 1986), p. 597. For the second view, see Cui Shu, *Cui Dongbi yishu*, ed. Gu Jiegang (Shanghai: Shanghai Guji, 1983), pp. 205–6; Liu Qiyu, "Zhou chu de Sanjian yu Bei Yong Wey sanguo ji Wey Kangshu fengdi de wenti," *Lishi dili* 2 (1982), 66–81. Modern scholars have not been able to solve this issue.

[113] We have three accounts on this point. (1) The newly discovered Jinhou Su *bianzhong* 晉侯蘇編鐘 (JL: 35–50) records that it took a Zhou king forty-four days, from day *wuwu* (no. 55 in the sixty-day *ganzhi* circle) in the first month to day *renyin* (no. 39) in the second, to travel from the capital Hao to Chengzhou. See Ma Chengyuan, "Jinhou Su bianzhong," *Shanghai bowuguan jikan* 7 (1996), 1–17. Jaehoon Shim, "The 'Jinhou Su *Bianzhong*' Inscription and Its Significance," *Early China* 22 (1997), 49. (2) The Ling *fangyi* records that Mingbao traveled the same distance in fifty-six days from *dinghai* (no. 24) in the eighth month to *guiwei* (no. 20) in the tenth month. (3) The "Shaogao" chapter in the *Shangshu* records that the Duke of Shao completed the trip between the two capitals in fourteen days from *yiwei* (no. 32) in the second month to *wushen* (no. 45) in the third month. See *Shangshu*, 15, p. 211 (Legge, *The Shoo King*, pp. 420–33). The two inscriptional accounts roughly agree with Shaughnessy's reconstruction of the Zhou conquest campaign which took the Zhou troops sixty days to reach the Shang capital; see Shaughnessy, "'New' Evidence on the Zhou Conquest," pp. 70–71. The third account will agree if there was an intercalary month between the second and third months, and that is likely.

Rivers; and Chengzhou located to the east of the Chan River.[114] Lending
support to this idea, the ancient geographers identified Luoyi with the site
of Henan County 河南縣 and Chengzhou with the site of Luoyang County
洛陽縣 of the Former Han dynasty (206 BC–AD 8), which was located some
20 kilometers to the east, roughly corresponding with the Later Han (AD 25–
220) capital Luoyang (Map 7).[115] However, the Luoyang archaeologists who
are working in the field overwhelmingly suggest that Luoyi and Chengzhou
were virtually one city, and that it must have been located on the banks
of the Chan River in the east.[116] While this seems to have been supported
by the current archaeological evidence that is mainly concentrated on the
two banks of the Chan River, the locally discovered early Western Zhou
inscription on the Ling *fangyi* (JC: 9901) says quite explicitly that the
minister Mingbao performed sacrifices in both Chengzhou and Wang 王,
which reasonably refers to Wangcheng. The inscriptional evidence seems to
work well with the ancient geographical works to suggest that Wangcheng
and Chengzhou were different cities. Therefore, scholars working with
inscriptions tend to think that they were twin cities in the Luoyang region
during the Western Zhou.[117] Perhaps the specific location of Chengzhou
has to await future archaeological discovery.

Discovering the regional Zhou states

What had given the Western Zhou state a new geopolitical structure and
a real stabilizing power was the establishment of the Zhou regional states,
widely distributed on the eastern plain and its surrounding areas that were
either formally Shang or non-Shang strongholds. The discovery of some
of these regional states ranked among the most important archaeological
findings of the 1980s and 1990s, and the important point for the present
study is that, when taken together, they show us how these regional polities

[114] The "Luogao" chapter of the *Shangshu* says that before carrying out the construction the Zhou
performed divination at two locations: one between the Jian River and the Chan River and the
other to the east of the Chan River. In both places, the result was auspicious provided that the
future cities would be constructed near the Luo River; *Shangshu*, 15, p. 214 (Legge, *The Shoo King*,
pp. 434–52). Sun Xingyan, one of the best Qing classicists of the eighteenth century, considered that
Wangcheng was constructed by the Duke of Shao, and Chengzhou to the east of the Chan River
was constructed by the Duke of Zhou; see Sun Xingyan, *Shangshu jinguwen zhushu*, pp. 404–5.

[115] See *Hanshu*, 28, p. 1,555. The sixth-century geographer Li Daoyuan also indicated two separate sites,
but he was himself confused about which should be called Wangcheng and which should be called
Chengzhou. See *Shuijing zhu*, 15, pp. 495–96.

[116] See Ye Wansong and Yu Fuwei, "Guanyu Xi Zhou Luoyi chengzhi de tansuo," in *Xi Zhou shi yanjiu*
(Monograph of *Renwen zazhi* 2; Xi'an, 1984), pp. 317–20; *Luoyang Beiyao Xi Zhou mu*, p. 369.

[117] See Tang Lan, *Tang Lan xiansheng jinwen lunji*, p. 11. Among other paleographers, for example,
Chen Mengjia accepted Tang's reading of "Wang" as Wangcheng, and systematically examined
the problem and concluded that there must have been two different towns; see Chen Mengjia,
"Xi Zhou tongqi duandai," 2, pp. 90, 135–38. For recent analyses of the inscriptional and textual
evidence for the two cities, see Chen Gongrou, "Xi Zhou jinwen zhong de Xinyi Chengzhou yu
Wangcheng," pp. 386–97; Zhou Yongzhen, "Guanyu Luoyang Zhou cheng," in *Luoyang kaogu sishi
nian*, ed. Ye Wansong (Beijing: Kexue, 1996), pp. 227–29.

fit both into the historical context of the great early Western Zhou expansion and into the landscape of East China of which they soon became an integral part.

As early as 1932–33, more than eighty Western Zhou tombs and chariot-burials were excavated by the Academia Sinica at Xincun 辛村, Xunxian 濬縣, on the east bank of the Qi 淇 River, about 40 kilometers from the former Shang capital Anyang.[118] These include eight large tombs with ramps, indicating the high status of their occupants. The bronzes from these tombs bear inscriptions that indicate "Ruler" (*hou* 侯) and "Wey" 衛, the local state; one from a large late Western Zhou tomb (no. 5) bears an inscription that was cast by the "Lady of Wey" (*Wey furen* 衛夫人). More interestingly, an inscription from tomb no. 60 mentions the official visit of a Wey ruler to the Zhou capital in Shaanxi.[119] While these discoveries explicitly identify the cemetery with one of the Zhou regional states, Wey 衛, the received textual records explain to us about the state's origin. The state of Wey was granted to Kangshu Feng 康叔封, a younger brother of King Wu. The appointment was so important, mainly because of its location near the former Shang capital with the mission to govern the recently reconquered Shang subjects, that two authentic Western Zhou chapters in the *Shangshu* are devoted to the documentation of the appointment.[120] Moreover, we actually have an inscription, the Kanghou *gui* 康侯簋 (JC: 4059), that states explicitly that after the king attacked the Shang capital he granted Kanghou a territory in Wey.[121] As for the location of the state of Wey, the received textual records constantly point to the areas along the Qi River in northern Henan,[122] and the Han dynasty geographers located it in the territory of the Zhaoge County 朝歌縣 of Han, which corresponds approximately with present-day Qixian 淇縣, the neighboring county of Xunxian.[123] In fact, the cemetery in Xincun is located right on the section of the Qi River that runs on the border between the two counties. Only 1 kilometer to the west of Xincun, at Pangcun 龐村, an early Western Zhou tomb containing

[118] See *Xunxian Xincun* (Beijing: Kexue, 1964), pp. 1, 72. This book, though incomplete because the artifacts were shipped to Taiwan when the author was still in the midst of writing, is the only archaeological report on the cemetery. The artifacts were also published in another book: *Xunxian yiqi* (Henan tongzhi guan, 1937), pp. 1–75.

[119] See *Xunxian Xincun*, pls. 60–61, 66, 69.

[120] These are the "Kanggao" 康誥 and "Jiugao" 酒誥 chapters; *Shangshu*, 14, pp. 202–7 (Legge, *The Shoo King*, pp. 381–412).

[121] Among the transmitted bronzes, besides the Kanghou *gui*, there were also Kanghou *fu* 康侯斧 (JC: 11778) and Kanghou *dao* 康侯刀 (JC: 11812); both were found in Xunxian long before the excavation in Xincun. See *Jinwen fenyu bian*, p. 3.12.

[122] For instance, the poems in the "Weyfeng" 衛風 section of the *Shijing*, presumably gathered from the state of Wey, constantly mention the Qi River and the Yellow River. See *Shijing*, 3.2–3, pp. 320–28 (Waley, *The Book of Songs*, pp. 84–89). The *Shiji* says that Wey was located between the Qi River and the Yellow River. See *Shiji*, 37, p. 1,589. The *Zuozhuan* (second year of Duke Min) also mentions that, defeated by the Di 狄 troops in 660 BC, the Wey refugees crossed the Yellow River and fled to the east; see *Zuozhuan*, 11, p. 1,788.

[123] See *Hanshu*, 28, p. 1554.

fifteen bronzes was discovered in 1961, probably also related to the state of Wey.[124]

To the north, in southern Hebei, multiple Western Zhou sites have been excavated at Xingtai 邢台, at Handan 邯鄲, and at two locations in Cixian 磁縣.[125] In 1978, a mid-Western Zhou tomb was found at Xizhangcun 西張村, about 70 kilometers to the north of Xingtai. The inscription of the Chenjian *gui* 臣諫簋 (JC: 4237) from this tomb mentions a battle in which the ruler of the state of Xing 邢 engaged the Rong people at a place called Di 軧.[126] In fact, the tomb was located about 20 kilometers to the north of the present-day Zhi 泜 River, and close to the north bank of the ancient course of the Zhi River. Given the apparent similarities between the two graphs and the geographical coincidence, it can hardly be a mistaken conclusion that the modern name Zhi maintains the locale's archaic name Di that was used during the Western Zhou,[127] as the modern name Xingtai was certainly derived from the name of the ancient state Xing. These are good examples of the transmission of place-names from the Western Zhou to modern times. The particular discovery supports the location of Xing in the present-day Xingtai area, where a bronze cast by the "Wife of the Ruler of Xing" (*Xinghou furen* 邢侯夫人) in the northern Qi dynasty (AD 550–577) was discovered.[128] Important evidence was brought to light again in 1993 when over 200 tombs, mostly of Western Zhou date, were excavated at Gezhuang 葛莊, on the western edge of Xingtai City. Owing to the heavy looting in historical times before the exacavation, very few inscribed bronzes could still be found in the tomb pits, but given the previous discovery of Xing-related bronzes from the area and in the surroundings, it is very likely that the cemetery belonged to the state of Xing, and the four large tombs with ramp-ways are probably burials of Xing rulers and their spouses. The majority of the Gezhuang tombs can be dated to the early and mid-Western Zhou, with a few to the late Western Zhou.[129] The state of Xing is known to have been founded by a son of the Duke of Zhou (see below, p. 71), and there has been a strong and continuing textual tradition that locates Xing in the area of present-day Xingtai.[130] Importantly, some of the tombs discovered in Xingtai can be securely dated to the very early phase

---

[124] See *Wenwu ziliao congkan* 3 (1980), 35–38.

[125] For these findings, see *Wenwu* 1960.7, 69; *Kaogu* 1959.10, 534–35; *Kaogu xuebao* 1975.1, 99–110; *Kaogu* 1974.6, 363.

[126] See *Kaogu* 1979.1, 23–26.

[127] Or perhaps the character *di* referred to a place or settlement, while the character *zhi* referred to the river that ran by it. See Li Xueqin, *Xinchu qingtongqi yanjiu*, p. 65.

[128] See *Jinwen fenyu bian*, p. 2.12.

[129] I had the opportunity to observe these new materials in summer 1998, and therefore am able to note my primary reflections on them. However, since the Gezhuang materials have not been fully published, detailed comments are to be avoided.

[130] For example, the "Geographical Records" chapter of the *Hanshu* says that Xing was located in Xiangguo County 襄國縣 of the state of Zhao 趙 during the Han dynasty. In his commentary to the *Zuozhuan*, Du Yu (AD 222–284) indicates that Xing was located in Xiangguo County of the Guangping Commandery 廣平郡 of his time. Put on a historical map, both places correspond well

Fig. 12 Cemetery of the state of Ying in Pingdingshan (photograph by the author)

of the early Western Zhou; this supports the date of Xing's establishment at the beginning of the dynasty, probably during the regency of the Duke of Zhou.

In the southern half of the eastern plain, the most sizeable archaeological excavation relevant to the Western Zhou period has been carried out on an earth ridge located to the west of Zhiyangzhen 滍陽鎮 in the western district of Pingdingshan City (Fig. 12). Between 1979 and 1984, four Denggong *gui* 鄧公簋 vessels were found in the cemetery; the bronzes were cast by the ruler of Deng for his daughter Ying Man 應嫚 as marriage gifts, indicating that the local cemetery probably belongs to her husband's state named Ying 應, as indicated by her name.[131] This point became quite clear in 1982 when a mid-Western Zhou tomb was excavated at the same site, containing bronzes cast by an "Official of Ying" (Ying Shi 應事).[132] From 1986 to 1992, archaeologists excavated more than 130 tombs at the site.[133] Three of these tombs, nos. 1, 84, and 95, have been formally reported. Judging from the bronzes and pottery unearthed from these tombs, no. 1 should be dated to the beginning of the Eastern Zhou. Tomb no. 95, which is clearly earlier

with present-day Xingtai. See *Hanshu*, 28, p. 1,631; *Zuozhuan*, 3, p. 1,727. On the location of Xing, see also Zhu Youzeng, *Shi dili zheng*, in *Huang Qing jingjie* 1039–45 (1829), p. 1,078; Chen Pan, *Chunqiu dashi biao lieguo juexing ji cunmie biao zhuanyi* (Taipei: Academia Sinica, 1969), p. 183.

[131] See *Kaogu* 1981.4, 370; *Kaogu yu wenwu* 1983.1, 109; *Kaogu* 1985.3, 284. There were a number of rules governing the way in which a woman was referred to during the Western Zhou. While these rules will be discussed in detail in chapter 3 (see note 126 on p. 186), it will suffice here to note that when a father names his married daughter, he normally calls her by the name of her husband's state or lineage (to be differentiated from other married daughters he may have), followed by her (and his) own surname.

[132] See *Wenwu* 1984.12, 29–31.

[133] See *Huaxia kaogu* 1988.1, 30–44; 1992.3, 92–102; *Wenwu* 1998.9, 4–17.

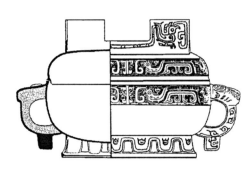

Fig. 13 Bronze *xu* cast by the Ruler of Ying from tomb no. 84 in Pingdingshan
(from *Wenwu* 1998.9, 11, fig. 10; 12, fig. 11)

than no. 1, should be dated to the end of the mid-Western Zhou, containing
five bronzes cast by Ying Bo 應伯 with others by *gong* 公 and four by *hou* 侯.
Tomb no. 84, in which five bronzes cast by either Yinghou Cheng 應侯再
or Cheng 再 were found (Fig. 13), is much earlier, and can be dated to
the early phase of the mid-Western Zhou. The archaeologists noted that
the cemetery is very close to a local landmark traditionally known as the
"Town of Ying" (Yingcheng 應城) located at the edge of Zhiyangzhen,
in the area suggested by Han dynasty geographical works for the state of
Ying.[134]

The locations of the above three states in the areas indicated by archaeology are certainly not random. The state of Wey, located in the vicinity
of the former Shang capital Anyang, was established with the purpose of
converting the Shang subjects into obedient new citizens of the Zhou state,
an objective that is clearly stated in the Zhou texts. The location of Xing
in the north section of the Taihang–Yellow River belt blocks the way to
Wey, and protected the Central Plain from northern attacks as so manifestly demonstrated by the inscription on the locally excavated Chenjian

---

[134] See *Huaxia kaogu* 1988.1, 43–44. The "Geographical Records" chapter of the *Hanshu* says that there
was a Yingxiang 應鄉 located in Fucheng County 父城縣 of Yingchuan Commandery 潁川郡 of
the Han dynasty, which was located to the west of present-day Pingdingshan. However, the Jin
commentator Du Yu says that Ying was located in Chengfu County 城父縣 of Xiangyang 襄陽 in
Hubei province. See *Hanshu*, 28, p. 1,560; *Zuozhuan*, 15, p. 1,817. Modern scholars have noted that
Du Yu was wrong while the *Hanshu* was right; see Zhou Yongzhen, "Xi Zhou shiqi de Ying guo,
Deng guo tongqi jiqi dili weizhi," *Kaogu* 1982.1, 49–50.

Table 1.1 *The regional Ji states established during the early Western Zhou according to the* Zuozhuan *(twenty-fourth year of Duke Xi).*

Sons of	Regional states
King Wen	Guan 管, Cai 蔡, Cheng 郕, Huo 霍, Lu 魯, Wey 衛, Mao 毛, Dan 聃 Gao 邵, Yong 雍, Cao 曹, Teng 滕, Bi 畢, Yuan 原, Feng 酆, Xun 郇
King Wu	Yu 邘, Jin 晉, Ying 應, Hann 韓
Duke of Zhou	Fan 凡, Jiang 蔣, Xing 邢, Mao 茅, Zuo 胙, Zhai 祭

gui. The state of Ying, on the other hand, was located near the exit of the Ying River valley connecting with the Luoyang plain and right at the entrance to the Nanyang basin, controlling the road to the middle Yangzi region. Putting this into historical context with respect to the landscape of the eastern plain, one can hardly overlook their strategic significance. These three states happened to be the only regional states in their areas for which sizeable archaeological excavations were conducted, but they were certainly not the only regional Zhou states that existed in their time on the eastern plain. Although it is indeed hard to determine how many such regional states were established at the beginning of the Western Zhou, our sources agree on the simple point that their number must have been quite large. An account in the *Zuozhuan* (twenty-eighth year of Duke Zhao) states that forty regional states of the Ji 姬 – a surname marking them as of royal descent – were established at the beginning of the Western Zhou.[135] Another account in the *Xunzi* text suggests that seventy-one regional states were established during the regency of the Duke of Zhou, of which fifty-three were ruled by royal descendents.[136] There is little ground at present for us to evaluate the accuracy of these two figures, which could be much exaggerated. In comparison, our third account from the *Zuozhuan* (twenty-fourth year of Duke Xi) may be closer to reality because it gives a much smaller number and mentions them one after another by their specific names (see Table 1.1).[137]

A total of twenty-six such states, including the above three, are mentioned here as states founded by members of the two generations of the Zhou royal family. Among them, sixteen, Cai, Cheng, Lu, Wey, Gao, Yong, Cao, Teng,

[135] "Ji" is the surname of the Zhou royal lineage; See *Zuozhuan*, 52, p. 2119.
[136] See *Xunzi*, 4, p. 300.
[137] This account is found in a speech purportedly given by Fu Chen 富辰, a minister at the court of King Xiang of Zhou (r. 651–619 BC), admonishing the king not to carry out military attack on the Ji state Zheng. Therein, the establishment of the Zhou regional states was looked back upon as a historical precedent that illustrates to the speaker the brotherly relationship between the many Ji-surnamed states. See *Zuozhuan*, 15, p. 1,817. Although the reliability of the speeches in the *Zuozhuan* has been recently questioned by Schaberg, the specific list given here would qualify as that kind of "detailed information in historical anecdotes . . . whose accuracy we have little reason to doubt"; see Schaberg, *The Patterned Past*, p. 26.

Yu, Ying, Fan, Jiang, Xing, Mao, Zuo, and Zhai (exclusive of Guan which was eliminated by the Duke of Zhou during the second conquest), were probably located on the eastern plain and its peripheral areas, while the rest were located in either the Fen River or the Wei River valley. Except for the above-mentioned three states whose excavation provided a solid focal point to the reconstruction of this possible network, few of them have been subject to serious archaeological research. Therefore, our information on their location is largely derived from scattered and unplanned archaeological discoveries of inscribed bronzes, assisted by the ancient geographical records. For some of these states, until archaeological excavations bring to light definite evidence, what we can say here is meant only as "probabilities." However, the actual archaeological excavations of the above three states as well as many others located beyond the Central Plain (see examples in appendix 1) have already testified to the value of the early geographical records, especially records passed down from the Han dynasty, in pinpointing quite accurately the areas in which these states were located. Putting this into a larger historical context that is shared by the archaeological evidence we already have, these early geographical records can help us significantly to understand the geopolitical construction of the eastern plain. In fact, I believe that the locations of these sixteen states, when taken together, reveal some very interesting patterns, carefully constructed into the landscape of East China.

First, in the former Shang capital area in the Taihang–Yellow River belt, besides the state of Wey, which was ruled by a younger brother of King Wu, two other states, Fan and Zuo, ruled by two sons of the Duke of Zhou, were established in Huixian 輝縣 and Yanjin 延津.[138] In fact, the two states may have served as satellites of Wey, ruled by an uncle of their own founders, forming an interesting triangle. In the southernmost section of the Taihang–Yellow River belt, which had also been the former stronghold of the Shang, a number of Western Zhou sites have been reported but not formally excavated.[139] According to the ancient geographical records, three Ji states were established in this area: a son of King Wu was installed at the site of the former Shang state Yu in Qinyang; to either side of Yu, two of King Wu's brothers were established at Yuan and Yong, probably to assist their nephew.[140] These three states not only guarded the north gate of Luoyi

[138] In his commentary to the *Zuozhuan* (seventh year of Duke Ying) that mentions both states, Du Yu says that Fan was located to the east of Gong County 共縣 in Ji Commandery 汲郡, pointing to present-day Huixian; see *Zuozhuan*, 4, p. 1,732. As for Zuo, Du Yu says that it was to the southwest of Yan County 燕縣 of Dong Commandery 東郡. See *Zuozhuan*, 15, p. 1,817. From Du Yu's commentary, the Qing scholar Jiang Yong (AD 1681–1762) indicates that Zuo was in the former Zuocheng County 胙城縣, which was then incorporated into Ji County 汲縣 during Qing, pointing to the area to the east of present-day Xinxiang 新鄉 and north of Yanjin. See Jiang Yong, *Chunqiu dili kaoshi*, in *Huang Qing jingjie* 252–255 (Guangzhou: Xuehaitang, 1829), 253, p. 8.

[139] See, for instance, the Beipinggao 北平皋 site in Wenxian 溫縣; *Wenwu* 1982.7, 7.

[140] Du Yu says that Yong was in Shanyang County 山陽縣 of Henei Commandery 河內郡 of the third century, which is present-day Xiuwu 修武; *Zuozhuan*, 15, p. 1,817. Regarding Yuan, Du Yu says it was to the west of Qinshui County 沁水縣; *Zuozhuan*, 4, p. 1,737. The Qing scholar Jiang Yong

and Chengzhou, but also blocked the way into the Fen River valley (see below, pp. 83–84), from which attacks could also be made on the Wei River valley.

A bronze *gui* of the Spring and Autumn period cast by a member of the state of Cao, Caobo Di 曹伯狄 (JC: 4019), was found in an unknown location in the adjacent Shandong region,[141] and another bronze *pan* of the same period cast probably by the ruler of Cao as dowry for his daughter was found in Huaiyang 淮陽.[142] These bronzes were probably carried away from their place of origin in Cao, which according to the geographical records was located in present-day Dingtao 定陶.[143] In fact, Cao was one of the three Ji states located in the eastern part of the eastern plain mentioned in the *Zuozhuan* list; they displayed a triangle in the south of the ancient Juye Marsh. While Cao and Gao were granted to two brothers of King Wu, the third state, Mao 茅, was granted to their nephew, a son of the Duke of Zhou.[144] These three states were located midway to the Shandong region, and probably had in their time provided footholds for the Zhou troops and officials traveling frequently between Luoyi and the Zhou "Far East." The historical records show that during the Eastern Zhou period this road was frequently taken by the envoys going back and forth between the Zhou court and the eastern states.[145] Along this road to the east and extending to the foothills of western Shandong, field archaeological works have confirmed the locations of two Ji states in the *Zuozhuan* list: Lu, in present-day Qufu 曲阜, was established by the eldest son of the Duke of Zhou; Teng, in present-day Tengxian 滕縣, was ruled by an uncle of the ruler of Lu. To the north of Lu, the geographical records indicate that another state, Cheng, also included in the *Zuozhuan* list, was located in Ningyang 寧陽, being ruled by another uncle of the Lu ruler (see appendix 1).

In the southern part of the Central Plain, the state of Ying was located in Pingdingshan. To its west, a group of early Western Zhou bronzes was found in Lushan 魯山 in 1951.[146] About 40 kilometers to the east, another

suggests that the Yuanxiang 原鄉 located to the northwest of Jiyuan 濟源 was the site of Yuan; Jiang Yong, *Chunqiu dili kaoshi*, 252, p. 9. Yuan was annexed by the state of Jin in 635 BC, recorded in the *Zuozhuan*.

[141] See Chen Banghuai, "Caobo Di gui kaoshi," *Wenwu* 1980.5, 27, 67.

[142] See *Zhongyuan wenwu* 1981.2, 59.

[143] The "Geographical Records" chapter of the *Hanshu* says that Dingtao County 定陶縣 of Jiyin Commandery 濟陰郡 of the Han dynasty was the state of Cao, where a younger brother of King Wu, Zhenduo 振鐸, was established; *Hanshu*, 28, p. 1,571. Jiang Yong indicates that the ancient town of Cao is 2 kilometers to the northwest of Dingtao; see Jiang Yong, *Chunqiu dili kaoshi*, 252, p. 12.

[144] Du Yu says that the ancient town of northern Gao was to the southeast of Chengwu County 城武縣 of Jiyin Commandery in the third century; *Zuozhuan*, 5, p. 1,741. See also Chen Pan, *Chunqiu dashi biao ji lieguo juexing*, p. 196. As for the location of Mao, Du Yu says that it was in Maoxiang 茅鄉 to the west of Changyi County 昌邑縣 of his time; see *Zuozhuan*, 5, p. 1,817. Jiang Yong indicates that the town of Changyi is 20 kilometers to the northwest of present-day Jinxiang 金鄉; Jiang Yong, *Chunqiu dili kaoshi*, 253, p. 8.

[145] See Shi Nianhai, *Heshanji*, vol. 1 (Beijing: Sanlian, 1963), p. 71.

[146] See *Wenwu cankao ziliao* 1958.5, 73.

early Western Zhou tomb was excavated at Huozhuang 霍庄 in Xiangxian 襄縣 in 1975.[147] Since these bronzes lack identifiable inscriptions, their home state is unknown.[148] In addition to Ying, the ancient geographical records locate two other Ji states, Cai and Jiang, to the southern part of the plain. In 1956, an early Western Zhou tomb containing nine bronzes was excavated in Shangcai 上蔡, about 20 kilometers from the ancient town believed to be the center of Cai.[149] As for Jiang, founded by another son of the Duke of Zhou, the ancient geographical records point to present-day Huaibin 淮濱.[150] The decision to establish these states in the upper Huai River region must have been made in view of the enemies of Zhou in the lower Huai River region.

These sixteen Ji-surnamed states, when put on a map, display some very interesting settlement patterns (Map 6). First, they were located in groups of three, forming four discernible triplets, either as triangles or in linear formation. Second, they tended to be situated at the edge of the alluvial plain where the richest agricultural land was located, rather than at the center of the plain where the flood of the Yellow River very much affected the life of man. As indicated earlier, there may have been other Ji states that the *Zuozhuan* list does not include, such as Eastern Guo located at the east gate of Luoyi,[151] but the fact that the above sixteen states are mentioned together in a list suggests that they may have belonged to the same class, or were of comparable importance. As long as we recognize the list as a single and integrated record, we cannot dismiss these patterns. Moreover, the *Zuozhuan* text does not suggest any preconceived context in which the geopolitical triplets can be used to support the speaker's political agenda; it is only when we examine the list against our geographical records that the patterns become evident. The historical geographer Tan Qixiang has noted that from the Neolithic era down to the Spring and Autumn period

---

[147] See *Wenwu* 1977.8, 13–16.

[148] Ma Shizhi considers that Ying's territory stretched from Pingdingshan to Xiangxian, Baofeng 寶豐, Lushan, and Xiexian 葉縣 areas, suggesting that these bronzes could be related to the state of Ying. But there is no proof of this. See Ma Shizhi, "Ying guo tongqi jiqi xiangguan wenti," *Zhongyuan wenwu* 1986.1, 60.

[149] See *Wenwu cankao ziliao* 1957.11, 63, 66–69. According to the *Shiji* genealogy, the founder of Cai was a son of Caishu who joined Guanshu in rebellion against the Zhou court and was exiled; *Shiji*, 35, p. 1,565. The "Geographical Records" chapter of the *Hanshu* says that Cai was located in Shangcai 上蔡縣 of Runan Commandery 汝南郡 and this location is accepted by most historical geographers; see *Hanshu*, 28, p. 1,562; Chen Pan, *Chunqiu dashi biao ji lieguo juexing*, p. 25. The local archaeologists of Henan report that the ancient town of Cai is located on the west side of the town of present-day Shangcai, but no excavation has been conducted. See *Henan sheng zhi: wenwu zhi*, p. 117.

[150] Du Yu suggests that Jiang was located in Qisi County 期思縣 of Yiyang Commandery 弋陽郡 of the third century, which is present-day Huaibin; see *Zuozhuan*, 15, p. 1,817. The local archaeologists of Henan identify a walled enclosure as the site of Qisi of the third century, located 15 kilometers to the southeast of present-day Huaibin; see *Henan sheng zhi: wenwu zhi*, p. 116.

[151] Eastern Guo is said to have been founded by one of King Wen's brothers; the history of Guo will be discussed in detail in chapter 5. The "Geographical Records" chapter of the *Hanshu* indicates that Eastern Guo was in Xingyang County 榮陽縣 of Henan Commandery 河南郡 of the Han dynasty; see *Hanshu*, 28, p. 1,549.

there had continuously been a vacuum of human habitation on the great plain of southern and central Hebei; it was only from the Warring States period that some settlements began to appear in the area.[152] Although this may not be exactly true in the southern part of the plain where Neolithic–Shang sites were found on some originally high mounds now buried underground,[153] there seems little doubt that the center of the alluvial plain was much less favorable for human habitation than the transitional belt on its periphery.

It is in the central area of the Central Plain in eastern Henan that the ancient geographical records locate a concentration of some non-Ji states such as Song 宋, Qi 杞, Ge 葛, and Dai 戴, and in the southwest part, Chen 陳, Xu 許, and Kuai 鄶.[154] The recent archaeological excavations jointly conducted by Harvard University and the Institute of Archaeology, CASS, in 1996–97 uncovered a large Eastern Zhou walled enclosure buried 10 meters below the surface of Shangqiu City, and the archaeological team identified it with the capital of Song.[155] Although this does not prove that Song must have been located in the same place during the Western Zhou as the geographical records would suggest, it argues strongly for it. Nonetheless, a very major archaeological discovery was brought to light in 1997 at Daqinggong 大清宮 in Luyi 鹿邑, about 60 kilometers to the south of Shangqiu. In a well-preserved large tomb of 9 × 6.63 meters with two long ramp-ways originally dug into a low mound, a total of eighty-five bronze vessels along with thirty-two bronze weapons and 197 pottery wares were excavated, showing us the image of a rich burial that archaeologists had previously had the chance to experience only in such central sites as Anyang.[156] Certainly the excavation revealed a strong link to the Shang capital, as the majority of the bronzes are typically of late Shang style and ornamentation, and the burial of a large number of human victims both as death companions and as sacrifices indicates Shang practice. What is even more significant is that the more than one hundred pottery wares also show an unmistakeable Anyang tradition. On the other hand, the stylistic features of the two bronze *gui* with four ears and perhaps also the bronze *you* and some of the *li* vessels would put the date of the burial undoubtedly into the Western Zhou, and not even to the beginning of it, but to the middle

[152] See Tan Qixiang, "Xi Han yiqian de Huanghe xiayou hedao," *Lishi dili* 1 (1981), 49–50.
[153] In fact, many historical sites in the area have been buried deep underground by the deposits of the Yellow River. For instance, the city of Julu 巨鹿 in Hebei has been buried as deep as 6 meters since AD 1108; the Dingtao 定陶 area in western Shandong was buried 8 meters deep beginning in the fourteenth century. See Zeng Zhaoxuan, *Zhongguo de dixing*, p. 281.
[154] According to these records which I will not detail here, Song was located in present-day Shangqiu 商丘, Qi was in Qixian 杞縣, Dai was in Minquan 民權, Ge was between Song and Qi, Chen was in Huaiyang 淮陽, Kuai was in Mixian 密縣, and Xu was in Xuchang 許昌.
[155] See Kwang-Chih Chang and Zhang Changshou, "Looking for City Shang of the Shang Dynasty in Shangqiu: A Brief Report of a Sino-American Team," *Symbols* (1998, Spring), 5–10.
[156] See *Kaogu* 2000.9, 9–23. For the formal report, see *Luyi Daqinggong Changzi Kou mu* (Zhengzhou: Zhongzhou guji, 2000), pp. 21–199.

part of the early Western Zhou.[157] Therefore, it has been strongly suggested that Changzi Kou 長子口, the apparent occupant of the tomb whose name is inscribed on as many as thirty-seven bronze vessels, should be identified with Weizi Qi 微子啓, the founder of the state of Song in the textual tradition.[158] Considering the phenomena recovered by archaeology at the burial site and the often hard-to-define distinction between the graphs *chang* 長 and *wei* 微 in paleography, the identification is indeed very probable. At least, the discovery strongly evidences the activity of Shang remnants in the area that is traditionally known to have been the base of Song.

No inscribed Western Zhou bronzes have been found in the areas where the other non-Ji states were located, owing probably to the thick sediment left by the Yellow River. But, because these non-Ji states were the marriage partners of the Ji states located on the periphery of the alluvial plain, this provided a context in which their bronzes may be found outside of the plain. This is certainly the case with the discovery of a bronze *hu* in Shandong, cast by the ruler of Chen for his daughter.[159] In 1977, a bronze *ding* cast by the ruler of Qi 杞 for his wife from the state of Zhu 邾 was found in Tengxian 滕縣, Shandong.[160] The origins of these states, except for a few,[161] remain largely obscure, although later sources such as the *Shiji* trace their ancestries back to the former dynasties or even to mythical figures. What is most likely is that they were pre-existing communities that were incorporated into the overall regional system of the Western Zhou state, or whose rights as local states were recognized by the Zhou court.[162] But we have every reason to believe that their locations in the center of the alluvial plain reflect their political disadvantage in the Zhou state, if not the deliberate arrangement by the Zhou founders.

Cultural integration of the east and the west

To the general geopolitical structure of the Western Zhou state in the east analyzed above, we should add yet another cultural layer. This cultural layer will allow us to see the process through which the west and the east were

[157] See *Luyi Daqinggong Changzi Kou mu*, pp. 79, 81, 108. The two *gui* vessels are almost identical to the famous Yihou Ze *gui* 宜侯夨簋 (JC: 4320), and are also very similar to the Eshu *gui* 鄂叔簋 (JC: 3574), except for the square base of the latter bronze. For the two bronzes, see *Zhongguo qingtongqi quanji* (Beijing: Wenwu, 1993–99), 6, pp. 104, 115.

[158] See Wang Entian, "Luyi Daqinggong Xi Zhou damu yu Weizi feng Song," *Zhongyuan wenwu* 2002.4, 41–45; Matsumaru Michio, "Kanan Rokuyū ken Chōshi Kō bo o meguru sho mondai: kobunken to kōkogaku tono kaikō," *Chūgoku kōkogaku* 4 (2004), 219–39.

[159] See *Wenwu* 1972.5, 9–10.

[160] See *Wenwu* 1978.4, 94–95. Another group of ten bronzes cast by the ruler of Qi 杞 was found in Xintai 新泰, not very far from Tengxian. In his long essay on the inscriptions, Wu Shifen argued that this group of bronzes was produced after the state of Qi moved to Xintai in northwestern Shandong; see *Jungu lu jinwen* (1895), 2, pp. 2, 24, 43–50.

[161] For instance, most modern scholars credit the *Shiji*'s attribution of the founding of the state of Song to Weizi Qi 微子啓, a Shang royal descendent reportedly settled in the area by the Zhou court after the second conquest. See *Shiji*, 38, p. 1,261.

[162] On this point, see Hsu and Linduff, *Western Chou Civilization*, p. 152.

integrated into a whole and how the common interests of the Western Zhou state were built on diverse local traditions in the diversified geographical unit.

As a matter of fact, the artistic features of the bronze vessels found along the edges of the alluvial plain from Yuanshi in the north to Pingdingshan in the south are remarkably unified with bronzes found in the Wei River valley. In fact, such a strong adherence to the metropolitan Zhou standards can be observed even on bronzes from regions lying far beyond the Central Plain, for instance from Beijing in the north and the middle Yangzi in the south. Through the entire early Western Zhou and most of the mid-Western Zhou, although very occasionally local pottery types could be cast in bronze, the bronze culture as a whole was highly coherent, guided by standards established in the Zhou heartland in the Wei River valley, and facilitated by a single system of writing. Such a high degree of uniformity has encouraged Jessica Rawson to observe the following:

It may be surmised that a well-developed organization of bronze casting must have existed in the early Zhou period. The inscriptions underline this need. Whether bronzes were transported from centralized foundries, for example, at Feng, Hao, or Chengzhou, or whether foundries capable of highly sophisticated casting were located in several areas, close contact between the royal household and the owner of the bronzes is implied . . . In both the situations suggested, trained scribes in close contact with foundries would have been essential. If all such casting was centralized, then close communication would have been necessary between the centers in Xi'an and Luoyang and the more distant cities in Yan near Beijing, or Yu near Baoji. If casting of inscribed bronzes was not centralized, then close communication between different centers would have been needed to ensure the adoption of standard language and calligraphy. In either case, a formidable unity of purpose and practice seems to have linked the diverse parts of the Zhou realm in its early phases.[163]

In fact, as I have recently shown, we have good evidence that bronzes of the same styles found in the Zhou central areas not only were cast in the regional states of Zhou cultural descent, but were imitated and sometimes closely reproduced in the peripheral regions by communities that had their own unique cultural traditions and that might not even be politically a part of the Western Zhou state.[164] The issue was certainly how to maintain close communications between the center and the periphery, and by whatever means the bronze inscriptions show that such communication was certainly carried out in considerable volume during the early Western Zhou (see chapter 2, pp. 113–14, 117–19). In short, the archaeological evidence shows a strong bond in the elite culture that reflected the political integration of the eastern plain with the Wei River valley.

[163] See Rawson, "Western Zhou Archaeology," pp. 365–66.
[164] See Li Feng, "Literacy Crossing Cultural Borders: Evidence from the Bronze Inscriptions of the Western Zhou Period (1045–771 BC)," *Bulletin of the Museum of Far Eastern Antiquity* 74 (2002), 210–42.

By contrast, pottery wares found in the east seem to have been much
more closely tied to the pre-conquest local eastern traditions than to the
Zhou culture that radiated from the Wei River valley. Thanks to the relatively recent publication of materials from two areas, Luoyang and Xingtai,
supplemented by the materials from a more distant site, Liulihe 琉璃河 in
Beijing, belonging to the state of Yan 燕 (discussed in appendix 1), we are
now in a much better position than before to address this issue.[165] However, space here allows only a summary of what we can learn from the new
materials on a topic that deserves at least a chapter-long treatment. To lay
the ground for this discussion, let me first try to characterize the typological features of the pottery assemblage from the Zhou capital region in the
Wei River valley, contemporary with the early Western Zhou (Fig. 14). The
Zhou pottery tradition was centered on two types: a tripod cooking vessel
called *li* 鬲 and a small-mouthed jar called *guan* 罐. The *li*-tripod pottery
in the Zhou capital area shows clearly the merging of three discernible traditions that can all be traced back to the pre-dynastic period: the first has
a sunken but joint crotch (14.1); the second has a divided crotch and three
breast-like hollow legs (14.2); the third has a relatively long and straight
neck. The *guan*-jars, though differentiated by the shape of their shoulders
(round or carinated), are characterized by their narrow mouths (14.3–5).
In the residential sites, another commonly seen type was the straight-sided
deep basin, wider at the top than at the bottom, named *pen* 盆 (14.6). Two
other types were probably adopted from the Shang pottery tradition but
had already been fully naturalized into the Zhou culture: a high-base plate
called *dou* 豆 (14.7–9) and a low-base small basin called *gui* 簋 (14.10–11).
The above types constituted the basic menu of the pottery wares frequently
found in the Wei River valley during the early Western Zhou and the early
phase of the mid-Western Zhou.

Except for the last two types that may have had a Shang origin, none of
the typical Zhou types of pottery was found in Luoyang.[166] On the contrary,

[165] The materials from the site of the bronze workshop at Beiyao in Luoyang were previously analyzed
in two articles by Ye Wansong and Yu Fuwei, while the materials from the earlier excavation of the
Beiyao cemetery have been recently published; see Ye Wansong and Yu Fuwei, "Luoyang Beiyao Xi
Zhou yizhi taoqi de fenqi yanjiu," *Kaogu* 1985.9, 834–42; "Zhongyuan diqu Xi Zhou taoqi de chubu
yanjiu," *Kaogu* 1986.12, 1,104–11, 20; *Luoyang Beiyao Xi Zhou mu*, pp. 62–65, 197–201, 277–79. The
formal report on the excavation in Xingtai has not been published, but some materials from the site
are included in two articles by members of the excavation team; see Jia Jinbiao, Ren Yashan *et al.*,
"Xingtai diqu Xi Zhou taoqi de chubu yanjiu," in *Sandai wenming yanjiu* (Beijing: Kexue, 1999),
pp. 65–75; Shi Congzhi, Li Enwei *et al.*, "Xingtai diqu taoli chubu yanjiu," in *Sandai wenming
yanjiu* (Beijing: Kexue, 1999), pp. 76–85. For materials from Liulihe, see mainly *Liulihe Xi Zhou
Yan guo mudi 1973–77* (Beijing: Wenwu, 1995), pp. 79–100.
[166] Ye Wansong and Yu Fuwei give an incomplete *li*-tripod from Beiyao (T2H80:1) as an example of
the Zhou-style sunken-crotched *li* and another piece (C5M91:2) as an example of the breast-legged
li. However, the first is quite different from the Zhou style and the second actually resembles the
F-type *li* of the western region of Anyang. See Ye Wansong and Yu Fuwei, "Zhongyuan diqu Xi
Zhou taoqi de chubu yanjiu," pp. 1,109, 1,106, fig. 2: 9, 14. For typical Shang pottery types, see
Kaogu xuebao 1979.1, 111.

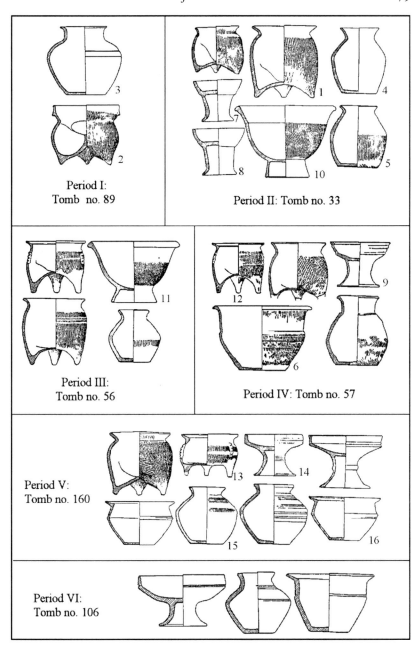

Fig. 14 Periodized examples of Zhou burial pottery from Zhangjiapo (based on *Kaogu xuebao* 1980.4, 249, 283–85)

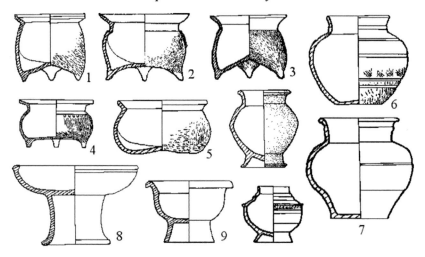

Fig. 15 Early Western Zhou pottery from Beiyao in Luoyang (based on *Luoyang Beiyao Xi Zhou mu*, pp. 63–65)

almost every type found in Luoyang can be traced back to a prototype at Anyang, suggesting that the pottery tradition once associated with the Shang remained predominant in the Luoyang area even after the Zhou conquest (Fig. 15). These include mainly the various sub-types of the *li*-tripod with an extremely low body and divided crotch, commonly featuring also a raised ridge around the rim (15.1–5). The large-mouthed *guan*-jar with rings and sometimes small buttons on its narrow shoulder (15.6–7) and the straight-bodied *zun* 尊 container were other types inherited from the Shang, in addition to the *dou*-plate (15.8) and the *gui*-basin (15.9) that were common between the Shang and Zhou traditions (although stylistically they could also be differentiated from Zhou types). Because of the similarities with Anyang pottery, some of the tombs excavated in the 1950s used to be called the "tombs of the Shang people,"[167] but by our current standards they are early Western Zhou tombs in the Luoyang region. However, the Shang tradition did not persist in the region without changes. One of the changes can be identified in the complete lack of wine-serving pottery containers such as *jue* and *gu* that were originally based on bronze types and figured so prominently in the pottery assemblage from Anyang. But the important point is that while the Luoyang region as the eastern administrative center of Zhou was fully integrated politically with the west, as evident in the bronze culture and the inscriptions, the non-elite local culture presents us with an almost complete separation from the Wei River tradition.[168]

[167] See *Kaogu xuebao* 9 (1955), 102–5.

[168] In a more recent analysis of pottery from Luoyang, Liu Fuliang tried to regionalize these two traditions in the Luoyang region. He suggested that the Shang-style pottery wares are mainly from the east side of the Chan River, while larger tombs containing bronzes are located between the

The same trend is evident also in the pottery wares recently excavated in Xingtai. The Xingtai pottery assemblage is much simpler because most samples are from tombs, which usually show a narrower or more selective range of typological variants. But the available pieces show quite clearly that, as suggested also by the archaeologists of Hebei, the pottery culture of Xing overwhelmingly adhered to Shang tradition. This is most evident in the large number of low-crotched *li*-tripods and the almost equally high number of large-mouthed *guan*-jars, not to mention the *dou* and *gui*, that together constituted the basic menu of local burial pottery.[169] Similar also to Luoyang, the wine containers *jue* and *gu* are lacking from the Xingtai burials. However, different from Luoyang, the early Xingtai pottery also contains, though in very small numbers, some unmistakable Zhou types commonly found in the Wei River valley. These include a sunken-crotched *li*-tripod found in tomb no. 172, and another straight-necked *li*-tripod found in tomb no. 4.[170] Whether these two samples were locally produced or brought to the site by Zhou immigrants can still be debated, but they show clearly the arrival of Wei River pottery tradition.

In short, the archaeological excavations suggest that while the Zhou elite in the east enjoyed a highly developed bronze culture identical to that which is found in the Wei River valley, the pottery workshops on the eastern plain continued to produce old types of pottery according to local standards that had their origins in Shang. As suggested above, from the very beginning the Western Zhou state faced a west–east division that emerged as the result of the Zhou conquest. The study of pottery shows that, decades after the Zhou conquest, such division still remained very significant at the non-elite level of Western Zhou culture. However, the situation began to change some time during the mid-Western Zhou when the Zhou pottery types were gradually introduced to the eastern plain. This is fully evident in a *li*-tripod decorated with jutting flanges, as often seen on Zhou-style bronze *li*, belonging to Period II of the bronze workshop site in Beiyao excavated in 1974 (similar to Fig. 14.12).[171] Some other Zhou-style pieces were found in tomb no. 167 in Xiayaocun.[172] In the northern part of the eastern plain, Zhou-style *li*-tripods (14.12) and a new type of *dou*-plate with a ridge at the middle of its high base (14.14), evidently developed in the west, were found in Xiguanwai 西關外 in Xingtai.[173] On the other hand, pottery types in the Wei River valley had also undergone significant changes

---

Chan and Jian rivers. See Liu Fuliang, "Luoyang Xi Zhou taoqi mu yanjiu," *Kaogu yu wenwu* 1998.3, 62–67. Liu's analysis is evidently inspired by the textual tradition that Chengzhou on the east side of the Chan River accommodated a large Shang population. However, the analysis is not very successful because very few Wei River types can be identified even in the area between the Chan and Jian rivers.

[169] See Jia Jinbiao, Ren Yashan, *et al.*, "Xingtai diqu Xi Zhou taoqi de chubu yanjiu," pp. 73–74.
[170] See Jia Jinbiao, Ren Yashan, *et al.*, "Xingtai diqu Xi Zhou taoqi de chubu yanjiu," p. 72.
[171] See *Wenwu* 1981.7, 58, figs. 11 and 12.   [172] See *Kaogu xuebao* 9 (1955), 100, fig. 10: 9, 8, 1.
[173] See *Wenwu* 1960.7, 69, figs. 2 and 7.

during the mid-Western Zhou, especially in the design of the *li*-tripod, that gradually became lower and was finally not clearly differentiable from the pottery *li*-tripod found in the east that continued the Shang tradition.

The process of cultural integration between west and east was largely accelerated during the late Western Zhou. For instance, in Luoyang the bronzes cast by the famous Zhou noble Shaobo Hu 召伯虎 were excavated together with a pottery *li*-tripod identical to those found in the Wei River valley (similar to Fig. 14.13).[174] Typical late Western Zhou pottery types were excavated in relatively larger numbers from Xinzheng 新鄭,[175] and from two sites in Cixian 磁縣, Hebei.[176] Pottery wares from the three sites include most types from the contemporary Wei River valley: besides the *li*-tripod and high *dou*-plate already mentioned,[177] the small-mouthed *guan*-jars with a sharp shoulder (14.15)[178] and the small *yu*-basin are typical of the late Western Zhou period (14.16).[179] The complete merging of the two pottery traditions during the late Western Zhou reflects the eventual integration of the two regions, guided by a unified elite culture introduced soon after the Zhou conquest.

THE FEN RIVER VALLEY DURING THE WESTERN ZHOU

The Fen River valley of southern Shanxi, though not far removed in distance from the Luoyang region, is effectively blocked off from the eastern plain by the Taihang Mountains and Zhongtiao 中條 Mountain. However, given its easy access to the Zhou heartland in the Wei River valley, the region played an important part in late Western Zhou history and in the transition to the Eastern Zhou. Therefore, it is appropriate to provide an overview of the region here.

Landscape features

To the west of the Taihang Mountains lies the Fen River valley in southern Shanxi. It is, in fact, a huge geological fault between the Taihang in the east and the Lüliang 呂梁 Mountains in the west. The valley is wide and flat, with loess steps extending on both sides of the Fen River, which turns west near Houma 侯馬 and soon enters the Yellow River (Map 1). The upper Fen River valley, normally called the Taiyuan 太原 Basin, is an open area at an elevation of 700–900 meters.[180] Today, this is a rich agricultural area and the center of the Shanxi province. To the north,

---

[174] See *Kaogu* 1995.9, 788–91.   [175] See *Wenwu ziliao congkan* 2 (1978), 45–68.

[176] See *Kaogu xuebao* 1975.1, 73–111; *Kaogu* 1974.6, 356–63.

[177] For example, see *Wenwu ziliao congkan* 2 (1978), 46, fig. 3: 2, 8; *Kaogu xuebao* 1975.1, 104–6, fig. 26: 3, fig. 27: 3, 4; *Kaogu* 1974.6, 363, fig. 10: 1.

[178] See *Wenwu ziliao congkan* 2 (1978), 46, fig. 3: 5.   [179] See *Kaogu xuebao* 1975.1, fig. 26: 6, 7.

[180] See Zhao Songqiao, *Physical Geography of China*, p. 119.

the valley gradually gives way to ranges of hills and mountains towards the Mongolian Plateau. To the south, the valley is separated by Huoshan 崔山 Mountain from the lower Fen River basin. Much lower in elevation than the Taiyuan basin, the lower Fen area is extensively covered by loess, and is fertile and abundant in water resources. Therefore, through the historical period, the lower Fen River valley was more often the economic center of Shanxi province than was the Taiyuan basin in the north. Further south, the region was divided between two valleys: the Fen River valley turns west, leading to the Yellow River; the Su 涑 River flows southwest, along the north edge of the high and narrow Zhongtiao 中條 Mountain, forming another small triangular basin. The Zhongtiao range lies on the north bank of the Yellow River, separating the entire Fen River valley from the Yellow River, and the hinterland of Shanxi from the open plain in Henan. The Fen River valley is closely linked to the Wei River valley in the west; together they form a lowland area in the middle reaches of the Yellow River.

Routes out of the Fen River valley

Throughout history, the Fen River valley provided an alternative route of communication between the Wei River valley in the west and the eastern plain. As the two river valleys are open to each other on either side of the Yellow River, no major obstacles separate them, except for the effort that people have to make to cross the river. However, the river was not always a mere geographical divide between the two provinces; it was also used as a channel of communication. As the Warring States sources show, people could sail from the Wei River, along a short section of the Yellow River, and into the Fen River to reach the heartland of the powerful local state of Jin. During a famine that ravaged the Fen River valley in 647 BC, the neighboring state Qin provided Jin with a huge quantity of grain carried in boats that are said to have lined up in the rivers all the way from the Qin capital to the Jin capital. The next year, when Qin had a famine, the Jin ruler refused to lend help.[181] The real obstacle to communication through the Fen River valley lies in the eastern section where the road has to traverse the steep Zhongtiao Mountain, traditionally referred to as the "Road of Zhi" from the location of Zhi County 軹縣 (near present-day Jiyuan 濟源) at its exit during the Han dynasty. During the Western Zhou, as mentioned earlier, the position was probably occupied by the state of Yuan. This road goes east, entering the mountains along the Su River, and then turns southeast by way of Yuanqu 垣曲 and Gucheng 古城, to Jiyuan in the east (Map 6).[182] During the hegemony of Duke Wen of Jin in the seventh century BC, the state of Jin reportedly bribed the so-called

---

[181] This was called the "Floating Boat Campaign," see *Zuozhuan*, 13, p. 1,803; 14, p. 1,805.
[182] See Lu Yun, "Zhanguo shiqi zhuyao lulu jiaotong chutan," in *Lishi dili yanjiu*, 1, pp. 40–41.

"barbarians" in the eastern mountains controlling these paths and reconstructed this road, which then became the superhighway for Jin connecting
the Fen River valley and the eastern plain.[183] However, a recent archaeological study of local resources suggests that the road was evidently in use
much earlier, during the nineteenth through the sixteenth centuries BC. In
the early Shang period, with the construction of a walled city at Yuanqu on
the middle section of the road, it had certainly played a major role in communication between the Shang centers and the Fen and further Wei River
valleys in the west.[184] To the west, there was another minor path through
the valleys of the Zhongtiao Mountain to Pinglu 平陸 on the north bank of
the Yellow River, crossing the river to Sanmenxia. This was the road taken
by the Jin army to conquer the state of Guo and Yu in 655 BC. Both roads
were used for transporting salt out of the Fen River valley during the later
historical period.[185]

The archaeology of the Fen River valley

The lower Fen River valley was the focus of Western Zhou archaeology
during the early 1990s, centering on the discovery of the state of Jin. The
research carried out by Beijing University in the 1970s was originally aimed
at recovering the pre-conquest Zhou remains, as Professor Zou Heng of the
university was of the opinion that the Fen River valley was the homeland of
the Zhou people before their move west into the Wei River valley. However,
the project subsequently led to the discovery of the large site in the areas
of Tianma 天馬 and Qucun 曲村,[186] which was then under continuous
excavation during the 1980s. The burial ground of the rulers of Jin was
discovered in 1991 when fourteen of the original sixteen bronze bells in a
set, the Jinhou Su *zhong* 晉侯蘇鍾 (JL: 35–50), were looted by grave robbers
from a tomb at the same site. Then, seventeen large tombs (fourteen with
ramps) in eight groups were excavated between 1992 and 1994.[187] In late
2000, another pair of tombs with ramp-ways were excavated in the central
row of the burial ground, after an initial looting in 1998.[188] These nine
groups of tombs (usually in pairs) were arranged in three rows (Fig. 16),

[183] See Shi Nianhai, *Heshanji*, 1, pp. 69–70.
[184] See Liu and Chen, *State Formation in Early China*, p. 73. For the archaeological discoveries at
Yuanqu, see Tong Weihua, "Shanxi Yuanqu gucheng wenhua yizhi de fajue," in *Jin wenhua yanjiu
zuotanhui jiyao* (Houma, Shanxi: Shanxi sheng kaogu yanjiusuo, 1985), pp. 28–29; *Wenwu* 1997.12,
4–15. See also Jim Railey, "Neolithic to Early Bronze Age Sociopolitical Evolution in the Yuanqu
Basin, North-Central China," unpublished PhD thesis, Washington University (1999), pp. 198–213.
[185] See Liu and Chen, *State Formation in Early China*, pp. 54–56. Today this road still serves as the
major transportation route linking the two provinces.
[186] See *Wenwu* 1982.7, 1–4.
[187] For the excavations, see *Wenwu* 1993.3, 11–30; 1994.1, 4–28; 1994.8, 22–23, 68; 1994.8, 1–21; 1995.7,
4–38. See also Jae-hoon Shim, "The Early Development of the State of Jin: From its Enfeoffment
to the Hegemony of Wen Gong (r. 636–628 BC)," unpublished PhD thesis, University of Chicago
(1998), pp. 51–88.
[188] See *Wenwu* 2001.8, 4–21.

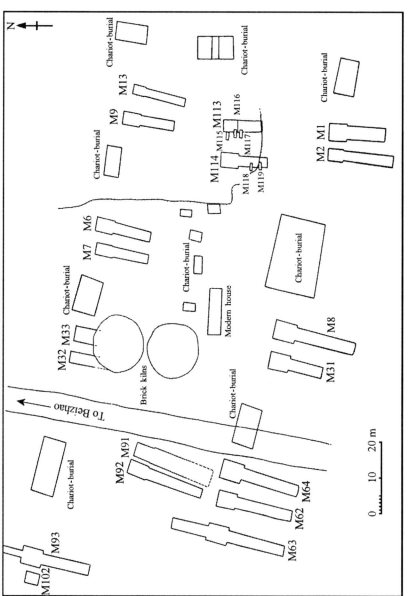

Fig. 16 The burial ground of the rulers of Jin at Beizhao (based on *Wenwu* 2001.8, 4)

and the inscriptions from the tombs suggest that they were burials of nine Jin rulers and their spouses. According to the published sources, the earliest tombs, for instance tomb no. 7, can be dated to the early phase of the mid-Western Zhou, while the latest, tomb no. 93, can be dated to the early Spring and Autumn period. Among the large number of inscribed bronzes excavated from the Jinhou cemetery, the 355-character inscription on the sixteen bells from tomb no. 8 is extremely important.[189] The inscription documents a joint military campaign between the state of Jin and the Zhou court against a people called Suyi 夙夷, most likely located in northern Anhui or southern Shandong.

The complete chronology of the Jin rulers is known from both the *Bamboo Annals* and the *Shiji*, and therefore the discussion since the discovery has been centered on the identification of those names of the Jin rulers appearing on the bronzes with what the two texts offer, and hence the chronology of the tombs in which the bronzes were discovered. To this end, a number of different ways to interpret the tombs have been proposed.[190] Because of the discrepancy between the received records and the inscriptions with respect to the length of reigns of some Jin rulers contemporary with the late Western Zhou, the discovery has led to significant reconsideration of the dates of the Zhou kings as well as the order in which the Jin rulers came to rule.[191] But for the purpose of the present study, it is important above all that the discovery has actually fixed the location of the state of Jin, mentioned in the *Zuozhuan* list of the regional Zhou states. The *Shiji* attributes the founding of the state of Jin to Shu Yu 叔虞, a younger brother of King Cheng, at the site of a former state called Tang 唐, that Sima Qian himself said was located to the east of both the Yellow River and the Fen River.[192] The geographical location of Jin in this position is important above

---

[189] See Ma Chengyuan, "Jinhou Su bianzhong," pp. 1–17. See also Shim, "The 'Jinhou Su *Bianzhong*' Inscription and Its Significance," pp. 43–75.

[190] The excavation team proposed that the process of burial began at the northeastern corner of the burial ground and moved west, and then turned to the south, continuing in two rows. Finally, it turned back to the northwestern corner and ended up with tombs nos. 93 and 102. See *Wenwu* 1995.7, 37–38; Li Boqian, "Tianma-Qucun yizhi fajue yu Jin guo shifengdi de tuiding," in *Zhongguo qingtong wenhua jiegou tixi yanjiu* (Beijing: Kexue, 1998), pp. 117–18. However, this has been contested by other scholars who proposed an entirely different arrangement. See, for example, Lu Liancheng, "Tianma-Qucun Jinhou mudi niandai ji muzhu kaoding," in *Dingcun wenhua yu Jin wenhua kaogu xueshu yantaohui wenji* (Taiyuan: Shanxi gaoxiao lianhe, 1996), pp. 138–51; Zhang Changshou, "Guanyu Jinhou mudi de jige wenti," *Wenwu* 1998.1, 41–44. It should be noted that all of these arrangements were proposed before the discovery of the last pair of the tombs in the central row of the burial ground, by which the overall organization of the tombs has been significantly changed.

[191] See for instance Wang Zhankui, "Zhou Xuanwang jinian yu Jin Xianhou mu kaobian," *Zhongguo wenwu bao* 1996.7, 7; David Nivison and Edward Shaughnessy, "The Jin Hou Su Bells Inscription and Its Implications for the Chronology of Early China," *Early China* 25 (2000), 29–48.

[192] See *Shiji*, 39, pp. 1,635–36. The *Kuodizhi* of the Tang dynasty (quoted in the "Zhengyi" commentary to the *Shiji*) says that the town of Tang was 10 kilometers to the west of Yicheng County 翼城縣 of Jiang Prefecture 絳州 of the Tang period, which is very close to present-day Yicheng; this points

all because it controlled the road coming into the Fen River valley from Yuanqu and at the same time blocked the way down the Fen River valley from the north, protecting the Wei River valley from attacks from both directions (Map 6).

Besides the Tianma–Qucun site, another important Western Zhou site in the Fen River valley is Yongningbu 永凝堡. In 1957, a group of early Western Zhou bronzes was excavated at the site.[193] In 1980, twenty-two Western Zhou tombs were excavated there, dating from the early Western Zhou to the late Western Zhou.[194] The ancient geographical records locate the state of Huo, also mentioned in the *Zuozhuan* list, in this area.[195] The third state that is mentioned in the list is Hann which, according to the geographical records, was located near the confluence of the Fen River and the Yellow River.[196] There were probably two other states mentioned in the historical records, but not in the *Zuozhuan* list, the states of Geng 耿 and Wei 魏. Geng was located very close to Hann, and Wei was located along the southern side of the Zhongtiao Mountains.[197] The actual location of these states will have to wait for confirmation by archaeology, but so far as our current information permits, two points are important regarding the geopolitical configuration of the Fen River valley. First, no significant non-Ji states are known to have been installed by the Zhou in this region. Instead, the region was divided almost entirely into states granted to the royal descendents of Zhou. This seems to indicate an intimate relation between the region and the Wei River valley and reflects a possible Zhou strategy that perceived the Fen River valley to be politically different from the eastern plain. Second, the Zhou states were concentrated in the lower

fairly accurately to the Tianma–Qucun site that is located some 12 kilometers to the west of Yicheng. There are other locations suggested by geographers after Tang, but the archaeological excavation has proved that both the *Shiji* and the *Kuodizhi* accounts are correct. For an analysis of the various geographical records on Jin, see Li Boqian, "Tianma-Qucun yizhi fajue," pp. 114–23. Later, Li Boqian has identified Shu Yu, the founder of Jin, with Shu Ze 叔夨, the caster of a square bronze *ding* from tomb no. 114, excavated in early 2001. See Li Boqian, "Shu Ze fangding mingwen kaoshi," *Wenwu* 2001.8, 39–42.

[193] See *Wenwu cankao ziliao* 1957.8, 42.   [194] See *Wenwu* 1987.2, 1–16.

[195] Du Yu indicates that Huo was located near Huotaishan 霍太山, northwest of Yong'an County 永安縣, which is present-day Huoxian 霍縣; *Zuozhuan*, 11, p. 1,786. Jiang Yong further notes that the ancient town of Huo was located 8 kilometers to the west of Huoxian; Jiang Yong, *Chunqiu diming kaoshi*, 252, p. 22.

[196] Du Yu notes that Hann was in the territory of Hedong Commandery 河東郡; *Zuozhuan*, 14, p. 1,805; 15, p. 1,817. However, later commentators have mistakenly located this Hann in Hancheng 韓城, Shaanxi. It is likely that this Hann was the Hanyuan 韓原 mentioned in the *Zuozhuan* (fifteenth year of Duke Xi), where the states of Qin and Jin fought the famous battle of 645 BC. The Qing scholar Jiang Yong suggests that Hanyuan was located between Hejin County 河津 and Wanquan County 萬泉, to the east of the Yellow River. See Jiang Yong, *Chunqiu diming kaoshi*, 253, p. 4. In a study Shen Changyun argues convincingly that the Hann mentioned in the *Zuozhuan* (twenty-fourth year of Duke Xi) must have been located in Shanxi and not Shaanxi. But Shen locates it in Ruicheng 芮城, to the south of the Zhongtiao Mountains. See Shen Changyun, "Xi Zhou er Hann guo diwang kao," *Zhongguo shi yanjiu* 1982.2, 135–36.

[197] See Chen Pan, *Chunqiu dashi biao ji lieguo juexing*, pp. 205, 281.

Fen River basin, indicating that, for much of the Western Zhou, Zhou control had not gone beyond Huoshan Mountain into the Taiyuan basin in the north.

Cultural relations

The intimate relationship between the Fen River valley and the Wei River valley suggested by the historical and geographical records corresponds well with the cultural relationship between the two regions recovered by archaeology. This is particularly true in the study of pottery from the lower Fen River valley. Although pottery wares from the region have not been systematically published because of the attention given almost entirely to the bronzes, the available materials are adequate for an assessment of the basic features of the local pottery. These sources show quite clearly that the Fen River pottery had descended from the same tradition that underlay the pottery production in the Wei River valley; this situation was very different from both the Luoyang region and the vast eastern plain. The Shang oracle-bone inscriptions register a cluster of pro-Shang polities located by scholars in the Fen River valley.[198] If there had indeed been a cultural affiliation between the region and the Shang east, then there would have been a major break in the local tradition, replaced soon after the conquest by a system of pottery production that was overwhelmingly Zhou in character. According to the chronological table published by the Beijing University team in 1982, the development of pottery types in the Fen River valley followed the same course of typological evolution evident in the Wei River valley.[199] Central to this tradition were the various sunken-crotched *li*-tripods and the small-mouthed *guan*-jars, and this point was confirmed by groups of pottery subsequently published from 1980.[200] However, the pottery tradition developed in the Wei River valley was not transplanted to the Fen River valley without changes. This can be seen in the lack of the breast-legged *li*-tripods and the more frequent appearance of the container *zun* in the Fen River valley. Another type of pottery, large round-bodied *weng*-jars with three hollow legs, which probably originated in northern Shanxi, showed up more often in the Fen valley than in the Wei valley. But, overall, the similarities between the two regions are very impressive.

CONCLUSION

The Western Zhou state was the product of negotiation between political ambition and geographical reality. From the very beginning, the Zhou, as a

[198] See Chen Mengjia, *Yinxu buci zongshu*, pp. 291–98.
[199] See *Wenwu* 1982.7, 3.   [200] See especially, *Wenwu* 1987.2, 10; 1995.7, 11; 2001.8, 18.

people in the inland basin of the west and isolated from the heartland of the previous Shang civilization, faced the challenge of overcoming a west–east division that was both geopolitical and cultural. The attempt to overcome such division had guided the dynastic policy through much of the first century of the period and thereafter continued to influence the fortunes of the Western Zhou state. The construction of Luoyi (and/or Chengzhou) as the eastern administrative and military center was clearly a strategy to offset the geographical disadvantages of the Western Zhou capitals being located in the west, far removed from the regions of primary threat and possibilities for expansion. This resulted in the creation of an axis of power that linked the two regions through the difficult mountains of western Henan, providing the Western Zhou state with a crucial stabilizing power. It is also evident that the deployment of the regional Zhou states, at least the Ji states in the eastern plain, extending from this power axis and fully integrated with the landscape of the region, was the outcome of systematic planning based on far-sighted geopolitical considerations: not only were they located along the main transportation lines in positions that could effectively control the roads, but they were also situated in the agriculturally most favorable areas in the transitional belt between the mountains and the alluvial plain. It is plausible that the establishment of the regional states was not just a random process to give out land to royal kinsmen and the various local leaders, but was a process through which the Western Zhou state carefully constructed its geographical space, hence strengthening its political foundation.[201]

To return to the Wei River valley in the west, the archaeological and inscriptional evidence shows that the royal domain was integrated through a network of administration with multiple central sites as its supporting points. The royal cities were at the same time residential sites for the aristocratic families. Depending on the social connections of the aristocratic families, the network further extended from the central sites to lineage centers located in the more rural areas. The paramount importance of the Wei River valley as the heart of the Western Zhou state is suggested by many important archaeological discoveries, especially the discovery of government-related bronze inscriptions. The Wei River valley also served as

---

[201] In 1935, riding on a current of the *Gushibian* movement in China, Fu Sinian argued that many regional states such as Lu, Yan, and Qi were originally established in other places and only later moved to the locations suggested by the geographical records. Fu's idea was accepted by his student Chen Pan, who produced a long list including more than seventy states that he thought had moved at least once during the early Western Zhou. Chen's thesis was then accepted by Cho-yun Hsu, who gave twenty-one states to exemplify such movement. Archaeological discoveries have proven Fu wrong at least on the original location of Yan; the evidence suggested by Fu for the relocation of Lu and Qi is also very weak. See Fu Sinian, "Dadong xiaodong shuo," in *Fu Mengzhen xiansheng ji* (Taipei: Taiwan daxue, 1952), pp. 1–13; Chen Pan, *Chunqiu dashibiao ji lieguo juexing*, pp. 16–17; Hsu and Linduff, *Western Chou Civilization*, pp. 158–63. It is not likely, based on the information we have today, that the regional states could freely move out of their assigned localities, unattached to the land.

a base for further Zhou expansion into the adjacent upper Jing River region and for military adventures into the Loess Plateau of northern Shaanxi and the upper Wei River valley in southeastern Gansu. As these outlying regions were culturally integrated with the Wei River valley, they also provided a dimension of protection for the Zhou heartland. The Western Zhou state could work only when the Wei River valley was secured, but the Wei River valley could not be secured without firm political and military holdings in its outlying regions.

CHAPTER 2

Disorder and decline: the political crisis of the Western Zhou state

The preceding chapter has shown the rapid growth of the Western Zhou state during the first century following the conquest. The Zhou achievement in this period, known as the "Cheng-Kang Peace," was much admired by later historians as one of the politically most accomplished periods in Chinese history.[1] However, the issue that remains here is not so much the Zhou's ability to expand as their ability to maintain what they had already accomplished. In that regard, the Zhou appeared indeed quite incompetent. As soon as the mid-Western Zhou phase began, a new trend set in which was to drive the dynasty through a long process of gradual decline. In the hundred years after the death of King Mu (r. 956–918 BC), central control over the eastern regions increasingly weakened and the Western Zhou state faced both internal crisis and serious external threats. The problems had accumulated so enormously that in a showdown that stormed the Zhou capital in 842 BC King Li (r. 857/53–842/28 BC) was violently dethroned by the rebels and was forced into exile in the Fen River valley from which he was never to return. A dying dynasty would take much more than just the dethronement of an "unworthy" king to cure, but even the ambitious and to some extent successful policies adopted by the next king, Xuan (r. 827/25–782 BC), could serve only to postpone its final days.

What really happened in the Western Zhou state to cause the disorder and decline? The present chapter proposes a twofold theory that I think most logically explains Zhou's decline. The problem was first of all a structural crisis that had its origin in the process by which the Western Zhou state was created. In the Zhou case, I believe we can see clearly the historical effect of a political organization that was suddenly expanded to the extent that the maintenance of the fruit of such expansion demanded the inevitable and excessive dispersion of its limited resources to stabilize a large geopolitical unity. As such, the bond that connected its numerous

---

[1] "Cheng" refers to King Cheng (r. 1042/35–1006 BC) and "Kang" to King Kang (r. 1005/3–978 BC). Such reputation can be seen in Sima Qian's description that in the time of King Cheng and King Kang the world was in good order and corporal punishment was not used for as many as forty years; *Shiji*, 4, p. 134 (Nienhauser, *The Grand Scribe's Record, 1*, p. 66). Another dynastic history, the *Sanguo zhi* 三國志 (Records of the Three Kingdoms), also alludes to the so-called "Cheng-Kang Peace": see *Sanguo zhi*, 65, p. 1,459.

local branches, namely the regional Zhou states, was too weak and condi-
tional to bring back constant replenishment of the power center by local
resources. Quite to the contrary, the political and administrative autonomy
granted to the regional rulers provided a centrifugal power that with the
passage of time gradually undermined the willingness of the regional rulers
to support the center, and even encouraged them actually to go against it.
The problem was also the result of the mismanagement of the state core
by the Zhou king. The central government operated on the principle of
"favors for loyalty" as the Zhou officials received no regular stipend on
a quantified basis determined either by the length of their service or by
the substance of their work. Instead, they received occasional royal gifts
of various kinds, and most importantly in the form of landed property.
Since such property had to be sliced out from the royal possessions located
mainly in the limited space of the Wei River valley, the more the king gave
out land to his officials, the less possible was it for him to continue to do so.
This "suicide" method of government inevitably resulted in the weakening
of the economic basis of the Western Zhou state and the poverty of the
Zhou royal house. Both of these problems were rooted in the fundamental
political system of the Western Zhou state and they worked together to
weaken it from inside, especially at a time when outside threat also began
to take hold on the Western Zhou.

The present chapter examines the crisis and decline of the Western Zhou
as an issue separate from its fall, the subject of chapter 4. The distinction
between the two issues has been eloquently put by Arther Ferrill with regard
to the Roman Empire: "The Romans began their gradual decline at such a
high level of wealth and power that they were able to decline for centuries
before they were in danger of falling."[2] Compared to a fall, decline is a
much longer process of gradual weakening marked by a chain of crises
and disorders across many aspects of a society. At the same time, political
problems often lead to and are manifest in spatial crisis, as most political
organizations occupy a space which they dominate with their strength.
Therefore, the present study also explores the spatial implications of the
weakening of the Western Zhou state. This involves two issues: first, the
gradual internal disintegration of the Western Zhou state as the result of
the conflict in its supporting structure; and second, the incursion by foreign
powers into its peripheral or even core areas.

EMERGENCE OF POLITICAL DISORDER AND DECLINE

How do we know that the Western Zhou state declined? What was the
extent of the decline? By "decline," I am in particular referring to the

[2] See Arther Ferrill, *The Fall of the Roman Empire: The Military Explanation* (London: Thames and
Hudson, 1986), p. 8.

weakening of royal power as the organizing authority and the focal point of the Western Zhou state, but not to the demise of any constituting parts of it such as the regional states, many of which were actually growing in power as royal authority declined. Moreover, historians of decline have reminded us of the need to differentiate conceptually between the symptoms of a decline and the causes of it, although a symptom in one period could be the cause of further decline in another.[3] Therefore, we must first identify signs of Zhou's decline in order to investigate its causes. The purpose of this section is to survey the signs of Zhou's decline on the basis of our current evidence, highlighting some key issues to be explored further in the next two sections.

Signs for the "early" decline of the Western Zhou

It is probably fair to say that the Western Zhou dynasty started with a series of crises: the death of King Wu almost immediately after the conquest, the split of the Zhou court, the revolt of the Zhou armies stationed in the east, and the revolt of the conquered Shang people. But the crises provided opportunities for the rise of the strong leadership of the Duke of Zhou who, through the second conquest, step by step consolidated the Zhou regime. The crises that we are looking for here are those that the Zhou could not overcome successfully and those that had contributed to the weakening of Zhou royal power in the long run. When we take this line of investigation, the first recognizable sign of crisis in Western Zhou history would appear to be the disastrous southern campaign conducted by King Zhao (r. 977/75–957 BC).

In the nineteenth year of his reign, after an initial successful attack on Chu three years earlier,[4] King Zhao embarked on another major military campaign into the middle Yangzi region. I believe that the move marked a major shift of focus of expansion from the east to the south. The inscription of the Huan *you* 覂卣 (JC: 5407), which is self-dated to the nineteenth year, indicates that before the campaign took place the king was in a place called An 斤, somewhere on the Wei River plain, probably in preparation for the military operation.[5] Some scholars consider that three other inscriptions

---

[3] See Solomon Katz, *The Decline of Rome and the Rise of Medieval Europe* (Ithaca, NY: Cornell University Press, 1955), p. 74.

[4] We have a number of bronzes cast by individuals who personally followed the king in this initial campaign against Chu, commemorating the capture of metals in the south that seemingly suggests a victorious campaign: the Yiyu *gui* 𫊣𣪍簋 (JC: 3976), Guobo *gui* 過伯簋 (JC: 3907), Cai *gui* 䈕簋 (JC: 3732), and Hongshu *gui* 唯叔簋 (JC: 3950). The dating of this group of bronzes to the time of King Zhao is generally agreed. See Tang Lan, *Tang Lan xiansheng jinwen*, pp. 280–81; Ma Chengyuan, *Shang Zhou qingtongqi mingwen xuan*, 4 vols. (Beijing: Wenwu, 1986–90), 3, pp. 73–76. The artistic features of these bronzes correspond well with the general characteristics of the late phase of the early Western Zhou. See Li Feng, "Huanghe liuyu Xi Zhou muzang chutu qingtong liqi de fenqi yu niandai," *Kaogu xuebao* 1988.4, 387–88, 407–17.

[5] Chen Mengjia dates the Huan *you* to the reign of King Cheng, while Tang Lan dates it to the reign of King Zhao; see Chen Mengjia, "Xi Zhou tongqi duandai," 2, p. 117; Tang Lan, *Tang Lan*

that record awards of land by the king to officials were probably also cast on the same occasion.[6] Many aspects of this campaign remain obscure in history, but all received textual records agree that it turned out to be disastrous. Both the *Ancient* and the *Current Bamboo Annals* say that King Zhao was himself killed and the royal Six Armies that he brought on the campaign entirely vanished in the Han River.[7] Owing to the lack of detail in our sources, it is hard to estimate how much damage the disastrous campaign may have done to the power of the Western Zhou state, but at least there is one way to measure its damage to the Zhou military. Throughout the Western Zhou the Zhou royal forces were composed of the Six Armies and the Eight Armies.[8] The Six Armies was stationed in the Zhou capital region in the Wei River valley and therefore was called the "Six Armies of the West" (*Xi liushi* 西六師) while the Eight Armies was stationed in the eastern capital Chengzhou and was hence called the "Eight Armies of Chengzhou" (*Chengzhou bashi* 成周八師). The loss of the Six Armies in a single campaign would imply that nearly half of the royal forces were destroyed in the nineteenth year of King Zhao. And there seems no doubt that this was an overwhelming military setback as well as a political defeat. But perhaps what was even more serious was the far-reaching impact that the inauspicious death of the Son of Heaven at the hands of the southern "barbarians" made on the psychology of the Zhou people, who had so far seemed forever victorious. To its enemies, the Western Zhou state ceased to be an undefeatable military giant, and they would not hesitate to test its strength whenever possible. In the long run, the disastrous southern campaign in King Zhao's nineteenth year put an end to the era of early Western Zhou expansion. Thereafter, the Zhou never again ventured farther south into the middle Yangzi region. In the east, after the death of King

---

xiansheng jinwen, p. 303. My own analysis of the burial bronzes of the Western Zhou period suggests that the Huan *you* and Huan *zun* must have been cast during the late phase of the early Western Zhou, corresponding more probably with the time of King Zhao, but not King Cheng. See Li Feng, "Huanghe liuyu Xi Zhou muzang," pp. 412–13. For the Huan *you*'s relationship to the southern campaign, see Lu Liancheng, "An di yu Zhaowang shijiu nian nanzheng," *Kaogu yu wenwu* 1984.6, 75–79; see also Shirakawa, "Kinbun tsūshaku," 5.22:236.

[6] See Tang Lan, *Tang Lan xiansheng jinwen*, pp. 292–94; Lu Liancheng, "An di yu Zhao Wang," p. 75. These bronzes are the Shao *huanqi* 盠圜器 (JC: 10360), Zhong *fangding* 中方鼎 no. 1 (JC: 2785), and Qian *you* 趞卣 (JC: 5402). All three bronzes were cast in the thirteenth month and their day-numbers are also compatible with each other. It is very possible that they were from the thirteenth month of the same year. The Qian *you* mentions that the king was in An 序 on the *gengyin* day (no. 27); the Zhong *fangding* no. 1 mentions the king in Hanshu 寒眿 on the *xinmao* day (no. 28). This may suggest a connection with the Huan *you*, which mentions that the king was in An before the southern campaign in the nineteenth year. However, none of these bronzes has a year number or a reference to the southern campaign. Another bronze, the Zhong *fangding* no. 2 (JC: 2751), cast by the same Zhong, records a southern campaign led by Nangong 南宮, but the enemy under attack was Hufang 虎方. See Shirakawa, "Kinbun tsūshaku," 14.71:791.

[7] Fan Xiangyong, *Guben Zhushu jinian jijiao dingbu* (Shanghai: Xinzhishi, 1956), pp. 25–26; *Zhushu jinian*, 2, p. 8 (Legge, *The Shoo King*, Prolegomena, p. 149).

[8] For the military organization of the Six Armies and the Eight Armies, see Li Xueqin, "Lun Xi Zhou jinwen zhong de Liushi Bashi," *Huaxia kaogu* 1987.2, 207–10; Li Feng, "'Offices' in Bronze Inscriptions," p. 35.

Zhao, campaigns against the indigenous societies in the hinterland of the Jiaodong peninsula, referred to by the Zhou in their bronze inscriptions as "Dongyi" 東夷, also seem to have entered a period of stagnation.

In the next reign, that of King Mu, the Six Armies was evidently reestablished because it was again mentioned in the inscriptions of the Li *fangzun* 盠方尊 (JC: 6013) and Li *fangyi* 盠方彝 (JC: 9899), and royal authority was restored.[9] There are many bronzes and bronze inscriptions cast during this reign that offer us the overall impression of a period of reorganization and transition in Western Zhou society. The reign seems to have been the starting point of some important changes that gradually showed their effect during the subsequent reigns of the mid-Western Zhou. One of these changes took place in the operation of the Zhou central government, giving rise to the "Appointment Inscriptions" that are the manifestation of a routinely maintained and somewhat rationalized government administration.[10] In the area of bronze art, the most apparent change was perhaps

---

[9] The Li bronzes have been variously dated by earlier scholars. For instance, Guo Moruo dates them to the reign of King Yih (r. 899/97–873 BC), while Li Xueqin and Ma Chengyuan date them to King Xiao (r. 872?–866 BC). See Guo Moruo, "Li qi ming kaoshi," *Kaogu xuebao* 1957.2, 6; Li Xueqin, "Meixian Lijiacun tongqi kao," *Wenwu* 1957.7, 58; Ma Chengyuan, *Shang Zhou qingtongqi*, 3, pp. 228–29. Although the stylistic features of the Li *fangyi* and Li *fangzun* depart from the *fangyi* and *fangzun* vessels cast during the early Western Zhou period, their delicate ornament still maintains early tradition. The Mugong 穆公 mentioned on the Li bronzes is probably the caster of another bronze, the Mugong *guigai* 穆公簋蓋 (JC: 4191), that bears the big-bird pattern typical of the early mid-Western Zhou period, and is mentioned also on the Yin Ji *li* 尹姞鬲 (JC: 754), a bronze that by its stylistic features must be assigned to the late phase of early Western Zhou. Therefore, I think the most appropriate date for the Li bronzes would be the reign of King Mu. This point has been made very clear by the recent discovery of the Lai *pan* 逑盤, which mentions the caster's ancestor Lifu 盠父, whom many identify with the caster of the Li bronzes, as having served both King Zhao and King Mu. It is worth noting that, although the Lai *pan* is reported as from Yangjiacun and the Li bronzes from Lijiacun, they were discovered at the large site to the north of the Meixian train station (see chapter 1, p. 48). For the image of the Mu Gong *guigai*, see *Kaogu yu wenwu* 1981.4, 27. For the Lai *pan*, see *Wenwu* 2003.6, 4–42. For the identification of Lifu with Li, see "Shaanxi Meixian chutu jiaocang qingtongqi bitan," *Wenwu* 2003.6, 43–65. With the double connections through Mu Gong and Li/Lifu, we can now safely date the Li bronzes to the early part of the mid-Western Zhou, or, most appropriately, the reign of King Mu.

[10] Two "Appointment Inscriptions" are almost certainly from the reign of King Mu, the earliest time we see such inscriptions. The first is the Li *fangzun* (*fangyi*) mentioned above. The second is the Hu *gui* 虎簋, whose connection with the Shi Hu *gui* 師虎簋 (JC: 4316), probably cast in the first year of King Yih (see below, pp. 101–2, note 33), and whose high year number (thirtieth year), for no other mid-Western Zhou king ruled that long, would certainly date it to the reign of King Mu. For the Hu *gui*, see *Kaogu yu wenwu* 1997.3, 78–80; for its relation with the Shi Hu *gui*, see Li Feng, "Succession and Promotion: Elite Mobility during the Western Zhou," *Monumenta Serica* 52 (2004), 1–35. A number of scholars have argued for the bureaucratization of the Western Zhou government starting in the early mid-Western Zhou. For instance, Hsu and Linduff suggest that the process seems to have begun with the roles associated with the Secretariat and then extended to other branches of the Western Zhou government, while Shaughnessy, taking the inscription of the Li *fangyi* as an example, associates the process with the organizational development of the Zhou military which then extended to non-military offices; see Hsu and Linduff, *Western Chou Civilization*, pp. 245–49, 54–56; Shaughnessy, "Western Zhou History," pp. 325–26. In two recent studies, I have shown in detail that not only were some bureaucratic rules developed in the way the central administrative body was divided during the Western Zhou, but the selection and promotion of officials for higher services also seem to have followed some bureaucratic rules. The reader is invited to read these studies for details. See Li Feng, "'Offices' in Bronze Inscriptions," pp. 1–72; "Succession and Promotion," pp. 1–35.

the maturity of the Zhou-style decoration characterized by various types of magnificent bird patterns placed in prominent positions on the bronzes, marking a complete break from the traditionally dominant animal masks originating in Shang.[11] Moreover, it has also been suggested that, in the realm of literature, poems that were to be performed by a collective body of celebrants of the ancestral rites gave way to poems that were sung by ritual specialists before an audience.[12] However, the most profound change came in a way that was neither intended nor initiated by the Zhou: it was in the reign of King Mu that the Zhou experienced the first major foreign invasion in the hundred years after their conquest of Shang. This incident is fully evident in a series of contemporaneous bronze inscriptions. Three inscriptions indicate that the Zhou royal forces under the command of Shi Yongfu 師雝父 were deployed in the Gu 古 garrison.[13] The frontline of Gu was formed by the polity of Dao 道, located near present-day Runan 汝南 in Henan province, and the polity of Hu 戲 (Hu 胡), located near Fuyang 阜陽 in Anhui province, and the inscription of the Yu *ding* 歔鼎 (JC: 2721) mentions that Shi Yongfu subsequently inspected Dao and arrived in Hu.[14] According to the Dong *gui* 戜簋 (JC: 4322), a major battle seems to have been fought in a place called Yulin 棫林, located to the east of present-day Xiexian 葉縣, Henan, most likely near the Gu garrison, implying a possible breakthrough by the enemies of the Zhou frontline (Map 6).[15] The inscriptions make perfectly clear that the threat was from the lower reaches of the Huai River, and the Lu Dong *you* 彔戜卣 (JC: 5419) indeed mentions the enemies by the name Huaiyi 淮夷. The invasion was clearly also memorialized in the received textual records, as the *Current Bamboo Annals* records that in King Mu's thirteenth year the Xurong 徐戎, traditionally known as part of the Huaiyi, invaded the Luo River region, threatening the Zhou eastern center Luoyi.[16] There are still some problems in the historical-geographical reconstruction of this war, but there seems little doubt that this was an invasion through the valleys of the Ying and the Ru rivers, aiming at the capture of Luoyi.

Edward Shaughnessy has made two observations regarding this war between the Zhou and the Huaiyi. First, this was a war initiated by the

---

[11] For an analysis of this change, see Jessica Rawson, *Western Zhou Ritual Bronzes from the Arthur M. Sackler Collections* (Washington, DC: Arthur M. Sackler Foundation, 1990), pp. 75–83.

[12] See Edward Shaughnessy, *Before Confucius: Studies in the Creation of the Chinese Classics* (Albany, NY: State University of New York Press, 1997), pp. 175–87.

[13] These inscriptions are Yu *yan* 歔甗 (JC: 948), XX *you* 稻卣 (JC: 5411), and Jian *zun* 臤尊 (JC: 6008). Another inscription, on the Lu Dong *you* 彔戜卣 (JC: 5419), suggests that an official named Dong 戜 was commanded to lead the marshals of Chengzhou to defend the Gu garrison.

[14] For the identification of Hu 戲 with the polity of Hu 胡, see Li Xueqin, *Xinchu qingtongqi yanjiu*, p. 265; Qiu Xigui, *Gu wenzi lunji* (Beijing: Zhonghua, 1992), pp. 386–93. For the location of the polities of Dao and Hu, see also Xu Shaohua, *Zhou dai nantu lishi dili yu wenhua* (Wuhan: Wuhan daxue, 1994), pp. 157, 213.

[15] For the location of Yulin, see Qiu Xigui, *Gu wenzi lunji*, p. 388.

[16] See *Zhushu jinian*, 2, p. 9 (Legge, *The Shoo King*, Prolegomena, p. 150).

Huaiyi and not the Zhou, and therefore the Zhou "victory" in expelling the enemy suggests at best a successful defense. Second, the likely location of the battleground at Yulin in present-day Xiexian, about 140 kilometers from Luoyi, suggests that the Huaiyi at that time were able to launch attacks not only on the peripheral regions of the Western Zhou state, but into its core area, threatening the Zhou center in the east.[17] Evidently, the invasion by the Huaiyi during the reign of King Mu was an important watershed in Western Zhou history – the beginning of Zhou's gradual decline. From this time on the Zhou position in foreign relations began to change from that of invaders to that of defenders. In domestic politics, the Western Zhou state also began to show signs of disorder and conflict. Not only was the basic organizing principle of the Western Zhou state challenged – political unity maintained through the submission of the regional rulers to the Zhou king. Even the principle of royal succession, which had never been a problem since the beginning of the dynasty, was also seriously questioned.

We have a number of sources that show disorders and conflicts in the Western Zhou state in the post-King Mu period of the mid-Western Zhou. The bronze inscriptions suggest that in this period disputes occurred between the Zhou court and some of its old political allies on the border. For instance, the Guaibo *gui* 乖伯簋 (JC: 4331) records a campaign led by Duke Yi (Yigong 益公) against Mei'ao 眉敖, ruler of the state of Guai, whose ancestors had assisted the Zhou since the time of King Wen and King Wu. The state of Guai was regarded by the Zhou king as a foreign ally and was probably located somewhere in the upper Jing River region.[18] If this inscription is still not sufficient to demonstrate the disorder in the political system of the Western Zhou state, then another inscription, the Fifth Year Shi Shi *gui* 五年師事簋 (JC: 4216), would suggest that this was definitely the case. This inscription, discovered in the area of the Zhou capital Feng, records a campaign that took place in the ninth month of the fifth year of a Zhou king. In this campaign, Shi Shi, the caster of the bronze, was commanded by the Zhou king to attack the state of Qi in

---

[17] See Xia Hanyi (Edward Shaughnessy), *Wengu zhixin lu: Shang Zhou wenhua shi guanjian* (Taibei: Daohuo, 1997), pp. 153–54.

[18] The Guaibo *gui* mentions that Duke Yi was sent to attack Mei'ao on the *jiayin* day (no. 51) in the ninth month of the ninth year (9/9/51); on the *jiwei* day (no. 56) in the second month of the following year (10/2/56), Mei'ao appeared at the Zhou court. The bronze must have been cast close in time to the Ninth Year Qiu Wei *ding* 九年裘衛鼎 (JC: 2831), which mentions Mei'ao sending envoys to the Zhou court. However, the two dates recorded in the Guaibo *gui* would require the ninth month to have included days *jiashen* (no. 21) to *jiayin* (no. 51). So, the first month of the same year would not have *gengchen* (no. 17), which is the day recorded in the Ninth Year Qiu Wei *ding*. This suggests that the Guaibo *gui* and the Ninth Year Qiu Wei *ding*, both cast in the ninth year, were probably from different reigns. The Ninth Year Qiu Wei *ding* is generally considered to be from the time of King Gong, so the Guaibo *gui* would be possibly from the reign of King Yih. For the background of Mei'ao and the date of the Guaibo *gui*, see Li Feng, "Literacy Crossing Cultural Borders," pp. 210–42.

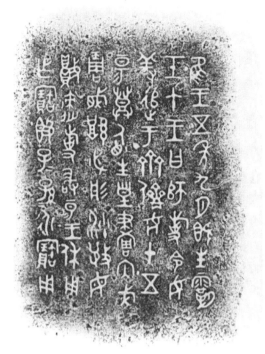

Fig. 17 The Fifth Year Shi Shi *gui* discovered at Zhangjiapo (JC: 4216.2; *Shaanxi qingtongqi*, p. 115)

Shandong (Fig. 17).[19] It is quite surprising that the state of Qi, one of the prominent Zhou regional states, founded by the Grand Duke who was said to have commanded the Zhou troops during the conquest campaign, was the target of Zhou royal attack! The situation is so unusual that we must look into the received textual records for more background information. Not accidentally, both the *Ancient* and the *Current Bamboo Annals* record that in his third year King Yi (r. 865–858 BC) summoned the many regional rulers to the Zhou capital and boiled Duke Ai of Qi in a huge caldron.[20] The *Shiji* gives more details about this incident. After killing Duke Ai, King Yi appointed the duke's brother, Duke Hu, to rule the state of Qi. Soon after, another brother of Duke Ai by the same mother killed Duke Hu and established himself as the ruler of Qi – Duke Xian.[21] It is very likely that the state of Qi experienced some major turmoil during the late mid-Western Zhou period that brought it into a series of conflicts with the Zhou royal will. Because the campaign was recorded in the Fifth Year Shi Shi *gui* as two years later than the execution of Duke Ai of Qi recorded in

[19] On the finding of the Fifth Year Shi Shi *gui*, see *Chang'an Zhangjiapo Xi Zhou tongqi qun*, pls. 14–16.
[20] See Fan Xiangyong, *Guben zhushu jinian jizheng*, p. 30; *Zhushu jinian*, 2, p. 12 (Legge, *The Shoo King*, Prolegomena, p. 153).
[21] See *Shiji*, 32, pp. 1,481–82.

the *Bamboo Annals*, it could be a punitive action carried out by the Zhou court to remove the self-appointed Qi ruler.[22] But if that is the case, since Duke Xian continued to rule for another seven or eight years until the time of King Li, it would seem that the campaign had possibly resulted in a military failure, if not a humiliating defeat of the royal army at the hands of the regional troops.

However, the received textual records tell us more than this, and the larger picture they present of the mid-Western Zhou period is quite consistent with what we can construct from the bronze inscriptions. But perhaps the most important piece of information that is missing from the bronze inscriptions is relevant to a possible succession dispute that occurred at the Zhou court on the death of King Yih (r. 899/97–873 BC). According to the *Shiji*, for the first time since the Regency of the Duke of Zhou at the beginning of the dynasty, the royal heir was left aside and power was passed back to one of King Mu's sons, King Xiao (r. 872?–866 BC), uncle of the deceased King Yih.[23] The historical background of this very strange succession is unknown, but whatever the case was, the accession of King Xiao clearly violated the normal pattern of royal succession and this could not have been done without causing conflict among the court officials. The fact that King Yih's son was reestablished as king after the death of King Xiao suggests that the rule of King Xiao was eventually regarded as illegitimate in Zhou tradition. In general, the presentation of the mid-Western Zhou period in the received textual records emphasizes the increasing weakness of royal authority and the incompetence of the Zhou kings. We read in the *Shiji* that "in King Yih's time, the royal court declined, and the poets wrote critical poems."[24] And the *Current Bamboo Annals* suggests that King Yih may have moved his residence out of the capital to a place called Huaili 槐里.[25] For his son King Yi, there was a tradition in the *Zuozuan* (twenty-sixth year of Duke Zhao) that he was physically ill,[26] and the *Current Bamboo Annals* indeed says that he died of an illness in his eighth year.[27] In the later Confucian text *Liji*, King Yi is said, probably rumored, to have had to descend from the audience hall to meet with the regional rulers on equal ground.[28] Some of the details in these accounts may not be reliable, and there is no way that we should take them at face value, but these late sources seem to reflect a strong and persistent tradition that the mid-Western Zhou was a period marked by political

---

[22] The stylistic features of the Fifth Year Shi Shi *gui* and its dating in relation to the turmoil in the state of Qi have already been discussed in some detail by Shaughnessy; see Shaughnessy, *Sources of Western Zhou History*, pp. 267–78. For the inscription, see also Shirakawa, "Kinbun tsūshaku," 25.141:236.

[23] See *Shiji*, 4, p. 141 (Nienhauser, *The Grand Scribe's Records*, 1, p. 70). Unfortunately, the *Shiji* is the only source for this unusual succession. However, while no scholar has ever doubted this, the record is itself peculiar enough to suggest the possibility that Sima Qian may have based his account on some earlier sources.

[24] See *Shiji*, 4, p. 140 (Nienhauser, *The Grand Scribe's Records*, 1, p. 70).

[25] See *Zhushu jinian*, 2, p. 11 (Legge, *The Shoo King*, Prolegomena, p. 152).

[26] See *Zuozhuan*, 52, p. 2,114.   [27] See *Zhuzhu jinian*, 2, p. 12.   [28] See *Liji*, 25, p. 1,447.

instability and royal incompetence; this image fits well with what we can learn about the period from the inscriptional sources such as the Fifth Year Shi Shi *gui* on the royal campaign against Qi. The political instability is also suggested by and may have been closely related to the shortness of the mid-Western Zhou reigns: it has been made perfectly clear by the recent discovery of the inscription of the Lai *pan* that the four mid-Western Zhou kings, put together, ruled for a total length of time that was equal to only two generations in Lai's family.[29]

In a very vivid sense, however, a unique mid-Western Zhou inscription, the Mu *gui* 牧簋 (JC: 4343), informs us of the political chaos that is also evident in the textual records, and a full translation of it is given here.[30]

惟王七年十又三月，既生霸，甲寅。王在周，在師汸（湯?）父宮。格太室，即位。公
ᴿ（尹）絹入右牧，立中庭。王呼內史吳冊命牧。王若曰："牧！昔先王既命汝作嗣土。
今余唯或啻改，命汝辟百寮（僚）。□（厥?）有ᴵ（同?）事，卣（迺）逎多啇（亂），不用
先王作井（型），亦多虐庶民。厥訊庶右蓉（鄰），不井（型）不中，ᴼ（迺?）厌（侯?）
止ᴸ（稻）ᴵᴵ（人?）。今，ᴮ嗣富（偪=逼?）厥皋（辜?）召（招）故。"王曰："牧！
汝勿敢□（不?）□（用?）先王作明井（型）。用雩（于）乃訊右蓉（鄰），勿敢不明不中不井
（型）；乃申政事，勿敢不尹丌（其）不中不井（型）。今余唯繭罍乃命，錫汝秬鬯一卣，

金車：ᴬ（賁?）較畫輯，朱虢（鞹）囨（鞃）斳（靳），虎䡇（韓）熏（纁）裏，旆（旗），
余（騂）[馬]四匹。取□[鍰]（賵 = 專?）□[?]受（守）。敬夙夕，勿廢朕命。"牧拜稽首，
敢對揚王丕顯休。用作朕皇文考益伯寶尊簋。牧其萬年壽考，子子孫孫□[永]寶用。

It was the king's seventh year, thirteenth month, after the growing brightness, *jiayin*. The king was in Zhou, in Shi Zifu (Tangfu?) Gong. [He] entered the grand chamber and assumed position. The Duke-Governor XX entered and accompanied Mu to his right, standing at the center of the courtyard. The king called out to the Interior Scribe Wu to command Mu with a written document. The king said to the effect: "Mu! In the past, the previous king already commanded you to serve as Supervisor of Land.[31] Now, I am to further change the order, and command you to rule the hundred bureaus. In their affairs, [they] would (?) therefore cause many disorders; [they] do not use the model created by the former kings, and also abuse the common people a great deal. [When] they question the many neighbors,[32]

---

[29] See *Wenwu* 2003.6, 26.

[30] This long inscription was discovered in the Northern Song dynasty (AD 960–1126) and has not been fully understood in earlier scholarship. I have recently examined all textual versions of this inscription and have suggested the above reading. For more details, see Li Feng, "Textual Criticism and Western Zhou Bronze Inscriptions: The Example of the Mu Gui," in *Essays in Honour of An Zhimin*, ed. Tang Chung and Chen Xingcan (Hong Kong: Chinese University of Hong Kong, 2004), pp. 280–97. For a transcription and interpretation of the Mu *gui* inscription, see also Shirakawa, "Kinbun Tsūshaku," 19.104:364.

[31] Some scholars read this term as "Supervisor of Officers" (*sishi* 嗣士), as some of the transmitted hand-drawings of the inscription seem to suggest; see Zhang Yachu and Liu Yu, *Xi Zhou jinwen guanzhi yanjiu* (Beijing: Zhonghua, 1986), pp. 38–39. However, since there is no other example of such an office in the entire corpus of Western Zhou bronze inscriptions, *sishi* may be a mistake made by the Song artist who actually transcribed the inscription from the bronze to paper. Therefore, I maintain the more common term "Supervisor of Land" (*situ* 嗣土).

[32] Here, my reading departs from the previous readings that more often read *xun* 訊, *shuyou* 庶右, and *lin* 蓉 as three official titles. See Ma Chengyuan, *Shang Zhou qingtongqi*, 3, p. 188; Shirakawa, "Kinbun Tsūshaku," 19.104:365. When *xun* appears for the second time in the inscription, it appears

[they] do not model [themselves on the former kings] and are not moderate; therefore, [they] hostilely (or hastily?) arrive in *dao*-ing the people (?). Now, [they] X work to force their criminals to confess [their] faults." The king said: "Mu! Don't you dare [not to take] the former kings to be your illustrious models. Therefore, in your questioning the many neighbors, don't [you] dare not to be bright and moderate, and not to model [yourself on the former kings]; [when you] conduct administration, don't you dare not to control those who are not moderate and do not model [themselves on the former kings]. Now, I am to extend your mission, awarding you one *you* of fragrant wine, a bronze-fitted chariot, which has decorated side-rails, patterned axle-coverings, a covering of the front-rail and chest-trappings made of scarlet leather, a tiger-skin canopy with brown lining, a banner, and four fine [horses] from the north. Take [five?] *lüe* [of *tuan*-metals]. Be respectful morning and evening, and do not fail my command." Mu bowed with [his] head touching the ground, and dares to extol the king's greatly illustrious beneficence. [Mu] herewith makes for my august cultured deceased-father Yi Bo [this] treasured sacrificial *gui*-vessel. May Mu for ten thousand years enjoy longevity, and his sons' sons and grandsons' grandsons [eternally] treasure and use [it]!

Different from all other Western Zhou inscriptions, which record honorable matters, this rare inscription speaks about the dark side of the Zhou government and administration through the mouth of a Zhou king. According to the royal words, those officials in the "hundred bureaus," a generic term referring to the Zhou government as a whole, had together caused many disorders. They not only betrayed the teachings of the former kings, but also abused the common people a great deal. This was especially serious when they dealt with civil disputes in the neighborhood; they would not conduct careful investigation, but possibly used force to extort criminal confessions. Because of this, Mu, previously Supervisor of Land, was recalled and put in a position responsible for disciplining the officials in the central government. The long inscription leaves us with the impression that by the mid-Western Zhou the Zhou bureaucracy had become an abusive and oppressive body of corrupt officials. The royal lament over the lack of spirit and discipline in government service tells us exactly about the political disorder in the Western Zhou state. After all, it is quite possible that the Zhou king who was condemning the disorderly officials in this inscription was King Xiao, the king who had possibly usurped royal power upon the death of King Yih.[33]

in the phrase *yu nai xun you lin* 霁乃訊右叠 which runs in exact parallel with the phrase *nai shen zheng shi* 乃申政事, and the sentences following them are exactly the same. Therefore, *xun* must be read as a verb meaning "to question" or "to interrogate." As this is very clear, the first *xun* should also be read as a verb. While reading *shuyou* and *lin* as two official titles is not impossible, "many neighbors" (*shu youlin* 庶右叠) works much better with the preceding sentence that talks about the "common people."

[33] The Mu *gui* mentions Neishi Wu 内史吳, who also appears in the Shi Hu *gui* 師虎簋 (JC: 4316) and Shi Yun *gui* 師𤩴簋 (JC: 4283). In all three "Appointment Inscriptions," Wu played the role of announcing the royal command to the appointees, suggesting that the three bronzes must have been close in time. Most scholars date the Shi Hu *gui* to the first year of King Yih (899 BC), in relation to the Fifth Year Qiu Wei *ding* 五年裘衛鼎 (JC: 2832) and in conjunction with the solar eclipse that occurred in that year; in fact, the inscription has been used as one of the fixed points for the reconstruction of the Western Zhou calendar. See Shaughnessy, *Sources of Western Zhou*

In short, our current evidence suggests that the mid-Western Zhou was a period of significant changes. Evidently, the Western Zhou state was taking a downturn both in its relations with the outside world and in its domestic political system, showing clear signs of disorder and decline. Certainly the changes that occurred during the mid-Western Zhou were manifold and needed to be addressed, besides the political changes analyzed here as evidence of the decline of royal power, in other social and cultural contexts. To art historians, the period represents a complete change both in the way the bronzes were ornamented and in the way they were used, a change that some have termed "Ritual Revolution" or "Ritual Reform."[34] Most notably, the various types of bird decoration fashionable in the early mid-Western Zhou were replaced by the more abstract and bold patterns that can often be described in geometric terms.[35] In the way the bronzes were used, especially in the ritual context of burials, a major shift gradually took place at least in central Shaanxi during the late mid-Western Zhou: the traditional combination of burial bronzes centered on wine vessels gave way to a new assemblage that was essentially devoid of wine vessels.[36] While the issue cannot be discussed in detail here, given the purpose of the current analysis to identify signs of Zhou's decline, the phenomenon was certainly the material manifestation of an underlying sociocultural change that had evidently taken place during the mid-Western Zhou.

The late Western Zhou crisis: the exile of King Li

If the mid-Western Zhou was a period of increasing political instability and military weakness, then it is certainly true that, at the beginning of the late Western Zhou, the Western Zhou state was running into a total crisis. By "total crisis" I mean that troubles had spread to all aspects of Western Zhou society and had intensified to the degree that even the survival of the

History, pp. 257–58; Ma Chengyuan, *Shang Zhou qingtongqi*, 3, pp. 167–68; *Xia Shang Zhou duandai gongcheng*, pp. 25–26. Shaughnessy notes further that, since the full date of the Mu *gui* is incompatible with the Shi Hu *gui* in the same calendar, the Mu *gui* is likely to have been cast in the next reign, probably in the seventh year of King Xiao; Shaughnessy, *Sources of Western Zhou History*, pp. 259–61. For more discussion on the stylistic features of the Mu *gui* and its possible date, see Li Feng, "Textual Criticism and Western Zhou Bronze Inscriptions," pp. 283–93.

[34] See Jessica Rawson, "Statesmen or Barbarians? The Western Zhou as Seen through Their Bronzes," *Proceedings of the British Academy* 75 (1989), 89–93; Rawson "Western Zhou Archaeology," pp. 433–40. See also Luo Tai (Lothar von Falkenhausen), "Youguan Xi Zhou wanqi lizhi gaige ji Zhuangbai Weishi qingtongqi niandai de xin jiashe-cong shixi mingwen shuoqi," in *Zhongguo kaoguxue yu lishixue zhi zhenghe yanjiu* (Taipei: Academia Sinica, 1997), pp. 651–75; "Late Western Zhou Taste," *Études Chinoises* 18 (1999), 155–64. It should be noted that while Rawson now pinpoints this change within the confines of the mid-Western Zhou, particularly in the reigns of Kings Yih, Xiao, and Yi, from 899/97 to 858 BC, Falkenhausen insists on calling it the "Late Western Zhou Ritual Reform," a transformation that he thinks occurred around 850 BC; see Rawson, "Western Zhou Archaeology," p. 434; Falkenhausen, "Late Western Zhou Taste," pp. 150–51, especially note 14 on p. 151.

[35] For a recent discussion on this topic, see Falkenhausen, "Late Western Zhou Taste," pp. 155–74.

[36] See Rawson, *Western Zhou Ritual Bronzes*, p. 102. For earlier observations on this phenomenon in archaeology, see Guo Baojun, *Shang Zhou tongqiqun zonghe yanjiu* (Beijing: Wenwu, 1981), pp. 62–63; Li Feng, "Huanghe liuyu Xi Zhou muzang," p. 392.

dynasty was called into question. This was clearly the situation in the reign of King Li.

In foreign relations, Zhou's security was simultaneously threatened on two fronts: the Huaiyi in the southeast and the Xianyun in the northwest. After the war that took place during the reign of King Mu, the Huaiyi continued to be formidable adversaries in the southeast, and military contest between them and Zhou had never stopped. So it was understandable that the Huaiyi continued to be the target of military campaigns in the time of King Li. The Ehou Yufang *ding* 鄂侯馭方鼎 (JC: 2810), cast most likely during the reign of King Li or slightly earlier,[37] mentions that the king attacked Jiao 角 and Yu 鄱; on the way back he had an audience with the ruler of the state of E, probably located in the Nanyang basin of southern Henan, at a place called Pei 坏 and richly rewarded him.[38] The king indeed treated the Ruler of E with great courtesy and entertained him with archery ritual and a banquet, and then richly rewarded him. It was this Ehou, one of only two people in the inscriptions identifiable as having had the honorable title "Border Protector" (*yufang* 馭方), who soon rebelled against Zhou, and this touched off extensive disturbances among the Huaiyi in the Huai River region and the Dongyi in the Shandong region. According to the Yu *ding* 禹鼎 (JC: 2834), the Huaiyi and the Dongyi launched attacks along almost half of the perimeter of the Western Zhou state. It can hardly be an exaggeration that this put the Zhou in a very dangerous situation, comparable to that of the rebellion of the "Three Overseers" and Wu Geng at the beginning of the dynasty. To deal with the situation, the court not only sent the Eight Armies into the field but also moved the Six Armies stationed on the Wei River plain to the east. However, they failed. Finally, Yu was sent out with Duke Wu's private army, and he managed to capture Ehou the Border Protector (Fig. 18).[39] Another inscription, the Wu *gui* 敔簋 (JC: 4323), apparently cast in the same period and also mentioning Duke Wu as the superior commander at the Zhou court, says that the Southern Huaiyi reached

---

[37] The Ehou Yufang *ding* can be dated in relation to the Yu *ding* (JC: 2834) that mentions Ehou Yufang's rebellion. The Yu *ding* names a number of Yu's ancestors and, more importantly, Wu Gong 武公, a very influential figure in the early late Western Zhou court who provides links to many other bronzes; on this basis, the scholars unanimously date the bronze to the reign of King Li. See Xu Zhongshu, "Yu ding de niandai jiqi xiangguan wenti," *Kaogu xuebao* 1959.3, 53–67; Ma Chengyuan, *Shang Zhou qingtongqi*, 3, p. 281; Shaughnessy, *Sources of Western Zhou History*, p. 179; Shirakawa, "Kinbun tsūshaku," 27.162:451–52. I have recently suggested that the Ehou Yufang *ding*, as a bronze cast in a cultural environment different from that of Zhou, presents a mixture of early Western Zhou body design and late mid-Western Zhou ornament. See Li Feng, "Literacy Crossing Cultural Borders," pp. 222–31.

[38] The two place-names appear as Jiaohuai 角𩰫 and Tongyu 桐遹 on the Miaosheng *xu* 翏生盨 (JC: 4459), in the context of a royal campaign against the Southern Huaiyi. For the identification of these names in the Huai River region and the historical background of the Miaosheng *xu*, see Ma Chengyuan, "Guanyu Miaosheng xu he Zhujian zhong de jidian yijian," *Kaogu* 1979.1, 60–62. See also Shirakawa, "Kinbun tsūshaku," 25.142:260–67.

[39] For an English translation of the Yu *ding* inscription, see Edward Shaughnessy (ed.), *New Sources of Early Chinese History: An Introduction to the Reading of Inscriptions and Manuscripts* (Berkeley: Society for the Study of Early China, 1997), pp. 82–84.

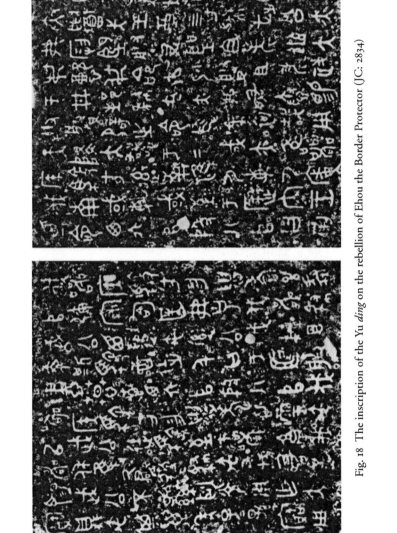

Fig. 18 The inscription of the Yu *ding* on the rebellion of Ehou the Border Protector (JC: 2834)

as far as the Luo and Yi river valleys in the vicinity of the Zhou eastern capital.[40]

In the northwest, particularly in the upper Jing River valley, war between the Zhou and the Xianyun broke out some time during the mid-Western Zhou. By the reign of King Li, the Xianyun had apparently gained the upper hand and launched frequent attacks on Zhou polities and communities in the upper Jing region. One of these attacks was recorded in some detail in the inscription of the Duoyou *ding* 多友鼎 (JC: 2835). The war with the Xianyun was more critical than that with the Huaiyi because failure in the upper Jing region could lead directly to invasion of the Wei River valley. However, this critical war will be examined in detail in the next chapter.

Domestically, the political struggles at court and social unrest in the capital area became white-hot around 842 BC. During a revolt in the capital, the royal palace was attacked by the rebels and King Li was forced into exile. Fourteen years later, he died in exile at Zhi 彘 in the Fen River valley of Shanxi. This unusual incident had a very complex social and political context which will be discussed below (see pp. 131–34). The traditional account, presented mainly in the *Guoyu* and adopted into the *Shiji*, blames King Li for this political crisis. According to this account, King Li was a brutal tyrant who abruptly extorted wealth to enrich the royal house.[41] In the *Guoyu*, King Li is also accused of having reformed the traditional institutions.[42] King Li's policy is said to have met with protest from the so-called *guoren* 國人, or "people of the capital," but he adopted severe measures to deal with the criticism. This angered the people even more until they staged a large-scale rebellion in 842 BC, forcing King Li to flee. The general historical outline regarding King Li's exile can be confirmed by other sources such as the *Bamboo Annals* and is supported also by the bronze inscriptions. The *Ancient* version of the text, while supporting the historicity of the exile, states that it was a person named Gongbo He 共伯和 who had actually interfered with the position of the king, and is thus quite different from the *Shiji* account.[43] It seems more likely that the narrative in the *Guoyu* and *Shiji* about the people overthrowing the king was a direct reflection of Eastern Zhou social reality that such mass movements frequently happened in the regional states.

One piece of positive evidence for this dramatic political change in the Zhou court comes from the inscription of the Shi Hui *gui* 師毀簋 (JC: 4311):[44]

---

[40] In this case, the inscription explicitly mentions the Luo and Yi river valleys as places that the Southern Huaiyi had reached during their invasion.

[41] See *Guoyu*, 1, pp. 9–10; *Shiji*, 4, pp. 141–42 (Nienhauser, *The Grand Scribe's Records*, 1, pp. 70–71).

[42] See *Guoyu*, 3, p. 110.   [43] See Fan Xiangyong, *Guben zhushu jinian*, p. 30.

[44] For the inscription of the Shi Hui *gui*, see also Shirakawa, "Kinbun tsūshaku," 31.186:740.

惟王元年正月初吉丁亥，伯龢父若曰: 師毀，乃祖考有𤉡（勳）于我家。汝有惟小子，余
命汝死我家，𤔲嗣我西隔東隔僕駿、百工、牧、臣、妾，東（董）𢦏（裁）內外。毋敢否
善。錫戈戥戥、□柲、彤𥎓十五，錫鐘一，磬五全。敬乃夙夜，用事。毀拜頓首，對揚皇
君休。用作朕文考乙仲𤖺簋。毀其萬年子子孫孫永寶用享。

It was the king's first year, first month, first auspiciousness, *dinghai* day; Bo Hefu
said to the effect: Shi Hui! Your grandfather and father had accomplishment in
our family.[45] Although you are but a young man, I command you to serve our
family diligently, in charge of the servant chariot-drivers, the hundred craftsmen,
the herders, and the male and female slaves in our western district and eastern
district, interrogating and judging both internal and external affairs. Don't dare to
be not good! [I] award [you] fifteen dagger-axes with carved ends, XX-handles, and
red tassels, one bell made of red metal, and five sets of stone chimes. Be respectful
morning and night in serving [your] affairs. Hui bowed with his head touching
the ground; [he] extols the beneficence of the august monarch. [I] herewith make
for my cultured deceased father Yizhong [this] *gui*-vessel. May Hui's sons' sons
and grandsons' grandsons for ten thousand years eternally treasure and use it in
offering.

Guo Moruo identified this Bo Hefu with Gongbo He 共伯和, head of the
Gong lineage, who is said then in the *Bamboo Annals* to have stepped in to
rule in the king's position after the exit of King Li until his death in 828 BC,[46]
and this identification is generally accepted by scholars.[47] Other scholars
further note that the use of the term *ruoyue* 若曰 in the inscription, generally
reserved for quotations of the king, suggests that Gongbo He did indeed
rule from the position of the Zhou king. But it is above all significant that
this is one of the only two inscriptions that record official appointments
announced by a minister, while all other "Appointment Inscriptions" record
the Zhou king as the host of such ceremonies. Moreover, Shaughnessy notes
that the full date recorded in the inscription matches exactly the calendar
of the first month of 841 BC.[48] It seems to me that on the current evidence
the historicity of Gongbo He's regency can firmly be established, and so
can the exile of King Li that occasioned the rule of Gongbo He.

However, from inscriptional evidence, I consider that Gongbo He's role
may have been greater than simply an official who ruled in the king's
absence. The inscription of the First Year Shi Dui *gui* 元年師兌簋 (JC:
4274) records the appointment of the caster as an assistant to Shi Hefu
師龢父 who was in charge of the military units called "Masters of Horses"
(*zouma* 走馬) in the Left and Right Camps of the capital and the "Masters
of Horses" in the five major cities in the Wei River valley. Two years later,
according to the Third Year Shi Dui *gui* 三年師兌簋 (JC: 4318), Shi Dui was

45 The reading of the graph 𤉡 as *xun* 勳 (accomplishment) follows Yang Shuda; see Yang Shuda,
    Jiweiju jinwen shuo (supplemented) (Beijing: Zhonghua, 1997), p. 119; see also Shirakawa, "Kinbun
    tsūshaku," 31.186:747. Some scholars read it as *jue* 爵 taking it to mean *ke* 恪 (to respect); see Ma
    Chengyuan, *Shang Zhou qingtongqi*, 3, p. 263.
46 See Fan Xiangyong, *Guben zhushu jinian*, p. 30; *Zhushu jinian*, 2, p. 13 (Legge, *The Shoo King*,
    Prolegomena, p. 154).
47 See Guo Moruo, *Liang Zhou jinwen ci daxi tulu kaoshi* (Beijing: Kexue, 1958), p. 114.
48 See Yang Shuda, *Jiweiju jinwen shuo*, p. 119; Shaughnessy, *Sources of Western Zhou History*, pp. 272–73.

promoted to take over Shi Hefu's office in full capacity.[49] The inscriptions suggest that Shi Hefu was once commander of the praetorian troops in the Zhou capital region and probably had some important influence on the Zhou court prior to the downfall of King Li. It is possible that he may not just have benefited from the king's fall, but possibly also played a part in it. The prominence of Gongbo He can also be seen in another inscription, the Shi Li *gui* 師釐簋 (JC: 4324.2). The inscription on the vessel part of the Shi Li *gui* mentions that when Shi Hefu died, Li, the principal caster of the bronze, reported it to the king in mourning dress and the king thus rewarded the caster. The presence of the king in this inscription suggests that it should be dated not to the Interregnum of Gongbo He, but to the early years of the next King, Xuan (r. 827/25–782 BC).[50] The fact that the caster was rewarded by the king for a report he made on the death of Shi Hefu suggests reasonably that the deceased was a very important political figure at the Zhou court.

STRUCTURAL CONFLICT AND THE ORIGINS OF POLITICAL ANTAGONISM

It has become clear from the above discussion mainly based on inscriptional evidence that through much of the mid-Western Zhou and the early phase of the late Western Zhou there had developed a general trend towards the weakening of royal power in the face of the spreading political disorder and foreign invasions. The crises were both internal and external, but more

---

[49] On the promotion of Shi Dui, see Li Feng, "Succession and Promotion," p. 14.

[50] The four bronzes, though arguably from the late Western Zhou period to judge from the artistic features they exhibit, have been variously dated by previous scholars. For instance, Guo Moruo dates the Shi Dui *gui* to the reign of King You and Ma Chengyuan dates it to King Xiao; see Guo Moruo, *Liang Zhou jinwen ci daxi*, pp. 154–56; Ma Chengyuan, *Shang Zhou qingtongqi*, 3, pp. 200–2. Rather than dating them as individual bronzes, I think that it is important first to comprehend the internal connections suggested by their inscriptions. On the basis of the identification of Bo Hefu with Shi Hefu, I believe that the four inscriptions themselves suggest a sensible historical sequence: while the Shi Li *gui* was cast at the death of Bo Hefu, providing an end point of the sequence and hence dating later than all other bronzes that mention him, the First Year and Third Year Shi Dui *gui* are more likely to have been cast during Bo Hefu's early career prior to his regency; the Shi Hui *gui*, in which he speaks like a king, on the other hand, was probably cast during his regency. The presence of the king in the Shi Li *gui*, where the death of Shi Hefu is reported, almost certainly dates it to the reign of King Xuan, particularly in his eleventh year (817 BC, taking 827 BC as his first year), a date that is supported also by other evidence. The inscription mentions another figure, Zai Zhou Sheng 宰周生, a superintendent of the royal household and the principal caster of the Zhou Sheng *gui* 周生簋 (or Shaobo Hu *gui* 召伯虎簋; JC: 4292–93) and Zhou Sheng *dou* 周生豆 (JC: 4682), generally dated to the reign of King Xuan. As for the two Shi Dui *gui*, they certainly cannot be dated too far apart from the date of the Shi Li *gui* in the eleventh year of King Xuan, but in addition they certainly cannot be put in the Gonghe interregnum, because the king is active in the inscriptions. Therefore, the most suitable time for it is the reign of King Li. In fact, on the basis of calendric studies, Shaughnessy has already suggested that the two bronzes should be placed in the reign of King Li. More support for this date is the appearance of Tong Zhong 同中 in both the First Year Shi Dui *gui* and the Jifu *hu* 幾父壺 (JC: 9721), cast probably in the time of King Yi or King Li. See Shaughnessy, *Sources of Western Zhou History*, pp. 281–86. On the date of the Jifu *hu*, see Chen Gongrou, "Ji Jifu hu Zha zhong jiqi tongchu de tongqi," *Kaogu* 1962.2, 88–101; *Fufeng Qijiacun qingtongqi qun* (Beijing: Wenwu, 1963), pp. 7–8.

fundamentally internal in the political and social structure of the Western Zhou state. For a long time, the Western Zhou state was apparently unable to overcome these problems that had accumulated in an enormous destructive force undermining the foundation of the Zhou regime.

The problem of explanation

What were the origins of the political disorder and crisis analyzed above? Could the Zhou have avoided these problems if better policies were implemented in time? What were the real causes of Zhou's gradual decline? These questions have been repeatedly asked with regard to a large number of ancient civilizations or states such as the Indus civilization, the Assyrian Empire, the Maya, and, most intensively perhaps, the Roman Empire. In an attempt to understand the general pattern and dynamics of decline and collapse, Joseph Tainter has developed a universal model that he thinks can explain the collapse of all complex societies.[51] In his view, human societies are problem-solving organizations that need continuing investment of energy for their maintenance. The basic strategy of complex societies to deal with stress is to increase their complexity, which means increased costs of investment. At first, the most general, most accessible, and least expensive solutions are attempted, and therefore the investment yields a favorable return of benefit. However, continuing stresses and unanticipated challenges force the societies to invest more, and once the least costly solutions have been exhausted, the societies must invest in a more costly way by expanding hierarchy and specialization. At some point the marginal return of benefit per unit of investment would begin to decline. A society that cannot counter this curve between an increased cost and a decreased benefit would inevitably decline, and when the stresses become insurmountable the society will collapse.[52] Drawing his information exclusively from Herrlee Creel, Tainter considers that Western Zhou society matches this pattern of decline, and writes: "The increasing costliness of ensuring loyalty of feudal officials seems to have coincided with an upswing in barbarian incursions. There was thus a pattern of increasing costs of integration and of containing stress surges, imposed on a situation where returns for such costs may not have increased at all."[53]

There are probably some merits in Tainter's theory of decline and collapse, for the simple fact that all past complex societies in human history, be it an empire, a kingdom, or a republic, have fallen, and the economic "law of diminishing returns" seems to account for this universal process. And as far as the Western Zhou is concerned, the mention of hierarchization and specialization as costly strategy with negative impact to deal with

[51] Joseph A. Tainter, *The Collapse of Complex Societies* (Cambridge: Cambridge University Press, 1988). [52] See *ibid.*, pp. 119–127, 195. [53] See *ibid.*, p. 203.

increasing problems is especially appealing, since we know that that was exactly what was going on during the mid-Western Zhou period. However, many historians would find Tainter's theory too general and simplistic to account for any historical specificity. If all complex societies eventually fell as they did, then the real question is not why they fell but when. Even if the "law of diminishing returns" worked to cause all falls in history, it is still left to the historian to find out when and for what particular reasons such a "law" began to bring a society to decline. Answers to such questions must account for historical oddities and can only be found in each subject area.[54] When looking into the problem of decline and fall, the historian should be more interested in locating specific factors that contributed to a society's weakening and in the way these factors interacted with each other, but not in a universal model that does not say very much.

In world context, and with respect to specific regions, the possibility of historical explanation of decline and fall has been explored to the fullest extent possible in the case of Rome. According to some unsympathetic statistics, as many as 210 factors have been suggested by scholars as causes of Rome's fall.[55] One of the primary lessons we learn from such scholarship is that as an enormously complex process the decline of a political power cannot and should not be explained by only one factor, because each factor acted with and upon every other factor.[56] Therefore, it is my understanding that rather than trying to determine the "ultimate cause," it would be more meaningful to try to demonstrate how a factor interacted with other factors. At the same time, we must draw a distinction between factors that are inherited in the general political and socioeconomic system and those factors that happened only accidentally to weaken a political power.

It seems to me that the crisis of the Western Zhou state was the result of changes gradually and simultaneously taking place in two fundamental relationships: (1) the relationship between the royal court and the regional states in the east; (2) the relationship between royal power and the power of the aristocratic families in the royal domain of Shaanxi. From the standpoint of institutional history, these changes were quite natural if not inevitable because they had their roots in the sociopolitical structure of the Western Zhou state. From the mid-Western Zhou onward, the Zhou king lost control of both of these relationships and therefore the foundation of the Western Zhou state was seriously undermined. In the following, I will analyze these changes and explain their origins.

---

[54] It should be noted that, as examples, Joseph Tainter analyzed three societies: the Roman Empire, the Maya, and the Chacoan; see *ibid.*, pp. 127–92.

[55] See Ferrill, *The Fall of the Roman Empire*, p. 12. For a volume that gathers some of the most important writings on the topic, see Donald Kagan (ed.), *Decline and Fall of the Roman Empire: Why Did It Collapse?* (Boston: D.C. Heath and Company, 1962).

[56] See Katz, *The Decline of Rome*, p. 74.

The "Fengjian" institution as a source of conflict

Before we can discuss factors for Zhou's weakness in the political system of the Western Zhou state, we need first to clarify the fundamental features of that system. For a long time, the interpretation of the Western Zhou state has been troubled by discussions of so-called "Western Zhou feudalism," which entails a comparison with the "feudal" system of medieval Europe.[57] In a recent study, I have systematically discussed problems with this identification and the inapplicability of "feudalism" to Western Zhou China.[58] As a matter of fact, in the last two decades "feudalism" has come under serious criticism even by scholars of medieval European history and has ceased to be an adequate way to describe the unique institutions of medieval Europe.[59] The doctrine of "Western Zhou feudalism" is based on misunderstandings of the Western Zhou state and its government, and of some non-feudal elements of medieval Europe as the essential features of "European feudalism."

The system that has been identified as "feudalism" was termed in the native Warring States tradition as "Fengjian" 封建, which means literally "to establish by means of marking boundaries."[60] It is impossible to offer here a detailed discussion of the Zhou institution named "Fengjian," which would demand a long study to clarify. But, for the very purpose of beginning to understand problems that arose later, possibly from the system, we can perhaps highlight some of the important features of it to the extent that they have become clear to us at this point. It should be noted first that the Warring States conception of Western Zhou "Fengjian" was probably a combination, perhaps mistakenly, of two original sets of regulations

---

[57] Both of the only two general histories of the Western Zhou period in the English language adopted "feudalism" as the basic frame of interpretation of the Western Zhou states; see Creel, *The Origins of Statecraft*, pp. 317–87; Hsu and Linduff, *Western Chou Civilization*, pp. 126–29, 147, 171–83. It must be noted also that all of these studies are different from the theory of "Western Zhou feudalism" advocated by the Marxist historians.

[58] See Li Feng, "Feudalism and Western Zhou China: A Criticism," *Harvard Journal of Asiatic Studies* 63.1 (2003), 115–44.

[59] The two most important critics of medieval European feudalism are Elizabeth A. R. Brown and Susan Reynolds. Reynolds mounted the most recent and massive attack on the concept of European feudalism, rejecting terms such as "feudalism," "feudal institution," and "feudal relation." See Elizabeth A. R. Brown, "The Tyranny of a Construct: Feudalism and Historians of Medieval Europe," *American Historical Review* 79.4 (1974), 1,063–88; Susan Reynolds, *Fiefs and Vassals: The Medieval Evidence Reinterpreted* (Oxford: Clarendon Press, 1994), pp. 11–12.

[60] The term *"Fengjian"* first appears in the *Zuozhuan*, where it is used in its verbal form. It is possible that the term was a Warring States creation to describe a Western Zhou institution by combining the two characters *feng* 封 and *jian* 建, which both appear in the Western Zhou bronze inscriptions. The original meaning of *feng* was "to plant trees in defining boundaries" as is obvious in the inscription of the Sanshi *pan* 散氏盤 (JC: 10176). The character *jian* has only recently been deciphered by Professor Qui Xigui to mean "to establish," appearing in the inscription of the Xiaochen X *ding* 小臣𦥑鼎 (JC: 2556), clearly in the context of a regional state being established: "The Duke of Shao established the state of Yan" (*Shao Gong jian Yan* 召公建燕). This point has been proven by the recent discovery of the Forty-Second Year Lai *ding* 四十二年逨鼎, on which the same character *jian* is used to describe the establishment of the ruler of Yang. See Qiu Xigui, *Gu wenzi lunji*, pp. 353–56; *Wenwu* 2003.6, 6, 18. Inscriptions such as the Yihou Ze *gui* 宜侯夨簋 (JC: 4320) and the Ke *lei* 克罍 (JL: 987) show that the action of establishing a person as ruler was also termed *hou* 侯 in the verbal sense.

that were implemented at the beginning of the Western Zhou but had become indistinguishable after the fall of the dynasty. One set of rules regulated the political relations between the royal court and the east where the numerous regional states were established, and the other was applied to the royal domain in the Wei River valley under the direct administrative control of the Zhou court. This bifurcated structure of the Western Zhou state has become increasingly clear from recent archaeology and is also evident in the received texts of Western Zhou date.[61] The division was both political and geographical, and it is certainly reflected in the language of the contemporary bronze inscriptions in which the rulers of the regional states in the east were customarily called *hou* 侯, while the heads of the aristocratic lineages in the royal domain in Shaanxi were called by their seniority order, very often *bo* 伯, the first-born of the family. Furthermore, it is likely that while the term *jian* is used to describe the establishment of the regional states, *feng* is used mostly in cases where landed properties were given to or transferred between two aristocratic lineages. In other words, *jian* and *feng* by their origins were associated with different institutional rules in different geopolitical settings. The term "Fengjian," according to its Warring States usage, will be used here to refer to the establishment of the regional states in the eastern half of the Western Zhou state.

In any event, the regional states were the most important constituting units of the Western Zhou state, as the relationship between the Zhou king and the regional rulers was the most important political relationship of the time. The essence of the "Fengjian" institution was that the function of the Western Zhou state was carried out by its numerous local agents, who were replicas of the Zhou central government and were centered on lineages as branches of the Zhou royal house or as marriage partners of it. As clarified in the preceding chapter, the rise of the regional states was a direct result not so much of the Zhou conquest of Shang as of the second conquest led by the Duke of Zhou to suppress the rebellions of the already conquered eastern population. As such, each regional state constituted an autonomous geopolitical entity located in a specific area, and was equipped with a small but complete government that enjoyed the combined rights of civil administration, legal punishment, and military authority. This is why in both the received texts and the excavated bronze inscriptions, the granting of the regional states was often accompanied by the granting of people.[62] In this regard, the regional Zhou states were very different from the "fiefs" of medieval Europe, which were essentially land "stipends" with

---

[61] For a detailed discussion of evidence for this division in the Western Zhou state, see Li Feng, "Transmitting Antiquity: The Origin and Paradigmization of the 'Five Ranks'," in *Perceptions of Antiquity in China's Civilization*, ed. Dieter Kohn (Monograph of *Monumenta Serica*), forthcoming.

[62] Itō Michiharu has compared the circumstances of the establishment of the states of Lu, Wei, and Jin in the *Zuozhuan* (fourth year of Duke Ding), and that recorded in the Yihou Ze *gui* on the establishment of the state of Yi, pointing out that the granting of people was an indispensable part of establishing a regional state. This point was again illustrated by the discovery of the inscription on

no political and legal authority but with specifically defined obligations in the form of military service.

However, this does not mean that the regional states were independent from Zhou royal authority. As I have recently shown, the relationship between the Zhou king and the regional rulers as his subjects was much closer and more dictatorial than the contracted ties between the "lord" and his "vassal" under the "feudo-vassalic" institution of medieval Europe.[63] In the absence of such contracted political ties, there were a number of ways in which political authority was achieved in the Western Zhou state. In the past, scholars talked a great deal about the institution of "Lineage Law" (*Zongfa* 宗法).[64] Zhao Guangxian was probably one of the few scholars of the Marxist school who was able to go beyond the debate generated by different readings of the *Liji* phrases to look for the implications of the system in Western Zhou sources, including the bronze inscriptions. He suggested that the Zhou king, who was normally succeeded by his eldest son by his primary wife, represented the "Primary Line" (*Dazong* 大宗), while the regional rulers, descended from the minor sons of the Zhou kings, founded the "Minor Lines" (*Xiaozong* 小宗). The heads of the minor lines were required by the "Lineage Law" to submit to the great line in the capital, which was therefore called Zongzhou 宗周.[65] This differentiation not only was practiced by the royal lineage, but also, perhaps more important, was pertinent to other aristocratic lineages that were not organized through an administrative structure as was the royal lineage. In this case, sons of the primary wife of a lineage were differentiated by their seniority as *bo* 伯, *zhong* 仲, *shu* 叔, and *ji* 季, and under normal condition only *bo* would succeed as the head of the lineage and were therefore referred to as the "First son of the primary line" (*zongzi* 宗子). The essence of the "Lineage Law" was to regulate inheritance of political authority and property through a kinship structure. Since the inscription of the Shan *ding* 善鼎 (JC: 2820) clearly mentions the *zongzi*, and the inscriptions of the Zhou Sheng *gui* 琱生簋 (JC: 4293) mention the "Head of the primary line" (*zongjun* 宗君), such a differentiation between the primary line and minor lines seems to have been practiced during the Western Zhou. However, a "law" without enforcement can hardly be a law. Although the system had probably created

the Ke *lei*, which shows that six groups of people were granted to the new ruler of Yan in present-day Beijing. See Itō Michiharu, *Chūgoku kodai kokka no shihai kōzō* (Tokyo: Chūō kōronsha, 1987), pp. 78–83, 98–105. For the Kei *lei*, see Li Feng, "Ancient Reproductions and Calligraphic Variations: Studies of Western Zhou Bronzes with Identical Inscriptions," *Early China* 22 (1997), 4–15.

[63] For the nature of the Western Zhou regional states and their differences from medieval European fiefs, see Li Feng, "Feudalism and Western Zhou China," pp. 125–32.

[64] Just to list a few, Zhao Guangxian, *Zhou dai shehui bianxi* (Beijing: Renmin, 1982), pp. 99–110; Jin Jingfang, *Gushi lunji* (Jinan: Qilu, 1982), pp. 111–40.

[65] See Zhao Guangxian, *Zhou dai shehui bianxi*, p. 102. For an interpretation of the system, see also Hsu and Linduff, *Western Chou Civilization*, pp. 163–71; Barry B. Blakeley, "Regional Aspects of Chinese Socio-political Development in the Spring and Autumn Period (722–464 BC): Clan Power in a Segmentary State," unpublished PhD thesis, University of Michigan (1970), pp. 16–21.

a strong sense of obligation among the regional rulers and psychological superiority of the Zhou king as long as the familial ties connecting them remained strong, it is indeed difficult to estimate how effective the "Lineage Law" was in the real political scene in subjugating the regional rulers to the particular Zhou kings. As mentioned in the preceding chapters, there were also many regional rulers who were not descendents from the royal lineage and therefore not subject to the same "Lineage Law" that governed the royal lineage.

But, on the basis of our current evidence, there were perhaps two other measures taken by the Zhou court to secure the political authority of the king, and each probably constituted some kind of institution. The first was the practice of the hereditary office of the "Overseers of the States" (*jianguo* 監國) that the royal court installed in the regional states, serving as "watchdogs" for the king. This system must be differentiated from the "Three Overseers" installed by King Wu to watch over the Shang subjects right after the conquest; instead, the mission of the "Overseers of the States" was to watch over the regional Zhou rulers distant from the capital. It is traditionally known from the *Zuozhuan* that in the state of Qi, the Guo 國 and Gao 高 families, referred to as the "two royal watchmen," were commissioned by the Zhou king to occupy high offices and to report back to the Zhou capital.[66] The bronze inscriptions suggest the probability that the system was not only applied to the non-Ji states such as Qi, but was commonly applied to regional Zhou states, both Ji and non-Ji. The Zhong Jifu *gui* 仲幾父簋 (JC: 3954) mentions that an official of Zhong Jifu was sent out on a mission to see the "many regional rulers" (*zhuhou* 諸侯) and also to meet with the "many overseers" (*zhujian* 諸監), probably stationed in the states of the many regional rulers. The fact that the "many overseers" are mentioned as counterparts of the many regional rulers suggests that their political status was relatively high; at least, they were very important for the Zhou court. Some of these overseers in the regional states also cast bronze inscriptions that have been discovered. For instance, a bronze *yan* cast by Yingjian 應監 (JC: 883), "Overseer of the State of Ying," was discovered in 1958 in Jiangxi province.[67] Ying was an important Ji state in present-day Pingdingshan. Another late Western Zhou inscription from the state of Shen 申, the Zhong Chengfu *gui* 仲再父簋 (JC: 4188), suggests that the "Overseer" of the state of Shen was a close descendent of the Zhou royal family, a son of King Yi, and his family held high positions in the local state.[68]

[66] For a detailed discussion on the status and origin of the Guo and Gao families, see Melvin Thatcher, "A Structural Comparison of the Central Government of Ch'u, Ch'i, and Chin," *Monumenta Serica* 33 (1977–78), 148–51.

[67] See Guo Moruo, "Shi Ying Jian yan," *Kaogu xuebao* 1960.1, 7–8.

[68] The inscription was cast by Zhong Chengfu, the "Grand Superintendent" of the state of Shen in Nanyang, for his father Jianbo 監伯 and grandfather King Yi. On the discovery of the bronze in Nanyang, see *Zhongyuan wenwu* 1984.4, 13–16.

Fig. 19 The Yanhou Zhi *ding* and its inscription on the Ruler of Yan's visit to the Zhou
capital (JC: 2628; *Sen'oku hakko kan* (catalogue), p. 15)

The second measure was the visit of the regional rulers to the Zhou capital
upon their assuming power. Three early Western Zhou inscriptions – the
X *zun* 隙尊 (JC: 5986), Mai *zun* 麥尊 (JC: 6015), and Yanhou Zhi *ding*
匽侯旨鼎 (JC: 2628) – record the visits by the regional rulers to the Zhou
capital in the Wei River valley. The X *zun* was excavated in the cemetery of
the state of Wey and it records the ruler of Wey's visit from northern Henan
to the honorable Zhou capital Zongzhou.[69] The Yanhou Zhi *ding* records
the ruler of Yan's first visit to the Zhou king from present-day Beijing,
very likely upon his accession to power (Fig. 19). The Mai *zun*, which
records the ruler of Xing's visit to the Zhou king from present-day Hebei,
provides more details about such visits. According to the inscription, he
made the visit only about two months after being established as Ruler of
Xing by the Zhou king.[70] When he arrived at the Zhou capital Zongzhou,
the king was away in the capital Pang. The Ruler of Xing thus went on to
see the king in Pang where the king held the ritual of archery to entertain
him. Thereupon, the Ruler of Xing was richly furnished by the king with
a long list of gifts, including even a royal chariot and 200 households of
servants. The treatment accorded to the ruler of Xing by the Zhou king
was very generous and cautious. Given the repeated mention of such visits
in the inscriptions, it is likely that visits by regional rulers, especially newly
established ones, were probably a regulation or at least a common practice
during the early Western Zhou.

[69] See *Xunxian xincun*, pl. 14.
[70] For an interpretation of the inscription, see Shirakawa, "Kinbun tsūshaku," 11.60: 631.

The above inscriptional evidence suggests, at the most conservative level, that the issue of maintaining political control over the regional rulers was an important royal concern. The regional rulers, though equipped with full authority over civil, economic, and military affairs within their states, were not left completely free to rule. This in another way suggests that their states were not independent sovereign kingdoms, but were integral parts of the Western Zhou state. At a very fundamental level, it was the presence of a strong royal military in the eastern center that provided the relationship between the central court and the regional states with a crucial stabilizing power. Therefore, the issue is clearly not that there were no methods to control the regional states, but whether such methods could stand the test of time.

In theory, as proclaimed by the poem "Beishan" 北山 (no. 205) in the *Book of Poetry*,[71] the Zhou king had the sovereign right to all land and its population under Heaven, but in practice such rights were mediated by the rulers of the regional states; the Zhou king ruled through the rules of the regional rulers. In other words, by giving out the vast eastern territories under the authority of the regional rulers, the Zhou king actually renounced his own administrative right as well as duty to these territories, although it was legitimate for him to impose his will on the regional rulers. But legitimacy does not mean that he could always do so. As the numerous "Appointment Inscriptions" suggest, the sphere of the Zhou court's direct administrative control was limited to the royal domain in Shaanxi and the small area around the eastern center Luoyi. This seems to have created a structural or even strategic contradiction: on the one hand, the Zhou court clearly perceived the security of the whole realm of the Western Zhou state, including both the east and the west, as its responsibility, as indicated by a number of inscriptions showing that the royal armies were sent to counter foreign attacks on the distant and peripheral Zhou states; and on the other hand, the resources that it could always be sure to depend on to support such operations were derived only from the royally administered area. How much military assistance based on local resources that the regional states would provide to the king in such operations was dependent on the will of the regional rulers and on the king's ability to command them. Although such ability varied from king to king, in the long run it tended to weaken as the regional states, when extending their roots in the local areas, became competitors of the Zhou royal court and their rulers tended more often to put their local interests before the royal ones. In a political system where the central power is mediated by local authorities, the move towards regional autonomy is only a matter of time.

The natural disadvantage of political control through kinship structure was that such control tended to weaken over time as the positions of the agents became more and more distant in the structure from their main

---

[71] See *Shijing*, 13.1, p. 463 (Waley, *The Book of Songs*, pp. 189–90).

line of derivation. In the *Liji* description of the "Zongfa" system, after five generations the minor sons would no longer be recognized as members of the ancestral lineage.[72] It is hard to tell whether such a strict rule described by later ritual books was implemented during the Western Zhou, but separated from the main line of the Zhou house by at least seven or eight generations, the regional rulers of the middle and late Western Zhou would have found themselves little akin to the Zhou king, and would have had less and less interest in going back to the royal court in Shaanxi. As will be shown below, among the increasing number of inscriptions of this period from the cemeteries of the eastern states such as Lu, Qi, and Ying, or even those from Shanxi, we find no mention of visits in either direction between the Zhou court and the local states, in sharp contrast to those early Western Zhou inscriptions that frequently mention such visits. I believe that this phenomenon in the inscriptions indicates an important change in the relationship between the Zhou court and the regional states in the east. When the blood ties were weakened, the high degree of autonomy granted to the regional states under the "Fengjian" system began to change these states into independent powers that would no longer act at the will of the Zhou king. Such was probably the case with the state of Qi and the state of Lu (see below, p. 138), both having a history of going against the royal court. In theory, the system of the "Overseers of the States" could have provided a mechanism to curb the tendency of the regional states to "drift away" from central authority. But, in reality such a system could remain effective over time only when the overseers were occasionally transferred from state to state in the hope of creating among them a strong sense that their welfare was dependent on the royal will. Unfortunately, the likely situation is that the overseers were hereditary lineages appointed by the king, with their permanent residences in their designated states. As such, although they may have continued to provide a channel of communication between the central court and the regional states, after generations of residence in their host state their interest could become identified with that of the regional states where they lived, rather than with that of the central court.

Archaeological approaches to the "drift-away" of the regional states

The question is, if it had taken a considerably long time for a decentralization tendency to develop and to spread in the Western Zhou state, what was its material manifestation? Can we actually see the drift-away of the regional states in the archaeological records? Although archaeology need not necessarily reflect political changes, changes that took place in the political sphere across a large geographical area and that developed into a general tendency over a long period of time should have had their impact on the material culture. While this proposition should be acceptable to most scholars, the issue is how we can demonstrate it.

[72] See *Liji*, 21, p. 1,508.

About thirty years ago, Itō Michiharu attempted to show the weakening of Zhou royal control over the east by comparing the wide geographic distribution of early Western Zhou bronzes with that of the late Western Zhou period which by then was confined to the Wei River valley.[73] However, besides the limited material on which Itō based his observations in contrast to the tremendous amount of material we have today, there are some methodological defects in his using archaeological data to make political claims. In general, it is valid that the spatial expansion and retreat of the Zhou culture were related to, though not exactly coincident with, the rise and decline of Zhou power. However, given the general political circumstances during the late Western Zhou, the weakening of the Western Zhou state does not have to entail the weakening of the regional states; on the contrary, as recent archaeology shows, the eastern states achieved steady growth and produced a large number of bronzes during the late Western Zhou, when royal power was clearly declining. Therefore, to demonstrate the drift-away of the regional states as a factor of royal weakening, we must adopt a more complex approach which includes two steps. As the first step, we must demonstrate whether there was a shrinkage in the distribution, not of Western Zhou bronzes in general, but of the inscribed bronzes that show clear links to the Zhou royal court and of those that suggest direct communications between the two regions.[74] As the second step, we must decide whether there was a general centrifugal tendency in the Zhou archaeological culture or a tendency towards localization manifest in the regional sites distant from the Zhou capital. Corresponding to changes in their political status, if the archaeological culture, especially the elite culture, of the regional states shows increasing local features, this should certainly be considered as an indication of the weakening influence of central power.

Three inscriptions, the X *zun*, Mai *zun*, and Yanhou Zhi *ding*, have already been discussed above as evidence of visits by the regional rulers to the Zhou capital in Shaanxi during the early Western Zhou. Two other inscriptions, the Jin *ding* 堇鼎 (JC: 2703) and Yu *you* 圉卣 (JC: 5374), unearthed in the cemetery of Yan in Beijing, mention visits by Yan officials to the Zhou capitals Zongzhou and Chengzhou.[75] Moreover, the Qi *zun* 啟尊 (JC: 5983) and Qi *you* 啟卣 (JC: 5410), discovered in Huangxian 黃縣, Shandong, record the caster's experience in accompanying the Zhou king on a southern campaign (Fig. 20).[76] Recently, still in the Shandong region, a bronze *ding* cast by Wang Jiang 王姜 was excavated from a tomb at Liutaizi 劉台子, near Jinan.[77] As the caster Queen Jiang is well known as

---

[73] See Itō Michiharu, *Chūgoku kodai ōchō no keisei* (Tokyo: Sōbunsha, 1975), pp. 307–8, 310.

[74] Musha Akira noted that the court-related "Appointment Inscriptions" were found only in Shaanxi and the Luoyang area; therefore, the individuals appointed by the Zhou king to government service, mainly during the middle and late Western Zhou, were only to work in the royal domain; see Musha Akira, "Sei Shū satsumei kinbun bunrui no kokoromi," in *Sei Shū seidōki to sono kokka*, ed. Matsumaru Michio (Tokyo: Tōkyō daigaku, 1980), pp. 315–16.

[75] See *Liulihe Xi Zhou Yan guo mudi*, pp. 106, 187.

[76] For the discovery of the two bronzes, see *Wenwu* 1977.4, 68.　　[77] See *Wenwu* 1996.12, 8–11.

Fig. 20　The Qi *zun* and Qi *you* (inscription on the *you*; based on *Wenwu* 1972.5, 6, pl. 7)

the spouse of King Kang in a number of later early Western Zhou bronzes, the discovery certainly suggests a strong connection between the local site and the Zhou court.[78] Moreover, far to the south, at Lutaishan 魯臺山 near Wuhan, four bronze *ding* cast by the "Duke Grand Scribe" (*gong taishi* 公太史) were excavated from an early Western Zhou tomb.[79] We certainly know this person as a prominent official at the court of King Kang or King Zhao and he is mentioned on other bronzes such as the Zuoce Hu *you* 作冊魌卣 (JC: 5432). All of these inscriptions were cast during the early Western Zhou and are strong evidence of communication between the eastern and southern states and the Zhou royal court in Shaanxi.[80] They indicate that the Zhou court had maintained strong connections with the

---

[78] On the status of Queen Jiang and bronzes that mention her, see Shaughnessy, *Sources of Western Zhou History*, pp. 208–9.

[79] See *Jianghan kaogu* 1982.2, 37–50.

[80] To these we may add the newly discovered Zhabo *gui* 柞伯簋 from the cemetery of the state of Ying in Pingdingshan, Henan, describing an archery ritual held by the Zhou king. The reporters of the bronze suggest that the Zhabo *gui* was cast by the ruler of the state of Zuo, located in northern Henan, and was brought to the state of Ying as a present. It is also possible that Zhabo was a noble

regional states during the early Western Zhou period. In contrast, for the period from the accession of King Gong to the end of King Li (917/15–842/28 BC), we have only one such inscription – the Yinghou *zhong* 應侯鐘 (JC: 107), discovered in Lantian in the Wei River valley – recording that the ruler of Ying presented tribute to the Zhou king in the capital upon the king's return from the east.[81] To this may be added the Ehou Yufang *ding*, already discussed above, recording a meeting the Ruler of E had with the king when he was on campaign in the east. Among the increasing number of middle and late Western Zhou inscriptions discovered in the eastern states such as Ying, Lu, and Qi, there is no mention of a visit in either direction between the Zhou court and these states.[82] So, the conclusion we can draw from this is that there is a sharp decline in our inscriptional sources on the communication between the Zhou royal court in Shaanxi and the eastern states. This phenomenon indicates that there was at least some relaxation in Zhou royal control over the regional states.

Next, we need to put the issue in a larger archaeological context. Shandong is the area where we have systematic sources that suggest the rise of a local bronze culture. As mentioned earlier, two major states, Qi and Lu, had contested royal power during the middle and late Western Zhou. The Shandong region witnessed the emergence of some local-style bronzes and a new pottery inventory during the late Western Zhou. Early Western Zhou bronzes from the Shandong region such as those from Liutaizi and from the state of Teng show a high degree of uniformity with bronzes found in the Zhou metropolitan area. However, during the late Western Zhou some distinctive bronzes appeared, most typically in two types of *hu*-vessels, decorated with a local zigzag net pattern combined with typical Zhou-style ornamentation (Fig. 21). The first type has a bag-like body hanging down, with four or sometimes two ring-like handles on it.[83] The second type has

---

in the royal domain and that the bronze was brought from Shaanxi to the state of Ying. In any event, this is a court-related inscription that was discovered in a regional state in the east. See Yuan Junjie, Jiang Tao, and Wang Longzheng, "Xin faxian de Zhabo gui jiqi mingwen kaoshi," *Wenwu* 1998.9, 54.

[81] For the discovery of the Yinghou *zhong*, see *Wenwu* 1975.10, 68. For a discussion and English translation of this inscription, see Lothar von Falkenhausen, *Suspended Music: Chime-Bells in the Culture of Bronze Age China* (Berkeley, CA: University of California Press, 1993), pp. 58–59. The inscription, since it mentions an important court figure Rongbo 榮伯 who was active in the time of King Gong and King Yih, can be dated roughly to the same period. See Ma Chengyuan, *Shang Zhou qingtongqi*, 3, pp. 163–64.

[82] A special case is the discovery of the vessel part of the Buqi *gui* 不娶簋 (JC: 4328) in Tengxian, Shandong, probably from a tomb belonging to the state of Teng. However, since the inscription records a battle with the Xianyun in the upper Jing River valley, it must have been cast by an individual at the Zhou court and have been brought to Shandong for some reason. For the discovery of the Buqi *gui*, see *Wenwu*, 1981.9, 25–29.

[83] This type of bronze *hu* was found in Qufu tombs nos. 30 and 48 belonging to the state of Lu, and in Laiyang 萊陽; the Laiyang *hu* bears an inscription cast by the ruler of the state of Ji (Jihou 己侯).[83] See *Qufu Lu guo gucheng*, pls. 80:4, 81; *Wenwu* 1983.12, pl. 3:1. Another *li*-vessel, found in Huangxian and also cast by the ruler of Ji, is clearly adapted from the local pottery *li*-tripod; see *Wenwu* 1983.12, pl. 3:5.

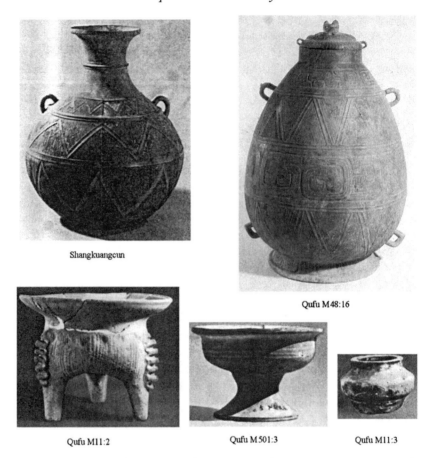

Fig. 21 Local bronze and pottery types from Shandong (from *Wenwu* 1972.5, pl. 7.3; *Qufu Lu guo gucheng*, pls. 8.1, 60.4, 35.2, 62.5)

a round body and a trumpet mouth.[84] Local characteristics are even more obvious in the late Western Zhou pottery inventory from the Lu capital Qufu. As suggested in the preceding chapter, the eastern plain and the Wei River valley were not integrated at the non-elite cultural level until the beginning of the mid-Western Zhou, when Wei River types of pottery were introduced to the east. Many of the types certainly made their way to the Shandong region. But by the beginning of the late Western Zhou, even those types originally introduced from the Wei River valley began to show definitely local features in Shandong. The situation is very typical in Qufu, the capital of the state of Lu, where a distinctive group of pottery

---

[84] This type of bronze *hu* was found in Yantai 煙臺 (Shangkuangcun) and Laiyang; see *Wenwu* 1972.5, pl. 7:3; *Wenwu* 1983.12, pl. 3:2. Interestingly, a *hu*-vessel found in Suixian, Hubei, in the middle Yangzi region, matches exactly the Yantai piece, and was probably imported from the coastal region of Shandong; see *Wenwu* 1973.5, pl. 4:4; see also Colin Mackenzie, "Chu Bronze Work: A Unilinear Tradition, or a Synthesis of Diverse Sources?" in *New Perspectives on Chu Culture*, ed. Thomas Lawton (Washington, DC: Smithsonian Institution, 1991), p. 117.

types was repeatedly found in many late Western Zhou to early Eastern Zhou tombs, including: a shallow *li*-tripod with a wide rim and slender legs; a high *dou*-plate with a trumpet-like base; a shallow *gui*-basin on a narrow and trumpet-like base; and a small plain-surfaced or polished *guan*-vessel with a wide mouth. In fact, we have little difficulty in differentiating the pottery assemblage found in Shandong from the general Zhou types found in the eastern plain on which the Shandong types were based. There was clearly a localization process going on in the material culture of the Shandong region during the late Western Zhou.

In short, it seems evident that both in the elite inscriptions and in the non-elite material culture there was a general "drift-away" of the regional states from the Zhou political and cultural center. This must have worked to undermine the foundation of the Western Zhou state and to dissolve its basic geopolitical unity. The system implemented in the early decades of the dynasty suited the special circumstances of the immediate post-conquest era and contributed positively to the political stability of the Western Zhou state. However, for the reasons stated above, the system instead presented a situation destructive to the integration of the Western Zhou state during its middle and late periods. However, had the Zhou royal court been politically and militarily strong enough, it would still have been possible to keep the regional states in line against the emerging regionalism. Unfortunately, the Zhou royal court was itself weakened by a number of internal factors that are explored further below.

ARISTOCRATIC POWER AGAINST ROYAL AUTHORITY

The royal domain in Shaanxi constituted the political core of the Western Zhou state and was under the direct administrative control of the Zhou court. As has been clarified in the preceding chapter, there were multiple royal centers distributed over the Wei River valley that were hubs of Zhou administration, extending from there to the rural regions along the branches of the Wei River. The bronze inscriptions suggest that there were probably two types of local administration, *li* 里 and *bang* 邦, managed by *lijun* 里君 and *bangjun* 邦君 respectively.[85] The small area surrounding the eastern center Luoyi probably had a similar administrative structure controlled by the king. They together provided most of the revenue for the royal court, with which it covered the expenses of the royal household and financed the Zhou armies. However, the Wei River valley was also home to numerous aristocratic families who, while holding residences in the royal centers, lived on estates widely scattered over the Wei River plain, side by side with the royal possessions managed by officials appointed by the Zhou king. However, the divide between the two types of ownership was rather fluid, and the transfer between them was not only possible but also intended.

---

[85] On this point, see Li Feng, "'Offices' in Bronze Inscriptions," p. 25.

Land-granting and the reduction of royal property

The royal government was staffed by members of the aristocracy. It has been traditionally believed that such offices were hereditary, but my recent analysis shows that although the opportunity for service was reasonably limited to the social elite – the aristocracy – the selection of officials was quite fluid, allowing certain bureaucratic elements to prevail in the body of the Zhou government.[86] However, the officials were not on the payroll of the central government, that mainly used its revenue from the royal domain to support the royal household and the military, but lived on the estates that they themselves or their ancestors had received from the Zhou king.[87] The middle and late Western Zhou "Appointment Inscriptions" suggest that royal gifts frequently accompanied official appointments, but such gifts did not constitute salary because they were related neither to the period of the service nor to the quantity of it. It has also been previously argued that some of the royal gifts were indeed accouterments that the officials used during the period of their service, and would then be returned to the royal court.[88] The landed properties figured importantly among the items of granting from the king to his officials, and it seems they were granted as a royal favor on a rather random basis. Quite consistent with this practice is the situation that there does not seem to have been a centralized financial system involving also the regional states in the east that could provide a basis for an institutionalized wage or salary. There is no evidence, at least for most of the Western Zhou period, that regular taxation was imposed by the royal court on the aristocratic families in the Wei River valley or the regional states in the east, although occasional tributes may have been presented by the regional rulers to the king.[89]

---

[86] This can be seen most explicitly in the fact the many young officials were first appointed assistants to senior officials and then, after some years of service, were promoted to senior positions. The fact of promotion is quite consistent with the statistics that more officials were appointed without acknowledged previous family history of service in the royal government. See Li Feng, "Succession and Promotion," pp. 1–35.

[87] Creel has correctly noted that the Zhou officials were not paid directly for their government service, but derived emolument from their estates, or "fiefs" in Creel's terminology; see Creel, *The Origins of Statecraft*, p. 117.

[88] See Virginia Kane, "Aspects of Western Chou Appointment Inscriptions: The Charge, the Gifts, and the Response," *Early China* 8 (1982–83), 14–28.

[89] Creel has written a chapter on royal finance in which he hypothesized that a centralized financial administration involving the "feudal lords" must have existed; see Creel, *The Origins of Statecraft*, pp. 134, 154–55. However, the only "solid" evidence that Creel could offer is the inscription of the Maogong *ding* 毛公鼎 (JC: 2841), in which the Duke of Mao is commanded by the Zhou king "to establish small and great *chufu* 楚賦." The meaning of *chufu* has been hotly debated: while some consider that it referred to "tax," others take it to be a generic term referring to "officials." For the first opinion, see Guo Moruo, *Liang Zhou jinwen ci daxi*, pp. 137–38; Shirakawa, "Kinbun tsūshaku," 30.181:668–69. For the second opinion, see Yang Shuda, *Jiweiju jinwen shuo*, p. 14; Ma Chengyuan, *Shang Zhou qingtongqi*, 3, p. 319. It seems reasonable to me that *chufu* refers to some kind of levy, and this, given the generally accepted date of the bronze to King Xuan, seems to agree with an entry under King Xuan's first year in the *Current Bamboo Annals*: "levy on land (*tianfu* 山賦) was restored";

This suggests, therefore, that the Zhou government actually operated on a "favor for loyalty" basis, and the landed properties provided an important economic link between the Zhou king and the aristocratic officials. Given the lack of evidence for a systemized taxation, and for the very reason that the value of such lands as "royal favors" rested on the economic benefit they would bring to the receivers, it seems quite reasonable to think that when a piece of landed property was passed from royal possession to an aristocratic family it would become no longer productive for the king. Scholars of the Marxist school have long debated about the so-called "Well Field" (*jingtian* 井田) system attributed by the Warring States philosophers to the Western Zhou as a way to levy labor-tax.[90] However, such a system, if it ever existed, only regulated the economic relationship between the land owners and the peasants, but not the relationship between the land owners and the Zhou state.

The bronze inscriptions suggest that throughout the Western Zhou the Zhou king continued to grant land to the aristocratic officials who served in the central government. There are about fourteen inscriptions that record such land grants by the Zhou king. Early Western Zhou examples are the Shao *huanqi* 𤯍圜器 (JC: 10360), Qian *you* 趞卣 (JC: 5402), and Zhong *fangding* 中方鼎 no. 1 (JC: 2785); as mentioned above, all three bronzes were cast in the late phase of the early Western Zhou, and possibly on the verge of the nineteenth-year campaign of King Zhao. Shao was given the land of Bi 畢, measuring fifty square *li* 里; Qian was given an estate named X 趞; Zhong was given the land of X 褮 to be his estate. Most likely, these are grants of large tracts of land. The mid-Western Zhou inscriptions continue to record land-granting: the Yong *yu* 永盂 (JC: 10322) mentions that the official Shi Yong 師永 was given fields in the valley of the Luo River, a major branch of the Wei River in Shaanxi; the Mao *gui* 卯簋 (JC: 4327) records that Mao received four fields in four different locations; the Da Ke *ding* 大克鼎 (JC: 2836) records the king giving multiple pieces of field to Ke in seven different locations, including some of the fields that originally belonged to the powerful Jing lineage. Among the late Western Zhou inscriptions that

see *Zhushu jinian*, 2, p. 14 (Legge, *The Shoo King*, Prolegomena, p. 155). However, the issue is its implication for Zhou institutions. First, it is not clear whether such a levy was instituted in the time of King Xuan or before. I am inclined to think that, as the context of the inscription appears to suggest, this was a policy related to King Xuan's restoration program (see below, pp. 135–38). Second, it is not clear whether the levy was imposed on the aristocratic families in the royal domain, or the eastern states, or the foreign subjects. Only the last possibility is supported by our sources at present. The Xi Jia *pan* 兮甲盤 (JC: 10174), also cast in the reign of King Xuan, mentions that Xi Jia was put in charge of the tributes that came from the four directions into the eastern capital Chengzhou, and therefore he travelled to the Southern Huaiyi to collect a variety of items including silk, agricultural products, and slaves. For the inscription, see Shirakawa, "Kinbun tsūshaku," 32.191:790–93. The contribution of rare and precious items by the regional states to the Zhou king may have been practiced, but it does not seem that such contributions could have constituted a significant part of the regular revenue controlled by the royal court.

[90] For such debate, see Gao Heng, "Zhou dai dizu zhidu kao," *Wenshizhe* 1956.10, 42–44; Lin Jianming, "Jingtian he yuantian," *Renwen zazhi* 1979.1, 69–70.

record land-granting by the king, the largest amount is recorded in the Wu *gui* 敄簋 (JC: 4323): Wu was given one hundred fields located in two places as reward for his contribution in defeating the Southern Huaiyi. The Buqi *gui* 不嬰簋 (JC: 4328) mentions that, after defeating the Xianyun, Buqi was given ten fields with locations unspecified. The Da *gui* 大簋 (JC: 4298) mentions the king giving the official Da land that originally belonged to another official.

Some of these grants were made to military commanders who made their contributions in foreign warfare, and others were to civil administrators at the royal court. The point is that land constituted an important item of royal favor given to the civil and military officials on whose shoulders the burden of the Zhou government rested. Certainly it must also be noted that many of the court officials may have come from lineages whose history went back all the way to the pre-conquest period when their ancestors received such grants of landed properties from the Zhou rulers. In the "favor for loyalty" relationship, in order to maintain the loyalty of the officials, the Zhou king must continue to grant such favors. Joseph Tainter's theory about the collapse of complex societies may be applied here: the king could not just grant land at the same level; he must increase the level of granting because the return of loyalty tended to be ever diminishing.[91] At some point, the investment of royal favor would even stop bringing any return of loyalty, and when that happened, the Western Zhou dynasty would be on the verge of collapse. However, the real dilemma here is that the more land the Zhou king granted to his officials, the less possible it was for him to continue to do so. Given the historical circumstances that the large territory in the east was already sliced up and put under the control of the numerous regional states, the pool available to the king for land-granting to the royal officials was only the Wei River valley and the small area around Luoyi, which certainly had a limit. When a piece of land was granted, it would disappear from royal possession and would become the property of and productive only to the aristocratic family that received it. In other words, the Zhou king was giving out his capital to his economic competitors close to home. As long as land continued to pass into the hands of the aristocratic families, such a policy of land-granting must have contributed enormously to reducing the size of the royal estate and to undermining the economic foundation of the Western Zhou state.

It would be ideal if we could measure how much land was transferred as royal favor into the possession of the aristocratic lineages in each given period of time on a statistical basis, but such methodology cannot be applied to the Western Zhou period because no such statistics were left behind. However, we have a number of indications of the possible consequences of land-granting by the Zhou king. This can be seen from the changing size

---

[91] See Tainter, *The Collapse of Complex Societies*, pp. 5–6, 92, 203.

of lands granted by the Zhou king in the bronze inscriptions. During the early Western Zhou, we see more often the granting of an entire unit of territory bearing a single place-name such as those recorded in the Qian *you* and the Shao *huanqi*. However, such records rarely appear in middle and late Western Zhou bronze inscriptions where, instead, we see only the "piecemeal granting" of land as exemplified by the inscriptions of the Mao *gui* and the Da Ke *ding*. In fact, even the expression of such grants in the inscriptions changed over time: in the early Western Zhou bronzes, the land granted was referred to as "land" (*tu* 土), while from the mid-Western Zhou, it was referred to as "field" (*tian* 田), which undoubtedly referred to a much smaller area. This point has acquired new support from the recently discovered Meixian bronzes; the inscription on the Forty-Second Year Lai *ding* 四十二年逨鼎 records that the king (Xuan) granted a total of fifty "fields," divided between two locations.[92] Clearly, a major change in the system of land had taken place during the mid-Western Zhou. Itō Michiharu once suggested that this change indicates a transition from the estate-economy that characterized the early Western Zhou to the small-scale land ownership that flourished during the late Western Zhou.[93] "Small-scale land ownership" here means not that the total area of land owned by a lineage became smaller during the middle or late Western Zhou, but that the land was owned in the form of small pieces.

In this regard, the inscription of the Fifth Year Qiu Wei *ding* 五年裘衛鼎 (JC: 2832) provides us with some sense of such small pieces of land called "field" and the possible social values attached to them. The inscription mentions the transfer of five fields from a local administrator called Bangjun Li 邦君厲 to Qiu Wei, the caster of the bronze. However, it is interesting that in the actual process of demarcation, only four fields were handed over to Qiu Wei, while another field was probably substituted by a residential area yielded to Qiu Wei in Bangjun Li's settlement. The four fields that Qiu Wei received, as diagrammatized by Itō, were actually located in the midst of the fields owned by Li and other aristocrats.[94] This inscription, together with that on the Qiu Wei *he* 裘衛盉 (JC: 9456), suggests that during the mid-Western Zhou, if not before, land had become such a transferable commodity in small parcels that were privately owned and sold at the free will of the holders.[95] Moreover, as shown by the inscription of the Hu

---

[92] Given the high number of the year recorded on the bronze, all scholars agree that the bronze, and probably also other pieces from the same cache, was cast during the reign of King Xuan. See *Wenwu* 2003.6, 14–15.

[93] See Itō, *Chūgoku kodai ōchō no keisei*, pp. 53–54; Itō, *Chūgoku kodai kokka no shihai kōzō*, pp. 193, 205, 213–16, 390.

[94] See Itō Michiharu, "Kyūei shoki kō – Sei Shū ki tochi shoyū keitai ni kansuru shiken," *Tōyōshi kenkyū* 37.1 (1978), 35–58.

[95] For more discussions on land transfer and ownership, see Laura Skosey, "The Legal System and Legal Tradition of the Western Zhou, ca. 1045–771 BCE.," unpublished PhD thesis, University of Chicago (1996), pp. 17–19, 103–10; Constance Cook, "Wealth and the Western Zhou," *Bulletin of the School of Oriental and African Studies* 60.2 (1997), 269–73.

ding 曶鼎 (JC: 2838), land was used as an item to pay for failed lawsuits.[96] Thus, there seems little doubt that these fields were privately owned by the aristocratic lineages during the mid-Western Zhou, and the assertion that all lands were the king's in the poem "Beishan" was probably only political idealism that had very little economic effect.[97] Such was probably the socioeconomic setting in which the Zhou king continued the granting of small pieces of land which would also become such privately owned properties.

But I think our current inscriptional evidence shows more than just that. There are two circumstances under which the "piecemeal granting" of fields could become an established practice, and in an extreme case, such as the Da Ke *ding*, seven pieces of such fields could have been located in seven different locations. First, the royal properties had already become such "piecemeal" holdings during the mid-Western Zhou and had to be granted in such fashion. But, considering that the royal house was reasonably the largest land holder and the original source from which all of the privately held lands were derived, the royal land holding could have got into such a condition only through competition with and incursion by the private lineage owners. In general, as indicated by the many land disputes recorded in the legal inscriptions, the competition for land in the Wei River valley during the middle and late Western Zhou was quite intensive. Second, such fields granted in "piecemeal" fashion were probably marginal lands newly exploited with royal resources. But the "piecemeal" marginal lands would be exploited when the regular and large-size royal lands became unavailable for granting. In both cases, our current evidence points to the insufficiency of royal land during the middle and late Western Zhou. Although we cannot measure the actual extent to which the royal possessions were drained by such land-granting to the officials, there seems little doubt, as long as the king continued to give out land as he apparently did, it must have contributed significantly to the economic weakening of the Zhou royal house, and hence of the power of the Western Zhou state. Here, I believe, we can see one of the fundamental reasons for the decline of the Western Zhou.

The growing power of the Wei River aristocracy

The relationship between royal authority and aristocratic power was twofold: on the one hand, the strength of royal power rested on the support of the aristocracy; and on the other, the growth of the political and economic power of the aristocracy could endanger royal authority. This,

---

[96] For an interpretation of this inscription, see Matsumaru Michio, "Sei Shū kōki shakai ni mieru henkaku no meiga – Ko tei mei kaishaku mondai no shobōteki kaiketsu," in *Higashi Ajia shi ni okeru kokka to nōmin* (Tokyo: Yamakawa, 1984), pp. 52–54.

[97] See *Shijing*, 13.1, p. 463 (Waley, *The Book of Songs*, pp. 189–90).

however contradictory it may be, was the inescapable dynamic of court politics in the Western Zhou state.

Many of the aristocratic lineages of Zhou had a very long duration, and we have sufficient reason to believe that most of them had achieved steady growth during the early Western Zhou expansion. During their long history these lineages accumulated both political resources by serving in the royal court generation after generation, and economic resources by enlarging their estates and establishing new branches. Let us take the Nangong 南宮 (or Nan 南) lineage as an example, to see how the aristocratic lineages accumulated their fortune. Since the acquiring of landed property has been discussed above, here we will just talk about the way they acquired people. This brings us to a famous inscription, the Da Yu *ding* 大盂鼎 (JC: 2837), that has been treated by most scholars as a standard vessel of the reign of King Kang (r. 1005/3–978 BC), cast in the twenty-third year of the king.[98] The inscription records a royal gift to Yu of the Nangong lineage that was composed of the following:[99]

錫汝鬯一卣，冂，衣，市，舄，車馬。錫乃祖南公旂，用遊（狩）。錫汝邦嗣 四伯，人 鬲自馭至于庶人六百又五十又九夫。錫夷嗣王臣十又三伯，人鬲千又 五十夫。迺（率）遷自厥土。

[I] award you a *you*-jar containing wine, a cap, a jacket, a pair of knee pads, a pair of shoes, and a chariot with horses. [I] award you the flag of your grandfather the Duke of Nan; use it in hunting. [I] award you four *bo* who are officials of the *bang* units, with 659 slaves from chariot-riders to commoners. [I] award you thirteen *bo* of the "barbarian" officials who are the royal servants, with 1,050 slaves. Order them to immediately [also] move from their land.

This is certainly an impressive list. Mentioned first was a set of official accouterments that was then to appear frequently in the "Appointment Inscriptions" from the mid-Western Zhou accompanying the various official appointments. The mention of Yu's ancestral flag traces the family line back to an ancestor called the "Duke of Nan" (Nan Gong 南公), to whom the vessel was actually dedicated; there is good reason to identify him with Nangong Kuo 南宮括, mentioned in the "Jun Shi" 君奭 chapter of the *Shangshu* as one of the advisers to King Wen.[100] A total of seventeen *bo*, heads of families, together with 1,709 slaves, were given to the Nangong family. They included, interestingly, four *bo* who were local

---

[98] The inscription is self-dated to the twenty-third year. Since the Xiao Yu *ding* 小盂鼎 (JC: 2839) has clear reference to the worship of kings Wen, Wu, and Cheng, there seems little doubt that Yu spent most of his career under King Kang. For the date of the Yu bronzes, see Ma Chengyuan, *Shang Zhou qingtongqi*, 3, pp. 37–44; Shaughnessy, *Sources of Western Zhou History*, pp. 111, 243.

[99] For a reading of this inscription, see Ma Chengyuan, *Shang Zhou qingtongqi*, 3, pp. 38–41. See also Shirakawa, "Kinbun tsūshaku," 12.61:666–73.

[100] See *Shangshu* 16, p. 224 (Legge, *The Shoo King*, p. 481). On the identification of the Duke of Nan, see Li Xueqin, "Da Yu ding xinlun," *Zhengzhou daxue xuebao* 1985.3, 54–55. On the status of Nangong Kuo, see also Edward Shaughnessy, "The Duke of Zhou's Retirement in the East and the Beginnings of the Minister–Monarch Debate in Chinese Political Philosophy," *Early China* 18 (1993), 57.

officials of Zhou, and thirteen *bo* who were by origin foreigners and who were to be transferred from the direct possession of the royal house to the Nangong lineage. The inscription gives us a realistic sense of what constituted the property of an aristocratic lineage in the Western Zhou and how it acquired it. However, they were not merely receivers of royal fortune, but also contributors to royal possessions. In the Xiao Yu *ding* 小盂鼎 (JC: 2839), cast only two years later, Yu is said to have captured more than 13,000 people along with a large number of domestic animals and chariots in two campaigns against the Guifang, and presented them to the king.[101] The inscriptions suggest that during the late Western Zhou the Nangong family continued to produce prominent military officers like Nangong Liu 南宮柳 and civil administrators like Nangong Hu 南宮呼.[102]

Although we have no statistics on the number of lineages represented by the late Western Zhou bronze inscriptions that had descended from ancestors at the beginning of the dynasty, there are certainly other lineages, such as Guo 虢, Shao 召, Rong 榮, Mao 毛, and Wei 微, whose history can be traced back to figures who lived in the pre-conquest era. This list represents probably only the most prominent lineages of the Wei River aristocracy. For instance, the Guo lineage, as will be detailed in chapter 5, was founded by Guoshu 虢叔, a brother of King Wen, also mentioned in the "Jun Shi" chapter, who was granted land in the present-day Baoji area. By the time of the conquest, the Guo lineage had developed at least three sub-lineages, one of which was transferred to the east to found the state of Eastern Guo 東虢. Through the entire Western Zhou, the Guo lineage maintained its prestige and its members continued to occupy important offices. The bronze inscriptions suggest that besides its base in the Baoji area, Guo also held residences in major cities like Zhou and Zheng.[103] Another important lineage was Jing 井, whose base was somewhere in the Fengxiang area.[104] The lineage history of Jing can be traced back to a prominent official called "Duke Mu" (Mu Gong 穆公) who was active in the early mid-Western Zhou.[105] After Duke Mu, the lineage seems to have

[101] As suggested in chapter 1 (see p. 54), Guifang was probably located in northern Shaanxi and Shanxi. For details of Yu's campaigns, see Ma Chengyuan, *Shang Zhou qingtongqi*, 3, pp. 42–43; Shirakawa, "Kinbun tsūshaku," 12.62:690–94.

[102] The Nangong Liu *ding* (JC: 2805) mentions Nangong Liu as an officer in charge of the pastoral land and hunting ground belonging to the Six Armies. In the Nangong Hu *zhong* (JC: 181), Nangong Hu addresses himself as "Supervisor of Land." On the Nangong family, see also Zhu Fenghan, *Shang Zhou jiazu xingtai yanjiu* (Tianjin: Tianjin guji, 1990), pp. 361–62.

[103] For more details on the Guo lineage, see chapter 5. For previous studies of Guo, see Li Xueqin, *Xinchu qingtongqi yanjiu*, pp. 85–87; Zhu Fenghan, *Shang Zhou jiazu*, pp. 374–75; Li Feng, "Guo guo mudi tongqi qun de fenqi jiqi xiangguan wenti," *Kaogu* 1988.11, 1041–42.

[104] The Jing lineage must be differentiated from the state of Xing 邢 in Hebei; see Chen Mengjia, "Xi Zhou tongqi duandai," 6, pp. 107–9. For the location of Jing in the Wei River valley, see Lu Liancheng, "Xi Zhou Ze guo shiji kaolue jiqi xiangguan wenti," in *Xi Zhou shi yanjiu* (Monograph of *Renwen zazhi* 2) (Xi'an, 1984), pp. 232–48.

[105] Duke Mu is mentioned in a number of inscriptions, including the Yinji *li* 尹姞鬲 (JC: 754) and Li *fangzun* (JC: 6013).

divided between his two sons, Jingbo 井伯 and Jingshu 井叔, and was prosperous throughout the mid-Western Zhou. The Jingshu sub-lineage was further divided into two branches: the Jingshu of Zheng and the Jingshu of Feng, respectively holding residences in the two major cities.[106] Inscriptional evidence suggests that the Jing lineage began to decline during the late Western Zhou when its estates were annexed by other lineages. But one of the lineage members, the caster of the Yu *ding* (JC: 2833), served in military offices and played an important role in the suppression of the rebellion of Ehou the Border Protector.

I hope the above discussion has highlighted the basic features of the Wei River aristocracy and clarified its developmental logic. Through the years, the lineages accumulated both political influence and economic power as their members continued to serve in the government and as the royal land continued to flow into their possession. In his study of the Western Zhou families, Zhu Fenghan pays attention to the relationship between the growth of aristocratic power and the decline of the Western Zhou dynasty, admitting that aristocratic power damaged royal authority.[107] In the received written records, there is little direct mention of a struggle between royal power and the power of the aristocracy. However, in the bronze inscriptions, I believe that there are indications of a prominent aristocratic power that sometimes overshadowed Zhou royal authority and hence created a continuing tension between the two poles of power.

Let us begin with a late Western Zhou case, the Zha *zhong* 柞鐘 (JC: 133), a set of eight bells:[108]

惟王三年四月初吉甲寅，中太師右柞，柞錫載，朱黃，鑾，䦣五邑佃人事。柞拜手，對揚仲太師休，用作大龢鐘，其子子孫孫永寶。

It was the king's third year, fourth month, first auspiciousness, *jiayin*. Zhong Taishi accompanied Zha to his right, and Zha was awarded purple [kneepads], a red demi-circlet, jingle-bells, [and was commanded] to be in charge of the affairs of peasants in the five cities. Zha bowed and in response extols the beneficence of Zhong Taishi, herewith making the grand *lin*-chimes. May my sons' sons and grandsons' grandsons eternally treasure it.

[106] The cemetery of the branch of Jinshu of Feng was found in 1984 in the area of the capital Feng; see *Kaogu* 1986.1, 22–27. For the lineage history of Jing, see also Zhu Fenghan, *Shang Zhou jiazu*, pp. 368–69.
[107] However, Zhu thinks that throughout the dynasty the king maintained absolute power over the aristocracy that never grew strong enough to challenge it. Instead, reasoning in a tortuous way, Zhu suggests that it was the struggle among the aristocratic families over political rights and economic resources that dissolved the solidarity of the aristocracy on which royal power was based, and therefore contributed to the fall of the dynasty. See Zhu Fenghan, *Shang Zhou jiazu*, pp. 412–13, 422, 427.
[108] For the inscription, see also Shirakawa, "Kinbun tsūshaku," 33.198:898. The Zha *zhong* was initially attributed by Guo Moruo to the King Yi–King Li period, but was dated by others to the third year of King You (779 BC) on the basis of the calendric information in the inscription. See *Fufeng Qijiacun tongqigun*, pp. 4–5; Ma Chengyuan, *Shang Zhou qingtongqi*, 3, p. 323; Shaughnessy, *Sources of Western Zhou History*, p. 285. Besides this, there is no other evidence to date the bells. But it is safe to say that they were from the late Western Zhou period.

The inscription mentions that Zha was commanded to be in charge of the peasants of the "Five Cities." Since Zhong Taishi in this inscription was only the *youzhe*,[109] according to the procedure of appointment ritual commonly known from other inscriptions, it is almost certain that the Zhou king hosted this appointment ceremony. Although, as I have argued elsewhere, the superior officials at the court may have played an important role in the decision of royal appointment,[110] in all cases it was the Zhou king who was considered the origin of all appointments and to whom all appointees expressed their gratitude. Standing apart from all inscriptions, the Zha *zhong* here presents a unique case in which Zha extols only the beneficence he has received from Zhong Taishi, who may well have been the initiator of Zha's appointment. By contrast, the king is not even mentioned in the inscription. I believe that the Zha *zhong* is a good example of aristocratic power encroaching on royal authority.

However, what really evidences the power of the aristocracy is the role of Duke Wu (Wu Gong 武公), as reflected in a group of late Western Zhou inscriptions including the Wu *gui* 敔簋 (JC: 4324), Nangong Liu *ding* 南宮柳鼎 (JC: 2805), Yu *ding* 禹鼎 (JC: 2834), and Duoyou *ding* 多友鼎 (JC: 2835). As mentioned above, Duke Wu was in a critical position when Ehou the Border Protector rebelled against Zhou. According to the Yu *ding*, the king sent out the Six Armies and Eight Armies to attack E but the royal armies failed. Then, Duke Wu sent out his private chariotry and infantry under command of Yu, and succeeded in capturing the rebels. An army that could change the balance of war and save the dynasty at the critical moment must not have been a small army. In another inscription, the Duoyou *ding*, it was again Duke Wu who sent out his private chariotry commanded by Duoyou to attack the invading Xianyun and protected the Zhou capital. An army with such superior capability but in private hands could be a source of serious threat to the Zhou king. The philosopher Mencius once remarked that in a state that has 10,000 chariots those who murder their rulers must be from the family that has a thousand chariots.[111] Mencius knew well that private military capability was not in the interest of the state. In this regard, the most interesting point in the Duoyou *ding* is the official hierarchy it exhibits. A full translation of this inscription will be given in chapter 3 (see pp. 147–49) in connection with the Xianyun war; a selection of paragraphs reflecting the bureaucratic ladder should suffice here:[112]

---

[109] *Youzhe* is the official who guides the candidate into the courtyard and introduces him to the Zhou king. Since by convention he always stands to the right of the candidate during the appointment ceremony, he is called *youzhe*, the "one on the right." For the appointment procedure and the role of *youzhe*, see Li Feng, "'Offices' in Bronze Inscriptions," pp. 29–42.

[110] See *ibid.*, pp. 48–51.

[111] See *Mencius*, trans. David Hinton (Washington, DC: Counterpoint, 1998), p. 3.

[112] See Tian and Luo, "Duoyou ding de faxian," pp. 115–18.

〔王〕命武公："遣乃元士，羞追于京𠂤（師）！" 武公命多友："衒（率）公車，羞追于京𠂤(師)！"
… 多友迺獻孚（俘）、𩲸（馘）、𫢛〔訊〕于公，武公迺獻于王。〔王〕迺曰武公曰："女（汝）
既靜京𠂤（師），𤲷（釐）女（汝），易（錫）女（汝）土田。" … 公𥄳（親）曰多友曰："余肈
（肇）事（使），女（汝）休！不𨒪（逆），有成事，多禽（擒），女〔汝〕靜京𠂤（師）。易（錫）女
（汝）圭𤪌… 湯（鍚）鍾一𦘺（肆）、鐈（鐈）鋚百匀（鈞）。"

The king commanded Duke Wu: "Dispatch your most capable men and pursue
at Jingshi!" Duke Wu commanded Duoyou: "Lead the ducal chariots and pursue
at Jingshi!" . . . Duoyou contributed the captured, the heads, and the prisoners to
the duke, and Duke Wu then contributed [them] to the king. [The king] therefore
addressed Duke Wu and said: "You have pacified Jingshi; [I] enrich you and
award you lands" . . . The duke personally addressed Duoyou and said: "I initially
assigned [you the task], and you have done well! [You] have not disobeyed, and
have accomplished [the deed and] have taken many captives. You have pacified
Jingshi. [I] award you one *gui*-XX, one set of bells made in finest bronzes and one
hundred *jun* of the *jiaoyou*-copper."

The order of campaign was given by the king to Duke Wu, who then
commanded Duoyou to go into the field. When the war was over, Duoyou
contributed his captures to the duke, and the duke in turn contributed
them to the king. However, the royal award only reached the duke, who
had never been to the battleground but had earned the reputation as one
who brought peace to the frontier. While the duke received the royal gift
of landed property, Duoyou, who had commanded the actual battle, was
rewarded by the duke with a ritual jade, a set of bronze bells and some metals.
Although we do not know the actual value of these items in contrast to
the landed property received by Duke Wu, there can be little doubt that
this was a highly hierarchical relationship and perhaps also an unfair play
in which Duke Wu controlled both the king's access to the military forces
and the military commander's access to the king. Certainly the new land
assigned to Duke Wu had to be transferred from the royal estate to the
possession of the duke, which would further strengthen Duke Wu's power
and weaken the Zhou king's. I think that the Duoyou *ding* provides an
excellent example of how an aristocratic family strengthened its own power
by capitalizing on foreign warfare conducted by the Zhou court.

Understanding this power balance, we can now reconsider the implications of the historical issue of King Li's exile in 842 BC, and it just so
happened that the powerful Duke Wu was in office during the reign of
King Li.[113] The historical event of 842 BC that resulted in King Li's exile

---

[113] The critical point here is the date of Duke Wu in relation to the Duoyou *ding*, but this requires a
review of all relevant inscriptions. It is generally agreed that Duke Wu's prominence overlapped in
time the reign of King Li, based on: (1) the very close stylistic and decorative similarities between
the Yu *ding* and the Da Ke *ding* 大克鼎 (JC: 2836) and Xiao Ke *ding* 小克鼎 (JC: 2797), which
from the fact that Ke's grandfather once served King Gong (and also on the appearance of a person
named Shen Ji who started his career in the time of King Gong) were commonly put in the late
part of the mid-Western Zhou, for instance the reign of King Xiao; (2) the identification of Rongbo

and Gongbo He's Regency has been taken by Marxist historians as an epic-making victory of plebeian or serf revolution against an exploiting aristocratic class.[114] This view misinterprets the real political dynamic in this historical conflict, and has recently been questioned by a number of scholars.[115] The most serious charge that was cast on King Li by the historiographical tradition represented by the *Guoyu* and the *Shiji* accused him of "monopolizing the profit" (*zhuanli* 專利); or, and by extension, it was Duke Yi of the Rong family who was accused of advising the king to pursue his personal ambitions.[116] The inscription of the Wu *gui* actually says explicitly that all the prisoners Wu brought back to the capital from the battlefield were handed over to the care of Rongbo, head of the Rong family, identified by many scholars with Duke Yi. This may not be significant, but may suggest that Rongbo was in charge of the booties of war, a position that might have easily exposed him to criticisms that should have been directed at the king. In any event, a Zhou king, as the principal possessor of all under Heaven, should not have been blamed for accumulating fortune unless such action ran into conflict with the interests of some social groups. The bronze inscriptions provide us with some evidence as to what he may have

榮伯 who appears in the Wu *gui* as probably a subordinate of Duke Wu (different from the Rongbo of the King Gong–King Yih period, mentioned by the Qiu Wei bronzes) with Rong Yigong 榮夷公 known from the texts as King Li's minister. On the relationship between the Yu *ding* and the Ke bronzes, see Li Xueqin, *Xinchu qingtongqi yanjiu*, pp. 129–30. For the Da Ke *ding* and Xiao Ke *ding*, see *Shanghai bowuguan cang qingtongqi* (Shanghai: Renmin, 1964), nos. 47–48. On their dates, see Ma Chengyuan, *Shang Zhou qingtongqi*, 3, pp. 215–17; Shaughnessy, *Sources of Western Zhou History*, p. 111. On the status of Rongbo, see Xu Zhongshu, "Yu ding de niandai," pp. 56–57. However, problems arose when the Duoyou *ding* was discovered in 1980 because the name Duoyou can be related to You 友, also called Duofu 多父, a younger brother of King Xuan. Therefore, some scholars proposed dating the Duoyou *ding* to the reign of King Xuan, causing an extension of Duke Wu's service from the time of King Li to the time of King Xuan. See Liu Yu, "Duoyou ding de shidai yu diming kaoding," *Kaogu* 1983.2, 152–57; Edward Shaughnessy, "The Date of the 'Duo You *Ding*' and Its Significance," *Early China* 9–10 (1983–85), 55–69. I think that it is first important to recognize, as most scholars would do, the high degree of similarity in the status of Duke Wu in all three inscriptions, the Yu *ding*, Wu *gui*, and Duoyou *ding*; this is reinforced by the appearance of Xiangfu 向父 in the Duoyou *ding* who is undoubtedly Yu, the caster of the Yu *ding*. Therefore, the three bronzes must have been cast very close to each other in time. Dating the Duoyou *ding* to King Xuan would indicate that Duke Wu maintained such high dominance over the Zhou court from the reign of King Li across the fourteen years of the regency of Gongbo He and well into the middle part of King Xuan's reign to allow the king's young brother (if he was indeed Duoyou) to grow up as a capable military commander. This seems at least very unnatural in a time when the Western Zhou dynasty experienced the most dramatic political change – the fall of King Li and the regency of Gongbo He. This certainly also causes problems in the reconciliation of the historical role of Gongbo He and that of Duke Wu if the latter had indeed continued to dominate the court after the fall of King Li. Furthermore, as pointed out by Li Xueqin, Duoyou in the Duoyou *ding* acted more like a subordinate of Duke Wu, rather than a royal prince. In short, the King Xuan dating of the Duoyou *ding* poses a number of problems in fitting the role of Duke Wu into the historical context of late Western Zhou. Therefore, I maintain that the Duoyou *ding* should be dated to the reign of King Li.

[114] Typical of this view, see Guo Moruo, *Zhongguo shigao* (Beijing: Renmin, 1976), pp. 285–87; Sun Zuoyun, *Shijing yu Zhou dai shehui yanjiu* (Beijing: Zhonghua, 1966), p. 219.

[115] See He Fan, "Guoren baodong xingzhi bianxi," *Renwen zazhi* 1983.5, 76–77; Hao Tiechuan, "Xi Zhou de guoren yu Zhi zhi luan," *Henan shida xuebao* 1984.1, 39–42; Zhang Pingche, "Xi Zhou Gonghe xingzheng zhenxiang jiemi," *Xibei shida xuebao* 1992.4, 51–54.

[116] See *Guoyu*, 1, pp. 12–13.

done to invite such accusation that had since become a persistent part of the historiographical tradition. The Da *gui* 大簋 (JC: 4298) was probably cast during the reign of King Li:[117]

惟十又二年三月既生霸丁亥，王在𥴦佚宮。王呼吳師召大錫越𤔲里。王命善夫豕曰越𤔲曰：“余既錫大乃里。”𤔲賓豕璋，帛束。𤔲命豕曰天子：“余弗敢婪。”豕以𤔲履大錫里。大賓豕凱璋，馬兩，賓𤔲凱璋，帛束。大拜頓首，敢對揚天子丕顯休，用作朕皇考烈伯之尊簋。其子子孫孫永寶用。

It was the twelfth year, third month, after the growing brightness, *dinghai*, the king was in Yizhen Gong. The king called out to Wushi to summon Da and to award (him) the *li* of Ci Kui. The king commanded Provisioner Shi to tell Ci Kui: "I have already awarded Da your *li*." Kui presented Shi with a jade-tablet, and a roll of silk. Kui asked Shi to tell the Son of Heaven: "I would not dare to be greedy." Shi and Kui then surveyed the *li* awarded to Da. Da presented Shi with a *huo*-jade-tablet, and two horses, and presented Kui with a *huo*-jade-tablet, and a roll of silk. Da bowed with his head touching the ground, and dares to extol the illustrious beneficence of the Son of Heaven, herewith making (for) my august deceased father Liebo (this) sacrificial *gui*-vessel. May my sons' sons and grandsons' grandsons eternally treasure and use it.

The inscription records that the king awarded his official Da land that was once owned by a person named Ci Kui. Although Ci Kui from whom the land was taken showed his obedience to the royal decision, this is learned entirely from the records kept by Da and cast on Da's bronze. The actual response of Ci Kui towards this land transaction could have been significantly different from what Da described. The simple fact is that, despite Ci Kui receiving a jade tablet and a roll of silk from Da who acquired the land, exactly the same as what Ci Kui himself had to present to Shi, the royal messenger, there was no compensation from either Da or the king for what he had lost. Clearly the Da *gui* is a case where King Li simply took land away from someone and gave it to another person. In the inscription on the newly discovered Wuhu *ding* 吳虎鼎, Wu Hu was granted a unit of land described as the "old territory." Again, this unit was not from the royal estate but was previously owned by another individual named Wu Wu 吳𤔲.[118] The Wu Hu *gui* was apparently cast in the eighteenth year of King Xuan, for the inscription says explicitly that the granting to

---

[117] For the inscription of the Da *gui*, see also Shirakawa, "Kinbun tsūshaku," 29.175:571–80. It is first to be noted that the two surviving Da *ding* 大鼎 (JC: 2806–7), one in the Palace Museum, Beijing, and the other in its counterpart in Taipei, both show clear late Western Zhou features, most typically in their deep hemispherical bodies and their legs that are thinner in the middle. Shaughnessy has suggested that the full dates recorded in the two inscriptions cannot fit in the calendar of King Xuan, so they must not be from the reign of King Xuan; see Shaughnessy, *Sources of Western Zhou History*, pp. 279–80. On the other hand, the "fifteenth" year number on the Da *ding* would fit neither the reign of King You which lasted eleven years nor that of Gongbo He which lasted fourteen. So the only possible reign for the Da bronzes is that of King Li. This is also the date for the Da bronzes adopted by the recent Xia–Shang–Zhou Chronology Project; see *Xia Shang Zhou duandai gongcheng*, p. 33.

[118] See *Kaogu yu wenwu* 1998.3, 69–70.

Wu Hu of the territory previously owned by Wu Wu was the unfulfilled will of King Li.

Although there is a danger in generalizing on the basis of these two inscriptions, the land transactions sanctioned by King Li, quite unusual among the many land-related inscriptions, may well have been among the things that he was blamed for. The two inscriptions suggest that King Li had probably confiscated the estates of some aristocratic lineages and then given them to others, and this could have been a tactic to consolidate royal power. We need to keep in mind the ongoing problems of the period: the Xianyun repeatedly invaded the northwestern frontier and the Dongyi and Huaiyi attacked the eastern states. We need also to be reminded of the probable consequences of the land-granting policy that had been practiced for 200 years – the possible impoverishment of the royal house in the face of a dominating aristocratic power represented by Duke Wu. Put in such context, King Li's alleged misconduct of "monopolizing profit" would appear merely as an effort to strengthen the royal finances in the hope of saving the dynasty from downfall. But this could not be done without competition with the powerful Wei River aristocracy. He probably had done it too quickly, and caused widespread unrest and criticism. Although the situation is far from being clear, sorting out all the pieces of information from the reign and considering them in a shared historical context, I believe that the best reading of the events of 842 BC would point to a major struggle between royal power and some of the influential lineages that had probably forced King Li out of power, but not to a revolution in which the people overthrew their tyrant. As mentioned before, such a narrative of people overthrowing the king was more probably a reflection of Eastern Zhou reality. Therefore, rather than a victory of the exploited class over the aristocratic class, the rebellion in 842 BC was more likely a victory of the aristocracy over royal authority, or a failure of royal power to restore its strength.

THE LAST STAND OF ZHOU ROYAL POWER: THE RESTORATION OF KING XUAN

After fourteen years in exile, King Li died in 828 BC. It became no longer necessary for a regent to rule in the king's name. The transition to the next reign seems to have been rather peaceful, with Gongbo He abdicating from power and King Xuan established with support from both the Duke of Shao and the Duke of Zhou.[119] The inscription of the Shi Li *gui* in fact alludes to a friendly relationship between Gongbo He and the new king, who took quite seriously the message of the death of the senior official.

---

[119] The *Bamboo Annals* says that Duke Ding of Zhou and Duke Mu of Shao assisted the new government. It should be noted that both the "Duke of Zhou" and the "Duke of Shao" were inherited titles. See *Zhushu jinian*, 2, p. 14.

Perhaps because of this peaceful transition, the new reign started off in a positive direction with recognition by Gongbo He's faction and also support by the two most important lineages, those of the Duke of Zhou and the Duke of Shao. With this new departure, the first thirty years of King Xuan's forty-six-year reign seem to have been successful, regarded by later historians as the "Restoration of King Xuan" – the last stand of Zhou royal power.[120] While there seems to have been no major dispute about the way in which King Xuan came to power, do we really have evidence that his reign represented a resurgence of the Western Zhou state? What were the strategies adopted by the new court to achieve such a "restoration"? In this section, I will review our current evidence for the reign of King Xuan and highlight the historical developments of this period.

It seems likely that the "restoration" program, if there was one, started with the northwestern frontier in the hope of securing the Zhou heartland. As will be discussed in detail in chapter 3, the operation was carried out in a series of campaigns aimed at reestablishing Zhou dominance over the upper Jing River and upper Wei River valleys. This included two major battles recorded in the bronze inscriptions against the Xianyun that took place in 823 BC and 816–815 BC; the first battle seems to have been started by the Zhou side, and not the Xianyun. Quite consistent with this effort in the upper Jing region, an earlier attack was launched by the Qin people with royal backup into the upper Wei River region in 825 BC but they were not successful until many years later.[121] These military actions were not without great danger, but it is likely the Zhou–Qin forces succeeded in reestablishing strongholds in the two regions, hence securing the Zhou capitals on the Wei River plain.

Perhaps the most important battle was fought in the southeast, aiming at holding back the pressure from the long-time enemy Huaiyi. We have two bronze inscriptions that allude to Zhou's relations with the Huaiyi during the reign of King Xuan. The Shi Yuan *gui* 師袁簋 (JC: 4314) mentions a major campaign against the Huaiyi that was so extensive that even troops from the states of Qi and Ji 冀 (= Ji 紀) and others in the Shandong region were enlisted to fight alongside the Zhou royal armies (Fig. 22).[122] The inscription on the Jufu *xu* 駒父盨 (JC: 4464) mentions that in King Xuan's eighteenth year (810 BC) a Zhou envoy was sent by Nan Zhong to the

---

[120] See for instance, *Hanshu*, 22, p. 1,071; *Houhan shu*, 86, p. 2,830.

[121] Qin was an allied polity established by the Zhou court during the mid-Western Zhou in the upper Wei River valley. The early history of Qin will be discussed in chapter 5.

[122] For the inscription of the Shi Yuan *gui*, see also Shirakawa, "Kinbun tsūshaku," 29.178:600. The Shi Yuan *gui*, together with the Yuan *pan* 袁盤 (JC: 10172) which is self-dated to the twenty-eighth year, are now commonly dated to the reign of King Xuan. See Ma Chengyuan, *Shang Zhou qingtongqi*, 3, p. 307; Shaughnessy, *Sources of Western Zhou History*, p. 285. This date has acquired new support from the Meixian bronzes because Scribe Yu 減 who is mentioned in the Yuan *pan* is also mentioned in the Forty-Second Year Lai *ding* and Forty-Third Year Lai *ding*. The high year numbers leave us with little doubt that they were from the long reign of King Xuan. See *Wenwu*, 2003.6, 6, 16.

Fig. 22 The Shi Yuan *gui* and its inscription (*Shanghai bowuguan cang qingtongqi*, 53, p. 49)

Southern Huaiyi by way of Cai to collect tribute, and that he was well received by the Southern Huaiyi.[123] This inscription seems to suggest that some kind of peaceful settlement may have been reached as a result of Zhou's military effort in the early years of King Xuan. Since the enemies at this time are commonly referred to as the "Southern Huaiyi," it is very likely that the Zhou operation had aimed at areas to the south of the Huai River. The Zhou operation in the south recorded in the bronze inscriptions certainly left its traces in the literary tradition as it is the subject of at least two poems in the *Book of Poetry*: "Changwu" 常武 (no. 263), which celebrates a campaign conducted by King Xuan who himself led the royal Six Armies under the field command by Nan Zhong (mentioned in the Jufu *xu*) and Huangfu 皇父 to attack the state of Xu in the Huai River valley, traditionally known as a part of the Huaiyi;[124] and "Jianghan" 江漢 (no. 262) that celebrates the contribution of the Duke of Shao, Hu 虎, mentioned in the Zhousheng *gui* 琱生簋 (JC: 4292–3) and indisputably the caster of the Shaobo Hu *gui*

---

[123] For this interpretation, see Huang Shengzhang, "Jufu xu gai mingwen yanjiu," *Kaogu yu wenwu* 1983.4, 53; Wang Hui, "Jufu xu gai mingwen shishi," *Kaogu yu wenwu* 1982.5, 59. A different reading suggests that it records an equal exchange of presents between the Zhou and the Huaiyi; see Xia Hanyi (Edward Shaughnessy), *Wengu zhixin lu: Shang Zhou wenhua shi guanjian* (Taibei: Daohuo, 1997), pp. 160–65. For the inscription, see also Shirakawa, "Kinbun tsūshaku," 48.ho8:226–27.

[124] See *Shijing*, 18.5, pp. 576–78 (Waley, *The Book of Songs*, pp. 281–83).

召伯虎簋 excavated in Luoyi,[125] in restoring order to the southern lands.[126] In the *Current Bamboo Annals*, this campaign against the Huaiyi is dated to the sixth year of King Xuan (822 BC).[127] The inscriptions and the textual tradition combine well in this case to report a historical process that can be logically contextualized with the politics of the reign of King Xuan.

The textual tradition points also to the middle Yangzi as a region of Zhou initiatives during the reign of King Xuan, and this seems to have centered on the relocation of some states such as Shen 申 in the Nanyang basin. The event is the subject of the poem "Songgao" 崧高 (no. 259) in the *Book of Poetry*, which gives quite a lot of details,[128] and another tradition, the *Current Bamboo Annals*, dates the event in King Xuan's seventh year (821 BC).[129] The historical-geographical issues involving Shen's move will be examined in chapter 4 (see pp. 221–28); it will suffice here to note that Shen was originally probably located in the upper Jing River region, and its transfer to the Nanyang basin implies that some kind of reorganization of the Zhou defense in the north may have taken place. But more likely, I believe, the relocation of Shen together with another state Lü 吕 in the Nanyang basin was carefully planned by the Zhou court to strengthen Zhou defense in the middle Yangzi: after the rebellion of Ehou the Border Protector during the reign of King Li, there was a Zhou power vacuum in the middle Yangzi; it was necessary to establish a stronghold in the region with men the king could trust. The archaeologically excavated inscriptions, though they do not confirm the move itself, confirm well the location of Shen in the Nanyang basin during the late phase of the Western Zhou.

Besides military operations, the textual tradition concerning the reign of King Xuan seems to reflect also a systematic diplomatic effort to restore relations with the distant regional states. The poem "Hanyi" 韓奕 (no. 261) was written with regard to an important visit by the ruler of the state of Hann from the northern Hebei plain.[130] On this trip, the ruler of Hann was not only warmly received and richly rewarded by the king, but also brought home a new consort who was the daughter of Juefu 蹶父 and a niece of King Li.[131] The *Current Bamboo Annals* records that, in fact, before the ruler's visit, in the fourth year of King Xuan (824 BC), Juefu was sent by

[125] For the discovery of the Shaobo Hu *gui*, see *Kaogu* 1995.9, 788–91.
[126] See *Shijing*, 18.4, pp. 573–75 (Waley, *The Book of Songs*, pp. 280–81).
[127] See *Zhushu jinian*, 2, p. 14 (Legge, *The Shoo King*, Prolegomena, p. 155).
[128] See *Shijing*, 18.3, pp. 565–66 (Waley, *The Book of Songs*, pp. 272–74).
[129] See *Zhushu jinian*, 2, p. 14 (Legge, *The Shoo King*, Prolegomena, p. 155). As for the location of Shen, the "Geographical Records" chapter of the *Hanshu* indicates that Shen was located in Wan County 宛縣 of Nanyang Commandery 南陽郡 of the Han dynasty, which is present-day Nanyang city; see *Hanshu*, 28, p. 1,563.
[130] See *Shijing*, 18.4, pp. 570–73 (Waley, *The Book of Songs*, pp. 277–79).
[131] The poem describes the new wife of Hann as a niece of *fenwang* 汾王, whom most commentators identify with King Li who, after the rebellion of 842 BC, resided at Zhi in the Fen River valley. For this interpretation, see Chen Huan, *Shi Maoshi zhuan shu*, 3 vols. (Beijing: Zhongguo shudian, 1984), 25, p. 45.

the king on a diplomatic trip to Hann, probably with an invitation to the Hann ruler.[132] As suggested in appendix 1, the Hebei plain seems to have been cut off from contact with the Zhou court during the long period of the mid-Western Zhou. The mutual visits and the new marriage relationship between the Zhou court and Hann were above all significant probably as a strategy adopted by the Zhou court to reassert royal influence over the peripheral regions.

Quite consistent with these diplomatic efforts in the north, it is evident that the Zhou court also made efforts to reestablish royal authority in the east. The poem "Zhengmin" 烝民 (no. 260) describes Zhong Shanfu's 仲山父 mission to the state of Qi in Shandong, that was once in a hostile relationship with the Zhou court in the time of King Yi.[133] The inscription of the Shi Yuan *gui* suggests that Qi assisted King Xuan in his military operation against the Huaiyi. The *Current Bamboo Annals* says that in the seventh year (821 BC) Zhong Shanfu was commanded by King Xuan to fortify the capital of the state of Qi with assistance from the ruler of Fan 樊.[134] The following year, according to the *Shiji*, King Xuan interfered in the succession of the state of Lu. When Duke Wu of Lu paid a visit to the Zhou court, bringing along his two sons, Kuo 括 and Xi 戲, King Xuan chose the younger son Xi to be the heir of Lu. This led eventually to the murder of Xi by Kuo's son, Boyu 伯御, nine years after the death of Duke Wu. Then, in the thirty-second year of King Xuan, the royal army attacked Lu and killed Boyu.[135]

While the inscriptions do confirm some of the royal actions celebrated in the Zhou literary tradition, for instance the campaign against the Southern Huaiyi and the location of Shen, they do not and cannot be expected at present to confirm every historical detail told in Zhou literature. However, since these actions are also dated in the historical texts such as the *Bamboo Annals*, there seems no ground to doubt that they had actually taken place. What is more important is that these seemingly isolated events that happened in different directions of the Zhou realm, including the upper Jing region where the inscriptions indicate that royal campaigns were carried out, seem to reflect a series of well-coordinated initiatives, and very likely such initiatives were generated from a unified strategy adopted by the Zhou court to reassert royal prestige along the perimeter of the Zhou world through the combined use of military force and diplomacy. This was probably the result of an activist government that had characterized the early decades of King Xuan and contributed to a reign of forty-six years, the longest in Western Zhou history. It can be well established on the available evidence that for at least a period of

[132] See *Zhushu jinian*, 2, p. 14 (Legge, *The Shoo King*, Prolegomena, p. 155).
[133] See *Shijing*, 18.3, pp. 568–69 (Waley, *The Book of Songs*, pp. 275–77).
[134] See *Zhushu jinian*, 2, p. 14 (Legge, *The Shoo King*, Prolegomena, p. 155).
[135] See *Shiji*, 33, pp. 1,527–28.

time Zhou royal military strength was restored in some distant regions and the relationship between the central court and the regional states was improved.

However, for the later part of the reign of King Xuan, our historical records present a series of unsuccessful royal attempts. An entry in the *Current Bamboo Annals* says that in the thirty-third year (795 BC), the royal army attacked the Rong of Taiyuan 太原 but did not succeed. In the thirty-eighth year (790 BC), the royal army was defeated by the Tiaorong 條戎 and Benrong 奔戎 in the Fen River valley of Shanxi. In the next year, the royal army was again defeated by the Jiangrong 姜戎 at a place called Qianmu 千畝; even the newly recruited troops from the southern states were destroyed in this battle.[136] These records suggest that in the last two decades of King Xuan, royal power was again set on a trend towards sharp decline from which it never recovered.

CONCLUSION

Compared to many later imperial dynasties in China, the Western Zhou seems to have begun to show weaknesses at a much earlier stage and hence had a longer history of decline. Putting aside the disastrous southern campaign conducted by King Zhao, from the reign of King Mu the Western Zhou state experienced a number of political disputes involving both the royal court in Shaanxi and the regional states in the east, showing the relaxation of political control and the weakening of royal authority. Outside, the security of the Western Zhou state was challenged by the rising powers mainly in two directions: the Xianyun in the northwest; the Huaiyi in the southeast. Serious damage had been done to Zhou power especially by the rebellion of some former Zhou allies such as Ehou the Border Protector. The accumulation of problems eventually led to a total crisis in the time of King Li. But the exile of King Li was not so much the result of a struggle between the aristocracy and the lower class in the capital, as the result of a failed attempt to restore power to the royal house in the face of a dominating aristocracy.

The problem was by and large structural. The Western Zhou state was formed on the principle of submission of the regional rulers to the Zhou king through a common ancestral cult. However, after a hundred years, such blood ties tended to weaken naturally and the high degree of autonomy granted to the regional states under the "Fengjian" institution began to move them towards independence. The archaeological evidence shows that communications between the Zhou royal court and the regional states were frequent during the early Western Zhou but were interrupted in the middle

---

[136] See *Zhushu jinian*, 2, p. 16. The *Ancient Bamboo Annals*, however, dates the first campaign two years earlier, to the thirty-first year (797 BC), and the second campaign to the thirty-sixth year (792 BC) of King Xuan. See Fan Xiangyong, *Guben zhushu jinian*, p. 32.

part of the dynasty. It also shows that, by the late Western Zhou, local cultural traditions began to take hold on both the elite and non-elite levels in some of the distant regional states. But the weakening of Zhou power had another root in the royal management of resources. The "favor for loyalty" exchange characterized the relationship between the Zhou king and the official aristocrats at the central court. When the period of great expansion ended, the continuing royal grant of landed properties functioned to drain the royal house and contributed to the growing power of the Wei River aristocracy. Since land cannot be reproduced, the more land the king gave out to his officials, the less able he was to do so. With such a suicidal method of government in the "favor for loyalty" game, the Zhou king was inevitably moving to the losing side.

It is evident that in the two most fundamental relationships of the Western Zhou state – that between the central court and the regional states and that between royal power and the aristocracy – the Zhou king lost his control and the foundation of the Western Zhou state was seriously undermined.

CHAPTER 3

Enemies at the gate: the war against the Xianyun and the northwestern frontier

In the preceding chapter, I have analyzed problems in the sociopolitical structure of the Western Zhou state. Now, I turn to Zhou's relationship with the outside world and examine external pressures that may have accelerated the political disintegration of the Western Zhou state. However, this is not to offer a general survey of Zhou's foreign relations; instead, the present chapter will concentrate on a particular region, the upper Jing River valley, as the battleground between the Zhou and their northwestern enemies who had directly threatened the Zhou heartland in the Wei River valley. By focusing on one region, we will have a better chance of actually demonstrating the geopolitical crisis facing the Western Zhou state and its possible responses. The study will further enhance our understanding of the degree to which the internal and external problems had profoundly perplexed the Zhou regime.

As demonstrated in chapter 1, the Wei River valley in central Shaanxi was the heartland of the Western Zhou state and the locus of Zhou royal administration. However, if we look at a map of the Zhou realm, we find that the Zhou capitals Feng and Hao were not located in the geographical center of the Zhou state, where the eastern center Luoyi was favorably located, but were close to the western border. Through much of the dynasty, the Zhou effort to expand was focused on the east, but this could not be done without the core being secured from attacks from the west. The location of the Zhou capitals on the Wei River plain in the west – separated by some 400 kilometers or 40–60 days of travel from the geographical center – had important implications: while the numerous regional states in the east could at least absorb foreign invasions until the royal army arrived on the scene to win a decisive battle, in the west any attacks by the enemies would fall directly on the royal domain and would require immediate response by the royal forces.

This geographical disadvantage of the Zhou capitals was fully exposed during the late part of the mid-Western Zhou when their enemies in the northwestern highlands gained the upper hand and launched frequent invasions into Zhou territory. From this time on, the Zhou had to fight very hard in a war that took place in the vicinity of the Zhou capital, an area so critical to the survival of the dynasty. However, the historian should throw

141

no blame on the Zhou founders for having created such a dangerous geopolitical situation; no dynastic founders had ever prepared their regimes to decline. Indeed, the Zhou were capable enough during their early years, not only to hold the frontier firm against enemies but also to carry out aggressive expeditions into enemy territory. It was the effect of history that when their vigor was gone and their position changed from offense to defense, the Zhou found themselves hopelessly within the immediate reach of their enemies. Understanding this prolonged warfare in the northwestern frontier will provide us with a necessary background to understand the eventual fall of the Western Zhou state.

A HISTORY OF THE ZHOU–XIANYUN WAR

All this is about a people or society that was called the "Xianyun" by the Zhou. For a very long time, the Xianyun presented the most intimidating threat to the security of the Zhou regime, and the war with them had a long-lasting impact both on Western Zhou society and on the psyche of the Zhou people, who continued to be haunted by the experience even at a time when the war had already become a part of the past. The new archaeological discoveries enable us not only actually to locate this war in the landscape of the Zhou west, but, by doing so, to provide for it a broad sociocultural context.

Who were the Xianyun?

We should perhaps begin by asking, who were the Xianyun? But there is no easy, if any, answer to this very basic question. In fact, the identity of any people who lived outside of the literary tradition of civilization can potentially be a subject of hot debate. In this particular case, there is not even enough textual evidence for an informed debate about the early history of the Xianyun people. Nevertheless, on the basis of information currently available we can attempt a sketch of their power and cultural dimensions as well as the historical context from which they had emerged.

In traditional historiography, the discussion on Xianyun has taken place mainly in the framework provided by the first-century BC historian Sima Qian in the "Genealogical Account of the Xiongnu" of his *Shiji*. In this document, Sima Qian simply lists a number of ancient peoples such as the Shanrong 山戎, Hunyu 葷粥, Xianyun 獫狁, Quanyi 畎夷, Xirong 西戎, and Quanrong 犬戎, as perhaps the cultural progenitors of the Xiongnu 匈奴.[1] The account of these people was by no means an anthropological or an ethnographical documentation by modern standards, but was only a retrospective synthesis of pre-existing textual records concerning peoples who had once reportedly inhabited the same section of the known world.

---

[1] See *Shiji*, 110, pp. 2,879–81.

Therefore, it amounts to suggesting at best a common political relation with the Shang and Zhou states in which these various groups of people had subsequently taken part. It is in this context, and also in the "Basic Annals of Zhou," that Sima Qian tells the story of Zhou's early relations with these northern peoples. Accordingly, the Ancient Duke of Zhou (Gugong 古公; grandfather of King Wen), also called "Great King" (Taiwang 太王), he writes, used to live with his people in a place called Bin 豳, close to the land of the Xunyu 薫育, who repeatedly attacked him. Having exhausted all ways to appease the enemies, the Ancient Duke had no choice but to leave his homeland and migrated to Qiyi, located in the Wei River valley.[2] Sima Qian also narrates the end of the Western Zhou, which was reportedly caused by the attack by the Quanrong people.

Starting with Wang Guowei's famous essay that brought into discussion terms such as Guifang 鬼方, Kunyi 昆夷, Xunyu 獯鬻, and Xianyun 獫狁 from the various pre-Qin texts, modern scholars have poured into the enterprise a great deal of effort to identify these names.[3] In the West, the identification of the Hunyu and Xianyun with the Xiongnu, and further with the European Huns, was once strongly advocated by some scholars, but was sharply criticized by others.[4] While these are merely arguments about names, as far as such discussion goes I think that there are only two clear points: (1) Xianyun 獫狁 and Xunyu 薫育 are terms that appeared only in the Han dynasty and are respectively the graphic equivalents of the terms Xianyun 獫狁 and "Xunyu" 獯鬻 that appear in the pre-Qin sources;[5] (2) the term Quanrong was an Eastern Zhou invention to denote the Xianyun 獫狁 in Western Zhou sources (this point is fully explained in appendix 2). As far as their relations with the later Xiongnu are concerned, Pulleyblank has pointed out that none of them has anything to do with the Xiongnu.[6] While the term "Xianyun" almost certainly carried with it an ethnic and even cultural identity, as it was probably originally used by the Xianyun people to refer to themselves in a language foreign to the Zhou, the bronze inscriptions show clearly that the Xianyun could be simply called "Rong" 戎, a purely Zhou term that meant "warlike foreigners." When the word

---

[2] See *Shiji*, 4, pp. 113–14; 110, p. 2,881 (Nienhauser, *The Grand Scribe's Records*, 1, p. 56). On the Zhou migration to the Wei River valley and their possible location prior to the move, see chapter 1 (see note 28 on p. 41).

[3] See Wang Guowei, "Guifang Kunyi Xianyun kao," in *Guantang jilin* (1923; reprinted Shijiazhuang: Hebei jiaoyu, 2001), pp. 369–83. See also Meng Wentong, *Zhou Qin shaoshu minzu yanjiu* (Shanghai: Longmen, 1968), pp. 8–14; Liu Xueyao, *Xiongnu shilun* (Taipei: Lantian, 1987), pp. 3–8.

[4] See Omeljan Pritsak, "Xun: Der Volksname der Hsiung-nu," *Central Asiatic Journal* 5.1 (1959), 27–34. For a criticism of this identification, see Otto Maenchen-Helfen, "Archaistic Names of the Hsiung-nu," *Central Asiatic Journal* 6.4 (1961), 249–61.

[5] This can be seen in the textual origins of Sima Qian's account that is clearly based on two earlier sources: (1) the poem "Mian" 綿 (no. 237) in the *Book of Poetry* that mentions the Zhou's migration to Qiyi under the Ancient Duke; (2) *Mencius*, which mentions that the Great King had submitted himself to serve the Xunyu 獯鬻. See *Shijing*, 16.2, p. 510 (Waley, *The Book of Songs*, pp. 232–33); *Mencius*, pp. 24–25.

[6] See E. G. Pulleyblank, "The Chinese and Their Neighbors in Prehistorical and Early Historical Times," in *The Origins of Chinese Civilization*, ed. David N. Keightley (Berkeley: University of California Press, 1983), p. 449.

"Rong" was used, certainly not limited to the Xianyun, it was very often prefixed with a place-name that differentiated them from other locations.

There are also scholars who have looked for the origins of the Xianyun outside of the context of Chinese history. It was once suggested by Jaroslav Průšek that the Xianyun were probably migrants from the Altai region in Central Asia, the heartland of the nomadic culture, on the sole basis that they are likely to have been mounted horse-nomads who suddenly attacked China at the end of the Western Zhou dynasty and had since suddenly and completely disappeared from Chinese history.[7] A number of scholars have already rejected Průšek's misconceptions regarding the origin and war techniques of the Xianyun.[8] The discovery of the Duoyou *ding* in 1980 has made it perfectly clear that the Xianyun were not mounted nomads but fought from chariots in the same way the Zhou conducted their warfare; this also cleared the misconception that the so-called "barbarians" were foot raiders against the Chinese chariotry.[9] On the contrary, our current evidence suggests that the Xianyun were a society of considerable size and high concentration of power that was able to field hundreds of war chariots in a single battle against the Zhou. And certainly the possession of bronze technology that could support long-term warfare with the Zhou with advanced weaponry was a must. If we put the Xianyun in a geographical setting, as will be shown below, the fact that they could conduct warfare against the Zhou simultaneously in different directions across a large area suggests that their society may have been composed of various units or groups with shared cultural traditions and ethnic background that were able to coordinate among themselves against a common enemy.

On all accounts, they are likely to have been the indigenous inhabitants of the broad northern highlands stretching from the Yellow River bend to the upper Yellow River regions. In a very subtle way, they may have been cultural successors to the bronze culture of Ordos that was prosperous during the late Shang period but had diminished since the beginning of the Western Zhou. They may not have been nomads at all, but may have been, as most societies in the so-called "Northern Zone Complex" were, widely distributed communities of farmers and pastoralists.[10] According to Nicola Di Cosmo, during the Shang–Western Zhou period the Northern

---

[7] See Jaroslav Průšek, *Chinese Statelets and the Northern Barbarians in the Period 1400–300 BC* (New York: Humanities Press, 1971), pp. 130–34.

[8] See Pulleyblank, "The Chinese and Their Neighbors," p. 499; Di Cosmo, "The Northern Frontier in Pre-Imperial China," in *The Cambridge History of Ancient China: From the Origins of Civilization to 221 BC*, ed. Michael Loewe and Edward L. Shaughnessy (Cambridge: Cambridge University Press, 1999), p. 920.

[9] See Creel, *The Origins of Statecraft*, pp. 266–69. For the discovery of the Duoyou *ding*, see Tian and Luo, "Duoyou ding de faxian," pp. 115–18.

[10] The "Northern Zone Complex" was a cultural complex with shared characteristics different from those of the Shang and Zhou cultures. Geographically, the "Northern Zone" comprises the vast interlocking desert, steppe, and forest regions from Heilongjiang and Jilin in the east to Xinjiang in the west, to the north of Shaanxi, Shanxi, and Hebei provinces. For the definition of the "Northern Zone Complex," see Di Cosmo, "The Northern Frontier in Pre-Imperial China," pp. 885, 893.

Zone was inhabited mainly by such communities of shepherds and farmers who also practiced extensive hunting, even though throughout the period pastoral elements gradually became more and more dominant.[11] In the next period, from the sixth or even seventh to the fourth century BC, as the archaeological evidence shows, a shift from an agropastoralist economy to pastoral nomadism had completely overtaken the entire Northern Zone.[12] In this cultural chronology, when the Xianyun attacked Zhou during the ninth century BC, their lifestyle had probably not been much altered by the transition to nomadism that was already going on in the heartland of the Northern Steppe, and they had probably shown themselves to be not much different from the Zhou people, who may also have practiced pastoralism, though to a lesser degree.

The early war period

What had triggered the long confrontation between the Zhou and the Xianyun was probably a campaign that is said to have been conducted by King Mu of Zhou (r. 956–918 BC) against the "Quanrong," a name that is used in texts of Warring States and Han times for the Xianyun (see appendix 2). The story was told in the *Guoyu* and was copied character by character into the *Shiji*.[13] It takes the form of a long speech put into the mouth of the Duke of Zhai 祭, who admonished King Mu not to use force against the Quanrong if it was for the pure purpose of displaying military power. In this speech, the Duke of Zhai noted that the Quanrong, since the death of their chiefs Dabi 大畢 and Boshi 伯士, had often paid homage to the Zhou king and acknowledged the supremacy of Zhou, and there was no reason to attack them. Despite the awkward moral position it might put him in, and going against the precedence of the Duke of Zhou who is said to have preferred virtue over military power, King Mu attacked the Quanrong anyway, and captured four white wolves and four white deer.[14] The campaign is also recorded in the *Bamboo Annals* (under the twelfth year of King Mu); in both the *Current* and the *Ancient* versions of the text, it is said that King Mu captured the five kings of the Quanrong and moved them to a place called "Great Plain" (Taiyuan 太原).[15] The location of Taiyuan can be confirmed in a slightly later historical context in relation

[11] *Ibid.*, pp. 888–90; Nicola Di Cosmo, *Ancient China and Its Enemies* (Cambridge: Cambridge University Press, 2002), pp. 44–54.

[12] Di Cosmo, *Ancient China and Its Enemies*, pp. 74–80.

[13] See *Guoyu*, 1, pp. 1–8; *Shiji*, 4, pp. 135–36 (Nienhauser, *The Grand Scribe's Records*, 1, pp. 67–68).

[14] Di Cosmo considers that this campaign opened a new phase in Zhou expansion under King Mu, and the discourse itself represents a contradistinction between political ambition and philosophical idealism in the pre-imperial discussions on relations with the non-Chinese states. See Di Cosmo, *Ancient China and Its Enemies*, p. 108.

[15] See Fan Xiangyong, *Guben zhushu jinian*, pp. 26–27; *Zhushu jinian*, 2, pp. 9–10 (Legge, *The Shoo King*, Prolegomena, p. 150). The campaign was further fictionalized in the Warring States novel *Mu tianzi zhuan*, excavated together with the *Bamboo Annals* in AD 281, in which the attack on the Quanrong was one of the sequential events that took place on King Mu's journey to the unknown world of the northwest. See *Mu tianzi zhuan*, 1, p. 4; Loewe, *Early Chinese Texts*, pp. 342–46.

to the Xianyun war, as the lineage of the persuader, the Duke of Zhai, is well known from the bronze inscriptions.[16] But what is more important is that the narrative portrays King Mu as a reckless ruler, in contrast to the Quanrong who are described as being honest, following the ancient virtues, and remaining committed to their faith. This is certainly different from all Eastern Zhou presentations of the Zhou–"barbarian" relationship (see chapter 6) and suggests that, in the historical memory of the Zhou, King Mu must have taken the blame for altering the relations on the northwestern border hitherto favorable to the Zhou, if not for all the subsequent invasions that the Zhou had to suffer. Thus, although the details of the speech in the *Guoyu* may have been constructed (or reconstructed) centuries later, based probably on a persisting Zhou tradition regarding King Mu's relation to the west, the campaign, as a part of that relation, may have actually taken place and can well be explained in the context of the historical development of the Western Zhou.[17] The *Guoyu* concludes that since this campaign, the Rong people in the wild world never appeared at the Zhou court.[18]

As already shown in the preceding chapter, after the reign of King Mu the Western Zhou state underwent a long process of internal disorder and decline. An entry under the twenty-first year of King Yih (r. 899/97–873 BC) in the *Current Bamboo Annals* suggests that the Duke of Guo 虢 led an army to attack the Quanrong in the north but was defeated.[19] Then, in the reign of King Yi (r. 865–858 BC), the *Ancient Bamboo Annals* reports, the Zhou court sent out the Six Armies of the West, the major field troops stationed on the Wei River plain, under command of the Duke of Guo (who may or may not be the earlier Duke of Guo on campaign), to attack the Rong at Taiyuan. The royal armies are said to have marched as far as a place called Yuquan 俞泉 and captured a thousand horses. This major military operation against the Quanrong was put under the seventh year of King Yi in the *Current Bamboo Annals*.[20] If this campaign went well, as the historical sources suggest, it would indicate that for a certain period of time during the mid-Western Zhou, despite the weakening royal power, the Zhou were still able to maintain the upper hand over the enemies on the northwestern border by taking a number of military initiatives against them, though perhaps not all the operations had ended in success.

---

[16] In a recent article, Professor Li Xueqin has demonstrated convincingly that the graph 瀙 in the inscriptions is indeed the archaic form of *zhai* 祭. We know of a number of individuals such as Zhaigong 瀙公, Zhaizhong 瀙仲, and Zhaiji 瀙季, all from the Zhai lineage, but during the early Western Zhou. See Li Xueqin, "Shi Guodian jian Zhaigong zhi guming," *Wenwu* 1998.7, 44–45.

[17] This happened at a time when Zhou expansion in the south was blocked at the end of King Zhao's reign. It seems reasonable for the Zhou to have turned their attention back to the west that had been left aside during the early Western Zhou expansion, in search of new lands to conquer.

[18] See *Guoyu*, 1, p. 8.   [19] See *Zhushu jinian*, 2, p. 11 (Legge, *The Shoo King*, Prolegomena, p. 152).

[20] Fan Xiangyong, *Guben zhushu jinian*, p. 30; *Zhushu jinian*, 2, p. 12 (Legge, *The Shoo King*, Prolegomena, p. 153).

However, the situation began to change significantly thereafter. During the next reign, that of King Li (r. 857/53–842/28 BC), it was now the Xianyun, and not the Zhou, who began to take the offensive, launching repeated attacks into the Zhou territory. The inscription of the Duoyou *ding* (JC: 2835) informs us about one of the battles in a very exceptional way (Fig. 23):[21]

唯(惟)十月,用嚴(玁)狁(狁)放(方)巤(興), 廣(廣)伐京自(師), 告追于王。〔王〕命武公: "遣乃元士, 羞追于京自(師)!" 武公命多友: "衛(率)公車, 羞追于京自(師)!"
癸未, 戎伐筍, 衣孚(俘)。 多友西追。 甲申之臂(晨), 博(搏)于郗(漆), 多友有折首、 執(執)噤(訊)。凡已(以)公車折首吾(二百)又口又五人, 執(執)噤(訊)廿(二十)又三人, 孚(俘)戎車百乘一十又七乘, 衣匋(復)筍人孚(俘)。或博(搏)于龔, 折首卅(三十)又六人, 執(執)噤(訊)二人, 孚(俘)車十乘。從至, 追博(搏)于世, 多友或有折首、 執(執)噤(訊)。 乃軼(軼)追至于楊冢, 公車折首百又十又五人, 執(執)噤(訊)三人。唯孚(俘)車不克, 已(以)焚, 唯馬歐(歐)盡。 匋(復)奪(奪)京自(師)之孚(俘)。
多友逎獻孚(俘)、 罘(馘)、 噤(訊)于公, 武公逎獻于王。〔王〕逎曰武公曰: "女(汝)既靜京自(師), 叡(釐)女(汝), 易(錫)女(汝)土田。" 丁酉, 武公才(在)獻宮。逎命向父钬(召)多友, 〔多友〕逎延(延)于獻宮。 公親(親)曰多友曰: "余肇(肇)事(使), 女(汝)休! 不逆(逆), 有成事, 多禽(擒), 女(汝)靜京自(師)。 易(錫)女(汝)圭瓚一、 湯(鍚)鍾一膳(肆)、 鐈(鐈) 鋚百匀(鈞)。"多友敢對錫(揚)公休, 用乍(作)障(尊)鼎, 用匐(朋)用萱(友), 其子子孫孫永寶用。

It was in the tenth month, because the Xianyun greatly arose and broadly attacked Jingshi, [it] was reported to the king. The king commanded Duke Wu: "Dispatch your most capable men and pursue at Jingshi!" Duke Wu commanded Duoyou: "Lead the ducal chariots and pursue at Jingshi!"

On the *guiwei* (no. 20) day, the Rong attacked Xun and took captives. Duoyou pursued to the west. In the morning of the *jiashen* (no. 21) day, [he] struck [them] at Qi. Duoyou had cut off heads and captured prisoners to be interrogated: in all, using the ducal chariots to cut off 2[X]5 heads, to capture 23 prisoners, and to take 117 Rong chariots; [Duoyou] liberated the Xun people captured [by the Xianyun]. Furthermore, [Duoyou] struck at Gong; [he] cut off 36 heads and captured 2 prisoners and took 10 chariots. Following [the Xianyun], [Duoyou] pursued and struck at Shi; Duoyou again had cut off heads and taken prisoners. Thereafter, [Duoyou] rapidly pursued [them] and arrived at Yangzhong; the ducal chariotry cut off 115 heads and captured 3 prisoners. It was that [they] could not capture the [Rong] chariots; they burnt [them]. And it was their (the Xianyun's) horses that they wounded gravely. [Duoyou] recaptured the Jingshi captives.

---

[21] For the discovery of the Duoyou *ding*, see Tian and Luo, "Duoyou ding de faxian," pp. 115–18. It should be noted that there are two different views on the date of the Duoyou *ding*. The first view dates it to the reign of King Li, and the second to King Xuan. In the preceding chapter, I have fully discussed the date of the Duoyou *ding* in relation to the power of Duke Wu and concluded that the bronze should be dated to the reign of King Li (see note 113 on pp. 131–32). For more discussion of this date, see Li Xueqin, *Xinchu qingtongqi yanjiu*, pp. 129–31; Zhang Yachu, "Tan Duoyou ding mingwen de jige wenti," *Kaogu yu wenwu* 1982.3, 64–68; Li Zhongcao, "Yeshi Duoyou ding mingwen," *Renwen zazhi* 1982.6, 95–99.

Fig. 23 The Duoyou *ding* and its inscription (inscription from the author; vessel from
Shaanxi qingtongqi, p. 69)

Duoyou contributed the captured, the heads, and the prisoners to the duke,
and Duke Wu then contributed [them] to the king. [The king] therefore addressed
Duke Wu and said: "You have pacified Jingshi; [I] enrich you and award you lands."
On the *dingyou* (no. 34) day, Duke Wu was in the *Xian*-hall. [He] commanded
Xiangfu to summon Duoyou, and [Duoyou] entered the *Xian*-hall. The duke
personally addressed Duoyou and said: "I initially assigned [you the task], and you
have done well! [you] did not disobey, but have accomplished [the deed and] taken

many captives. You have pacified Jingshi. [I] award you one jade tablet, one set of bells made in finest bronzes and one hundred *jun* of the *jiaoyou*-copper." Duoyou dares to respond to the duke's beneficence, and herewith makes [this] sacrificial *ding*-vessel, with which to entertain friends; may my sons' sons and grandsons' grandsons eternally treasure and use it!

Clearly, this battle was not an ordinary "frontier" skirmish but was rather a sizeable and organized attack by the Xianyun on the Zhou towns inside the frontier. The Xianyun first attacked a place called Jingshi 京師, apparently a Zhou settlement, and the message of war soon reached the Zhou capital. In response to the Xianyun's attack, the Zhou king ordered Duke Wu to handle the matter and Duke Wu subsequently sent out Duoyou to counterattack the invading Xianyun. While the Zhou troops were perhaps still on their way west to the battlefield, the Xianyun advanced to plunder another Zhou settlement named Xun 筍 on the day *guiwei* (no. 20), and had apparently taken its people prisoner.[22] On the next morning, the Zhou troops arrived on the scene and engaged the Xianyun in a major battle at Qi 漆 where hundreds of the Xianyun were killed and more than a hundred Xianyun chariots were captured together with the Xun people taken back by the Zhou forces. Successive battles took place at Gong and at Shi 世 when the Xianyun were retreating from the Zhou territory. The Zhou troops pursued the Xianyun uninterruptedly to the west and finally concluded the battle with another major strike at a place called Yangzhong 楊冢, where more Xianyun were killed and the Zhou people they had taken from Jingshi were liberated by the Zhou army. After the battle, Duoyou submitted the prisoners to Duke Wu, who than gave them over to the king. When the awards came down to the duke, Duoyou was also rewarded for his military contributions which were concurrently commemorated on this bronze.

The inscription of the Duoyou *ding* is important both in the details its composer offers us within a spatial dimension in which the battles are clearly marked by places, and in the exposition of the Zhou military-political power structure in which the campaign was conducted. The lively description of the war gives us a vivid sense of how a foreign invasion could be contained by a superior military force of the Zhou and what actually the Xianyun and the Zhou soldiers might do on the battlefield, such as capture and recapture the residents of the frontier towns. The inscription tells us that the Zhou army won a complete victory over the Xianyun, and certainly it ought to be so, for otherwise the inscription would not have been composed and cast. However, we should not forget that the victory was one of defense, for the Xianyun were on the attacking side; there may well have been battles

---

[22] There have been some previous misunderstandings about the process of this war. For a new reading and reconstruction of the war, see Li Feng, "Tayūtei meibun o meguru rekishi chiri teki mondai no kaiketsu: Shū ōchō no seihoku keiryaku o kaimei suru tameni, sono ichi," in *Chūgoku kodai no moji to bunka* (Tokyo: Kyūko shoin, 1999), pp. 181–88.

that the Zhou could not win that easily. Considering the general problems of the period – the Zhou were troubled by domestic political disputes and the rebellion of Ehou the Border Protector in the south – their position in the war must have been quite difficult.[23] In 840 BC, the second year of the regency of Gongbo He, the *Current Bamboo Annals* reports that the Xianyun again broke into Zhou territory and raided the western approaches to the capital Hao.[24] But there is no further information on this battle.

Progression of the war under King Xuan

The ascendance of King Xuan (r. 827/25–782 BC) to power after a long period of political instability may have reenergized Zhou foreign policy in some ways. As I have suggested in chapter 2, a systematic effort seems to have been made by the Zhou court under King Xuan to reestablish political order in the Western Zhou state, and it is very likely that the restoration program began with an attempt to regain control over the upper Jing River region. Indeed, only after the northwest border was secured would the Zhou be able to carry out further actions in the distant east. This new plan developed in the Zhou court provided the state of Qin with the best chance to rise in power. As the prologue of the successive actions, according to the *Current Bamboo Annals*, in the third year of King Xuan (825 BC), Qin Zhong 秦仲, the ruler of the state of Qin, was sent by the Zhou king to attack the Western Rong, a term that refers to the Rong people who lived probably in the upper Wei River region, most likely a part of the Xianyun. Since the state of Qin was located near present-day Tianshui in the upper Wei River valley, this campaign would seem to have been a flanking attack on the Western Rong or Xianyun.[25] This campaign partly overlapped in time King Xuan's personal campaign into the upper Jing River valley. However, Qin Zhong failed in the mission and was killed by his enemies in the sixth year of King Xuan (822 BC). Thereafter, the Zhou court did not abandon the effort, but summoned the five sons of Qin Zhong and gave them 7,000 Zhou troops to attack the Rong, and the Zhou–Qin coalition was eventually victorious. We learn more details about these early encounters between the Qin people and the Rong people from the "Basic Annals of Qin" in the *Shiji*, which I will discuss at length in chapter 5.

As far as the Zhou are concerned, we previously knew three bronze inscriptions whose dating to early in the reign of King Xuan is generally accepted, and three poems from the *Book of Poetry* that record the war

---

[23] It is significant to note that the war was fought by Duoyou with the *gongche* 公車, the chariotry that belonged to Duke Wu, but not the Six Armies. The Six Armies was sent east to attack the state of E and is not mentioned in connection with the Xianyun war thereafter.

[24] See *Zhushu jinian*, 2, p. 13 (Legge, *The Shoo King*, Prolegomena, p. 154).

[25] See *Zhushu jinian*, 2, p. 14 (Legge, *The Shoo King*, Prolegomena, p. 155). Qin Zhong's campaign against the Western Rong is dated to King Xuan's fourth year in the *Ancient Bamboo Annals*, as quoted in the *Houhan shu*; see Fan Xiangyong, *Guben zhushu jinian*, p. 31.

against the Xianyun and can be reasonably related to the inscriptions. The recent discovery in Meixian offered us yet another important document on the war with the Xianyun as it was continued towards the end of the reign. Combining these poems and the inscriptions we can learn a good deal about the war itself, as we learn through the war about the general politics of the long reign of King Xuan. Moreover, the analysis of these sources will also show how specific information contained in the poems can be used in relation to the inscriptions to reconstruct scenarios that might have provided a basis for both the inscriptional and the textual recording and interpretation. The best connections can be made between the inscription on the Xi Jia *pan* 兮甲盤 (JC: 10174) and the poem "Liuyue" 六月 (no. 177). The inscription says:[26]

佳（惟）五年三月既死霸庚寅，王初各伐厰（玁）狁于蕾盧。兮甲從王，折首，執眔（訊）。休，亡啟。王易（錫）兮甲馬四匹，駒車…兮伯吉父作盤，其眉壽，萬年無疆。子子孫孫永寶用。

It was the fifth year, third month, after the dying brightness, *gengyin*-day (no. 27); the king for the first time approached and attacked the Xianyun at Tuyu. Xi Jia followed the king, cutting off heads and taking prisoners. Well done, no harm. The king awarded Xi Jia four horses and a colt chariot . . . Xibo Jifu makes [this] *pan*-basin. May [he] have abundant longevity, for ten thousand years without limit. May [his] sons' sons and grandsons' grandsons eternally treasure and use it.

In the poem "Liuyue" (Sixth Month) we read (Waley's translation):[27]

1	六月棲棲，	In the sixth month all is bustle,
2	戎車既飭。	We put our war-chariots in order,
3	四牡騤騤，	Our four steeds are in good fettle,
4	載是常服。	We load our bow-cases and quivers.
5	玁狁孔熾，	The Xianyun are ablaze,
6	我是用急。	We have no time to lose.
7	王于出征，	The king is going out to battle,[28]
8	以匡王國。	To set aright the king's lands.
9	比物四驪，	Our team of blacks is well-matched,
10	維之維則。	A pattern of perfect training.
11	惟此六月，	It is the sixth month;

[26] For the inscription of the Xi Jia *pan*, see Shirakawa Shizuka, "Kinbun tsūshaku," 32.191:785–99. The Xi Jia *pan* is one of the very few bronzes that were discovered in the Northern Song dynasty and passed down to the modern day. The bronze was traditionally and commonly dated by the scholars to the reign of King Xuan, on the basis of its very mention of Jifu. Scholars working on calendars also noted that its full date fits well into the known calendar of the fifth year of King Xuan (823 BC) See Ma Chengyuan, *Shang Zhou qingtongqi*, 3, p. 305; Shaughnessy, *Sources of Western Zhou History*, pp. 141–42, 205.

[27] See *Shijing*, 10.2, pp. 424–25 (Waley, *The Book of Songs*, pp. 150–51).

[28] Here and in line 15, Waley gives "We are going out to battle." There seems no way to translate *wang* 王 to "we", and my revision here is based on traditional commentaries by Kong Yinda and Chen Huan; see *Shijing*, 10.2, p. 424; Chen Huan, *Shi Maoshi zhuan shu* (Beijing: Zhongguo shudian, 1984), 17, p. 15.

12	既成我服,	We have finished all our field-work.
13	我服既成,	We have finished all our field-work
14	于三十里。	Throughout the thirty leagues.
15	王于出征,	The king is going out to battle
16	以佐天子。	We help the Son of Heaven.

17	四牡脩廣,	Our four steeds are tall and broad,
18	其大有顒。	Hugely high they stand.
19	薄伐玁狁,	We fall upon the Xianyun,
20	以奏膚公。	We do great deeds,
21	有嚴有翼,	So stern, so grim
22	共武之服。	We fulfill the tasks of war,
23	共武之服,	Fulfill the tasks of war
24	以定王國。	That the king's land may be at rest.

25	玁狁匪茹,	The Xianyun were scornful of us,
26	整居焦穫。	They encamped at Jiaohuo.
27	侵鎬及方,	They invaded Hao and Fang.
28	至于涇陽。	As far as the north bank of the Jing.
29	織文鳥章,	With woven pattern of bird blazonry
30	白旆央央。	Our silken banners brightly shone.
31	元戎十乘,	Big chariots, ten of them,
32	以先啓行。	Went first, to open up a path.

33	戎車既安,	Those war-chariots were well balanced
34	如輊如軒。	As though held from below, hung from above.
35	四牡既佶,	Our four steeds were unswerving,
36	既佶且閑。	Unswerving and obedient.
37	薄伐玁狁,	We smote the Xianyun,
38	至于太原。	As far as Taiyuan.[29]
39	文武吉甫,	Mighty warrior is Jifu,
40	万邦為憲。	A pattern to all the peoples.

41	吉甫燕喜,	Jifu feasts and is happy;
42	既多受祉。	He has received many blessings from Heaven:
43	來歸自鎬,	"Here I am, back from Hao;
44	我行永久。	I have been away a long time
45	飲御諸友,	And must give a drinking-party to my friends,
46	炰鱉膾鯉。	With roast turtle and minced carp."
47	侯誰在矣,	And who was with him?
48	張仲孝友。	Zhang Zhong, pious and friendly.

In the third month of his fifth year (823 BC), when the Qin people were probably fighting the Xianyun in the upper Wei River valley, according to the Xi Jia *pan*, King Xuan personally set out on a campaign, attacking the Xianyun at a place called Tuyu. The character *chu* 初 in the inscription

---

[29] Here, Waley gives "Great Plain." But as other textual records show, Taiyuan is a specific place-name.

suggests accurately that this was the first major military operation carried out by King Xuan against the Xianyun since he was established as king. Xi Jia, who referred to himself also as Xibo Jifu 兮伯吉父 at the end of the inscription, followed the king on the campaign, during which he cut off many enemy heads and took many prisoners. There seems little doubt that this Jifu can be identified with the Zhou minister Jifu 吉甫 in the poem "Liuyue" (lines 39, 41) which celebrates the contribution of the latter on a campaign alongside the king against the Xianyun in the sixth month. This campaign, according to the *Current Bamboo Annals*, also took place in the fifth year of King Xuan.[30] The poet speaks very emotionally about the Xianyun's offensive deep into Zhou territory. It is clearly mentioned that the Xianyun took the path of the Jing River and soon occupied a place called Jiaohuo 蕉獲 and then, aiming at the Zhou capitals Hao and Fang 方 (the capital Pang), marched as far as Jingyang 涇陽 (lines 25–28). As the geographical reconstruction will show below, the Xianyun had actually moved to within about 40 kilometers of the Zhou capitals. Finally, King Xuan went personally on campaign and Jifu led the Zhou troops, pursuing the Xianyun back as far as Taiyuan (lines 37–38). Since this campaign recorded in the poem "Liuyue" took place three months later than the campaign recorded in the Xi Jia *pan*, it seems very likely that the overwhelming attack launched by the Xianyun in the summer was a retaliation on the Zhou after an early assault by the Zhou royal forces in the spring, or perhaps the two battles may be viewed as two phases of a war that lasted for more than three months. Evidently, this was a long and difficult war, and the final victory the Zhou had over their enemies in 823 BC must have been very significant to the young king ruling over a recently restored royal court.

Connections have also been made between the Guoji Zibai *pan* 虢季子白盤 (JC: 10173) and the Buqi *gui* 不嬰簋 (JC: 4329) by Guo Moruo, who thinks that Zibai 子白, the caster of the *pan*, was the same as the Boshi 伯氏 mentioned in the latter bronze, since the characters *bai* 白 and *bo* 伯 are written the same in the inscriptions.[31] But this equation is no longer tenable when we consider that Zibai was a personal name while Boshi was an honorable designation.[32] The *pan* is self-dated to the first month of the

---

[30] See *Zhushu jinian*, 2, p. 14 (Legge, *The Shoo King*, Prolegomena, p. 155). In fact, the *Current Bamboo Annals* is the only place in the entire textual tradition where the campaign of Jifu is dated to the fifth year of King Xuan, collaborating well with the inscription on the Xi Jia *pan*. On this point, see Shaughnessy, "On the Authenticity of the *Bamboo Annals*," 152.

[31] See Guo Moruo, *Liang Zhou jinwen ci daxi*, pp. 106–7.

[32] Instead, I think that Boshi in the Buqi *gui* may refer to Xibo Jifu in the Xi Jia *pan*, or Jifu in the poem "Liuyue," who was evidently an eminent military commander in King Xuan's court and was the caster of a number of bronzes including the Bo Jifu *gui* (JC: 4035), Bo Jifu *ding* (JC: 2656), etc. For the two bronzes, see *Shaanxi chutu Shang Zhou qingtongqi*, 3 vols. (Beijing: Wenwu, 1979–84), 3, pp. 103–4.

Fig. 24 The inscription on the Buqi *gui* (JC: 4329)

twelfth year (816 BC), seven years after the battle of 823 BC; it mentions Zibai's battle against the Xianyun on the north bank of the Luo 洛 River in Shaanxi, where he cut off 500 heads and took fifty prisoners.[33] The Buqi *gui* is yet another important document of the Zhou–Xianyun war (Fig. 24):[34]

唯九月初吉戊申，白（伯）氏曰："不嬰馭（御）方！嚴（玁）允（狁）廣伐西俞，王令（命）我羞追于西。余來歸獻禽（擒）。余命女（汝）御追于曇，女（汝）已（以）我靷（車）宕伐噝（玁）允（狁）于高陵，女（汝）多折首、鞁（執）噝（訊）。戎大同，從追女（汝），女（汝）彶（及）戎大臬（敦）戟（搏）。女（汝）休，弗已（以）我靷（車）函（陷）于鞎（艱）。女（汝）多禽（擒），折首鞁（執）噝（訊）。"

[33] For the Guoji Zibai *pan*, see also Shirakawa, "Kinbun tsūshaku," 32.192:800. Guo Moruo used to date the Guoji Zibai *pan* to the reign of King Yi (r. 865–858 BC), but all other experts date it to the twelfth year of King Xuan (816 BC). See Guo Moruo, *Liang Zhou jinwen ci daxi*, pp. 104–6. While Tang Lan's long article initially published in 1950 already solved this problem, the later appearance of the Guo Xuangong Zibai *ding* 虢宣公子白鼎 (JC: 2637), cast apparently by the same Zibai who cast the *pan*, in the collection of the Summer Palace in Beijing, suggests, by its design and ornament, that the King Yi date is impossible; see Tang Lan, *Tang Lan xiansheng*, pp. 415–26. For the Zibai *ding*, see *Zhongguo qingtongqi quanji*, 6, p. 137.
[34] For the inscription of the Buqi *gui*, see also Shirakawa, "Kinbun tsūshaku," 32.193:814–40. The lid of the Buqi *gui*, now stored in the Museum of Chinese History, Beijing, has been known since the middle of the nineteenth century; see *Jungulu* 3, p. 25. In 1980, the vessel part of the Buqi *gui* was excavated from a late Western Zhou tomb in Tengxian, Shandong; see *Wenwu* 1981.9, 25–29.

白（伯）氏曰：“不娶，女（汝）小子！女（汝）肇（肇）誨（敏）于戎工，易（錫）女（汝）
弓一、矢束、臣五家、田十田，用從乃事。”不娶拜頴（稽）手（首），休。用乍（作）朕皇且
（祖）公白（伯）、孟姬障（尊）篹，用匄多福，眉（眉）壽無疆，永屯（純）霝冬（終）。
子子孫孫其用寶用宮（享）。

It was the ninth month, first auspiciousness, *wushen*-day (no. 45), Boshi said: "Buqi, the Border Protector! The Xianyun broadly attacked Xiyu, and the king commanded us to pursue to the west. I came back to send in the captives. I commanded you to defend and to pursue at Luo, and you used our chariots sweepingly attacking the Xianyun at Gaoyin; you cut off many heads and took many prisoners. The Rong greatly gathered and followed chasing you, and you and the Rong greatly slaughtered and fought. You have done well, and have not let our chariots get trapped in difficulty. You captured many, cutting off heads and taking prisoners."

Boshi said: "Buqi, you young man! You are nimble in warfare; [I] award you one bow, a bunch of arrows, five households of servants, ten fields of land, with which [you are] to take up your affairs." Buqi bowed with [his] head touching the ground, [and extols the] the beneficence. [Buqi] herewith makes for my august grandfather Gongbo and Mengji [this] sacrificial *gui*-vessel, with which to entreat much good fortune, longevity without limits, and eternal pureness without end. May [my] sons' sons and grandsons' grandsons eternally treasure and use [it] in offerings.

Anyone who reads through this inscription would be moved by the actual scene of the battle depicted in it. Boshi, the chief commander of the campaign, first pursued west, in response to the Xianyun's attack on Xiyu 西俞. When he came back from the field with captives, perhaps after an initial victory, the young Buqi was promptly sent to chase the Xianyun at Luo 霎. Buqi then stormed the enemy at a place called Gaoyin 高隆, probably deep in the enemy's territory. Unexpectedly, the Xianyun mustered more forces and pursued Buqi back, probably after beating him off. We might imagine that Buqi went through a hell of slaughtering and in the end managed to escape narrowly with his life and chariots. More importantly, the inscription suggests that the Xianyun were able to launch attacks simultaneously in at least two directions, so that Boshi's initial campaign in the west had to be followed by another campaign led by Buqi confronting the Xianyun at Luo that turned out to be the more difficult one.

The battle took place in the ninth month of an unknown year, and there is actually no solid ground to date the bronze precisely, since the identification of Boshi with Zibai seems unsound. But the very simple pattern of ornament and the proportions of its two handles compared to the vessel body suggest a late Western Zhou date; most scholars think that the battles it records are related to that appearing in the Zibai *pan* and hence date it to the reign of King Xuan.[35] In fact, Shaughnessy suggests that the Buqi *gui* was probably cast in 815 BC, the thirteenth year of King Xuan;[36] in the ninth month of that year, about twenty months after the battle in the first month of 816 BC,[37] Boshi made the speech regarding Buqi's battle. In this case, I believe that Buqi's battle could not have taken place much earlier than the time when Boshi made the speech. It is most likely that Buqi fought the Xianyun during the late summer of the year, if not actually in the ninth month.

The above inscriptions and poems suggest that the early decades of King Xuan probably saw the most intensive warfare between the Zhou and the Xianyun. Clearly, the Zhou had gone through a long series of battles, some initiated by the Zhou themselves and some in response to attacks by the Xianyun. As they were able to invade as far as Taiyuan and reestablished control over the upper Wei River valley, it seems likely, on the basis of the inscriptional and textual records available, that the Zhou had managed to hold back the Xianyun pressure, at least for a time. However, the Zhou may not have been always victorious as they say in their bronze inscriptions. According to the *Ancient Bamboo Annals*, in the thirty-third year of King Xuan (797 BC), the royal army was again sent to attack Taiyuan, but the campaign ended in failure.[38] Perhaps the recently discovered Forty-Second Year Lai *ding* can give us a better sense of the war between the Zhou and the Xianyun in the late years of King Xuan (Fig. 25):[39]

佳（惟）四十又二年五月既生霸乙卯，王在周康穆宮。旦，王各太室，即位。嗣工散右吴逨入門，立中庭，北鄉。尹氏受王釐（釐）書，王呼史淢冊釐（釐）逨。王若曰："逨！不（丕）顯文武膺受大令（命）， 匍有四方。則繇佳（惟）乃先聖祖考夾鹽（召）先王，盭（恪）堇（謹）大令（命）， 奠周邦。余弗叚（遐）望（忘）聖人孫子。余佳（惟）閈（聞）乃先祖

考有護于周邦。肄余作□□訽。余肇建長父侯于⬚（楊？）， 余令（命）女（汝）奠長父。休！女（汝）克奠于厥启（師）。 女（汝）佳（惟）克弗（井：型？）乃先祖考⬚

（？）嚴（嚴）□（狁）出戲（戲）于井阿，于曆巖。女（汝）不⬚戎；女（汝）⬚長父以追搏戎，乃即宕伐于弓谷。女（汝）執訊，獲馘，俘器，車馬。女（汝）敏于戎工，弗逆朕親令（命）。釐（釐）女（汝）矩鬯一卣，田于䵼三十田，于犀二十田。" 逨拜稽首，受冊釐（釐），以出⋯

[35] See Ma Chengyuan, *Shang Zhou qingtongqi*, 3, pp. 309–10; Shirakawa, "Kinbun tsūshaku," 32.193:833–40. It should be noted that Li Xueqin proposed the identification of Buqi with Duke Zhuang of Qin (r. 821–778 BC), a son of Qin Zhong who attacked the Rong in 825 BC and was killed in 822 BC This view was reiterated later by Wang Hui. However, apart from the fact that both Buqi and Duke Zhuang fought the Rong people, there is really no evidence for this identification. See Li Xueqin, "Qin guo wenwu de xin renshi," *Wenwu* 1980.9, 25–26; Wang Hui, *Qin tongqi mingwen biannian jishi* (Xi'an: Sanqin, 1990), pp. 1–6.

[36] See Shaughnessy, "The Date of the 'Duoyou *ding*'," pp. 59, 63.

[37] This is to count from the first month of 816 BC, the time when the Guoji Zibai *pan* was cast. But it is possible the battle recorded by the *pan* could have taken place a little earlier than the first month, some time at the end of the eleventh year (817 BC) or the beginning of the twelfth year (816 BC).

[38] See Fan Xiangyong, *Guben zhushu jinian*, p. 33.

[39] For the Lai *ding* and its inscription, see *Wenwu* 2003.6, 5–17.

Fig. 25 The Forty-Second Year Lai *ding* no. 2 and its inscription (from *Kaogu yu wenwu* 2003.3, 9; *Wenwu* 2003.6, 14)

矩㠪一卣，田于𢓊三十田，于降二十田。" 逨拜稽首，受冊賸（釐），以出…

It was the forty-second year, fifth month, after the growing brightness, *yimao*-day (no. 52); the king was in Kang Mu Temple in Zhou. At dawn, the king approached the grand chamber, and assumed position. Supervisor of Construction San accompanied Supervisor of Marshes Lai to his right entering the gate, standing at the center of the court, and facing north. The Chief [Document Maker] received the royal edict of rewards. The king called out Scribe Yu to command [with a written document] and to reward Lai. The king said to the effect: "Lai! The greatly illustrious King Wen and King Wu received the great Mandate, extending in possessing the four directions. It was your past sagely grandfather and father who supported the former kings, being faithful and cautious about the great Mandate, and consolidated the Zhou state. I have had no time to forget about the grandsons and sons of the sagely men. And I have heard that your past grandfather and father had contributions to the Zhou state. Therefore, I make X X consultation. I initially established Changfu ruler in Yang (?), and I commanded you to settle Changfu. Good! You were able to settle his troops. You were able to model (?) [yourself] on your grandfather and father.[40] X Xianyun emerged and attacked [us] in Jing'e, and in Lihan.[41] You did not X the Rong; you X Changfu to pursue and strike the Rong, and you thereupon broadly attacked [them] in Gonggu. You took prisoners, cut off heads, captured objects and chariots with horses. You were very capable in warfare and did not disobey my personal command. [I] award you one *you*-bottle of fragrant wine, land in Jie thirty fields, in Xi twenty fields." Lai bowed with his head touching the ground, receiving the document and awards, and coming out . . .

The "forty-second year" recorded at the beginning of the inscription would doubtless put the bronze at 786 BC, in the later reign of King Xuan, since he was the only Zhou king to have ruled that long. Owing to the relatively poor quality of the casting, some characters are eroded and hinder our understanding of the inscription. However, roughly speaking, it describes as its main subject a battle between the Zhou and the Xianyun in which Lai, the caster of the bronze, took part. It happened when Lai was sent on a trip to help Changfu, probably an important noble, to settle in his newly granted state – Yang (?). He had apparently accomplished his mission and helped to set up the camps for the troops. At this point, the Xianyun emerged and attacked two places: Jing'e and Lihan. Under royal command, Lai therefore moved on and subsequently fought the Xianyun in a place called Gonggu. Lai killed many enemies and captured prisoners, chariots, and horses, for which he was rewarded by the Zhou king with wine and fields. In short, the inscription suggests that, despite the campaigns the Zhou court conducted in the early years of King Xuan, the Xianyun continued to constitute a major threat throughout the reign.

LOCATING THE ZHOU–XIANYUN WAR

Above, I have examined in some detail the historical process of the war between the Zhou and the Xianyun. In order to understand fully the far-reaching impact of this war on Western Zhou society, especially the role it played in Zhou's decline, it is important to recover further its spatial dimension; that is, to locate the war in the actual terrain of Zhou China.

---

[40] The character *fu* 弗 in this sentence is most likely a miswriting for *jing* 井 (= 型), which means "to model on."
[41] The first graph of this sentence is read *bi* 鬭 by both Li Xueqin and Qiu Xigui, but it is very unlikely. See Li Xueqin, "Meixian Yangjiacun xinchu qingtongqi yanjiu," *Wenwu* 2003.6, 68; Qiu Xigui, "Du Lai qi mingwen zhaji sanze," *Wenwu* 2003.6, 76.

As already detailed in chapter 1, the regions that surrounded the Zhou heartland in the Wei River valley are predominantly occupied by mountains, loess plateaus, and deep valleys. Such mountainous conditions must have had some major impact on a war between any society that was based on the Wei River plain and its northwestern neighbors. War is above all an art of utilizing geography. It is true that some of man's great achievements were attained by overcoming natural limits, but it is also the tendency of man to use geography in the most favorable way. In this regard, we can see some clear similarities between the wars conducted during the Western Zhou and those that happened in later historical times. However, we must also be aware of the fundamental nature of the Zhou–Xianyun war as essentially chariot warfare, in contrast to the wars fought by the later Chinese dynasties using cavalry and heavy infantry against the mounted northern nomads. Since chariot warfare requires better road conditions and a relatively open area, it is to be expected that the Zhou–Xianyun war took place in much more limited areas throughout the region.

Locating the Zhou–Xianyun war involves a complex operation: on the one hand, any assumption must be based on a thorough understanding of the region's landscape, especially the main system of road communication in the better-documented later historical periods as demonstrated in chapter 1 (see pp. 35–40); on the other, we must fully understand the relationship between the place-names in the context of the relevant documents before they can be correlated to the actual locales on the basis of traditional geographical records. Writing in the early twentieth century, Wang Guowei suggested that the Xianyun had invaded Zhou from two directions: from the northwest through the Jing River valley; and from the east through the lower Fen River valley.[42] In his important study of the Xianyun problem, Jaroslav Průšek rejected the east road proposed by Wang and accepted Wang's northwest route through the Jing River valley.[43] The discovery of the Duoyou *ding* in 1980 has brought to light decisive new evidence to locate the Zhou–Xianyun war precisely, because the inscription mentions six place-names in its description of the battles. With this inscription, and also considering evidence in other inscriptions and from archaeology, we can now reexamine the route or routes by which the Xianyun invaded Zhou. Although there is still some disagreement regarding the location of some of these place-names,[44] I believe that the available evidence suggests beyond doubt that the upper Jing River valley was the main channel of this prolonged military encounter between the Zhou and the Xianyun. Let us start by examining the Duoyou *ding*.

---

[42] See Wang Guowei, "Guifang Kunyi Xianyun kao," pp. 370–71.

[43] See Průšek, *Chinese Statelets*, pp. 124–25.

[44] For instance, Huang Shengzhang and the reporters of the Duoyou *ding* hold that the battle took place in the lower Fen River valley; see Huang Shengzhang, "Duoyou ding de lishi yu dili wenti," in *Guwenzi lunji* (Kaogu yu wenwu congkan 2) (Xi'an, 1983), pp. 12–20; Tian and Luo, "Duoyou ding de faxian," p. 117.

The battle in the Duoyou ding

The first piece of evidence in the inscription of the Duoyou *ding* is the mention of Jingshi, which was attacked by the Xianyun in the early phase of the war. Jingshi as a place-name also appears in the inscription of the Ke *zhong* 克鐘 (JC: 204) in a context where it was apparently related to the Jing River:[45]

王才（在）周康剌宮。王乎（呼）士曶召克。王親令克遹涇東至于京皀（帥）。

The king was in Kang Lie Gong at Zhou. The king called out Shi Hu to summon Ke. The king personally commanded Ke to inspect the east side of the Jing River and to arrive at Jingshi.

Since Ke was commanded to inspect the east side of the Jing River and to arrive at Jingshi, Jingshi must have been somewhere very close to the Jing River, and probably located on the east side of it. As clarified in chapter 1, it is only between Binxian and Jingyang that the Jing River runs in a roughly northwest–southeast direction, and therefore, taking Zhou (Qiyi) where the command was given as his starting point, Ke must first have moved east to the lower Jing area near Jingyang and then have traversed a road roughly corresponding to the present-day interprovincial highway 211. Along this route, he would logically enter the upper Jing River basin in the Changwu–Binxian area.[46] In fact, we do know something more about this place-name: Jingshi appears in the poem "Gongliu" 公劉 (no. 250) in the *Book of Poetry*, in which it is clearly another designation of the place Bin 豳, the settlement of Gong Liu, one of the Zhou ancestors in the pre-dynastic era before the historical migration of the Zhou people to the Wei River valley.[47] Ancient geographical works unanimously locate this place in the area west of Xunyi and north of Binxian, to the north of the Jing River, and this is in close agreement with the geographical context described in the inscription of the Ke *zhong*.[48] Two later sources even give a specific location

---

[45] For this inscription, see Shirakawa, "Kinbun tsūshaku," 28.171:531–39.

[46] There is another reading of the inscription proposed by Liu Yu: "The king personally commanded Ke to inspect the Jing River, eastwardly arriving at Jingshi" (王親令克遹涇，東至于京師); see Liu Yu, "Duoyou ding de shidai yu diming," p. 156. This reading, assuming that Jingshi was the capital Hao at the south side of the Wei River, entails a journey from Zhou to the capital that cannot be geographically configured because such a trip would have nothing to do with the Jing River.

[47] See *Shijing*, 17.3, pp. 542–3 (Waley, *The Book of Songs*, pp. 252–53).

[48] For instance, the "Geographical Records" chapter of the *Hanshu* lists Binxiang 豳鄉 under Xunyi County 栒邑縣 of the Han dynasty; the site of the Xunyi County of Han was to the northeast of present-day Xunyi. Ban Gu himself explicitly says that this Binxiang in the county's territory was the location of Bin mentioned in the poem "Gongliu" of the *Book of Poetry*. See *Hanshu*, 28, p. 1547. The "Jijie" commentary to the *Shiji* quotes Xu Guang (third century AD) saying that there was a site called Binting 豳亭, located to the northeast of Qi County 漆縣 of Xinping Commandery 新平郡 of the later Han period, which is present-day Binxian; see *Shiji*, 4, p. 113. The two sources apparently point to the same area.

for Bin (Jingshi), but the precise figures they give may not be accurate.[49] However, since the valley of the Jing River is about 2.5 kilometers wide in the Binxian area, these sources would necessarily put Jingshi on the top of the high plain to the north of the Jing River (Map 8). As the Han dynasty dictionary *Shuowen jiezi* suggests, the term *jing* 京 indeed originally meant "high."[50]

Our evidence regarding the location of Xun, attacked by the Xianyun after the capture of Jingshi, is also very strong, and the war context described in the inscription of the Duoyou *ding* indeed suggests that the two settlements could not have been located very far from each other. Xun seems already to have been called "Settlement of Xun" ("Xunyi" 枸邑) during the Western Zhou, for the latter terms appears in the inscription on the Shichen *ding* 尸臣鼎, a Western Zhou bronze that was discovered in the Zhouyuan area during the Han dynasty.[51] Further evidence comes from the historical context of the founding of the Han dynasty as described in the *Shiji*: in 206 BC the Han troops commanded by the general Li Shang 酈商 defeated the troops of the former Qin general Zhang Han 章邯 at Xunyi.[52] These sources suggest that Xunyi as a place-name continued to exist from Western Zhou into the Han dynasty, when it was listed as a county in the "Geographical Records" chapter of the *Hanshu*.[53] It was located to the northeast of present-day Xunyi and it was the ancient location of Xun mentioned in the Duoyou *ding*.[54] Like present-day Xunyi, the ancient Xun was probably also located in the valley of the Malan River, one of the tributaries of the Jing River, and it was to the east of Jingshi.

Unlike Jingshi, the battlefield Qi was located in the bottom of the valley of the Jing River.[55] The "Geographical Records" chapter of the *Hanshu* lists a Qixian 漆縣, saying that to its west runs the Qi 漆 River.[56] From the geographical works composed during the medieval period, we know that the Qi River was roughly 4.5 kilometers to the west of the present-day

[49] For instance, the Tang dynasty work *Kuodizhi* (quoted by Wang Yinglin [thirteenth century AD]) says that there was a Bin Plateau (Binyuan 豳原) some 5 kilometers to the west of Sanshui County 三水縣 of Tang (present-day Xunyi), on which the town of Bin was located; see Wang Yinglin, *Shi dili kao*, in *Qingzhaotang congshu* vols. 41–42 (Chaoyi: Liu shi, 1835), p. 30. Another Tang dynasty work, the *Yuanhe junxian tuzhi*, says that the ancient town site of Bin was 15 kilometers to the west of Sanshui and some 19.5 kilometers to the northwest of Binxian; see *Yuanhe junxian tuzhi*, 2 vols. (Beijing: Zhonghua, 1983), pp. 60–62. The two sources do not necessarily contradict each other because the *Kuodizhi* is referring to a large geographical area called "Bin Plateau" in the Tang dynasty, while the latter source points to a specific location.
[50] See Duan Yucai, *Shuowen jiezi zhu* (Shanghai: Guji, 1981), p. 229.
[51] For the discovery of the Shichen *ding* and the identification of Xunyi with Xun 荀, see *Hanshu* 25b, p. 1,251; Shaughnessy, *Sources of Western Zhou History*, p. 6.
[52] See *Shiji*, 35, p. 2,661.   [53] See *Hanshu*, 28, p. 1,547.
[54] Regarding the location of Xunyi, *Yuanhe junxian tuzhi* says that it was 12.5 kilometers to the northeast of Sanshui County of the Tang dynasty (which is present-day Xunyi). If we trust the distance given in the Tang works, Jingshi and Xun would have been separated from each other by some 27.5 kilometers. See *Yuanhe junxian tuzhi*, p. 62.
[55] Regarding the reading of 祁 as Qi 漆, see Li Xueqin, *Xinchu qingtongqi*, pp. 131–32.
[56] See *Hanshu*, 28, p. 1,547.

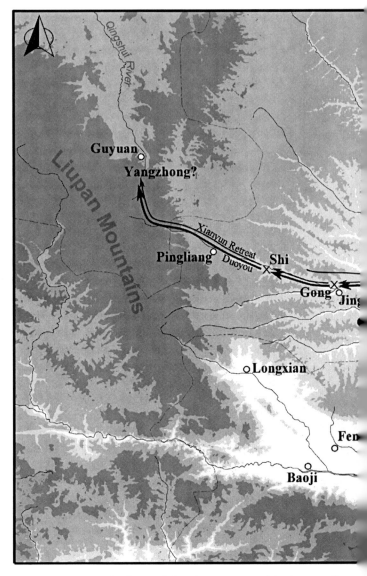

Map 8 The battle recorded in the inscription of the Duoyou *ding*
(topographical layers derived from "ESRI Data & Maps: 2004"; river
course based on "Harvard China Historical GIS Dataset, Version 2.0: August

Binxian.[57] Thus, writers of the local gazetteers of the late Qing and early
Republic identified this Qi River with the present-day Shuilian 水簾 River,
a small tributary entering the Jing River from the southwest at a place

---

[57] The Tang dynasty geographical survey, *Yuanhe junxian tuzhi*, says that the Qi River was 4.5 kilometers
to the west of Xinping County of the Tang dynasty, which was based on Qixian of the Han dynasty
and is present-day Binxian; see *Yuanhe junxian tuzhi*, p. 61.

presently called Shuilian 水帘, about 4.5 kilometers to the northwest of Binxian and 20 kilometers to the east of Changwu (Map 9).[58] Whether the Qi of the Duoyou *ding* was located near the Qi River or at the town of the Qixian County of Han cannot be decided, but it must have been

---

[58] See Liu Bida and Shi Bingzhen, *Binzhou xinzhi gao* (manuscript, 1929), pp. 22–23. In the *Changwu xian zhi*, Fan Shifeng and the famous classicist Hong Liangji record that the Qi River was 20 kilometers to the east of the town of Changwu. Since the distance between Changwu and Binxian is about 32 kilometers, this creates a 7.5 kilometers discrepancy from the location of the Qi River suggested by the Tang work. See Fan Shifeng and Hong Liangji, *Changwu xian zhi* (1783), p. 7.

somewhere on the southern bank of the Jing River between present-day Binxian and the confluence of the Jing River and the Hei River.

The name of Gong 龔(共) appears in the poem "Huangyi" (no. 241) already discussed in chapter 1 that reads: "The people of Mi are in revolt. They have dared to oppose the great kingdom. They have invaded Ruan and marched against Gong."[59] Regarding the location of Gong, there has been no dispute since ancient times. Zhu Xi (AD 1130–1200) indicated that it was located near the "Gong Pool" in Jing Prefecture 涇州 of the Song dynasty, which is present-day Jingchuan 涇川.[60] Zhu Youzeng of the Qing dynasty further specifies that it was 2.5 kilometers to the north of Jing Prefecture.[61] And the Qing local historian Zhang Yanfu states that to the north of Jing Prefecture an underground spring created a lake which was the Gong Pool of antiquity.[62] These works suggest that the name "Gong" probably survived from antiquity to the later time and was associated with the Jingchuan area at the confluence of the Jing River and the Rui River. The Gong of the Duoyou *ding* was probably located in this area. Mi, the state that attacked Gong, was located in the narrow valley of the Daxi River, about 37 kilometers to the south of Gong.

With the location of the above four place-names determined on the basis of the ancient geographical records, we still need to test them in the context of the war described in the inscription of the Duoyou *ding*. By comparing the spatial relationship between these places on the basis of the textual records and that which is suggested by the inscriptions, we can reconstruct the battle of the Duoyou *ding* in the landscape of the upper Jing River region (Map 8). At the beginning of the war, the Xianyun, as did all invaders in later history, first descended from the Qianshui Plateau of Changwu and drove into the valley of the Jing River. Passing by present-day Binxian along the bank of the Jing River, they then turned north and climbed the plateau to attack Jingshi because, as clarified in chapter 1, further southeast the valley would virtually close at a place called "Cutting off the Jing River." After capturing Jingshi, they marched about 25 kilometers east and attacked the Zhou settlement Xun on the *guiwei* day (no. 20).[63] Xun was not far from the road going down to the Wei River plain along the eastern side of the Jing River, corresponding to present-day interprovincial highway 211; it is not impossible that the Xianyun had actually intended to make further attacks on the Wei River plain, as they did later in the summer of 823 BC.

---

[59] See *Shijing*, 16.4, p. 521 (Waley, *The Book of Songs*, p. 238).
[60] See Zhu Xi, *Shi ji zhuan* (Shanghai: Guji, 1980), p. 185.
[61] See Zhu Youzeng, *Shi dili zheng*, in *Huang Qing jingjie, juan*: 1,039–45 (1829), p. 5.12.
[62] See Zhang Yanfu, *Jingzhou zhi* (1753), pp. 9–11.
[63] This was in fact the only possible road to attack Xun from the west. Since the Malan River enters the Jing River about 7.5 kilometers to the southeast of the "Cutting off the Jing River," the landscape made it impossible for the Xianyun to go down the Jing valley and then turn into the Malan valley.

Having perhaps heard of or encountered the Zhou troops marching from the capital to the upper Jing region in response to their attack on Jingshi,[64] the Xianyun began to retreat to the valley of the Jing River in the Binxian region. The next morning (*jiashen*, no. 21), the Xianyun were caught by the Zhou troops at Qi to the northwest of Binxian (Map 9). During this battle, the residents of Xun who had been captured by the Xianyun a day earlier were taken back by Duoyou. However, some of the Xianyun troops who had captured the residents of Jingshi apparently escaped Duoyou's initial attack and ran away across the Qianshui Plateau to the west. The location of Gong in the middle section of the upper Jing River, where the Xianyun were caught and defeated again by Duoyou, indicates that the Xianyun were proceeding through the wide and flat bottom of the valley of the upper Jing River after descending from the Qianshui Plateau at some point west of Changwu (Map 8). The topography of the region almost excludes any possibility other than that the Xianyun were moving towards the Xiao Pass (Map 2). This being so, then Shi and Yangzhong must also have been located in the valley west of Gong. At Yangzhong the residents of Jingshi were finally taken back by Duoyou. In short, there seems little doubt that the battle described by the Duoyou *ding* proceeded along the northern branch of the later "Road to Xiao Pass." It fits perfectly into the geographical context of the upper Jing River valley along the main transportation line, as we know from later historical campaigns through the region.

Taiyuan and the battle of 823 BC

Why did the Xianyun retreat west by way of Gong? This question cannot be fully answered until we have located Taiyuan, which was, as mentioned above, probably an important base of the Xianyun and was the farthest point ever reached by the Zhou royal army in previous reigns. This is the key point in reconstructing the geography of the Zhou–Xianyun war. In the past, many have followed Zhu Xi's commentary in locating it in Yangqu County 陽曲縣 of Taiyuan Superior-Prefecture 太原府 of the Song dynasty, which is present-day Taiyuan City, the capital city of Shanxi province.[65] Průšek correctly rejected this location, but was unable to suggest a specific location for it.[66] Indeed, Zhu Xi's thesis was rejected by most Qing scholars and commentators on the *Book of Poetry* that mentions Taiyuan as the headquarters of the Xianyun. Gu Yanwu, the founding father of Qing evidential scholarship, noting the close relationship between Taiyuan

---

[64] Since Binxian is 120 kilometers from the Zhou capital and Duoyou arrived in the Binxian region by day *jiashen* (no. 21), it is clear that Duoyou left the capital some days before the Xianyun advanced to attack Xun on *guiwei* (no. 20). Duoyou's march to the upper Jing River valley must have been mainly a response to the Xianyun's attack on Jingshi.

[65] See Zhu Xi, *Shi ji zhuan*, p. 115; Guo Moruo, *Liang Zhou jinwen ci*, p. 104.

[66] Průšek also rejected the location of Taiyuan suggested by Gu Yanwu; see Průšek, *Chinese Statelets*, pp. 124–5.

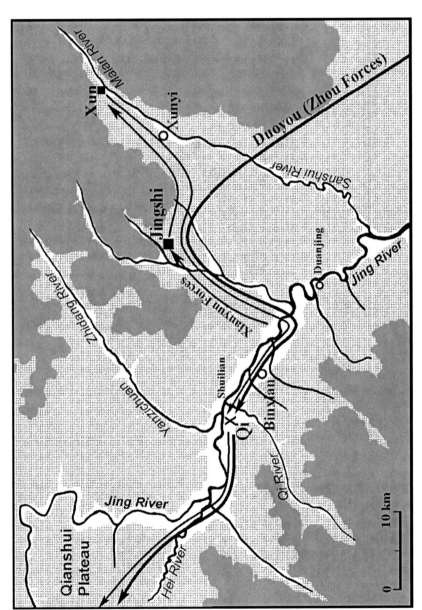

Map 9 The battle of the Duoyou *ding*: detail of progression in the Binxian area

and Jingyang in the battle of 823 BC, suggested that it was located in the Pingliang area. Gu also argued that the Yuan Prefecture 原州 of the Northern Wei dynasty (AD 386–534), which was located in present-day Guyuan of southern Ningxia Autonomous Region, must have derived its name from the ancient Taiyuan, although he did not himself locate Taiyuan in Guyuan.[67] Chen Huan, on the other hand, argued that Taiyuan was in Zhenyuan County 鎮原縣 of the Qing dynasty (present-day Zhenyuan), located to the north of Pingliang.[68] Differing from Gu and Chen, Hu Wei suggested that Taiyuan was actually in the same location as Guyuan, where the Yuan Prefecture of Northern Wei was located, and that the battle of 823 BC was one in which the Zhou troops chased the Xianyun all the way out of the Xiao Pass from Pingliang to the Guyuan plain.[69] It is not surprising to see the consistency between Hu's reconstruction of the battle of 823 BC and what we have learned from the Duoyou *ding*, because this was and still is the primary road going out from the upper Jing region – the so-called "Road to Xiao Pass."

Guyuan is an area of more than 80 square kilometers at an average elevation of 1,600 meters at the upper reaches of the Qingshui River, higher than all of the plateaus in the upper Jing River region, and is open in the north to the Yellow River plain of central and northern Ningxia (Fig. 26). Through the area runs the Great Wall built by the state of Qin during the Warring States period. As has been briefly mentioned in chapter 1 (see p. 52), at the southern edge of the area and outside the Great Wall of Qin, an early Western Zhou tomb and a contemporary chariot-burial were excavated in 1981 at Sunjiazhuang, about 7.5 kilometers to the west of the town of Guyuan (Map 5). Standard early Western Zhou bronze vessels and chariot fittings and a typical Zhou-style pottery *li*-tripod were excavated from the main pit (Fig. 10).[70] As the cultural identity of the tomb is beyond doubt, this extremely important discovery demonstrates that the "Road to Xiao Pass" was already in use during the early Western Zhou, and that the Zhou culture had extended from the upper Jing River valley into the Qingshui River valley. The high degree of cultural uniformity of the Sunjiazhuang findings with the Zhou central area, for both bronzes and pottery, completely different from the local steppe culture, strongly suggests that the Zhou had reached this region during the early Western Zhou.

The location of Taiyuan in the Guyuan area is further supported by two pieces of evidence. First, two Han dynasty works present the equation "*Gaoping* 高平 is called Taiyuan 太原";[71] in other words, in the interpretation held by the Han people, Taiyuan should refer to a place that

[67] See Huang Rucheng, *Ri zhi lu jishi* (Changsha: Yuelu shushe, 1994), 3, pp. 94–5.
[68] See Chen Huan, *Shi Maoshi zhuan*, 17, p. 19.
[69] See Hu Wei, *Yugong zhui zhi*, in *Huang Qing jingjie* (Guangzhou: Xuehaitang, 1829), 29, pp. 25–26.
[70] For the discovery, see *Kaogu* 1983.11, 982–83. In the Guyuan Museum, I was able to identify some Western Zhou-style pottery wares from other unspecified locations in the Guyuan area.
[71] These works are the *Chunqiu shuo tici* (quoted in the *Shuijing zhu* of the sixth century AD) and the *Xiao erya*. See *Shuijing zhu jiao*, 6, p. 200; *Xiao erya*, p. 4.

Fig. 26 The Guyuan plain at the Sunjiazhuang cemetery (photograph by the author)

is both high and flat on top. Although *gaoping* in these two Han sources is not a specific place-name but a generic description of a plateau, high and flat on top, which is called "Taiyuan," curiously enough Gaoping was the name of a county during the Han dynasty, and it was located precisely in present-day Guyuan.[72] The fact that the Guyuan area was named "Gaoping" indicates that the area was famous during the Han dynasty for such topography; for the same reason, the area could also be called Taiyuan. In fact, it has been strongly argued by the Qing scholar Song Xiangfeng that the name of "Gaoping County" of Han must have derived from the ancient "Taiyuan" in the same location.[73] Second, the poem "Gongliu" (no. 250) of the *Book of Poetry* mentions a place called the "Broad Plateau" (Boyuan 薄原) together with the "Hundred Springs" (Baiquan 百泉), suggesting the two were located close to each other.[74] By the meaning of the terms, there is no problem in identifying Boyuan with Taiyuan. As for the location of the "Hundred Springs," there were two possible places: one between Jingchuan and Pingliang in the valley of the Jing River, and the other 40 kilometers to the northwest of Pingliang, in the territory of the Yuan Prefecture of Northern Wei dynasty, which is present-day Guyuan.[75] During the Sui dynasty (AD 581–619), "Baiquan" then became the name of a county located only 20 kilometers to the southwest of Guyuan.

As far as the available sources show, I believe that the Guyuan area in the upper reaches of the Qingshui River was the most likely location of the Taiyuan to which the Xianyun fled from Zhou attacks, according to the Duoyou *ding*. Bearing this location in mind, we can now reconsider the battle of 823 BC described both in the inscription on the Xi Jia *pan* and in the poem "Liuyue" (Map 10). According to the Xi Jia *pan*, in the third month the Zhou attacked the Xianyun at Tuyu 斁盧, a place that cannot be identified.[76] Then, according to "Liuyue," three months later the Xianyun advanced to occupy a place called Jiaohuo 焦澤 (lines 25–26), the location of which, at the edge of the Zhongshan 中山 Mountain in present-day Jingyang to the east of the Jing River, has never been questioned.[77]

---

[72] See *Hanshu*, 28, p. 1,615.

[73] See Yang Jialuo, *Xiao erya xunzuan deng liuzhong* (Taipei: Dingwen, 1972), p. 27.

[74] See *Shijing*, 17.3, p. 542 (Waley, *The Book of Songs*, pp. 252–53).

[75] See Gu Zuyu, *Dushi fangyu jiyao* (Taipei: Letian, 1973), pp. 2,539, 2,554.

[76] Wang Guowei suggested that 斁 should be pronounced "Peng" 彭, therefore identifying it with Pengya 彭衙 near the Luo River, to the north of Baishui 白水; Wang Guowei, "Guifang Kunyi Xianyun kao," p. 379. If the graph should indeed be read "Peng," it would be better to identify it with the Pengyang 彭陽 of the Han dynasty (in present-day Zhenyuan). Pengyang was later moved upstream to present-day Pengyang, only 35 kilometers from Guyuan. But I think that neither of these two locations is strongly supported by the evidence.

[77] The *Erya* lists "Jiaohuo of Zhou" as one of the famous marshes in China. The authority on its location is Guo Pu's commentary on the *Erya* which identifies Jiaohuo with Huzhong 瓠中; see *Erya*, 7, p. 2615. The *Yuanhe junxian zhi* indicates that the Jiaohuo Marsh in Jingyang County 涇陽縣 of the Tang dynasty was also called Hukou 瓠口; see *Yuanhe junxian tuzhi*, p. 28. Huzhong or Hukou was famous for being the starting point of the famous Zheng Guo Canal 鄭國渠 of the state of Qin which connected the Jing River and the Luo River in the late third century BC; *Hanshu*, 28, p. 1,578. See also Chen Huan, *Shi Maishi zhuan shu*, 17, pp. 16–17.

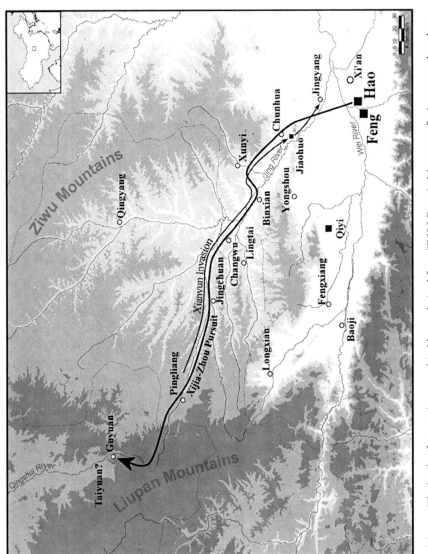

Map 10 The battle of 823 BC (topographical layers derived from "ESRI Data & Maps: 2004"; river course based on "Harvard China Historical GIS Dataset, Version 2.0: August 2003")

However, the next phrase (line 27) in the same poem "Liuyue," suggesting that the Xianyun invaded Hao 鎬 and Fang 方, has generated much dispute among the classicists. Ancient commentators tended to locate Hao and Fang somewhere in the upper Jing River region.[78] This was based upon locating the "north bank of the Jing" (Jingyang 涇陽) mentioned in the poem (line 28) to the west of Pingliang, where the Jingyang County of the Han dynasty was located. I believe that the context of the poem indicates quite clearly that the two places were located to the south of Jiaohuo and are most likely to be identified with the Zhou capitals Hao 鎬 and Pang 菶; the latter appears frequently in the bronze inscriptions (see chapter 1, p. 56). Průšek's reading of "Jingyang" as a general term referring to the northern bank of the lower Jing River, which turns east in present-day Jingyang, would seem acceptable.[79] This would put the battle of 823 BC on virtually the same road as that of the battle of the Duoyou *ding*, the only difference being that in 823 BC the Xianyun advanced even deeper south, all the way to the confluence of the Jing and Wei rivers, only about 40 kilometers from the Zhou capitals Feng and Hao. In the end, Zhou troops pushed the enemy back along the Jing River as far as Taiyuan, which was located in Guyuan in southern Ningxia Autonomous Region. The route of the battle also resembles the battle of 765 AD, during which the joint forces of the Tibetans and the Uighurs marched down from Binxian to Jingyang, forcing the Tang army to confront their enemies in the vicinity of the capital Chang'an (see p. 39 and map 2).

Other battles

Unlike the two battles discussed above, for which a systematic match of the inscriptional contexts and geographical records can be pursued, there are other battles for which the relevant place-names either are mentioned in isolation from one another or are not fully supported by the geographical records. Therefore, what we can say about them is more or less speculative. The first is the battle of 816 BC, recorded in the Guoji Zibai *pan*. Given the direction of the Luo River, the battleground "North of the Luo River" (Luo zhi Yang 洛之陽) can only have been located either in the upper Luo valley north of Ganquan 甘泉 or, possibly but less likely, near the confluence of the Wei and Luo rivers in Dali 大荔, because only in these two sections

---

[78] See *Shijing*, 10.2, p. 424 (Waley, *The Book of Songs*, pp. 150–51); Chen Huan, *Shi Maoshi zhuan shu*, 17, p. 17.

[79] But this reading seems to create problems in understanding the phrase "Here I am, back from Hao" (line 43), which was taken by some commentators as meaning that Jifu came back to the capital from a far distance (Hao); see Chen Huan, *Shi Maoshi zhuan shu*, 17, p. 17. In his study of the inscription of the Duoyou *ding*, Li Zhongcao has made a good point that the context of the particular section of the poem suggests that Jifu came back to his own town from the capital Hao where a celebration had already been held by the king after the campaign (lines 41–42), but not from the battlefield to the capital; see Li Zhongcao, "Yeshi Duoyou ding mingwen," p. 99.

does the Luo River flow in a roughly southeast direction (Map 3).[80] This
suggests that the battle may have taken place along the so-called "Road to
Yanzhou," and that the attack by the Xianyun may have been launched
from farther north, probably the Ordos region, through the valleys of the
Hengshan Mountains. As mentioned in chapter 1, recent archaeological
discoveries in northern Shaanxi suggest that this road was probably already
in use during the Western Zhou. If so, this would support the location of
the battleground "Luo zhi Yang" in the upper Luo River valley.

The battles described in the Buqi *gui* inscription pose a problem in the
geographical reconfiguration of the Zhou–Xianyun war, but I believe that
they took place to the north and west of the Zhou capitals. It has been
suggested by Guo Moruo that the place-name Xiyu 西俞, where Boshi
arrived in the early phase of the war, should be identified with the "Spring
of Yu" (Yuquan 俞泉) mentioned in the *Ancient Bamboo Annals*, which the
royal Six Armies commanded by the Duke of Guo had reached in pursuit of
the Rong of Taiyuan during the reign of King Yi. This certainly cannot be a
mere coincidence, and the textual context of the record suggests that Xiyu
and Taiyuan must have been in the same direction, if not next to each other.
Certainly the term "Xiyu" means the "Yu in the west," as the inscription says
explicitly that Boshi pursued to the west, and Taiyuan was indeed located
in the west. These connections would certainly put Xiyu or the "Spring
of Yu" near present-day Guyuan in southern Ningxia. The Han text *Erya*
lists a certain Xiyu 西俞 together with Yanmen 雁門 as in the northern
mountains of China, and Shi Nianhai notes that it must have been close to
the Yanmen Mountain located in the northeastern corner of Shanxi, near
Hebei.[81] This does not seem to fit the historical context because Boshi says
clearly that he pursued to the west from the Zhou capital. Alternatively,
there was another Yu 俞 Mountain located in the present-day Linyou 麟遊
and Fengxiang areas close to the valley of the Qian River.[82] However, since
the *Ancient Bamboo Annals* mentions that the Duke of Guo captured a
thousand horses at "Spring of Yu" on a campaign directed at Taiyuan, it is
not likely that this place could have been located in the lower Qian River
valley, not far from the capital. Another location for Yu was proposed by
Cen Zhongmian, who suggested that Xiyu refers to the same landmark
as the "Slope of Yu" (Yu zhi guan deng 隃之関隥) mentioned in the *Mu
tianzi zhuan* which, from the text, seems to be the slopes of the Liupan

[80] The upper Luo River runs southeastwards from Wuqi 吳旗 and then turns south in Ganquan. When
the river reaches Dali it turns again to the east, entering the Wei River. It seems unlikely that the
battle of 816 BC could have taken place on the lower reaches of the Luo River because traveling all
the way from the upper to the lower Luo River is extremely difficult and is not in the direction of
the Zhou capitals. The Luo River is also mentioned in the inscription of the Yong *yu* 永盂 (JC:
10322) and there can be no doubt that it refers to present-day Luo River in Shaanxi. Certainly, this
is not the Luo River flowing by present-day Luoyang. For the inscriptions, see Shirakawa, "Kinbun
tsūshaku," 48.ho3:192.

[81] See Shi Nianhai, *Heshanji*, 4, p. 408.

[82] See *Shuijingzhu jiao*, p. 556. To the south of Yushan was located the Yumi County 隃麋縣 of the
Han dynasty, which is present-day Qianyang 汧陽; *Hanshu*, 28, p. 1,547; *Shuijing zhu jiao*, p. 582.

Mountains;[83] in the foothills of the mountains there is located Guyuan, the ancient Taiyuan. If this identification is correct, it fits perfectly into the historical context of the Zhou–Xianyun war, as a long pursuit of the Xianyun west would necessarily lead to the Liupan Mountains. The two places Luo 畧 and Gaoyin 高隂, where Buqi himself fought the Xianyun, cannot be decided with certainty. Wang Guowei once identified Luo 畧 with Luo 洛, suggesting that it was related to the Luo River. He also identified Gaoyin with Gaoling 高陵 near Xi'an, on the northern bank of the Wei River.[84] If Wang is right, it must be inferred that a separate campaign into the Luo River valley was conducted by the Zhou army. However, I suspect that Luo 畧 should be identified with Luo 蛏, a place probably located in the lower Malian River valley, where a bronze cast by one Luobo 蛏伯 was excavated in Ningxian 寧縣.[85] If this is the case, Buqi's pursuit could have been through the Malian River valley to the north. But I think that we simply do not know the locations of the two battles.

The geography of the Zhou–Xianyun war can, however, be investigated with respect to the recently discovered Forty-Second Year Lai *ding*. It has been strongly argued by Wang Hui that the Yang (?) mentioned in the inscription should be identified with the state of Yang 楊 located in present-day Hongdong 洪洞 in the Fen River valley in southern Shanxi. This is based on medieval sources such as the *Xin Tangshu*, which says that the state of Yang was granted by King Xuan to his son Shangfu 尚父.[86] This would fit both the date of the Lai bronzes and the name Changfu 長父 since the characters *shang* 尚 and *chang* 長 were pronounced similarly and also connected in meaning. Since two bronze *hu*-vessels cast by a lady in the state of Yang were found in tomb no. 63 in the cemetery of the Jin rulers in Beizhao 北趙, it seems very likely that the Yang established in the forty-second year of King Xuan was located in the lower Fen valley.[87] Wang further suggests that the battle recorded in the inscription must have been fought in southern Shanxi or even northern Henan. The problem of this reconfiguration is that there is no reference at all to any of the places mentioned in the inscription (except Yang) in the lower Fen valley, and it would seem unnatural that a major combat with the Xianyun taking place in the lower Fen valley would not involve the prominent state Jin. Instead, Jing 井 (of Jing'e 井阿, "High Ridge of Jing") was a well-known place located in the Fengxiang area in the west part of the Wei River valley, and by its very location could be attacked by the Xianyun marching down the "Road of Huizhong" (see chapter 1). Ultimately, whether the battle took place in the lower Fen valley or in the west part of the Wei River valley

---

[83] See Cen Zhongmian, *Zhongwai dili kaozheng* (Hong Kong: Taiping, 1966), pp. 10–11.

[84] Wang Guowei, "Guifang Kunyi Xianyun kao," p. 378.

[85] See *Kaogu yu wenwu* 1983.3, 10; *Kaogu* 1985.4, 349.

[86] See Wang Hui, "Sishi'er nian Lai ding jianshi," in *Disijie guoji Zhongguo guwenzi xue yantaohui lunwen ji* (Hong Kong: Chinese University of Hong Kong, 2003), pp. 78–79.

[87] See *Wenwu* 1994.8, 12, 14. For a study of the bronze *hu*, see Wang Rencong, "Yang Ji hu ming shidu yu Beizhao 63 hao mu muzhu wenti," *Wenwu* 1996.5, 31, 32.

would have to depend on an interpretation of the character ▦ (?) standing between *ru* 汝 (you, Lai) and Changfu. If it means "and" or "assist," as Wang hopes to read it, the sentence would suggest that Lai and Changfu, the new ruler of Yang, together fought the Xianyun in areas near Yang. But it could also mean something like "leave" or "depart," and if so, the whole sentence could mean that Lai was recalled by the king from the state of Yang to fight the invading Xianyun in the west. Given the high uncertainty of this character, the best way to deal with the problem at present is perhaps to leave it as it is.

In short, the Jing River valley was the primary path of the Xianyun invasions of the Western Zhou. The straight and wide valley provided the Xianyun with an ideal channel to ride their chariots deep into Zhou territory. The Changwu–Binxian area, near which the towns of Jingshi and Xun were located, was the most critical point in defending the Wei River plain from the Xianyun. Our evidence also indicates that the Xianyun once made a flanking attack on the Zhou by way of the Luo River valley in northern Shaanxi, or even the Fen River valley farther to the east. Such a strategy was frequently adopted in later history by invaders such as the Tibetans and the Western Xia. So far as our current evidence goes, the Jing River valley was most important to the security of the Zhou capitals in the middle part of the Wei River valley.

SPATIAL CRISIS AND THE NORTHWESTERN FRONTIER OF ZHOU

The above study has shown that the military confrontation between the Zhou centered on the Wei River plain and the Xianyun based probably on the Ningxia region took place along the main valleys penetrating the northwestern frontiers of the Western Zhou state. This highland crescent stretching from the Loess Plateau of northern Shaanxi to the forested hills in southeastern Gansu is remarkable for its geographical diversity as well as its cultural complexity. In this section, I will further situate the prolonged military struggle in the broad sociocultural context of the northwestern frontier of Zhou. Only in such a context can we fully understand the cultural background of the Zhou–Xianyun war and evaluate its far-reaching historical impact.

In his recent book *Ancient China and Its Enemies*, Nicola Di Cosmo writes:[88]

Frontiers, however, are neither fixed nor exclusively defensive. With the expansion of civilization, the opening of new spaces to investigation, the acquisition of broader geographic and cultural horizon, frontiers acquire ever-different meanings. Because of their marginal yet critical status, frontiers are often gray areas, liminal zones where habitual conventions and principles can lose value, and new ones begin to

---

[88] See Di Cosmo, *Ancient China and Its Enemies*, p. 2.

appear. In this sense, the study of frontier often promotes a critical stance toward definitions of "community," "culture," or "civilization."

Not only can the meaning of a frontier change over time as a result of changes in the political relations between societies "in" and "out" of it, but, perhaps more often, the physical formation of the frontier can also vary in accordance with changes in the political configuration of the landscape and the balance between military powers. In another important recent frontier study, drawing heavily on Owen Lattimore's study of the Chinese frontier, C. R. Whittaker argues that ancient frontiers, in both China and the West, remained far more zonal than linear, and that the very existence of a physical linear border, even taking Hadrian's Wall in Britain and the Great Wall of China as examples, was mainly a limit of bureaucratic order and administration.[89] Whittaker further demonstrates with archaeological evidence the ethnic and cultural ambiguity or assimilation between the two sides of the physical border in Rome's frontier zones.[90] The concept of frontier as "zone" but not "line" has important implications for our study of pre-imperial frontiers in China before the rise of territorial states. It suggests that a frontier must have a certain "thickness" or "depth" in order to accommodate the many cultural variations. It is an intermediate or transitional zone where different cultures meet, different ethnic communities coexist, and different types of economies are mixed, in contrast to a line of political dichotomy separating the civilized population and the so-called "barbarians," as has been portrayed through much of the traditional historiography.[91]

Cultural and political relations in the northwestern frontier

The highland crescent that formed the northwestern frontier of Zhou is the western section of the broad region called by archaeologists the "Northern Zone Complex," located on the edge of the northern steppe.[92] Recent studies of the cultural ecology of the Northern Zone Complex have radically altered the received views that project the political antagonism between the Qin–Han empires and the mounted northern nomads back onto antiquity. By contrast, during the Shang–Western Zhou period, the Northern Zone was inhabited by mixed communities of shepherds and farmers who also practiced extensive hunting.[93] The following analysis will reveal the

[89] See C. R. Whittaker, *Frontiers of the Roman Empire: A Social and Economic Study* (Baltimore: Johns Hopkins University Press, 1994), pp. 71–73, 84.
[90] See Whittaker, *Frontiers of the Roman Empire*, pp. 222–37.
[91] For a criticism of perspective of the frontier in traditional Chinese historiography, see Di Cosmo, *Ancient China and Its Enemies*, pp. 6–7.
[92] For the definition of the "Northern Zone Complex," see Di Cosmo, "The Northern Frontier," pp. 885, 893.
[93] See Di Cosmo, "The Northern Frontier," p. 889; Di Cosmo, *Ancient China and Its Enemies*, pp. 48, 68. This well echoes a theory proposed by Lattimore more than a half century ago that the way of life of the northwestern tribesmen was not fundamentally different from that of the "Chinese"

cultural complexity of the northwestern frontier of Zhou as a back-ground for understanding the Zhou–Xianyun war and the related territorial conflict.

The most important cultural symbiosis on the northwestern frontier of Zhou is found between the Zhou culture and the Siwa 寺洼 culture. The Siwa culture was first developed in the upper Wei River and Tao River valleys in Gansu during the second half of the second millennium BC and moved east across the Liupan Mountains into the upper Jing River valley around the late pre-dynastic Zhou period (Map 11).[94] More than thirty sites are known to archaeologists, but only three, Xujianian 徐家碾, Lanqiao 蘭橋, and Jiuzhan 九站, have been formally excavated.[95] There is evidence that the Siwa communities practiced agriculture, as there are frequent impres-sions of grain on the bottoms of Siwa pottery vessels. However, the Siwa pottery wares were coarsely made and fired at a low temperature, and their styles were simple and limited, being technically and artistically less sophis-ticated than those of almost all Neolithic cultures that previously existed in the region (Fig. 27). Accompanying this pottery assemblage, there are large numbers of roughly made stone tools, but few well-polished stone implements. Clearly, Siwa society was an underdeveloped agricultural one. There is also evidence that the Siwa communities practiced hunting and sheep herding, but it is difficult to estimate the scale of such activities.[96]

Carbon-14 dating of human bones from Siwa tombs at Lanqiao points to 1335 ± 175 BC,[97] while bone samples from Xujianian are dated between 715 and 370 BC, leaving a major gap from the Lanqiao dating; the pottery assemblages from the two locations are in fact very similar to each other. However, the recent excavation at Jiuzhan by Beijing University leaves almost no doubt that the Siwa culture continued to exist in the region until the late Western Zhou, and even the early Eastern Zhou.[98] If so, we must recognize that the Siwa culture may have been the most dominant non-Zhou element in the region, and the northwestern frontier of Zhou was actually carved out of the territory of the Siwa culture in the process of Zhou expansion during the late pre-dynastic and early dynastic periods. As a matter of fact, the two cultures overlapped each other both temporally and spatially as their sites were often located side by side, together forming an important aspect of the landscape in these regions, although there was a tendency that, while the Zhou settlements concentrated on the main

in the early period; the only difference was that they did more herding and less farming while the "Chinese" did more farming and less herding; see Owen Lattimore, *Inner Asian Frontiers of China* (New York: American Geographical Society, 1940), pp. 55–58, 238–42.

[94] See *Wenwu kaogu gongzuo shi nian* (Beijing: Wenwu, 1990), p. 319. For the geographical distribution of the Siwa culture, see Li Feng, "Xian Zhou wenhua de neihan," pp. 278–80.

[95] See Hu Qianying, "Lun Siwa wenhua," *Wenwu jikan* 2 (1980), 118–24. For the excavations of the three sites, see *Kaogu* 1982.6, 584–90; 1987.8, 678–91; *Kaoguxue yanjiu* 3 (1997), 300–477.

[96] See Hu Qianying, "Lun Siwa wenhua," pp. 119–22.   [97] See *Kaogu* 1987.8, 691.

[98] See *Kaoguxue yanjiu* 3 (1997), pp. 300–460.

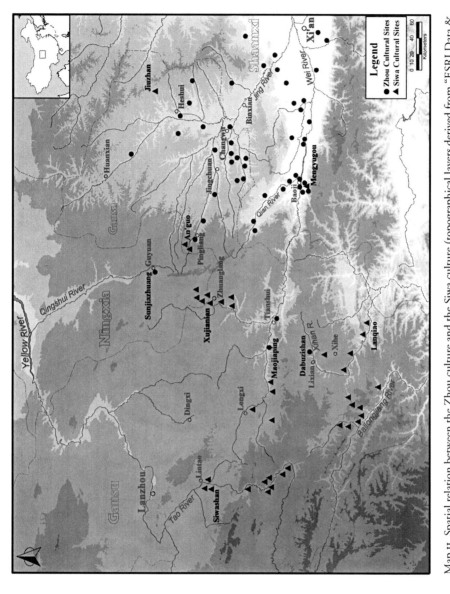

Map 11 Spatial relation between the Zhou culture and the Siwa culture (topographical layers derived from "ESRI Data & Maps: 2004"; river course based on "Harvard China Historical GIS Dataset, Version 2.0: August 2003")

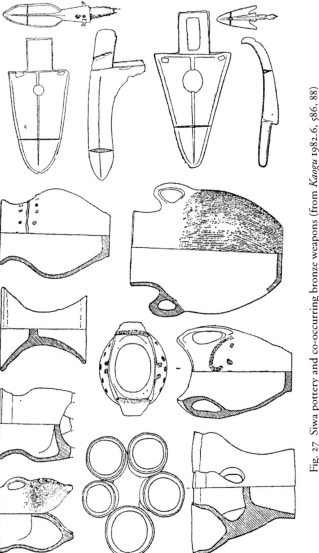

Fig. 27 Siwa pottery and co-occurring bronze weapons (from *Kaogu* 1982.6, 586, 88)

branches of the Jing and upper Wei rivers, the Siwa settlements tended to be located along their upper streams.[99]

The excavation at Jiuzhan further provides us with an excellent example of how two different cultures could coexist at a single site. Pottery wares from the settlement can be clearly differentiated according to the two traditions: Siwa and Zhou. But the two types of sherds were found together in each stratum and every unit. In the Jiuzhan cemetery, Zhou-style pottery vessels, though in much smaller numbers, were found in the same graves with Siwa pottery vessels.[100] The Jiuzhan settlement was probably occupied by a Siwa community that adopted Zhou cultural elements to a very significant degree; no doubt this community had close contact with the Zhou communities in its neighborhood. In addition, Zhou-style bronze weapons and pottery vessels were found in Siwa tombs at the sites of Xujianian and Lanqiao.[101]

In chapter 1, I discussed the distribution of the Western Zhou sites in the upper Jing region, showing that there was a high concentration in the Lingtai area where a relatively large number of high-ranking Western Zhou tombs were found. However, the Zhou bronze culture in the upper Jing River valley shows influence from another cultural tradition – that of the northern steppe. It has been noted by a number of scholars that a socketed beak-like hammer or axe from tomb no. 1 at Baicaopo was of steppe style, if not a product imported from the steppe.[102] So too perhaps were two bronze knives from the two tombs, one with an integrally cast rattle-pommel and the other with a tubular hilt (Fig. 28). The use of short-swords and helmets was rare among the Zhou, but was customary in areas to the north and west of Zhou. The use of socketed hammers or axes had a long history in the "Northern Zone Complex." Two similar bronzes were found in tombs nos. 1 and 2 in Zhongning 中寧, Ningxia, dated to the late Spring and Autumn or the early Warring States period; two other bronzes were found in Qin'an 秦安, Gansu, possibly dating from the same period.[103] The discovery of northern-style bronzes in Lingtai was not an isolated case. In 1982, four tombs were discovered at Heidouzui 黑豆嘴, Chunhua 淳化, on the southern slope of the Northern Mountain system, yielding, besides Shang-style bronze *jue* and *hu*, a large number of northern-style bronze knives, axes, and mirrors.[104] Again, in 1985 and 1987, a northern-style bronze axe and two knives were found in Chunhua County.[105] These were probably of late

---

[99] Certainly, this does not mean that all sites on the map were necessarily concomitant; such chronological correspondence cannot be known until all sites have been excavated and properly periodized. But the overall dates of the two cultures suggest that many of the sites must have coexisted during the Western Zhou.

[100] See *Kaoguxue yanjiu* 3 (1997), pp. 399, 446.   [101] See *Kaogu* 1982.6, 588; 1987.8, 687.

[102] See Wu En, "Yinmo Zhouchu de beifang qingtongqi," *Kaogu xuebao* 1985.2, 138; Du Zhengsheng, "Zhou Qin minzu wenhua Rongdi xing de kaocha: Jianlun Guanzhong chutu de beifangshi qingtongqi," *Dalu zazhi* 87.5 (1993), 9–10. For the bronze, see *Kaogu* 1987.9, 774, pl. 1; *Wenwu* 1986.2, 40.

[103] See *Kaogu* 1987.9, 774, pl. 1; *Wenwu* 1986.2, 40.

[104] See *Kaogu yu wenwu* 1986.5, 12–22.   [105] See *Kaogu yu wenwu* 1990.1, 53–57.

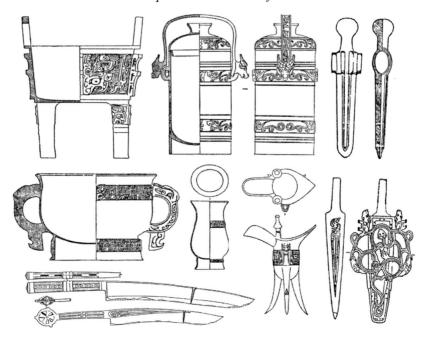

Fig. 28 Bronzes from tombs nos. 1 and 2 at Baicaopo in Lingtai, Gansu (based on *Kaogu xuebao* 1977.2, 107, fig. 7; 115, fig. 3.1–2; 116, fig. 15.5–6)

Shang date, but their very existence at the northern edge of the Wei River valley indicates the deep penetration of the Northern Zone bronze culture.

Different from the early Western Zhou tombs at Baicaopo in which Zhou elements are dominant alongside a small number of possible northern steppe imports, another later Western tomb containing twenty-two bronze objects found at Yucun 宇村, Ningxian, in the lower Malian River valley, perhaps illustrates an important cultural change that may have occurred during the late Western Zhou, at least in the northern half of the upper Jing River basin. A detailed discussion of this critical group of bronzes is needed here (Fig. 29):[106]

   1 Luobo *xu* 夆伯盨 (JC: 4346): a standard late Western Zhou bronze, inscribed: "Luobo makes [for] Zhongji 仲姞 [this] sacrificial [vessel]."
   2 Zhong Shengfu *li* 仲生父鬲 (JC: 729): standard late Western Zhou bronze, inscribed: "Zhong Shengfu makes [for] Jing Mengji 井孟姬 [this] treasured *li*."
   3 Cup: small, with dragon decoration. A similar cup was excavated at Chakou 岔口 in Yanchang 延长 near Yan'an, northern Shaanxi, together with a group of late Western Zhou bronzes and other "Northern Zone" objects.[107]

[106] See *Kaogu* 1985.4, 349–52, pl. 5; *Kaogu yu wenwu* 1983.3, 10.
[107] See *Kaogu yu wenwu* 1993.5, 8–12.

Fig. 29 Bronzes from the Yucun tomb in Ningxian, Gansu (from *Kaogu* 1985.4, 351, fig. 5–6, pl. 5)

4 Bronze tiger sculpture: 7.2 centimeters long, 2.5 centimeters high. The tiger is the most commonly seen motif later in the "Northern Zone." The shape of this particular piece resembles a bronze tiger plate from Maoqinggou 毛慶溝, Inner Mongolia.[108]

5 Three bronze tiger plates, with a belt-knob at the back of all three. This is the type of bronze plaque that later flourished in the "Northern Zone."[109]

6 Two bronze jars, each with two small knobs on the shoulder. This is a distinctive type of bronze; a bronze jar of the same type but having a handle on one side was among the group of bronzes from Yanchang.

7 Four bronze spoons, with round or elliptical heads and cord-shaped handles. These spoons are clearly different from the Zhou-style *bi*-spoons, but are undoubtedly the prototype of the cord-handled spoons of the "Northern Zone," e.g. those found in the Ordos region.[110]

8 A double-bladed short-sword, with an animal mask on each side of the hilt. A similar sword was excavated from an early Spring and Autumn tomb in Xigaoquan 西高泉, Baoji, but was considered by some to be a "northern-style" object.[111]

9 Small bronze bell: 2.5 centimeters high, resembling the standard bell objects found in the Ordos.[112]

10 Miscellaneous objects, including a U-shaped object and a small bronze hook. Both are alien to the Zhou culture.

Everything in this inventory, except the two inscribed bronzes, is alien to the Zhou bronze culture but has strong connections to the northern steppe bronzes; their shape and ornamentation indicate that they were contemporary with the two late Western Zhou-style bronzes found with them, and in that regard they are very important for recovering the cultural chain of the Northern Zone that has few finds datable to the late Western Zhou period.[113] The Yucun tomb presents a sharp contrast to the Baicaopo tombs in which, although "Northern Zone" elements are recognizable, the Zhou elements are overwhelming. The "Northern Zone" bronzes in the Yucun tomb are so prominent that we must reconsider the cultural identity of the possible occupant of the tomb – Luobo. The inscription on the Zhong Shengfu *li* indicates a strong connection to a prominent Zhou lineage – Jing 井, located in the Fengxiang area. Luobo may have been a new migrant from the northern steppe who adopted the Zhou bronze culture and cast

---

[108] See Tian Guangjin and Guo Suxin, *E'erduosi shi qingtongqi* (Beijing: Wenwu, 1986), p. 281, pl. 67.1.

[109] See *ibid.*, pp. 87, 89, 93.   [110] See *ibid.*, p. 144.

[111] See *Wenwu* 1980.9, 3; see also Du Zhengsheng, "Zhou Qin minzu wenhua," pp. 193–94.

[112] See Tian Guangjin and Guo Suxin, *E'erduosi shi qingtongqi*, p. 137.

[113] There is a lack of a comparable inventory of bronzes in the "Northern Zone Complex" contemporary with the middle and late Western Zhou. So far the dating of bronzes from the "Northern Zone" is largely based on their co-occurrence with Shang and Western Zhou-style bronzes. See Wu En, "Yinmo Zhouchu de beifang qingtongqi," p. 141.

bronzes according to Zhou standards; or the occupant of the Yucun tomb may have been an invader from the north who simply had buried with him bronzes he had looted from the nearby Zhou settlements. In any event, the presence of the Yucun bronzes in the region is significant. They suggest that, besides the Zhou and Siwa cultures, a strong third cultural tradition was present in areas to the north of the Zhou central region.

The influence of the Siwa culture reached as deep into the Zhou central area as Baoji, where a Siwa-style jar was found in the cemetery of the state of Yu in Zhuyuangou 竹園溝, and many more were discovered in nearby Mengyugou 濛峪溝, indicating very possibly that a Siwa community may have lived in the area (Map 11).[114] However, the Baoji area seems to have received more influence from the south, centered on the state of Yu. Archaeological excavations have revealed that although Yu adopted the standard bronze culture of Zhou, the material remains of Yu present a high degree of cultural mixing. For instance, the male nobles of Yu were buried in double-chambered trapezoidal pits, accompanied by their concubines, while the Zhou nobles were normally buried in a single rectangular pit. The pottery inventory of Yu is composed entirely of various types of jars, showing strong connections to the Sichuan region in the south.[115] The burial of short-swords with the dead is normally seen in the cemeteries of Yu, but was not a custom in the cemeteries of Zhou. Finally, even the Zhou-style bronzes do not overshadow the existence of a group of distinctive local-style bronzes, most notably the round-bodied *ding* and *gui*.[116] Because of such cultural mixing, many believe that the ruling family of Yu owed its origins to the Di 氐 or Qiang 羌 peoples in the mountains to the southwest of Baoji.[117] Although Yu was only 150 kilometers to the west of the Zhou capital, given the topography of the region, it was located at the foot of the high Qinling Mountains, the natural frontier of the Western Zhou state.

However, political relations in the frontier region could be just as complex as cultural relations. In this regard, our best evidence comes from tomb no. 1 at Yaojiahe 姚家河, Lingtai, where two early Western Zhou bronze vessels were found together with a Zhou-style pottery *li*-tripod (Map 3). The *ding*-vessel is inscribed with three characters indicating that the bronze was cast by a certain Guaishu 乖叔, the third-born of the Guai lineage or state.[118] This discovery provided an important clue to the long-pending issue regarding the provenance of a bronze called Guaibo *gui* 乖伯簋 (JC: 4331), evidently cast by another member of the Guai; the latter bronze provides

---

[114] See *Baoji Yu guo mudi* (Beijing: Wenwu, 1988), pp. 14, 140.

[115] See *Baoji Yu guo mudi*, pp. 454–55. For the southern connection in the Yu cemetery, see also Nishie Kyotaka, "Sei Shū jidai no Kanchū heigen ni okeru Gyo shūdan no ichi," in *Chūgoku kodai no moji to bunka* (Tokyo: Kyūko shoin, 1999), pp. 230–31.

[116] See, *Baoji Yu guo mudi*, pp. 446–56.

[117] See *ibid.*, p. 462; Zhang Changshou, "Lun Baoji Rujiazhuang faxian de Xi Zhou tongqi," *Kaogu* 1980.6, 526–29.

[118] See *Kaogu* 1976.1, 39–42.

Fig. 30 The Guaibo *gui* and its inscription (JC: 4331; *Shanghai bowuguan cang qingtongqi*, no. 54)

important information regarding Zhou's relationship to the communities on the northwestern frontier (Fig. 30):[119]

隹（惟）王九月甲寅，王命益公征眉敖，益公至告。二月，眉敖至見，獻賞。己未，王命中偯歸訣（乖）白（伯）狐（貔）裘。王若曰："訣（乖）白（伯），朕丕顯且（祖）文武應受大命，乃且（祖）克弇（奉）先王，翼自也（他）邦，有荋于大命。我亦弗兇（曠）苗（享）邦，易（錫）女（汝）狐（貔）裘。"訣（乖）白（伯）拜手頓首："天子休！弗望（忘）小愍（裔）邦。"歸夆敢對訊（揚）天子丕丕魯休，用乍（作）朕皇考武訣（乖）幾王隥（尊）簋，用好宗廟，苗（享）夙夕；用好朋友雩（與）百者（諸）鄧（婚）遘（媾）；用蘄（祈）屯（純）彔（祿）永命，魯壽子孫。歸夆其萬年日用苗（享）于宗室。

It was the king's ninth year, ninth month, *jiayin*-day (no. 51), the king commanded Duke Yi to campaign against Mei'ao, and Duke Yi arrived and reported. In the second month, Mei'ao arrived and presented himself [before the king], and contributed silk and shells. On *jiwei* (no. 56), the king commanded Zhong Zhi to return Guaibo with a badger coat. The king said to the effect: "Guaibo, when my illustrious ancestors, King Wen and King Wu, received the great mandate, your ancestors were able to assist the prior kings, and supported [them] from the other state, taking part in the great mandate. We also have not wasted enjoying the state, and award you a badger coat." Guaibo bowed with his head touching the ground: "Beneficent is the Son of Heaven! [You] have not forgotten the petty border state." Guifeng dares in response to extol the Son of Heaven's illustriously felicitous

---

[119] The Guaibo *gui* was discovered late in the nineteenth century, and was previously known also as "Qiangbo *gui*" 羌伯簋 or "Guijiang *gui*" 歸降簋. For its inscription, see also Shirakawa, "Kinbun tsūshaku," 25.145:282–95.

beneficence,[120] and herewith makes [for] my august deceased father, the Martial King Ji of Guai, [this] sacrificial *gui*-vessel, with which to accommodate in the ancestral temple, making offering morning and evening, and to accommodate [our] friends and the hundred nobles [through] marriage relations, and to entreat pure wealth and eternal mandate, longevity and descendents. May Guifeng for ten thousand years daily use [it] to make offering in the ancestral chamber.

Previous studies have concluded incorrectly that this bronze was cast in the state of Gui 歸, located in Zigui 秭歸, Hubei, in the Three Gorges region.[121] The discovery of the Guaishu *gui* suggests that Guai was probably located somewhere in the upper Jing region, if not actually in the Daxi River valley. The bronze can probably be dated to the reign of King Yih, and Duke Yi also appears in several other inscriptions cast during the mid-Western Zhou period.[122] According to the inscription, the Zhou king sent Duke Yi to attack Guai. It is likely that Duke Yi suppressed Guai and that this caused Guaibo's visit to the Zhou court five months later.

According to the Zhou king's words, the ancestors of Mei'ao, ruler of Guai, had assisted King Wen and King Wu to host the Heaven's Mandate, indicating that Guai was an old ally of the Zhou from pre-dynastic times. The Ninth Year Qiu Wei *ding* (JC: 2831) records that Mei'ao sent a delegate to the Zhou court in the first month of King Gong's ninth year, suggesting that Guai was previously on friendly terms with Zhou.[123] Interestingly, the Zhou king literally recognizes Guai as a "foreign state" (*tabang* 他邦), differentiated from the Zhou states. This is consistent with the fact that in the inscription Mei'ao refers to his father as "King Ji," equal in status to the Zhou king. Another factor that may reinforce the foreign origin of Guai is that the name Mei'ao seems to have been the Chinese transliteration of a foreign name. The message here is clear: the state of Guai, although politically associated with the Zhou, had maintained some independence and could stand on an equal footing with the Zhou. This relationship is fully manifest in the cautious dealing and exchange of gifts between the Zhou king and Mei'ao.

Mei'ao also cast another *gui* vessel: the Mei'ao *gui* 眉敖簋 (JC: 4213), currently in the Palace Museum, Beijing. The inscription relates that the Rong 戎 contributed one hundred carts of metal to Zi Yafu 子牙父, and Zi

---

[120] It should also be noted that some scholars, for instance Wu Hesheng and Yu Xingwu, read the term *gui feng* 歸夆 in connection with the preceding phrase as *gui xiang* 歸降, meaning "come to submit." See *Jijin wenlu*, 3, p. 7; *Shuangjian chi jijin wenxuan* (1933), 1, p. 3.7.

[121] This conclusion is entirely based on an arbitrary reading of *gui* 歸 as the name of Guaibo's native state; see Guo Moruo, *Liang Zhou jinwen ci*, pp. 147–48; Shirakawa, "Kinbun tsūshaku," 25.145:285–87. Since Guaibo is clearly the ruler of Guai, and his father is referred to as King of Guai, it is impossible to treat "Gui" as Guaibo's native state. Clearly, Guifeng was the personal name of Guaibo, who is also referred to as Mei'ao 眉敖 at the beginning of the inscription. In addition, the alleged location clearly does not fit the historical and archaeological context that Zhou domination in the middle Yangzi region was limited to the east of the Han River and the north of the Yangzi River (see appendix 1).

[122] For a detailed discussion of the date of the Guaibo *gui*, see chapter 2 (note 18 on p. 97). See also, Shaughnessy, *Sources of Western Zhou History*, pp. 117–19, 255–58.

[123] For the Ninth Year Qiu Wei *ding*, see Shirakawa, "Kinbun tsūshaku," 49.h011:267–73.

Yafu in turn rewarded Mei'ao. The inscription suggests that Mei'ao may
have in some way assisted the Zhou in frontier affairs in dealings with the
Rong people. The casting as well as the calligraphy of the inscription is
apparently unusual, and I have suggested in a recent study that it is most
likely to have been cast in the local bronze workshop of the state of Guai.
In fact, it is one of the few examples of inscriptions that were cast not
in the Zhou cultural setting, but in a non-Zhou cultural environment of
the frontier regions.[124] The Mei'ao case illustrates the complex and ever-
changing relationship between the Zhou court and the frontier polities.

   Another interesting case is the state of Ze 夨, located in the Longxian–
Qianyang region in the Qian River valley.[125] The surname of the ruling
family of Ze was Ji 姬, the same as that of the Zhou kings, suggesting
that they may have shared the same ancestry, as the material culture of Ze
is also indistinguishable from the Zhou culture.[126] However, in a number
of bronze inscriptions, the rulers of Ze refer to themselves or are referred
to by members of the state of Ze as "kings," being equal in status to the
Zhou king.[127] More important, on the Sanshi *pan* 散氏盤 (JC: 10176), a
bronze that records a land compensation made by Ze to its neighbor state –
San – that almost certainly cast the bronze, the "King of Ze" is also mentioned.[128] These inscriptions indicate that Ze was probably in a very special relationship with the Zhou: although Ze may have been akin to the

[124] For a detailed study of the Mei'ao *gui*, see Li Feng, "Literacy Crossing Cultural Borders," pp. 212–22.
[125] For the archaeological discovery of the state of Ze, see Lu Liancheng, "Xi Zhou Ze guo shiji kaolue,"
   pp. 233–36; *Wenwu* 1982.2, 48–57.
[126] There has previously been some confusion about the surname of Ze as well as about the general
   rules by which women are referred to in the Western Zhou bronze inscriptions. But I believe
   that this problem has been satisfactorily solved by Li Zhongcao, who laid down the following
   principles. (1) A woman is referred to by her sons or grandsons by her own surname name and
   her husband's lineage name, e.g. "Make for my august father Zhengbo and (mother) Zheng Ji"
   作朕皇考鄭伯鄭姬 (Zheng Ji was a woman from the Ji clan who married into the Zheng lineage).
   (2) When a married woman refers to herself, she does it by her surname and her husband's lineage
   name, e.g. "San Ji makes this sacrificial *ding*" 散姬作尊鼎 (San Ji was a woman from the Ji clan
   who married into the San lineage). (3) On bronzes cast as dowries, a ruler refers to his daughter
   by her (and his) surname and her husband's lineage name, e.g. "Ehou makes for Wang Ji marital
   gui" 鄂侯作王姞媵簋 (Wang Ji was a woman from the state of E of the Ji 姞 clan who married the
   Zhou king). (4) A ruler refers to his married daughter by her husband's lineage name or personal
   designation and her own surname name, e.g. "The king makes for Zhong Ji this treasured vessel"
   土作仲姬寶彝 (Zhong Ji was a royal princess who married a man who was *zhong* [second born] in
   his family). (5) When a husband casts a bronze for his wife, he refers to her by her own surname
   and her own lineage name, e.g. "Sanbo makes for Ze Ji this treasured *gui*" 散伯作夨姬寶簋 (Ze Ji
   was a woman from the state of Ze of the Ji clan who married the ruler of San). The issue of Ze is
   related to another lineage – Zheng 鄭 (non-Ji clan, as in the first instance), which will be discussed
   in some detail in chapter 5. The inscription of the Zewang *guigai* 夨王簋蓋 (JC: 3871) mentions
   that the King of Ze cast a bronze for Zheng Jiang 鄭姜, suggesting almost certainly that Zheng
   Jiang married into the state of Ze from Zheng which was of the Jiang 姜 clan. By the same token,
   the Sanbo *gui* 散伯簋 (JC: 3779) (above, fifth instance) suggests that Ze was of the Ji clan while San
   was not. Both bronzes were clearly not cast as dowries which must have the character *ying* 媵, but
   were bronzes that husbands cast for their wives. I believe this is the best we can conclude on this
   matter. See Li Zhongcao, "Xi Zhou jinwen zhong de funü chengwei," *Baoji wenbo* 1991.1, 35–39.
[127] For instance, the Zewang *ding* 夨王鼎 (JC: 2149), Zewang *zhi* 夨王觶 (JC: 6452), Zewang *guigai*
   夨王簋蓋 (JC: 3871), and Tong *you* 同卣 (JC: 5398). For a discussion of these bronzes, see Lu
   Liancheng, "Xi Zhou Ze guo shiji," pp. 236–37; Shirakawa, "Kinbun tsūshaku," 24.139:212–16.
[128] For the inscription, see Shirakawa, "Kinbun tsūshaku," 24.139:191–212.

Zhou in origin, it is likely that Ze was outside the political system of the Western Zhou state, being an independent polity located on the northwestern frontier of Zhou.[129]

The above study has shown that the northwestern frontier of the Western Zhou state was an extremely complex political and cultural system. Although the Zhou culture was predominant during the early Western Zhou as the result of Zhou expansion, the Siwa culture constituted another important cultural layer that coexisted with the Zhou culture throughout the entire Western Zhou period. Some of the non-Zhou elements in the bronze culture of the upper Jing region were clearly associated with the northern steppe region. And by the late Western Zhou, even tombs with overwhelming northern features began to appear in the region. Furthermore, a complicated political relationship is manifest in the bronze inscriptions from the region. These inscriptions suggest that there were clusters of Zhou communities or even military garrisons widely distributed along the main branches of the Jing River. There existed also polities of possible foreign origin such as Guai, which maintained its independence but sometimes probably also served Zhou interests. But there was an even larger number of Siwa villages widely distributed along the streams of the Jing River. It was into this frontier that the Xianyun launched frequent invasions which the Zhou had to fight hard to resist.

Spatial crisis and the impact of the Zhou–Xianyun war

In this multicultural and perhaps also multiethnic environment of the northwestern frontier of Zhou, can we actually identify any sites that may have been left by the historically known Xianyun? It has been suggested by Hu Qianying that the Siwa culture was the remains of the historically known Xunyu 薰育, which may in turn be related to the historically known Xianyun.[130] However, this identification suffers from the fact that the Siwa sites discovered so far all seem too small in size and low in subsistence level to have sustained an advanced society like the Xianyun that could field hundreds of chariots in battle against the Zhou. Although some bronze weapons were excavated from Siwa tombs, they were probably imports from Zhou; there is no evidence that the Siwa culture had ever developed its own bronze casting tradition. Until some central sites of the Siwa culture are discovered, there seems no strong link between the Siwa culture and the historical Xianyun. Considering further the historical geography of

---

[129] On the basis of the Sanshi *pan* and the Guaibo *gui*, Wang Guowei once proposed that the regional rulers of Zhou referred to themselves in accordance with Zhou institutions while in the Zhou court, but entitled themselves kings in their own domains. The cases of the Sanshi *pan* and Guaibo *gui* should be explained by the unique history of the two states, but this is not pertinent to other Western Zhou regional states. See Wang Guowei, "Gu zhuhou chengwang shuo," in *Guantang jilin* (Shijiazhuang: Hebei jiaoyu, 2001), p. 779.

[130] See Hu Qianying, "Lun Siwa wenhua," pp. 123–24.

the Zhou–Xianyun war, it is more likely that the Xianyun were a power that intermittently struck into the upper Jing River region from the north by way of Ningxia through the "Road to Xiao Pass." In this regard, the inscription of the Guoji Zibai *pan* is very important in pointing to the Luo River valley in northern Shaanxi as yet another channel of Xianyun invasion; in the meantime, it points to the north side of the Hengshan Mountains as the source of the invasion. From this, it seems likely that the Xianyun were a society that inhabited the large region stretching from the Ningxia plain east along the north side of the Hengshan Mountains. The discovery in Yanchang of a group of late Western Zhou bronzes occurring with northern-style bronzes similar to those found at Yucun suggests a cultural influence over the highlands of northern Shaanxi that clearly also had its sources in the north.[131] For this reason, it is plausible to consider that the Xianyun was one of the societies that shared the "Northern Zone" tradition, represented for the particular period of the middle to late Western Zhou by the Yucun and Yanchang bronzes. It is not impossible that the Xianyun were cultural heirs to the Bronze Age civilization of Ordos that was once prosperous during the later Shang. The Siwa culture, on the other hand, as an indigenous cultural tradition in the upper Jing and upper Wei valleys, may have been the cultural origin of many communities that had long collaborated with the Zhou.

In any event, the incursion by the Xianyun seems to have brought some major changes in the cultural ecology of the northwestern frontier, especially the upper Jing region. The inscription of the Duoyou *ding* records that the first Zhou town to have been attacked by the invading Xianyun was Jingshi, for which an initial report was sent to the Zhou king. It is interesting to note that Jingshi and Xun, the second town captured by the Xianyun, were located close to each other at the eastern edge of the upper Jing basin. This seems to suggest that by the time of Duoyou's war Zhou had probably already lost effective administrative control over the settlements along the Jing River to the west of Jingshi. At least, one may reasonably consider that most areas along the main branches of the Jing River were possibly turned into war-zones where the original Zhou as well as the Siwa communities, had they survived the onslaught by the Xianyun at all, would have to depend on themselves for their security. It has been shown earlier that during the early Western Zhou the Zhou not only firmly controlled the upper Jing valley, but probably also advanced beyond it into the Qingshui River valley in southern Ningxia. This situation is radically different from what we learn about the region during the late phase of the mid-Western Zhou to the early late Western Zhou. In contrast to the wide distribution of early Western Zhou sites and tombs in the upper Jing region, late Western Zhou remains were rarely reported from areas along the main branches of the

---

[131] See *Kaogu yu wenwu* 1993.5, 8–12.

Jing River.[132] In contrast, and it is not surprising, during the late Western Zhou we begin to see bronzes like those that were excavated at Yucun. It seems likely that the geopolitical system that the Zhou constructed in the upper Jing region during the early Western Zhou had collapsed towards the late phase of the mid-Western Zhou.

If the above assessment of the political situation in the upper Jing River region is correct, then we must consider that the incursion by the Xianyun into the region actually put the Zhou in a very dangerous situation. According to the inscription of the Duoyou *ding*, the first battle took place on the *jiashen* day (no. 21) at Qi in the Binxian area, only about 120 kilometers from the Zhou capital. Then, on day *dingyou* (no. 34), presumably still in the same month, Duoyou presented captives in the capital. Since Gong, the site of the second battle, was probably located in the Jingchuan area, about 70 kilometers from Qi, it is clear that Duoyou traveled at least 260 kilometers in thirteen days, at an average rate of 20 kilometers per day. If this rate was constant, it would suggest that Duoyou had only six days to reach the site of the first battle, from the capital. Since, after the battle at Gong, Duoyou fought two other battles before turning back to the capital, it actually took Duoyou much less than six days to move from the Zhou capital to the first battlefield at Qi.

If the Duoyou *ding* case represents the normal pace of Zhou response to Xianyun attack, the implication is that the Zhou must have always been prepared to bring a force into the battlefield within three to four days over a distance of 120 kilometers. In other words, if the Zhou failed to do so, the enemy chariots could ride down from the upper Jing region to make a direct attack on the Zhou capitals in just three or four days. Although we have no way of knowing whether the Duoyou *ding* is representative of all encounters between the Zhou and the Xianyun, it at least suggests that some of the battles may have been fought at very short notice. This extremely short line of defense certainly constituted a major pressure on the Zhou capital region in the Wei River valley. This contrasts sharply with the time needed for Zhou military operations in the east, in which a march from the Zhou capitals in the Wei River valley to the eastern center Chengzhou would take more than a month. One may argue that the mountainous terrain of the northwestern frontier was itself a protection for the Zhou, while the

---

[132] At present, the period from the late phase of the mid-Western Zhou in the upper Jing region is represented, besides the Yucun tomb mentioned above, by only two findings: a bronze *li* found at Penggong 彭公 in Changwu from an unknown context; the cover of a bronze *hu* found at Yangjiatai 楊家台 in Zhengning. See *Kaogu yu wenwu* 1981.1, 9; pl. 4.1; *Kaogu yu wenwu* 1983.3, 10. During my visit to five local museums in the upper Jing region in 1997, I was particularly concerned with the middle and late Western Zhou period. While early Western Zhou bronzes and pottery were disproportionately numerous in these collections, I encountered only one pottery *guan* from the late Western Zhou period. Since these pottery vessels were randomly gathered in the region, they do suggest a break in the upper Jing River valley during the late Western Zhou. In addition, some formally excavated cemeteries in the upper Jing region such as Yujiawan in Chongxin also show a similar break in their cultural sequence. See *Kaogu yu wenwu* 1986.1, 1–7; *Kaogu* 1976.1, 39–48.

eastern capital Luoyi was more open to attacks. But the reality is that the Xianyun were the major threat to the Western Zhou state and they were too close to the Zhou heartland. When they managed to overcome the geographical obstacles as they did, for which the Jing River valley provided an ideal channel, the Zhou capital would lie in their immediate reach. In one battle at least, that of 823 BC, the Xianyun evidently moved very close to the Zhou capitals.

In this regard, the poem "Caiwei" 采薇 (no. 167) in the *Book of Poetry* seems to speak best about the urgency the Zhou people actually felt to defend the Zhou state against the invasion by the Xianyun (Waley's translation):[133]

1 采薇采薇, We plucked the bracken, plucked the bracken
2 薇亦作止。 While the young shoots were springing up.
3 曰歸曰歸, Oh, to go back, go back!
4 歲亦莫止。 The year is ending.
5 靡室靡家, We have no house, no home
6 玁狁之故。 Because of the Xianyun.
7 不遑啓居, We cannot rest or bide
8 玁狁之故。 Because of the Xianyun.

9 采薇采薇, We plucked the bracken, plucked the bracken
10 薇亦柔止。 While the shoots were soft.
11 曰歸曰歸, Oh, to go back, go back!
12 心亦憂止。 Our hearts are sad,
13 憂心烈烈, Our sad hearts burn,
14 載飢載渴。 We are hungry and thirsty,
15 我戍未定, But our campaign is not over,
16 靡使歸聘。 Nor is any of us sent home with news.

17 采薇采薇, We plucked the bracken, plucked the bracken;
18 薇亦剛止。 But the shoots were hard.
19 曰歸曰歸, Oh, to go back, go back!
20 歲亦陽止。 The year is running out.
21 王事靡盬, But the king's business never ends;
22 不遑啓處。 We cannot rest or bide.
23 憂心孔疚, Our sad hearts are very bitter;
24 我行不來。 We went, but do not come.

25 彼爾維何, What splendid thing is that?
26 維常之華。 It is the flower of the cherry-tree.
27 彼路斯何, What great carriage is that?
28 君子之車。 It is our lord's chariot,
29 戎車既駕, His war-chariot ready yoked,

[133] See *Shijing*, 9.3, pp. 412–14 (Waley, *The Book of Songs*, pp. 139–41).

30 四牡業業。 With its four steeds so eager.
31 豈敢定居, How should we dare stop or tarry?
32 一月三捷。 In one month we have had three alarms.

33 駕彼四牡, We yoke the teams of four,
34 四牡騤騤。 Those steeds so strong,
35 君子所依, That our lord rides behind,
36 小人所腓。 That lesser men protect.
37 四牡翼翼, The four steeds so grand,
38 象弭魚服。 The ivory bow-ends, the fish-skin quiver.
39 豈不日戒, Yes, we must be always on our guard;
40 獫狁孔棘。 The Xianyun are very swift.

41 昔我往矣, Long ago, when we started,
42 楊柳依依。 The willows spread their shade.
43 今我來思, Now that we turn back
44 雨雪霏霏。 The snowflakes fly.
45 行道遲遲, The march before us is long,
46 載飢載渴。 We are thirsty and hungry,
47 我心傷悲, Our hearts are stricken with sorrow,
48 莫知我哀。 But no one listens to our plaint.

This poem speaks well of the grief of soldiers on campaign to defend the Western Zhou state against the incursion by the Xianyun. Reading through the lines, one can clearly see and feel a constant fear and anxiety that the Zhou people had about the Xianyun. The poem in a profound literary sense shows the psychological impact of the Xianyun invasion on the Zhou population and the social unrest it caused in the royal domain in Shaanxi. Or perhaps only in the historical and cultural context constructed here can the true meaning and implication of the poem be recognized and fully appreciated. As the poet says here, the Zhou soldiers must always be on high guard about an enemy who could strike into the heart of the Western Zhou state at any time (lines 39–40). However, the impact was probably not just psychological; in order to cope with the immediate threat from the Xianyun, the Western Zhou state must mobilize its resources in the best way to fight an enemy whom they could defeat but could not destroy.

CONCLUSION

The Xianyun were old enemies as well as neighbors of the Zhou people. Their political power was probably centered on the south edge of the northern steppe, stretching from the Ningxia plain to the north side of the Hengshan Mountains. From approximately the late part of the mid-Western Zhou on, the Xianyun launched frequent invasions into Zhou-controlled territory, altering the power balance in the northwestern frontier of the Western Zhou state. On the basis of new inscriptional evidence as well as received textual records, we can safely locate the main battleground of the Zhou–Xianyun war in the upper Jing River valley, in the immediate neighborhood of the Zhou heartland. In accordance with the landscape of the region, we can further reconstruct the process of a number of major battles between the Zhou and the Xianyun. This reconstruction runs an interesting parallel with many historically well-documented wars between the later Chinese dynasties and the northern nomadic power. The similarity suggests the important influence of geography on the political and military conduct of the Western Zhou state.

In a broader cultural context, the battles took place in an environment of high cultural mixture and symbiosis. The Siwa culture constituted the first cultural layer, originating in the west and stretching from the upper Wei River valley across the Liupan Mountains east to the upper Jing River valley. Throughout the entire Western Zhou, the Siwa communities had probably lived side by side with the Zhou communities in the region. Archaeological discoveries suggest that during the early Western Zhou the Zhou not only maintained tight control over the upper Jing region, but ventured onto the northern steppe, entering the Qingshui River plain in southern Ningxia. The archaeological evidence also shows that the Zhou bronze culture in the upper Jing River region received influences from the northern steppe, which seem to have increased towards the late Western Zhou, represented by the distinctive bronze objects from Yucun.

It has also been suggested that by the beginning of the late Western Zhou, the Zhou probably had already lost effective control over most of the upper Jing River valley. This exposed Zhou settlements in the Changwu–Binxian area at the eastern edge of the upper Jing basin, the most critical position for Zhou security, to the first attacks by the Xianyun. There were only 120 kilometers, or three to four days of marching, from the Changwu–Binxian area to the Zhou capitals at the center of the Wei River plain. Facing a very short line of defense, the Zhou must always be prepared to fight the Xianyun at a short distance from their capital. This dangerous situation coincided in time with the political disturbance developing at the Zhou court. As the Western Zhou state was internally weakened by a number of factors, it was threatened from outside by a formidable enemy who was determined to push the regime to the verge of perishing.

CHAPTER 4

The fall of the Western Zhou: partisan struggle and spatial collapse

In the spring of 771 BC, the Western Rong poured into the middle Wei River valley, plundering the Zhou capitals Feng and Hao and killing the last Zhou king, You (r. 781–771 BC). The Western Zhou dynasty came to an end. In many regards, the eventual downfall of the Western Zhou state was the last phase of the prolonged warfare between the Zhou and the Xianyun.[1] When the new king, Ping (r. 770–720 BC), was established after the death of his father, it was clearly impossible for him to maintain the Zhou court in the Wei River valley, in the immediate reach of the Xianyun who could renew their attacks at any time, much less to rule from it. Thus, King Ping decided to move the royal court to the eastern capital Luoyi, and thereby opened another era in Chinese history.

However, the "fall of the Western Zhou" meant much more than just the change in the geographical location of the Zhou capital. It put an end to the long-standing domination of Zhou royal power over the middle and lower Yellow River regions; the Western Zhou state as a complex political organism was extinguished. More significantly, the year 771 BC also marked the end of the long history of the early Chinese states that had sustained the largest society in East Asia since at least the founding of the Shang dynasty in the sixteenth century BC. For more than a millennium, royal power dominated political life and guided cultural development in North China, but the collapse of central authority in 771 BC gave rise to a long period of more than 500 years of interregional warfare, resulting in the annexation of the weak local states by their strong neighbors. From this interregional struggle, an imperial political structure gradually emerged in China.

What really happened in the years leading up to the final collapse? Was the fall a simple military disaster, or a political outburst promoted by tensions coming to a head in the Western Zhou state? In traditional historiography, the inauspicious fall is clouded by legend and complicated with documentary contradictions with regard particularly to the geographical positions of the parties involved. The bronze inscriptions from the last

---

[1] With the recent discovery of the Forty-Second Year Lai *ding*, we can be sure that the war with the Xianyun continued to the end of King Xuan's reign, and very possibly was fought also in the reign of King You, making a reasonable connection in time to the attack by the Western Rong in 771 BC.

reign of the Western Zhou are not only few, but also historically uninformative, leaving most of the story to the textual tradition. We will probably never have bronze inscriptions that would provide us with enough details on the dynastic downfall – such a disgraceful event would not be recorded by the Zhou elite on the bronzes that were used to commemorate glory and honor. In this chapter, I will conduct a systematic study of the eleven years of King You as the basis for a new interpretation of the dynastic downfall. I propose that the fall of the Western Zhou was provoked directly by a serious miscalculation, by which the Zhou royal armies were sent up the Jing River valley to attack some of the allied Zhou polities as a solution to the political dispute that had been building up for years at the Zhou royal court. The royal armies met the counter-attack by the Xianyun and collapsed, opening up the way for the enemies to march on the Zhou capital. I will begin by evaluating some traditional views on the historical downfall. Through clarifying chronological problems involving the reign, the thread of historical development through the eleven years can be gradually established. In the last part of the chapter, I will study two difficult geographical questions, and the answers to these questions will help us reconfigure the fall of the Western Zhou state in geographical terms.

VIEWS AND SCHOLARSHIP

In the 2,000 years after the Western Zhou dynasty, the historical downfall continued to be mentioned and discussed in the historiographical tradition of China. This was partly because of the high prestige that Confucianism invested in the dynasty as its honorable name came back alive repeatedly in Chinese history,[2] and partly because of the need to answer a question that was hovering around the prescribed prestige: if the Western Zhou dynasty was so perfect an age of good politics and institutions as Confucius tended to suggest, then why had it to fall, and to give rise to a time of political disorder and moral decline? The issue, though a historical one, clearly had significant moral and metaphorical implications for later politicians and historians.

In fact, even in the period not very far removed from the fall of the Western Zhou, there were already different opinions regarding the causes of the historical downfall. A reference to the incident of 771 BC is found in a political discourse that took place at the court of the state of Jin during the reign of Duke Xian (r. 676–651 BC), one hundred years after the fall of the Western Zhou.[3] In a campaign against the Lirong 驪戎, located in the Lishan area of Shaanxi, the Jin troops captured Li Ji 驪姬, a princess of the Lirong tribe. However, Li Ji soon became favored by the duke over

---

[2] There were a number of later Chinese dynasties that adopted the name "Zhou," including the Northern Zhou (AD 557–581), Wu Zhou (AD 690–704), and Later Zhou (AD 951–960).

[3] See *Guoyu*, 7, pp. 252–53.

his primary wife as well as his two earlier consorts, thus creating a political dilemma at the Jin court. The campaign is mentioned retrospectively in the *Zuozhuan* under the twenty-eighth year (666 BC) of Duke Zhuang of Lu.[4] According to the *Guoyu*, before the campaign a divination was conducted in the Jin court which was interpreted by the court historian Shi Su 史蘇 to be "victorious but inauspicious." On a later occasion, after the campaign, Shi Su explained his judgment that favorite concubines, for instance Li Ji, were "female weapons" that the conquered states would use to avenge their conquerors. To strengthen his position, Shi Su said: when King You of Zhou attacked the polity Bao 褒, the people of Bao made peace with Zhou by presenting a beauty named Bao Si 褒姒, who then became a lover of the king and bore him a son. She plotted the expulsion of the legitimate royal heir to the state of Shen 申, and Shen then called on the support of the Western Rong and destroyed Zhou. Since Bao Si caused the fall of the Western Zhou, Shi Su predicted that Jin was bound to fall because of the rise of Li Ji.[5]

Shi Su's theory was contested by another court official of Jin, Guo Yan 郭偃, who insisted: "The falls of the three dynasties were just appropriate! The rulers of the people indulged in evil but did not think it ill; (they) were extreme in extravagance and never ceased to enjoy it; (they) behaved according to their arbitrary wills which none was not sick of. Therefore, when approaching the time of their fall they still could not have learned from the fate of their preceding dynasties."[6] Rejecting Shi Su's rather fatalist interpretation of the fall of the Western Zhou which is used to anticipate the future civil war in Jin, Guo Yan's view brought out the moral issue of the rulers: it was King You's own misconduct, and not Bao Si, that caused the fall of the Zhou dynasty. Therefore, Guo argues, although Li Ji will cause turmoil in Jin, because of the support of the great families and the neighboring states, Jin will not be destroyed by her.

Both of these two pre-Qin views reported by the *Guoyu* on the dynastic downfall of the Western Zhou had exerted their influence on later historians, but Shi Su's view seems to have had more followers. Influenced by Shi Su, Sima Qian's presentation of the fall of the Western Zhou in the *Shiji* narrative was clearly centered on the role of Bao Si, although he also mentioned King You's use of an immoral minister, Guo Shifu 虢石父, probably the head of the Guo lineage. Sima Qian narrated at length the story of Bao Si's birth, suggesting that she was the incarnation of an ancient evil spirit "God/Goddess of Bao" from the Xia dynasty. In the *Shiji* version of the story, the mysterious Bao Si would not smile, nor would she even speak much. King You, who was seemingly haunted by her mysterious power, tried everything to please her. For her amusement, King You repeatedly teased the many regional rulers by lighting up the beacon fires to summon

4 See *Zuozhuan*, 10, p. 1781.   5 See *Guoyu*, 7, pp. 252–56.   6 See *Guoyu*, 7, p. 257.

them to defend the royal capital when there was no enemy at hand. When the Quanrong actually attacked the capital these rulers did not come to the rescue of the king, who was thereupon killed.[7] In this way, Sima Qian held Bao Si primarily responsible for the fall of the Western Zhou dynasty, while King You was only seduced by her mysterious power.

From the Tang dynasty, the *Shiji*'s presentation was followed in standard historical writings, for instance in Zheng Qiao's 鄭樵 (AD 1104–62) long narrative of Western Zhou history in his celebrated historical encyclopedia *Tongzhi*.[8] However, there were some progressive thinkers, for instance Liu Zongyuan 柳宗元 (AD 773–819) of Tang and Li Zhi 李贄 (AD 1527–1602) of Ming, who cast serious doubts on the story of Bao Si. The former, pursuing an argument somewhat similar to Guo Yan's, suggested that the cause of Zhou's fall must be sought in King You's own conduct, but to speak about "God/Goddess of Bao" is not appropriate for gentlemen. However, differing from the pre-Qin critic who thought King You was morally wrong, Liu tended to think that he adopted a wrong policy which resulted in the alienation of the wise advisers but offered opportunities for the immoral men.[9] This tradition of criticism was fully developed in an essay titled "Debating Bao Si" ("Bao Si bian" 褒姒辯), written by the Qing scholar Jiao Xun 焦循 (AD 1763–1820). Informed by the evidential textual scholarship developed by his predecessors and contemporaries, Jiao systematically exposed the internal contradictions in the logic as well as the historical sequence of the story of Bao Si. For instance Jiao Xun argued that, since the story in the *Shiji* says that Bao Si was conceived by a young concubine in the palace of King Li who then gave birth after fourteen years of pregnancy when the king was in exile, at the time when King Xuan was established, she must have been fifty when she came into King You's favor and sixty when the Quanrong attacked Zhou, too old for the king to fall in love with. Jiao concluded that the story is ridiculous and untrustworthy.[10]

However, the most systematic pre-modern study of the fall of the Western Zhou, or of Western Zhou history in general, was Cui Shu's 崔述 (AD 1740–1816) *Feng Hao kaoxin lu* 豐鎬考信錄 (Examining the Beliefs of Feng and Hao). Cui simply dismissed the story of Bao Si and looked for the causes of Zhou's fall in the politics of King You. Taking a position very similar to that of Liu Zongyuan, he suggested that the fall of the Western Zhou was first of all caused by King You's failure to choose men of dignity as ministers. Secondly, Cui considered the fall of the Western Zhou to be the result of the interaction of internal factors with external ones, seeing it as the final

---

[7] See *Shiji*, 4, pp. 147–49.   [8] See *Tongzhi*, 3, p. 52.

[9] See Liu Zongyuan, *Liu Hedong ji*, vol. 3 (Beijing: Zhenghua, 1961), p. 786. Li Zhi, on the other hand, sneered at the story of Bao Si as it is told in the *Shiji*; see Li Zhi, *Shigang pingyao* (Beijing: Zhonghua, 1974), pp. 33–34.

[10] See Jiao Xun, *Diaogu ji* (Shanghai: Shangwu, 1936), pp. 118–19. See also *Shiji*, 4, p. 147 (Nienhauser, *The Grand Scribe's Records*, 1, pp. 73–74).

outcome of the long-standing incursion by the so-called "barbarians," the history of which can be traced back to the reign of King Mu. In addition to these two factors, Cui believed that there was a society-wide decline in moral standards and respectable customs that also contributed to the fall of the Western Zhou.[11]

The above comments and studies reflect a continuous intellectual discourse regarding the dynastic downfall of the Western Zhou. It seems likely that the effort among the traditional scholars to explain the fall emphasized either the role played by the mysterious Bao Si or the impact of King You's wrong policy which blocked the service of worthy ministers. Particularly in this latter case, one can clearly see a reflection of the most important political concerns of the intellectuals about their own future in the scholar-bureaucratic system of imperial China. In this system, the fall of the Western Zhou is likely to have been encoded with a powerful symbolic meaning.

Modern historical scholarship, both in China and in the West, has produced little to add to these points already made by pre-modern scholars. The story of Bao Si continues to be told in many history books, often with careful noting of its legendary features. More cautious scholars have also tried to set the incident in the larger context of invasions by foreign enemies, especially the Xianyun, that took place during the last reigns of the Western Zhou dynasty.[12] However, not much effort has been made to address the complex historical questions involving both internal politics and outside pressures on the basis of a comprehensive examination of all textual as well as archaeological evidence. In recent decades, the important discovery of late Western Zhou tombs in the cemeteries of some regional states, most notably Jin, Guo, and Ying, has again raised scholarly interest in late Western Zhou history. A new view of the fall of the Western Zhou as the manifestation of the factional struggles at the Zhou court has been suggested by some young scholars. In an article published in 1986, Taniguchi Yoshisuke, working mainly on poems in the *Book of Poetry*, suggested that the fall had its origins in the succession dispute at the time of King You that was actually a struggle between two clans, the Si 姒 and the Jiang 姜, both being the traditional marriage partners of the Zhou royal house. Behind this was a struggle between two groups of regional Zhou states that were located in the west and east and derived their origins from the two named clans; the fall of the Western Zhou, in this view, was the victory of the Jiang clan over the Si.[13] In a more recent study of the early history of the state of Jin, Jae-hoon Shim compared different sources concerning the Western–Eastern Zhou transition and suggested that Zhou was divided between two factions, with King You, Bao Si's son Bo Fu 伯服, and the Guo 虢 lineage on one side, and Prince Yijiu 宜臼, the states of Shen 申, Zheng 鄭, and

[11] See Cui Shu, *Cui Dongbi yishu*, ed. Gu Jiegang (Shanghai: Shanghai Guji, 1983), pp. 246–47, 334–35.
[12] See Hsu and Linduff, *Western Chou Civilization*, pp. 259–60.
[13] See Taniguchi Yoshisuke, "Sei Shū metsubō no ichi sokumen," *Gakurin* 8 (1986), 11–12.

Lu 魯, and even the Western Rong, on the other.[14] The fall of the Western Zhou was the victory of the second faction over the first.

These new views, though they need to be refined with a more comprehensive understanding of the evidence, depart significantly from the traditional presentations of the fall of the Western Zhou that emphasize either the role of Bao Si or the misrule of King You. Instead, we should consider the fall rather as a natural or logical development from the internal politics of the Western Zhou state. In this perspective, the role played by external factors was merely an extension of Zhou's internal politics.

DISCOVERING THE FALL OF THE WESTERN ZHOU

In order to understand the historical process of the downfall of the Western Zhou dynasty and discover the real driving power behind the incident of 771 BC, a fully fledged analysis of the available information is needed. In this section, I will examine all the evidence on the period and propose a new reading of the political development involving both the Zhou court and some of the local polities leading up to the fall of the dynasty. However, the correct configuration of the politics of King You depends on the accurate sorting out of the sequence of the historical events that happened in his eleven years. This is done in appendix 3 on the basis of careful comparison of the basic chronicle of the reign found in the *Bamboo Annals* and other relevant textual records. Therefore, the reader is advised to consult the appendix closely when reading the following analysis.

The historiographical development of the role of Bao Si

Since the traditional presentation of the fall of the Western Zhou has long been clouded by the mysterious role of Bao Si, we must first try to solve this puzzle that is important to understanding all other puzzles of the period. As mentioned above, internal contradictions in the story of Bao Si's birth had already been pointed out by Jiao Xun 200 years ago, and there is no need to repeat these points here. On the other hand, I believe that, as our evidence shows, the role of Bao Si as presented by later historians was the result of a long evolution that took place in the historiography of ancient China. Therefore, the task here is to demonstrate how the Bao Si story evolved and took its form of presentation in later histories. And if we can discern these later strata in the legend, and therefore differentiate later fabrications from the original core of the story, we can probably reveal what her real historical role may have been, or whether there was such a role. The correct

---

[14] See Jae-hoon Shim, "The Early Development of the State of Jin: From Its Enfeoffment to the Hegemony of Wen Gong (r. 636–628 BC)," unpublished PhD thesis, University of Chicago (1998), pp. 139–50.

understanding of the situation will pave the way for a new interpretation of the fall of the Western Zhou.

Let us begin with the story in the "Zhengyu" chapter of the *Guoyu*, supposedly told by Shi Bo 史伯, a historian at the court of King You:[15]

且宣王之時有童謠曰：“檿弧箕服，實亡周國。”於是宣王聞之，有夫婦鬻是器者，王使執而戮之。府之小妾生女而非王子也，懼而棄之。此人也，收以奔褒。天命此久矣，其又何可為乎？《訓語》有之曰：“夏之衰也，褒人之神化為二龍，以同於王庭，而言曰：‘余，褒之二君也。’夏后氏卜殺之與去之與止之，莫吉。卜請其漦而藏之，吉。乃布幣焉而策告之，龍亡而漦在，櫝而藏之，傳郊之。”及殷、周，莫之發也。及厲王之末，發而觀之，漦流于庭，不可除也。王使婦人不幃而譟之，化為玄黿，以入于王府。府之童妾未及齓而遭之，及笄而孕，當宣王之時而生。不夫而育，故懼而棄之。為弧服者方戮在路，夫婦哀其夜號也，而取之以逸，奔于褒。褒人褒姁有獄，而以為入於王。王遂寘之，而嬖是女也，使至於為后而生伯服。天之生此久矣，其為毒也大矣，將使候淫德而加之焉。毒之酉臘者，其殺也滋速。

Moreover, there was a children's rhyme in the time of King Xuan, saying: "The bow of wild mulberry and the quiver of beanstalk will indeed destroy the Zhou state!" Thereupon, when King Xuan heard of a husband and his wife selling these items, [he] ordered them to be arrested and executed. A young concubine in the palace bore a daughter who was not the child of the king; she was frightened and abandoned her. This couple picked her up and fled to Bao. Heaven has commanded this a long time ago, so what can [you] do about it? The *Xunyu* says: "When the Xia declined, the God/Goddess of the Bao people turned into two dragons and together stopped at the royal court [of Xia], saying: 'We are the two lords of Bao.' The Xia emperor divined about whether he should kill them, or expel them, or keep them; none of these was auspicious. [He then] divined about requesting their saliva to be preserved; it was auspicious. Thus, [he] laid out jades and silk and presented the dragons with a document written on bamboo strips. The dragons vanished and left their saliva there. [The emperor] concealed the saliva in a wooden box and successively worshiped it outside the capital". In Yin and Zhou times, the box was never opened. But at the end of King Li's reign, [he] opened the box and saw it. The saliva overflowed in the court and could not be cleaned up. When the king ordered women to strip naked and yell at it, it then turned into a huge black reptile and entered the royal chamber. A young girl in the royal palace who had not yet completely lost her baby teeth encountered it and became pregnant by the time she was old enough to pin her hair up; she gave birth to a child at the time of King Xuan. Bearing [a child] with no husband, [she] was frightened and abandoned the girl. The couple who sold the bow and quiver were on their way to flee. They could not bear the night-screaming [of the girl], and thus picked her up and fled to Bao. Bao Ju, a man of Bao, had a lawsuit; he thus sent her to the king. The king received her and fell in love with her; he established her queen and she bore [for the king] Prince Bo Fu. Heaven created it a long time ago and its poison is great! [Heaven] will let [her] wait until [the king] fully abused virtue and then she will add to it [more crimes]. When the poison is fully developed, death is also imminent.

This long narrative appears in the midst of the historian Shi Bo's criticism of King You's misrule. In this narrative, Shi Bo quotes two sources, a children's

---

[15] See *Guoyu*, 16, p. 519.

rhyme and a lost book called *Xunyu* 訓語. However, neither of these quotes seems to have much to do with Bao Si, nor do they readily justify Shi Bo's portrayal of her as an evil woman. From another point of view, it was possibly Shi Bo, as long as he was the speaker, or perhaps the composer of the *Guoyu* text, who had correlated the two sources to create a fascinating but self-contradictory story.

However, there is another narrative mentioning Bao Si, a much shorter one by Shi Su, in the "Jinyu" chapter of the *Guoyu*. Differing from the "Zhengyu" account that Bao Si was actually paid to King You as a fine perhaps for a failed lawsuit, the "Jinyu" had a campaign undertaken by King You against the polity of Bao which, in the speaker's view, was a close analogy to Duke Xian's campaign against the Lirong. According to this the people of Bao made peace with the king by presenting him with Bao Si. The account goes on to say that she came into the favor of the king and bore him prince Bofu. Then, she plotted with the evil minister Guo Shifu 虢石父 to expel the royal heir, Yijiu 宜臼.[16] The Shi Su version of the story is different not only in its simplicity but in its underlying philosophy: Bao Si was the means by which the conquered exacted revenge on the conquerors – "a female weapon." But in the Shi Bo version of the story, she was the incarnation of an ancient spirit, evoked by Heaven in time to punish the Zhou king for his wrong-doings and to bring the Zhou dynasty down. It has been suggested by some scholars that the "Zhengyu" chapter was probably composed later than the "Jinyu" chapter of the *Guoyu*.[17] If this is indeed true, the differences between the two versions may reflect a change in the perception of the fall of the Western Zhou among the historians and philosophers of the Warring States period. But they may simply represent two competing traditions of the life story of Bao Si.

These two versions were certainly both known to Sima Qian, but in the *Shiji* he clearly adopted the narrative details from the Shi Bo version of Bao Si, while taking Shi Su's position on her causing the fall of the Western Zhou dynasty. In fact, Sima Qian not only copied the Shi Bo version, but added to it another part, in some ways the most famous part of the story. It seems very likely that this particular part was copied and modified from the *Lüshi chunqiu* 呂氏春秋, compiled even later than the "Zhengyu," in about 239 BC:[18]

周宅酆鎬近戎人，與諸侯約為高葆，置鼓其上，遠近相聞。即戎寇至，傳鼓相告，諸侯之兵皆至救天子。戎寇嘗至，幽王擊鼓，諸侯之兵皆至，褒姒大說喜之。幽王欲褒姒之笑也，因數擊鼓，諸侯之兵數之而無寇。至於後，戎寇真至，幽王擊鼓，諸侯兵不至，幽王之身乃死於驪山之下，為天下笑。

---

[16] See *Guoyu*, 7, p. 255.
[17] See Wei Juxian, *Gushi yanjiu*, vol. 1 (Shanghai: Shangwu, 1934), p. 164; see also Loewe, *Early Chinese Texts*, p. 264.
[18] See *Lushi chunqiu*, 22, pp. 712–13. For the date of composition of the text, see Loewe, *Early Chinese Texts*, p. 324.

The homes of the Zhou, Feng and Hao, were near the barbarians. [The king] agreed with the many rulers to build up a high fortress and to set up a drum on it, which could be heard from a distance. When the barbarians were present, the beating drums would inform the many rulers, whose troops would all come to rescue the Son of Heaven. Once when the barbarians came, King You beat the drum and the troops of the many rulers all rushed in, Bao Si was greatly amused by this. King You wanted Bao Si to smile, so [he] repeatedly beat the drum, and the troops of the many rulers repeatedly came but there were no barbarians. Later on, when the barbarian really came, King You beat the drum but the troops of the many rulers did not come. King You therefore died at the foot of Lishan Mountain, and was laughed at by all people under Heaven.

In the *Shiji*, the story becomes:[19]

褒姒不好笑，幽王慾其笑萬方，故不笑。幽王為烽燧大鼓，有寇至則舉烽火。諸侯悉至，至而無寇，褒姒乃大笑。幽王說之。為數舉烽火。其後不信，諸侯亦不至 … 申侯怒，與繒、西夷犬戎攻幽王。幽王舉烽火徵兵，兵莫至。遂殺幽王驪山下，虜褒姒，盡取周賂而去。

Bao Si did not like to smile, and King You tried ten thousand ways to make her smile, but still she did not smile. King You built a beacon-fire tower with a great drum on it, and lit the beacon-fire whenever there was an enemy presence. [Once] the many rulers all came, but there were no enemies, and Bao Si then burst out laughing. King You was pleased, so he repeatedly lit the fire. After this he lost the trust of the many rulers, who, more and more, would not come again . . . The Ruler of Shen was enraged, so he, together with Zeng and the western barbarian Quanrong, attacked King You. King You lit the beacon-fire to summon the troops, but the troops did not come. [The enemies] then killed King You at the foot of Lishan Mountain, captured Bao Si, and went away with all the treasures of Zhou.

The "beacon-fire" was clearly Sima Qian's invention, because the *Lüshi chunqiu* only says "drum"; there is hardly any evidence that such an alarm system of beacon-fires existed in pre-Qin times, not to mention during the Western Zhou. More importantly, Sima Qian bestowed on Bao Si a more mysterious feature: she would not smile, nor would she even speak. In such a way, her evil power "demanded" that King You try to please her by whatever means. This is certainly not the way Bao Si appears in the *Lüshi chunqiu* or in the *Guoyu*. While in the *Lüshi chunqiu* the story was merely used to show how reckless a ruler could be to confuse his subjects, Sima Qian used it to show how evil and ill-willed Bao Si was to cause the fall of the Western Zhou dynasty. Given the great influence of the *Shiji* on later historical writings, the *Shiji* version thus became the mainstream story of Bao Si. However, the development of the story did not stop with the *Shiji*; by the twelfth century AD, Bao Si had acquired an additional strange habit: listening to the sound of silk tearing. According to the *Tongzhi*:[20]

褒姒好聞裂繒之聲，王發繒，裂之以適其意。

Bao Si liked to hear the sound of tearing silk. The king therefore levied silk and tore it in order to comply with her wishes.

---

[19] See *Shiji*, 4, pp. 148–49 (Nienhauser, *The Grand Scribe's Records*, 1, p. 74).
[20] See *Tongzhi*, 3, p. 52.

I suspect that this new development probably had something to do with the name of the state of Zeng 鄑, written in the *Guoyu* and the *Shiji* as Zeng 繒, which, according to the *Current Bamboo Annals*, was attacked by the Zhou troops in 780 BC.[21] It is very likely that this new element is based on a misreading and misinterpretion of the meaning of the character *zeng* 繒. As demonstrated in appendix 3, the attacked state was written probably in the tomb version of the *Bamboo Annals* as *zeng* 鄑; the character *zeng* 繒 (literarily meaning "silk") in the *Guoyu* for the same state, then copied into the *Shiji*, was clearly a graphic variant of the character *zeng* 鄑 in a different textual tradition. By the medieval period, the original character *zeng* 鄑 in the tomb version of the *Bamboo Annals* had already been misquoted as *kuai* 鄶, causing confusion with another state denoted by the character Kuai 鄶 located in a different region. Therefore, the connection between *zeng* 鄑 and *zeng* 繒 was lost, and the meaning "silk" associated with the latter character gave rise to the story of Bao Si being fond of listening to the sound of tearing silk. I think that here careful textual analysis can clearly explain the origin of the new fictional account transmitted by the *Tongzhi*.

This development of the Bao Si story owes a great deal to an ancient belief that evil women caused the fall of dynasties. Although evil men would have had many more chances to cause the fall of a dynasty, when a woman was involved in dynastic turmoil, even if her role was insignificant, such a role would be exaggerated, and the woman would be demonized in history. The development of the story of Bao Si as shown above was typically a long process of the gradual demonization of Bao Si. Such a perception of women's role in history, which is deeply rooted in men's objection to women's involvement in politics, has a long history in a world that has always been dominated by men. In the "Mushi" 牧誓 chapter of the *Shangshu*, King Wu cited an ancient proverb: "The hen does not announce the morning. The crowing of a hen in the morning indicates the subversion of the family!"[22] In the poem "Zhan yang" 瞻仰 (no. 264) in the *Book of Poetry*, the poet asserts: "No, disorder does not come down from Heaven, rather it is the spawn of these women!"[23] Notably, a mysterious story regarding the fall of the Shang dynasty, with Da Ji 妲己 as the evil woman, developed in very much the same way as the Bao Si story.[24]

However, in perhaps a more profound sense, through the demonization of Bao Si, the contradiction between the prestige of the Western Zhou dynasty and its humiliating end can be properly reconciled. By finding someone to blame for the fall of the dynasty, the later historians and politicians were also able to work out a psychological balance that enabled them to continue to perceive the Western Zhou dynasty as the model dynasty. As the following discussion will further demonstrate, these later fabrications

---

[21] See *Zhushu jinian*, 2, p. 16 (Legge, *The Shoo King*, Prolegomena, p. 157).
[22] See *Shangshu*, 11, p. 183 (Legge, *The Shoo King*, p. 302).
[23] See *Shijing*, 18.5, p. 577 (Waley, *The Book of Songs*, p. 284).   [24] See *Shiji*, 3, p. 105.

regarding Bao Si's birth, her mysterious conduct, and her role in causing
King You to cheat the many regional rulers and to bring the dynasty down
were constructed around some core information preserved in the *Book of
Poetry* that shows that she probably did play a political role in King You's
reign and was an ideal person to be blamed for the dynastic downfall. If her
name was indeed Bao Si, which we have no grounds to doubt, she may have
been from the mountainous area of southern Shaanxi, as Bao was located
in present-day Mianxian 勉縣 in the upper Han River valley.[25] However,
in order to understand the real history of the fall of the Western Zhou, we
must first of all liberate ourselves from the influence of the legends.

Partisanship and political struggle at the Zhou court

The historiographical tradition attributes to King You a number of inauspicious features. According to a story cited in the *Taiping yulan*, King You was
born prematurely and was nearly abandoned by his father King Xuan. It was
only because King Xuan had no other children that You was left to live and
went on to succeed to royal power.[26] The eleven-year reign of King You was
an eventful and deeply troubled period in Chinese history. The situation
was especially complicated by the interweaving of the political struggle in
the royal court with the court's conflict with some regional states, and also
by the interplay between political crises and natural disasters. But the root
of the political chaos that eventually brought the dynasty down was in the
transition of power from the court of King Xuan to the court of King You.

In the first five years after King You came to power, the politics of the
Zhou court involved a very important historical figure called the "August
Father" (Huangfu 皇父). According to the *Current Bamboo Annals*, in his
first year (781 BC), King You bestowed on Huangfu a royal command,
appointing him "Grand Marshal and Chief" (*Taishi yinshi* 太師尹氏).[27]
This entry suggests that Huangfu probably exercised authority over both
the field armies and the court. It is very important to note, however, that
Huangfu's power and prestige probably began much earlier than King You's
succession, for he was already appointed Grand Marshal by King Xuan in
his second year (826 BC), forty-four years before his reappointment to the
same position by King You. Then in the sixth year of King Xuan (820 BC),

[25] The "Geography" chapter of the *Hanshu* records that there was a Baozhong County 襄中縣 in
Hanzhong Commandery 漢中郡 during the Han dynasty. See *Hanshu*, 28, p. 1,596. The Bao River
valley, where Bao was probably located, runs through the Qingling Mountains south into the Han
River, providing an important transportation route between the Wei and Han valleys.
[26] See *Taiping yulan*, 85, p. 403.
[27] See *Zhushu jinian*, 2, p. 16 (Legge, *The Shoo King*, Prolegomena, p. 157). Most scholars agree that in
the middle and later Western Zhou bronze inscriptions, *yinshi* is the abbreviation of "Chief Interior
Scribe" (*Neishiyin* 內史尹) or "Chief Document Maker" (*Zuoceyin* 作冊尹), or more likely the two
combined as the head of the various secretarial officials at the Zhou court. See Zhang Yachu and
Liu Yu, *Xi Zhou jinwen guanzhi yanjiu* (Beijing: Zhonghua, 1986), pp. 56–57.

the *Current Bamboo Annals* reports that he served as an eminent military commander on a royal campaign against the Xurong 徐戎 in the Huai River region. This campaign is the subject of the poem "Changwu" 常武 (no. 263) in the *Book of Poetry*.[28] The high status of Huangfu can also be seen in his title "August"; in the entire corpus of Western Zhou inscriptions, the only other person to have been called by the title was the Duke of Shao, the most eminent official at the later court of King Cheng and that of King Kang.[29]

The historicity of Huangfu can be fully confirmed by Western Zhou bronze inscriptions for he was apparently the principal caster of a group of bronzes, discovered in 1933 in the Qiyi (Zhouyuan) area (Fig. 31).[30] Given his extremely long career and eminent position during the reign of King Xuan, by the time he was reappointed "Grand Marshal and Chief" by King You, Huangfu must have been at least near the age of seventy. And given his seniority and previous glory as the Grand Marshal for forty-four years, there can be no doubt that Huangfu was the central figure in the Zhou court at the time of King You's accession to power.

However, the *Current Bamboo Annals* reports, confirmed also by the poem "Shiyue zhi jiao" 十月之交 (no. 193) in the *Book of Poetry*, that in the fifth year of King You (777 BC) Huangfu constructed for himself a new residence at a place called Xiang 向, located to the north of Luoyi, in present-day Jiyuan 濟源, Henan, and permanently left the capital to spend the rest of his life in Xiang on the eastern plain.[31] This is certainly a very unusual political event, not because a senior official had to retire but because, for whatever reason, he had to leave the royal domain in Shaanxi and move his permanent residence to the distant east. The only analogy in Western Zhou history was probably the Duke of Zhou's residence in the east at the beginning of the dynasty as the result of a major political dispute between the duke and the young King Cheng (r. 1042/35–1006 BC) who had the Duke of Shao at his back.[32] It is interesting, as our chronological analysis in appendix 3 shows, that in the same year the legitimate royal heir Yijiu

---

[28] See *Zhushu jinian*, 2, p. 14 (Legge, *The Shoo King*, Prolegomena, p. 155); see also *Shijing*, 18.5, p. 576 (Waley, *The Book of Songs*, pp. 281–83).

[29] For instance, the Duke of Shao is referred to as "August Heavenly Chief the Grand Protector" (*Huangtian yin taibao* 皇天尹太保) in the inscription of the Zuoce Da *fangding* 作冊大方鼎 (JC: 2758).

[30] This includes the two Han Huangfu *ding* 函皇父鼎 (JC: 2548, 2745), the four Han Huangfu *gui* 函皇父簋 (JC: 4143), and the Han Huangfu *pan* 函皇父盤 (JC: 10164). Unfortunately, the content of the inscriptions on these bronzes is very simple. See *Qingtongqi tushi* (Beijing: Wenwu, 1960), pp. 20–21, pls. 61–6.

[31] This Xiang is mentioned together with other settlements in the *Zuozhuan* (eleventh year of Duke Ying), all located at the southwest end of the Taihang–Yellow River belt, crossing the river to the north from Luoyang. The commentators and historical geographers commonly locate Xiang in Zhi County 軹縣 of the Han dynasty which is present-day Jiyuan. See *Zuozhuan*, 4, p. 1,737; Jiang Yong, *Chunqiu dili kaoshi*, p. 10.

[32] For an excellent analysis of this issue, see Edward Shaughnessy, "The Duke of Zhou's Retirement in the East and the Beginnings of the Minister–Monarch Debate in Chinese Political Philosophy," *Early China* 18 (1993), 64–72.

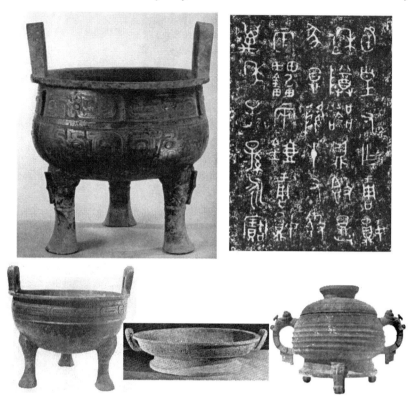

Fig. 31 The Han Huangfu bronzes from Zhouyuan (from *Shaanxi qingtongqi*, p. 66; *Qingtongqi tushi*, pp. 59–64)

宜臼 was forced out of the capital and took refuge in the state of Shen. This is another very unusual development. I believe that this was an important turning point in the history of the reign of King You, the beginning of the end of the Western Zhou. Does the retirement of Huangfu in the east mark the peaceful and honorable abdication of the respected court official Huangfu from power, or a disgraceful defeat at the hands of his political enemies? Unfortunately, our historical texts do not provide details on the retirement of Huangfu, but the Zhou literature offers us some important clues to understand what was outlined in rather a simplistic way in the historical texts. Our sources suggest that the latter is more likely to have been the case. Huangfu's retirement in the east is the subject of the poem "Shiyue zhi jiao" in the *Book of Poetry* (Waley's translation):[33]

1	十月之交，	With the alignment in the tenth month,
2	朔日辛卯。	On the first day, *xinmao* of the cycle,
3	日有食之，	The sun was eclipsed,

---

[33] See *Shijing*, 12.2, pp. 445–47 (Waley, *The Book of Songs*, pp. 170–72).

4 亦孔之醜。	And it was so very frightening.
5 彼月而微,	First the moon grew dim,
6 此日而微。	Then the sun grew dim too.
7 今此下民,	All of the folk here below
8 亦孔之哀。	Were in great lament.

9 日月告凶,	The sun and moon foretell disaster
10 不用其行。	When they do not follow their normal path.
11 四國無政,	No state in the realm is well-governed
12 不用其良。	When it fails to use its good men.
13 彼月而食,	The eclipse of the moon,
14 則維其常。	Is something often seen.
15 此日而食,	But this eclipse of the sun!
16 于何不臧。	Where have we gone astray?

17 爗爗震電,	Slashing was the lightning with its thunder
18 不寧不令。	Nothing was settled, nothing well run,
19 百川沸騰,	All the streams boiled and overflowed,
20 山冢崒崩。	Mountaintops crashed and tumbled down.
21 高岸爲谷,	High ledges became deep valleys,
22 深谷爲陵。	And valleys rose up into ridges.
23 哀今之人,	Take pity on people now;
24 胡憯莫徵。	Why does no one stop this?

25 皇父卿士,	Huangfu was Prime Minister,
26 番維司徒。	Fan was Master of Multitudes,[34]
27 家伯爲宰,	Jiabo was Superintendent of the royal household;
28 仲允膳夫。	Zhong Yun, the Provisioner
29 聚子內史,	And Zouzi, Interior Scribe,
30 蹶維趣馬。	Jue was Master of Horses,
31 楀維師氏,	Yu was the Marshal.
32 艷妻煽方處。	The lovely consort, so resplendent, had just taken her position.

33 抑此皇父,	Come now, Huangfu,
34 豈曰不時。	How can things be so untimely?
35 胡爲我作,	Why do you send us off to labor
36 不即我謀。	Without considering our pressing needs?
37 徹我墻屋,	Fallen down are our walls and houses,
38 田卒汙萊。	The fields unkept and overgrown,

[34] Some of the official titles in this stanza are rendered here differently from Waley's original translation which has: "Minister of Land" (*Situ* 司徒), "Chief of Officials" (*zai* 宰), "Steward of the Table" (*shanfu* 膳夫), "Royal Scribe" (*neishi* 內史), "Master of the Stables" (*quma* 趣馬), and "Captain of the Guard" (*shishi* 師氏). The revision here is based on the functions and differentiation of their equivalents in the bronze inscriptions. For instance, "Minister of Multitudes (*Situ* 司徒) is different from "Minister of Land" (*situ* 司土), "Interior Scribe" (*neishi* 內史) is different from "Scribe" (*shi* 史). For translations of these titles, see Li Feng, "'Offices' in Bronze Inscriptions," pp. 14–42.

39 曰予不戕,	And you say, "I am not mistreating you,
40 禮則然亦。	These are just the rules."
41 皇父孔聖,	Huangfu, you are so very wise;
42 作都于向。	Choosing Xiang as your new city site,
43 擇三有事,	You select three ministers to serve,
44 亶侯多藏。	Truly many are stores and treasures.
45 不憖遺一老,	You were unwilling to leave even one senior man behind,[35]
46 俾守我土。	Whereby to protect our king.
47 擇有車馬,	You selected those with carriages and horses
48 以居徂向。	To resettle them off in Xiang.
49 黽勉從事,	Hard you have worked in your service,[36]
50 不敢告勞。	Daring not complain about the toil.
51 無罪無辜,	Without offense, you are quite innocent,
52 讒口囂囂。	But slanderous mouths clamor on.
53 下民之孽,	The hardships of the folk here below
54 匪降自天。	Are not brought on by Heaven;
55 噂沓背憎,	No, nice to meet, then a stab in the back,
56 職競由人。	Violence comes from the acts of men.
57 悠悠我里,	Unending is my malady,
58 亦孔之痗。	Making me so very pained.
59 四方有羨,	Abundance fills every land,
60 我獨居憂。	I alone am lost in grief
61 民莫不逸,	The people all are slipping away,
62 我獨不敢休。	I alone do not dare take rest.
63 天命不徹,	The Mandate of Heaven is unfathomable;[37]
64 我不敢 傚我友自逸。	Yet I dare not imitate my colleagues and slip away myself.

As noted in the introduction, we do not know when the poem was actually composed, or by whom. However, since all scholars can agree on the mid-sixth century BC as the date for the latest poems in the *Book of Poetry* (mainly in the "Airs of the States" section) and on a Western Zhou date for at least some of the relatively earlier poems, especially those from the "Hymns" and "Odes" sections, this would give a rough date of composition of the

---

[35] Here Waley has "old guard" for *lao* 老, which certainly does not have to be guard, but more likely refers to senior officials.

[36] Here Waley has "we" instead of "you" as the subject of the line, as for line 51 where he uses "I am" instead of "you are." But this does not seem to connect well with the following line about clamor. I think, with respect to lines 11–12, these two lines are clearly talking about Huangfu.

[37] Waley has "Decrees of Heaven" for *tianming* 大命, which is more practically translated as "Mandate of Heaven."

poem not very far removed from the last reign of the Western Zhou of which it speaks. In fact, a significant point in the poem is that it includes a list of official titles (lines 25–31) that accurately summarizes the most significant offices in the Zhou government during the later Western Zhou as we know them from the bronze inscriptions; in fact, the "Superintendent" was not important until the mid-Western Zhou and the "Provisioner" not until the late Western Zhou.[38] This presentation of late Western Zhou institutions in the poem suggests strongly that, whenever the poem was composed, whoever composed it must have had accurate knowledge about later Western Zhou politics and personnel. The great earthquake did not occur in the particular year of Huangfu's abdication but, according to the *Current Bamboo Annals* and the *Guoyu*, in the second year of King You (780 BC);[39] in the same year or one year earlier, as some modern scientific studies show, there was indeed a solar eclipse visible in the Zhou capital area, showing again the historical value of the poem.[40]

However, previous interpretations of the poem have all followed the "Preface to the Poetry," traditionally attributed to Confucius' disciple Zi Xia, and the commentary by Zheng Xuan of the Han dynasty in supposing that the poem was a general criticism of the politics of the reign of King You.[41] Reading the poem in its historical context, I believe that the main subject of the poem is clearly the retirement of Huangfu, and not just the misrule of King You. The poem indeed reveals a serious political split between the eminent Huangfu and the newly rising King You, and this political conflict eventually resulted in the retirement of Huangfu from the capital. The poet relates the natural phenomena such as earthquake

---

[38] For a general discussion of these titles, see Hsu and Linduff, *Western Chou Civilization*, pp. 230–49. For a tentative reconstruction of late Western Zhou government, see Zhang Yachu and Liu Yu, *Xi Zhou jinwen guanzhi*, p. 110.

[39] See *Zhushu jinian*, 2, p. 16 (Legge, *The Shoo King*, Prolegomena, p. 157). The great earthquake reportedly caused the collapse of Qishan Mountain, and the three major rivers in Shaanxi, the Wei, Jing, and Luo, to dry up. In the *Guoyu*, this was taken by Bo Yangfu 伯陽父 as a very bad omen, anticipating the fall of the Western Zhou. See *Guoyu*, 1, pp. 26–27.

[40] The date of the solar eclipse mentioned in the poem is an important issue in the study of Western Zhou chronology. The traditional date for this solar eclipse is the sixth year of King You (776 BC). However, modern astronomical studies show that there was no solar eclipse in that year visible from the Zhou capital area. Instead, some identify this eclipse with one that occurred in 734 BC, a date that apparently contradicts the historical content of the poem "Shiyue zhi jiao." On the other hand, Fang Shanzhu has argued, as most scholars now accept, that this eclipse can be identified with the eclipse that occurred in 780 BC (Julian ephemeris day number 1436318), visible from the Zhou capital. On Stephenson and Houlden's historical maps of eclipses, this eclipse is dated to −780, corresponding to 781 BC See Joseph Needham, *Science and Civilisation in China*, vol. 3 (London: Cambridge University Press, 1959), p. 409; Fang Shanzhu, "Xi Zhou niandai xue shang de jige wenti," *Dalu zazhi* 51.1 (1975), 21–22; F. R. Stephenson and M. A. Houlden, *Atlas of Historical Eclipse Maps: East Asia 1500 BC–AD 1900* (Cambridge: Cambridge University Press, 1986), p. 89.

[41] In this view, all the people listed in the poem, including Huangfu, the beautiful wife (certainly Bao Si), and the king, are criticized by the poet. See *Shijing*, 12.2, pp. 445–46 (Waley, *The Book of Songs*, pp. 170–72). This view fails to explain the reason for Huangfu's retirement in the east, which is clearly the subject of the poem. Also, by treating Huangfu and the other four officials all as associates of Bao Si, it fails to see the actual power structure in the Zhou court. Historically, considering Huangfu's background, I believe there was little ground for him to join hands with Bao Si.

and solar eclipse that happened in the years previous to the retirement of Huangfu, which in his view was just as disastrous as the earthquake. The poet complains about Huangfu because, from his perspective, Huangfu irresponsibly left the king unguarded, and his move to the east caused disturbance in the capital area and drainage of its resources. At the same time, the poet is apparently sympathetic towards Huangfu, suggesting that he was the victim of the slanders of his enemies (lines 52–56) and of distrust by the king (lines 11–12). Importantly, lines 42–48 indicate that a number of senior officials (the old) had in time followed Huangfu in retiring from the Zhou court and in moving to the east, perhaps implying a breakup between the generation left over from King Xuan's time and a newly rising faction fostered by the king. Lines 45–46, "You were unwilling to leave even one senior man behind, whereby to protect our king," particularly suggest that Huangfu left the capital in anger.

In the personnel described in the poem (lines 25–32) where it names the six officials Fan 番, Jiabo 家伯, Zhong Yun 仲允, Zouzi 棸子, Jue 蹶, and Yu 楀, we see another strong link between the poem and the historical context in which the poet places his story. Besides Huangfu himself, the caster of the Han Huangfu bronzes, notably Jue, was probably Juefu who, as mentioned in chapter 2 (see p. 137), was on a diplomatic mission to the state of Hann in northern Hebei in the fourth year of King Xuan and is mentioned in the poem "Hanyi" of the *Book of Poetry*. Zhong Yun may have been from the same family, if not actually the same person, as Zhong Shanfu, who was also active during the preceding reign and was sent by King Xuan on a trip to the state of Qi in Shandong. Fan was probably the offspring of Fansheng 番生, an important official at the time of King Xuan, and the principal caster of the famous Fansheng *gui* 番生簋 (JC: 4326).[42] I believe that most of these officials were probably the political allies of Huangfu, but not, as Zheng Xuan's commentary suggests, the followers of Bao Si (in this view, Huangfu was also a follower of Bao Si). At the end of this list, the poet says that the "beautiful wife" – almost certainly, as all commentators agree, referring to Bao Si – was at this time just gaining power; this is consistent with the date in our chronological table that Bao Si came into King You's favor only two years earlier, in 779 BC (see appendix 3).

I believe that the new reading proposed above most reasonably explains the internal logic of the poem and is most consistent with the historical context in which the poem was placed. It always happens in the history of mankind that a new ruler will want to consolidate his power by replacing the older generation of eminent officials with his own men. In his struggle

---

[42] Guo Moruo identified this Fan with Fansheng; see Guo Moruo, *Liang Zhou jinwen ci daxi*, p. 133. However, in the Fansheng *gui* 番生簋, which is necessarily earlier than the time of King You, Fansheng was apparently the head of the entire court bureaucracy, in a higher position than Fan who was only the Minister of Multitudes. Therefore I consider them to be different individuals. For the Fansheng *gui*, see Shirakawa, "Kinbun tsūshaku," 27.160:422.

with Huangfu, King You may have had the assistance of his young wife Bao Si, who probably had her own ambition to become the future queen. Furthermore, this new reading is strongly supported by another poem, "Jie nanshan" 節南山 (no. 191) in the same section of the *Book of Poetry*, and the contents of the two poems are clearly connected. In fact, this is one of the few poems in the *Book of Poetry* that actually names the poet, in this case a person called Jiafu 家父. There is good reason to identify this Jiafu with Jiabo 家伯, the Superintendent and one of the possible associates of Huangfu mentioned in the "Shiyue zhi jiao," because there are examples in the bronze inscriptions that a person can be called by both terms.[43] If Jiafu was indeed Jiabo, this identification could suggest that the poem may have been composed before the fall of the dynasty, but it is certainly also possible that a later poet could speak through the mouth of an earlier politician. While the issue should be left open here, the important point is that, whoever the composer was, the poem itself apparently speaks from the standpoint of the Huangfu party, while sharply criticizing the opposition party associated with King You:[44]

1	節彼南山,	High-crested are those southern hills,
2	維石巖巖。	With rocks piled high and towering.
3	赫赫師尹,	Majestic are you, Marshal and Chief,[45]
4	民具爾瞻。	To whom all the people look.
5	憂心如惔	Grief is burning in their hearts.
6	不敢戲談。	But they dare not even speak in jest.
7	國既卒斬,	The state lies in ruins,
8	何用不監。	Why do you not see to this?
9	節彼南山,	High-crested are those southern hills,
10	有實其猗。	Filled with tortuous terrain.
11	赫赫師尹,	Majestic are you, Marshal and Chief,
12	不平爲何。	Why is your heart unsettled?[46]
13	天方薦瘥,	Heaven has sent a plague down upon us,

---

[43] Just to give two examples of this kind from the bronze inscriptions, in the inscription of the Ban *gui* 班簋 (JC: 4341), Maofu 毛父 is also called Maobo 毛伯. The Zheng Yibo 鄭義伯 in the Zheng Yibo *xu* 鄭義伯盨 (JC: 4391) is called Zheng Yi Qiangfu 鄭義羌父 in the Zheng Yi Qiangfu *xu* 鄭義羌父盨 (JC: 4392); but he is also called Zheng Qiangbo 鄭羌伯 in the Zheng Qiangbo *li* 鄭羌伯鬲 (JC: 659).

[44] See *Shijing*, 12.1, pp. 440–41 (Waley, *The Book of Songs*, pp. 165–67).

[45] Waley here has "Master Yin," which is apparently a misreading. *Shiyin* appearing in lines 3 and 11 is clearly the abbreviation of Yinshi taishi 尹氏太師 in line 17. Under the second year of King Xuan, the *Current Bamboo Annals* reports that the king commanded "Grand Marshal the August Father" (Taishi Huangfu 太師皇父); under the first year of King You, it says that the king commanded "Grand Marshal and Chief the August Father" (Taishi yinshi Huangfu 太師尹氏皇父). It is very likely that Huangfu's role under King Xuan was "Grand Marshal," and under King You he was entrusted with an additional role – "Chief." There seems no doubt that the *Shiyin* here refers to Huangfu. See *Zhushu jinian*, 2, pp. 14, 16 (Legge, *The Shoo King*, Prolegomena, pp. 155, 157).

[46] Waley has "unfair" for the term *buping* 不平, which appears also in line 57 as a description of Heaven. In the latter case, the term clearly parallels *buning* 不寧 in line 58. So "unsettled" is a better translation here.

14	喪亂弘多。	Death and destruction are everywhere.
15	民言無嘉,	The people's words are full of spite,
16	憯莫懲嗟。	Why does no one stop this sadness?

17	尹氏太師,	The Chief, Grand Marshal,
18	維周之氐。	You are the bedrock of Zhou,[47]
19	秉國之均,	Hold the state's even balance,
20	四方是維。	Control all these lands,
21	天子是毗,	Aid the Son of Heaven himself;
22	俾民不迷。	Thereby the people will not go astray.
23	不弔皇天,	Mighty Heaven, now unkind,
24	不宜空我師。	Do not take away our Marshal.[48]

25	弗躬弗親,	You have not attended to this yourself,
26	庶民弗信。	Thus the common folk have no trust.
27	弗問弗仕,	You do not investigate, do not serve,
28	勿罔君子。	Then at least do not neglect the noble ones.
29	式夷式已,	Be impartial, be resolute,
30	無小人殆。	Then there will be no danger from petty men,
31	瑣瑣姻亞,	And trivial relatives and sycophants
32	則無膴仕。	Will not hold high office again.

33	昊天不傭,	Mighty Heaven now inconstant,
34	降此鞠訩。	Brings down on us this hardship;
35	昊天不惠,	Mighty Heaven now uncaring,
36	降此大戾。	Brings down on us this great pain.
37	君子如屆,	If you, sir, were strict in rule,
38	俾民心闋。	The people's hearts would be relieved.
39	君子如夷,	If you, sir, brought peace to reign,
40	惡怒是違。	Evil and anger would be sent away.

41	不弔皇天,	Now inconstant is mighty Heaven,
42	亂靡有定。	Disorder is forever on the land,
43	式月斯生,	Month upon month it arises,
44	俾民不寧。	And people live unsettled lives.
45	憂心如酲,	Grief fills their hearts like bad wine,
46	誰秉國成。	Who will control state's good order?
47	不自為政,	If one does not himself take over,
48	卒勞百姓。	Our families will long toil and suffer.

| 49 | 駕彼四牡, | Driving forth those four steeds, |
| 50 | 四牡項領。 | Four steeds with thick necks stretched. |

[47] Waley uses "Be" instead of "You are" and therefore treats lines 18–22 as the wish of the poet. I think that they are rather a statement of the important role of the Grand Marshal.

[48] Waley translate this line as "Do not oppress our people so," based on the previous reading of the character *kong* 空 as *qiong* 窮. But since the character *shi* 師 may refer to the Grand Marshal as in line 3, it is more likely that this line suggests the declining power of the Grand Marshal.

51 我瞻四方,   I look out over the four quarters,
52 蹙蹙靡所騁。Increasingly troubled, I have no place to ride.

53 方茂爾惡,   When your cruelty is in full form,
54 相爾矛矣。   We will indeed meet your spears;
55 既夷既懌,   But if you are constant and kind to us,
56 如相醻矣。   Then we shall pledge ourselves to you.
57 昊天不平,   Mighty Heaven is now unsettled,
58 我王不寧。   Our king is not at peace,
59 不懲其心,   He does not take heed his own heart,
60 覆怨其正。   And turns on those who correct him.[49]

61 家父作誦,   Jiafu made this ballad
62 以究王訩。   To delve the King's disorder.
63 式訛爾心,   If you would change your heart,
64 以畜萬邦。   The myriad states would be well-nourished.

The traditional interpretation of this poem as political sarcasm directed against Huangfu and therefore extending the criticism to King You (since he appointed Huangfu) not only is misleading but also totally ignores the historical context. The identification of Jiafu with Jiabo, no matter whether he was or was not the author of the poem, would itself overturn this theory because the same theory treats Jiabo and Huangfu equally as associates of Bao Si. It seems very clear to me that lines 1–24 emphasize the importance of Huangfu to the stability of the Zhou state and express sorrow about his falling from power. Lines 25–36 accuse Huangfu's enemy of hoodwinking the king and of putting his/her followers and relatives (*yinya* 姻亞) in office.[50] Lines 37–48 complain about King You for allowing the anger and hatred among the people to grow, and for allowing the evil ones to gain power. The last part of the poem (lines 53–64) is perhaps the most important. Here the poet calls for reconciliation between Huangfu and the king, which is indeed the stated purpose of the poem. Jiafu, the named composer of the poem, was probably himself unable to escape the political strife (as implied by lines 49–52), but tried to persuade Huangfu to compromise with the king and to remain in the capital.

There seems little doubt that the poem "Jie nanshan" presents a sharply partisan view of late Western Zhou politics. This view is even more evident in the poem "Zhengyue" 正月 (no. 192), which presents a harsh and open criticism of Bao Si, partly translated below (Waley's translation). The poet speaks evidently from the standpoint of a man (probably one of the previous

---

[49] Another possible reading of the character *zheng* 正 is "officials." But Waley's reading of it as "complain" seems unfounded.

[50] Lines 25–32 were previously read as critiques of Huangfu. I think this part is clearly a criticism directed to Huangfu's enemies, most likely pointing to Bao Si and her partners.

associates of Huangfu) who was forced out of the court after he failed to accommodate the new faction.[51]

1	瞻彼阪田,	See how on that barren, hilly field
2	有菀其特。	The rich grain rises above all others.
3	天之扤我,	Heaven beat me down,
4	如不我克。	But it could not overcome me.
5	彼求我則,	First they took me as model,
6	如不我得。	But they could not reach that high;
7	執我仇仇,	Then they treated me as enemy,
8	亦不我力。	But they too could not overpower me.
9	心之憂矣,	Alas, the grief in my heart
10	如或結之。	Feels like it is tied in knots.
11	今茲之正,	How can these officials now[52]
12	胡然厲矣。	Be so very vicious?
13	燎之方揚,	When the flames are first rising high,
14	寧或滅之。	How can they be extinguished?
15	赫赫宗周,	Majestic was the capital of Zhou,
16	襃姒滅之。	But Lady Bao Si destroyed it!
17	終其永懷,	Till the end is this ever-lasting worry,
18	又窘陰雨。	And we are beleaguered by a driving rain.
19	其車既載,	After the carriage is already loaded,
20	乃棄爾輔。	You then toss the side-boards away,
	. . .	
21	彼有旨酒,	There are those with tasty wine,
22	又有嘉殽。	And they also have fine dishes.
23	洽比其鄰,	They gather together with their neighbors,
24	婚姻孔云。	Their relatives are very numerous.
25	念我獨兮,	To think of me all alone,
26	憂心慇慇。	My grieved heart is deeply pained.

In short, although the satirical function suggested by the "Preface to the Poem" that was followed by all traditional commentators is probably untrue, the political orientation of the above poems is very clear. Evidently, these poems were composed not for pure literary pleasure or aestheticism, but with clear political objectives. They speak jointly about an underlying historical context or process that actually allows us to read them as a group and that is also evidenced by the historical texts. But differing from the often oversimplified outlines found in historical texts such as the *Bamboo Annals*, the poems convey a profound sense of political judgment and historical realism that had become an important part of the cultural memory

---

[51] See *Shijing*, 12.1, pp. 441–43 (Waley, *The Book of Songs*, pp. 167–70).
[52] Waley here has "rulers" instead of "officials," but it is probably not right.

of the Zhou people. They suggest that there was a fierce political struggle taking place in the Zhou court during the early years of King You that had resulted in Huangfu's retirement or exit to the east. It was probably a struggle between the young king and the senior officials carried over from his father's court for control of court policy, entangled with another struggle between two women, the legitimate Zhou queen Shenhou 申后 and the rising Bao Si, for the succession of their sons to royal power. It is important to recall that, according to the *Current Bamboo Annals*, the legitimate Prince Yijiu was forced into exile *in the same year as Huangfu's retirement from power*. I consider that these two events were necessarily related, simultaneously stemming from the same political defeat of the Huangfu party by the King You–Bao Si party. Under such circumstances, to stay away from trouble was probably the best choice for an old man. Without the political support of the Huangfu party, to flee into exile was probably the only choice for the royal prince.

Returning to our historical records, we find that from the fifth year until the eighth year (777–774 BC), the Zhou court went through an important period of power restructuring and government reorganization. The "Zhengyu" chapter of the *Guoyu* mentions a pro-King You minister called Guo Shifu, the head of the Guo lineage, who was elevated to the status of "Prime Minister" (*qingshi* 卿士), previously held by Huangfu. We do not know when exactly the appointment was made, but since, according to the *Current Bamboo Annals*, Guo attacked the state of Jiao 焦 in present-day Sanmenxia in the seventh year of King You (775 BC),[53] it is possible that he began to play an important role in the Zhou court soon after Huangfu's departure. We also know that in the eighth year of King You (774 BC), as a chronicle part at the end of the "Zhengyu" chapter of the *Guoyu* tells us, Duke Huan of Zheng 鄭 was appointed the new Minister of the Multitudes.[54] More importantly, in 774 BC, three years after the legitimate heir, Yijiu, went into exile, Bo Fu (or Bo Pan 伯盤), son of Bao Si, was formally established as the royal heir. Our chronological table in appendix 3 indicates that since Bao Si became favored by King You in 779 BC, Bo Fu was probably only a three- or four-year-old child when he was established.[55] It is very likely that Bo Fu's establishment as royal heir was a step taken to secure the political status of Bao Si.

I think that our historical records, though mainly from texts that were put in their current forms possibly during the Warring States period, are quite consistent with early poems in telling of a major political transition at the Zhou court. They suggest that, by 774 BC, a new power structure had emerged in the Zhou court, with four figures, the king, Bao Si, Guo Shifu, and Duke Huan of Zheng, as the major players. According to the

[53] See *Zhushu jinian*, 2, p. 17 (Legge, *The Shoo King*, Prolegomena, p. 157).   [54] See *Guoyu*, 16, p. 524.
[55] See *Zhushu jinian*, 2. p. 17 (Legge, *The Shoo King*, Prolegomena, p. 157).

Lüshi chunqiu, the Duke of Zhai, Dun (Zhaigong Dun 祭公敦), mentioned together with Guo Shifu, was possibly also a member of this new government, but no other sources support this account.[56] The opposition party of the seniors was completely eliminated, and the king gained full control over the policies of the Zhou court. A general critique of the politics of King You is found in the *Guoyu*, as a part of Shi Bo's speech addressed to Duke Huan of Zheng. Besides the personal attacks on Bao Si and Guo Shifu, the attributed historian raised a philosophical question regarding the relationship between harmony and unity. According to Shi Bo, King You eliminated the harmony at the Zhou court that was based on the reconciliation of different opinions, and he specially sought for unity among the officials.[57] This, according to Shi Bo, was a very bad thing that would cause the extinction of the Zhou state. This interesting point reflects at least how the political problems of King You's court were viewed by the politicians and historians in the post-Western Zhou era.

To conclude, the above analysis of the political development at the court of King You differs significantly from Taniguchi's simple supposition of a struggle among the in-laws, with Bao Si's family backed up by the lineage of Guo against the family of Shenhou backed up by the lineage of Shen. It is also different from the overall political divide drawn by Shim between the faction of King You, Bo Fu (son of Bao Si), and Guo and the faction of Prince Yijiu, Shen, Zheng, Lü, and the Western Rong.[58] Instead, my interpretation looks for the origin of political antagonism that disturbed King You's court and eventually resulted in the dynastic downfall in the generational power transition across the last two Western Zhou reigns. It was a partisan struggle centered on the role of Huangfu and King You, which was entangled with the succession dispute involving the two royal ladies and their sons. In this process, with the defeat of the Huangfu party, the struggle gradually led to the power restructuring of the Zhou government probably along a different line of policy under the full control of King You. But the victory of the king over his political enemies provided not just a chance to restore power to the royal house, but also the starting point of the dynastic downfall.

Alliances and the sack of the Zhou capital

The consolidation of the power of King You and Bao Si at the Zhou court certainly had an important impact beyond the capital, and what happened in the following years from 773 to 771 BC can be regarded as an extension of the political struggle at the Zhou court. However, this time the struggle

---

[56] See *Lüshi chunqiu*, 2, p. 634.   [57] See *Guoyu*, 16, pp. 515–16.
[58] It should be noted that neither author has mentioned the role of Huangfu that is critical in the political development of the reign of King You. See Taniguchi, "Sei Shū metsubō no ichi sokumen," pp. 10–12; Shim, "The Early Development of the State of Jin," p. 139.

was elevated to a diplomatic level, taking the form of alliances among the local states. The conflict involved mainly two local polities and a foreign power near the northwestern border, and, as it progressed, extended to pull in even some states in the distant east.

The state of Shen was the natal home of the legitimate Zhou queen, Shenhou, and therefore the safest asylum for the royal prince Yijiu after he fell from power. For six years, from 777 to 771 BC, according to the entries in the *Current Bamboo Annals*, Prince Yijiu remained at Shen under the protection of his maternal grandfather, the ruler of Shen (Shenhou 申侯). The ruler of Shen was certainly unhappy about his grandson's expulsion from the capital and his daughter's loss of royal favor. The *Shiji* says in a simplistic way that he was enraged and subsequently led the Quanrong and the polity of Zeng in an invasion of the Zhou capital.[59] The actual situation, I believe, was probably very different from this account in the *Shiji* that was then made the orthodox story of the fall of the Western Zhou in traditional Chinese historiography. Apparently, the ruler of Shen did not take any action until the fourth year after he received Prince Yijiu. A very important entry is preserved in the *Current Bamboo Annals* under the ninth year of King You (773 BC):[60]

（幽王）九年，申侯聘西戎及鄫。

In the ninth year (of King You), the Ruler of Shen sent an envoy to Western Rong and Zeng.

The term here is *pin* 聘, used frequently in texts such as the *Zuozhuan*, referring to the official interstate visit. The Western Rong is an alternative way to say the Quanrong because they were geographically located to the northwest of Zhou (see appendix 2). Zeng, as analyzed in appendix 3, was the same state that was attacked by the Zhou royal army under the command of Prince Duofu (Duke Huan of Zheng) with the assistance of Ruler Wen of Jin in the second year of King You (780 BC). Although the reason for the campaign is unknown, it was doubtless that, as a result of its conflict with the Zhou court, the Zeng would have been in a position to be willing to lend their help to the Shen. The timing of the establishment of this alliance in 773 BC, only one year after the King You–Bao Si party consolidated control over the court, encourages us to consider that this was mainly a response to the threat from the royal court, which from the perspective of Shen and Zeng was now completely in the hands of their political enemies. In any event, by 773 BC the frontline had become clearer than ever and a military confrontation on a large scale would have become inevitable. In this regard, Shi Bo's speech in the *Guoyu* provides us with an "anticipatory" political analysis of the situation:[61]

---

[59] See *Shiji*, 4, p. 149 (Nienhauser, *The Grand Scribe's Records*, 1, p. 74).
[60] See *Zhushu jinian*, 2, p. 17 (Legge, *The Shoo King*, Prolegomena, p. 157).   [61] See *Guoyu*, 16, p. 519.

申、繒、西戎方強，王室方騷，將以縱慾，不亦難乎？王慾殺太子以成伯服，必求之申。申
人不畀，必伐之。若伐申，而繒與西戎會以伐周，周不守矣！繒與西戎方將襲申，申、呂方
強，其隩愛太子亦必可知也。王師若在，其救之亦必然也。王心怒矣，虢公從矣，凡周存
亡，不三稔矣！

Shen, Zeng, and the Western Rong are now ascending in power, and the royal house is disordered; so even if [the king] wants to indulge himself in what he desires, would it not be difficult? If the king wants to kill the prince in order to secure the succession of Bo Fu, he must demand him from Shen. If the people of Shen do not hand him over, [the royal army] must attack Shen. If it attacks Shen, then Zeng and the Western Rong will jointly attack Zhou, and Zhou will not be able to defend itself! Zeng and the Western Rong are going to lend favor to Shen. Shen and Lü are ascending in power; their love for the prince must be understandable. When the royal army appears on the scene, it is unavoidable that they (Western Rong and Zeng) will come to rescue it (Shen). The heart of the king is enraged, and the Duke of Guo will follow him in action. The fall of Zhou will not be farther off than three years!

What followed in the next three years was just as Shi Bo "predicted." More probably, considering the late date of composition of the text, this "prophesy" was retrospectively constructed on the model of the actual historical events that had happened after the year 774 BC, to which Shi Bo's speech is dated in the *Guoyu*. Whatever the case might be, the *Guoyu* records are consistent with other sources, especially the *Bamboo Annals*, while different from the *Shiji* narrative on the point that it was the royal court that took the first offensive move against Shen and not the Shen who took the initiative to attack the royal capital. While it is not impossible the *Shiji* account was based on a different historiographical tradition, it is the *Guoyu* account correlating with the *Bamboo Annals* that seems to fit much better into the historical context of the time. However, before the breakout of the final combat, another important event may have taken place in 772 BC. The *Zuozhuan* (fourth year of Duke Zhao) says:[62]

商紂為黎之蒐，東夷叛之。周幽為太室之盟，戎狄叛之。皆所以示諸侯汰也，諸侯所由棄命
也。

Zhou of Shang hunted at Li, then the Eastern Yi defected. King You of Zhou made the covenant of alliance on Taishi Mountain, then the Rong and Di defected. This was all to show the many rulers excessiveness, and was the reason why the many rulers abandoned the royal charge.

In the *Current Bamboo Annals*, we read:[63]

（幽王）十年春王及諸侯盟于太室。

In the tenth year (of King You), spring, the king and the many rulers swore covenant of alliance on Taishi Mountain.

---

[62] See *Zuozhuan*, 42, p. 2,035.
[63] See *Zhushu jinian*, 2, p. 17 (Legge, *The Shoo King*, Prolegomena, p. 157).

The *Zuozhuan* account comes out of the context of a speech made by the Chu official Jiao Ju 椒舉 who admonished the hegemonic Chu king who had just displayed ritual excessiveness in an interstate conference that took place in the summer of 538 BC. The notion of the account, which may reflect the view of Eastern Zhou politicians, appears to be self-contradictory. On the one hand, it says that the "barbarians" defected from Zhou; and on the other, it suggests that the meeting on Taishi Mountain was the reason for the many rulers to betray Zhou. The political logic behind the *Zuozhuan* lines is that when the king, who by his kingship would command unconditional support of the local rulers, decided to swear a "covenant of alliance" (*meng* 盟), a political ritual regularly performed in the interstate conferences between the equals of the Eastern Zhou period, he actually exposed his weakness to the local rulers, who would therefore neglect the royal command. "Taishi" refers to present-day Songshan Mountain, located about 60 kilometers to the east of Luoyang; it was the reputed central mountain in the later Chinese world. The *Current Bamboo Annals* dates this conference to the spring of the tenth year of King You (772 BC). While the event has a unique meaning for Warring States politicians who would use it as a historical precedent to support their agenda, for us the account seems to suggest that King You traveled east to meet with the many regional rulers, and this is, in a very interesting way, related to the establishment of the alliance between Shen, Zeng, and the Western Rong only a year earlier, and to the final combat that was to take place only a few months later. In the historical context of the final years of King You, it is very possible that King You would have taken such a step to consolidate his relationship with the eastern states and to bring them to his side before the showdown with Shen. If so, he probably had done so in an unusual way by putting himself on equal ground with the local rulers in the relationship of covenants of alliance. In any event, later in the year, King You decided to go ahead with the final combat with Shen.

The *Current Bamboo Annals* records that in the ninth month of the same year (772 BC) the royal army was sent out to attack Shen. To understand this final phase of Western Zhou history, it is necessary to compare the two entries for King You in the *Ancient Bamboo Annals* and the *Current Bamboo Annals*. The *Ancient* records:[64]

（文侯九年）幽王十年，九月，桃杏實。
（文侯十年）伯盤與幽王俱死于戲。先是，申侯、魯侯及許文公立平王于申。幽王既死，而虢公翰又立王子余臣于攜。周二王並立。
二十一年，攜王為晉文公所殺。

(In the ninth year of Ruler Wen of Jin), in the tenth year of King You, ninth month, the peach and apricot trees bore fruits.

---

[64] The ninth year entry was copied from the *Taiping yulan* quotation; the tenth year entry was copied from Kong Yingda's commentary on the *Zuozhuan* (twenty-sixth year of Duke Zhao). See Fan Xiangyong, *Guben zhushu jinian*, p. 34.

(In the tenth year of Ruler Wen of Jin) Bo Pan and King You died together at Xi. Before this, the Ruler of Shen, the Ruler of Lu, and Duke Wen of Xu established King Ping at Shen. After King You had died, then the Duke of Guo, Han, again established Prince Yuchen at Xie. Zhou had two kings reigning at the same time. In the twenty-first year, the King of Xie was killed by Duke Wen of Jin.

In the *Current* version:[65]

（幽王十年）秋九月，桃杏實，王師伐申。

（幽王）十一年，春正月，日暈。申人、鄫人及犬戎入宗周，弒王及鄭桓公。犬戎殺王子伯服，執褒姒以歸。申侯、魯侯、徐男、鄭子立宜臼于申，虢公翰立王子余臣于攜。

（平王）二十一年，晉文侯殺王子余臣于攜。

(In the tenth year of King You) Autumn, ninth month, the peach and apricot trees bore fruits. The royal army attacked Shen.

In the eleventh year (of King You), spring, first month, the sun had a corona. The people of Shen, the people of Zeng, and the Quanrong entered Zongzhou, killing the king and Duke Huan of Zheng. The Quanrong killed Bo Fu, captured Bao Si, and left for home. The Ruler of Shen, the Ruler of Lu, the Ruler of Xu, and the prince of Zheng established Yijiu at Shen, while the Duke of Guo, Han, established Prince Yuchen at Xie.

In the twenty-first year (of King Ping), Ruler Wen of Jin killed Prince Yuchen at Xie.

According to the *Current Bamboo Annals*, the invasion of the Zhou capital by Shen, Zeng, and the Quanrong was very much a counterattack on the Zhou after the royal army apparently failed to capture Shen, the geographical location of which will be discussed in the next section. The *Ancient Bamboo Annals* does not have this campaign. We have to keep in mind the nature of the *Ancient* version as a text reconstructed from fragments of quotations by medieval authors; if an entry on the campaign was not quoted, there is no way for it to show up in the reconstructed *Ancient* version. But more importantly, the *Current* version seems to agree with a tradition also transmitted by the *Guoyu* as shown by Shi Bo's "prediction" that once the Zhou royal army appeared on the scene to attack Shen, Zeng and the Western Rong would come to the rescue of Shen. What is more, the process of the fall as suggested by the *Current Bamboo Annals* and the *Guoyu* runs a very close parallel to the battle of 823 BC in an early year of King Xuan, which has been reconstructed and mapped out in chapter 3 (see p. 169). It seems very likely that the joint forces of Shen, Zeng, and the Quanrong defeated the royal army in an early engagement somewhere near Shen, and then marched on the Zhou capital, which instantly fell into the hands of the enemies. In addition, the *Ancient Bamboo Annals* reports that King You and Bo Fu died at a place called Xi 戲, located at the foot

---

[65] See *Zhushu jinian*, 2, p. 17 (Legge, *The Shoo King*, Prolegomena, pp. 157–58).

of Lishan Mountain, about 50 kilometers to the east of the capital Hao.[66]
If this was indeed true, it would suggest that King You and Bo Fu were
retreating from the capital to the east when they were caught and killed by
the Quanrong.

Perhaps the most important difference between the *Ancient* and *Current*
versions regarding this final stage of Western Zhou history is the date of
the establishment of Prince Yijiu as King Ping: while the term *xianshi* 先是
in the *Ancient* version dates it before the death of King You, the *Current*
version dates it after that. If the *Ancient* version is accurate, we must consider
King You's attack on Shen to be a suppression of the usurpation by Prince
Yijiu. We need to look into this matter more carefully. The entry in the
reconstructed *Ancient Bamboo Annals* was retrieved from Kong Yingda's
commentary to the *Zuozhuan* (twenty-sixth year of Duke Zhao); a full
citation of the Kong Yingda version of this entry is given in appendix 3.
However, in the Song dynasty, this particular entry was again quoted by
two sources, the *Tongzhi* and the *Zizhi tongjian waiji*, in exactly the same
way:[67]

幽王死，申侯、魯侯及許文公立平王于申，虢公翰立王子余，而王並立。余為晉文侯所殺，
是為攜王。

After the death of King You, the Ruler of Shen, the Ruler of Lu, and Duke Wen of
Xu established King Ping at Shen, and the Duke of Guo, Han, established Prince
Yu, and so two kings were reigning at the same time. Yu was killed by Ruler Wen
of Jin; this was the King of Xie.

Since the wording of these quotes is different from Kong Yingda's commentary which was copied into the reconstructed ancient version, it is likely
that the quotes were not based on the Kong commentary, but were possibly
direct quotations from the tomb version of the *Bamboo Annals*. Liu Shu (AD
1032–78) and even Zheng Qiao (AD 1104–62), authors of the two texts, may
have had direct access to the tomb text. They simply indicate that King
Ping was established after the death of King You, consistent with the *Current* version.[68] By contrast, the Kong Yingda version of the passage appears
explanatory and narrative. This certainly exposes the problem in using the
Ancient Bamboo Annals that has been analyzed in appendix 3. In fact, both
Wang Guowei and Fan Xiangyong noted possible textual intrusions in the
Kong Yingda version of the entry.[69] I think, however, the term *xianshi* is
also a later intrusion that was created by Kong Yingda when he quoted the

[66] As for the location of Xi, the "Junguo zhi" chapter of the *Houhan shu* locates it in Xinfeng County 新豐縣 of Later Han; see *Houhan shu*, 19, p. 3,403. The *Shuijing zhu* mentions a Xi River that originated in Lishan Mountain and flowed northward into the Wei River through the territory of Xinfeng; see *Shuijing zhu*, 19, p. 616.
[67] See *Tongzhi*, 3b, p. 52; *Zizhi tongjian waiji*, 3, p. 32.
[68] The fact that the prince of Zheng was involved in the establishment process in the *Current* version certainly indicates that it must have taken place after the death of Duke Huan of Zheng.
[69] See Wang Guowei, *Guben zhushu jinian jijiao*, p. 11; Fan Xiangyong, *Guben zhushu jinian*, p. 34.

tomb version of the *Bamboo Annals* in his commentary. In short, King Ping was not established until the death of his father King You.

If the preceding reconstruction of the historical process of the fall of the Western Zhou is correct, this fall would appear first of all to be the result of a serious military miscalculation, motivated by a desire in the Zhou court to eliminate the banished royal heir in the hope that this would secure the future succession of the new heir to power. This was done when the opposition party at the court was defeated and King You gained full control over the court's policy. Nevertheless, had the Zhou been strong enough, they would have taken the prince into custody by defeating the joint enemy forces. But the Zhou court was already too weakened by political struggles in the early years of King You, and the enemies were apparently strong enough to resist the initial attack by the Zhou and to carry the battle back to the Zhou capital, overthrowing the Zhou regime. Under such dangerous circumstances, a miscalculation had turned out to be a major disaster.

LOCATING THE FALL OF THE WESTERN ZHOU

Above, I have presented an interpretation that I think, on our current evidence, most consistently explains the political dynamics in the historical development leading up to the fall of the Western Zhou. However, the interpretation needs to be connected to the landscape in spatial dimensions, and this actually involves a number of difficult issues. The most important are questions regarding the locations of the states of Shen and Lü that had played a crucial role in the downfall of the Western Zhou dynasty as simultaneously a historical process and a geographical process. We cannot fully understand the historical fall until we can solve these geographical problems.

The location of the state of Shen

In appendix 2, I demonstrate that the Quanrong (Western Rong) who joined Shen to overthrow the Zhou dynasty can be reasonably related to the Xianyun, the traditional adversaries of the Zhou regime. I have also demonstrated in chapter 3 that the upper Jing River valley, the so-called "Road to Xiao Pass," was the main channel through which the Xianyun invaded Zhou, and that Taiyuan, probably located near Guyuan in southern Ningxia, was a main base of Xianyun power. Perhaps by the time of King You these people were already widely distributed in southern Ningxia and the regions to the west of the Liupan Mountains in eastern Gansu. Our chronological table in appendix 3 shows that the Western Rong were also enemies of the state of Qin, in the present-day Tianshui area of eastern Gansu. The Taiyuan area may have served as a gathering place for them, the place from which they launched repeated attacks on the Zhou (Map 12).

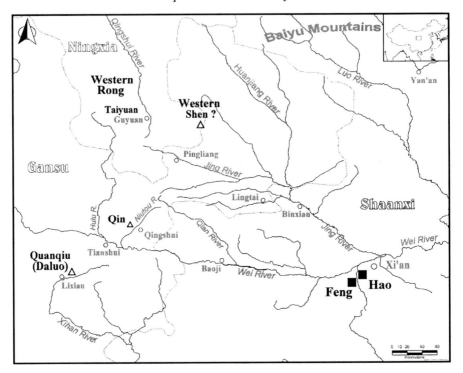

Map 12 The possible location of Western Shen and Western Rong

In later history, although the center of their power was located farther to the southwest, the Tibetans also took this road to invade Tang, and this was mainly because of the topography of the land of the northwestern region.

It has long been the belief of many scholars that Shen was located in the Nanyang basin in southwestern Henan, to the southeast of the Zhou capitals in the Wei River valley. There was indeed a Shen in the Nanyang area and its establishment in the reign of King Xuan is celebrated in the poem "Songgao" (no. 259) of the *Book of Poetry*.[70] The "Geographical Records" chapter of the *Hanshu* indicates that Shen was located in the Wan County 宛縣 of Nanyang Commandery of the Han dynasty, which is present-day Nanyang city.[71] Seemingly supporting this location of Shen are the locations of two other states, Zeng and Lü, mentioned together with Shen in Shi Bo's political analysis quoted above from the *Guoyu*. The authority on the location of Lü is the commentary to the *Shiji*, saying that it was located to the west of Nanyang.[72] As for the location of Zeng,

---

[70] See *Shijing*, 18.3, pp. 565–68 (Waley, *The Book of Songs*, pp. 272–74).   [71] See *Hanshu*, 28, p. 1,563.
[72] See *Shiji*, 32, p. 1,477. Furthermore, the Tang geographical survey *Kuodi zhi* (cited in Zhu Youzeng, *Shi dili zheng*), provides information regarding the specific locations of Shen and Lü: Shen was 15 kilometers to the north of Nanyang, while Lü was 20 kilometers to the west of it. See Zhu Youzeng, *Shi dili zheng*, pp. 32–33.

later commentators identified it with another state Zeng 繒, located in the Shandong region and active during the early Spring and Autumn period.[73] Differing from this, the Qing scholar Gao Shiqi suggested that Zeng must have been somewhere near Shen and identified it with the Zeng Pass 繒関 mentioned in the *Zuozhuan* (fourth year of Duke Ai), which was located near present-day Fangcheng, to the northeast of Nanyang.[74]

These locations of Shen, Zeng, and Lü as suggested by traditional scholars would necessarily lead to the conclusion that the fall of the Western Zhou resulted from a political and military conflict between the Zhou court in the Wei River valley and a cluster of regional states in the Nanyang basin of southwestern Henan. However, this contradicts the location of the Western Rong, which had to be in the "west" and was almost certainly in eastern Gansu and southern Ningxia. The Qing historian Cui Shu was the first scholar to cast serious doubts on the alliance between the Western Rong and Shen, on the basis of their geographical locations:[75]

Shen was more than a thousand *li* (500 kilometers) to the southeast of Zhou, while the Rong were to the northwest of Zhou. Separated by such a great distance, why would the Ruler of Shen have jumped over Zhou and attached himself to the Rong? Huang and Xuan attached themselves to Qi because they were located to the northeast of Chu. Even so, when Chu destroyed them, Duke Huan of Qi was unable to rescue them because they were distant (from Qi). When the royal army attacked Shen, how could the Rong come to rescue it?

Of course, Cui Shu here is mainly concerned with the historicity of the political alliance between Shen and the Western Rong. However, since the *Guoyu* and the *Current Bamboo Annals* both testify to the existence of the alliance, there seems no ground to reject it, and hence reject the involvement of either the Western Rong or Shen in the fall of the Western Zhou. The problem is the locations of these polities, most importantly the location of Shen. It should be mentioned that Qian Mu has tried to solve this contradiction by locating the Western Rong in the large area stretching roughly from Xingping 興平 in the middle of the Wei River valley in Shaanxi to Nanyang in southwestern Henan, based on the textual records that some Rong people were active in the region during the early Eastern Zhou.[76] However, by locating the Rong people who attacked the Zhou capital in 771 BC in eastern Shaanxi and western Henan, Qian totally ignored the historical context, because the Rong people moved into eastern Shaanxi and western Henan from the northwest only after, and as the result

---

[73] For instance, the "Zhengyi" commentary to the *Shiji* suggests that it was in Cheng County 承縣 of Yi Prefecture 沂州, to the south of present-day Zaozhuang 棗庄; see *Shiji*, 4, p. 149.

[74] On the location of Zeng Pass, see Gao Shiqi, *Chunqiu diming kao lue*, 14, p. 1; Jiang Yong, *Chunqiu diming kaoshi*, 254, p. 34.

[75] See Cui Shu, *Cui Dongbi yishu*, p. 246.

[76] See Qian Mu, "Xi Zhou ronghuo kao," in *Gushi dili luncong* (Taibei: Dongda tushu, 1982), p. 154.

of, the fall of the Western Zhou. Qian took the result to be the reason, and therefore failed completely in his study of late Western Zhou history.

Clearly, the problem does not lie in the location of the Rong people, as we now have contemporaneous inscriptional evidence that they must have been located to the north and west of the Zhou royal domain; the problem lies in the location of the states that joined the Rong to attack the Zhou capital in the traditional records. In some regards, the records themselves are not wrong, because the states of Shen and Lü were evidently located in the Nanyang region and were soon after annexed by the southern state Chu. It is the early history of these states that had become obscured in the received traditional geographical records. A number of more recent scholars, for instance Tong Shuye and Shi Quan, have already rejected the location of Shen in Nanyang, suggesting that Shen must have been located somewhere in Shaanxi, near the Western Rong.[77] Although these scholars could not point to an approximate location for Shen, their argument was developed in the right direction. In light of the new analysis of late Western Zhou history presented above, I believe that our current sources do offer some important clues to the missing history of early Shen.

Regarding the exile of Prince Yijiu, the *Ancient Bamboo Annals* says that he took refuge in Western Shen (Xishen 西申), and not simply Shen. This implies that there was another Shen that existed in the western region of Zhou at the time of King You. There seems to have been a continuous historiographical tradition on this Western Shen because it is mentioned not only in the *Bamboo Annals* but also in another text – the *Yi Zhoushu* – that, though composed during the Warring States period, probably contains some earlier materials.[78] In the "Wanghui" 土會 chapter of the latter text, Western Shen was mentioned as one of the northwestern peoples (most likely, Rong) who presented themselves in a meeting in the eastern center Chengzhou during the reign of King Cheng.[79] This seems to agree with another record in the "Zhouyu" chapter of the *Guoyu* where it is stated that the establishment of the four states, Qi 齊, Xu 許, Shen 申, and Lü 呂, was due to the marriage between the Great King of Zhou, the grandfather of King Wen, and Taijiang 太姜, a lady from the Jiang clan. This record suggests that these four states or polities were probably all established during the early Western Zhou, having their origins in the same Jiang clan that undoubtedly originated in the west.[80] Furthermore, an excerpt from the

[77] See Tong Shuye, *Chunqiu shi* (Hong Kong: Taiping, 1962), p. 47; Shi Quan, *Gudai Jing Chu dili xintan* (Wuhan: Wuhan daxue, 1988), p. 88.

[78] On the content and textual history of the *Yi Zhoushu*, see Loewe, *Early Chinese Texts*, pp. 229–33. It was suggested by Shaughnessy that, for instance, the "Shifu" chapter of the text was most likely an early Western Zhou document that was originally collected in the *Shangshu*; see Edward Shaughnessy, "'New' Evidence on the Zhou Conquest," *Early China* 6 (1981–82), 57–79.

[79] See *Yi Zhoushu*, 7, p. 9.

[80] The relationship between these states and the Jiang clan in the west has been studied in great detail by Gu Jiegang; see Gu Jiegang, "Cong guji zhong tansuo woguo de xibu minzu – qiangzu," *Shehui kexue zhanxian* 1980.1, 122–23.

"Basic Annals of Qin" in the *Shiji* suggests that Shen was also in a close relationship with the state of Qin 秦, also located in the west:[81]

昔我先酈山之女，為戎胥軒妻，生中潏，以親故歸周，保西陲，西垂以其故和睦。今我復與大駱妻，生適子成。申駱重婚，西戎皆服，所以為王。

In the past my ancestor Lishan's daughter married Xuxuan of Rong and gave birth to Zhongjue, who because of the marriage submitted himself to Zhou and guarded the Western March; for this reason the Western March was at peace. In the present days, I again gave a daughter to be Da Luo's wife who gave birth to Cheng (the legitimate heir). Shen and Luo had two marriages between them, for which reason the Western Rong are all obedient, therefore allowing [you] to be the king.

While the historical context of this quote will be examined in detail in chapter 5, it will suffice here to note that this passage suggests that Shen had been a traditional marriage partner of the Qin lineage (Xuxuan of Rong and Da Luo were both ancestors of the Qin people), located in the present-day Tianshui region in eastern Gansu, and this marriage relationship became the foundation for the security of the western border of the Western Zhou state. The context of this excerpt suggests strongly that Shen was located near both Qin and the Western Rong, and therefore its alliance with Qin through marriage could serve as a crucial factor to stabilize the western border of Zhou.

The bronze inscriptions of the mid-Western Zhou also testify to the early existence of Shen prior to the reestablishment of Shen in the Nanyang basin in the time of King Xuan. The Fifth Year Qiu Wei *ding* (JC: 2832) mentions an individual named Shenji 䤔季 who, by the inscriptional practice that a man is called by the name of his lineage or polity, is most likely to have been from Shen. In two other inscriptions, Shenji is mentioned as having performed the role of the official who introduces the candidates to the Zhou king in the appointment ceremonies taking place in the Zhou court.[82] Since these bronzes all pre-date the reign of King Xuan, they certainly suggest that Shen must have existed before the establishment of the Shen in Nanyang in 821 BC as a part of the restoration program initiated by King Xuan, and this Shen was most likely the Western Shen.[83] It is very probable that Shen was originally located in the west, and was then split or relocated by royal order in the south. A very important archaeological discovery was made in Nanyang City in 1981. From a late Western Zhou tomb, two bronzes cast by a person called Zhong Chengfu 仲再父, the Grand Superintendent of the ruler of "Southern Shen" (Nan Shen 南䤔), were excavated.[84] This

---

[81] See *Shiji*, 5, p. 177 (Nienhauser, *The Grand Scribe's Records*, 1, p. 89).

[82] These two inscriptions are the Da Ke *ding* 大克鼎 (JC: 2836) and the Yi *gui* 伊簋 (JC: 4287). For the career development of Shenji, see Li Feng, "Promotion and Success," pp. 1–35.

[83] See *Zhushu jinian*, 2, p. 14 (Legge, *The Shoo King*, Prolegomena, p. 155).

[84] See *Zhongyuan wenwu* 1984.4, 15. The identification of the character *shen* 䤔 in the inscriptions with the character *shen* 申 in the texts was first proposed by Professor Qiu Xigui in his analysis of the inscription of the Shi Qiang *pan* 史墻盤 (JC: 10175), and is now generally accepted; see Qiu Xigui, *Gu wenzi lunji*, pp. 375, 382–83.

discovery not only confirmed the specific location of the Shen at Nanyang contemporaneous with the bronzes, but, more importantly, shows also that this Shen was called "Southern Shen" during the late Western Zhou. I believe that the west–south distinction of the Shens (but not symmetrical: north–south or west–east) that we can see in this case suggests that the geographical directions of the two Shens were *viewed from the standpoint of Zongzhou (capital Hao), and not from that of each other.*[85] In other words, Southern Shen was located to the south of Zongzhou, and Western Shen was located to the west of it, which corresponds to the way the Western Rong were named.

Moreover, there is other evidence that this Western Shen continued to exist even after the establishment of Southern Shen in Nanyang. Most obviously, the *Ancient Bamboo Annals* says that Prince Yijiu took refuge in Western Shen in 777 BC. Even earlier, for reasons unknown, Shen (most likely Western Shen) found itself in military conflict with the Zhou court in the thirty-ninth or forty-first year of King Xuan (789/787 BC); a campaign against Shen was recorded for the year in both the *Current* and *Ancient* versions of the *Bamboo Annals*. The *Current* version says:[86]

（宣王）四十一年，王師敗于申。

In the forty-first year (of King Xuan), the royal army was defeated by Shen.

However the *Ancient* version says:[87]

（宣王）三十九年，王伐申戎，破之。

In the thirty-ninth year (of King Xuan), the king attacked the Shenrong, and defeated them.

Not only is the result of the battles reported differently in the two sources, the way in which Shen was referred to is also different. Given their possible location close to and their long-time involvement with the Rong people, it would be understandable that the Shen could be called "Rong of Shen" (Shenrong 申戎) when their relations with Zhou turned bad. However, there is another possibility: if the Shen in Nanyang was established by

---

[85] Conflicting with this interpretation is the theory that another Shen, "Eastern Shen," was located at Xinyang 信陽, Henan. This theory was first proposed by Gu Tiefu and has been followed by a number of scholars; see Gu Tiefu, "Xinyang yihao Chu mu de diwang yu renwu," *Gugong bowuyuan yuankan* 1979.2, 77. Some have even suggested that this "Eastern Shen" at Xinyang was the original location of the Shen in Nanyang, which they called the "Western Shen"; see Ai Yanding, "Shen guo zhi mi zhi wojian," *Zhongyuan wenwu* 1987.3, 109; Wu Xifei, "Yetan Xi Zhou Shen guo de youguan wenti," *Hangzhou daxue xuebao* 1992.1, 30–31. However, Xu Shaohua has shown quite convincingly that the Shen at Xinyang did not exist until the early Spring and Autumn period. In other words, after the conquest of Shen (in Nanyang) by the state of Chu, the remnants of Shen were relocated by Chu to Xinyang, which was then called "Eastern Shen." Xu also argues that before the establishment of Shen in Nanyang, there was only one Shen, the Western Shen in Shaanxi. See Xu Shaohua, *Zhou dai nantu lishi dili*, pp. 28–29, 35.

[86] See *Zhushu jinian*, 2, p. 16 (Legge, *The Shoo King*, Prolegomena, p. 156).

[87] See Fan Xiangyong, *Guben zhushu jinian*, p. 32.

the ruling elite of Western Shen who had migrated to the south, it may well be possible that a new group of the Rong people moved in to occupy Western Shen and was therefore called "Rong of Shen." In this case, the Western Shen that the Zhou were dealing with in their last years would have been historically very different from the Shen that was moved to the south in the early time of King Xuan. But there is no proof for this. In any event, the timing of this campaign appears a little problematic: the Zhou attacked Shen only about seven years before the daughter of the Ruler of Shen was established as the queen of King You. However, political relations between two peoples could rapidly change, and it was not uncommon in Chinese history for marriage alliances to be made with former enemies in a newly established good political relation. I would like to suggest that it was this Western Shen, not the Southern Shen in Nanyang, that allied itself with the Western Rong and Zeng and resisted the aggressive move by the Zhou court.

The location of Western Shen had apparently become unknowable by the Han dynasty, and thereafter was absent from all ancient geographical works. Perhaps because the Shen in Nanyang entered the main stream of the geographical tradition, the Shen that was located in the west was ignored. Fortunately, in the Warring States part of the text *Shanhai jing* (Classic of Mountains and Seas), which by later standards was not a real geographical work, there are traces of this Western Shen. In this text, there is a mountain that is literally called the "Mountain of the fountainhead of the Shen River" (Shenshou zhi shan 申首之山), probably located somewhere in the Pingliang region, near the headwaters of the Jing River. The "Western Mountains" section of the text says:[88]

西二百五十里，曰白於之山...洛水出其陽，而東流注于渭；夾水出于其陰，東流注于生水。

Two hundred and fifty *li* to the west [of Yushan] is Baiyu Mountain . . . The Luo River originates on its south side and flows eastward into the Wei River; the Jia River originates on its north side and flows eastward into the Sheng River.

西北三百里，曰申首之山 . . . 申水出于其上，潛于其下。

Three hundred *li* to the northwest [of Baiyu Mountain] is Shenshou Mountain . . . The Shen River originates on it but flows under it.

又西五十五里，曰涇谷之山，涇水出焉，東南流注于渭。

Another fifty-five *li* to the west [of Shenshou Mountain] is the mountain of Jinggu, where the Jing River originates, and flows southeastward into the Wei River.

Although many of the mountains and some of the directions or distances given in the *Shanhai jing* are subjects of controversy, in this particular case we are fortunate to have two important landmarks, Baiyu 白於 Mountain and the headwaters of the Jing River, the existence and geographical locations of which are beyond question. Some historical geographers have

---

[88] See *Shanhai jing*, p. 1,348.

already noted the accuracy of the geographical information regarding these two landmarks in the *Shanhai jing*, although the same text also mentions many other landmarks that are illusive or even fictional.[89] Since the "Jing River" section of the *Shuijing zhu* text of the sixth century had long been lost, this information on the upper Jing region is of considerable importance. Baiyu Mountain, also known as the west section of the Hengshan Mountains, is located in northern Shaanxi, where it joins with the Ziwu mountain ranges that run along the eastern edge of the upper Jing River basin. The Jing River, as mentioned in chapter 1, originates on the east side of the Liupan Mountains in present-day Longde 隆德, Ningxia Autonomous Region, about 250 kilometers to the southwest (not northwest, as the text says) of Baiyu Mountain.[90] Accordingly, Shenshou Mountain, which literally means the mountain at the headwaters of the Shen River, was located between Baiyu Mountain and the headwaters of the Jing River.

This suggests that in the geographical conception of the *Shanhai jing* there were a Shen River that was probably a minor tributary of the Jing River, and a certain Shenshou Mountain that was probably one of the mountains standing at the northwestern edge of the upper Jing River basin. By the same concept, the distance (55 *li* or 27.5 kilometers) between the headwaters of the Jing River and the named Shenshou Mountain suggests that at the very least they were located close to each other, possibly in the north part of the Pingliang region (Map 13). Since ancient states often derived their names from those of mountains or rivers nearby, and *vice versa*, it is likely that Western Shen was located near Shenshou Mountain and the Shen River. Although this piece of information is from a text that is generally of doubtful reliability, the geographical location of Shen it suggests can be confirmed within the text itself and also fits perfectly into the historical context that requires Western Shen to have been located to the west of the Zhou capital, close to both the Western Rong and the state of Qin. This is not likely to be a mere coincidence. Pingliang is about 75 kilometers to the southeast of Guyuan, a main base of the Xianyun, and is about 130 kilometers northeast of Tianshui where the state of Qin was located. I believe that, as far as the available evidence shows, this was the most likely location of Western Shen.

The location of Lü

In locating the fall of the Western Zhou, we also need to consider the geographical position of Lü, mentioned together with Western Shen in the *Guoyu*. There is a general agreement that Lü was located to the west

---

[89] See Wang Chengzu, *Zhongguo dili xue shi* (Beijing: Shangwu, 1982), pp. 24–25.
[90] This discrepancy between the direction given in the text and the actual geography is due to a systematic distortion of the direction of mountains in the "Western Mountains" section of the *Shanhai jing*.

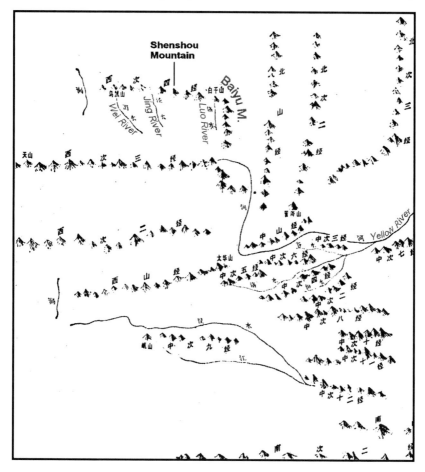

Map 13 Location of the Shen River in the *Shanhai jing* (based on Wang Chengzu, *Zhongguo dili xue shi* [Beijing: Shangwu, 1982], p. 19; fig. 2)

of Nanyang during the early Spring and Autumn period. However, Xu Shaohua has suggested that Lü was not located in the Nanyang basin until very late in the Western Zhou, and that it probably moved there from Shanxi.[91] Western Zhou inscriptions suggest that the lineage or polity of Lü had played a much more active role than Shen did in the Zhou court. In the Lü Xing *hu* 呂行壺 (JC: 9689), probably cast in the time of King Kang or Zhao, Lü Xing is said to have been on a northern expedition.[92] In the Jing *gui* 靜簋 (JC: 4273), a certain Lü Gang 呂剛 accompanied the

---

[91] See Xu Shaohua, *Zhou dai nantu lishi dili*, p. 41.

[92] The Lü Xing *hu* belongs to the group of bronzes all mentioning the military commander Bo Maofu 伯懋父 that by their design and ornamentation were undoubtedly cast in the late part of the early Western Zhou to the early years of King Mu. The *hu* itself is typical of early mid-Western Zhou *hu*-vessels, excavated from many tombs. See Li Feng, "Huanghe liuyu Xi Zhou muzang," pp. 389, 403, 414.

Zhou king on a campaign.[93] In a more important inscription, the Ban *gui* 班簋 (JC: 4341), Lübo 呂伯, the head of the Lü lineage, was commissioned by King Mu to assist Maobo 毛伯 in a military campaign in the east. In the Lü Fuyu *pan* 呂服余盤 (JC: 10169), another mid-Western Zhou bronze, Lü Fuyu was ordered by the king to serve in the royal Six Armies.[94] All of these inscriptions are evidence that Lü existed long before the Lü in Nanyang was founded, and it is very likely that it was located near or in the Zhou royal domain. But these inscriptions provide no information regarding where Lü was located during the early and mid-Western Zhou.

Of all the Lü bronzes that can be dated to the Western Zhou, the provenance of only two is known: the Lü Jijiang *hu* 呂㡴姜壺 (JC: 9610), reportedly discovered in the capital Feng or Hao during World War II;[95] and the Lü Jiang *gui* 呂姜簋 (JC: 3348), a typical King Mu period vessel, excavated from a tomb in Lingtai 靈臺 in the upper Jing River region.[96] The discovery of the Lü Jiang *gui* strongly suggests Lü's relation to the upper Jing River region where Western Shen was probably located. It is also possible that Lü was related to the Pu 蒲 River, since Lü is also called Fu 甫 in a chapter in the *Shangshu*.[97] There are two Pu Rivers in the upper Jing River region, the northern one a tributary of the Jing River, and the southern one being a tributary of the Daxi 達溪 River which is in turn a tributary of the Jing River (Map 2). While the name of the northern Pu River did not appear until after the Ming dynasty, the southern Pu River had a much earlier origin, being recorded in a phrase quoted in the *Taiping huanyu ji* (late tenth century AD) from the already lost "Jing River" chapter of the *Shuijing zhu*.[98] The tomb in which the Lü Jiang *gui* was found is located only a few kilometers from the entrance to the southern Pu River. Moreover, the *Shuijing zhu* also mentions that the upper Qian 汧 River in present-day Longxian area was called the Pu River.[99] Both of these Pu Rivers mentioned in the *Shuijing zhu* are very close to the Pingliang area where Western Shen is likely to have been located.

From the above analysis, we can now set the historical downfall of the Western Zhou dynasty into the landscape of the northwestern frontier of Zhou. In the ninth month of the tenth year of King You (772 BC), the royal

---

[93] The Jing *gui* mentions Lü Gang together with Wu Hui 吳卉 as companions of the king in an archery ritual. Since the Ban *gui* mentions Lübo along with Wubo 吳伯, some scholars believe that they were the same as Lü Gang and Wu Hui in the Jing *gui*. These bronzes, both by their design and by the connection through their inscriptions, were undoubtedly cast during the early mid-Western Zhou. See Ma Chengyuan, *Shang Zhou qingtongqi*, 3, pp. 108–11. For the date of the two bronzes, see also Shaughnessy, *Sources of Western Zhou history*, pp. 250–52.

[94] The *pan*, by its deep basin and decorative pattern, is typical of the mid-Western Zhou period. For its discovery and date, see *Wenwu* 1986.4, 1–7, pl. 1.

[95] For the discovery of the Lü Jijiang *hu*, see *Wenwu* 1982.10, 43.

[96] For the discovery of the Lü Jiang *gui*, see *Kaogu* 1976.1, 41–42.

[97] For instance, some scholars have identified Lübo in the Ban *gui* with Fuhou 甫侯, said to be the author of the "Lüxing" 呂刑 (or "Fuxing" 甫刑) chapter in the *Shangshu*. See Shirakawa, "Kinbun tsūshaku," 15.79:46. See also *Shangshu*, 19, p. 247 (Legge, *The Shoo King*, pp. 588–612).

[98] See *Taiping huanyu ji*, 32, p. 11. [99] See *Shuijing zhu*, 2, p. 581.

army of Zhou set out to attack Western Shen, probably located in the valley of a tributary of the upper Jing River, and demanded Prince Yijiu from the Ruler of Shen. Determined not to hand the prince over, Western Shen called on its allies for help. In response to this call, the Western Rong broke into the Jing River valley from the Guyuan region and engaged the Zhou troops in an initial battle, probably near Shen. Apparently the royal army was defeated by the joint forces of Western Shen, the Western Rong, and Zeng. Pursuing the fleeing Zhou royal army, the allies marched down the Jing River and reached the Zhou capital in the first month of the eleventh year of King You (771 BC). Unable to resist the invasion by the joint forces, King You and the court officials including Duke Huan of Zheng then fled the capital, probably in the hope that they could escape to the eastern capital Chengzhou. But they were caught and killed by the Western Rong at the foot of Lishan Mountain. The Western Zhou dynasty thus fell. The whole process was very similar to the battle of 823 BC in the fifth year of King Xuan, but with a very different result.

CONCLUSION

Much of what we know about the political history of the last years of the Western Zhou is based on the received textual records, but the bronze inscriptions do provide us with some important references to the individuals and polities that had played a significant role in the historical development of the late Western Zhou. They also provide us with some crucial links between the political history and its geographical setting. Helped by the links through bronze inscriptions, the careful analysis of textual records in a historical context that logically extends from the preceding period has enabled us to achieve a coherent understanding of the interplay by the many powers in the common process of the dynastic downfall.

It is likely that the problems that eventually led to the fall of the dynasty had their origins in the politics of the Zhou court, particularly in the generational power transition straddling the reigns of King Xuan and King You. Differing from all previous views on the matter, my reading of the three poems in the "Minor Odes" section of the *Book of Poetry* in connection with the historical texts reveals a major political conflict between the party of senior officials centered around Huangfu and the newly established King You. The king was in turn aided by his new consort Bao Si, who was trying to attain the status of legitimate Zhou queen by putting her own son in the position of royal heir. In 777 BC, Huangfu was probably defeated and left the capital for the east, and the legitimate Prince Yijiu was forced into exile in Western Shen, probably located in the Pingliang area in the upper Jing River valley. Thus, King You attained full control over the policy of the Zhou court.

However, the consolidation of King You's power led the Zhou court to adopt an aggressive policy towards Western Shen, the patron of Prince Yijiu. To protect itself, Western Shen established an alliance with the polity of Zeng and the Western Rong, who can be reasonably related to Zhou's traditional enemy – the Xianyun. The joint forces of Western Shen, Western Rong, and Zeng first defeated the Zhou royal army in a battle probably near Western Shen, and then marched down the Jing River valley and sacked the Zhou capital. In an immediate sense, the fall of the Western Zhou appears to have been the result of a serious miscalculation by the Zhou court of the power balance between Zhou and its enemies. In this regard, the Zhou dynasty might have lasted some years longer had King You not triggered the final combat by attacking Western Shen. But at a fundamental level, the fall was the result of the long process of Zhou's gradual weakening, by factors that I have discussed in the preceding chapters, and by the political struggle that took place during the early years of King You.

CHAPTER 5

The eastward migration: reconfiguring the Western Zhou state

The aftermath of the fall of the Zhou capitals in the Wei River valley was chaotic and devastating. The *Shiji* says that the Western Rong, after killing King You at the foot of Lishan Mountain, returned home to the west with Bao Si and all the valuables from the Zhou treasury.[1] The real situation may have been more complicated. It is likely that many settlements on the Wei River plain were plundered by the invaders, resulting in widespread social panic as well as economic destruction. The Western Shen and the Zeng probably no longer presented themselves as serious threats to the Zhou people since their political rivals at the court had already been eliminated. But the Western Rong, who may have allied with the Shen for a totally different purpose, had become the greatest destructive power.

The real implication of all this is that the Wei River plain was no longer a safe place suitable for the continuous development of the Zhou metropolitan society and culture. The strategic vulnerability of the Wei River plain was fully exposed by the events of 771 BC, and the Western Rong, who had successfully captured the Zhou capital once, could easily do so again. It was no longer possible for the Zhou court, now reestablished under the leadership of King Ping (Prince Yijiu), to survive on the Wei River plain. So a decision was made to move the court east to Luoyi on the Luo River plain in western Henan – the beginning of the "Eastern Zhou."[2] The migration of the Zhou center to the east had far-reaching impact on Chinese history. It initiated a process of geopolitical reconfiguration of the Western Zhou state, involving the transformations of many aristocratic lineages originally located in the west into new regional states in the east. This transition further gave rise to new political antagonisms and new social relations, and therefore redirected political life in China for the next 500 years, during

---

[1] See *Shiji*, 4, p. 149 (Nienhauser, *The Grand Scribe's Record*, 1, p. 74).

[2] The Zhou court lasted in the eastern capital for more than five centuries until its extermination by the state of Qin in 256 BC The Eastern Zhou period is further divided into two parts. The first part is called the "Spring and Autumn period" (Chunqiu 春秋) because it corresponds roughly with the time covered by the *Spring and Autumn Annals* which actually begins only at 722 BC The second part is called the "Warring States period" (Zhan'guo 戰國), a name taken from the *Stratagems of the Warring States* that runs until the unification by Qin in 221 BC As for the dividing point between the two parts, it is conventionally placed either in 481 BC, the year in which the Tian family replaced the Jiang family as ruler of the state of Qi, or in 403 BC the year that the three new states, Hann, Wei, and Zhao, were formally sanctioned by the Zhou court.

which time the Zhou king and his court were gradually marginalized. It certainly also gave rise, owing to the disappearance of central power, to new political norms and strategies that were needed for achieving political authority in a new era.

To an even larger extent, the eastward migration opened a new era of great cultural and ethnic mixing. During the Eastern Zhou, the Zhou states found themselves confronted by the various Rong people not on the former borders of the Western Zhou, but among them in central China. This resulted from a long process of migration and penetration of the Rong people into the Zhou territory, following the eastward move of the Zhou court. Thus, how to accommodate the so-called "barbarians" had become a critical social issue for the native Zhou states in the 200 years following the move. What is more significant is the migration of the state of Qin 秦, originally located in southeastern Gansu, into the Wei River plain, by fighting the various Rong people. This move transformed the Wei River plain into a new power base, the cradle of China's future empire.

The present chapter addresses this complex process of geopolitical reconfiguration as well as social transformation of the Zhou state. It first examines the historical records on the move of the Zhou court to the east. Then, I turn to the eastward migration of the Zhou aristocratic lineages, focusing on the history of two important lineages – Zheng 鄭 and Guo 虢 – for which we not only are better informed by the textual records, but also have new archaeological evidence. The third part of this chapter discusses the crucial relationship between Zhou and Qin, and examines how the Qin people established themselves as new masters of the west.

THE RELOCATION OF THE ZHOU COURT IN THE EAST

As already demonstrated earlier, the Wei River valley in Shaanxi was the political center of the Zhou state, but not its geographical center, which lay on the Luo River plain in western Henan. Beginning with the relocation of the Zhou court in Luoyi, China entered a new period during which the structure of political power was significantly different from that of the Western Zhou. By its physical existence in Luoyi, the Zhou court continued to serve as the center of political struggles among the regional rulers who competed for guardianship to the Zhou king in the first century after the historical move.

Geopolitical setting of the eastern capital

In order to understand Luoyi as the new site of political struggle, we must first understand its geographical setting. The Luoyang plain enjoys a natural environment similar to the Wei River plain in central Shaanxi; however, compared with the more open Wei River plain, the Luoyang plain is much smaller. By relocating the royal capital on the Luo River plain, the major geographical obstacles in western Henan, as analyzed in chapter 1 (see pp. 60–61), were turned into an effective protection for the royal court from enemies in the west. To its south, the Funiu Mountain system separates it from the Nanyang basin and from the upper Huai River region. To its east, the high Songshan Mountain is a natural barrier, protecting it from the open plain further east. To its north, the Yellow River forms another natural barrier. Owing to these geographical advantages, Luoyang has been the capital of nine dynasties in Chinese history; it is especially worth noting that two other major dynasties – the Han and the Tang – had capitals on the Wei River plain at the peak of their power and then moved to Luoyang during their decline, as did the Zhou dynasty.

However, it is more important here to know how the Zhou people perceived the importance of Luoyi in their geopolitical perception of the Zhou world. This takes us back to an important discourse in the *Guoyu* that is said to have taken place in 774 BC at the court of King You. When Duke Huan of Zheng reportedly inquired where he should move the lineage property of Zheng to in order to avoid the disaster of the dynastic downfall, the court historian Shi Bo presented him with the following analysis:[3]

王室將卑，戎狄必昌，不可偪也。當成周者，南有荊蠻、申、呂、應、鄧、陳、蔡、隨、唐；北有衛、燕、狄、鮮虞、潞、洛、泉、徐、蒲；西有虞、虢、晉、隗、霍、楊、魏、芮；東有齊、魯、曹、宋、滕、薛、鄒、莒。是非王之支子母弟甥舅也，則皆蠻、荊、戎、狄之人也。非親則頑，不可入也。其濟、洛、河、潁之 間乎？

The royal house will diminish, while the Rong and Di must become prosperous; this is what you cannot go against. Those that are located around Chengzhou are, in the south, Jingman, Shen, Lü, Ying, Deng, Chen, Cai, Sui, and Tang; in the north, Wey, Yan, Di, Xianyu, Lu, Luo, Quan, Xu, Pu; in the west, Yu, [Western] Guo, Jin, Wei, Huo, Yang, Wei, Rui; in the east, Qi, Lu, Cao, Song, Teng, Xue, Zou, Ju. These, if not the royal offspring, the princes, and the royal in-laws, were all people of Man, Jing, Rong, and Di. They are either the royal relatives or the stubborn, [and therefore, you] cannot enter among them. Isn't it the area between the Ji, Luo, He, and Ying rivers [to which you should go]?

In this paragraph, Shi Bo suggested that since the "four directions" of Chengzhou (Luoyi) were all occupied by either the royal relatives or the "barbarians," the only place where the lineage of Zheng could possibly be relocated was the area between the four rivers: Ji, Luo, He (Yellow River), and Ying; this area approximately corresponds to present-day Xingyang 滎陽, Mixian 密縣, and Xinzheng 新鄭 in the core area of the Central Plain, to the immediate east of Luoyi (Map 6). Although states such as Eastern Guo 東虢 and Kuai 鄶 were already located there, they were not regarded by Shi Bo as significant powers.

[3] See *Guoyu*, 16, p. 507.

As has been mentioned before, the "Zhengyu" chapter of the *Guoyu* was probably composed some time in the late Warring States period.[4] Besides the date of composition of the text, there are also issues of the date of the materials it contains, and the date of the geographical perception the materials reflect. These are certainly valid questions that should be asked about an ancient text. On the last point, I think we can find some clues in a comparison of the states list here with the known histories of these states. For instance, in the west states such as Yu, Western Guo, Huo, and Rui no longer existed after 640 BC. The southern state Chu annexed Deng in 678 BC, Chen in 478 BC, and Cai in 447 BC. The state of Cao in the east was annexed by Song in 487 BC.[5] In all, at least eight states mentioned here no longer existed after the mid-fifth century BC, and I think that this is a strong indication that the speech reflects a geopolitical perception that can be traced back to the first half of the Spring and Autumn period. Even if the speech itself may have taken its current form in the late Warring States, its composer must have had good knowledge of early Spring and Autumn period political geography, or at least have made an effort to try to reconstruct it.

In this typical *shifang* (four quarters)–center model of the geopolitically conceived Zhou world, Chengzhou was given the central position.[6] To the south of Chengzhou were located the state of Ying at Pingdingshan, Southern Shen, Lü, Deng, and Tang in the Nanyang basin, and Chen and Cai in the upper Huai River region (which were actually to the southeast of Luoyi). These states served as a barrier between Chengzhou and the southern power Jingman (Chu) in Hubei and the Huaiyi in the middle and lower Huai River regions. To the north of the capital were located the states of Wey in northern Henan and Yan in Beijing. To the west of Chengzhou were located the states of Jin, Huo, and Yang in the Fen River valley, and Wei, Yu, Rui, and Western Guo in the narrow pass of the Yellow River between Shanxi and western Henan. To the east, were located the states of Song, Cao, Qi, Lu 魯, and Teng in eastern Henan and western Shandong. These Zhou states formed a huge web that could protect the royal capital at its center against invasions from outside if they functioned as intended by the Zhou rulers. This network was largely the outcome of early Western Zhou expansion, though partly too the result of late Western Zhou consolidation under King Xuan, discussed in chapter 2. It was certainly the case in the Di invasion of 662–659 BC, during which the Zhou states in eastern Henan and western Shandong united themselves

[4] For the date of composition of the *Guoyu*, see Wei Juxian, *Gushi yanjiu*, p. 164; Loewe, *Early Chinese Texts*, p. 264.

[5] On the extinction of these states, see Chen Mengjia's fundamental study: Chen Mengjia, *Xi Zhou niandai kao* (Shanghai: Shangwu, 1945), pp. 57–59.

[6] For a recent discussion of the "*shifang*–center" cosmology in early China, see Aihe Wang, *Cosmology and Political Culture in Early China* (Cambridge: Cambridge University Press, 2000), pp. 23–74.

against the invaders moving towards the royal capital.[7] However, the quoted paragraph also indicates that on the periphery of the network the original Zhou states had already become mixed with some non-Zhou polities. This is especially the case in the north, where several polities related to the Di and Rong, including Xianyu, Lu 潞, and Luo in central Hebei, are mentioned. However, there is no mention of the important northern state Xing that was conquered by the Di people in 662 BC. This may be an indication that the speech could not have been made by Shi Bo at the court of King You.

From the fall to the relocation of the Zhou court

Although historians consent to the importance of the relocation of the Zhou court in Luoyi as the beginning of a new era, what really happened in the interval between the downfall of the Zhou capital in the west in 771 BC and its relocation in the east in 770 BC has long been obscured in history. In order to understand early Eastern Zhou politics, it is important to examine the available evidence for this transitional period. Let us begin by reading the poem "Yu wuzheng" 雨無正 (no. 194) from the *Book of Poetry*, which in all likelihood speaks of the situation in the Zhou homeland after the fall of the Zhou capital to the invading Quanrong (Waley's translation).[8]

1	浩浩昊天,	Broad and vast is mighty Heaven,
2	不駿其德。	Yet it keeps its grace from us,
3	降喪饑饉,	But rather brings death and famine,
4	斬伐四國。	War and destruction to all the states.
5	昊天疾威,	Foreboding Heaven is a cruel affliction,
6	弗慮弗圖。	It does not ponder, does not plan.
7	舍彼有罪,	It pays no attention to the guilty,
8	既伏其辜。	Who have admitted their crimes.
9	若此無罪,	But the ones who are innocent,
10	淪胥以鋪。	These, without exception, suffer.

11	周宗既滅,	The Zhou capital was already destroyed,[9]
12	靡所止戾。	There was no place to rest or reside.
13	正大夫離居,	The great officials scattered across the land,
14	莫知我勩。	No one knew how we toiled.
15	三事大夫,	The three high ministers
16	莫肯夙夜。	All refuse to serve at dawn or at dusk.

[7] The expedition has been described in detail by Průšek; see Průšek, *Chinese Statelets*, pp. 145–48. However, the irony is that during the long period of Eastern Zhou some of these states also engineered foreign attacks on the royal capital or attacked it themselves. This shows the changing relationship between the Zhou court and regional states during the Eastern Zhou period.

[8] See *Shijing*, 12.2, pp. 447–48 (Waley, *The Book of Songs*, pp. 172–74).

[9] Waley here has the "House of Zhou" for the term *Zongzhou* that also appears in the poem "Zhengyue" (no. 192) where he translates it as the "Capital of Zhou." The term appears in many bronze inscriptions clearly referring to the Zhou capital Hao.

17 邦君諸侯，	Territorial administrators and regional rulers[10]
18 莫肯朝夕。	All refuse to meet in the morning or at night.
19 庶曰式臧，	One wished they could be good,
20 覆出為惡。	But no, they continue their wayward ways.
21 如何昊天，	How can it be, mighty Heaven,
22 辟言不信。	That the word of rule is untrue?
23 如彼行邁，	Like those who walk along,
24 則非所臻。	With no place in the end to go.
25 凡百君子，	You, our many lords,
26 各敬爾身。	Take special care of yourselves.
27 胡不相畏，	How could you not fear the others,
28 不畏于天。	Or hold no fear of Heaven?
29 戎成不退，	There is war, but we do not withdraw;
30 饑成不遂。	There is famine, but we do not progress.
31 曾我暬御，	I am but a common attendant
32 憯憯日瘁。	Deeply saddened, exhausted every day.
33 凡百君子，	You, our many lords,
34 莫肯用訊。	All refuse to take counsel.
35 聽言則答，	When words are well-considered, you respond;
36 譖言則退。	When words are slanderous, then withdraw.
37 哀哉不能言，	How pitiful I am, unable to speak.
38 匪舌是出，	Not that my tongue has problems,
39 維躬是瘁。	But rather I am exhausted.
40 哿矣能言，	To be able to speak would be good indeed;
41 巧言如流，	Then the clever words would flow,
42 俾躬處休。	And I would finally find some rest.
43 維曰于仕，	"Go serve in office," is what they say;
44 孔棘且殆。	But it is so difficult, so full of danger.
45 云不可使，	Some orders cannot be carried out,
46 得罪于天子。	And thus you incur the Son of Heaven's blame.
47 亦云可使，	Other orders can be carried out,
48 怨及朋友。	But rancor can reach even to your friends.
49 謂爾遷于王都，	They say you should return to the royal city,
50 曰予未有室家。	But you say, "There I have no house or home."
51 鼠思泣血，	So lonely I weep till my eyes bleed;
52 無言不疾。	Of these words not one does not pain.

---

[10] Waley here has "Princes and feudal lords"; corrections are made in accordance with our current understanding of Western Zhou institutions; see Li Feng, "'Offices' in Bronze Inscriptions," pp. 28–29.

53 昔爾出居，　　　In the past when you moved away,
54 誰從爾作室。　Who was there to build a house for you?

The poem is explicitly not a composition for pure literary pleasure, but one that was written with deep political concerns. Reading through the lines, everyone can get a vivid sense of sorrow and hopelessness about a state of affairs that can be properly described as "anarchy." Qu Wanli has suggested that the poem was composed at the time of the eastward migration of the Zhou court.[11] Whether this date is valid can still be debated, but that is evidently the point of time the poem is speaking of, as most explicitly indicated by lines 11–12: "The Zhou capital was already destroyed; there was no place to rest or reside." The poem appears to suggest that concomitant with the fall of the Zhou capital a serious drought hit the Wei River plain and spread to the whole world, resulting in a great number of deaths. This may be true, or it may also be a literary exaggeration or a metaphor of the great disaster that brought the dynasty down. Despite the literary nature of the poem, there are clearly visible historical specificities in it from which we can draw some useful information regarding the aftermath of the dynastic downfall.

First, the poet appears to suggest that the impact of the dynastic downfall went far beyond just punishing the criminals (lines 7–8), the term probably referring in a broad sense to those who had caused the fall of the dynasty. It resulted in a large number of deaths and long-lasting suffering among the Zhou people. Another poem, "Zhaomin" 召旻 (Mao 265), which I believe also speaks about the same period, says that the area of the Zhou state was being reduced daily by 100 *li* (50 kilometers),[12] implying that the fall of the Zhou capital was followed by large-scale incursions into the Zhou territory by the Rong peoples. This situation is different from the *Shiji*'s statement that the Quan Rong went immediately home with the Zhou treasury after they captured the Zhou capital.[13] This point acquires further proof in the fact that many of the Rong people actually founded their own polities on the former Zhou sites such as the capital Hao and continued to be active in the region during the next half-century, as will be discussed later in this chapter. Second, lines 13–18 and 49–54 suggest that many people, including presumably some official aristocrats, had lost their homes in the incident and had sought asylum elsewhere. For this reason, when they were asked to return to the capital, they could excuse themselves for having no house or home in the royal capital (line 50). Third, the poem strongly suggests that the Zhou administrative machine was paralyzed by the foreign invasion bringing the dynasty down and throwing Zhou society into complete chaos. It is above all significant that the poet draws up a bureaucratic ladder of the

---

[11] See Qu Wanli, *Shijing quanshi* (Taipei: Lianjing, 1983), p. 362.　[12] See *Shijing*, 18.5, p. 580.
[13] See *Shiji*, 4, p. 149 (Nienhauser, *The Grand Scribe's Records*, 1, p. 74).

Zhou government from the eminent chief ministers (great officials, as Waley translates) to the minister of three affairs (land, construction, and horses), and then to the local administrators and regional rulers, quite consistent with the bureaucratic hierarchy we learn of from the bronze inscriptions. In this regard, it says that the chief ministers had left the capital and the three ministers of affairs would not conduct their administrative duty. (It is very interesting to see the expression "at dawn or at dusk" [*suye* 夙夜] here; it appears at the end of many "Appointment Inscriptions" where the Zhou king demanded that the officials be "Respectful at dawn and at night.") The local administrators and the regional rulers would not be respectful while the hundred gentlemen, referring probably to the many aristocrats, would not even bother to ask about state affairs (lines 33–34). From the point of view of the poet, it is the responsibility of the aristocrats and ministers to move the government forward even during the catastrophic period; but to his complete dissatisfaction, they all tried to stay away from the government and refused to be involved in politics. Fourth, and probably most important, in an explicit way lines 43–48 suggest the rise of a new political tension between the king (who must be the newly established King Ping, given the post-Western Zhou chronology the poem describes) and many nobles whom the poet refers to as "friends." There is the difficult choice facing the aristocrats between serving the new king, probably in the new capital (line 49), and incurring the blame of the "friends." As will be shown soon below, this certainly has its own unique historical context in which the lines can only be fully understood.

It is true that the poem only allows us to view the dynastic catastrophe through the eyes of its composer, as do any historical sources, including the bronze inscriptions; nonetheless, such a poetic view may be a fresh and truthful reflection of historical reality. In general, the poem suggests that the attack on the Zhou capital by the Western Rong in 771 BC had caused great destruction to Western Zhou society in central Shaanxi. It threw the Wei River plain into a state of long-lasting disorder and anarchy, in which the common people could only put their hopes in the hands of former officials who sought asylum for themselves elsewhere. One important testimony to this destruction has been provided by archaeology. In all of the three major cities on the Wei River plain – Feng, Hao, and Qiyi – there is a definite disruption in the sequence of their archaeological remains, and this disruption coincides well with the end of the Western Zhou. In Feng and Hao, Warring States layers are sometimes superimposed on the Western Zhou stratum, but more often it is the Han deposits that lie directly over it; deposits from the Spring and Autumn period which, if anything might suggest a continuing occupation of the sites from the Western Zhou period, have never been found.[14] In Qiyi (Zhouyuan) there is normally a disturbed stratum post-dating the Han dynasty that overlies the Late Western Zhou

[14] See *Fengxi fajue baogao* (Beijing: Wenwu, 1962), pp. 17–18, 70–71.

stratum.[15] Archaeological evidence strongly suggests that all three cities were simultaneously ruined at the end of the Western Zhou. It has also been suggested by some scholars that owing to the sudden attacks by the Western Rong a large number of bronze vessels were buried underground in Zhouyuan and the capital Feng and have been preserved until today.[16]

For the historical context in which this archaeologically visible phenomenon actually took place, and referring to which the poems mentioned above were written, we must turn to the historical records. In this regard, the *Zuozhuan* (twenty-sixth year of Duke Zhao) offers us a unique statement. In 516 BC, after King Jing of Zhou was installed by the regional rulers at Chengzhou, Prince Zhao 朝, who was defeated in the political struggle with the new king, sent a long message to the many rulers to explain his own position. In this he alluded to the historical developments following the death of King You:[17]

至于幽王，天不弔周，王昏不若，用愆厥位。攜王奸命，諸侯替之，而建王嗣，用遷郟鄏，則是兄弟之能用力于王室也。

Arriving at the time of King You, Heaven had no mercy on the Zhou; the king was muddleheaded and therefore lost his position. The King of Xie usurped the mandate, but the many rulers removed him and established the royal successor; therefore, (the court) was moved to the area of Jia and Ru. This is the proof that the brothers were able to use their power with respect to the royal house.

The passage says that after King You lost his position, it was the King of Xie who usurped the mandate. But he was then displaced by the many regional rulers who established the legitimate heir of the former king and moved the Zhou court to the land of Jiaru, referring to Luoyi. Although this statement comes in the middle of Prince Zhao's speech, which has its own political agenda, a simple fact such as the existence of a nominal "king" does not seem to have been forged by a later author because such would only serve to undermine the power of the speech. A speech, in order to be persuasive, has to be credible on basic historical facts. There has been some disagreement regarding the identity of this rival king; for instance, Du Yu identified him with Bo Fu, who was a son of King You and Bao Si.[18] This mistake has already been corrected by a number of scholars.[19] Certainly, the *Zuozhuan* is not the only source that mentions this rival king; the *Bamboo Annals* has slightly more to say about the circumstances under which this king was established. Full citations of the relevant paragraphs in both the *Ancient* and *Current Bamboo Annals* have already been given in

---

[15] For instance, see *Wenwu* 1979.10, 27–28.
[16] This view was first suggested by Guo Moruo; see *Fufeng Qijiacun qingtongqi qun* (Beijing: Wenwu, 1963), pp. 5–6. The burial condition of these caches containing bronzes was systematically examined by Luo Xizhang, who concluded that most caches, but not all, were buried when the Quanrong attacked the Zhou capital; see Luo Xizhang, "Zhouyuan qingtongqi jiaocang jiqi youguan wenti de tantao," *Kaogu yu wenwu* 1988.2, 44–47.
[17] See *Zuozhuan*, 52, p. 52, 2,114.   [18] *Zuozhuan*, 52, p. 2,114.
[19] See Lei Xueqi, *Zhushu jinian yizheng*, 27, p. 210; Chen Fengheng, *Zhushu jinian jizhu*, 35, pp. 17–19.

chapter 4, pp. 218–19. According to these paragraphs, both the *Current* and *Ancient* versions indicate that Bo Fu was killed by the Quanrong, probably together with King You at Xi. They also suggest that it was another prince – Yuchen 余臣 – who was established king in a place called Xie 攜 by the Duke of Guo, Han 翰, while the legitimate heir of King You, Yijiu, who had been in exile in Western Shen since 777 BC, was established king by the many rulers, including the rulers of Shen, Lu, Xu, and probably also Zheng, at the state of Shen, certainly the Western Shen. However, as I will demonstrate in appendix 3, the lines that explain the reasons why King Ping was called "Heavenly King" and the rival king was called "King of Xie" in the *Ancient* version were later intrusions into the *Bamboo Annals*. From the genuine parts of both the *Ancient* and *Current* versions, it is clear that because Prince Yuchen was established at Xie, he was referred to as the "King of Xie." Unfortunately, ancient geographical works provide no information on the location of Xie, though there seems little doubt that it was in the Wei River valley.[20]

To understand this succession struggle upon the death of King You, we need to contextualize these facts within the general setting of late Western Zhou politics. Here, the Duke of Guo, Han, is a key figure. As has been shown in chapter 4, the Duke of Guo, Gu 鼓, mentioned in the *Lüshi chunqiu*, or Guo Shifu mentioned in the *Guoyu*,[21] was a political ally of Bao Si in her struggle against Huangfu and served in the most eminent position at the Zhou court during the last four years of King You's reign. Given their closeness in time, I consider that the Duke of Guo, Han, and the Duke of Guo, Gu, were the same person; I strongly suspect that the character *han* 翰 in the *Bamboo Annals* was a mistranscription of the character *gu* 鼓 in the original tomb text.[22] Whether or not this identification is correct, the ruler of Guo, given the important role the state of Guo played at King You's court, was in the most authoritative position to choose a new king as the legitimate successor to King You. In this regard, the succession struggle between the King of Xie and King Ping upon the death of King You was indeed the continuation of the political struggle from the court of King You. It marked the complete split of the Zhou aristocracy into two factions.

---

[20] On the basis of phonetic similarities, some scholars identified Xie with Xi, where King You and Bo Fu were killed by the Quanrong; see Chen Faren, *Chunqiu zuoshi zhuan diming tukao* (Taipei: Guangwen, 1967), p. 242. According to the *Houhan shu* and *Shuijing zhu*, Xi was located on the bank of the Xi River flowing north into the Wei River from Lishan Mountain; see *Houhan shu*, 19, p. 3,403; *Shuijing zhu*, 19, p. 616.

[21] See *Lüshi chunqiu*, 2, p. 634; *Guoyu*, 16, p. 518.

[22] There are clear similarities between the two characters. For instance, the character *gu* is written on the Yan'er *zhong* 沇儿鍾 (JC: 203), an Eastern Zhou bronze, as 鼓, while the character *han* is written 翰 on the same bronze; for the inscription, see also Shirakawa, "Kinbun tsūshaku," 40.228:572. The inscription has been translated into English by Mattos; see Gilbert Mattos, "Eastern Zhou Bronze Inscriptions," in *New Sources of Early Chinese History: An Introduction to the Reading of Inscriptions and Manuscripts*, ed. Edward Shaughnessy (Berkeley: Society for the Study of Early China, 1997), pp. 100–1. Chronologically, since the establishment of the King of Xie by the Duke of Guo, Han, took place in 771 BC, only four years after the Duke of Guo, Gu, became minister in the Zhou court, it is highly unlikely that there were two dukes from the state of Guo.

It is likely that the news of the fall of the Zhou capital was soon carried throughout the Zhou world, and some regional rulers may have gone west to help the Zhou court against the Quanrong. The *Current Bamboo Annals* lists three: the Ruler of Lu, Duke Wen of Xu, and the Prince of Zheng. According to the "Genealogical Account of Wey" in the *Shiji*, Duke Wu of Wey also seems to have gone west to help the Zhou court.[23] However, these rulers did not submit themselves to the King of Xie chosen by the state of Guo, but instead joined hands with the Ruler of Shen, who had played a very important role in bringing the dynasty to an end. They jointly established the previously legitimate heir Yijiu as King Ping at Western Shen. Western Shen, as noted in the preceding chapter, was probably located in the upper Jing River region. Some have questioned why the many rulers who would have fought the Rong should have cooperated with the Ruler of Shen who had joined the Rong to overthrow the Zhou dynasty, and why King Ping, who became king as a result of his political rivals having been eliminated by Western Shen and the Western Rong, should have ever regarded the Rong as a threat.[24] But this is not a serious problem; the Western Rong may have joined Western Shen through their own motives and the relationship between them could have changed rapidly after the capture of the Zhou capital and the killing of King You. By the same token, King Ping's attitude towards the Rong after he became the Zhou king could also have been different from that of the time when he was expelled by the Zhou court.

In the *Shiji*'s simple narrative of the transition, the threat from the Western Rong was given as the sole reason for the eastward migration of the Zhou court under King Ping. This is probably true because compared to the Wei River plain, which by this time had already been opened to attacks by the Western Rong, the Luoyang area, with its geopolitical advantages as shown above, offered the new king an ideal refuge. By moving to Luoyang, he could go under the immediate protection of those regional rulers who established him at Western Shen. Furthermore, one may conjecture about another factor that may also have played an important role in the eastward migration of the Zhou court – the existence of the court of the King of Xie on the Wei River plain. By moving to the east, King Ping could avoid running into immediate conflict with the King of Xie, who was supported by the state of Guo, which had by this time already established its new base in the Sanmenxia region (see below, pp. 255–8). Here again, we must consider the impact of the landscape. Sanmenxia is located at a crucial point controlling east–west communication, which the new court under King Ping must rely on for support of the many rulers in the east. In order to overcome the obstacle of the Guo lineage, it would be wise for King Ping to leave the Wei River valley and to go east under direct protection of the eastern rulers. But by doing so, he had left the Wei River valley in the

---

[23] See *Shiji*, 37, p. 1,591.
[24] For instance, see Yoshimoto Michimasa, "Shūshitsu tōsen kō," *Tōyō gakuhō* 71.3.4 (1990), 36; Song Xinchao, "Lishan zhi yi ji Pingwang dongqian lishi kaoshu," *Renwen zazhi* 1989.4, 75–79.

hands of the King of Xie and the lineage of Guo. I believe that this is the real historical dynamic in the transition of the Zhou court to the east.

We have very little information regarding King Ping's actual trip from Shaanxi to Luoyang. But it is likely that he was escorted by a number of regional rulers. The *Current Bamboo Annals* says:[25]

（平王）元年辛未，王東徙洛邑，錫文侯命。晉侯會衛侯、鄭伯、秦伯以師從王入 于成周。

In the first year (of King Ping), *xinwei*, the king moved east to Luoyi and entrusted to Ruler Wen [of Jin] the royal command. The Ruler of Jin together with the Ruler of Wey, Zhengbo, and Qinbo escorted the king with their troops entering Chengzhou.

According to this passage, the Ruler of Jin, the Ruler of Wey, Zhengbo, and Qinbo escorted King Ping all the way to Luoyi. This may indicate that the trip east was probably accompanied by dangers and difficulties, in addition to possible assault from the Rong people. Without the company of the eastern rulers, it would be impossible for King Ping to make his way east out of the Wei River valley. A passage in the *Zuozhuan* (tenth year of Duke Xiang) suggests that seven lineages followed King Ping on the trip to Luoyang.[26] Another passage in the "Zhouyu" chapter of the *Guoyu* highlights the role of the states of Jin and Zheng in the eastward migration of the Zhou court, saying: "When we, the Zhou, moved to the east, it was the Jin and Zheng on whom we relied."[27] The "Basic Annals of Qin" in the *Shiji* also mentions that Duke Xiang of Qin helped the Zhou court to move east.[28] Since Qin was located, as will be demonstrated later in this chapter, in the Tianshui area of eastern Gansu, to the west of the Longshan Mountains, Duke Xiang's long-distance expedition to secure the successful relocation of the Zhou court in the east seems very remarkable.

Above, I have tried to clarify the historical development from the fall of the Zhou capital to the relocation of the Zhou court in Luoyang. I suggest that through extensive search and careful analysis of textual sources, we can recover some hidden facts in this historical transition and can achieve a logical and better contextualized interpretation than the simple narrative offered by the *Shiji*. Although many aspects of this critical period remain unknown, it has been shown that the transition was not a smooth one but was accompanied by political struggles between the remnants of the King You–Bao Si party at the court of the King of Xie and the new court of King Ping supported by the many regional rulers. It has also been shown that, despite the continuing existence of the "Zhou court" at Xie, the Wei River plain probably went through a long period of panic and anarchy following the dynastic downfall. In this regard, the new court of King Ping, which was first established at Western Shen and was then moved

[25] See *Zhushu jinian*, 2, p. 18 (Legge, *The Shoo King*, Prolegomena, p. 158).
[26] See *Zuozhuan*, 31, p. 1,949.　　[27] See *Guoyu*, 2, p. 45.
[28] See *Shiji*, 5, p. 179 (Nienhauser, *The Grand Scribe's Records*, 1, p. 90).

to Luoyang by the regional rulers, represented more a break with than a continuation of the Western Zhou court. The King of Xie ruled for at least eleven years before finally dying at the hands of Ruler Wen of Jin.[29] Nothing is known about relations between the court of King Ping and the court of the King of Xie during these eleven years. The above-quoted passage from the *Zuozhuan* suggests that he was eventually removed by the many rulers. The killing of the King of Xie was a very important event in early Eastern Zhou politics because it secured the position of King Ping. It also marked the final completion of the transition from the Western to the Eastern Zhou.

THE MIGRATION OF THE ARISTOCRATIC LINEAGES

Seeing the eastward migration as a massive movement, we must admit that the process may have begun even before the evacuation of the Zhou court from the Wei River valley. Cho-yun Hsu has noted that during the reign of King You there was a general atmosphere that many people had anticipated the downfall of the dynasty and thought that it would be wise to escape.[30] In this regard, the move east of Huangfu to Xiang after his political defeat at the hands of the King You–Bao Si party, discussed in chapter 4, is a very good example. Among the many aristocratic lineages that had possibly moved to the east in the Western–Eastern Zhou transition, two – Zheng 鄭 and Guo 虢 – are most important as the defining elements in this process. This is because both Zheng and Guo were deeply involved in the politics of the Zhou court of King You, and even after the migration they continued to form, from their new locations in the east and with the relocated Zhou court in between, the axis of political struggle in the eastern plain during much of the eighth to the early seventh centuries BC. Therefore, in order to understand the eastward migration of the Zhou elite, we must first clarify the translocations of the Zheng and Guo lineages, which actually reveal some general patterns of population relocation as well as lineage development in pre-imperial China. In both cases, there are long-pending puzzles regarding their origins as well as their subsequent historical development. However, by carefully analyzing our current archaeological,

---

[29] According to the *Current Bamboo Annals*, the King of Xie was killed by Ruler Wen of Jin in the twenty-first year of King Ping; see *Zhushu jinian*, 2, p. 18 (Legge, *The Shoo King*, Prolegomena, p. 158). In the *Ancient Bamboo Annals* (quoted by Kong Yingda in his commentary to the *Zuozhuan*), as shown above, the "twenty-first year" is given without reign title, so it is difficult to know whether it refers to the twenty-first year after the death of King You, or to the twenty-first year of Ruler Wen of Jin, which would be the eleventh year of King Ping. In addition, Kong Yingda misquoted "Ruler Wen of Jin" 晋文侯 as "Duke Wen of Jin" 晋文公. See *Zuozhuan*, 52, p. 2,114; Fan Xiangyong, *Guben zhushu jinian*, p. 35. Some believe that the "Wenhou zhi ming" 文侯之命 chapter of the *Shangshu* records King Ping's bestowal of the royal command along with an award on Ruler Wen of Jin, and that this was particularly to honor his contribution in eliminating the rival court in Shaanxi; see *Shangshu*, 20, pp. 253–54; Qu Wanli, "Shangshu Wenhou zhi ming zhucheng de niandai," *Zhongyang yanjiuyuan lishi yuyan yanjiusuo jikan* 29 (1958), 510–11.
[30] See Xu Zhuoyun, "Zhou dongqian shimo," in *Qiugu bian* (Taipei: Lianjing, 1982), pp. 104–5.

inscriptional, and textual evidence, I believe that the puzzles can now be solved.

The origin and migration of the lineage of Zheng

As for the heritage of Zheng, the "Genealogical Account of Zheng" chapter of the *Shiji* says that Duke Huan of Zheng, You 友, founder of the lineage of Zheng, was the youngest son of King Li and a brother of King Xuan.[31] This account is supported by a passage from the *Zuozhuan* (second year of Duke Wen) saying that the lineage of Zheng regarded King Li as its founding ancestor.[32] Despite some traditional confusion concerning You's (also called Duofu 多父) position in the genealogy of the Zhou royal clan,[33] it is safe to say that Duofu, a son of King Li, was established in a place called Zheng in the twenty-second year of King Xuan (806 BC) and therefore started the history of the new lineage of Zheng as a branch of the Zhou royal clan.

Where was Zheng located? Most ancient historians cited the "Geographical Records" chapter of the *Hanshu* to locate Zheng in the Zheng County 鄭縣 of the Qin and Han dynasties, which is present-day Huaxian 華縣 at the east end of the Wei River valley in Shaanxi.[34] However, it has been suggested by Lu Liancheng that Zheng was originally located in the Fengxiang area near the west end of the Wei River valley, to the west of Qiyi, based on the location of the Great Zheng Palace 大鄭宮 in the capital of the state of Qin in the area during the Spring and Autumn period.[35] There is also another connection that seems to support this point: the *Shiben* 世本, a lost pre-Qin text (quoted by Tang dynasty commentators), says that Duke Huan of Zheng lived in a place called Yulin 棫林,[36] a place-name that appears also in the *Zuozhuan* (fourth year of Duke Xiang), and that in the summer of 559 BC, in a joint expedition against Qin, the troops of the eastern states crossed the Jing River and then arrived at Yulin, indicating undoubtedly that Yulin was to the west of the Jing River, and therefore

---

[31] See *Shiji*, 42, p. 1,757.   [32] See *Zuozhuan*, 18, p. 1,839.

[33] Some scholars previously considered that Duofu was a son of King Xuan, on the basis of three sources. First, a passage from the *Zuozhuan* (twenty-fourth year of Duke Xi) says that Zheng was kin to King Li and King Xuan; but this does not indicate that Duke Huan was a son of King Xuan because brothers can also be regarded as kin. Second, a passage from the *Guoyu* says that Zheng originated (*chuzi* 出自) from King Xuan; but this could simply mean that Zheng was established by King Xuan. Third, an entry for King Xuan in the *Current Bamboo Annals* refers to Duke Huan as prince (*wangzi* 王子) and therefore these scholars think that he must have been the son of King Xuan. In fact, another entry for King You also refers to Duke Huan as *wangzi*, and there is plenty of evidence in the *Zuozhuan* that princes were referred to as such after the death of their fathers. For these three sources, see *Zuozhuan*, 28, p. 1,918; *Guoyu*, 2, p. 50; *Zhushu jinian*, 2, p. 15. For views regarding Duofu as a son of King Xuan based on these sources, see Chen Pan, *Chunqiu dashi biao lieguo juexing*, pp. 53–56; Matsui Yoshinori, "Shūō shitei no hōken: Tei no shihō tōsen o megutte," *Shirin* 72.4 (1989), 4–6.

[34] See *Hanshu*, 28, p. 1,544.

[35] See Lu Liancheng, "Zhou du yu Zheng kao," in *Guwenzi lunji* (Monograph of *Kaogu yu wenwu* 2) (Xi'an, 1983), pp. 9–10; Wang Hui, "Zhou jinei diming xiaoji," pp. 26–27.

[36] See *Zuozhuan*, 47, p. 2,080; *Shiji*, 42, p. 1,758.

in the west part of the Wei River valley.[37] This Yulin can be related to the Yuyang Palace 棫陽宮, also located in the capital of Qin, and this has already been proved by the discovery of some eaves tiles in the target area.[38] Perhaps Yulin was very close to Zheng, if not actually a part of the area referred to as Zheng. Both connections indeed point to the west part of the Wei River valley as the location of the lineage of Zheng.

However, Zheng was a site very well known from the bronze inscriptions and it existed long before it became the base of Duke Huan of Zheng in 806 BC. The bronze inscriptions indicate that Zheng was a very important city of royal activities during the middle and early late Western Zhou. Three inscriptions, the Mian *zun* 免尊 (JC: 6006), the Third Year Xing *hu* 三年興壺 (JC: 9726), and the Da *gui* 大簋 no. 1 (JC: 4165), mention that the king conducted business in Zheng. Two other inscriptions indicate that the Zhou court directly appointed officials to manage properties located in Zheng and its vicinities. In addition to being a site of royal activity, Zheng seems also to have comprised residences that belonged to other aristocratic lineages. For instance, one branch of the Jing 井 lineage was apparently located in Zheng and was therefore called Zhengjing 鄭井, differentiated from the branch Fengjing 豐井 located in the Zhou capital Feng.[39] By the time of King Yih (r. 899/97–873 BC) and King Xiao (r. 872?–866 BC), the city of Zheng had probably already developed a degree of complexity similar to that of the capital Feng and Qiyi, where many aristocratic families held their residences side by side with the royal properties.[40] I suspect that the royal and aristocratic interests in the site of Zheng were probably promoted by King Mu's ambition in the west. However, except for the Da *gui*, which may be dated to the twelfth year of King Li, none of the bronzes mentioning Zheng can be dated later than the mid-Western Zhou, indicating that the city of Zheng had probably lost its significance after the period of its prosperity during the mid-Western Zhou. Interestingly, this decline paralleled in time the decline of the Jing lineage, as demonstrated by Itō Michiharu many years ago.[41] During the late Western Zhou, Zheng does not appear to have been a significant site of royal activity, so it was probably granted to Prince Duofu as the base of his new lineage.

Not only does the city history of Zheng go back to a time before the founding of the lineage of Zheng by Prince Duofu in 806 BC, but it had also served as the base for an earlier lineage that bore the same name "Zheng."

[37] See *Zuozhuan*, 32, p. 1,956.
[38] Eaves tiles inscribed "*yuyang*" 棫陽 or "*yu*" 棫 were discovered near Majiazhuang 馬家庄, Fengxiang, in the territory of the Qin capital. See *Wenwu* 1963.5, 69–70; Lu Liancheng, "Zhou du Yu Zheng kao," p. 10.
[39] See Chen Mengjia, "Xi Zhou tongqi dunadai," 6, pp. 108–9.
[40] For an analysis of inscriptional evidence on Zheng, see Matsui Yoshinori, "Sei Shū ki Tei no kōsatsu," *Shirin* 69.4 (1986), 24–31. Because of the significance of the city of Zheng during the mid-Western Zhou, there is a theory in the traditional sources that King Mu had once moved the Zhou capital to Zheng; see commentaries to the "Geographical Records" chapter of the *Hanshu* in *Hanshu*, 28, p. 1,544.
[41] See Itō, *Chūgoku kodai kokka*, p. 179.

The transition between the two Zhengs is a missing piece of Western Zhou history and we can now reconstruct it on the basis of the bronze inscriptions. The inscription of the Zewang *guigai* 矢土簋蓋 (JC: 3871) says that the King of Ze makes for Zheng Jiang 鄭姜 a sacrificial *gui*-vessel.[42] Zheng Jiang was a woman from the Zheng lineage (surname: Jiang) who married into the state of Ze, whose surname was Ji.[43] As the bronze can be properly dated to the late mid-Western Zhou by its design and ornament, evidently long before the founding of the Zheng lineage of Duofu, there is little doubt that the Zheng lineage mentioned in the Zewang *guigai* was different. This point acquires further support from the inscription of the Yuan *pan* 袁盤 (JC: 10172), in which Yuan claims to make for his father Zhengbo 鄭伯 and mother Zheng Ji 鄭姬 a sacrificial vessel.[44] Since the Yuan *pan* was almost certainly cast in the twenty-eighth year of King Xuan – only five years after the establishment of the new lineage Zheng – and by that time both Zhengbo and Zheng Ji were already dead, clearly this was an earlier Zheng lineage different from that of Duofu, who was to live until 771 BC when he died with King You. Needless to say, Duofu was not the Zhengbo mentioned in the Yuan *pan*.[45] Since Zhengbo's wife is referred to as Zheng Ji, this earlier Zheng lineage clearly did not belong to the Ji clan according to the marriage taboo commonly practiced by the Zhou that prohibited marriage between families of the same surname, and was almost certainly the Zheng of the Jiang surname mentioned by the Zewang *guigai*. Chen Pan has suggested that the site of Zheng was previously occupied by an earlier Zheng lineage and was later taken over by Duke Huan to establish his new lineage – Zheng.[46] This is most likely the case.

However, the biggest debate in traditional historiography concerning Zheng has been whether it was Duke Huan of Zheng who attacked and annexed the state of Kuai and subsequently moved the state of Zheng east

---

[42] Since the state of Ze was located in the Baoji–Longxian region along the Qian River, this inscription also indicates that Zheng was located in the neighboring area of Ze in the western part of the Wei River valley.

[43] On the assumption that Zheng mentioned in this inscription is the Zheng of Duofu (surname Ji), some scholars have treated Zheng Jiang as a woman who married into Zheng from the state of Ze that they assume to be of Jiang surname. But this is wrong. For discussions on the rules by which women are referred to in the Western Zhou inscriptions, see chapter 3 note 126 on p. 186.

[44] The Yuan *pan* is self-dated to the twenty-eighth year. Since King You reigned only eleven years, the *pan* cannot be dated later than the twenty-eighth year of King Xuan. The date of the Yuan *pan* has acquired another recent proof: Scribe Yu 減 who announces the royal command in the Yuan *pan* played exactly the same role in both the Forty-Second and Forty-Third Year Lai *ding* 逨鼎. Owing to the high year numbers (42 and 43) recorded in the later bronzes, it is very unlikely that Scribe Yu could have played the same role for more than forty-three years, starting before King Xuan came to power. This almost definitely fixes the Yuan *pan* to the twenty-eighth year of King Xuan. For the inscription of the Yuan *pan*, see Shirakawa, "Kinbun tsūshaku," 29.177:594. For the Lai *ding*, see *Wenwu* 2003.6, 6–16.

[45] Certainly the bronze could not have been cast by Duke Huan of Zheng for his father and mother, who were the Zhou king and queen and could not be referred to as Zhengbo and Zheng Ji.

[46] See Chen Pan, *Chunqiu dashi biao ji lieguo juexing*, pp. 62–65. Since the designation Zhengbo is different from designations such as Zheng Jingshu 鄭井叔, which entails a lineage that held residence in Zheng but derived its lineage name from another settlement named Jing, it is likely the lineage of Zhengbo was an earlier occupant of Zheng and therefore it took on the place as its lineage name.

to the Central Plain, or whether it was his son, Duke Wu of Zheng, who accomplished this transition.[47] In other words, did the eastward migration of Zheng take place before the downfall of the Zhou capital or after it? Much of the debate was provoked by two entries in the *Ancient Bamboo Annals* (under the second year of Ruler Wen of Jin) and the *Current* version (under the second year of King You) on Duofu's attack on the polity of Zeng 鄫 (Kuai 郐 in the *Ancient* version) which are examined in detail in appendix 3 (see pp. 351–4).

The ancient version, since it has the wrong graph *kuai* 郐 for the attacked state, seems to suggest that in 779 BC. Duke Huan of Zheng attacked the state of Kuai, which then became the new site of Zheng. However, two other sources suggest that Kuai was attacked and was made a part of Zheng in the early years of King Ping's reign, and I demonstrate in appendix 3 that: (1) the eastward migration of Zheng could not have taken place before Duke Huan of Zheng became the Minister of Multitudes at the Zhou court in 774 BC (it is likely that he sent the treasury of Zheng to the states of Kuai and Eastern Guo in 773/72 BC); (2) it was Duke Wu of Zheng who annexed Kuai and Eastern Guo in 769 and 767 BC, respectively; and (3) the state of Kuai 郐 in the ancient version is probably a misquote of Zeng 鄫 in the original tomb version of the *Bamboo Annals*, the state that later went into alliance with Western Shen and the Western Rong to attack the Zhou capital in 771 BC. This misquote of Zeng as Kuai caused great confusion with the state of Kuai that was later attacked and made the territory of Zheng by Duke Wu. Without reexamining the evidence here, we can simply conclude that the state of Zheng was reestablished by Duke Wu in the territories of the states of Kuai and Eastern Guo during the first few years of King Ping's reign.

As already studied in chapter 1, the state of Eastern Guo was located in present-day Xingyang.[48] As for Kuai, although traditional sources locate its capital to the northeast of Mixian 密縣, on the basis of a field survey two archaeologists have identified it with a walled site at Dafanzhuang 大樊莊, to the southeast of Mixian.[49] The new capital of Zheng was located in the immediate vicinity of Xinzheng, and is known as the "Old Town of Zheng and Han" because it was occupied by the state of Han after 375 BC (Map 14). Rich archaeological remains have been excavated in this immense walled site during the last four decades.[50] This site is only about 10 kilometers to

---

[47] For a summary of these arguments, see Zhang Yiren, "Zheng guo mie Kuai ziliao de jiantao," *Zhongyang yanjiuyuan lishi yuyan yanjiusuo jikan* 50.4 (1979), 615–25.

[48] For more details, see also Chen Pan, *Chunqiu dashi biao ji lieguo juexing*, p. 158.

[49] See Jiang Yong, *Chunqiu diming kaoshi*, 253, p. 12; Xu Hongpan, *Fangyu kaozheng* (Jining: Huajiange, 1932), 28, p. 33. For the new archaeological studies, see Ma Shizhi, "Kuai guo shiji chutan," *Shixue yuekan* 1984.5, 30–34; Liang Xiaojing, "Kuai guo shiji tansuo," *Zhongyuan wenwu* 1987.3, 103–4. See also *Henan sheng zhi: wenwu zhi*, pp. 114–15. Since ancient geographical works indicate that the state of Mi 密 was also located in the same area, whether the site in Dafanzhuang is the site of Kuai or Mi still needs further study.

[50] For a summary of the discoveries at Xinzheng, see *Xin Zhongguo de kaogu faxian*, p. 274; *Henan kaogu sishi nian* (Zhengzhou: Henan renmin, 1994), pp. 231–34.

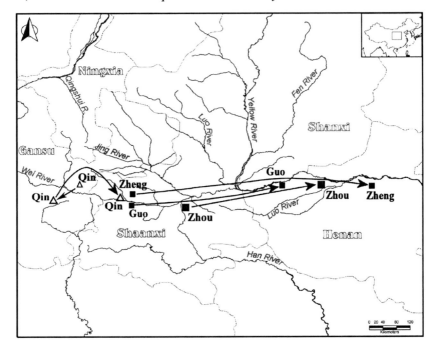

Map 14 The migration of Zhou, Zheng, Guo, and Qin

the southeast of Dafanzhuang, the proposed site of the capital of the state of Kuai. However, there is another tradition suggesting that Duke Wu of Zheng may have lived in a place called Liu 劉 prior to his eventual move to Xinzheng.[51] This, if reliable, would fill in the short period from the year 770 BC, when the Zhou court and Zheng moved east, to the relocation of Zheng in Xinzheng after the annexation of Kuai and Eastern Guo in 769 and 767 BC.

In short, the state of Zheng was originally located in the Fengxiang area near the west end of the Wei River valley. Anticipating the fall of the Western Zhou dynasty, between 773 and 772 BC, Duke Huan of Zheng sent the lineage property of Zheng and some of its population east to the territories of the states of Kuai and Eastern Guo. After the fall of the Zhou capital, Duke Wu of Zheng followed King Ping east and temporarily lived in Liu. Finally, Duke Wu annexed Kuai in 769 BC and Eastern Guo in 767 BC, and reestablished the state of Zheng in present-day Xinzheng.

---

[51] See *Gongyang zhuan*, 5, p. 2,220. There have been two locations suggested by scholars for this Liu. The first is Chen Liu 陳留 of the Han dynasty, near Kaifeng 開封, about 55 kilometers to the northeast of Xinzheng; see Chen Pan, *Chunqiu dashi biao lieguo juexing*, pp. 70–71. The second is a settlement that later became the site of the state of Liu 劉 near Luoyi, located in present-day Yanshi 偃師; see Chen Huan, *Shi Maoshi zhuan shu*, 6, pp. 18–19. For a recent archaeological study of Liu, see Liang Xiaojing, "Liu guo shiji kaolue," *Zhongyuan wenwu* 1985.4, 67–69.

The eastward migration of Western Guo

The history of Guo and its move to the east present another piece of the puzzle in early Chinese history, and the discoveries in the cemetery of the state of Guo in Sanmenxia during the 1990s have raised renewed interest among the scholars in this issue. This is a very complex question because it mingles historical-geographical issues with anthropological ones concerning the general rules of lineage segmentation in early China. Also, unlike the case of Zheng, here we have a considerable number of inscribed bronzes cast by the elite of Guo, and many of them have been archaeologically excavated; therefore, the textual records can be closely related to archaeological findings. Below I will discuss first the origin and segmentation of Guo, and then its possible locations; finally, I will examine the process of the eastward migration of Guo.

The origin and segmentation of Guo

On the issue of origins, there has been a long tradition that polities were founded separately by Guozhong 虢仲 and Guoshu 虢叔, two brothers of King Wen.[52] One of them, Guoshu, is mentioned in "Jun Shi" 君奭, a Western Zhou chapter in the *Shangshu*, as one of the virtuous former advisers to King Wen.[53] The "Jinyu" chapter of the *Guoyu* says that King Wen was very respectful and friendly towards the two Guo polities.[54] Furthermore, Shi Bo in his long speech in the "Zhengyu" chapter of the *Guoyu*, part of which is cited at the beginning of this chapter, clearly mentions two Guo polities, one among the states located to the west of Chengzhou, and the other, that of Guoshu, located in the central land between the four rivers and proposed by Shi Bo as a target state that Zheng should conquer.[55] By the extension of logic, it is implied that the Guo in the west was probably the one that was founded by Guozhong.

I have long doubted this historiographical tradition that the two Guo polities were founded by King Wen's two brothers, for three reasons: (1) if "Guo" was the name of a polity from the very beginning, the chance of King Wen's two brothers being established simultaneously at two different locations bearing the same lineage name "Guo" without differentiation would be very slight; (2) it would be impossible for either Guozhong or

---

[52] See *Zuozhuan*, 12, p. 1,795. As already discussed in chapter 2, in the *Zongfa* system of Zhou, sons born by the primary wife in a lineage were differentiated by their seniority as *bo* 伯, *zhong* 仲, *shu* 叔, and *ji* 季. Only the first-born *bo* would succeed his father as the head of the lineage, while the younger brothers, as allowed by the size of the lineage property, would be sent out to found sub-lineages, or, in the case of the royal house, local polities or states. For an explanation of this practice, see Hsu and Linduff, *Western Chou Civilization*, pp. 164–71; Blakeley, "Regional Aspects of Chinese Socio-Political Development," pp. 19–21.

[53] See *Shangshu*, 16, p. 224 (Legge, *The Shoo King*, pp. 481–82). Guoshu is also mentioned in the *Yi Zhoushu* where he is called "Guoshu" 郭叔; see Zhu Youzeng, *Zhoushu jixun jiaoshi* (Guiyanzhai, 1846), 7, p. 6.

[54] See *Guoyu*, 10, p. 387.   [55] See *Guoyu*, 16, pp. 507, 518.

Guoshu, if they were King Wen's brothers, to be established in Eastern Guo in the eastern plain at a time when the region was still under Shang control;[56] and (3) both the *Shangshu* and the *Yi Zhoushu* mention only Guoshu as a contemporary of King Wen, and do not mention Guozhong. It seems clear to me that the tradition transmitted by the *Zuozhuan* and *Guoyu* on the concomitant founding of two Guo states totally misinterpreted the historical context. A logical explanation is that only Guoshu, a brother of King Wen, was initially granted land at a place called Guo before the conquest and thus became the founder of the Guo lineage. After the conquest, the Guo lineage was split up and a younger Guoshu, son of the senior Guoshu who founded the original Guo lineage, was probably sent to the eastern plain to establish the state of Eastern Guo as the *de facto* sub-lineage of Guo. Certainly, the senior Guoshu should also have had as his sons Guobo 虢伯, the successor to the "Primary Line" (*dazong* 大宗) of Guo, and Guozhong and Guoji 虢季, who may also have founded their own sub-lineages. Hypothetical though it may be, I think this theory not only explains the distinction between the two Guo states bearing the same name, but also explains why, besides Guozhong and Guoshu, there was also a Guoji branch, which seems to have been more important during the middle and late Western Zhou than the other sub-lineages of Guo, and the archaeological evidence will sufficiently illuminate this point below.

When the original Guo lineage was divided into a number of sub-lineages (those of Guozhong, Guoshu, and probably also Guoji), the personal designations such as "Guozhong," "Guoshu," and "Guoji" then became the titles of the newly established sub-lineages of Guo. In other words, the terms *zhong, shu,* and *ji* no longer signified order of seniority, but became marks that were used to differentiate the positions of the sub-lineages with respect to the "Primary Line." It has been a general understanding that such titles would be held by the heads of the corresponding sub-lineages in every generation, and would be used in inscriptions preceding their personal names. This is certainly not a phenomenon unique to Guo, but perhaps reflects the general pattern of lineage segmentation during the Western Zhou. Thus, for example, the third-born son of the Guoshu sub-lineage would have to refer to himself as "Guoshu Shu X," with *shu* doubled in his name. This is actually the case, and the theory acquired strong support from the excavation of the burial ground of the Jingshu 井叔 sub-lineage of the Jing lineage in 1984–85.[57]

[56] According to the *Zuozhuan* and the *Guoyu*, both Guoshu and Guozhong were simultaneously active during the reign of King Wen, implying both Guo polities were already established in the time of King Wen. But this seems quite impossible.

[57] This burial ground is a part of the cemetery located to the south of Zhangjiapo 張家坡 in the central area of the capital Feng. Bronze inscriptions indicate that tomb no. 157, located to the west, is the burial of Jingshu Shucai 井叔叔采; tomb no. 152, located in the middle, is the burial of Jingshu Da 井叔達; tomb no. 170, located to the east, is the burial of an anonymous Jingshu. They were the heads of three different generations of the Jingshu family. The reporters also think that tomb

Thus, the situation is very complicated: without clear archaeological context and such cautious wording as appears in the Jingshu bronzes, it would be difficult to determine whether the "Guoshu" or "Guozhong" in an inscription designates a sub-lineage or a person of second or third birth. And there is evidence in the texts, as already noted by some scholars, that the rulers of the Western Guo actually used both of these titles.[58] The archaeological evidence suggests, on the other hand, that Guoji was the title of a sub-lineage of Guo. But there is no solid evidence in the inscriptions that either Guozhong or Guoshu was used as the title of a Guo sub-lineage that may actually have existed.

The location of Guo(s)

Where were Guo or the Guos located? The discovery of inscribed bronzes and archaeological sites relevant to Guo provides us with solid grounds to answer this question. In connection with the Zhou–Xianyun war, I have already discussed the Guoji Zibai *pan* (JC: 10173), showing that the Guo elite was playing an important role in the defense of the Zhou royal domain. The bronze was actually found in a place called Guochuan 虢川 in the Baoji area during the early nineteenth century (Fig. 32).[59] Another bronze *pan* cast by Guoji shi Zizu 虢季氏子組 was reportedly discovered in the territory of Fengxiang Superior-Prefecture, which by the administrative division of Qing also covers the Baoji area.[60] These discoveries strongly relate Guo to the present-day Baoji–Fengxiang region at the west end of the Wei River valley; they also suggest that their caster was from the Guoji sub-lineage of Guo. The textual records actually locate the Western Guo in the Baoji

no. 168, a smaller tomb with a ramp, located between tombs nos. 152 and 170, is the burial of the Jingshu in another generation. According to the reporters, the chronological sequence of these tombs is 157–152–170. The discovery in tomb no. 157 of a bronze bell cast by Jingshu Shucai (the graph *shu* 叔 is cast with repetition mark), the third son of the Jingshu sub-lineage, is most significant. This crucial inscription verifies the simultaneous use of *shu* as both a seniority signifier and a sub-lineage mark. For the excavation in Zhangjiapo, see *Kaogu* 1986.1, 11, 22–27; 1990.6, 504–10; Zhang Changshou, "Lun Jingshu tongqi: 1983–86 nian Fengxi fajue ziliao zhi er," *Wenwu* 1990.7, 32–35. For a more detailed description of these tombs, see *Zhangjiapo Xi Zhou mudi* (Beijing: Zhongguo da baike quanshu, 1999), pp. 18–35. It should also be mentioned that an alternative sequence, 152–170–157, was proposed by Lu Liancheng, one of the main excavators in Zhangjiapo. See Lu Liancheng, "Zhangjiapo Xi Zhou Jingshu mudi de zhaomu pailie," *Zhongguo wenwu bao* 1995.3.5, 3.

[58] According to the *Zuozhuan*, the ruler of Western Guo in Sanmenxia could have been referred to as either "Guoshu" or "Guozhong," although it is now very clear that they belonged to the Guoji sub-lineage. See Higuchi Takayasu, "Kaku koku dōki ko," *Tōhōgaku* 20 (1960), 10; Uehara Tadamichi, "Kaku koku iseki shutsudo no seidōki meibun ni tsuite," *Kōkotsugaku* 8 (1960), 642–43.

[59] The bronze was reported to have been found in Guochuansi 虢川司 of Baoji by the Qing administrative division, but the site of this discovery cannot be specified. Some scholars have located the site 60 kilometers to the southeast of Baoji City 寶鷄市; see Tang Lan, *Tang Lan xiansheng*, p. 415. Guochuan is a river located about 75 kilometers to the southeast of Baoji County of Qing (present-day Baoji City), deep in the Qinling Mountains; see Qiang Zhenzhi et al., *(Chongxiu) Baoji xian zhi* (1922), 2, p. 16. However, according to the *Taiping huanyu ji* of the tenth century, there was a place called Taoguochuan 桃虢川 in present-day Baoji County; see *Taiping huanyu ji*, 30, p. 13; Gu Zuyu, *Dushi fangyu jiyao*, pp. 2,414, 2,419. It is possible that the bronze was found in the latter area but was misreported by antique dealers as having been found in Guochuansi.

[60] See *Zhou jinwen cun* (1916), 4, pp. 8–9; Shirakawa, "Kinbun tsūshaku," 34.200: 64.

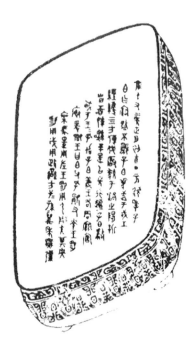

Fig. 32 The Guoji Zibai *pan* and its inscription (JC: 10173; Guo Moruo, *Liang Zhou jinwen ci daxi tulu kaoshi*, p. 18, no. 152)

area. The "Geographical Records" chapter of the *Hanshu* identifies Western Guo with the Guo County 虢縣 in the administrative jurisdiction of Right Fufeng 右扶風, which basically covered the western half of the Wei River valley during the Han dynasty; it also notes that there was a certain Guo Palace 虢宮 during the former Qin dynasty.[61] The name "Guo County" certainly survived through the medieval period, as two Tang dynasty sources continued to register it in the same area, pointing to the walled site presently called "Guozhen" 虢鎮, the base of modern-day Baoji County 寶雞縣.[62] It is quite safe to say that, on the basis of current textual and inscriptional evidence, the locus of Guo power was in the area of present-day Baoji County.

As did many other aristocratic families in Shaanxi, the Guo lineage held residence in the royal site Qiyi (Zhouyuan). In 1974, a group of seven inscribed bronzes was excavated from a cache in Qiangjiacun 強家村, in

---

[61] See *Hanshu*, 28, pp. 1,547, 1,549.

[62] The *Yuanhe junxian tuzhi* identifies Western Guo with the Guo County of Tang; see *Yuanhe junxian tuzhi*, p. 43. The *Kuodi zhi* (quoted in the "Zhengyi" commentary to the *Shiji*) says that the "Town of Guo" 虢城 was located 20 kilometers to the east of Chencang County 陳倉縣 of Tang (present-day Baoji City), pointing to the walled town of present-day Baoji County. About 5 kilometers to the west of Guozhen, there was another town, also called "Town of Guo." See *Shiji*, 5, p. 183.

the central area of Zhouyuan, including most importantly the Shi Cheng *zhong* 師承鐘 (JC: 141) and the Shi Zai *ding* 師訇鼎 (JC: 2812), from which a genealogical list of four to five generations of the Guoji sub-lineage can be drawn up, dating from roughly the reign of King Gong to approximately the reign of King Yi or King Li.[63] Besides these bronzes, another *li*-vessel cast by Guozhong 虢仲 was excavated in Jingdang 京當, also in the Zhouyuan area.[64]

Outside of the Zhou royal domain in Shaanxi, another concentration of Guo bronzes comes from the Sanmenxia area in western Henan. In 1957, as many as 234 tombs (thirty-eight containing bronzes) were excavated in Sanmenxia. The cemetery is located on a gradual slope on the south bank of the Yellow River. The most important discovery in terms of the historical geography of Guo is a *li*-vessel cast by Guoji shi Zizhi 虢季氏子 (JC: 683) from tomb no. 1631.[65] This inscription not only identifies the cemetery with the Guoji sub-lineage, but also relates it to the many Guoji bronzes discovered in the Wei River valley. The cemetery certainly contains some high-ranking tombs of the Guo elite such as tomb no. 1052, the inscription on a *ge*-dagger-axe from which identifies the occupant as the "Prince of Guo." Because many tombs were preserved intact, it is possible to analyze them in a system of ranking based on the number of the graduated *ding*-vessels, roughly corresponding to the size and furnishing of the tombs.[66] On the other hand, the Sanmenxia cemetery comprises tombs of apparently different dates. In 1988, I proposed the first periodization of the tombs containing bronzes from the cemetery into three consecutive periods, dating

---

[63] This genealogical list includes Guoji Gonggong 虢季宽公, Youshu 幽叔, Deshu 德叔, and Shi Cheng 師承 himself who cast the Shi Cheng *zhong*. The Shi Zai *ding* 師訇鼎 mentions two ancestors: Gong Shangfu 公上父 and Guoji Yifu 幸 (虢) 季易父. Professor Li Xueqin divided the term "Guoji Gonggong" to represent two Guo ancestors, Guoji 虢季 whom he identified with Guoji Yifu in the Shi Zai *ding*, and Gonggong 宽公 with Shi Zai, caster of the Shi Zai *ding*. But the identifications are still open to question. As for the date of the bronzes, the Shi Zai *ding* offers a solid point of reference to the eighth year of King Gong because the reigning king who appears in the inscription refers to King Mu as his father. Other bronzes from the same cache are later, but were all cast in a time from the mid-Western Zhou to early late Western Zhou. See Li Xueqin, *Xinchu qingtongqi yanjiu*, pp. 85–87. For the excavation, see *Wenwu* 1975.8, 57–62. For the inscriptions in question, see also Shirakawa, "Kinbun tsūshaku," 49.ho10:237–46.

[64] See Wang Guangyong, "Jieshao xin chutu de liangjian Guo qi," *Guwenzi yanjiu* 7 (1982), 185–86.

[65] See *Shangcunling Guo guo mudi* (Beijing: Kexue, 1959), p. 32, pl. 41.1.

[66] As a result of the analysis, five grades were proposed by the archaeologists, including tombs with seven *ding*, five *ding*, three *ding*, or one *ding*, and tombs without bronze vessels at all. See *Xin Zhongguo kaogu faxian he yanjiu*, pp. 283–85; Lothar von Falkenhausen, "The Waning of the Bronze Age," in *The Cambridge History of Ancient China: From the Origins of Civilization to 221 BC*, ed. Michael Loewe and Edward L. Shaughnessy (Cambridge: Cambridge University Press, 1999), pp. 470–76. Starting in the mid-Western Zhou, but more common during the late Western Zhou, bronzes were often cast in standard sets that typically included an odd number of *ding*-vessels in reducing size but with the same design and ornament, accompanied by the next lower even number of *gui*-vessels of a unified size and design. This phenomenon, called the *lieding* 列鼎 institution by archaeologists, is observed widely in many late Western Zhou as well as Eastern Zhou tombs. For a systematic analysis of the phenomenon, see Yu Weichao and Gao Ming, "Zhou dai yong ding zhidu yanjiu," *Beijing daxue xuebao* 1978.1, 84–89 (part I); 1978.2, 84–97 (part II); 1979.1, 83–96 (part III). See also Lothar von Falkenhausen, "The Waning of the Bronze Age," p. 489.

to a time from the late Western Zhou to 655 BC when Guo was finally annexed by its northern neighbor Jin. The suggested sequence as fully evident in the evolution of designs of the bronzes from the cemetery makes an important bridge between the Western Zhou bronzes and the Eastern Zhou bronzes.[67]

Important new evidence was brought to light again by the excavation of eighteen additional tombs (twelve published) in the same cemetery in the early 1990s.[68] Tomb no. 2001 contained seven graduated *ding* and six *gui*, showing a combination very similar to tomb no. 1052, excavated in 1957. Twenty bronzes from this tomb bear inscriptions cast by Guoji 虢季 (Fig. 33).[69] Tomb no. 2011 also contained seven graduated *ding* and a bronze axe cast by the "Primary Prince of Guo."[70] Another unpublished tomb, no. 2009, is said to have had nine graduated *ding* and eight *gui*, indicating an even higher status than tombs nos. 2001 and 1052, and bronzes from the tomb bear inscriptions cast by Guozhong 虢仲.[71] It is very possible that these are the burials of the Guo rulers.[72] Some have argued that both Guoji and Guozhong on these newly excavated bronzes are personal designations rather than lineage titles,[73] but the inscription on one bronze *ding* (M2001: 345) leaves us in no doubt that the Sanmenxia cemetery belonged to the Guoji sub-lineage of Guo; *ji* 季 in the term "Guoji" here refers to the particular sub-lineage of Guo that occupied the Sanmenxia cemetery, but is not a seniority marker:[74]

虢季作寶鼎, 季氏其萬年子子孫孫永寶用亨

Guoji makes [this] treasured *ding*-vessel, may the Ji sub-lineage for ten thousand years sons' sons and grandsons' grandsons eternally treasure and use [it] in offering.

---

[67] I date Period I (nos. 1820, 1810, 1601, 1602) to the late Western Zhou with a time span from King Xuan to King You, and Periods II (nos. 1052, 1689) and III (nos. 1705, 1721) to the early and late phases of the early Spring and Autumn period, respectively. See Li Feng, "Guo guo mudi tongqi qun de fenqi jiqi xiangguan wenti," *Kaogu* 1988.11, 1035–41. Some other views on the date of Sanmenxia cemetery should also be mentioned. The reporter of the excavations dated thirty-one of the tombs to the time of King Xuan; see Lin Shoujin, "Shangcunling Guo guo mudi buji," *Kaogu* 1961.9, 505–7. In an important analysis of the materials, the Japanese archaeologist Higuchi Takayasu reached the same conclusion; see Higuchi, "Kaku koku dōki kō," pp. 1–21. However, there are also scholars who think that all tombs in the cemetery should be dated to the early Spring and Autumn period. See Guo Baojun, *Shang Zhou tongqiqun zonghe yanjiu* (Beijing: Wenwu, 1981), pp. 70–78; Li Xueqin, *Eastern Zhou and Qin Civilizations*, trans. K. C. Chang (New Haven: Yale University Press, 1985), p. 84.

[68] See *Sanmenxia Guo guo mu* (Beijing: Wenwu, 1999), p. 9.

[69] See ibid., pp. 33–75; *Huaxia kaogu* 1992.3, 106–12.

[70] See *Sanmenxia Guo guo mu.*, p. 344.   [71] See ibid., pp. 245–49.

[72] It is likely that tombs no. 2001 and 2009 are both burials of the dukes of Western Guo, while tomb no. 2011 is considered to have belonged to a crown prince of Guo. Tombs nos. 2012 and 2006, judging from the burial goods they contain, are probably the burials of the consorts of two anonymous dukes of Guo.

[73] See Li Xueqin, "Sanmenxia Guo guo mudi xin faxian yu Guoguo shi," *Zhongguo wenwu bao* 1991.2.3, 3.

[74] See *Huaxia kaogu* 1992.3, 106.

Fig. 33 Newly discovered bronzes from tomb no. 2001 in Sanmenxia (from *Sanmenxia Guo guo mu*, pls. 5.1, 9.2, 10.1–2, 15.1, 16.1, 3, 18.2, 19.1, 3)

The Guo in Sanmenxia is mentioned a number of times in the *Zuozhuan* and was conquered by the state of Jin in 655 BC.[75] The "Geographical Records" chapter of the *Hanshu* says clearly that the Shan County 陝縣 of the Han dynasty (present-day Sanmenxia) was the ancient state Guo;[76] there has never been a debate on the basic fact that a Guo state was once located at the narrow pass of Sanmenxia. As mentioned above, another Guo (Eastern Guo) was located in present-day Xingyang in the eastern plain.[77] However, confusion had occurred, beginning in the Later Han dynasty, as to which of the Guo states was located in the Sanmenxia area. While some scholars suggested that the Guo in Sanmenxia (Western Guo) was founded by Guoshu and the Guo in Xingyang (Eastern Guo) was

---

[75] See *Zuozhuan* 12, pp. 1,795–96. [76] See *Hanshu*, 28, p. 1,549.
[77] On the location of the Eastern Guo, see *Hanshu*, 28, p. 1,549.

founded by Guozhong, other scholars advocated the opposite.[78] The situation was further complicated by a differentiation in the textual tradition between Southern Guo, which is another way to refer to the Guo in Sanmenxia, and Northern Guo in Pinglu 平陸, Shanxi, facing each other across the Yellow River at a distance of no more than 10 kilometers (Fig. 34).[79] However, the new archaeological discoveries have proved that the Guo in Sanmenxia was founded neither by Guozhong, the alleged brother of King Wen, nor by Guoshu, but evidently belongs to the Guoji sub-lineage that segmented later from the primary Guo lineage founded by the senior Guoshu. As for the relationship between the Southern Guo and the Northern Guo, I believe that a careful reading of the records in the *Zuozhuan* sufficiently clarifies that they were two parts of the same state – Western Guo in Sanmenxia. As I have pointed out in a previous study, it was only because the two parts were separated by the Yellow River that they were referred to as Southern Guo and Northern Guo by later historians and geographers.[80]

The move of Western Guo

While a full archaeological analysis of these tombs should be given in another study when the materials from the cemetery are sufficiently published, the issue here is: what do the archaeological materials tell us about the migration of Guo to the east? In order to understand the real implications of the archaeological findings, we must consider them in relation to the textual records on Guo. Apparently, the inscriptional evidence introduced above relates the Sanmenxia area and the Baoji area in the west as two bases of the Guoji sub-lineage. To understand this relationship, a paragraph from the *Shuijing zhu* is very significant:[81]

(雍縣)《〈晉書地道記〉》以為西虢地也,《〈漢書地理志〉》以為西虢縣。《〈太康地記〉》曰: "虢叔之國, 有虢宮。平王東遷, 叔自此之上陽, 為南虢矣。"

The "Didao ji" chapter of the *Jinshu* says that (Yong County) was the land of Western Guo; the "Geographical Records" chapter of the *Hanshu* says that it was the western Guo County. The *Taikang diji* says: "[Yong County] was the state of Guoshu; there was Guo Palace. When King Ping moved to the east, [Guo]shu went from here to Shangyang, which was Southern Guo."

---

[78] For the first position, for instance, Jia Kui of the Han dynasty (cited by Kong Yingda in his commentary to the *Zuozhuan*) suggested that Guozhong was established in Eastern Guo (Xingyang), while Guoshu was established in Western Guo; see *Zuozhuan*, 12, p. 1,795. For the second position, for instance, Fan Ye in the "Junguo zhi" chapter of the *Houhan shu* suggested that the Guo in Xingyang was founded by Guoshu, while the Guo in Shan County (Sanmenxia) was founded by Guozhong; see *Houhan shu*, 19, pp. 3,389, 3,401.

[79] Ma Rong of the Han dynasty (quoted in the "Zhengyi" commentary to the *Shiji* and in Kong Yingda's commentary to the *Zuozhuan*) suggested that Guozhong was established in Xiayang 下陽 (Pinglu) and Guoshu was established in Shangyang 上陽 (Sanmenxia). See *Shiji*, 39, p. 1,640; *Zuozhuan*, 12, p. 1,795.

[80] See Li Feng, "Guo guo mudi chutu tongqi qun," p. 1041.   [81] See *Shuijing zhu*, 18, p. 587.

Fig. 34 The Yellow River at Sanmenxia (photograph by the author)

This paragraph first identifies the Yong County 雍縣 of the sixth century, which covers roughly present-day Baoji–Fengxiang, with the Guo County mentioned by Ban Gu in the "Geographical Records" chapter of the *Hanshu*, and credits the *Jinshu*, another dynastic history, with identifying the area with Western Guo. Then, it cites the *Taikang diji*, a lost text composed in the third century, as suggesting that Western Guo, originally located in the Baoji area, was moved from there to the narrow pass in western Henan and relocated its capital at Shangyang (present-day Sanmenxia) at the end of the Western Zhou. While wrongly identifying Western Guo as the state founded by Guoshu, the paragraph explains well the occurrence of the Guoji related bronzes in both the Baoji and the Sanmenxia areas. Although this source offers us a reasonable explanation of the phenomenon in archaeology, we must consider this point more carefully in relation to the dates of the bronzes from the two areas, and in so doing, we can also put an outline of Guo history into perspective.

The Guoji Zibai *pan* from Baoji used to be dated by Guo Moruo to the reign of King Yi, or by others to as late as the Spring and Autumn period.[82] But I believe, as demonstrated convincingly by Tang Lan, that it was cast in the twelfth year of King Xuan (816 BC).[83] There is little doubt that Guoji Zibai 虢季子白 in this inscription should be identified with Duke

---

[82] See Guo Moruo, *Liang Zhou jinwen ci*, pp. 104–6. For the latter view, see Gao Hongjin, "Guoji Zibai pan kaoshi," *Dalu zazhi* 2.2 (1951), 7–9; Ogata Isamu and Hirase Takao, *Chūka bunmei no tanjō* (Tokyo: Chūō kōron sha, 1998), pp. 123–24.

[83] See Tang Lan, *Tang Lan xiansheng jinwen*, pp. 415–20; see also Shaughnessy, *Sources of Western Zhou History*, p. 285.

Xuan of Guo, the caster of the Guo Xuangong Zibai *ding* 虢宣公子白鼎 (JC: 2637), preserved in the imperial Summer Palace, Beijing.[84] Importantly, this identification suggests that at latest by the time of King Xuan the Guoji sub-lineage was already the ruling party of the Guo lineage, because Zibai as a member of the Guoji sub-lineage clearly assumed the title "Duke Xuan of Guo." It also suggests that in the early decades of King Xuan, Western Guo was still located in the Baoji area, while the Guoji bronzes from Qiyi, including the Shi Zai *ding* discussed above, suggest Guo presence in the Wei River valley through much of the mid-Western Zhou. The next generation after Duke Xuan of Guo (Zibai) was probably Duke Wen of Guo, who lived through the reign of King Xuan. The *Current Bamboo Annals* says that in his fifteenth year (813 BC) King Xuan bestowed on Duke Wen of Guo a royal command, indicating that his predecessor Duke Xuan may have died between 816, the year the Zibai *pan* was cast, and 813 BC.[85] This Duke Wen of Guo seems to have been a very important political figure in the later decades of King Xuan and is mentioned also in the *Guoyu*.[86] He is also evident in our bronze inscriptions as he is almost certainly the caster of the three Guo Wengong Zizhi *ding* 虢文公子㺇鼎 (JC: 2634–6), and very interestingly, this Zizhi is also the caster of the Guoji shi Zizhi *li* 虢季氏子㺇鬲 excavated from tomb no. 1631 in Sanmenxia in 1957.[87] These inscriptions suggest that Duke Wen was from the Guoji sub-lineage and, since the bronze was found in Sanmenxia, there is a good possibility that late in the reign of King Xuan the Guoji sub-lineage had already founded its new base in the east.

On the basis of the date of the bronzes from Sanmenxia, I suggested in 1988 that the eastward migration of Western Guo had probably taken place some time during the reign of King Xuan, when Duke Wen was the ruler of Guo.[88] On the basis of the newly excavated tombs in Sanmenxia, I still think that this is the most likely time for Western Guo's move to the east, and the date given by the *Taikang diji* for the eastward move is mistaken.[89]

---

[84] For the inscription, see also *Shang Zhou jinwen luyi* (Beijing: Kexue, 1957), p. 23. The bronze was photographed recently in *Zhongguo qingtongqi quanji*, 6, p. 137.

[85] See *Zhushu jinian*, 2, p. 15.

[86] Duke Wen of Guo is said to have admonished King Xuan not to abandon the ancient ritual of Spring Plowing; see *Guoyu*, 1, p. 15.

[87] See *Shangcunling Guo guo mudi*, pp. 31–32, pl. 41. See also Guo Moruo, "Sanmenxia chutu tongqi er san shi," *Wenwu* 1959.1, 13–15.

[88] Li Feng, "Guo guo mudi chutu tongqi qun," p. 1,042.

[89] The archaeologists in Henan strongly advocate that most, if not all, newly excavated tombs in Sanmenxia should be dated within the limits of the Western Zhou; see *Henan kaogu sishi nian* (Zhengzhou: Henan renmin, 1994), p. 249; Xu Yongsheng, "Cong Guo guo mudi kaogu xin faxian tan Guo guo lishi gaikuang," *Huaxia kaogu* 1993.4, 95. Indeed, most bronzes from tomb no. 2001 show late Western Zhou features; however, the seven graduated *ding*-vessels seem rather later, indicating that the tomb may have been constructed at the beginning of the Eastern Zhou although it contains some earlier bronzes. Bronzes from tomb no. 2011 show clear late Western Zhou features and should be dated to the late Western Zhou. As for tomb no. 2006, bronzes from it suggest that it was probably buried some time towards the end of the Western Zhou. All of these tombs including no. 2012 are evidently earlier than tombs nos. 1052 and 1689 excavated in 1957 that belong to Period II of the cemetery.

During the reign of King You, as has been shown in chapter 4, Western Guo was a strong supporter of the King You–Bao Si party and played an important role at the Zhou court. The *Current Bamboo Annals* suggests that in the seventh year of King You (775 BC), Guo annexed the small state Jiao 焦, the original residents in the Sanmenxia area,[90] and probably also at this time Guo began to expand its territory to the north bank of the Yellow River. There seems no doubt that the Duke of Guo, Gu 鼓, was the ruler of Western Guo; most likely the same duke established prince Yuchen as king at Xie after the fall of the Western Zhou.

Perhaps owing to the early involvement with the King You–Bao Si party and the subsequent patronage to the King of Xie, the relationship between Western Guo and the Zhou court reestablished under King Ping was very bad; the king, as the *Guoyu* says, mainly relied on support from the states of Jin and Zheng. However, late in his long reign, King Ping wished to use Western Guo to counterbalance the dominance of Zheng over his court, and therefore the Duke of Guo, known by the name Jifu 忌父, began to play an active role at the Zhou court in Luoyang,[91] On behalf of the Zhou court, the next Duke of Guo, Linfu 林父, also known as Guozhong, invaded Zheng in 707 BC, and attacked the junior branch of Jin in Quwo 曲沃 in 703 BC. After 681 BC, Linfu's role at the Zhou court was taken over by another Duke of Guo, Chou 醜, also known as Guoshu 虢叔. During the time of Chou, Guo went through a series of conflicts with the rising state of Jin, and also provided asylum for some banished Jin princes.[92] In 658 BC the troops of Jin with assistance from Guo's neighboring state Yu 虞 captured the part of Guo territory to the north of the Yellow River. Then, in 655 BC, Jin troops captured the Guo capital Shangyang in Sanmenxia, and the state of Western Guo was eliminated.

To conclude, through the analysis of Guo, we can reveal a pattern of lineage segmentation during the Western Zhou. It was probably Guoshu, a brother of King Wen, who was given properties in the present-day Baoji–Fengxiang area and thus founded the lineage of Guo prior to the Zhou conquest of Shang. During the first wave of Zhou migration to the east following the conquest, a son of the senior Guoshu was sent to the eastern plain by royal order to found the regional state of Eastern Guo as a sub-lineage of Guo; thereafter there were two Guo polities known to the historians. Splitting off from the "Primary Line" of Guo, there was the Guoji sub-lineage. And owing to the very existence of the "Ji" sub-lineage founded by the fourth son, there may also have been the Guozhong sub-lineage, while the primary lineage of Guo was passed down through the line

---

[90] See *Zhushu jinian*, 2, p. 17 (Legge, *The Shoo King*, Prolegomena, p. 157).

[91] For a discussion of the political struggle between Guo and Zheng, see Uehara Tadamichi, "Kaku no rekishi oyobi Tei to To Kaku to no kankei," *Kodaigaku* 6.2 (1957), 124–43; "Keishi o meguru arasoi oyobi Teihaku shōōsetsu no kentō," *Tōkyō daigaku kyōyōbu jinbun kagaku kiyō* 14 (1958), 6–19.

[92] For the political situation in Jin at this time, see Shim, "The Early Development of the State of Jin," pp. 170–89.

of Guobo. However, we have no solid evidence for a Guozhong sub-lineage
or for the activities of the primary lineage of Guo ruled by Guobo. What
is probably the situation is that, at some point during the Western Zhou,
the Guoji sub-lineage had established itself as the dominant line of Guo
in the west, and its leaders continued to serve in the Zhou royal court.
During the reign of King Xuan, the Guoji leaders found for themselves a
new base in the Sanmenxia area. Towards the end of the Western Zhou,
the Guoji further enlarged their territory in the Sanmenxia area by victimizing the local polity Jiao and by expanding to the north side of the Yellow
River.

THE RISE OF QIN AND QIN MIGRATION INTO THE ZHOU HEARTLAND

Among the many moves that we can observe in the historical sources relevant to the transitional period from the Western to the Eastern Zhou, the
one move that was destined to change the history of China was that of the
state of Qin 秦 from its homeland in southeastern Gansu into the former
Zhou heartland in the Wei River valley of central Shaanxi. By relocating
themselves on the fertile Wei River plain of Shaanxi, the Qin acquired
new potentials for growth, and eventually contributed to China the first
great centralized bureaucratic empire. In this section, I will systematically
examine Qin's relationship with Zhou and its move east after the fall of the
Zhou capital.

The search for the early Qin

The early history of Qin and its relationship with Zhou is one of the
most important issues in late Western Zhou history. In this regard, a
paragraph from the "Basic Annals of Qin" in the *Shiji* that has already
been partly discussed in chapter 4 provides us with the most valuable
information:[93]

非子居犬丘，好馬及畜，善養息之。犬丘人言之周孝王，孝王召使主馬于汧渭之 間，馬大蕃
息。孝王欲以為大駱適嗣。申侯之女為大駱妻，生子成為適。申侯乃言孝王曰：“昔我先酈
山之女，為戎胥軒妻，生中潏，以親故歸周，保西垂，西垂以其故和睦。今我復與大駱妻，
生適子成。申駱重婚，西戎皆服，所以為王。王其圖之。”於是孝王曰：“昔伯翳為舜主畜，
畜多息，故有土，賜姓嬴。今其後世亦為朕息馬，朕其分土為附庸。”邑之秦，使復續嬴氏
祀，號曰秦嬴。亦不廢申侯之女子為大駱適者，以和西戎。

Feizi lived at Quanqiu and was a lover of horses and other domestic animals, being
good at breeding them. The people of Quanqiu told this to King Xiao, who then
summoned him and put him in charge of horses between the Qian River and
the Wei River. The horses greatly proliferated. King Xiao wanted to establish him

---

[93] See *Shiji*, 5, p. 177 (Nienhauser, *The Grand Scribe's Records*, 1, p. 89).

the heir of the Daluo lineage. The daughter of the Ruler of Shen was a wife of Daluo and gave birth to Cheng who was the legitimate heir of Daluo. Therefore, the Ruler of Shen spoke to King Xiao: "In the past my ancestor Lishan's daughter married Xuxuan of Rong and gave birth to Zhongjue, who because of the marriage submitted himself to Zhou rule and guarded the Western March (Xichui); for this reason the Western March was at peace. In the present days, I again gave a daughter to be Daluo's wife who gave birth to the legitimate heir Cheng. Shen and Luo have two marriages between them, for which reason the Western Rong are all obedient, therefore allowing [you] to be the king. King, please think about it." Thus, King Xiao said: "In the past, Bo Yi took charge of domestic animals for Emperor Shun and the animals were proliferous; therefore he received land and was awarded the surname Ying. Now, his descendent also breeds horses for me. I will divide my land and make him a dependent [of Zhou]." [King Xiao] settled him (Feizi) at Qin, and let him carry on sacrifice of the Ying clan; [Feizi] was called Qin Ying. [King Xiao] also did not abandon the heir of the Daluo lineage who was a son of the Ruler of Shen's daughter, in order to harmonize the relationship with the Western Rong.

This is a fairly informative source for the history of the Daluo lineage and the establishment of Qin as its sub-lineage. But different from the case of Guo, the segmentation of Qin involved the Zhou royal will. According to this paragraph, the forerunner of Qin was the lineage of Daluo located at a place called Quanqiu 犬丘, that had double marriages with Shen (Western Shen), the state that itself was, as has been mentioned in chapter 4, an old marriage partner of Zhou. The Zhou–Shen alliance reportedly goes back to the time of the Grand King and Taijiang, the grandparents of King Wen. The first Shen–Daluo marriage was between Xuxuan of Rong, an ancestor of Qin, and a daughter of the Lishan tribe, probably a part of the Rong people to which the state of Shen owed its origin. Because of their marriage relationship with the Shen, the people of the Daluo lineage submitted themselves to Zhou rule. The second marriage was between Daluo and the daughter of the Ruler of Shen, the purported speaker in the paragraph; the legitimate heir of the Daluo lineage – Cheng 成 – was born of this marriage. However, because Feizi, a secondary son of Daluo and direct ancestor of the later Qin rulers, won the favor of King Xiao of Zhou (r. 872?–866 BC), the king attempted to establish him as the heir of the Daluo lineage while abandoning Cheng. This plan met strong objection from the Ruler of Shen – Cheng's grandfather-in-law – who made it clear to the Zhou king that it would endanger the Shen–Daluo relationship which was the foundation of the security of the western frontier of Zhou. Finally, King Xiao gave up his original plan and sought a compromise by establishing Feizi as ruler in another place – Qin 秦. The state of Qin was thus born as the result of political maneuver at the Zhou court. Literally, before this time, we should not use the term "Qin" for the Qin people.

Since the textual records seem to locate both Quanqiu and Qin in the upper Wei River valley in southeastern Gansu, as will be examined below, this provides a basis for the archaeological search for early Qin.[94] In the first chapter, I have mentioned the discovery of a bronze *gui* in Dongquanxiang, Tianshui, and the excavations at Maojiaping to the west of Tianshui (see p. 54).[95] The *gui* from Dongquanxiang is a typical early Western Zhou bronze, indicating the presence of Zhou culture in the upper Wei River valley. The excavations at Maojiaping in 1982–83 yielded important results, providing us with a chance to look at the actual archaeological remains in southeastern Gansu contemporaneous with the Western Zhou. The deposition of substratum 4B at Maojiaping can be properly dated to the early Western Zhou, yielding different types of deep sunken-crotched *li*-tripods and deep *pen*-basins. Substratum 4A yielded a large number of joint-crotched *li*-tripods with a low body, shallow *yu*-basins, and shallow high *dou*-plates with a slim base, for which a middle through late Western Zhou date was suggested by the reporter (Fig. 35).[96] In addition to the occupational remains, twenty-two of the thirty-three tombs from which pottery vessels were excavated were divided into five different periods with a time span from the mid-Western Zhou to the early Warring States. Tombs of periods I (nos. 6, 1, 2, 4, 10) and II (nos. 3, 9, and TM5) yielded a pottery assemblage roughly contemporary with that of substratum 4A.[97] Not only are these pottery vessels typologically similar to those found on the Wei River plain of central Shaanxi (see p. 78), but the way in which they were grouped in burials is also identical to that of the contemporary Zhou tombs in Shaanxi.[98] On the other hand, in my view, the Maojiaping pottery manifests a certain degree of simplicity when compared with that from the Zhou capital region.[99] This may be due in some degree to the small size of

---

[94] There have been two schools on the ethnic origins of the Qin people. Wang Guowei suggested that the reliable history of Qin began only with Zhongjue 中潏 at the end of Shang who lived to the west of Longshan Mountain. Therefore, Wang traced the origin of the Qin to the Rong people in the west. Similarly, Meng Wentong also argued that the Qin were a part of the Rong and were most closely related to the Quanrong. The theory of the western origin of Qin has been influential especially among archaeologists; see Wang Guowei, "Qin duyi kao," in *Guantang jilin* (Shijiazhuang: Hebei jiaoyu, 2001), p. 335; Meng Wentong, "Qin wei Rong zu kao," *Yugong* 6.7 (1936), 17; Yu Weichao, *Xianqin Lianghan kaoguxue lunji* (Beijing: Wenwu, 1985), pp. 187–88; Liu Qingzhu, "Shilun Qin zhi yuanyuan," in *Xianqin shi lunwen ji* (Monograph of *Renwen zazhi*) (Xi'an, 1982), pp. 176–78. However, the other theory insists that the Qin people originally lived in eastern China and were related to Dongyi communities in the Shandong region. See Xu Xusheng, *Zhongguo gushi de chuanshuo shidai* (Beijing: Wenwu, 1985), p. 205; Lin Jianming, *Qin shi* (Taipei: Wunan, 1992), pp. 21–28; Duan Lianqin, "Guanyu Yizu de xiqian he Qinying de qiyuandi zushu wenti," in *Xianqin shi lunji* (Monograph of the *Renwen zazhi*) (Xi'an, 1982), p. 175; Han Wei, "Guanyu Qinren zushu ji wenhua yuanyuan guanjian," *Wenwu* 1986.4, 23–27; Wang Yuzhe, "Qinren de zuyuan jiqi qianxi luxian," *Lishi yanjiu* 1991.3, 32–39. For a recent discussion of the issue, see Falkenhausen, "The Waning of the Bronze Age," pp. 496–97.

[95] See *Wenwu cankao ziliao* 1955.6, 117–18; *Kaogu xuebao* 1987.3, 359–96.

[96] See *Kaogu xuebao* 1987.3, 388.

[97] See *Kaogu xuebao* 1987.3, 387–88; Zhao Huacheng, "Gansu dongbu Qin he Qiangrong wenhua de kaoguxue tansuo," in *Kaogu leixingxue de lilun yu shijian*, ed. Yu Weichao (Beijing: Wenwu, 1989), pp. 153–62.

[98] The standard set of pottery in the middle–late Western Zhou tombs includes typically: *li*-tripod, high *dou*-plate, and *guan*-jar; or *li*-tripod, high *dou*-plate, *yu* (*pen*)-basin, and *guan*-jar.

[99] For instance, the hollow-legged *li*-tripod and *gui*-basin (early Western Zhou), and the bronze-style *li*-tripod, *li*-tripod with lumps at the end of the hollow legs, and high *dou*-plate with a ridge on

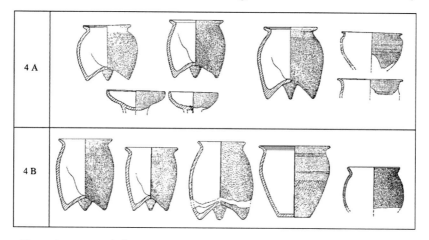

Fig. 35 Pottery vessels from stratum 4 at Maojiaping in Tianshui (*Kaogu xuebao* 1987.3, 367–38, 70)

the excavation at Maojiaping, but in all likelihood it is characteristic of the site.

What does this say about early Qin? While the excavation clarified the basic point that the pottery assemblage from the upper Wei River valley can be properly characterized as a local variation of the same material culture that was centered on the Zhou capitals in central Shaanxi,[100] it says little about Qin.[101] The question remains whether it is appropriate to try to define this pottery assemblage as "Qin culture" contemporaneous with the Western Zhou, for the simple reason that other pro-Zhou polities or communities with similar burial practices may also have been located in the upper Wei River region. However, decisive evidence identifying Qin was brought to light in the Lixian 禮縣 area, in a valley deep in the mountains about 55 kilometers to the south of Tianshui (Fig. 36). In June 1994, a pair of bronze *hu*-vessels appeared in a catalog published by the J. J. Lally Company, New York. The two *hu* were both inscribed as: "The Duke of Qin makes and casts this sacrificial *hu*" (*Qin gong zuo zhu zun hu* 秦公作鑄尊壺).[102] At about the same time, eight large gold plates which are most likely decorations from coffins appeared in Paris, reportedly from Lixian, Gansu.[103] Six other bronzes cast by the Duke of Qin, including

its base (middle–late Western Zhou), all common in the Zhou capital area, do not appear in Maojiaping.

[100] See Niu Shishan, "Qin wenhua yuanyuan yu Qinren qiyuan tansuo," *Kaogu* 1996.3, 45.

[101] In fact, a connection exists between Maojiaping and later Qin burials in the way the dead body was treated. In most tombs in Maojiaping, the dead body was placed in a flexed posture. This contrasts sharply with the Zhou burial practice that the dead body is stretched and facing up, but is similar to the characteristic Qin burial practice in the Spring and Autumn period. See *Kaogu xuebao* 1987.3, 376.

[102] See J. J. Lally & Co., *Archaic Chinese Bronzes, Jades and Works of Art* (New York: J. J. Lally & Co., 1994), no. 54.

[103] See Han Wei, "Lun Gansu Lixian chutu de Qin jinbo shipian," *Wenwu* 1995.6, 4–11.

Fig. 36 The upper Xihan River valley near Lixian, Gansu (photograph by the author)

four *ding* and two *gui*-vessels, were purchased and brought back to the Shanghai Museum from the antiques market in Hong Kong and were subsequently published in 1996 (Fig. 37).[104] Besides these bronzes that have already been published, a number of bronzes are also stored at the Bureau of Public Security, Lixian, confiscated from tomb robbers. As will be analyzed below, this is a group of bronzes cast probably during the late Western Zhou through the early Spring and Autumn period. The rescue excavation carried out at Dabuzishan 大堡子山 confirmed four tomb pits, almost certainly including two main burials and their accompanying chariot-burials.[105] This is the most important discovery in Qin archaeology in recent years; the inscriptions suggest that the center of Qin was probably located in the Lixian area in the upper Xihan 西漢 River valley.

To explain the location of these Qin tombs deep in the mountains far off the main course of the Wei River, we must turn to the received geographical records which actually identify the area with Quanqiu, the site of the Daluo lineage mentioned in the *Shiji*. The *Shuijing zhu* says explicitly that the old town of Xi County 西縣 (Han dynasty), located to the northeast of present-day Lixian, was the land of Quanqiu, the previous residence of the Daluo lineage.[106] There are also other possible locations for Quanqiu, suggested

---

[104] See Li Chaoyuan, "Shanghai bowuguan xinhuo Qingong tongqi yanjiu," *Shanghai bowuguan jikan* 7 (1996), 23–33.
[105] See Han Wei, "Lun Gansu Lixian chutu de Qin jinbo shipian," pp. 7, 11.
[106] See *Shuijing zhu*, 20, p. 643.

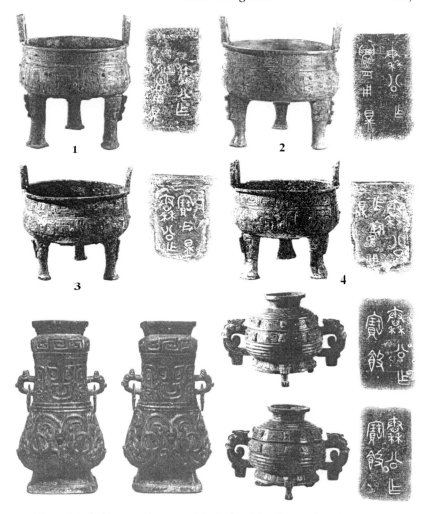

Fig. 37 Newly discovered bronzes of the Duke of Qin from Dabuzishan in Lixian
(from Li Chaoyuan, "Shanghai bowuguan xinhuo," pp. 24–27: Lally, *Archaic Chinese
Bronzes*, no. 54)

by the various geographical works,[107] but the *Shuijing zhu* corresponds
better in this case with the recent archaeological discoveries. As a matter
of fact, a recent archaeological report shows that the Dabuzishan cemetery
is located about 10 kilometers to the northeast of present-day Lixian, and
on the bank of the Xihan River. Crossing the river east from Dabuzishan,

[107] For instance, the "Geographical Records" chapter of the *Hanshu* mentions that the Huaili County
槐里縣 of the Han dynasty (present-day Xingping 興平, 20 kilometers to the west of the capital
Hao) was called Quanqiu; see *Hanshu*, 28, p. 1,546. The "Zhengyi" commentary to the *Shiji* thus
identifies this as Feizi's residence. See *Shiji*, 5, p. 177. The improbability of this location of Quanqiu
in the vicinity of the Zhou capital is obvious; it also contradicts the historical context as will be
analyzed below.

four Qin tombs of the middle to late Spring and Autumn period have been
excavated in 1998–2000 (Map 15).[108]

The problem is that while the geographical record points to the Lixian
area as the location of Quanqiu, the base of the Daluo lineage, the archaeological discoveries show that the Dabuzishan cemetery belongs to the rulers
of Qin, who should have lived in a separate settlement granted by King
Xiao. However, our historical records will fully explain this point below.
As for the location of Qin, the ancient geographical works point to the
area of present-day Qingshui 清水 in the Niutou 牛頭 River valley, about
100 kilometers northeast of Lixian and 40 kilometers east of Tianshui
(Map 12).[109] This actually puts Qin in the neighborhood of Quanqiu in
Lixian, which was in the valley of the upper Xihan River, where the original Daluo lineage was located. The term "Qin" appears in the inscriptions of the Xun *gui* 詢簋 (JC: 4321) and the Shi You *gui* 師酉簋 (JC:
4288), which mention Qinyi 秦夷 or Qinren 秦人 among other groups
of foreigners who lived in the Zhou capital area. Since these two bronzes
possibly pre-date the reign of King Xiao,[110] the time of the establishment
of the polity of Qin as given in the *Shiji*, these inscriptions may suggest
that, similar to the circumstances surrounding the founding of the polity of
Zheng analyzed above, a pre-existing community in the target settlement
bearing a single name "Qin" was granted by the Zhou king to Feizi as its new
ruler.

The Zhou–Daluo–Qin triangle

As suggested in chapter 1, the upper Wei River region to the west of the
Longshan Mountains was the westernmost part of the Zhou culture realm.
During the later pre-dynastic and early Western Zhou, the Zhou had exercised full control over the upper Jing River region and had extended their
power into the northern steppe of southern Ningxia and the upper Wei
River valley. In this historical context, the encounter between the Zhou
and the Daluo lineage may well have been a result of the westward expansion of the Zhou state. However, such an encounter could have taken
different forms, both political and cultural. The *Shiji* paragraph translated

---

[108] See *Wenwu* 2005. 2, 4.
[109] For instance, the *Kuodi zhi* (quoted in the "Zhengyi" commentary to the *Shiji*) says that Qingshui
清水 of Qin Prefecture 秦州 of Tang was originally named Qin, which was the settlement of Yingshi
嬴氏 (Feizi); see *Shiji*, 5, p. 178. The Qing historical-geographer Gu Zuyu identifies Qin with the
site of the ancient town of Qingshui, located to the west of present-day Qingshui; Gu Zuyu, *Dushi
fangyu jiyao*, p. 2,598.
[110] Most scholars consider that the two bronzes were cast by a father and his son. The appearance of
Duke Yi 益 in the Xun *gui* and Scribe Qiang 牆 in the Shi You *gui* would date them to a period
from King Gong to King Yih, prior to the establishment of Qin by King Xiao. For the date of
the Xun *gui*, see also Shaughnessy, *Sources of Western Zhou History*, p. 255. For the inscriptions, see
Shirakawa, "Kinbun tsūshaku," 31.182:701; 29.173:553.

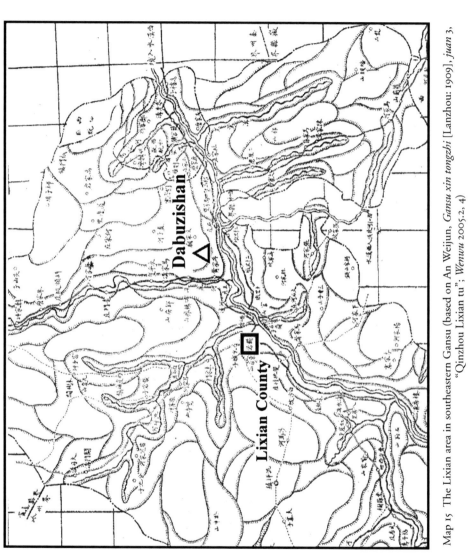

Map 15 The Lixian area in southeastern Gansu (based on An Weijun, *Gansu xin tongzhi* [Lanzhou: 1909], *juan* 3, "Qinzhou Lixian tu"; *Wenwu* 2005.2, 4)

above suggests that the Daluo lineage submitted to the political authority
of Zhou because of their marriage relationship with the Shen, who were an
old ally of the Zhou. As suggested in chapter 4, Shen was probably located
in the Pingling area in the upper Jing River valley, and both Shen and Qin
were strategically important to the defense of the Zhou world. During the
long period of the early and mid-Western Zhou, the Zhou–Shen–Daluo
triangle may have served as the foundation of the security of the Zhou's
western frontier (Map 12). Through the close ties between these two states
and the Rong people, the Zhou were able to maintain a relatively peaceful
relationship with the Rong.

By installing the state of Qin in the upper Wei River valley, separate
from the Daluo lineage in the Xihan River valley, the Zhou created for
themselves a new Zhou–Daluo–Qin triangle. Throughout the rest of the
mid-Western Zhou, the state of Qin had coexisted with the original Daluo
lineage in Quanqiu, both being allies of Zhou. However, during the late
Western Zhou, the situation on the northwestern frontier of Zhou changed
dramatically. The *Shiji* says that at the time of King Li (r. 857/53–842/28 BC),
when the Western Rong rebelled against the royal house of Zhou, they
attacked the Daluo lineage in Quanqiu and extinguished it.[111] An entry in
the *Current Bamboo Annals* says that in the eleventh year of King Li the
Western Rong entered Quanqiu, implying the conquest of Quanqiu by
the Western Rong.[112] The mother-lineage of Qin was thus eliminated. We
should, however, see this attack on the Daluo lineage by the Western Rong
as a part of the extensive movement of the Xianyun into conflict with the
Zhou world in the time of King Li. From this time on the Qin people
went through a long period of military confrontation with the Western
Rong. When King Xuan came to power a systematic effort was made by
the Zhou court to reestablish Zhou dominance in the northwestern regions.
As a part of this effort, Qinzhong 秦仲, the ruler of Qin, was given the
position of Minister by the Zhou court and was sent to attack the Western
Rong in the third year of King Xuan (825 BC), two years prior to the royal
campaign of 823 BC against the Xianyun in the upper Jing River region.[113]
However, Qinzhong was unsuccessful and was killed by the Western Rong
in 822 BC. Then, there came the most heroic and most important period
in early Qin history. The Zhou court summoned Duke Zhuang 莊 of Qin,
a son of Qinzhong, with his four younger brothers to attack the Western
Rong. It is said that the troops of Duke Zhuang were reinforced with 7,000
soldiers from the Zhou royal army.[114] The campaign was a great success;

---

[111] See *Shiji*, 5, p. 178 (Nienhauser, *The Grand Scribe's Records*, 1, p. 90).

[112] See *Zhushu jinian*, 2, p. 13 (Legge, *The Shoo King*, Prolegomena, p. 153).

[113] See *Zhushu jinian*, 2, p. 14 (Legge, *The Shoo King*, Prolegomena, p. 155); *Shiji*, 5, p. 178 (Nienhauser,
The Grand Scribe's Records, 1, p. 90).

[114] This figure would seem too large when compared with other records of wars against the Xianyun,
such as the inscription of the Duoyou *ding*.

the Zhou–Qin allied forces not only defeated the Western Rong, but also managed to capture the Quanqiu area. After the campaign, the Zhou court appointed Duke Zhuang the "Minister of the Western March" (Xichui 西垂) and formally granted him the land around Quanqiu. Thus, Duke Zhuang moved his residence from Qin to Quanqiu, which then became the center of Qin power. Riding on the tide of the restoration under King Xuan, the Qin people thus established themselves as an important power on the western limits of the Zhou world. Duke Zhuang reigned from Quanqiu for forty-four years, the most prosperous period in early Qin history, and died in the fourth year of King You (778 BC). In short, the early history of Qin was closely intertwined with later Western Zhou history, especially with Zhou's war with the Xianyun. Only when we view it from the overall strategy of Zhou will we be able to understand the emergence of Qin as a regional power.

This historical development, as informed by our textual records, explains well why the rulers of Qin should have been buried in Dabuzishan, in an area identified with Quanqiu, the residence of the original Daluo lineage. But the issue then is who was buried there? In the five years following the discovery of the Qin bronzes from Dabuzishan, a large number of studies have been published, and all the known Qin rulers from Qinzhong (d. 822 BC) to Duke Xian 憲 (r. 715–704 BC) across a century were recommended as candidates for these burials.[115] Partly responsible for this scholarly chaos is the currently poor condition of the sources; it is not even clear whether the eight bronzes were from one tomb or from different tombs. Therefore, a careful examination of the grouping and date of these bronzes is necessary for interpreting their implications for late Western Zhou history.

Some have attempted to divide the eight bronzes into two groups, suggesting that bronzes on which the character *qin* is written as ▨ (*ding* nos. 3 and 4; *gui* nos. 1 and 2) were cast by Duke Xiang, and bronzes on which it is written as ▨ (*ding* nos. 1 and 2; *hu* nos. 1 and 2) were cast by Duke Wen.[116] However, such a distinction means very little, since a character

---

[115] It was first suggested by Li Xueqin and Sarah Allan that the two *hu* of Lally's should be attributed to Duke Zhuang of Qin, who died in 778 BC; see Li Xueqin and Ai Lan, "Zuixin chuxian de Qingong hu," *Zhongguo wenwu bao* 1994.10.30. Then, Han Wei argued that the tombs were burials of Qinzhong (d. 822 BC) and Duke Zhuang; Han Wei, "Lun Gansu Lixian chutu de Qin jinbo shipian," p. 8. Since 1996, six more scholars have published studies on these bronzes, four identifying them with Duke Xiang 襄 (r. 777–766 BC) and (or) Duke Wen 文 (r. 765–716 BC); see Chen Zhaorong, "Tan xinchu Qingong hu de shidai," *Kaogu yu wenwu* 1995.4, 64–70, 69; Bai Guangqi, "Qingong hu yingwei Dongzhou chuqi qi," *Kaogu yu wenwu* 1995.4, 71; Li Chaoyuan, "Shanghai bowuguan xinhuo," p. 29; Wang Hui, "Yetan Lixian Dabuzishan Qingong mudi jiqi tongqi," *Kaogu yu wenwu* 1998.5, 93. The other two identify them with Duke Wen and (or) Duke Xian 憲 (r. 715–704 BC); see Lu Liancheng, "Qin guo zaoqi wenwu de xin renshi," *Zhongguo wenzi* 21 (1996), 64; Chen Ping, "Qiantan Lixian Qingong mudi yicun yu xiangguan wenti," *Kaogu yu wenwu* 1998.5, 86.

[116] See Wang Hui, "Yetan Lixian Dabuzishan," p. 90.

can be written differently even on a single bronze.[117] On the other hand, I believe for four reasons that *ding* nos. 1 and 2 and *ding* nos. 3 and 4 clearly belong to different sets: (1) the technique of casting the inscriptions appears different, with the edge of the inscribed block clearly visible on *ding* nos. 3 and 4 but not on *ding* nos. 1 and 2; (2) on *ding* nos. 3 and 4 the term *bao* 寶 is used, while on *ding* nos. 1 and 2 the term *zhu* 鑄 is used in the same context; (3) the decoration on *ding* nos. 3 and 4 is executed differently from that on *ding* nos. 1 and 2; and (4) there is a difference between the heights of *ding* nos. 3 and 4 (25.9 and 24.2 cm) and those of *ding* nos. 1 and 2 (47 and 38.5 cm). It is clear to me that the four *ding*-vessels belong to two different sets of graduated *ding*-vessels. Since each tomb normally can have only one set of *ding*, it is probable that the four *ding* were from two different tombs.

It is also evident that *ding* nos. 3 and 4 are slightly earlier than *ding* nos. 1 and 2; while *ding* nos. 3 and 4 have a round bottom, *ding* nos. 1 and 2 have a flat bottom, being the prototype of the flat-bottomed *ding* of the later Spring and Autumn period. The similarity between *ding* nos. 3 and 4 and other late Western Zhou bronzes such as the Xiao Ke *ding* 小克鼎 is clear.[118] The date of the pair of *hu*-vessels from Lally is the focus of current discussions among scholars. Compared with the Song *hu* 頌壺 and the *hu* in the Art Institute of Chicago (nos. 24.233–4),[119] the two *hu* are apparently later, as is evident in their slimmer belly and in the execution of their interlacing dragon motif; however, there is not a great gap in time between them. Compared with the *hu* of the same type from tomb no. 1 in Songcun 宋村,[120] which is generally dated to the late phase of the early Eastern Zhou, the Lally *hu* is much closer to the Song *hu*. It should also be noted that, since the character *zhu* 鑄 is used in the inscription, the Lally *hu* probably belong to the same group as *ding* nos. 1 and 2. As for the two *gui*-vessels, their relationship with the two groups of *ding* is unclear, but their shape is very common during the late Western Zhou. In short, these two groups of bronzes were probably cast during the late Western Zhou or perhaps during the early Spring and Autumn period, but surely they cannot be dated later than the early phase of the early Spring and Autumn period.

The possibility of Qinzhong being buried in one of the Dabuzishan tombs can first be excluded. Qin moved to occupy the Quanqiu area only after Duke Zhuang defeated the Western Rong with help from Zhou. It is very unlikely that Qinzhong was buried in Quanqiu if he had a tomb at

---

[117] For examples of such graphic variation, see Li Feng, "Ancient Reproductions and Calligraphic Variations: Studies of Western Zhou Bronzes with Identical Inscriptions," *Early China* 22 (1997), 38–39.

[118] For the design of the Xiao Ke *ding*, see *Shanghai bowuguan cang qingtongqi*, no. 48.

[119] For the *hu* in Chicago, see Charles Fabens Kelley and Ch'en Meng-chia (Chen Mengjia), *Chinese Bronzes from the Buckingham Collection* (Chicago: The Art Institute of Chicago, 1946), pls. 34–35.

[120] For the *hu* from Songcun, see *Wenwu* 1975.10, 55–67.

all; according to the *Shiji*, he was killed by the Rong. At the same time, I believe that a Duke Xian date would be too late for these bronzes. Duke Xian died in 704 BC, almost seventy years after the eastward migration of the Zhou court; the bronzes do not show such a distance in time from the well-known late Western Zhou bronzes. Even a Duke Wen (d. 716 BC) date would appear to be too late for these bronzes. Although there is no clear record as to where Duke Zhuang was buried, since he reigned forty-four years at Quanqiu, it is very likely that he was buried somewhere in the Quanqiu area. The same is true for Duke Xiang; the *Shiji* says that Duke Xiang was buried in the Western March (Xichui). The problem is the location of the tomb of Duke Wen. While the "Basic Annals of the First Emperor of Qin" says that Duke Wen was buried in the Western March,[121] the "Basic Annals of Qin" says that he was buried at Western Mountain (Xishan 西山); another duke who is also said to have been buried at Western Mountain was Duke Xian. It has been strongly argued by Li Ling that Duke Wen was not buried in Western March but rather in the Baoji area, because by his time the center of Qin had already been moved east to the Wei River plain of central Shaanxi.[122] In his fourth year (762 BC), Duke Wen moved the capital of Qin from Quanqiu to the confluence of the Wei and Qian rivers and settled there for the next forty-six years until his death in 716 BC. It is not likely that after nearly half a century on the Wei River plain of central Shaanxi, Duke Wen could have been sent back to be buried in Gansu.

The historical records inform us that there were only two rulers of Qin, Duke Zhuang and Duke Xiang, who ruled from the Quanqiu area and also died in the area. There are only two groups of bronzes from the two main burials at Dabuzishan. I think the answer is quite clear. Duke Zhuang died in 777 BC, seven years before the fall of the Zhou capital, and Duke Xiang died in 766 BC, four years after the historical fall. These dates are most consistent with the date of the bronzes from Dabuzishan.

The eastward campaign of Qin into the Zhou heartland

In the military struggle between the Zhou and the Western Rong, Qin had played a very important role. However, the collapse of the Western Zhou dynasty and the subsequent evacuation of the Zhou court under King Ping from the Wei River plain (and the termination of the court under the King of Xie) left the polity of Qin in a sea of Rong people. In this regard, the eastward migration of Qin to Shaanxi would appear to have been an escape from this dangerous situation, rather than an expansion of its power as the *Shiji* seems to suggest. In the decades that followed, the Qin people

---

[121] See *Shiji*, 6, p. 285 (Nienhauser, *The Grand Scribe's Records*, 1, p. 170).
[122] See Li Ling, "Shiji zhong suojian Qin zaoqi duyi zangdi," *Wenshi* 20 (1983), 19–23.

fought very hard to resist pressure from the Rong and gradually moved their political center from the Quanqiu area in southeastern Gansu to the Wei River plain in central Shaanxi, which was the homeland of the Zhou. The "Basic Annals of Qi" in the *Shiji* says:[123]

西戎犬戎與申侯伐周，殺幽王酈山下。而秦襄公將兵救周，戰甚力，有功。周避犬戎難，東徙雒邑，襄公以兵送周平王。平王封襄公為諸侯，賜之岐以西之地，曰："戎無道，侵奪我岐豐之地，秦能攻逐戎，即有其地。"與誓，封爵之。

The Quanrong of Western Rong and the Ruler of Shen attacked Zhou and killed King You at the foot of Lishan Mountain. However, Duke Xiang of Qin led his troops to rescue Zhou; [he] fought very hard and gained merit. To avoid the disaster brought by the Quanrong, the Zhou moved east to Luoyi, and Duke Xiang led his troops to escort King Ping of Zhou. King Ping granted Duke Xiang the status of regional ruler and gave him the land to the west of Qiyi, saying: "The Rong have no virtue; [they] deprived us of the land of Qiyi and Feng. If Qin can attack and drive the Rong away, Qin may possess the land." He swore an oath with [Duke Xiang] and conferred on him the rank.

This paragraph is very often cited by scholars to explain why the Qin campaigned repeatedly into the Wei River plain in central Shaanxi and finally established themselves as new masters of the Zhou homeland. However, there are also scholars who doubt the historicity of the paragraph, arguing that it was meant only to justify Qin's invasion of the Wei River plain. The real situation was probably that, after the collapse of Zhou central power, the Qin had to bear more pressure from the Rong. Moving east to the Wei River plain would distance them from the center of Rong power, with at least the Longshan Mountains as a natural barrier in the west, and would enable them to maintain contact with other Zhou states in the east. After all, the natural condition of the Wei River plain in central Shaanxi was much more favorable than that of the Tianshui area in Gansu.

Before discussing the eastward campaigns of Qin, I should comment briefly on the political landscape of the Wei River plain after the eastward migration of the Zhou court. The fall of the Zhou dynasty stirred up a large-scale migration of the Rong people into Zhou territory. This situation is also described in the poems "Yu Wuzheng" and "Zhaomin" in the *Book of Poetry*, but is more evident in the location of Rong communities during the early Spring and Autumn period. Some of these Rong people were traceable in the historical record. For instance, at the site of former Western Guo in Baoji was located the polity of Minor Guo (Xiaoguo 小虢) that is said to have been a separate branch of the Qiang 羌 people from the far west.[124] In the vicinity of the former Zhou capital Hao was located the polity of Bo 亳 (also called Dangshe 蕩社), probably a community that derived its origin from the Western Rong.[125] In the Lishan area was located the Lirong,

---

[123] See *Shiji*, 5, p. 179 (Nienhauser, *The Grand Scribe's Records*, 1, pp. 90–91).
[124] See *Shiji*, 5, pp. 182–83 (Nienhauser, *The Grand Scribe's Records*, 1, p. 93).
[125] See *Shiji*, 5, p. 181 (Nienhauser, *The Grand Scribe's Records*, 1, p. 92).

a campaign against whom by the state of Jin in 672 BC was recorded by the *Guoyu*.[126] In the eastern part of the Wei River plain were located the Rong of Dali 大荔 and the Rong of Pengxi 彭戲.[127] Moreover, the *Zuozhuan* mentions a campaign in 660 BC against the Quanrong in the Wei River valley by the state of Western Guo located in Sanmenxia.[128] These records, when taken together, are enough to suggest a Rong dominance of the Wei River valley after the move of the Zhou court to the east. However, it is important to note that the eastward migration of Qin and the migration of the Rong people into central Shaanxi should not be viewed as two processes separated by time. Instead, they are more likely to have been simultaneously going on during the first century of the Eastern Zhou. The point is that after the Zhou moved east, Qin had to cope not only with pressure from the west, but also with the Rong in the east. To move into the Zhou homeland in central Shaanxi meant fighting their way into it.

In 766 BC, four years after the eastward migration of the Zhou court, Duke Xiang 襄 led the Qin army east to attack the Rong and reached as far as Qiyi. The *Shiji* says that Duke Xiang died on this campaign. It is very likely that the Qin carried out military actions through the Qian River valley. During the late 1970s and early 1980s, several tombs of early Spring and Autumn date were excavated in Bianjiazhuang 邊家莊, Longxian, and these are generally associated with Qin activities in the region.[129] As it is located between Quanqiu in the west and the later Qin capital Yong 雍 in Fengxiang, the cemetery in Bianjiazhuang imposes itself both spatially and temporally between the tombs at Dabuzishan and those Qin tombs on the Wei River plain.[130] The next reign (Duke Wen) was an important period during which the Qin established their base in the western part of the Wei River plain. According to the *Shiji*, in his third year (763 BC) Duke Wen set out on a campaign to the east with 700 soldiers and arrived at the confluence of the Wei River and the Qian River. He divined and constructed a new settlement near the confluence.[131] Duke Wen resided at this site for forty-six years until his death in 716 BC.

Having consolidated their control over the Baoji area at the western end of the Wei River plain, the Qin then carried out aggressive campaigns against the Rong people in the central and eastern parts of the Wei River

---

[126] See *Guoyu*, 7, p. 253.
[127] See *Shiji*, 5, pp. 182, 199 (Nienhauser, *The Grand Scribe's Records*, 1, pp. 92, 106).
[128] See *Zuozhuan*, 11, p. 1,786.　　[129] See *Kaogu yu wenwu* 1986.6, 15–21; *Wenwu* 1988.11, 14–23.
[130] For two general studies of the cemetery in Bianjiazhuang, see Zhang Tian'en, "Bianjiazhuang Chunqiu mudi yu Qianyi diwang," *Wenbo* 1990.5, 227–31; Liu Junshe, "Bianjiazhuang Qin guo mudi fajue de zhuyao shouhuo jiqi yiyi," *Baoji wenbo* 1991.1, 12–14.
[131] The Tang geographical survey indicates that the old town of Chencang 陳倉 was located 10 kilometers to the east of Baoji County (present-day Baoji City) and was constructed by Duke Wen of Qin. It further says that the town of Chencang comprised two towns, the upper being the town built by Duke Wen of Qin. This is accepted by scholars as the location of Duke Wen's residence at the confluence of the Wei and Qian rivers. See *Yuanhe junxian tuzhi*, pp. 42–43. See also Li Ling, "Shiji zhong suojian Qin zaoqi duyi zangdi," p. 20.

plain. A summary of these campaigns is given below. The *Shiji* says that in his sixteenth year (750 BC), twelve years after the relocation of the Qin capital to Baoji, Duke Wen attacked the Rong and defeated them. This battle seems to have occupied an important position in Qin history because the *Shiji* says that after the battle the Qin expanded their land all the way to Qiyi and took over the remnants of the Zhou people as subjects of Qin. It is very likely that through this battle the Qin established their dominance over the western part of the Wei River plain.

Duke Wen was succeeded by his grandson, Duke Xian (or Ning 寧). During the reign of Duke Xian, the Qin moved their capital further east and relocated it to Pingyang 平陽, near the town of present-day Yangping 陽平, about 30 kilometers to the east of their previous capital in Baoji. As soon as he settled in this new location, Duke Xian sent out troops to attack the Rong kingdom – Bo, located in present-day Chang'an County. The King of Bo was defeated and his kingdom eliminated. Through this campaign, the Qin recovered the former capital area of Zhou and pushed their frontline to the middle portion of the Wei River plain. After the interim rule of Chuzi 出子 and the accompanying political disturbance at the Qin court, Duke Wu 武 was established in 697 BC. The *Shiji* says that in his first year the Qin attacked the Rong of Pengxi 彭戲 and arrived at the foot of Huashan 華山 Mountain. This campaign indicates that the Qin had pushed further into the eastern part of the Wei River plain. To consolidate control over the newly acquired territories, in 687 BC Qin created two counties – Zheng 鄭 and Du 杜 – as administrative units directly responsible to the Qin court. Zheng was located in present-day Huaxian near Huashan Mountain; Du was almost certainly located on the site of the previous Rong kingdom – Bo. In the next year, Qin annihilated Minor Guo in present-day Baoji County. At the same time, the effort of Duke Wu to consolidate Qin control was directed to the west: in 688 BC, Qin troops attacked the Rong of Gui 邽 and the Rong of Ji 冀, both located in the Tianshui area. After this campaign, both Gui and Ji were made counties of Qin.[132]

In short, after coming to the Wei River plain, the Qin gradually developed from a small polity into one of the major powers in north China. By the end of the reign of Duke Wu, Qin had evidently established its dominance over the entire sphere of the Wei River plain in central Shaanxi and had begun to exercise influence beyond the region. The Wei River plain – the homeland of the Zhou people – after eighty years of chaos and military and cultural conflicts following the fall of the Western Zhou dynasty, once again fell under the control of a single power and was reborn as the center of another round of historical development eventually leading to the unification of China.

---

[132] See *Shiji*, 5, p. 182 (Nienhauser, *The Grand Scribe's Records*, 1, p. 92).

CONCLUSION

In this chapter, I have discussed in detail the eastward migration of the Zhou court from the Wei River plain of Shaanxi to the Luo River plain of Western Henan, and the segmentation and migration of two important aristocratic lineages – Zheng and Guo – that had played an important role in the Western–Eastern Zhou transition. It has been shown that Zheng was originally located in the western part of central Shaanxi and moved from there to central Henan, reestablishing itself in present-day Xinzheng. Also located in the western part of the Wei River plain, the polity of Western Guo moved from there to present-day Sanmenxia in the narrow pass of western Henan. Correlating the migration of these two lineages with the relocation of the states of Shen and Lü probably from the upper Jing River region to the Nanyang basin during the reign of King Xuan, and considering also the eastward move of the Huangfu family to Xiang during the reign of King You, we can probably view the late Western Zhou through the early Eastern Zhou as one of the most important periods of population dislocation and relocation in early Chinese history. To this picture, of course, we should add the eastward migration of the state of Qin and the migration of "many Rong" communities who were running in front of the Qin from the northwestern regions into central Shaanxi.

So, what was the significance of such migration? For the Zhou court, the change was dramatic and fundamental. The authority of the Zhou king sharply diminished and policies of the royal court fell completely into the hands of the regional rulers. In the course of history, some states even declared war on the Zhou court and humiliatingly defeated the royal army. In a strict sense, from this time on we need to use the term "former Zhou states" for the many regional states which were once parts of the common Zhou state. Behind this, there was probably a major change in royal finance brought about by the loss of the Wei River plain, from which the Zhou court had drawn most of its revenue. The small area of the Luo River plain could only provide enough revenue for the Zhou court to maintain a small army; the renowned Six Armies and Eight Armies of the Western Zhou simply faded into history during the Eastern Zhou. The eastward migration of the Zhou states greatly changed the political landscape of the eastern plain. The relocation of these "new" states intensified competition in the eastern plain for both political and economic resources. There seems little doubt that such conflict was first centered on states such as Zheng and Western Guo who were trying to consolidate their new bases by victimizing other native states. Gradually, the strong regional powers on the periphery of the Zhou world such as Qi, Lu, Yan, Jin, and Chu, were drawn into battles in the plain by their connections with those inner states. Thus, a new era of interstate military conflict was inaugurated.

In the west, the withdrawal of the Zhou court left the Wei River plain in central Shaanxi open to competition between the remaining Zhou communities and the Rong people, and between the Rong polities and the rising state of Qin. Textual and new archaeological evidence show that Qin was originally located in the upper Wei River valley in southeastern Gansu, and had for centuries assisted the Zhou in fighting the Western Rong. After the fall of the Western Zhou dynasty, Qin was isolated by Rong power and therefore attempted to move east. During the early years of Duke Wen, the Qin had established for themselves a new base in the Baoji area. From this time to the end of the reign of Duke Wu, the Qin gradually eliminated the Rong polities from central Shaanxi and established themselves as masters of the west. The Wei River plain was once again transformed by the Qin into a new center of political power, and became, after many centuries, the heartland of China's first centralized bureaucratic empire.

CHAPTER 6

The legacy of the Western Zhou

Given 1045 BC as the year of the Zhou conquest of Shang, the Western Zhou dynasty would have lasted 274 years, just about the same length of time as the Ming dynasty (276 years: AD 1368–1644). However, after the downfall of the Western Zhou dynasty, the Zhou court continued to exist in Luoyi for another 515 years, making the history of the Zhou royal house much longer than that of any other royal or imperial lineage that ever ruled China. Compared to other major dynasties in Chinese history, the strength and glory of the Western Zhou dynasty seem to have passed too early and the course of its weakening seems to have been extraordinarily long. But the very fact that the royal line could persist for nearly 800 years indicates also the unique power of the Zhou system. The Western Zhou state declined as the result of being perplexed by internal problems under outside pressures, and fell as the outcome of a "sudden" foreign attack joined by some of Zhou's former allies. It was the growth of the regional states that deprived the Western Zhou state of its energy and resources; it was also this growth that preserved a Zhou world and a long-lasting royal line. The Western Zhou state was itself a contradiction – a contradiction that inevitably brought it to a disastrous end.

As the last of the early royal dynasties in China, the Western Zhou state left its clear imprint on later Chinese history. To some extent, the succession of the Qin and Han empires followed directly upon the Western Zhou state because there had not been another dominating cultural tradition separating them despite there being many competing regional powers in the interregnum of five centuries. It has been noted by previous scholars that the Western Zhou state had left behind it the core of the ancient Chinese Classics, namely the essential elements in the *Book of Poetry, the Book of Documents*, and the *Book of Changes*, which testify to its great cultural wealth and speak of its historical development.[1] Although the association of these texts with the Confucian tradition seems to have been something of a historical accident, through the able agent of Confucianism they have been built deeply into the foundation of the Chinese civilization. The Zhou dynasty's influence through these core texts on later Chinese culture

[1] See Creel, *The Origins of Statecraft in China*, p. 43.

in the fields of political ethics, governmental practice, literary estheticism, philosophy, and even military strategy can hardly be exaggerated. However, rather than taking this conventional line of investigation, this chapter will introduce a cultural and political approach to the legacy of the Western Zhou, analyzing the most fundamental contributions of the Western Zhou state to the formation of Chinese civilization. The aim is not to produce a list of political and cultural elements in later Chinese civilization that may have originated in the Western Zhou period. Instead, I will focus on the following subjects. In the first section, I will discuss the important lessons that the Qin and Han empires had learned from the Western Zhou in shaping the imperial structure of the Chinese state. In the second section, I will discuss the rise of the distinction between the collective "Hua" 華 or "Xia" 夏 nation and the collective "barbarian" world, a cultural self-realization among the people in the northern China plain during the Spring and Autumn period that had its deep roots in their common Western Zhou experience. In the third section, in the light of archaeology, I will discuss the far-reaching impact of the Western Zhou state on the cultural integration of the population of pre-Qin China.

LESSONS FOR THE EMPIRE

In closing his long concluding chapter in the *Cambridge History of Ancient China*, the respected senior British sinologist Michael Loewe writes:[2]

The empires had yet to work out an elusive compromise that was achieved only too rarely: the viable balance between a rigorous, disciplined mode of government and attention to the ethical values of the humanities. From the outset they faced one question, seen indeed before the days of empire had dawned, but not fully resolved over twenty centuries. Each dynastic house would need to choose between two principles that lay behind its way of government. Emperors could either rely on the ties of kinship to their own ancestors so as to ensure loyalty in the face of ambition, or they could exercise their government by controlling the appointments of their chief advisers on the ground of merit. Neither principle was wholly effective.

Loewe sounds towards the end very much like Creel, who with respect to the Western Zhou state argued that, faced with the choice between presiding over quasi-independent feudal states or over a carefully organized official hierarchy, the Zhou kings found neither acceptable, and accepted neither. In Creel's view, the Zhou government was a hybrid between "feudalism" and centralized royal control.[3] As I have noted elsewhere, this "dilemma" that Creel attributed to the Western Zhou state is probably illusory. On the one hand, no such thing as "feudalism" was ever practiced by the Western

---

[2] See Michael Loewe, "The Heritage Left to the Empire," in *The Cambridge History of Ancient China: From the Origins of Civilization to 221 BC*, ed. Michael Loewe and Edward L. Shaughnessy (Cambridge: Cambridge University Press, 1999), p. 1,031.

[3] See Creel, *The Origins of Statecraft in China*, pp. 423–24.

Zhou state; political relations in the Western Zhou state were defined by a set of rules quite different from those that were adopted in the "feudo-vassalic institution" of medieval Europe. The regional rulers, as agents of the Western Zhou state and subjects of the Zhou king, were fully expected to perform their duty, and the insurance for this was provided through a carefully constructed kinship structure backed up by an overwhelming royal military power.[4] On the other hand, while internal control of the royal domain was entrusted to a bureaucracy of limited size that had evidently emerged by the mid-Western Zhou, a centralized control over its whole realm through a "carefully organized official hierarchy" had never been attempted by the Western Zhou state.[5] In other words, the Zhou had never had to choose between a system of local rulers set up on kinship principles and a state-wide centralized bureaucratic machine that was not known to China until many centuries later.

However, when we move beyond the confines of the Western Zhou and view Chinese history in the long term, we find that there was indeed a dilemma – a sway between a government that was based on kinship ties and a government that achieved its goals through a disciplined bureaucracy. This sway profoundly influenced dynastic policies and guided the course of Chinese history. It cannot be denied that the "Fengjian" system implemented by the Zhou founders was a great success under the special circumstances of the early Western Zhou. The system worked well on the assumed and justly expected loyalty of the regional rulers, who were mostly close kinsmen or relatives of the king. These regional Zhou states with their political and military flexibility served as an effective means of royal control over the rebellious local population in the eastern plain and beyond. It was because of the existence of these regional states that the Zhou dynasty was able to achieve the so-called "Cheng-Kang Peace," and because of the support of these regional states that further Zhou expansion was possible. Also thanks to their protection, the Zhou court could choose enemies to attack rather than confronting enemies in all directions at all times. However, as analyzed in chapter 2, from the mid-Western Zhou the dark side of the "Fengjian" system began to expose itself: the increasing power of the regional states and their granted autonomy became more and more obstructive to the enforcement of royal rule throughout the realm of the Western Zhou state.

During the 500 years after the fall of the Western Zhou dynasty, interstate warfare completely destroyed the hope for political unity that the "Fengjian" institution was originally designed to achieve. As sole winner of this protracted interstate warfare, the Qin rulers learned an important lesson from the failure of the Western Zhou state. The "commandery–county" (Junxian 郡縣) system of Qin that was extended to the whole of the Qin

[4] See Li Feng, "'Feudalism' and Western Zhou China," pp. 142–44.
[5] See Li Feng, "'Offices' in Bronze Inscriptions," pp. 51–54.

Empire was evidently created with the "Fengjian" institution of the Western Zhou as a point of reference. The strong awareness of the Qin rulers not to repeat the historical tragedy of the Western Zhou is fully demonstrated by a court discourse that took place in 221 BC, changing the course of Chinese history once and for all:[6]

丞相綰等言：「諸侯初破，燕、齊、荊地遠，不為置王，毋以填之。請立諸子，唯上幸許。」皇帝下其議於群臣，群臣皆以為便。廷尉李斯議曰：「周文武所封子弟同姓甚眾，然後屬疏遠，相攻擊如仇讎，諸侯更相誅伐，周天子弗能禁止。今海內賴陛下神靈一統，皆為郡縣，諸子功臣以公賦稅重賞賜之，甚足易制。天下無異意，則安寧之術也。置諸侯不便。」始皇曰：「天下共苦戰鬥不休，以有侯王。賴宗廟，天下初定，又復立國，是樹兵也，而求其寧息，豈不難哉！廷尉議是。」

Wan, the Chancellor, and the others said: "The many lords have just been destroyed and the lands of Yan, Qi, and Jing are remote; if [we] do not establish kings [there], [we] will have nothing to fill the vacuum. Please establish the many princes. May the Sovereign kindly approve this." The First Emperor sent down their proposal to the officials [at court], and the officials all considered it appropriate. Li Si, the Superintendent of Trials, deliberated: "King Wen and King Wu of Zhou established many princes of the same surname as local rulers. Yet their descendents became alienated and attacked one another like enemies. The many rulers repeatedly attacked and killed each other, and even the Son of Heaven in the Zhou court was unable to stop it. Now, thanks to Your Majesty's divine sagacity, all lands within the seas have been united and became commanderies and counties. If [you] richly reward the many princes and the meritorious officials with state revenue, it will be sufficient and easy to control. All under Heaven have no disputes; this is the method to achieve peace. It is not appropriate to establish the many rulers." The First Emperor said: "All under Heaven had suffered enough from the unceasing wars and battles, because there were rulers and kings. With blessing from my ancestral temple, the world has now just been pacified. If [we] again establish regional states, it is to cause war. Then, if we still want peace, will it not be difficult? The Superintendent's argument is on the mark."

As the result of this debate, the First Emperor divided the new empire of Qin into thirty-six commanderies, put under centralized bureaucratic control. Interestingly, however, even at this time the Zhou system was still regarded by most officials at the imperial court as the norm of state, for the simple reason that it was the only way they had known in the past to achieve political unity over a large territory. However, the "commandery-county" system was the new political alternative to manage the huge area falling under the control of the empire, and it was Li Si and the First Emperor who were determined to abandon the Zhou system for the sake of perpetual political unity. Instead of sending the Qin imperial princes to govern remote areas, the First Emperor sent out well-disciplined bureaucrats who could never build their roots into the local societies they governed and could be removed from their positions at any time. Li Si provided the

[6] See *Shiji*, 6, pp. 238–39 (Nienhauser, *The Grand Scribe's Records*, 1, p. 137).

Qin Empire with an "effective" remedy to prevent the enlarged territory from falling under the control of future warlords. However, ironically, the remedy that Li Si prescribed to cure the empire's future potential illness could not save it from its immediate failure – after only fifteen years, the Qin Empire collapsed under attack neither by external forces, nor by its regional governors, but by a massive force of rebels made up of the peasants and the remnants of the old Warring States aristocracy.

The early collapse of the centralized Qin Empire demonstrated that the Qin system had serious problems. At the same time, it demonstrated the bright side of the Zhou system: when the Western Zhou dynasty fell, the Zhou court and worship of the Zhou ancestors survived for another 500 years because of the help of the regional rulers. This is fully manifest in the eastward migration of the Zhou court, as suggested in chapter 5. Although these regional rulers occasionally challenged the royal authority, it was the support or at least the recognition by the Zhou king in Luoyi, still the royal capital, that the regional rulers looked upon as the source of their legitimacy. But when the Qin capital was taken by Liu Bang in 206 BC, the entire Qin Empire vanished almost overnight. Nobody was determined to help the imperial house out of trouble, because the officials were otherwise unrelated to it except through the bureaucratic system that was already paralyzed. Here, we can clearly see the importance of the "ethical value of the humanities" described by Loewe, and in this regard the Qin system was not a perfect system either. The Qin system concentrated all power in the imperial court in Xianyang, and when that center was struck down the entire system of empire was paralyzed.

Before the emperors of the Han Empire there were two models of state and government: that of Zhou and that of Qin. The Han system was a typical hybrid: the Han Empire maintained the basic administrative structure (commandery–county) of the Qin Empire, mainly in its western half, but added to it Western Zhou features, mainly in the eastern half. But even this east–west split echoes the geopolitical division of the Western Zhou state into the royal domain in the west and the regional states in the east. Coexisting with the commanderies located mainly in the western half of empire, there were multiple kingdoms ruled by hereditary kings, and many of these were of the same size as large commanderies. Some of these kingdoms were founded by Liu Bang's own generals and others by descendents of the ruling houses of the former warring states who had restored their lost kingdoms during the rebellion against the Qin Empire. There was at one time a political tendency to go back to the multistate system of the Eastern Zhou, and the Han Empire simply incorporated these kingdoms into its territory by granting them imperial recognition.[7] However, one after

---

[7] In the first month of 201 BC, after the death of the hero Xiang Yu, Liu Bang officially took on the title "Emperor" and recognized the following kings: the King of Chu 楚, the King of Liang 梁, the

another, these kings rose against the Han court or were accused of doing so, and were replaced by imperial relatives. Finally, Emperor Gaozu (Liu Bang; r. 206–195 BC) swore an oath with his generals that if anyone who was not a member of the Liu family sought again to be established king, all people under Heaven should rise to eliminate him.[8] By the end of Gaozu's reign, nine kings from the Liu family were established, while the kings who were not members of the Liu family were mostly eliminated. This appears to have been a further move from the multistate system of the Warring States period back to the Western Zhou "Fengjian" institution characterized by the establishment of the regional states ruled by the royal kinsmen of Zhou. In other words, kinship that was essential to the Western Zhou system was built into the Han system of regional kingdoms. The Han emperor would probably have thought that by balancing the commanderies with kingdoms in the hands of imperial kinsmen, the empire could last forever.

However, even these "Liu" kingdoms did not wait too long to strengthen themselves against the empire. The Han court had to fight very hard to maintain control over them. Under Emperor Wen (r. 179–157 BC), the kingdoms of Zhao and Qi were first divided and given to a number of princes of the two kingdoms. Then, during the reign of Emperor Jing (r. 156–141 BC), the court adopted Chao Cuo's 晁錯 proposal to reduce the territory of the states of Wu and Chu, and this led to the extensive rebellion of the seven "Liu" kingdoms, whose armies jointly marched west against the imperial capital Chang'an. Under pressure from the rebels, the emperor ordered the execution of Chao Cuo and then sent troops east to crush the rebellious kings, replacing them with princes of a younger generation, again from the imperial Liu house. This incident brought the decisive destruction of the power of the regional kings. During the next reign, that of Emperor Wu (r. 140–87 BC), imperial power further crushed the rebellion of the kingdoms of Huainan 淮南 and Hengshan 衡山. Meanwhile, a new policy called "Extending the imperial favor" (*tuien* 推恩) was adopted by the court to reduce regional powers systematically by allowing the kings to establish their sons as secondary rulers, and therefore slicing their kingdoms into ever smaller pieces. Thereafter, regional kings were only given a few towns with tax allotments from state revenue, rarely associated with a sizeable territory.

This new status of regional "kings without kingdoms" became the norm of the imperial structure of almost every later Chinese dynasty. It

---

King of Hann 韓, the King of Changsha 長沙, the King of Huainan 淮南, the King of Yan 燕, and the King of Zhao 趙. In fact, few of these kings were still related to the original founders of these kingdoms by blood; they were warlords who once allied themselves to Xiang Yu or Liu Bang. At the end of the year, Liu Bang established his two brothers and one son kings of Chu (after eliminating Han Xin), Qi 齊, and Jing 荊. See *Shiji*, 8, pp. 380, 384 (William Nienhauser [ed.], *The Grand Scribe's Record*, vol. 2: *The Basic Annals of Han China* [Bloomington: Indiana University Press, 2002], pp. 66, 71).

[8] See *Shiji*, 9, p. 406 (Nienhauser, *The Grand Scribe's Records*, 2, p. 127).

simultaneously satisfied the need to enforce imperial bureaucratic rule and the need to construct blood ties throughout the empire. By granting imperial kinsmen the status of king superior to all bureaucrats, a super-privileged class was created, and this class could in turn secure the ruling position of the imperial family. This created, to use Loewe's expression again, a balance between a disciplined bureaucracy and "the ethical value of the humanities"; it was also, perhaps more importantly, a balance between the legalist measures of Qin and the kinship approach of the Western Zhou to achieve political unity. This balance was the result of a long historical process that began in the Western Zhou and went through various adjustments and adaptations. Because of the Zhou lesson, the imperial structure of China was always different from that of imperial Rome, where the great Roman Empire went on uninterruptedly for centuries while imperial authority constantly shifted from one family to another. However, the issue of imperial control was by no means fully settled; whenever central power was weakened, regional governors could pursue their own interests and move towards independence. Even those kings without a kingdom could still constitute a threat to imperial power, as they did in the so-called "Turmoil of the Eight Kings" in the Jin dynasty (AD 265–317). Nevertheless, the advantage of the balance worked out by the Han Empire, and hence the historical value of the Western Zhou lesson, can be fully seen in the fact that few dynasties after Han had declined as a result of the growing regionalism (except Tang, which was weakened by provincial military commissioners along the northern border); on the contrary, more often the growth of regional powers was the outcome of dynastic decline.

THE COMMON WESTERN ZHOU EXPERIENCE

Perhaps the most important impact the Western Zhou state had on China and its people through the historical period was more cultural and psychological than political. The self-awareness of a people is an important cultural phenomenon that can be best explained by historical reasons. In the centuries after the fall of the Western Zhou dynasty, we actually witness in China the rise of such cultural self-awareness, as represented by the concept "Huaxia" 華夏 that came quite close to what is meant by the term "Chinese" as it is used in modern Western historiography.[9] What was the real cultural and philosophical implication of "Huaxia"? What was special about the time context in which the concept arose? In the answers to these questions, we find that the common Western Zhou experience of the people in North China had played a very important part.

It is true that there was a distinction between the Zhou and the Rong 戎 or Yi 夷, both terms frequently appearing in the Western Zhou bronze

---

[9] On this issue, see also Di Cosmo, *Ancient China and Its Enemies*, pp. 93–94.

inscriptions as well as in the received Western Zhou texts. However, during the Western Zhou period, as the term "Rong" meant something like "warlike foreigners" and the term "Yi" came very close to "foreign conquerable," the distinction was probably more political than cultural or ethnic. In the present study, I have provided sufficient evidence that the Western Zhou state was a heterogeneous complex, embracing not only the Zhou, but peoples of various ethnic backgrounds and cultural traditions. Within such a political perimeter, ethnicity could have played a very limited role. This point can also be seen in terms of Shang–Zhou relations. Although the Zhou were cultural successors of the Shang, and indeed the evidence in the Zhou oracle-bone inscriptions shows quite clearly that the Zhou in their late pre-dynastic time worshiped the deceased Shang kings,[10] there is no evidence that the Zhou ever regarded themselves and the Shang as ethnically or even culturally the same, as opposed to the Rong and Yi peoples. Quite to the contrary, when their relations became hostile, the Zhou did not hesitate to use the word "Rong" for the Shang, as is evident in three genuine Western Zhou chapters of the *Shangshu* alluding to the conquest campaign. In this context, the Zhou straightforwardly called their Shang enemies "Rong Yin" 戎殷 or "Rong Shang" 戎商.[11] As the term "Rong" is often used in bronze inscriptions to mean "warfare," it is likely that when a people was called "Rong" the Zhou considered them as political and military adversaries rather than as cultural and ethnic "others." As for Yi, its inscriptional graph is similar to but also differentiated from *ren* 人 (human) by its kneeling gesture, clearly implying a population that was deemed a potential source of slaves or servants.[12]

However, the rise of self-awareness of the people in North China had led to the construction of a cultural divide between the "Huaxia" population and the totality of "Rongdi" 戎狄, which by the middle Spring and Autumn period had clearly gained a meaning similar to "barbarian" as the word is used in English.[13] "Xia" 夏 is the name of the first dynasty in the Chinese tradition that evidently goes back to the early Western Zhou writings;[14] its

---

[10] See Shaughnessy, "Zhouyuan Oracle-Bone Inscriptions," pp. 159–61.

[11] For instance, in the "Kanggao" chapter, the Shang people are referred to as "Rong Yin" 戎殷; see *Shangshu*, 14, p. 203 (Legge, *The Shoo King*, pp. 381–82). The same term also appears in the "Shifu" chapter of the *Yi Zhoushu*, which is probably the lost chapter "Wucheng" 武成 in the original *Shangshu*; see *Yi Zhoushu*, 4, pp. 9–12. For the identification of the "Shifu" with the original "Wucheng," see Shaughnessy, "'New' Evidence on the Zhou Conquest," pp. 57–79. In addition, in a phrase quoted by the *Guoyu* from the original "Taishi" 泰誓 chapter of the *Shangshu*, the term "Rong Shang" 戎商 is used; this phrase does not exist in the current "Taishi"; see *Guoyu*, 3, p. 100.

[12] For instance, in the Shi Yu *gui* 師酉簋 (JC: 4288), the characters *yi* and *ren* both appeared multiple times but are clearly differentiated. In the inscription of the Xi Jia *pan* 兮甲盤 (JC: 10174), the Southern Huaiyi were expected to contribute people to the Zhou, besides other material items.

[13] On the emergence of this distinction, see also Okura Yoshihiko, "I i no toriko: Saden no Ka I kannen," *Chūgoku kodaishi kenkyū* 2 (1965), 14–21.

[14] For instance, "Xia" as a dynastic name before Shang appears in the "Shaogao" chapter of the *Shangshu*. The Xia dynasty is also mentioned in other chapters of Western Zhou date such as "Duofang," suggesting that the tradition on Xia was certainly a Western Zhou one. This point has

use as a part of the term "Huaxia" certainly reflects a consciousness of unity among the people in the Zhou world and their quest for a homologous cultural and ethnic origin. The term "Hua" 華 was derived from Huashan 華山 Mountain, located at the central point of the political power axis of the Western Zhou state connecting the capitals Feng and Hao in the Wei River valley and Luoyi in the east. At the same time, the term "Rong" came to designate a people who were both culturally and ethnically, even morally, different from the "Huaxia" people. No matter how hostile the relationship was between the "Huaxia" or Chinese states, they never called each other "Rong." By the same token, no matter how intimate the relation was between a Rong people and a Chinese state, the distinction between them remained, nevertheless, fundamental. Such a sharp contrast is evident throughout the *Zuozhuan* text, and is best illustrated by the following two incidents.

In 569 BC, when the Rong state of Wuzhong 無終 in present-day Hebei sent an envoy to the state of Jin, asking for peace, the following discussion took place at the Jin court:[15]

無終子嘉父使孟樂如晉，因魏莊子納虎豹之皮，以請和諸戎。晉侯曰："戎狄無親而貪，不如伐之。"魏絳曰："諸侯新服，陳新來和，將覦於我。我德則睦；否則攜貳。勞師於戎，而楚伐陳，必弗能救，是棄陳也。諸華必叛。戎，禽獸也。獲戎失華，無乃不可乎！"

The chief of Wuzhong, Jiafu, sent Meng Yue to Jin, and submitted skins of tiger and leopard through Zhuangzi of Wei (Wei Jiang) to the Jin court, with which he asked for peace for the "Many Rong." The Ruler of Jin said: "The Rong and Di have no affinity and are greedy; it would be better that we attack them." Wei Jiang said: "The many rulers have just recently submitted [to Jin] and Chen recently came for peace; they will observe us. If we are virtuous, they will be in harmony; if not, they will betray us. If we belabor our troops with the Rong, when Chu attacks Chen, we will certainly be unable to rescue it; this is to abandon Chen. The Many Hua will certainly rebel against us. The Rong are birds and beasts. To gain the Rong but lose the Hua; surely this is not allowable!"

In this conversation, the Ruler of Jin regards the Rong and Di as having no feelings for humanity and being greedy, while the Jin minister Wei Jiang draws a clear distinction between the "Many Hua," whom he considers akin to Jin, and the "Many Rong," whom he deems inhuman. The logic that lies behind this deliberation is that the failure to rescue Chen, a "Hua" state in southern Henan, if it were attacked by Chu, would, even for the profit that Jin might possibly gain from the conquest of a Rong state in the north, serve to undermine Jin's credit among the many "Hua" states, and

---

acquired strong support from the recently discovered inscription of the Bingong *xu* 燹公盨, a late mid-Western Zhou bronze cast to commemorate the virtue of Great Yu, the attributed founder of the Xia dynasty. For the Xia dynasty mentioned in the *Shangshu*, see *Shangshu*, 15, p. 213; 17, p. 228 (Legge, *The Shoo King*, pp. 427, 497). For the Bingong *xu*, see Li Xueqin, "Lun Suigong xu jiqi zhongyao yiyi," *Zhongguo lishi wenwu* 2002.6, 4–12.

[15] See *Zuozhuan*, 29, p. 1,933.

this is something that must be avoided. A passage in the *Guoyu* even gives a "reason" for the inhuman nature of the Rong people: their blood and *qi* 氣 (breath) are not well configured.[16] This amounts to an accusation that the Rong were not only culturally and morally[17] but even physically wrong, and different from the "Huaxia" people.

In 559 BC, when their right to participate in an interstate conference held among the Chinese states was boldly rejected by the Jin minister, the chief of the Rong of Jiangshi 姜氏, named Juzhi 駒攴, is reported to have made the following speech:[18]

昔秦人負恃其眾，貪于土地，逐我諸戎。惠公蠲其大德，謂我諸戎，是四嶽之裔胄也，毋是
翦棄。賜我南鄙之田，狐狸所居，豺狼所嗥。我諸戎除翦其荊棘，驅其狐狸豺狼，以為先君
不侵不叛之臣，至于今不貳。昔文公與秦伐鄭，秦人竊與鄭盟，而舍戍焉，於是乎有殽之師。
晉御其上，戎亢其下，秦師不復，我諸戎實然。譬如捕鹿，晉人角之，諸戎掎之，何以不
免？自是以來，晉之百役，與我諸戎相繼于時，以從執政，猶殽志也，豈敢離逷！今官之師
旅，無乃實有所闕，以攜諸侯，而罪我諸戎！我諸戎飲食衣服不與華同，贄幣不通，言語不達，
何惡之能為？不與於會，亦無瞢焉。

In the past, the Qin, taking advantage of the great number of their people, desired our land and drove away our "Many Rong." Duke Huai [of Jin], manifesting his great virtue, said that we the "Many Rong" are the descendents of the Four Mountains (ancestral gods), and should not be cut off and thrown away. [He] awarded us land in the southern periphery [of Jin] where foxes lived and wolves howled. We the "Many Rong" cut off thistles and thorns, and drove away foxes and wolves, becoming the never-offending and never-betraying servants of the previous rulers [of Jin]. Until now, this has not been changed. In the past, when Duke Wen [of Jin] and the people of Qin jointly attacked Zheng, the people of Qin secretly made alliance with the Zheng and stationed their troops to guard for Zheng. Therefore, there was the battle of Xiao. The Jin defended above and the Rong fought below, so that the troops of Qin could not return home. Our "Many Rong" had achieved this. It was like catching a deer – the Jin people caught her horns, and the "Many Rong" dragged her legs. Why were the Rong not excluded at that time? Since that time [of the battle of Xiao], in the hundred battles that the Jin fought, our "Many Rong" continued to take part. [We] have followed the policy-makers [of Jin] with the aspiration we demonstrated in the battle of Xiao, and have never dared to stay away! Now, the ministers [of Jin] actually have shortcomings in their own conduct and therefore cause the many rulers to be alienated [from Jin]; how can you accuse us, the "Many Rong"! Our "Many Rong" have different food, drink, and clothes from the Hua, and are not in communication [with the many rulers]; even our language is not comprehensible [to the Hua]. What bad things could we do? Even if we do not take part in the conference, we will have no regret about it!

---

[16] See *Guoyu*, 2, p. 62.

[17] Such a moral attack on the Rong people can also be seen in a comment purportedly made by the Prince of Zheng: "The Rong [troops] are hasty and disorganized; [they are] greedy and have no sense of affinity. When they win a victory, they do not yield to each other; when they are defeated, they do not help each other"; see *Zuozhuan*, 4, p. 1,734. Elsewhere in the *Zuozhuan*, the Di are said to have had no sense of shame about running off from a battle; see *Zuozhuan*, 13, p. 1,799.

[18] See *Zuozhuan*, 32, p. 1,956.

According to this paragraph, the Rong of Jiangshi were allowed to settle in Jin territory and fought for the Jin against Qin in the famous battle of Xiao 崤 in 627 BC. Thereafter, they had served as auxiliary troops of Jin in a series of battles. However, despite their long service to Jin, they remained culturally and linguistically distinctive from the "Many Hua," and therefore were politically discriminated against by the Jin ministers. Certainly the deep cultural meaning of this speech can be explored in a more complex way in which one may question whether it was Juzhi who really did make the speech, or whether it was the composer of the anecdote who put such words in his mouth. However, the anecdote reflects well a profound understanding of the true relationship between the Rong tribes and the native Zhou states that could have been simultaneously intimate and distant.[19] Politically, the Zhou states could form alliances of various kinds with the Rong communities, but culturally the Rong remained distinguishable from and discriminated against by the native Zhou states.

The distinction is certainly not merely an intellectual fanaticism for cultural superiority in the textual tradition of the Warring States, but is supported by evidence from the contemporaneous bronze inscriptions, for instance the Qingong *gui* 秦公簋 (JC: 4315), cast by the ruler of Qin during the middle Spring and Autumn period. The opening lines of the inscription read (Mattos' translation):[20]

秦公曰： "不顯朕皇祖受天命，鼏宅禹賣（跡）。十又二公，在帝之坏（坏）。嚴龏夤天命，保鼏（業）厥秦，虩事蠻夏…

The Duke of Qin said: "Greatly illustrious were my august ancestors; [they] received Heaven's mandate and tranquilly dwelled in Yu's tracks. Twelve dukes are on God's mound (?). [They] reverently respected and revered Heaven's Mandate, protected and regulated their [state of] Qin, and vigilantly attended to the Man and the Xia . . ."

The term "Man" used in the inscription is a cultural equivalent of "Rong" or "Di." The inscription presents the "Man" and the "Xia" as two opposing worlds and says that the ancestors of Qin carefully attended both. As has been fully discussed in chapter 5, Qin was originally a small polity installed by the Zhou court on the northwestern frontier. The Qin had long experience in dealing with the Rong population of the northwest and successfully survived their challenges. After the evacuation of the Zhou court from the Wei River valley, the Qin moved into the region and established their new base by absorbing the Rong population. Therefore, it is quite understandable that in this inscription the ruler of Qin pronounced his predecessors

---

[19] For a discussion of the multifaceted relationship between the Zhou and the Rong and Di peoples, see Di Cosmo, *Ancient China and Its Enemies*, pp. 107–26.

[20] See Mattos, "Eastern Zhou Bronze Inscriptions," pp. 114–19. For an interpretation of the inscription, see also Shirakawa, "Kinbun tsūshaku," 34.199:1.

as mediators between the two opposing worlds: that of the "Man" and that of the "Xia."

The cultural prejudice and discrimination manifest in these incidents against the Rong people are obvious and need not be emphasized. However, behind these unjust attacks on the "Rong" and "Di" peoples, there was actually an underlying process through which the native population in North China reconstructed their cultural identity and redefined their position in the cosmos at a time when the belief in the Mandate of Heaven had utterly collapsed. There may have been a number of reasons for the self-awareness of the people in North China having to take this form of dichotomy of "Huaxia" versus "Rongdi," but we must first of all consider the special context of the Spring and Autumn period. In chapter 5 (see pp. 274–5), I have noted that the fall of the Western Zhou dynasty was followed by a wave of the Rong people moving into the Zhou world. In the west, "many Rong" people moved to settle on the Wei River plain; in the north and northeast, the Di people founded many small polities along the edge of the Taihang Mountains after wiping out the former Zhou states Xing and Wey.[21] Towards the end of the seventh century BC, even those states in the core area of the Zhou world had come under attack by the Rong and Di peoples, who founded their own states or polities in their neighborhood. The native states fought very hard to keep these newcomers out of their territory. Thus, the concept of "Hua" or "Xia" arose as a political ideology or strategy to unite the native Chinese states against their common enemies. When the native states were geographically interspersed with the Rong and Di polities, it was their common heritage from the Western Zhou state that differentiated them from the Rong and Di polities. This was particularly true when the Di broke into the Central Plain from the north in 661 BC, destroying the states of Xing and Wey. Guanzhong 管仲, who was credited by Confucius with having saved the Chinese world,[22] urged Duke Huan of Qi to rescue Xing, and this led to the formation of a Chinese league including Qi, Lu, Song, Cao, and Zheng in the following years. According to the *Zuozhuan*, Guanzhong is said to have persuaded Duke Huan of Qi with the following speech:[23]

戎狄豺狼，不可厭也；諸夏親暱，不可棄也。宴安酖毒，不可懷也。詩云："豈不懷歸？畏此簡書。"簡書，同惡相恤之謂也。請救邢以從簡書。

The Rong and Di are jackals and wolves who cannot be satisfied; the "Many Xia" are close relatives who cannot be abandoned. Banqueting and comfort are poisons that [you] cannot be infatuated with. The *Book of Poetry* says: "We do indeed long to return; but we fear the writing on the strips." The "Writing on the strips" means that people who have common enemies should help each other. Please follow the "Writing on the strips" to rescue the state of Xing.

---

[21] For the migration of the Di people, see Průšek, *Chinese Statelets*, pp. 136–83.
[22] See *The Analects of Confucius*, p. 185.   [23] See *Zuozhuan*, II, p. 1,788.

Here, Guanzhong makes a clear distinction between the Rong and Di, whom he condemned as jackals and wolves, and the many Xia states whom he considered akin to Qi, to obligate the duke to rescue the state of Xing. Interestingly, he quotes the poem "Chuche" (no. 168) in the *Book of Poetry*, which I have reproduced with English translation in appendix 2 with relation to the Xianyun, as his textual authority, suggesting that, according to this Western Zhou tradition, neighboring states must help each other in the face of a common enemy.

Another reason for the rise of the concept of "Huaxia" is probably that a contrast in lifestyle between the "Many Xia" and the "Many Rong" had become increasingly clear during the Spring and Autumn period. It has been suggested by Di Cosmo that the so-called "Northern Zone" during the Shang and Western Zhou periods was essentially populated with mixed communities of shepherds and farmers who also practiced extensive hunting and fought in war from chariots.[24] This way of life was not completely different from that of the Shang and Zhou peoples, who were also to some extent involved in hunting and even sheep-herding. The difference was probably only that between intensive agriculture, in Owen Lattimore's term, and non-intensive agriculture.[25] This may explain why in Western Zhou sources the term "Rong" was so freely applied, having little sense of cultural or ethnic discrimination. However, in the course of history, this broad "Northern Zone" – the home of the "Rong" and "Di" peoples – gradually disappeared between the intensive agricultural people in the Zhou world and the newly rising nomadic people in the northern steppe and Central Asia, bringing the Zhou world into direct conflict with the northern nomads.[26] According to some scholars, this process of cultural transition in the "Northern Zone" was not completed until the fourth century BC, or the Warring States period.[27] In the written records, there is evidence that the Rong and Di peoples of the Spring and Autumn period were different in lifestyle from the people of the Zhou world. While such a difference is clearly stated in Juzhi's speech translated above, in another place in the *Zuozhuan* the Rong are described as a people who treasured material goods over land, so that their land could be easily bought.[28] The term "*jianju*" 荐居 that is used to describe their settlements is also used in the *Hanshu* to describe the migratory lifestyle of the Xiongnu.[29] It is difficult to decide from these records whether the Rong and Di of the sixth century BC were already nomads; probably not, because in another place in the *Zuozhuan*

---

[24] See Di Cosmo, "The Northern Frontier," pp. 889, 920–1.
[25] See Lattimore, *Inner Asian Frontiers of China*, pp. 60–1.
[26] See *ibid.*, pp. 277–8, 331–4, 410. See also Di Cosmo, "Ancient Inner Asian Nomads: Their Economic Basis and Its Significance in Chinese History," *Journal of Asian Studies* 53.4 (1994), 1,117.
[27] See Lattimore, *Inner Asian Frontiers of China*, p. 55; Di Cosmo, "The Northern Frontier," p. 887.
[28] See *Zuozhuan*, 29, p. 1,933.
[29] See *Hanshu*, 64, p. 2,815; for an interpretation of *jianju*, see also Yang Bojun, *Chunqiu Zuozhuan zhu*, 4 vols. (Beijing: Zhonghua, 1990), 3, p. 939.

they are described as foot-soldiers.[30] Nevertheless, it is clear that by the Spring and Autumn period they had already come to present a visible contrast to the lifestyle of the Zhou people. The profound cultural change in the northern steppe towards nomadism did have some major impact on the Rong and Di peoples, as well as on the ongoing political-cultural antagonism between them and the Zhou population. On the other hand, we should not forget changes in the social life of the Zhou people; after nearly 300 years of acculturation under the Western Zhou, the people in the Zhou world had become more and more exclusively agricultural and urbanized.

However, the most fundamental reason for the formation of the concept of "Huaxia" must be sought in the internal structure and social life of the Zhou world. In this regard, it may be noted first that the club of the so-called "Many Hua" or "Many Xia" was never ethnically homogeneous; on the contrary, it included states of diverse origins. This is suggested by the number of peoples who are reported to have followed the Zhou on their conquest campaign.[31] It has been noted in chapter 1 that after the conquest many different peoples had followed the Zhou elite to their new states in the east, and compared to the great masses of the Zhou world the Zhou elite was perhaps only a small fragment. Besides the Ji states, there were many non-Ji states ruled by lineages of different ethnic origins. It is above all significant that the state of Chen, regarded as a critical element of "Huaxia" in Wei Jiang's speech quoted above (p. 287), was not a Ji state at all, but was reportedly founded by the descendents of the legendary emperor Shun 舜, and was possibly related to the Dongyi. The state of Song was evidently founded by the descendents of Shang and maintained worship of the Shang ancestors; but Song was a member of the Chinese league formed by Duke Huan of Qi in 661 BC in the face of the Di invasion from the north. Another state, Qi 杞, was reportedly established by the descendents of Xia and continued to worship the Xia ancestors. The state of Qi, leader of the "Many Xia" for some decades, and the states of Shen and Lü were ruled by the descendents of the Jiang 姜 clan from the west, who were probably distantly related to the later Rong of Jiangshi mentioned above. However, during the 274 years of Western Zhou rule, the Western Zhou state gradually brought to the people of the Zhou world a sense of cultural and ethnic unity under the guidance of a unified elite culture. These Zhou states, no matter whether their ancestors were Xia, Shang, or even Rong or Yi, had come to recognize each other as colleagues within the same unity and identified themselves with a common cultural tradition that was conceived of as having passed through Xia, Shang, and Zhou.

---

[30] See *Zuozhuan*, 4, p. 1,734.
[31] According to the "Mushi" 牧誓 chapter of the *Shangshu*, eight different groups of people, including the Yong 庸, Shu 蜀, Qiang 羌, Mao 髳, Wei 微, Lu 盧, Peng 彭, and Pu 濮, followed the Zhou to attack the Shang capital. See *Shangshu*, p. 183 (Legge, *The Shoo King*, pp. 300–1).

To be more specific, the Western Zhou state had achieved such assimilation of the originally diverse population by extending the royal Ji clan geographically and by promoting intermarriages between the Ji elite and non-Ji elite who were parts of the common Western Zhou state. Consequently, although the blood ties between the reigning Zhou kings in the capital and the Ji elite in the regional states became ever looser, contributing to the weakening of royal power, the elite of the Zhou world at large, including both the Ji and the non-Ji lineages, had become one that was closely bound by blood connections. It was this cultural and ethnic unity, gradually developed during the Western Zhou and fully recognized during the Eastern Zhou – in contrast with the "Rong" and the "Di" – that then became the ethnic core of China and, in the course of history, drew more and more people into it. In this regard, the Western Zhou state had contributed to the people of the Zhou world a new cultural identity – "Huaxia" – and provided a main source on which the Chinese elite of the Eastern Zhou period drew for support in the face of new pressures from the outside world. Certainly, this common Western Zhou heritage can also be seen in the archaeological records of the Eastern Zhou period.

THE BACKGROUND OF REGIONAL CULTURES

Archaeological study of the Spring and Autumn period during the past few decades has been characterized by searches for various regional cultures, for instance "Chu culture," "Wu culture," "Jin culture," and "Yan culture," as material representations of the political regionalism of the period.[32] However, an insightful observation on the overall cultural development of the Spring and Autumn period has recently been made by Lothar von Falkenhausen in his chapter in the *Cambridge History of Ancient China*:[33]

Recent work on earlier chronological segments of the Chinese Bronze Age suggests that the extent of centralized political control exercised by the early royal dynasties in the Yellow River valley may have been greatly exaggerated in traditional historiography. Evidence presented in this chapter shows that, conversely, the often vaunted fragmentation of the Zhou political structure after 770 BC should not be overemphasized. Western Zhou and Spring and Autumn period cultural patterns are but reverse sides of the same coin – the outcome of enduring trends that had evolved over many centuries and that had found their culminating systemic expression in the Later Western Zhou Ritual Reform. As established structures underwent increasing stress, piece-meal modifications occurred; but even the thoroughgoing cultural transformation of the Warring States period left crucial parts of the Bronze Age heritage intact . . . The encompassing trends toward homogenization we have

---

[32] For a discussion situating such studies in the broad regionalistic approach to cultural origins that had overtaken Chinese archaeology since the 1980s, see Lothar von Falkenhausen, "The Regionalist Paradigm in Chinese Archaeology," in *Nationalism, Politics, and the Practice of Archaeology*, ed. Phillip L. Kohl and Clare Fawcett (Cambridge: Cambridge University Press, 1995), pp. 198–217.

[33] See Falkenhausen, "The Waning of the Bronze Age," p. 543.

observed in archaeological materials of the Spring and Autumn period undoubtedly manifest the implementation, throughout the Zhou realm, of the new standards. Such a trend very probably reflects an even more self-conscious awareness of the defining criteria of Zhou civilization on the part of its elite participants, as is also evinced by the early Confucian texts.

Falkenhausen's statement makes the important point that the process of cultural assimilation, or the "homogenization process," did not end with the downfall of the Western Zhou state in 771 BC, but, taking a slightly different path, continued for many centuries during the Eastern Zhou period. I have noted in chapter 2 that during the late Western Zhou some regions in the periphery of the Zhou world, for instance Shandong, began to produce distinctive types of bronzes modeled on local types of pottery; by the mid-Spring and Autumn period, many regions had developed bronzes of unique patterns of shape and ornament that can be differentiated without much difficulty from their counterparts in other regions. But this is only one part of the story. During the Spring and Autumn period, we begin to observe the implementation of the Zhou sumptuary system throughout the whole realm of the Zhou world, regulating the number of major types of bronzes such as *ding* and *gui* to be used in accordance with the owner's social status. Indeed, only by the Spring and Autumn period had the status of the Zhou elite in every corner of the Zhou world become comparable to each other through the use of standard sets of vessels. Such widespread adherence to a single system of ritual regulation manifest in burial bronzes could not be observed during most of the Western Zhou period, but had to wait to appear gradually after the fall of the dynasty in 771 BC. There was certainly no central drive, given the political reality of the period, in this spreading of sumptuary rules; rather, what we can see is probably a spontaneous process in which the common Zhou cultural tradition was revered and followed in the newly rising regional political centers. Thus, despite political disunity, shared cultural values bound the elite of the Zhou world closer than ever.

This phenomenon is clearly visible in materials excavated throughout the Zhou world. In the core area, for instance in Guo tombs at Sanmenxia and Wey 衛 tombs at Liulige 琉璃閣, the practice of matching an odd number of graduated *ding* set with an even number of identical *gui* set was firmly established during the Spring and Autumn period. In the Fen River valley, particularly in the Shangma 上馬 cemetery of the state of Jin, tombs can also be ranked according to the same standard of *ding* sets. In the west, although Qin tombs were characteristic for their west–east orientation, flexed burial of human bodies, and the use of bronze replicas (*mingqi* 明器), the bronze assemblages they contain clearly comply with Zhou sumptuary rules practiced by the central states. In the eastern part of the Zhou world, not only are such rules clearly demonstrable in the cemetery of Xue 薛, but even states such as Jü 莒 and Yu 邮 which probably owed their origins to the Dongyi were no exception to it. Most telling is the situation in the south, where the Zhou sumptuary rules were adopted even by the state of Chu, which for a long time had been hostile to the Western Zhou state, if not to the entire Zhou tradition. During the Spring and Autumn period, Chu developed some distinctive types that came to be referred to as "Chu-style bronzes," most typical being a type of flat-bottomed shallow *ding* called by the name *sheng* 卅. This type of *ding* then became an indicator of status in high-ranking Chu tombs, and its number adheres to the Zhou sumptuary system.[34]

Falkenhausen views this widespread acceptance of the Zhou sumptuary system as a reflection of "an underlying shared system of politicoreligious values, as well as homologies in the social organization of elites."[35] In my view, the continuing cultural assimilation during the Eastern Zhou was but the material reflection of the ethnic assimilation brought about by the Western Zhou state through the extension of the Ji clan and the intermarriage between the Ji and non-Ji elites. Indeed, as examples provided in this book show, such marriages were themselves often accompanied, in a material way, by the exchange of bronzes between different states. In addition to Falkenhausen's observations on burial bronzes, one may further note that the Zhou sumptuary system did not stop at the elite level; from the mid-Spring and Autumn period, it began to affect the locally based non-elite cultures. The change began with the adoption into the burial inventory of two types of pottery vessels – *ding* and *hu* – that were hitherto available only in bronze (with some exceptions) and were used only by the Zhou elite. Combined with the pottery high *dou*-plate, the use of which had had a long history throughout the Shang and Western Zhou periods, the set of *ding* + *dou* + *hu* became prevalent in small tombs during the Warring States period.

It is not very clear where this process was initiated, but what is clear is that this transition was simultaneously going on in almost every part of the Zhou world, including Chu. In the state of Chu, although the high *dou*-plate was not as significant as it was in the northern states, the modified set of *ding* + *dui* + *hu* was dominant throughout its territory.[36] The only state that was left out of this new wave of "homogenization" of burial pottery was Qin, where people conservatively continued to bury traditional "usable" types centered on the *li*-tripod and *guan*-jar in their tombs. This contributed to a new west–east distinction in the local cultures of China, in contrast to the north–south distinction that had long been visible both politically and culturally. The change was very fundamental and needs to be explored further in another context, but it undoubtedly brought the Zhou world culturally closer than ever. One may note that this trend

[34] See *ibid.*, pp. 471–525.   [35] See *ibid.*, p. 544.
[36] For a general discussion of the burial pottery inventory of the Spring and Autumn and the Warring States periods, see *Xin Zhongguo de kaogu faxian he yanjiu* (Beijing: Wenwu, 1984), pp. 286–314.

towards homogenization through "aristocraticization" of the burial pottery inventory all over the Zhou world (except Qin) was not unrelated to the process of popularization of ritual practice that was hitherto monopolized by the Zhou ruling elite. But the origin of this ritual practice was in the Western Zhou, as the *ding* and *hu* types were essential to the bronze sets of the Western Zhou period.

In this sense, the Western Zhou state left to China not only an ethnic core, but also a cultural base that was crucial for the continued prosperity of the Chinese civilization during the next centuries and millennia under empire. To claim a connection between the Western Zhou state and the Qin and Han Empires entails a gap of more than 500 years. But cultural elements can survive such a long period. It is in the cultural and ethnic assimilation achieved under the Western Zhou state that we should look for the origins of China's great empires, and in the homogeneous cultural elements that the Western Zhou state had installed in every corner of the Zhou world that we should look for the foundation of China's later unification.

Conclusion

This book begins by investigating the geopolitical formation of the Western Zhou state, particularly its western part where the Zhou capitals were located. The investigation is further strengthened by an effort to recover the geopolitical perimeter of the Western Zhou through reconstructing its cultural and political periphery. The research integrates archaeological discoveries and inscriptional and textual records with the features of the landscape and presents us with a visible image of one of the pre-imperial states in China occupying a particular geographical space. It demonstrates that the deployment of the Western Zhou state both was conditioned by and responded to the limit and potential of the land. This thread of investigation runs through the whole book, providing us with a unique path to understanding the historical process of the weakening and fall of the Western Zhou.

It is suggested, therefore, that the crisis of the Western Zhou state can be meaningfully conceived as both a structural and a spatial one. The Western Zhou state was challenged in space by two forces: an internal force that moved its constituent parts away from its political core; and an external force that attacked the geographical perimeter of the Western Zhou state with ever increasing power. The responses to this spatial crisis, as so manifestly demonstrated during the decades of King Xuan's restoration, were directed at consolidating military defenses on the frontiers and at strengthening relations with the regional states in the east. In order to do so, the Zhou court probably even revived the institution of "Fengjian" that was originally constructed in the east after the second conquest by installing new regional rulers in the frontier areas. In the same way, the fall of the Western Zhou can also be investigated in geographical terms. It is demonstrated that the fall of the Zhou capital in 771 BC can be attributed to the destruction of the hitherto stable "Zhou–Shen–Qin" geopolitical triangle, and to King You's ignorance of the Xianyun's immediate threat through the Jing River valley. Furthermore, the eastward migration of the Zhou court and the Zhou aristocratic families was in fact a process of reconfiguring the geographical space of the Western Zhou state, which gave rise to new political dynamics and new norms.

It is in the ruling structure of the Western Zhou state that we find the roots of Zhou's gradual weakening, manifested in spatial crisis. It is suggested that the land-granting policy maintained by the Zhou king in the "favor for loyalty" exchange contributed substantially to weakening the economic foundation of the Zhou court and therefore to crippling the ability of the Western Zhou state. It is also suggested that a possible attempt made by King Li to restore the economic strength of the Zhou royal court was aborted in the face of resistance from aristocratic power, forcing the king into exile. This interpretation helps illuminate the real dynamics in the decline of Zhou royal power and opens a new way to look into the political life of the Western Zhou state.

However, the investigation of reasons for decline must consider as many factors as possible and must address the relationship between them. Our investigation of the causes of Zhou's weakening must go beyond the royal domain. It is argued that the high degree of civil and military autonomy granted to the regional rulers under the "Fengjian" institution underlay a basic contradiction in the political structure of the Western Zhou state that from the mid-Western Zhou began to develop into a major force, splitting the political unity of Zhou. The weakening of the Western Zhou state is further studied with relation to outside pressures, especially those cast on the Western Zhou state by the Xianyun. In order to cope with the increasing threat from the Xianyun, the Zhou court had to invest more resources into full-scale war that continued for decades during the middle and late Western Zhou. The war was won with increasing cost to the Zhou court, including the granting of landed property to military commanders as so manifest in the bronze inscriptions. In this way, outside pressures and internal problems interacted with each other to set the Western Zhou state on a path of continuing decline.

The fall of the Western Zhou is investigated as a separate matter from the weakening. However, the two issues were closely related to each other. In fact, the line of investigation of the fall of the Western Zhou runs through much of the book, gradually revealing a coherent historical understanding of the eventual fall: without studying the prolonged warfare between the Zhou and the Xianyun in chapter 3, we would be in no position to understand the cultural and historical background of the fall; without the geographical analysis of the Jing River valley in chapter 1, it would be difficult to reconfigure the Zhou–Xianyun war. The case is gradually built up through the book.

However, the present interpretation of the fall of the Western Zhou, while taking spatial configuration as its main approach, is based also on indepth research into the textual records in order to discover the political dynamics in that historical fall. The study reconstructs the process of the fall by solving many long-pending historical issues arising from textual contradictions. It is suggested that the political struggle leading eventually to the fall originated in a tension between the senior bureaucrats who had once served King Xuan and the supporting party of the newly established King You. This partisan struggle in the Zhou court eventually developed into a major military conflict between the court and some of the key frontier polities in the upper Jing River region. The defeat of the royal army, perhaps in a punitive campaign, by the joint forces of these frontier polities plus Zhou's long-time enemy Xianyun, opened the way to the Zhou capital. The Western Zhou fell as the immediate result of a disastrous political strategy and a military miscalculation.

The fall of the Western Zhou marked the eventual collapse of the political system of the early Chinese dynastic states characterized by the centrality of the royal court that exercised political control over a relatively large territory through the authority of administratively independent regional rulers. The eventual failure of the Western Zhou state suggests that, owing to the development of regional economic and political powers, such a political system could no longer entertain the idea of political unity in containing the new developments. The fall of the Western Zhou capitals in 771 BC and the subsequent migration of the Zhou court and the Zhou aristocratic lineages to the east gave rise to a situation in which the regional powers freely competed without central direction. A new system of control to achieve political unity had to be worked out through numerous political and military conflicts. Empire was the final answer.

The periphery: the Western Zhou state at its maximum geographical extent

Beyond the central areas – the Wei River plain and the eastern plain that formed the geopolitical axis – there lay the more distant peripheral regions of the Western Zhou state. These regions can be generally grouped into three sections: the Shandong region as the "Far East" of Zhou, the Huai–Yangzi River region in the south, and the northern Hebei plain to the east of the Taihang Mountains. These regions, combined with the upper Jing River valley in the west, formed the geographical perimeter of the Western Zhou state. The spatial division of the Western Zhou state suggested here corresponds roughly with the cosmological perception by the Zhou people of their own world as being divided into "Four Quarters" surrounding a core, fully evident in the bronze inscriptions as well as in Western Zhou texts.[1] By establishing strongholds in these more distant regions the Zhou had effectively secured their standing on the eastern plain and created for themselves demonstrably the largest ever geopolitical entity in China before the rise of the Qin Empire in 221 BC.

Continuing the same line of investigation that guided chapter 1, in this appendix I will explore the macro-geographical dimensions of the Western Zhou state, examining how Zhou's political organization and military conduct were interwoven with the landscape of these peripheral regions. I will demonstrate that, compared to the Zhou's quick victory in the eastern plain, constructing the geopolitical periphery entailed a much longer period of enterprise and a more complex operation, accompanied by many defeats and setbacks. This was not only because of the distance involved from the Zhou homeland in the west, but also because of the cultural and ethnic complexity of the regions that the Zhou entered. Some of these peripheral regions were formerly and partly colonized by the Shang, in which case the Zhou would have to deal with both a pro-Shang population and the indigenous people. By the later years of King Kang (r. 1005/3–978 BC), Zhou positions in these regions seem to have been fully solidified, although the process of expansion was still to go on thereafter, not so much under the

---

[1] For textual and inscriptional evidence for the "Four Quarters" theory of Zhou and its relationship with that of Shang, see Aihe Wang's recent discussion, *Cosmology and Political Culture*, pp. 57–74.

direct command of the Zhou court, but as the enterprise of the regional Zhou states located near the frontlines.

The study of the peripheral regions will give us a chance actually to delimit the geographical extent of the Western Zhou state, and to estimate its political and military might over time. However, it must be noted that, as opposed to the relatively stable geopolitical structure of the eastern plain, the periphery remained as constantly changing areas in terms of both their geopolitical layout and their cultural contexts. The purpose here is not to find a linear border encircling the Western Zhou state, but to define a series of peripheral zones in which the Western Zhou state *in its various capacities* exercised organized political dominance and interacted with the indigenous peoples. The study will also show how the Zhou adapted themselves to the landscape and cultural environment of the peripheral regions to create a high degree of cultural and ethnic mix, which then became the foundation of the regional cultures that flourished during the Eastern Zhou period.

ZHOU IN THE "FAR EAST"

For the Zhou, the Shandong region was the "Far East." As they were mainly an inland people, the expansion into the Shandong region brought the Zhou their first experience of coastal people and coastal culture. However, Shandong was a vast region of diverse landscape and complex cultural traditions. Throughout the Western Zhou, the Zhou and pro-Zhou communities managed to capture only a part of the peninsula, perhaps in its northern half, and therefore the region as a whole provides us with an ideal historical environment to study cultural confrontations and communications.

Landscape of the Shandong region

This region, east of the string of lakes that lie along the ancient Grand Canal, is predominantly hilly and mountainous.[2] It is estimated that about 70 percent of the peninsular part in the east consists of hills, and 60 percent of the whole territory of Shandong province is occupied by mountains and hills. In general terms, the Shandong region can be divided into two natural subregions: the Jiaodong 膠東 peninsula located to the east of the Jiaolai 膠莱 River and the mountainous central Shandong area (Map 16). The Jiaodong peninsula, which was the eastern limit of the world ever known to the Zhou, mainly consists of undulating hills of 200–300 meters in elevation. Igneous rocks produced by volcanic eruptions from the late Cretaceous period created a complex surface structure with no obvious ranges.[3] Owing to an intrusion by the sea in the Holocene epoch, the edge of the peninsula is narrow, leaving the shoreline rocky and perilous.[4] Although some mountains,

---

[2] See Zeng Zhaoxuan, *Zhongguo de dixing*, p. 227.   [3] See *Zhongguo ziran dili*, 2, p. 29.
[4] See Zeng Zhaoxuan, *Zhongguo de dixing*, pp. 232–33.

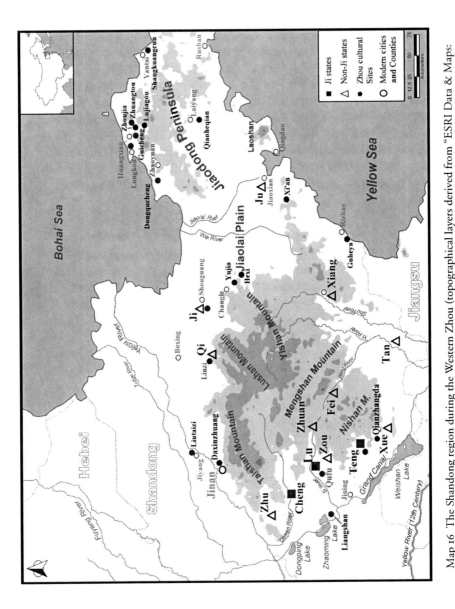

Map 16 The Shandong region during the Western Zhou (topographical layers derived from "ESRI Data & Maps: 2004"; river course based on "Harvard China Historical GIS Dataset, Version 2.0: August 2003")

Legend:
- ■ Ji states
- △ Non-Ji states
- ● Zhou cultural Sites
- ○ Modern cities and Counties

0 12.5 25 50 75
Kilometers

Bohai Sea

Yellow Sea

Jiaodong Peninsula

Jiaolai Plain

Hebei

Shandong

Jiangsu

Yellow River

Tuhai River

Fuyang River

Jiaolai River

Wei River

Shu River

Yi River

Sihe River

Si River

Zihe River

Daqing River

Yellow River (12th Century)

Grand Canal

Dongping Lake

Zhaoming Lake

Weishan Lake

Taishan Mountain

Lushan Mountain

Mengshan Mountain

Yishan Mountain

Nishan M.

Huangxian
Longkou
Guicheng
Zhaoyuan
Dongqucheng
Zhouija
Zhuangtou
Lujiagou
Yantai
Shangkuangcun
Laiyang
Rushan
Qianhequian
Laoshan
Qingdao

Ji
Shouguang
Changle
Yujia
Hexi
Ju
Jiaoxian
Xi'an
Xiang
Rizhao
Guheya

Boxing
Qi
Linzi

Liutaizi
Daxinzhuang
Jiyang
Jinan

Zhu
Cheng

Zhuan
Lu
Zou
Qufu
Jining
Liangshan

Fei
Teng
Xue
Qianzhangda
Nishan M.

Tan

e.g. the Laoshan 崂山 on the southern edge of the region, rise to 1,133 meters, most of the flat-topped hills are low, and the hill slopes, wide valleys, and basins are covered by deep layers of surface soil and thick vegetation with abundant surface water, favorable for diversified agriculture. This made the Jiaodong peninsula naturally richer and agriculturally more productive than the mountainous regions of central Shandong.[5] On the western edge of the hilly areas extends the Jiaolai plain, below 50 meters in elevation. The Wei River 潍河 and the Jiaolai River run though the middle of the plain; sediment is thin and flooding is always a problem.[6]

The process of tectonic mountain-building began later but had a more rapid pace in the west. This created an elevation of 500–600 meters on average, and some mountains, e.g. the Taishan 泰山 Mountain, rise as high as 1,524 meters. The Cambrian–Ordovician rock mass was cut by a series of major parallel faults running northeast or northwest, leaving six mountain ranges: the Taishan, Lushan 鲁山, and Yishan 沂山 ranges in the north, and the Motianling 摩天岭, Mengshan 蒙山, and Nishan 尼山 ranges in the south.[7] Most of these mountains are characterized by their exposed rocky surfaces, very different from the mountains and hills we see in northwestern China. Between these mountain ranges, the deep valleys provide three ideal channels for transportation through the region: the upper Dawen 大汶 River fault in the north between Taishan and Taipingding 太平顶–Lushan; the upper Si 泗 River and Beng 祊 River fault in the southwest between the Mengshan and Nishan ranges; and the upper Shu 沭 River valley in the southeast between the Yishan and the Wulianshan 五连山 ranges.

To the west of the central Shandong mountains and east to the strings of lakes, there extended a transitional belt, relatively higher in elevation than the heartland of the plain to the west of the lakes. Because this belt is relatively free of the floods that often overtook the plain in ancient times and is rich in water resources derived from the mountains to its east, this is a densely populated area and is highly productive in agriculture. It is also the main corridor of transportation connecting North China and southeastern China, especially the Yangzi delta.

Second conquest and colonization: Shandong during the early Western Zhou and early mid-Western Zhou

The early Western Zhou was an important period of Zhou expansion into the Shandong region in the "Far East." The material as well as inscriptional and textual evidence relevant to the region has by now accumulated to a degree that allows us to delineate this process of expansion. It also allows us to relate this historical process to the geography of the region, showing

[5] See Sun Qingji and Lin Yuzhen, *Shandong sheng dili* (Jinan: Shandong jiaoyu, 1987), pp. 358–59.
[6] See Zeng Zhaoxuan, *Zhongguo de dixing*, p. 233.   [7] See *Zhongguo ziran dili*, 2, pp. 29–30.

an interesting case of a political periphery constructed in relation to the topography.

Colonization of western Shandong

Let us begin with what we know from archaeology about the Shandong region during the early Western Zhou. Among the early archaeological discoveries in the Shandong region, one must first mention the so-called "Seven Bronzes from Liangshan 梁山," a group of early Western Zhou bronzes found at the foot of Liangshan Mountain in western Shandong during the Daoguang era of Qing (AD 1821–50).[8] Among them, three were cast by the Duke of Shao, and two others by his son Bo Xian 伯憲, who is said in the inscriptions to have been rewarded by the ruler of the northern state Yan (Yanhou匽 [燕] 侯). The location of these bronzes, far away both from the Zhou capital and from the state of Yan in present-day Beijing area, ruled by another son of the Duke of Shao as is definitely known from the inscriptions, poses a problem. Kaizuka Shigeki identified Yan 燕 with Yan 奄, a former pro-Shang state located in present-day Qufu 曲阜 in western Shandong, about 80 kilometers from Liangshan, arguing that the state of Yan 燕 was once located in the Qufu region and only later moved from there to the north.[9] Kaizuka has been proved wrong by recent excavations in Beijing which we will discuss below. There still remains a high degree of uncertainty about the circumstances surrounding the burial of these Yan-related bronzes as they may have made their way to the region through marriage, war, or other kinds of exchange; it is also possible that Bo Xian may have had his own domain in the Shandong region, separate from the state of Yan in the north. But the presence of these bronzes in Western Shandong, cast by clearly identifiable Zhou personnel, seems to reflect the fact that the region was integrated into the political system of the Western Zhou state.

An officially and recently excavated early Western Zhou site is Liutaizi 劉台子, Jiyang 濟陽, located some 40 kilometers to the north of Jinan. Several tombs have been found on a low mound and three were excavated between 1979 and 1985, dating to the late phase of the early Western Zhou.[10] A large number of bronzes were excavated from these tombs, showing features that are very similar to the bronzes found in the Zhou central area. From tomb no. 2, a *ding* cast by Ji 季 and two *gui* cast by Feng 夆 were

---

[8] See *Jining zhou jinshi zhi* (1845), I, pp. 10–16. The bronzes were soon dispersed through the hands of the antiquities dealers. For a study to recover the original set, see Chen Shou, "Taibao gui de fuchu he Taibao zhuqi," *Kaogu yu wenwu* 1980.4, 23–30.

[9] Kaizuka thinks that there was a military garrison in the Liangshan area that was under the command of Boxian, who was a brother of the Ruler of Yan, residing in Qufu. See Kaizuka Shigeki, "In matsu Shū sho no tōhō keiryaku ni tsuite," in *Kaizuka Shigeki chosaku shū*, vol. 2 (Tokyo: Chūō kōronsha, 1977), pp. 157–58.

[10] See *Wenwu* 1981.9, 18–24; 1985.12, 15–20. For the date of these tombs, see Li Feng, "Huanghe liuyu Xi Zhou muzang," p. 387.

unearthed. In tomb no. 3, a *ding* cast by Wang Ji 王季 (= 季) and a *gui* cast by Feng were found. The most important tomb is no. 6, from which twenty-four bronzes were excavated. Several bear the inscription "Feng," and a *ding* was cast by Wang Jiang 王姜 for a lady named Gongsi 龏姒.[11] Although these inscriptions do not clearly identify the local state to which they belonged, they do show strong connections to the Zhou court. In the time context in which the bronzes can be put, there seems little doubt that the "king" mentioned in these inscriptions refers to the Zhou king, and Wang Jiang was probably the spouse of King Cheng or King Kang, mentioned in many inscriptions from the Zhou central area.[12]

However, early Western Zhou bronzes that clearly identify their local states were excavated in the Tengxian 滕縣 area. In 1978, a bronze cast for the worship of the Duke of Teng (Tenggong 滕公) was found in a tomb about 2 kilometers from a walled site in Tengxian.[13] Four years later, in the same location, three bronzes cast by the Ruler of Teng (Tenghou 滕侯) himself were found in a large tomb which was probably the burial site of the Ruler of Teng.[14] These two groups of bronzes are both of early Western Zhou date, although the second group is slightly later than the first to judge from their designs and ornament. They identify the area with an important Zhou regional state, Teng, which is said in the *Zuozhuan* to have been granted to a brother of King Wu and is one of the three Ji-surnamed Zhou states in western Shandong (see p. 71). From ancient geographical works, it can be deduced that the capital site of the state of Teng was located to the southwest of the present-day town of Tengxian on the bank of the Jing 荊 River, corresponding closely with the location of these two groups of bronzes.[15] About 60 kilometers to the east of Tengxian, a group of early mid-Western Zhou bronzes was found at Jining 濟寧 City.[16]

[11] See *Wenwu* 1996.12, 4–25.

[12] In a recent analysis, Shang Zhiru, identifying Feng with Feng 豐, relates the Liutaizi site to the state of Feng 豐, mentioned in the inscription of the Ran *fangding* 塱方鼎 (JC: 2739), which he considers to be descendents of Fengbo Ling 逢伯陵 mentioned in the *Guoyu*; see Shang Zhiru, "Xi Zhou jinwen zhong de Feng guo," *Wenbo* 1991.4, 28–33. The reporter of tomb no. 6 also identifies the Liutaizi site with the state of Feng 夆; see *Wenwu* 1996.12, 23. In fact, there was a Fengshu *yi* 夆叔匜 (JC: 10282) discovered in Tengxian to the south; see *Tengxian jinshi zhi* (Beijing: Fayuansi, 1944), pp. 13–14. Despite these suggestions, whether the character *feng* on the Liutaizi bronzes is a personal name or the name of a state is still open to question, and the phonetic identification between Feng 逢 and Feng 豐 does not make a full case unless there is other evidence. The name of Wang Jiang appears in the Ling *gui* and other inscriptions, and is considered by Chen Mengjia to be the spouse of King Cheng, and by Tang Lan to be the spouse of King Kang; see Chen Mengjia, "Xi Zhou tongqi duandai," 2, p. 78; see also Tang Lan, *Tang Lan xiansheng jinwen*, p. 123. If so, the bronze may have been cast in the Zhou capital in Shaanxi and brought to the Shandong region. The same may be true also for the bronze cast by Wang Ji. Interestingly, these three published tombs are very close in time and should all be dated to the late phase of the early Western Zhou.

[13] See *Wenwu* 1979.4, 88–91.   [14] See *Kaogu* 1984.4, 333–37.

[15] The "Geographical Records" chapter of the *Hanshu* says that Teng was located in Gongqiu County 公丘縣 of Pei Commandery 沛郡, which was to the west of present-day Tengxian; see *Hanshu*, 28, p. 1,572. In addition, two other bronzes cast by the Ruler of Teng during the Spring and Autumn period were discovered to the east of the walled site; see *Kaogu* 1984.4, 337.

[16] See *Wenwu* 1994.3, 42–43.

Another important site in western Shandong is Qianzhangda 前掌大, located 25 kilometers to the south of Tengxian, where several large Shang tombs with ramp-ways were excavated from 1981 onwards. The excavation revealed an inventory of typical late Shang-style bronzes and pottery wares, with the co-occurrence of some local-style pottery vessels and a large number of glazed ceramics which possibly represent a southern tradition.[17] From my observation of these unpublished materials, there is no doubt that some small tombs at Qianzhangda can be dated to the early and even mid-Western Zhou. Qianzhangda is representative of pre-conquest sites under heavy Shang influence that continued to exist during the early Western Zhou. Two such sites were also found in the Jinan area at Wangfu 王府 and Daxinzhuang 大辛庄, and the recent discovery of inscribed oracle bones from the latter site demonstrates the area's close relationship with Anyang during the late Shang.[18] As the discoveries and the excavations at two other sites – Subutun 蘇埠屯 and Gucheng 古城 – in northern Shandong show, the Shandong region during the late Shang was undergoing a process of cultural assimilation with the Shang, and there seems little doubt that this was related to the Shang's vigorous expansion into the region, as is evident in the oracle-bone inscriptions as well as the written records.[19] But this process was interrupted by the Zhou conquest.

While the above archaeological findings are evidence of Shang–Zhou transition in the local Shandong region, their cultural and historical implications cannot be fully understood until we examine them in a historical context that can be constructed on the basis of both inscriptional and textual evidence. The historical outline we can construct from the textual records for the early Western Zhou period suggests that the Zhou had entered the Shandong region following the second conquest of Shang.[20] The great rebellion of Wu Geng and King Wu's brothers seems to have been

[17] See *Kaogu xuebao* 1992.3, 365–92, pls. 11–19.
[18] For the discovery of the oracle-bone inscriptions in Daxinzhuang, see "China Unearthed Shang Oracle Bones Again, 104 Years after the First Discovery," *People's Daily Online* (http://english.peopledaily.com.cn), April 9, 2003. See also *Chinese Archaeology* (Beijing) 4 (2004), 29–31.
[19] For the excavations at Subutun and Gucheng, see *Wenwu* 1972.8, 17–30; 1985.3, 1–11. For an analysis of bronzes from Subutun, see Yin Zhiyi, "Shandong Yidu Subutun mudi he Yachou tongqi," *Kaogu xuebao* 1977.8, 23–34. For analyses of both oracle-bone and textual evidence for campaigns undertaken by the Shang into the Shandong region against the Renfang 人方, see Dong Zuobin, "Jiaguwen duandai yanjiu li," in *Cai Yuanpei xiansheng liushi wu sui qingzhu lunwenji* (Monograph of *Guoli zhongyang yanjiuyuan lishi yuyan yanjiusuo jikan*) (Beiping: 1933), pp. 323–424; Shima Kunio, *Inkyo bokuji kenkyu*, pp. 392–403.
[20] In making this statement, one confronts the question of when the states of Qi and Lu were established. The *Shiji* attributes the establishment of the two states to King Wu; see *Shiji*, 4, pp. 127, 1,480 (Nienhauser, *The Grand Scribe's Records*, 1, p. 63). Debating the *Shiji* story that the Grand Duke (founder of Qi) had struggled with the Laiyi 萊夷 over his capital site, the Qing scholar Cui Shu notes that, had the establishment actually taken place in the reign of King Wu, there would have been preceding military actions taken in the time of King Wu in the Shandong region, but there were not; see Cui Shu, *Cui Dongbi yishu*, p. 341. No other sources support the *Shiji* account that the Zhou ever campaigned into the region under King Wu.

welcomed and joined by many states or communities in western Shandong and even the northern Jiangsu regions.[21] Among them, the pro-Shang state Yan 奄 was most important.[22] Whether this animosity in the "Far East" was the real cause of or was the excuse for Zhou's further military action, the evidence shows that the Zhou clearly marched east to bring the Shandong region under control. Two authentic chapters of Western Zhou date in the *Shangshu*, "Duoshi" 多士 and "Duofang" 多方, include references to King Cheng as having just come back from campaign against Yan.[23] Among the contemporaneous inscriptions the Qin *gui* 禽簋 (JC: 4041), for instance, mentions the king's attack on Gai 蓋 (= 奄 Yan); during the campaign, the Duke of Zhou served as the king's adviser while Qin (a son of the Duke of Zhou and the *de facto* founder of the state of Lu) served as the grand invocator.[24] The Ran *fangding* 塱方鼎 (JC: 2739) records a campaign conducted by the Duke of Zhou against the Dongyi 東夷 (a generic term referring to the various indigenous peoples in the east), Fengbo 豊伯, and Bogu 薄古 (Pugu 蒲古), and as the result, they were all conquered.[25] Correlating these sources, it can be well established that a series of campaigns against the former Shang allies as well as the indigenous communities in the Shandong region was launched by the Zhou court in the early years of King Cheng. In fact, a year-by-year account of this period is found in the *Current Bamboo Annals*, according to which the entire process of the second conquest took about three years.[26]

It can be estimated, as indicated by the locations of the historical sites mentioned in the texts and inscriptions, that through these military actions, however, the Zhou managed to capture only the transitional belt on the western and northern edges of the mountainous central Shandong, facing the Central Plain. But as soon as they found a foothold, the Zhou began to install regional states in the region. Bo Qin, the caster of the Qin *gui*, was established at Lu, at the site of former Yan in present-day Qufu, in front of the foothills of the Nishan 尼山 Mountains. As important as Lu, the state

---

[21] The *Yi Zhoushu* lists Xu 徐 and Yan 奄 as states that supported the rebellion; see *Yi Zhoushu*, 5, p. 7.

[22] Yan was traditionally considered to be in the same area as Lu (present-day Qufu), if not at the same site; see Jiang Yong, *Chunqiu diming kaoshi*, 254, p. 28.

[23] See *Shangshu*, 16, p. 220; 17, p. 227 (Legge, *The Shoo King*, pp. 453–63, 492–507).

[24] For the identification of Gai with Yan, see Chen Mengjia, "Xi Zhou tongqi duandai," 2, pp. 73–75; Shaughnessy, "The Duke of Zhou's Retirement in the East," p. 49.

[25] The "Geographical Records" chapter says that King Cheng exterminated Bogu and its territory was annexed by Qi; *Hanshu*, 28, p. 1,659. Chen Pan locates Bogu to the northeast of Boxing 博興; see Chen Pan, *Chunqiu dashi biao ji lieguo juexing*, 7, p. 662. Shaughnessy indicates that Feng was somewhere near Qufu and was the place where the Duke of Zhou spent the rest of his life in retirement; see Shaughnessy, "The Duke of Zhou's Retirement in the East," pp. 70–71.

[26] The *Current Bamboo Annals* gives the following chronology: in King Cheng's second year (which is in fact the second year of the Duke of Zhou's regency), Yan, Xu, and the Huaiyi rebelled; late in the year, Zhou set out on campaign. In the third year, the royal army exterminated Shang and killed Wu Geng; thereupon the Zhou attacked Yan, and exterminated Bogu. In the fourth year, the royal army attacked the Huaiyi, and thereupon entered Yan. In the fifth year, the king was in Yan, moving the Ruler of Yan to Bogu; in the summer, the king returned. See *Zhushu jinian*, 2, p. 4 (Legge, *The Shoo King*, Prolegomena, pp. 154–55).

of Qi was installed in a place called Yingqiu 營丘 and was to be ruled by the
Grand Duke. During the reign of King Yi of Zhou, the Qi capital was moved
to the site of former Bogu, and then, after a short while, to present-day
Linzi, in the foothills of the Boshan 博山 Mountains.[27] Two other Ji states,
Teng and Cheng 郕, were established by two of Bo Qin's uncles in present-
day Tengxian and Ningyang 寧陽, on evidence from ancient geographical
records.[28] Among these Zhou states, the archaeological discoveries have
already confirmed the location of the state of Teng for the early Western
Zhou period, while definite evidence is available also for the states of Lu
and Qi during the late Western Zhou (see below, pp. 314–15). The locations
of these states are first of all strategic: Lu and Cheng controlled the eastern
edge of the mountainous region and blocked the way from either the Si-
Beng corridor or the Dawen River valley; Qi controlled the road east along
the northern edge of the mountains; Teng controlled the road south to the
Huai River region. In short, the colonization of western and northwestern
Shandong, evidenced by both the written and the archaeological records,
provided the Zhou with a firm base for further expansion into the heartland
of the peninsula and into the lower Huai River region in the south.

Expansion into the eastern peninsula

The history of Zhou expansion or penetration into the hilly peninsula in
eastern Shandong is best substantiated by the discovery of two groups of
bronzes from Huangxian 黃縣.[29] The first group includes the famous Qi
zun 啟尊 (JC: 5983) and Qi *you* 啟卣 (JC: 5410), found at Xiaoliuzhuang
小劉莊, the inscriptions on which mention the caster's experience in accompanying a Zhou king on a southern campaign (Fig. 20).[30] Interestingly, the
context of these two inscriptions parallels closely the inscription on the
Shi Yu *ding* 師艅鼎 (JC: 2723) that actually describes the same campaign.
The second group includes ten bronzes, found at Jiangjia 姜家, dating to
the mid-Western Zhou. Even earlier, in 1896, the Yu *yan* 毃甗 (JC: 948)

[27] See *Shiji*, 32, pp. 1,481–82. The "Geographical Records" chapter of the *Hanshu* identifies Yingqiu
with Linzi and therefore says that the Grand Duke was established in Linzi County 臨淄縣 of Han,
in present-day Zibo City; see *Hanshu*, 28, p. 1,583; Chen Pan, *Chunqiu dashi biao lieguo juexing*, 1,
p. 85. Some modern scholars consider Yingqiu to be part of the later Qi capital Linzi; see Sekino
Takeshi, "Seito Rinji no chōsa: 1," *Kōkogaku zasshi* 32.4 (1942), 185. It should also be noted that Qi
was not a Ji state, but rather a Jiang 姜 state, a long-time ally of Zhou.

[28] As for the location of Cheng, Du Yu of the third century indicates that there was a place called
Chengxiang 郕鄉 in Gangfu County 剛父縣 of Dongping Commandery 東平郡, which is present-
day Ningyang; see *Zuozhuan*, 3, p. 1,727.

[29] For the discovery of the Qi *zun* and Qi *you*, see *Wenwu* 1972.5, 5–8.

[30] Tang Lan relates this campaign to King Zhao's southern campaign and therefore dates the vessels to
the reign of King Zhao; see Tang Lan, *Tang Lan xiansheng*, pp. 277–78. I would reject Tang's dating
for two reasons: (1) the shape of the two bronzes is characteristic of King Mu's reign but too early
for King Zhao's; and (2) Shi Yu 師艅, who participated in the same campaign, later cast the Shi Yu
gui 師艅簋 (JC: 4277), reasonably dated to the reign of King Gong or King Xiao. It is unlikely that
Shi Yu could have appeared in King Zhao's reign. A proper date for this group of bronzes would be
the early phase of the mid-Western Zhou.

was discovered in the Huangxian area, bearing an important inscription that mentions a campaign under the command of Shi Yongfu.[31] As already mentioned in chapter 2 (see p. 96), this belongs to the group of inscriptions cast in the time of King Mu by individuals who participated in the organized military defense of the Zhou state against the invasion by the Huaiyi. There may be different explanations regarding the background of Qi and Yu,[32] but the discovery of their bronzes in Huangxian in eastern Shandong fully testifies to the region's relationship to the Zhou royal court as well as the history of Zhou expansion into the peninsula. At the very least, they are evidence of personnel exchange between the eastern peninsula and the Zhou centers in a shared political system. To the south, in the adjacent Zhaoyuan 招遠, an early mid-Western Zhou bronze *gui* was excavated from a tomb in 1958; very interestingly, it was cast by Qizhong 齊仲, a member of the state of Qi located in western Shandong.[33] These locally excavated bronze inscriptions with explicit references to the Zhou royal court and to the regional Zhou state of Qi leave almost no doubt that the Zhou political network had extended to the eastern part of the peninsula by the beginning of the mid-Western Zhou. What is more important is the fact that, according to later excavations, these findings are associated with a large walled city at Guicheng 歸城 which is dated by local archaeologists to the late Western Zhou; the two groups of bronzes were actually found between the inner and outer walls encircling the settlement (Map 17).[34] Given the clear references to the Zhou court and Zhou personnel in the inscriptions excavated from the site, accompanied by clear Zhou cultural remains, it is very likely that the Huangxian region was a main base of Zhou activities in the eastern peninsula, between which and the Zhou centers and regional states in the west both people and materials flowed. It may be justified to compare the importance of the walled site at Guicheng to that of the Panlongcheng 盤龍城 site for Shang expansion into the south; it is potentially a hotspot in Western Zhou archaeology in the future.

Another important discovery was made in the early 1970s at Xi'an 西庵, Jiaoxian 膠縣, near the southeast coast of the peninsula, where a typical Zhou-style chariot was found buried with four horses and standard early Western Zhou bronze fittings and weapons (Fig. 38).[35] But the cultural context in which the chariot pit was found seems quite complex, for some small tombs found at the same site contain mainly local-style pottery. It is difficult to judge whether the chariot belonged to a local elite member who acquired it from Zhou, or to a Zhou noble who reached this region. But it undoubtedly indicates that Zhou influence had reached the southern

---

[31] On the provenance of the Yu *yan*, see *Zhensong tang jigu yiwen* (1931), 4, p. 21.

[32] For instance, they may have been Zhou commanders transferred from the west to the Shandong region after the respective campaigns, or indigenous persons from Shandong who had once served the Zhou king and in the Zhou army.

[33] See *Kaogu* 1994.4, 377–78.   [34] See *Kaogu* 1991.10, 910–18, pls. 6–8.   [35] See *Wenwu* 1977.4, 68.

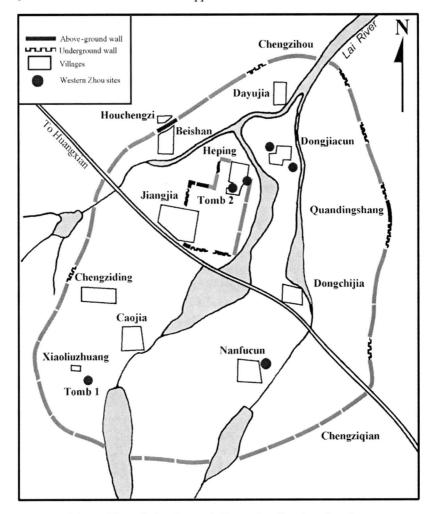

Map 17 The walled settlement in Huangxian, Shandong (based on
Kaogu 1991.10, 911, fig. 2)

coastal region. Since this region is so remote from the Zhou bases in western
Shandong, the discovery seems to speak well of the vigor of the Western
Zhou state and its material culture.

Just as the discovery of bronzes and bronze inscriptions reflects the process of Zhou penetration into the Shandong peninsula, pottery wares found
in the region also show a gradual spatial advance of the Zhou culture. So
far we have only two groups of pottery vessels in the published sources with
a certain early Western Zhou date. The first group was unearthed from
Liutaizi tombs nos. 2 and 6, along with early Western Zhou bronzes.[36]

---

[36] See *Wenwu* 1981.9, 22; 1996.12, 16–17.

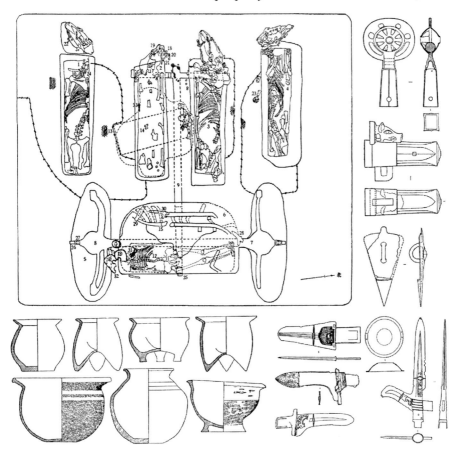

Fig. 38 Early Western Zhou chariot-burial at Xi'an in Jiaoxian, Shandong (bronze fittings and weapons from the chariot pit; pottery from tomb no. 1 at the same site; based on *Wenwu* 1977.4, 64–68)

While the sharp-shouldered *guan*-jar is distinctive, the *li*-tripod and the wide-mouthed *guan* are the same as those found in Luoyang, continuing the Shang tradition. The second group was from tomb no. 1 at Xi'an, from the same site as the chariot pit mentioned above.[37] The deep *gui*-jar is similar to those found in Henan, but the three plain-surfaced and bag-legged *li*-tripods are clearly different from those in Henan, representing a distinctive local tradition. Two groups of mid-Western Zhou burial pottery were excavated in Yujia 宇家 in Changle 昌樂 and Zhoujia 周家 in Huangxian.[38] Combined with a large number of pottery vessels found at Hexi 河西, Changle,[39] these sources offer us an overall image of the pottery culture in the northern half of the peninsula along the shore of the Bohai Sea from the

[37] See *Wenwu* 1977.4, 68.
[38] See *Haidai kaogu* 1 (1989), 299–302, 314–19.   [39] See *Haidai kaogu* 1 (1989), 294–97.

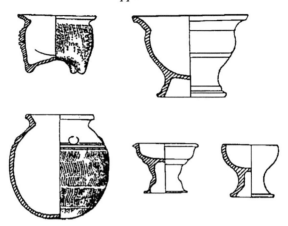

Fig. 39 Pottery vessels from tomb no. 1 at Yujia in Changle (from *Haidai kaogu* 1 [1989], 301, fig. 7.1, 2, 5, 6, 9)

state of Qi in the west to Huangxian in the distant east, the area that must have been most affected by Zhou expansion according to the discovered bronzes. There are clear similarities between this pottery assemblage and pottery vessels from the Wei River valley, most evident in such types as the high-based and wide-mouthed *gui*-basin, the high *dou*-plate with a strong base, and the mid-Western Zhou-type *li*-tripod that was modeled on the contemporaneous bronze *li* (Fig. 39). It is very likely that they were adopted from the Wei River valley at a time when Zhou pottery types were introduced into the eastern plain of Henan. Since the production of pottery is more closely tied to local traditions, the appearance of such unmistakeable Zhou pottery types in such a distant region fully suggests the prowess of Zhou cultural influence, supporting the records of Zhou activities on the inscribed bronzes.

However, coexisting with these Zhou types in this Zhou-affected region in Shandong are some local types of pottery, e.g. the plain-surfaced *li*, *guan*, and *ding*, and the cord-impressed *guan*-jar with a round body. These types, especially the plain-surfaced *ding*, are similar to those found in the stone-chambered tombs at Nanhuangzhuang 南黃莊 in Rushan 乳山, at the southern edge of the Jiaodong peninsula, clearly representing a local population.[40] In short, we see a very interesting phenomenon of cultural mixture between the Zhou culture and the indigenous culture across the Jiaodong peninsula. This indigenous culture can be plausibly related to the local population of the peninsula.

The phenomenon observed in the archaeology of Shandong, especially the distribution of Zhou-style bronzes and pottery, is but a reflection of

[40] See *Kaogu* 1991.1, 332–36, pls. 2–3; see also Wang Xiping, "Jiaodong bandao Xia Shang Zhou shiqi de Yiren wenhua," *Beifang wenwu* 1987.2, 22–23.

the ongoing historical process of Zhou expansion into eastern Shandong. Inscriptions from the reigns of King Kang and King Zhao include many references to the continuous fighting between the Zhou and the indigenous population in Shandong whom the Zhou referred to as the "Dongyi".[41] The X *ding* 窖鼎 (JC: 2741) mentions the Zhou king's personal involvement in a campaign against the Dongyi and an attack on a place called Yu 䑧, where the Zhou troops are said to have captured seashells.[42] The famous Minggong *gui* 明公簋 (JC: 4029) says that Duke Ming, probably a son of the Duke of Zhou, sent out three lineages to attack the eastern states and, especially interesting, the Ruler of Lu was called on for assistance in this military operation. The inscription provides a good example of how the Zhou central power and the regional Zhou states coordinated in warfare in the peripheral regions such as eastern Shandong.[43] The Xiaochen Lai *gui* 小臣謎簋 (JC: 4239) mentions that Bo Maofu 伯懋父 led the Eight Armies of Yin (*Yin bashi* 殷八師), the largest army stationed at the former Shang capital, to attack the Dongyi, pursuing them as far as the seashore; in concluding the campaign, Bo Maofu rewarded his soldiers with seashells captured on the campaign (Fig. 40).[44] These inscriptions are excellent testimony of Zhou expansion to the coastal areas in eastern Shandong and offer the best explanation for the archaeological findings of Zhou-style bronzes and pottery analyzed above.

In a larger historical context, the inscriptions suggest that during much of the early Western Zhou, the focus of Zhou military expansion was placed on the Shandong region. It has been suggested by Yang Kuan that through these campaigns the Zhou had subjugated the Dongyi people.[45] However, considering the immense size of the peninsula and the population implied by this very loose term "Dongyi" in the inscriptions, there seems no ground to argue that all the Dongyi were subjugated by the Zhou. Nevertheless, the entrance of the Zhou into eastern Shandong must have created a situation in which some of the Dongyi communities were subjugated and some became Zhou allies, while many others remained hostile to the Zhou state. On the basis of our current evidence, the best assessment is probably that during the late phase of the early Western Zhou the Zhou had achieved substantial

[41] For an extensive discussion of the textual and inscriptional evidence for the Dongyi, see David Cohen, "The Yueshi Culture, the Dongyi, and the Archaeology of Ethnicity in Early Bronze Age China," unpublished PhD thesis, Harvard University (2001), pp. 42–210.

[42] See Cheng Mengjia, "Xi Zhou tongqi dunadai," 1, pp. 174–75; Shirakawa, "Kinbun tsūshaku," 1.19:217.

[43] Minggong is identified with Mingbao in the Ling *fangyi* (JC: 9901), a son of the Duke of Zhou, who succeeded to his father's position at the Zhou court. Chen Mengjia identified this Lu ruler in the inscription with Bo Qin, the elder brother of Minggong and founder of the state of Lu; see Chen Mengjia, "Xi Zhou tongqi duandai," 2, pp. 69–70; Shirakawa, "Kinbun tsūshaku," 1.13:132.

[44] Some scholars identified Bo Maofu with Kangbo Mao 康伯毛, the second ruler of the state of Wey located near the former Shang capital, the base of the Eight Armies of Yin; see Chen Mengjia, "Xi Zhou tongqi duandai," 1, p. 170; Shirakawa, "Kinbun tsūshaku," 1.63:719.

[45] See Yang Kuan, "Xi Zhou Chunqiu shidai dui dongfang beifang de kaifa," *Zhonghua wenshi luncong* 1982.4, 116–17.

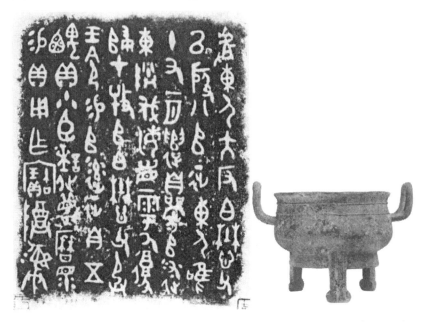

Fig. 40 The Xiaochen Lai *gui* and its inscription (JC: 4239; *Shanzhai yiqi tulu*, no. 70)

territorial gains in eastern Shandong and had probably established effective control over the Jiaolai plain. From the beginning of the mid-Western Zhou, the Zhou troops advanced further into the hilly regions to the east, mainly along the northern coastline, reaching as far as the northern tip of the peninsula and occupying the Huangxian region, as is well reflected in the archaeological findings.

Shandong during the late Western Zhou

For the two most important Zhou states in Shandong, Lu and Qi, we do not have solid archaeological evidence until the late Western Zhou period. Excavations indicate that the earliest part of the city wall of Qufu, now standing 6–10 meters high, was built during the late Western Zhou,[46] consistent in time with the extensive distribution of late Western Zhou remains within the walled enclosure.[47] More than fifty Western Zhou tombs

---

[46] See *Qufu Lu guo gucheng* (Jinan: Qilu shushe, 1982), pp. 34–35. The reporters speculate that some sections of the wall may be dated to the early Western Zhou because the techniques applied in building them were more primitive, but this has not been established with stratigraphic evidence; see *Qufu Lu guo gucheng*, p. 212.

[47] The reporters classified the burial pottery from Qufu into two groups (A and B), representing two different cultural traditions. Then, they divided group A into six periods, of which periods I–III are dated from the early to the late Western Zhou. Group B is divided into four periods and is also dated from the early to the late Western Zhou. Pottery vessels from settlements are also divided into six periods, corresponding to Group A burials. This dating is based on comparison with pottery

were excavated within the circuit of the wall. Among the fourteen bronzes found in tomb no. 48, seven were cast by the Minister of Multitudes of Lu, Zhongqi 仲齊, and one by the mother of the Lu ruler. In tomb no. 30 a bronze cast by Lu Boyu 魯伯悆 was found.[48] While these bronzes clearly identify the site as the center of the state of Lu, the reporters have ventured further to suggest that Qufu was inhabited from the time of Bo Qin's establishment, but this is based on a misdating of artifacts from the site.[49] Archaeological evidence suggests that the site was the Lu capital from the late Western Zhou. The walled city of the Qi capital Linzi is located in the northwestern part of Zibo city, between the Zi 淄 River and the Xi 系 River.[50] It has been reported that a late Western Zhou stratum was found in the center of the city, but so far no Western Zhou remains have been published to confirm the date.[51]

Another major state that had been deeply involved in Zhou expansion to the east was Ji 紀. Not far from the state of Qi, the state of Ji was thought to have been originally located in Shouguang 壽光, where the Jihou *zhong* 己侯鐘 (JC: 14) was found early in the nineteenth century.[52] However, recent discoveries of Ji-related artifacts seem to concentrate on the eastern part of the Jiaodong peninsula. In 1969, a late Western Zhou bronze cast by a brother of the Ruler of Ji (Jihou 異侯) and another by Ji Huafu 己華父 were excavated together with seven other bronzes in Shangkuangcun 上夼村 in Yantai, confirming that Ji 異 and Ji 己 were the same state.[53] Then in 1974, in Laiyang 萊陽 in the center of the hilly region of the Jiaodong peninsula, a local-style *hu*-vessel cast by the Ruler of Ji was found together with six other bronzes with clear late Western Zhou features.[54] Continuing excavations thereafter at the same site uncovered five more tombs and a chariot-burial,

---

vessels from the Hebei region or even the Wei River valley, which is methodologically questionable; the reporters' lack of experience with Western Zhou materials also caused them to date several late Western Zhou bronzes to the mid-Western Zhou. See *Qufu Lu guo gucheng*, pp. 80–85, 114–15, 183–86. The Qufu materials have been reexamined by Wang Entian and Cui Lequan, who indicate that most materials dated by the reporters to the early and mid-Western Zhou are late Western Zhou in date; see Wang Entian, "Qufu Lu guo gucheng de niandai jiqi xiangguan wenti," *Kaogu yu wenwu* 1988.2, 48–55; Cui Lequan, "Shandong diqu Dong Zhou kaoguxue wenhua de xulie," *Huaxia Kaogu* 1992.4, 73–97. For two more recent criticisms of the Qufu materials, see Falkenhausen, "The Waning of Bronze Age," pp. 497–501; Iijima Taketsugu, *Chūgoku Shū bunka kō kogaku kenkyū* (Tokyo: Dōseisha, 1998), pp. 219–28.

[48] See *Qufu Lu guo gucheng*, pp. 120, 46–50. Tomb no. 48 is misdated to the mid-Western Zhou. A proper date for the tombs would be the beginning of the Eastern Zhou. Tomb no. 30 is a little earlier than tomb no. 48, but still should be dated to the late Western Zhou. For the date of Qufu bronze groups, see Li Feng, "Huanghe liuyu Xi Zhou muzang," pp. 391, 404, 408.

[49] See *Qufu Lu guo gucheng*, pp. 211–12.   [50] See *Kaogu* 1961.1, 289–97; *Wenwu* 1972.5, 45–54.

[51] See *Wenwu* 1972.5, 45, 50. In 1984, an alleged "Western Zhou" tomb containing sixteen bronzes was excavated outside the north wall of Linzi. But in my view, this group of bronzes should be dated to the early Spring and Autumn period. See *Kaogu* 1988.1, 24–26.

[52] See *Jinwen fenyu bian*, 2, p. 20.

[53] See *Wenwu* 1972.5, 8–9; see also Li Xueqin, *Xinchu qingtongqi yanjiu*, p. 247. Judging from the shape and ornamentation of these two bronzes, they should be dated to the early phase of the late Western Zhou.

[54] See *Wenwu* 1983.12, 7–8.

and, interestingly, a pottery replica of a mid-Western Zhou bronze *he*-vessel was also found at the site, inscribed with fourteen characters.[55] In addition, in 1951, a set of four *xu*-vessels cast by a son of the Ruler of Ji, Renfu 妊父, and two other bronzes cast by the Ji ruler himself as dowry for his daughter were discovered in Huangxian.[56]

The three areas, Huangxian, Yantai, and Laiyang, where the bronzes inscribed by the members of Ji were found clearly mark a triangle as the base of Ji power during the late Western Zhou. The discovery in Laiyang is particularly significant in suggesting that Ji not only was able to cover the coastal area in the north, but was able to penetrate the complex terrain in the southern half of the peninsula traditionally inhabited by the Dongyi people. From these findings, some have proposed that Ji had a large territory stretching all the way from Shouguang in the west to Yantai in the east.[57] However, it would be better to assume that Ji, originally located in Shouguang in northwestern Shandong, had opened this new land in the distant east during the early mid-Western Zhou expansion. The political relation between Ji and the Zhou court is reflected in the inscription of the Shi Yuan *gui* 師衰簋 (JC: 4314) which says that in a campaign conducted by the Zhou court against the Huaiyi in the south, troops from Ji, along with those from the states of Qi and Lai 萊, fought side by side with the Zhou royal army under the command of Shi Yuan.[58] This evidently suggests that Ji, as certainly the most influential local state in the eastern part of the peninsula, was an active participant in the political system of the Western Zhou state. A later tradition transmitted by the *Shiji* portrays Ji as a strong competitor of the state of Qi for Zhou royal favor: by the words of the Ruler of Ji, King Yi of Zhou once summoned the Ruler of Qi to the Zhou capital and put him to death.[59] As a campaign against Qi at this time is evident in the inscription of the Fifth Year Shi Shi *gui* (see chapter 2, pp. 97–8), the *Shiji* tradition seems to reflect well the political relations between Ji, Qi, and the Zhou state.

The other state, Lai, mentioned in the Shi Yuan *gui* as a participant in the Zhou campaign, was located in Huangxian by most later historians,[60] but a set of four *li*-vessels cast by Libo 釐伯, identified with Laibo 萊伯, was excavated, together with ten other late Western Zhou bronzes, in Rizhao 日照, most probably from a tomb, very close to the south coast of Shandong.[61] It is very possible that Lai was founded originally by a Dongyi community

---

[55] See Chang Xingzhao and Cheng Lei, "Shilun Laiyang Qian Heqian mudi ji youming taohe," *Beifang wenwu* 1990.1, 20–25.

[56] See Wang Xiantang, *Shandong guguo kao* (Jinan: Qilu shushe, 1983), pp. 20–23, 38–49, 53–59.

[57] See Li Xueqin, *Xinchu qingtongqi yanjiu*, p. 248.

[58] For the inscription of the Shi Yuan *gui*, see Shirakawa, "Kinbun tsūshaku," 3.178:600.

[59] See *Shiji*, 32, p. 1,481.

[60] For the location of Lai, see Chen Pan, *Chunqiu dashi biao lieguo juexing*, 4, p. 391.

[61] The transcription given by the reporter reads: 釐伯□女子作寶鬲. The character after Libo 釐伯 is possibly *ying* 媵; in other words, the bronzes were probably cast by Libo as trousseaus for his daughter. See *Kaogu* 1984.7, 594–97. On the identification of the character Li 釐 with Lai 萊, see Chen Mengjia, "Xi Zhou tongqi duandai," 5, pp. 110–11.

under Zhou influence.[62] This naturally brings us to the question of what impact the Zhou state and it culture had on the life of the indigenous population of Shandong. Throughout the Western Zhou, there were many non-Ji states in the Shandong region. Some of them were geographically mixed up with the Ji-surnamed states in the transitional belt of western and northwestern Shandong, but many more states were located in the newly opened areas in the east. For instance, Xue 薛 and Zhu 鑄 (=祝), located in Tengxian and Ningyang on the western edge of the mountains, claimed to be descendents of the Yellow Emperor.[63] The state of Xiang 向 was in the area of Juxian 莒縣 in the Shu River fault and was said to have had Jiang 姜 as its surname.[64] Of a much larger number were states of obviously indigenous Shandong background that worshiped legendary figures such as Taihao 太皞 and Shaohao 少皞 as their ancestors:[65] Zhu 邾 (= Zou 鄒) was located in Zouxian 鄒縣, being a close neighbor of Lu and later annexed by Lu; Zhuanyu 顓臾 was located in the middle section of the Si-Beng River corridor; Tan 郯 was located at the southern edge of the mountainous region; Ju 莒 was located far to the east, in Jiaoxian, on the Jiaolai plain; Zeng 鄫 was probably located close to Zhu; and Biyang 偪陽 was located near present-day Zaozhuang 棗庄.[66] It is very likely that most of these small states were ethnically related to the so-called Dongyi.[67]

Most of these states survived into the Spring and Autumn period and therefore are frequently mentioned in the *Zuozhuan* as neighboring polities of Lu. However, for most of these states, there is no evidence as to whether or not they were established by Zhou royal order, or when they were founded. Their self-claimed ancestries are generally questionable. But, given the active role they played in the early Eastern Zhou, there seems little doubt that during the Western Zhou there was a move among the

---

[62] On the origin and location of Lai, see Chen Pan, *Chunqiu dashi biao lieguo juexing*, 4, pp. 388–93.
[63] For the heritage and locations of Xue and Zhu, see Chen Pan, *Chunqiu dashi biao lieguo juexing*, 2, pp. 128–30; 5, p. 445. Xue is identified with a walled site about 20 kilometers to the south of Tengxian that was excavated in 1978. The excavation confirms that the wall was constructed during the middle or late Spring and Autumn period, but according to a surface survey four Western Zhou sites have been located near the city. See *Kaogu xuebao* 1991.4, 449–95, esp. 451; *Kaogu* 1980.1, 32–44.
[64] On the heritage and location of Xiang, see Chen Pan, *Chunqiu dashi biao lieguo juexing*, 2, pp. 175–77.
[65] For a discussion on these legendary figures, see Cohen, "The Yueshi Culture, the Dongyi," pp. 255–62.
[66] On the heritage and locations of these four states, see Chen Pan, *Chunqiu dashi biao lieguo juexing*, 2, pp. 132–33, 136–38; 4, pp. 304–5, 319, 385–86; 5, pp. 442–43.
[67] There are some clear indications of this in the *Zuozhuan* and *Guoyu* for at least some of these small states because their "Dongyi" origin is sometimes recalled in the political scene of the Spring and Autumn period. For instance, in 529 BC Zhu together with Ju filed a complaint at the court of the hegemon Jin against their greater neighbor Lu; subsequently, Lu responded that Jin should not trust the accusation by the "barbarians" (Manyi 蠻夷; refers to Zhu and Ju). On another occasion (641 BC), Zhu captured the Ruler of Zeng, a small neighbor that also had a Dongyi origin, and made him a human sacrifice under order by the greater state Song whose ruler wanted to use that incident to intimidate the Dongyi people. In 525 BC, the Ruler of Tan 郯 paid a visit to the court of Lu where he recounted in detail the "bureaucracy" created by his ancestor Shaohao. Afterwards, Confucius is said to have remarked that "when the Son of Heaven lost his government, it must be sought among the four Yi." The Ruler of Biyang was captured by the troops of Jin in 563 BC and was made a human sacrifice called "Yi Prisoner" (*Yifu* 夷俘). See *Zuozhuan*, 46, p. 2,072; 14, p. 1,810; 48, pp. 2,083–84; 31, p. 1,947.

indigenous people in Shandong to form their own states, under the influence of the Zhou regional states as their immediate neighbors. This process
of state formation in the Shandong region, as well as the cultural and political mix, laid an important foundation for the region's continuing prosperity
and political importance throughout the Spring and Autumn period that
followed the Western Zhou.

ZHOU IN THE SOUTH

The south is a vast and diverse region, characterized by ranges of mountains
and a very complex system of rivers, marshes, and lakes. To the Zhou,
the south was both a region of great resources, especially materials such
as copper and tin that they needed to support their large-scale bronze
production,[68] and at the same time an unknown region of danger and
hostility. Throughout the entire Western Zhou, the south continued to
pose a problem and frequently tested the strength of the Western Zhou
state. If we were to point out an area where for the longest time the Zhou
court could not impose its will on matters, that was probably the south.

Mountains and rivers: geographical accessibility

The south can be divided into two general sub-regions: the middle and
lower Huai River valley combined with the Yangzi delta; and the middle
Yangzi region (Map 18). The area to the north of the Huai River is a natural
continuation of the eastern plain of Henan, with rivers flowing southeast
into the Huai. Most of these rivers have very long and slow channels, and
easily overflow in the wet season. However, the alluvial plain of the Huai
River is narrow on its south side, varying from 10 to 60 kilometers.[69] From
the eastern edge of the Dabie Mountains, a step of 40–80 meters in elevation
extends northeast as far as eastern Anhui, where it meets a hilly area. This
hilly area is sandwiched between the Huai and Yangzi rivers, and some of
its hills near Chuxian 滁縣 and Fengyang 鳳陽 rise to over 300 meters.[70]
To the east of these hills, in Jiangsu, the Huai River plain merges with the
Yangzi delta, forming a huge plain on China's east coast.

---

[68] In an important recent study, Li Liu and Xingcan Chen mapped out copper and tin deposits over
China, showing the middle Yangzi region as having one of the highest concentrations of copper
deposits in China. From the most recent archaeological discoveries, Liu and Chen suggest that from
late in the Erligang period (c. 1500–1400 BC) the Shang had come to rely heavily on the middle Yangzi
deposits which were intensively exploited after the exhaustion of surface deposit in the Zhongtiao
Mountain region in the north; see Li Liu and Xingcan Chen, *State Formation in Early China*, pp. 36–
44, 105, 116–17. Early archaeological excavation of one of the mining sites, Tonglushan 銅綠山 in
Hubei, suggested that the local deposit was exploited from the late Shang all the way through the
Han dynasty; see *Tonglushan gu kuangye yizhi* (Beijing: Wenwu, 1999), pp. 183–84.
[69] See Min Yuming *et al.*, *Anhui sheng dili* (Hefei: Anhui renmin, 1990), p. 47.
[70] See Min Yuming *et al.*, *Anhui sheng dili*, p. 49.

The middle Yangzi sub-region can be further divided into four units: the Nanyang basin, the Jianghan plain, the Dongting Lake plain, and the Poyang Lake plain. The Nanyang basin is an important buffer zone between the north and the south. The Funiu and Tongbai Mountains on its edge naturally break at Fangcheng 方城, providing an entrance into the basin from the Central Plain (Map 6).[71] The floor of the basin is undulating, inclining from its edge at an elevation of 140–100 meters to the center at 100–80 meters.[72] Influenced by this topography, rivers flow to the center of the basin and merge into a single channel, the Baitang 白唐 River, entering the Han River in the south. The Nanyang basin is connected with the Jianghan plain through two passages: the Han River valley in the west between the Jingshan 荊山 and the Dahong 大洪 Mountains, and the Sui-Zao 隨棗 corridor in the east between the Dahong and the Tongbai Mountains. Geologically, the Jianghan plain was from the Cretaceous period an area of continuous subsidence and deposition;[73] in pre-Qin times, a large proportion of it was still under the water of the famous Yunmeng 雲夢 Marsh, into which both the Yangzi and the Han flowed. Known in the text sometimes by its nickname "Great Marsh," the Yunmeng Marsh extended over 170 kilometers from Wuhan in the east to Jiangling in the west, leaving only the narrow margins between its shore and the Dabie, Dahong, and Jingshan Mountains appropriate for human habitation.[74] To the south of the Yangzi extends the marshy plain centered on the Dongting Lake. The plain was edged in the west and south by the Wuling 武陵 and Xuefeng 雪峰 Mountains, and in the east by the Mufu 幕阜 Mountains, which run to the bank of the Yangzi and separate the Dongting Lake plain from the Poyang Lake plain in the east.

The two sub-regions, the middle Yangzi and the Huai–Yangzi delta, are naturally connected by the river route of the Yangzi. However, Shi Nianhai has pointed out that ancient transportation between the two sub-regions was not along this waterway, but far to the north through the Huai valley.[75] In an important analysis of the invasion of the Chu capital by the army of the state of Wu in 506 BC, Shi Quan has reached the same conclusion.[76] In any

---

[71] The importance of this position can be seen in the construction of a "great wall," the Fangcheng, by the state of Chu to protect itself from the northern states during the Spring and Autumn period; see *Zuozhuan*, 12, p. 1,793; see also Jiang Yong, *Chunqiu diming kaoshi*, 253, p. 3. As mentioned above, the Zhou installed the state of Ying in Pingdingshan to control this entrance.

[72] See *Henan sheng zhi: Quyu jianzhi zhi, dimao shanhe zhi*, p. 28.

[73] See Zeng Zhaoxuan, *Zhongguo de dixing*, p. 297.

[74] For the location and extent of the ancient Yunmeng Marsh, see Tan Qixiang, *Zhongguo lishi dituji*, 1, pp. 25–26.

[75] This was because the innumerable marshes and river roads along the Yangzi between Jiangxi and Anhui provinces made transportation very difficult, if not impossible, for ancient people. Shi Nianhai also indicates that, although not as significant as the Nanyang road, transportation through the valleys of the Dabie Mountains was possible; see Shi Nianhai, *Heshanji*, 1, pp. 73–76.

[76] Shi Quan indicates that the Wu troops moved west from the Huai valley, but not the Yangzi, and reached the Chu capital in Jiangling from the Nanyang basin in its north; see Shi Quan, *Gudai Jing Chu dili xintan*, pp. 400–2.

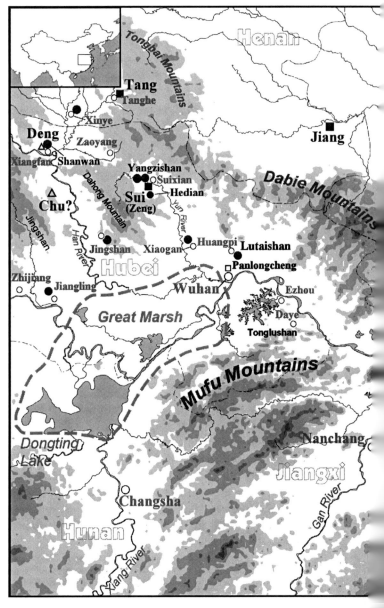

Map 18 The south during the Western Zhou (topographical layers derived
from "ESRI Data & Maps: 2004"; river course based on "Harvard China
Historical GIS Dataset, Version 2.0: August 2003")

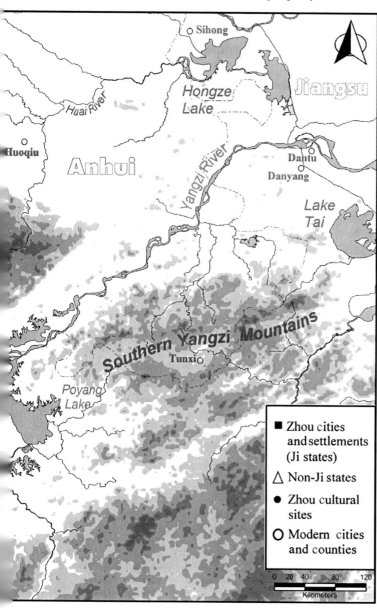

event, the route through the Nanyang basin was strategic; further south, the Sui–Zao corridor and the Wuhan–Huangpi 黄陂 area between the Yunmeng Marsh and the Dabie Mountains provided the most important road entering the Dongting plain and perhaps the only road entering the Poyang plain. On this strategic road, on the northern bank of the Yangzi, was located the Shang city of Panlongcheng 盤龍城. During the Western Zhou, the Jianghan plain was the southern extreme of the Western Zhou state, while the Dongting Lake plain and the Poyang Lake plain largely remained beyond the control of Zhou power.

Zhou ambition in the south during the early to mid-Western Zhou

The Huai River valley, despite its importance in Zhou's relations with the south, is almost blank in Western Zhou archaeology.[77] In the Yangzi delta, the most notable archaeological discovery is tomb no. 1 at Yandunshan 煙墩山, Dantu 丹徒, in which was found a group of bronzes including the famous Yihou Ze *gui* 宜侯矢簋 (JC: 4320), a bronze cast by the Ruler of Yi, whose name was Ze.[78] Evidently cast in the time of King Kang (r. 1005/3– 978 BC) since it mentions King Wu and King Cheng as two deceased kings, the inscription has been interpreted by many as describing the relocation of Ze, previously Ruler of Yu (Yuhou 虞侯), in his new state named Yi 宜, a place that is considered to be the locale where the bronze was found. If so, and given its explicit description of Yi as a regional state granted by the Zhou king, we must consider that the Western Zhou state had embraced at least a part of the Yangzi delta. Further connection has been suggested between Yi and the state of Wu, one of the southern states to have achieved hegemony during the Spring and Autumn period.[79] Against this prevailing view, Huang Shengzhang has demonstrated quite convincingly that Yi was not in the Yangzi delta but must have been located near the Zhou royal domain.[80] In other words, the Yihou Ze *gui* was a bronze produced in the north and was brought to the south; therefore, it by no means testifies to the Zhou expansion into areas south of the Yangzi.[81]

---

[77] The existence of Western Zhou sites in the Huai region was noted by Zeng Zhaoyu and Yin Huanzhang in the 1960s; see Zeng and Yin, "Gudai Jiangsu lishi shang de liangge wenti," in *Jiangsu sheng chutu wenwu xuanji* (Beijing: Wenwu, 1963), pp. 32–33. According to two later brief summaries, several "Western Zhou sites" were excavated during the 1980s in Huoqiu 霍邱, Chaoxian 巢縣, and Sihong 泗洪 in the Huai River valley; see *Wenwu kaogu gongzuo sanshi nian* (Beijing: Wenwu, 1979), pp. 105, 132. Since none of these sites has been formally reported, the cultural contents of these so-called "Western Zhou sites" are still unknown.

[78] See *Wenwu cankao ziliao* 1955.5, 58–69.   [79] See Tang Lan, *Tang Lan xiansheng*, pp. 69–70.

[80] Huang locates Yi at the present-day Yiyang 宜陽, to the southwest of Luoyang; see Huang Shengzhang, "Tongqi mingwen Yi Yu Ze de diwang jiqi yu Wu guo de guanxi," *Kaogu xuebao* 1983.3, 296–98. For the geographical implications of the Yihou Ze *gui* and a summary of Huang's arguments, see also Edward Shaughnessy, "Historical Geography and the Extent of the Earliest Chinese Kingdoms," *Asia Major* 2.2 (1989), 15–21.

[81] A very interesting discovery was made in Changzhi 長治, Shanxi, where six *ge*-daggers were excavated together from a single Warring States tomb (no. 14). The six *ge*-daggers were inscribed with three different inscriptions: (1) "Halberd of Yu" (虞之戟), (2) "Pricking halberd of Yi X" (宜之刺戟), and

Rather than looking for evidence in the text of the inscription, we should examine the archaeological context in which the bronze was found. In this regard, quite consistent with Huang's argument, the Yihou Ze *gui* was buried with a group of nine distinctive local-style bronzes.[82] In this region, standard Western Zhou bronzes were very often buried together with a much larger number of local-style bronzes. Such is the case of the tombs excavated at Muzidun 母子墩 in Dantu,[83] and other tombs in Tunxi 屯溪 and Danyang 丹陽.[84] The scarcity of standard Western Zhou bronzes compared with the local bronzes, often buried together, and the clear distinction between the two traditions suggest that the former were probably imported, and the latter, many modeled on the imported examples, were locally manufactured.[85] These locally manufactured bronzes from the Yangzi delta have been classified by the scholar Ma Chengyuan into two large categories: those imitating Western Zhou bronzes, and those of pure local design.[86] In all cases, bronzes were buried together with a large number of proto-porcelains, in mounds constructed above the ground, the so-called "mound-tombs" (*tudunmu* 土墩墓), very different from the earth pits dug into the ground in North China, the date of which is still being debated. Ma Chengyuan has strongly suggested that most types of the local bronzes, except those imported from the north, date to the Spring and Autumn period and perhaps even late in that period.[87] But others date the mound-tombs as contemporary with the Western Zhou bronzes they contain, that is the early Western Zhou or the early phase of the mid-Western Zhou.[88]

(3) "Wu X" (吳); see *Kaogu xuebao* 1957.1, 114. This discovery shows two things: first, since Yu, Yi, and Wu were phonetically interchangeable, the appearance of the three terms on bronzes from a single tomb indicates that they were probably used as phonetic variants for the same place-name; second, even though Changzhi is about 250 kilometers to the east of Pinglu 平陸 in the same province, where the state of Yu 虞 was once located, it is more convincing to relate these daggers to the site of ancient Yu in Pinglu than to the distant Yangzi delta.

[82] In this respect, the discovery of the Yihou Ze *gui* can be compared with that of the inscribed bronzes of the state of Xing (central Hebei) found in Huolinhe 霍林河, Inner Mongolia, together with artifacts of northern steppe tradition; see *Neimenggu wenwu kaogu* 2 (1982), 5–7.

[83] See *Wenwu* 1984.5, 3.   [84] See *Kaogu xuebao* 1959.4, pl. 5.1; *Wenwu* 1980.8, 7.

[85] The burial condition of these bronzes can be compared with that of Western Zhou bronzes found in tombs of the Upper Xiajiadian 夏家店 culture in northeast China, for instance in tomb no. 101 at Nanshangen 南山根, Ningcheng, but has no counterpart in the Shandong region or the middle Yangzi, not to mention the Central Plain; see *Kaogu xuebao* 1973.2, 27–39.

[86] See Ma Chengyuan, "Changjiang xiayou tudunmu chutu qingtongqi de yanjiu," *Shanghai bowuguan jikan* 4 (1987), 199–201.

[87] See *ibid.*, pp. 213–17.

[88] For such views, see Xiao Menglong, "Muzidun mu qingtongqi ji youguan wenti tansuo," *Wenwu* 1984.5, 14–15. There are some mound-tombs of a less questionable Western Zhou date. For instance, the Biedun 鱉墩 mound-tomb is dated by Carbon-14 to 2935 ± 130 BP (or 985 BC). The Fushan Guoyuan 浮山果園 mound-tomb is dated to 3025 ± 155 BP (or 1075 BC). Pottery *li*-tripods from Yandunshan 煙墩山 tomb no. 2 are considered as belonging to the early period of the local Hushu 湖熟 culture, generally dated to the late Shang and the early Western Zhou. Unfortunately no bronzes were found in these tombs. A similar pottery *li* was found in a tomb at Lishui 溧水, together with two proto-porcelains and a bronze *ding*-vessel. In short, the date of bronzes found in the mound-tombs in the Yangzi delta still awaits future evidence. See *Kaogu* 1978.3, 151–54; 1979.2, 107–18; *Zhongguo kaoguxue zhong tan shisi niandai shuji* (Beijing: Wenwu, 1983), p. 48; *Kaogu* 1976.4, 274.

It is beyond dispute that the Yangzi delta had received strong influence from the Zhou bronze culture in the north during the early Western Zhou. Communication between the north and the Yangzi delta through the Huai River region seems to have been frequent during the early Western Zhou, as evident both in the considerable number of the typical Zhou-style bronzes discovered in the delta such as the Yihou Ze *gui* and in the appearance of many proto-porcelain wares in tombs excavated in the Zhou central region.[89] It is important to note that only early Western Zhou bronze styles, but not those of middle and late Western Zhou bronzes, were incorporated into the design and ornament of the locally produced bronzes in the Yangzi delta. Despite Zhou influence on the region during the early Western Zhou, it is nevertheless clear that the Yangzi delta region was segregated from Zhou influence after the early phase of the mid-Western Zhou until the arrival of new influences from the north during the early Spring and Autumn period.[90] This discontinuity in receiving northern influence has encouraged some to suggest that it was the preference for proto-porcelains that inhibited the growth of bronze industries in the region after their brief florescence in the early and mid-Western Zhou.[91] But it seems more evident to me that, putting it in a larger historical context, the discontinuity in receiving northern influence owed much to the political situation in the Huai River region: the rebellion of the Huaiyi during the mid-Western Zhou.

Our textual records on Zhou relations with the Yangzi delta during the early Western Zhou are almost completely lacking. The only source is the "Genealogical Account of the House of Wu Taibo" in the *Shiji* that traces the founding of the state of Wu to two of King Wen's uncles.[92] However, in all likelihood, this genealogical relation with the Zhou royal house in the north was a fabrication by later historians, if not forged by the Wu elites themselves during the late Spring and Autumn period. On the other hand, we have solid information on a constant relationship between the Zhou and communities in the Huai River region that formed a buffer zone between the north and the Yangzi delta. The war between the Zhou and the Huaiyi during the early mid-Western Zhou period has already been discussed in some detail in chapter 2. It suffices here to point out that the prolonged warfare between the Zhou and the Huaiyi through much of the mid-Western Zhou probably blocked the communication between Zhou and the Yangzi delta. Hence, the historical context provides the most logical explanation for why the region seems to have discontinued in receiving northern influence after the early phase of the mid-Western Zhou.

[89] See, for example, *Zhangjiapo Xi Zhou mudi*, pls. 94–95; *Luoyang Beiyao Xi Zhou mu*, pls. 4–7.

[90] The new influence is most evident in a group of *ding*-vessels of early Spring and Autumn date, buried together with an early mid-Western Zhou *ding* and several local bronzes in early mid-Western Zhou styles in a tomb in Danyang 丹陽, Jiangsu; see *Wenwu* 1980.8, 3–8.

[91] See Virginia Kane, "The Independent Bronze Industries in the South of China Contemporary with the Shang and Western Chou Dynasty," *Archives of Asian Art* 28 (1974–75), 98.

[92] See *Shiji*, 31, p. 1,445.

Virginia Kane has suggested that there was no direct contact between the middle Yangzi region and the Yangzi delta in terms of the bronze production tradition during Shang and early Western Zhou times. This seems to agree with the assessment by the historical geographers of the ancient communication between these two sub-regions.[93] It is quite clear that a strong and distinctive bronze tradition like that of the Yangzi delta did not appear in the Nanyang basin or, as far as our sources indicate, in the Jianghan plain. Compared to the lower Yangzi, Zhou presence in the middle Yangzi region is much better documented in our archaeological records. As early as the Xuanhe reign (AD 1119–25) of the Song dynasty, a group of six bronzes was discovered in Xiaogan 孝感, including the Zhong *yan* 中甗 (JC: 949) and the three Zhong *fangding* 中方鼎 (JC: 2751–52, 2785).[94] While it is significant that these bronzes were buried at the south exit of the Sui–Zao corridor, on the main transportation route to the south and far away from the Zhou royal capital, the extremely interesting point is still that their inscriptions mention Zhou campaigns in the middle Yangzi region. In 1980, another group of eighteen bronzes was found in Suixian 隨縣, in the middle section of the Sui–Zao corridor.[95] By their design and ornament, this group of bronzes should be dated to the late phase of the early Western Zhou to which the Zhong bronzes from Xiaogan are generally dated.

However, the most important discovery was made in 1977 at Lutaishan 魯台山, Huangpi 黃陂, only about 50 kilometers to the east of Xiaogan and 10 kilometers from the Shang city Panlongcheng. Astonishingly, excavated here was a large wooden-chambered tomb (no. 30) with a ramp-way (Fig. 41), constructed exactly the same as the Jingshu tombs in the Wei River valley and the Jin ruler tombs in the Fen River valley. The tomb is located in a cemetery alongside many other tombs with clearly Zhou cultural contents. Thirteen bronzes were found in this tomb, including four square *ding* inscribed the "Duke Grand Scribe makes for Ji Yu this treasured sacrificial vessel" (公太史作姬𡥉寶尊彝) and another *ding* inscribed "Changzi Gou makes for his cultured father Yi this sacrificial vessel" (長子狗作文父乙尊彝). Standard Western Zhou bronzes were also excavated from four other tombs a few meters away.[96] There seems little doubt that Ji Yu 姬𡥉, as her surname Ji suggests, was a woman from the Zhou royal clan, implying that her husband was a person whose surname was not Ji.[97]

---

[93] See Kane, "The Independent Bronze Industries," p. 97. It has been suggested by Shi Nianhai and Shi Quan that a transportation system between the two regions through the Yangzi River was not in place during the Western Zhou.

[94] See *Jinwen fenyu bian*, 1, p. 3.   [95] See *Wenwu* 1982.12, 51–52, 54.

[96] See *Jianghan kaogu* 1982.2, 37–50. Among these five tombs, no. 28 could be dated a little earlier, to the reign of King Cheng or King Kang. Nos. 30 and 36 can be dated to the late phase of the early Western Zhou, most likely to the reign of King Zhao, according to the features of bronzes they contain.

[97] Zhang Yachu suggests that Changzi Gou, who may have been Ji Yu's husband, was probably a descendent of the Chang 長 clan, originally located in Shanxi; Zhang Yachu, "Lun Lutaishan Xi Zhou mu de niandai he zushu," *Jianghan kaogu* 1984.2, 23–28.

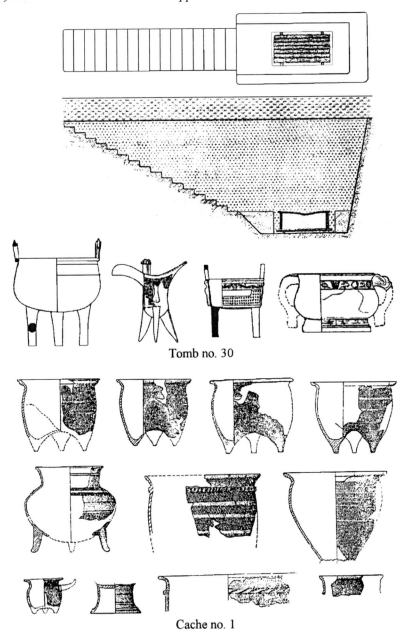

Tomb no. 30

Cache no. 1

Fig. 41 Tomb no. 30 at Lutaishan and the burial bronzes (pottery from cache no. 1 at the same site) (from *Jianghan kaogu* 1982.2, 42, fig. 3; 46, fig. 7.1, 3, 4–9, 12, 18, 24, 27; 47, fig. 8.1, 2, 4, 8)

But ethnic heritage is less important than the cultural and political relations manifest in this case. The caster "Duke Grand Scribe" (Gong Taishi 公大史) is mentioned also in the inscription of the Zuoce Hu *you* 作冊魖卣 (JC: 5433) and was evidently an important official at the Zhou court.[98] Their close relationship with the Zhou royal clan and the royal court as indicated by the inscriptions and the strong Western Zhou elements in the bronzes and burial structure, in contrast to those of the Yangzi delta, suggest that the local "state" to which the cemetery belonged was a participant in the political system of the Western Zhou state.

Relating the Lutaishan bronzes with the Suixian bronzes, and also with the Zhong bronzes found in Xiaogan at the southern entrance to the Sui–Zao corridor, we can clearly see that Zhou power had reached the northern bank of the Yangzi east of the Han River, through the Sui–Zao corridor. In this regard, Lutaishan probably functioned as a political and military base on the frontline of Zhou expansion, similar to the position of Panlongcheng (only 10 kilometers away) for the Shang in the same region. The closeness of the two prominent sites suggests strongly the impact of landscape: the Yangzi River presented a major obstacle and the Sui–Zao corridor limited the expansion of northern powers to a transitional strip along the eastern shoreline of the Yunmeng Marsh.[99] On the west side of the Han River, in 1961, a group of seventeen bronzes was found at Jiangling 江陵.[100] The fact that all of the major groups of bronzes from the region are dated to the late phase of the early Western Zhou suggests that the period was the time of the strongest Zhou presence in the middle Yangzi region.

In order to understand fully the implications of these archaeological finds in the middle Yangzi, we must put them in their historical context. In that regard, our textual and inscriptional records inform us that during the reign of King Zhao, while still fighting the Dongyi in the Shandong region, the Zhou royal court shifted its focus to the middle Yangzi region. The *Ancient Bamboo Annals* records that in his sixteenth year King Zhao attacked Chu and crossed the Han River; then, in his nineteenth year, King Zhao lost the royal Six Armies in the Han River, never returning to the capital.[101]

[98] Gong Taishi is identified with the Duke of Bi (Bigong 畢公) by Chen Mengjia; see Chen Mengjia, "Xi Zhou tongqi duandai," 2, pp. 111–12. Zhang Yachu considers that he was a son of either the Duke of Bi or the Duke of Shao; see Zhang Yachu, "Lun Lutaishan Xi Zhou mu," pp. 24–25.

[99] The significance of the Yangzi River in resisting political and cultural influence from the north can be seen also in the image of the bronze culture of the Hunan region. As demonstrated by Gao Zhixi, except for a few imported northern products, the bronze culture in the Hunan region south of Yangzi remained highly distinctive from Shang to the Western Zhou. The region was clearly beyond control by Zhou power. In contrast, bronzes in the Hubei region north of the Yangzi, at least as far as the early Western Zhou is concerned, are largely consistent with Zhou metropolitan tradition. For the bronze culture in Hunan during the Western Zhou, see Gao Zhixi, "Lun Hunan chutu de Xi Zhou tongqi," *Jianghan kaogu* 1984.3, 63–66. For the bronze culture in Hunan during the Shang, see Kane, "The Independent Bronze Industries," pp. 81–93.

[100] See *Kaogu* 1963.4, 224–25. Some bronzes in this group may be dated earlier, but the *ding* and the *zhi*-vessels certainly date the tomb to the end of the early Western Zhou.

[101] See Fan Xiangyong, *Guben zhushu jinian*, p. 25.

However, the inscription on the Shi Qiang *pan* 史墻盤 (JC: 10175) reflects
on the events in a more positive way, singling out that King Zhao attacked
the Chu and opened up the road to the south. More importantly, we have
a group of bronzes cast by individuals who had personally experienced
this campaign against Chu, in all likelihood that of the sixteenth year,
which was probably victorious: the Yiyu *gui* 馱駻簋 (JC: 3976), the Guobo
gui 過伯簋 (JC: 3907), the Cai *gui* 霂簋 (JC: 3732), and the Hongshu *gui*
㙴叔簋 (JC: 3950).[102] These inscriptions testify to the Zhou adventure in
the middle Yangzi region towards the later part of the early Western Zhou,
as reflected also in our archaeological records. The question is the location
of Chu during the Western Zhou, a major debate in the study of the early
cultural development of South China. Three possible locations have been
suggested for the early Chu center known as Danyang 丹陽: Xichuan 淅川,
Zhijiang 枝江, and Zigui 秭歸.[103] Since the campaign was clearly related
to the Han River, on which the Zhou were defeated, it seems reasonable
that Chu was located at this time somewhere southwest of the river.[104]
Of great importance in terms of geography are the Zhong bronzes from
Xiaogan, already mentioned above. The Zhong *yan* says that Zhong was
sent to inspect the southern states and to set up the king's camp at Zeng
曾 before the campaign actually took place. Consequently, he inspected
Fang 方 and Deng 鄧 and arrived at the E 鄂 garrison. At the same time,
Bo Maifu 伯買父 was on patrol along the Han River. According to the
Zhong *fangding* no. 1, cast by the same person and buried together with
the *yan*, this was a southern campaign against the Hufang 虎方, probably
located somewhere in the middle Yangzi region.[105] Importantly, the Zhong

---

[102] For a study of these inscriptions, see Tang Lan, *Tang Lan xiansheng*, pp. 280–92. The dating of
these four bronzes to the reign of King Zhao is now generally accepted. See, besides Tang Lan, Ma
Chengyuan, *Shang Zhou qingtongqi*, 3, pp. 73–75; Shaughnessy, *Sources of Western Zhou*, p. 246;
Shirakawa, "Kinbun tsūshaku," 14.68:772–74; 14.69:774–77; 14.70:778–81.

[103] Location 1 (Xichuan) seems to have won some recent support in both China and the West; see Shi
Quan, *Gudai Jing Chu dili xintan*, pp. 181–85; Barry Blakeley, "In Search of Danyang I: Historical
Geography and Archaeological Site," *Early China* 13 (1988), 116–52; Xu Shaohua, *Zhou dai nantu
lishi dili*, pp. 242–45. Shi Quan further argues that Danyang was originally located in Shangxian
商縣 in the upper Dan 丹 River valley and had moved to Xichuan during the reign of King Yi; see
Shi Quan, *Gudai Jing Chu dili xintan*, pp. 185–91.

[104] Barry Blakeley, who advocates that Danyang was in the Dan River valley at the time of the Shang–
Zhou transition, demonstrates that by the early Spring and Autumn period Chu had already been
relocated somewhere in the middle reaches of the Han River. On his map, Blakeley places Chu to
the west side of the Han River, but he does not indicate when Chu had moved to the area. See Barry
Blakeley, "On the Location of the Chu Capital in Early Chunqiu Times in Light of the Handong
Incident of 701 BC," *Early China* 15 (1990), 67, 70.

[105] For analyses of the Zhong bronzes, see Guo Moruo, *Liang Zhou jinwen ci*, pp. 17–19; Shirakawa,
"Kinbun tsūshaku," 14.71:791–93. Tang Lan reads Hu 虎 in the inscription of the Zhong *yan* as Jing
荊 and therefore sees the campaign as one directed against Chu, which is highly unlikely; Tang Lan,
Tang Lan xiansheng, p. 290. It seems to me that the southern campaign recorded by the Zhong *yan*
and Zhong *fangding* was probably the second campaign conducted by King Zhao in his nineteenth
year which had a different objective, against Hufang but not Chu, which was the target of his first
campaign three years earlier. Ding Shan 丁山 identifies the Hufang with Yihu 夷虎 in the *Zuozhuan*
(fourth year of Duke Ai), which was attacked by Chu, but mistakenly locates it in Shouxian 壽縣

yan also mentions two states – Zeng and Deng – that on the basis of our current evidence were both located in the middle Yangzi region. Deng was located to the northwest of Xiangfan City.[106] Zeng was probably the same as the state of Zeng during the late Spring and Autumn period and has been identified by many scholars with the Ji-surnamed state of Sui 隨 in the textual records, located to the west of Suixian in the middle section of the Sui–Zao corridor.[107] In the textual records, another Ji state was Tang 唐, located somewhere between Zaoyang 棗陽 and Tanghe 唐河 in the southern part the Nanyang basin.[108]

In short, the archaeological, inscriptional, and textual records together suggest that during the later part of the early Western Zhou the Zhou had tried vigorously to bring the middle Yangzi region under their control. It is very likely that they had indeed managed to establish political dominance over the region to the north of Yangzi and east of the Han River that was linked to the north through the Sui–Zao corridor and the Nanyang basin. This is probably why, despite his humiliating end, King Zhao was still commemorated in the Shi Qiang *pan* for his enterprises in the south.

The south during the late Western Zhou

The late Western Zhou period in the middle Yangzi region is represented by only some scattered discoveries of bronzes. As mentioned in chapter 1, four *gui*-vessels cast by the ruler of Deng for his daughter were found in the cemetery of the state of Ying in Pingdingshan, suggesting that the state of Deng continued to be active in the south. In 1981, a late Western Zhou *gui*-vessel cast probably by the ruler of Deng (in this case, Houshi 侯氏) for his wife Mengji 孟姬 was found in Shanwan 山灣, about 4 kilometers from the reported site of Deng in the geographical records.[109] Another *gui* cast by Mengji herself is in the collection of the city museum of Xiangfan.[110]

---

in the Huai region; see Ding Shan, *Jiaguwen suojian shizu jiqi zhidu* (Beijing: Zhonghua, 1988), p. 150. Since the Zhong *yan* clearly mentions such place-names as Zeng, Deng, and the Han River, Hufang must have been located somewhere in the middle Yangzi region, and a campaign against it would have had to be conducted through the Nanyang basin and, more importantly, through the Sui–Zao corridor where the bronzes were buried.

[106] For the location of Deng, see Shi Quan, *Gudai Jing Chu dili xintan*, pp. 106–11; Xu Shaohua, *Zhou dai nantu lishi dili*, p. 12.

[107] This equation was first proposed by Li Xueqin in 1978 soon after the discovery of the tomb of Zenghou Yi 曾侯乙. In 1979, Shi Quan suggested the same identification. See Li Xueqin, *Xinchu qingtongqi yanjiu*, pp. 146–50; Shi Quan, *Gudai Jing Chu lishi dili*, pp. 84–104; see also Xu Shaohua, *Zho dai nantu lishi dili*, pp. 71–75. As for the location of Sui, Du Yu of the third century says that it was located in Sui County 隨縣 of Yiyang Commandery 義陽郡, which is the present-day Suizhou City; see *Zuozhuan*, 6, p. 1,749.

[108] The "Geographical Records" chapter of the *Hanshu* indicates that Tang was in Chongling 春陵 County of Nanyang 南陽 Commandery of the Han dynasty, which is present-day Zaoyang; see *Hanshu*, 28, p. 1,564. Shi Quan suggests that Tang was located in present-day Tanghe 唐河, to the north of Zaoyang; see Shi Quan, *Gudai Jin Chun dili xintan*, pp. 360–66; Xu Shaohua, *Zhou dai nantu lishi dili*, p. 60.

[109] See Xu Shaohua, *Zhou dai nantu lishi dili*, pp. 12–13.   [110] See *Wenwu* 1986.4, 16.

These bronzes indicate that the local state Deng intermarried with the Ji states such as Ying in the Pingdingshan region. In 1974, a *ding* cast by Denggong Cheng 鄧公乘 was excavated from the same Shanwan site, dated to the Spring and Autumn period.[111] The Ji-surnamed state Sui (=Zeng) is represented by two groups of late Western Zhou bronzes: In 1966, ninety-seven bronzes were excavated at Jingshan 京山, on the southwest edge of the Dahong Mountains, including a set of nine *ding* and two *hu* cast by the Ruler of Zeng 曾侯 Zhongzi Youfu 中子游父.[112] In 1971, eight bronzes were found at Xinye 新野, at the northern entrance to the Sui–Zao corridor; one was clearly cast by the elite of the state of Zeng.[113]

However, through much of the mid-Western Zhou until the early phase of the late Western Zhou, the real power in the middle Yangzi seems to have been the state of E 鄂, on which the Zhou relied for the security of the south. Xu Shaohua has suggested that E was previously located near the Zhou capital Chengzhou and moved to the Nanyang basin by the end of the early Western Zhou.[114] The Ruler of E (Ehou 鄂侯) was one of the only two persons named in inscriptions as the "Border Protector" (Yufang 馭方).[115] According to the Ehou *gui* 鄂侯簋 (JC: 3929), currently in the Palace Museum in Taipei, E had marriage relationships with the Zhou king.[116] It is very likely that Ehou had played a very important role in Zhou's relations with the middle Yangzi region. However, the bronze culture of E shows some local characteristics. In 1975, a trumpet-mouthed *zun*-vessel was unearthed, together with four early Western Zhou bronzes in Suixian.[117] The *zun*, which was modeled on standard early mid-Western Zhou *zun* with local characteristics, was cast by a brother of Ehou, testifying to E's activities in the middle Yangzi region. Another *gui*-vessel bearing the same inscription was found in Luoyang and a *you*-vessel in the Shanghai Museum probably belonged to the same set.[118] These three bronzes, though clearly

---

[111] See *Jianghan kaogu* 1983.1, 52–53.   [112] See *Wenwu* 1972.2, 47–50.

[113] See *Wenwu* 1973.5, 14–16.

[114] See Xu Shaohua, *Zhou dai nantu lishi dili*, pp. 88–91. The "Geographical Records" chapter of the *Hanshu* records Xi'e County 西鄂縣 in Nanyang Commandery, which was located 25 kilometers to the north of present-day Nanyang; see *Hanshu*, 28, p. 1,565. Most scholars identify this Xi'e County as the location of the state of E. It should also be noted that some scholars locate E in present-day Ezhou City 鄂州市 in eastern Hubei on the southern bank of the Yangzi, but this is highly unlikely; see Liu Xiang, "Xi Zhou E guo kao," *Diming zhishi* 1982.3, 16–17; "Zhou Yiwang jingying Nan Huaiyi jiqi yu E zhi guanxi," *Jianghan kaogu* 1983.3, 45–46.

[115] Yufang 馭方 was often misinterpreted as Ehou's personal name. This new interpretation of Yufang as "Border Protector" was proposed by Edward Shaughnessy; see Xia Hanyi, *Wengu zhixin lu: Shang Zhou wenhua shi guanjian* (Taibei: Daohuo, 1997), p. 42; Edward Shaughnessy (ed.), *New Sources of Early Chinese History: An Introduction to the Reading of Inscriptions and Manuscripts* (Berkeley: Society for Study of Early China, 1997), pp. 82–83. The other person with the title "Border Protector" was Buqi, the caster of the Buqi *gui* 不嬰簋, who was defending the northwestern border of Zhou against the Xianyun in approximately the same period; see chapter 3 (see p. 155).

[116] The Ehou *gui* was cast by Ehou as a dowry for Wangji 王姑, a daughter of Ehou who married the Zhou king; see *Gugong tongqi tulu* (Taipei: Palace Museum, 1958), 2, pl. 183; Shirakawa, "Kinbun tsūshaku," 25.142:269.

[117] See *Kaogu* 1984.6, 512–13.

[118] See *Wenwu ziliao congkan* 3 (1980), 44. For the *you* in Shanghai, see *Wenwu* 1964.7, 10–14.

modeled on Zhou types, are quite distinctive from the Zhou tradition. They suggest that, although the state of E served as an ally and agent of the Western Zhou state, it probably had a distinctive cultural origin of its own.[119]

The Ehou Yufang *ding* 鄂侯馭方鼎 (JC: 2810), probably cast during the reign of King Yi or King Li, mentions that the king attacked Jiao 角 and Yu 鄱, and on the way back had an audience with the eminent Ehou at Pei 坏 and richly rewarded him.[120] The two place-names appear as Jiaohuai 角遌 and Tongyu 桐遹 on the Miaosheng *xu* 翏生盨 (JC: 4459), as locales of the Southern Huaiyi, thus making the campaign mentioned in the Ehou Yufang *ding* the same as the one directed to the lower Huai River region. However, it was Ehou the Border Protector who then led both the Huaiyi in the Huai River region and the Dongyi in the Shandong region in launching extensive attacks on Zhou's eastern and southern states during the reign of King Li, pushing the Western Zhou dynasty to the edge of collapse. In order to deal with the situation, the Zhou court sent out both the Eight Armies and the Six Armies to battle against the rebels, but they all failed. Finally Duke Wu sent out his personal armies under the command of Yu 禹, who reached E and captured the "Border Protector." The state of E was eliminated, but the damage the rebellion had done to Zhou power could not be repaired until sometime in the reign of King Xuan, who launched renewed campaigns into the Huai River region. This later historical development in the south has been described in chapter 2 (see pp. 135–7).

The local pottery culture of the middle Yangzi

Pottery wares from the Hubei region contemporary with the Western Zhou have been analyzed by Zhou Houqiang in two articles.[121] In general, owing to its origin, the Hubei pottery remained distinctive from that of the eastern plain throughout the entire Western Zhou period. This pottery assemblage is most characteristic for its small-mouthed *li*-tripod with a protruding shoulder and a high arching crotch, and for its high and narrow-based shallow *dou*-plate. The use of pottery *ding* in the middle Yangzi represented a strong local tradition that can be traced back to the Neolithic period. Although there were some variations as well as changes over time in each of these three types of pottery, their fundamental features remained unaltered for a very long time. On the other hand, Wang Jin emphasizes regional differences between the east and the west sides of the Han River, suggesting that the local culture to the east of the river was more influenced by the

[119] For a detailed study of the E bronzes and their cultural background, see Li Feng, "Literacy Crossing Cultural Borders," pp. 22–30.
[120] See Shirakawa, "Kinbun tsūshaku," 25.142:260–67.
[121] See Zhou Houqiang, "Xiaogan diqu Xi Zhou shiqi wenhua chuxi," *Jianghan kaogu* 1985.4, 65–74; "Hubei Xi Zhou taoqi de fenqi," *Kaogu* 1992.3, 236–44.

Zhou culture than was that to the west.[122] This is consistent with the fact that the discovery of Zhou-style bronzes was also largely limited to the east of the Han River, reflecting political and military advances of Zhou through the Sui–Zao corridor.

This is most evident in the adoption of the Central Plain-type *gui*-basin in the eastern region during the early part of mid-Western Zhou, and also in the shape of *li*-tripod found at Lutaishan which has a sunken crotch, characteristic of Zhou-style pottery *li*.[123] The Lutaishan pottery assemblage contemporaneous with the bronzes found at the same site can be taken to represent the local culture in the region under Zhou political domination (Fig. 41). Nevertheless, the Lutaishan pottery remained largely distinctive from the pottery assemblage found in the Central Plain or in the Wei River valley. Even this sunken-crotched *li* that was probably adopted from the north was very different from the standard *li*-tripod of the Zhou. Thus, it is likely that Zhou dominance in the east of Han and north of the Yangzi was built upon a distinctive local culture. In the Central Plain, the local tradition had merged with Zhou tradition by the late Western Zhou, but in the middle Yangzi region it seems to have remained distinctive much longer.

ZHOU IN THE NORTH

The northern periphery of the Western Zhou state, namely the northern Hebei plain edged by the Yanshan and Taihang Mountains as it is conceived in this study, used to be considered as having been located far beyond the reach of Zhou political authority.[124] However, the archaeological excavations in the 1980s and 1990s focusing on the state of Yan near Beijing have fundamentally changed this view. Therefore it is necessary to reconfigure the northern fringe of the Western Zhou state on the basis of the latest archaeological evidence.

Landscape of the northern Hebei plain

The northern Hebei plain is a natural extension of the Central Plain, and there are no major land obstacles between central Henan and the Beijing area near its northern limit (Map 19). Back in Shang–Western Zhou times, perhaps the most important geographical element that had great influence on the life of the peoples inhabiting the plain was the Yellow River. Unlike its present-day course that goes east from Zhengzhou, the river before

---

[122] See Wang Jin, "Dui Jianghan diqu Shang Zhou shiqi wenhua de jidian renshi," *Jianghan kaogu* 1983.4, 47–51.

[123] In Lutaishan, one such pottery *li*-tripod was buried together with Western Zhou bronzes in tomb no. 34; see *Jianghan kaogu* 1982.2, 46.

[124] See Shaughnessy, "Historical Geography and the Extent," pp. 21–22.

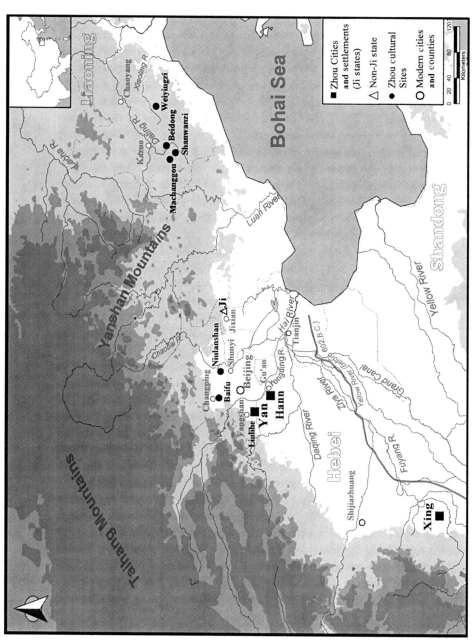

Map 19 The north during the Western Zhou (topographical layers derived from "ESRI Data & Maps: 2004"; river course based on "Harvard China Historical GIS Dataset, Version 2.0: August 2003")

602 BC ran almost straight north along the Taihang Mountains and turned
northeast near Shijiazhuang, entering the Bohai Sea at present-day Tianjin.
Between the Yellow River and the Taihang Mountains was a long and narrow
corridor of dense human habitation through which the Zhou extended their
political control all the way north. This is also the narrow belt in which
almost all pre-Qin archaeological sites on the Hebei plain are concentrated.

The Taihang Mountains, lying between Hebei and Shanxi, are one of the
oldest mountain systems in China and are often regarded as a part of the
Shanxi Plateau mainly shaped by the Yanshan tectonic movement during
the Mesozoic era. The Taihang has a naturally gentle slope in the west but
a clear and precipitous edge in the east.[125] The mountains have an average
height of 1000–1500 meters, with some peaks rising up to 3000 meters,
in contrast to the eastern plain that is below 100 meters above sea level.
Owing to its geological age, the calcareous rock of the Taihang has been
deeply cut by surface water, creating innumerable tortuous and dangerous
valleys.[126] The Yanshan Mountains, in the north, with an average height
below 1000 meters are the natural extension of Taihang, running from the
west to the shore of the Bohai Sea and segregating the Hebei plain from the
vast plain of Manchuria. Differing from the mostly calcareous formation
of the Taihang, the Yanshan Mountains in most sections are composed of
gneissic granite which forms more gentle slopes and wider valleys.

To the east of the Yellow River of ancient times lies the heartland of
the alluvial plain. According to an analysis by Tan Qixiang, most of the
plain was uninhabited until the Warring States period.[127] Certainly our
geographical records on the region before the Warring States are next to
nothing. Today, the landscape of the plain is still characterized by lowlands,
marshes, and the sand ridges that were left behind by old river courses. The
modern system of waterways on the Hebei plain is a very complex one,
formed by the five major tributaries of the Hai 海 River that enters the sea
at Tianjin. Among these tributaries, to the north flows the Yongding River,
passing by Beijing City; to the south, the Daqing 大清 River and the Ziya
子牙 River follow closely the course of the Yellow River before 602 BC.[128]

While the Taihang–Yellow River belt provided the most convenient
channel of communication between the north and the south, through
which most transportation lines still run today, there were also some ancient
roads connecting the two sides of the difficult Taihang Mountains. Two of
these roads were particularly important, and had been in use since at least
the Warring States period. The first was the "Road of Zhi" that, as already
mentioned in chapter 1 (see p. 83), starts at Jiyuan, going west through

[125] See Zhao Songqiao, *Physical Geography of China*, p. 118.
[126] See Zeng Zhaoxuan, *Zhongguo de dixing*, p. 37.
[127] See Tan Qixiang, "Xi Han yiqian de Huanghe xiayou hedao," pp. 48–51.
[128] See Wu Chen and He Naihua, "2 wan nian lai Huabei pingyuan zhuyao heliu de hedao bianqian,"
    in *Huabei pingyuan gu hedao yanjiu lunwenji*, ed. Wu Chen (Beijing: Zhongguo kexue jishu, 1991),
    p. 138.

the southern section of the Taihang by way of Yuanqu and entering the Fen River valley near Quwu. The second was the famous "Path of Jing" (Jingjing 井徑), connecting present-day Shijiazhuang and Taiyuan through the valleys in the northern section of Taihang, along which the modern railroad runs.[129] However, in Shang and Western Zhou times, the southern road was probably more important, linking the Shang capital Anyang and the lower Fen River valley, and the Wei River valley beyond in the west.

The northern state of Yan in archaeology

Archaeological excavations have confirmed that the capital of the state of Yan 燕 was located in a place called Liulihe 琉璃河, 43 kilometers to the southwest of Beijing. The site was discovered in the 1960s, with sizeable excavations being carried out from 1973 and continuing to the present.[130] First of all, a city wall 829 meters long on the north side (the other three sides have been partly or completely destroyed) has been found in Dongjialin 董家林. The stratigraphical evidence dates it to the beginning of the Western Zhou, and it is the only archaeological example of a city wall from that early Western Zhou period.[131] To its immediate east, sixty-one Western Zhou tombs were excavated between 1973 and 1977, and over 200 thereafter.[132] The most astonishing discovery came in 1985 when the archaeologists opened a large tomb (no. 1193) with four ramps. Two bronzes found in it, the Ke *lei* 克罍 (JL: 987) and Ke *he* 克盉 (JL: 942), bear inscriptions describing the establishment of Ke 克 in Yan as honor due to the "Grand Protector" (or the Duke of Shao) (Fig. 42).[133] For the first time in history a bronze inscription documenting the initial granting of a Western Zhou regional state by the Zhou king was excavated at the site of that state, and probably from the tomb of its founder. Besides this tomb, the archaeologists also excavated three other large tombs with ramps that were probably also burials of the subsequent Yan rulers or their spouses.

Moreover, inscriptional evidence identifying the local state came not only from the large tombs, but also from some middle-sized tombs. Several bronzes, e.g. the Boju *li* 伯矩鬲 (JC: 689), the Fu *ding* 復鼎 (JC: 2507), the Yu *fangding* 圉方鼎 (JC: 2505), and the You *gui* 攸簋 (JC: 3906), cast by individuals who were rewarded by the Ruler of Yan, were excavated from such tombs.[134] Two bronzes from tomb no. 253 are most illuminating

---

[129] See Lu Yun, "Zhanguo shiqi zhuyao lulu jiaotong chutan," in *Lishi dili yanjiu*, 1 (Shanghai: Fudan daxue, 1986), pp. 36–37.

[130] As early as 1867, a *ding*-vessel cast by the Ruler of Yan was discovered along with four other bronzes outside Beijing; see *Jinwen fenyu bian*, 2, p. 16.

[131] See *Liulihe Xi Zhou Yan guo mudi 1973–77* (Beijing: Wenwu, 1995), p. 3.

[132] The excavation between 1973 and 1977 was first reported in *Kaogu* 1974.5, 309–21, and then in the formal report, *Liulihe Xi Zhou Yan guo mudi*. Excavations after 1981 were reported briefly in *Kaogu* 1984.5, 404–16; 1990.1, 20–31; *Wenwu* 1996.6, 4–27.

[133] See *Kaogu* 1990.1, 20–25. For a discussion of the content of these inscriptions, see Li Feng, "Ancient Reproductions and Calligraphic Variations," pp. 6–8.

[134] See *Liulihe Xi Zhou Yan guo mudi*, pp. 102, 110, 135, 160.

Fig. 42 The Ke *lei* and its inscription from Liulihe, Beijing (from *Kaogu* 1990.1, 25, fig. 4;
Kaogu jinghua, p. 194.1)

regarding Yan's relations with the Zhou court in Shaanxi. The Jin *ding*
堇鼎 (JC: 2703) mentions that Jin was commanded by the Ruler of Yan to
contribute some kind of food or sweetmeat to the Grand Protector in the
Zhou capital in Shaanxi; the Grand Protector thereupon rewarded Jin. The
Yu *gui* 圉簋 (JC: 3825) says that Yu was rewarded by the Zhou king in the
eastern center Chengzhou when the king held a sacrificial ritual there.[135]
In view of the chronology of the whole cemetery, tombs such as nos. 253
and 251 must be dated to the early phase of the early Western Zhou, while
tombs such as nos. 17 and 13 are of an indisputably late Western Zhou date.
In short, the excavations have proven that the locale Liulihe was once the
Yan metropolis.

It should be noted that the initial establishment of Yan is not mentioned
in the pre-Qin sources; Yan is excluded from the list of Ji states given in
the *Zuozhuan* (twenty-fourth year of Duke Xi). The Han source *Shiji* says
that after the Zhou conquest of Shang, King Wu established the Duke of
Shao at Yan.[136] The Duke of Shao was the most important political figure
at the Zhou court during the reigns of King Cheng and King Kang. While
the new discoveries suggest instead that it was his son, Ke, not the Duke

[135] See *Liulihe Xi Zhou Yan guo mudi*, pp. 106, 151. The inscription of the Yu *gui* resembles the inscription
on the Yu *jue* 盂爵 (JC: 9104), which says that the king held the "*fen*"-sacrifice for the first time; see
Chen Mengjia, "Xi Zhou tongqi duandai," 2, pp. 118–19; Shirakawa, "Kinbun tsūshaku," 7.35:385.
[136] Historical records disagree also on the Duke of Shao's heritage. The *Shiji* mentions this in an
ambiguous way: the Duke of Shao was of the same surname as the Zhou and it was Ji. The
Guliangzhuan says that Yan was a "segmented son" (*Fenzi* 分子) of the Zhou. See *Shiji*, 34, p. 1,549;
Guliangzhuan, 6, p. 2,388.

of Shao himself, who was established ruler in Yan, they also confirm that, during the early Western Zhou, Yan maintained very close contact with the eminent duke and the Zhou court in Shaanxi. This is also indicated by the inscription of the Yanhou Zhi *ding* 匽侯旨鼎 (JC: 2628) that records the visit of another Ruler of Yan, Zhi, to the Zhou capital. The "Geographical Records" chapter of the *Hanshu* identifies the Ji County 薊縣 of Guangyang Commandery 廣陽郡 of the Han dynasty as the land of the ancient state Yan; this quite accurately points to present-day Beijing as the area where Yan was located. However, later commentators were confused about the name "Ji County" and argued that it was where the state of Ji 薊, another ancient state reportedly installed by Zhou, was located. Because of this, they instead located Yan in the area of Yuyang County 漁陽縣, about 75 kilometers to the east of Beijing. The archaeological excavations confirmed that the *Hanshu* is right on this point.[137]

The date of the artifacts from Liulihe suggests that Yan was established no later than the early years of King Cheng. This date also implies that after the conquest the Zhou very quickly extended their control to the northern limits of the Hebei plain. In chapter 2 (see p. 137), I have mentioned the reopening of relations between the Zhou court and the some of the regional states in northern Hebei such as Hann 韓 as a part of the restoration program initiated by King Xuan. While there seems good reason to locate Hann in present-day Gu'an 固安, to the southeast of Yan,[138] the uncertain point is about the time of its founding. The *Current Bamboo Annals* dates the establishment of Hann in the twelfth year of King Cheng, but the Mao commentary seems to suggest that it was founded in the reign of King Xuan during the late Western Zhou.[139] The *Current Bamboo Annals* suggests also that the city wall of Hann was constructed by the royal troops together with troops sent from Yan, an event that is also alluded to in the poem "Hanyi" in the *Book of Poetry*.

Although the locations of Ji and Hann have not been confirmed by archaeology, later discoveries suggest that Liulihe is certainly not the only site that presents clear Zhou cultural contents. Tombs that contain early Western Zhou bronzes were also found in Changping and Shunyi, at the foot of the Yanshan Mountains to the north of Beijing.[140] On the north

[137] See *Hanshu*, 28, p. 1,634; *Shiji*, 4, p. 128.
[138] There has also been some traditional confusion regarding this Hann in the Hebei plain and another Hann in the Fen River valley, listed in the *Zuozhuan* (twenty-fourth year of Duke Xi). Qing scholars such as Chen Huan and Jiang Yong have made clear that the Hann mentioned in the poem "Hanyi" must have been located somewhere near Yan. This is most evident in the poem's mention of northern tribes such as Zhui 追 and Mo 貊. These scholars suggested that Hann was located in present-day Gu'an, Hebei, about 50 kilometers to the south of Beijing. See Chen Huan, *Shi Maoshi zhuan shu*, 25, p. 41; Jiang Yong, *Chunqiu diming kaoshi*, 253, p. 8; see also Shen Changyun, "Xi Zhou er Hann guo diwang kao," *Zhongguo shi yanjiu* 1982.2, 137.
[139] See *Zhushu jinian*, 2, p. 5 (Legge, *The Shoo King*, Prolegomena, p. 146); *Shijing*, 18.4, p. 570.
[140] From the styles of the artifacts, the Shunyi tomb should be dated to the late phase of the early Western Zhou, while the Changping tomb should be dated to the early phase of the mid-Western Zhou; see *Kaogu* 1976.4, 228, 246–58; *Wenwu* 1983.11, 64–67.

side of the Yanshan Mountains, in the upper Xiaoling 小凌 River valley, eight tombs with wooden chambers were excavated in Weiyingzi 魏營子, Chaoyang. The burial structure of the tombs and the artifacts from them, including standard Zhou-style chariot fittings and horse harnesses, suggest undoubtedly that they belong to the Zhou bronze cultural menu, very similar to the tombs found in Changping near Beijing.[141] The discovery of these tombs is as important as the discovery of a Western Zhou tomb and chariot-burial in Guyuan in the northwest, examined in chapter 3 (see p. 167). But what is more important is that this is not an isolated discovery of Western Zhou remains in the region; only about 50 kilometers to the west of these tombs, four caches containing a total number of forty-one early Western Zhou bronzes were discovered in three locations in Kazuo 喀左 in the upper Daling 大凌 River valley.[142] Except for a spouted bronze bowl from cache no. 2 at Beidongcun 北洞村, and a long-necked *hu* and a duck-like *zun* from Machanggou 馬廠溝,[143] the rest of the bronzes are all standard early Western Zhou forms (some may be dated to late Shang).

The manner in which these bronzes were buried constitutes a sharp contrast to the stone-chambered tomb at Ningcheng 寧城, in which three standard late Western Zhou bronzes were buried together with a greater number of bronzes of the local Upper Xiajiadian 夏家店 culture.[144] While the Ningcheng case presents a close parallel to the "mound-tombs" in the Yangzi delta in which scattered Zhou bronzes imported from the north were buried in a local cultural environment, the Kazuo cases show a very different cultural context, a discontinuity from the non-Zhou local culture of southwestern Liaoning. Inscriptional evidence indicates an intimate relationship between the Kazuo bronzes and those found in the Yan cemetery in Beijing: a *yu* from Machanggou bears an inscription cast by the Ruler of Yan;[145] a *yan*-vessel from Shanwanzi 山灣子 bears an inscription cast by Boju 伯矩, whose bronzes were also found in Liulihe tomb no. 251;[146] a *fangding* from Beidongcun no. 2 bears the emblem "Ya Jihou" 亞其侯, which also appears on a *ding* from Liulihe tomb no. 253 (Fig. 43).[147] In addition, another Yu *gui* 圉簋 (JC: 3824) was found in Xiaobotaigou 小波汰溝 in Kazuo, bearing

---

[141] See *Kaogu* 1977.5, 306–9; *Wenwu kaogu gongzuo sanshi nian*, p. 90.

[142] See *Wenwu cankao ziliao* 1955.8, 16–27; *Kaogu* 1973.4, 225–26, 257; 1974.6, 364–72; *Wenwu* 1977.12, 23–33.

[143] See *Kaogu* 1974.6, 368; *Wenwu cankao ziliao* 1955.8, pls. 10, 12.

[144] See *Kaogu xuebao* 1973.2, 27–39, pls. 1–12.   [145] See *Wenwu cankao ziliao* 1955.8, 21.

[146] See *Wenwu* 1977.12, 24; *Liulihe Xi Zhou Yan guo mudi*, pp. 160, 197.

[147] See *Kaogu* 1974.6, 366; *Liulihe Xi Zhou Yan guo mudi*, p. 112. Kaizuka Shigeki suggested that "Jihou" was initially the head of a Shang lineage that was in close association with Yan after the conquest. The inscription of the Ya *he* 亞盉 (JC: 9439) which begins with this emblem says that Ya was rewarded by the Ruler of Yan; Kaizuka, Shigeki, "In matsu Shū sho no tōhō keiryaku ni tsuite," in *Kaizuka Shigeki chosaku shū*, vol. 2 (Tokyo: Chūō kōronsha, 1977), pp. 159–61. It has been noted earlier that another branch of the Ji lineage had evidently moved east to the Shandong region and established the state of Ji 其 (=紀 or 己) (see p. 315).

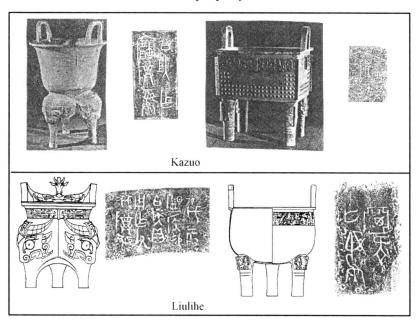

Fig. 43 Comparison of bronzes from Kazuo and Liulihe (from *Wenwu* 1977.12, 24, fig. 3; 32, fig. 52; *Kaogu* 1974.6, 366, fig. 3.2, pl. 7.3; *Liulihe Xi Zhou Yan guo mudi*, p. 111, fig. 74; p. 112, fig. 74c; p. 157, fig. 94; p. 160, fig. 94e)

exactly the same inscription as its peer from Liulihe tomb no. 253 (JC: 3825). Interestingly, the four caches in Kazuo are located within 10 kilometers of each other along the Daling River. Considering the concentration of these caches, their exclusive Western Zhou features, and their spatial relationship with the Western Zhou tombs found at Weiyingzi, it seems very likely that this was a base established by the state of Yan. Correlating these discoveries, I think that it is quite possible that the Zhou, or more precisely the Yan, had for a time colonized some areas along the Daling River in the southwest corner of Liaoning province.

But the time of Zhou presence in the region did not last very long, and the fact that these bronzes were buried in caches seems to suggest a sudden Yan withdrawal from the region, just as the Zhou did at the end of the Western Zhou from Zhouyuan in Shaanxi, where they left behind many caches. By the closing of the early Western Zhou, the Daling region had probably been integrated into the community of the Upper Xiajiadian culture, which imported bronzes from the Zhou polities on the south side of the Yanshan Mountains and at the same time developed its own bronze culture. Paralleling this development, there seems also to have been a cultural decline on the central site of Yan at Liulihe from the mid-Western Zhou; it is not clear whether the site still served as the Yan capital after the early Western Zhou period.[148] In the historical records, however, Yan seems to have lost any contact with the Zhou court after a short period during the early Western Zhou until Duke Hui's establishment, which was contemporary with King Li's exile in 841 BC; even the Yan genealogy before Duke Hui has been completely lost to history. Based on the historical record and with respect also to the fact that the state of Xing was fighting the Rong people from the north during the same period, the best supposition would be that the northern Hebei plain where the states of Yan and Ji were located was politically cut off from the Central Plain because of the intrusion of the Rong people. Such connection was probably not reestablished until the Ruler of Hann's visit to the Zhou capital following the Zhou official Juefu's diplomatic trip to northern Hebei, dated in the *Current Bamboo Annals* to the fourth year of King Xuan (824 BC).

The local pottery culture of Yan

An analysis of the pottery vessels from the Hebei plain has been conducted by Chai Xiaoming, whose chronological table agrees largely with the Liulihe report.[149] Chai pays particular attention to the formation of this pottery assemblage which, according to him, represents two different traditions: that of the Shang and that of the Zhou. The Shang elements are most evident in the shape of the low-crotched *li*-tripods and the wide-mouthed *guan*-jars; the Zhou elements are evident in such types as the joint-crotched *li*-tripod, and narrow-mouthed *guan*-jar with a round (or sharp) shoulder. Chai considers the Shang elements to be of the mainstream.[150] The fact that Chai's analysis is based on data gathered over a large area, including southern Hebei and even northern Henan, may have contributed to the impression of a stronger Shang tradition. If we limit our sight to the Liulihe site in the northern part of the Hebei plain, as far as the early Western Zhou is concerned, the Shang elements, while fully recognizable, are by no means dominant (Fig. 44). Compared with the Luoyang region, for instance, Liulihe seems to have had a stronger Zhou tradition. This is evident in the large number of narrow-mouthed *guan*-jars, and the presence of the *gui*-basins that, though of Shang origin, had developed a step under the neck, and the huge and deep *weng*-jars with three small hollow legs that appear more frequently in the Shaanxi and Shanxi regions. More significantly, the way in which the various pottery types were grouped in the burials adheres quite accurately to Zhou burial practice in the Wei River valley.

---

[148] It should be noted that no bronzes found so far in Liulihe can be dated later than the early phase of the mid-Western Zhou.

[149] See Chai Xiaoming, "Huabei diqu Xi Zhou taoqi chulun," in *Yan wenhua yanjiu lunwenji*, ed. Chen Guang (Beijing: Zhongguo shehui kexue, 1995), pp. 105–16; *Liulihe Xi Zhou Yan guo mudi*, p. 243.

[150] See Chai Xiaoming, "Huabei diqu Xi Zhou taoqi chulun," pp. 112–15.

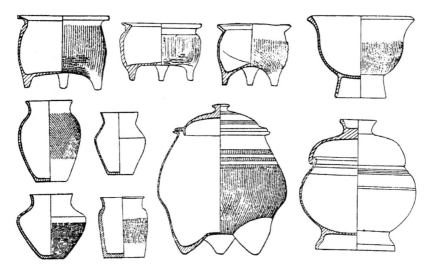

Fig. 44 Pottery from tomb no. 54 at Liulihe, Beijing (based on *Liulihe Xi Zhou Yan guo mundi*, p. 83, fig. 58.1; p. 85, fig. 59.3, 6; p. 88, fig. 62.2; p. 90, fig. 63.5; p. 93, fig. 65.7; p. 96, fig. 67.5, 7, 11; p. 99, fig. 69.8)

CONCLUSION

The discussion in this appendix has offered us some solid ideas about the geographical extent of the Western Zhou state based on current archaeological evidence, correlated with inscriptional and textual records. Particularly, the controlled archaeological excavation of bronze vessels from the peripheral regions bearing inscriptions that suggest unmistakeable connections with the Zhou central court has provided us with a firm ground to actually reconstruct the network of political control by the Western Zhou state. In that regard, these inscriptions are local marks of a huge political web that extended from the Wei River valley in Shaanxi to these remote areas. It has also been the focus of this appendix to show that such a network of political control by the Western Zhou state was never static, but changed from time to time. On the current evidence, we can conclude that this network had reached its maximum by the closing of the early Western Zhou as the result of the long-term expansion and the continuous practice of the "Fengjian" institution. At the beginning of the mid-Western Zhou, the political network of the Western Zhou state had expanded to the entire region of Henan, Hebei, a large part of Shandong, central Shaanxi, eastern Gansu, southern Shanxi, the southwestern corner of Liaoning, northern Anhui, and the Handong area of Hubei. Within this geographical area, the Western Zhou state embodied in the royal authority evidently exercised effective political control through the display of military forces and by commanding the regional states as its agents.

To be more specific, in the "Far East," the Zhou managed to capture only the western edge of Shandong during the reign of King Cheng; but by the end of the early Western Zhou they had pushed east, perhaps along the northern coastline, beyond the Jiaolai plain into the hilly Jiaodong peninsula. In the south, the Zhou probably controlled part of the Huai River region during the early Western Zhou, and extended cultural influence farther into the Yangzi delta. However, the Zhou seem never to have brought areas south of the Huai River under their control, although temporary expeditions into the region are possible. In the middle Yangzi region, the Zhou evidently controlled the Nanyang basin, from which they had pushed south through the Sui–Zao corridor to establish control over the area to the north of Yangzi and east of the Han River. In the north, while bringing the entire Hebei plain under control soon after the conquest, the Zhou had advanced, for at least a period of time during the early Western Zhou, beyond the Yanshan Mountains and controlled some areas in the southwestern corner of Liaoning. But in the Shanxi region, as mentioned in chapter 1, for the entire Western Zhou period the Zhou seem never to have gone beyond the lower Fen River basin (see the Topographical Map of China, p. xvi).

In the peripheral regions examined above, the advance of the Zhou led to the creation of a cultural mix. The elite Zhou culture represented by the bronzes from these regions shows a high degree of adherence to the metropolitan Zhou tradition in terms both of their artistic design and of their standard of literacy. In this regard, the early Western Zhou was undoubtedly the most important period in early Chinese history for the spreading of literacy over a large geographical area as a result of the migration of the Zhou elite to the periphery. However, the reaction of the local cultures to the advances of the Zhou culture varied from region to region. In the Shandong region, alongside the Zhou expansion some Zhou types of pottery were introduced into the local pottery assemblage that at that time already showed a strong Shang influence. The Handong area in the south adopted some types from the Central Plain, but throughout the Western Zhou period the local tradition remained strong and never fully merged with the northern tradition. Compared with the Central Plain where Shang influence was extremely strong during the early Western Zhou, the northern Hebei plain had a relatively stronger Zhou influence; but even there, the Shang elements continued to exist for a long time. The lower Fen River basin adopted the Zhou tradition with minor variations, and throughout the Western Zhou the two regions remained culturally very close to each other.

The relationship between the Quanrong and the Xianyun

One of the difficulties in the study of the Zhou–Xianyun war lies in the various ways in which the enemies are referred to in the Zhou sources, particularly in the relationship between the Quanrong 犬戎 and the Xianyun 獫狁. Here I discuss the origins of the two terms and clarify how they were related in early Chinese history. As we have seen in chapter 3, *xianyun* was a genuine Western Zhou term appearing both in the contemporaneous bronze inscriptions and in poems belonging to the "Minor Odes" section of the *Book of Poetry*. When these poems were quoted by the Han writers, for instance, the authors of the *Shiji* and *Hanshu*, the same term was written *xianyun* 獫狁. None of the Western Zhou sources mentions the name "Quanrong," which was in all likelihood a later expression. In two chapters, the "Zhengyu" and "Jinyu," of the *Guoyu*, "Western Rong" (*xirong* 西戎) is the term used to refer to the people who captured the Zhou capital along with Shen and Zeng, but another chapter, the "Zhouyu," mentions King Mu's campaign against the Quanrong 犬戎. In the *Current Bamboo Annals*, the terms *xirong* and *quanrong* are used interchangeably, both referring to the same people.[1] Finally, in his narrative history of the fall of the Western Zhou in the *Shiji*, Sima Qian created the term *xiyi quanrong* 西夷犬戎, apparently a combination of the terms *xirong* and *quanrong* used in different chapters of the *Guoyu*.[2] Thus, we can conclude first that Quanrong was also called the "Western Rong," and this was mainly because the Quanrong communities were located to the west of Zhou.

All of these sources in which the term *quanrong* is used were composed centuries later than the Western Zhou. This seems to suggest that *quanrong*

---

[1] For instance, under King You's ninth year, it mentions Shen's solicitation of Zeng and the Western Rong, and under King You's eleventh year, it mentions the attack on Zongzhou by the joint forces of Shen, Zeng, and Quanrong; see *Zhushu jinian*, 2, p. 17 (Legge, *The Shoo King*, Prolegomena, pp. 157–58).

[2] See *Shiji*, 4, p. 149 (Nienhauser, *The Grand Scribe's Records*, 1, p. 74). In the "Basic Annals of Qin," Sima Qian uses the term "*xirong quanrong*" 西戎犬戎; see *Shiji*, 5, p. 179 (Nienhauser, *The Grand Scribe's Records*, 1, p. 90).

was a term created in a later historical context and projected back onto an earlier people.[3] For this reason, Wang Guowei wrote:[4]

The Xunyu 薰育 or Xianyun 玁狁 of ancient times were all named Quanrong 犬戎 by the later people. Therefore, the Quanrong who had attacked King You and destroyed Zongzhou must have been the Xianyun of the time of King Xuan. Otherwise, the Xianyun who in the time between King Yih and King Xuan were still causing trouble would have had to disappear completely as soon as King You succeeded, and those who then destroyed Zongzhou would have had to be another ethnic group. This must be unreliable according to logic.

This equation between the Quanrong (or Western Rong) and the Xianyun has been accepted by many scholars.[5] In fact, the recently discovered Forty-Second Year Lai *ding* 四十二年逨鼎 has filled the chronological gap between the Xianyun and the Quanrong because it records that the Xianyun were invaders of Zhou until the final years of King Xuan.[6] However, Wang's argument is essentially deductive, and he did not provide solid evidence for such identification. I believe that there are at least three pieces of textual evidence that suggest a direct link between the Xianyun and the Quanrong. The first is found in the poem "Chuche" 出車 (Mao 168) in the *Book of Poetry* (Waley's translation):[7]

1	王命南仲,	The king has ordered Nanzhong
2	往城于方	To go and build a fort on the frontier.
3	出車彭彭,	To bring out the great concourse of chariots,
4	旗旐央央。	With dragon banners and standards so bright.
5	天子命我,	The Son of Heaven has ordered us
6	城彼朔方。	To build a fort on that frontier.
7	赫赫南仲,	Terrible is Nanzhong;
8	玁狁于襄。	The Xianyun are undone.
9	昔我往矣,	Long ago, when we started,
10	黍稷方華。	The wine-millet and cooking-millet were in flower.

[3] Průšek suggested that Quanrong can be identified with Quanhou 犬侯 in the Shang oracle-bone inscriptions. In his view, Quanrong and Xianyun were two different peoples: Quanrong were an indigenous people located at the edges of Shang and Zhou, while the Xianyun were a nomadic people who suddenly arrived on the borders of Zhou from Central Asia, historically inhabited by the Scythians; see Průšek, *Chinese Statelets*, pp. 19, 42–46, 130–35. Whether or not Quanrong can be identified with the Quanhou in the Shang inscriptions is a complex question. Ding Shan argues that the Quanhou mentioned in the Shang inscriptions was the ruler of an inner state of Shang but was not the chief of a people on the border, which was usually referred to as *fang*; therefore, the Quanhou of Shang had nothing to do with the later Quanrong. Furthermore, Ding Shan located this Quanhou at Quanqiu 犬邱 in eastern Henan, which is mentioned in the *Zuozhuan* (first year of Duke Xiang); see Ding Shan, *Jiaguwen suojian shizu*, pp. 116–17. As noted in chapter 3, a number of scholars have already rejected Průšek's misconceptions regarding the origins and war techniques of the Xianyun.

[4] See Wang Guowei, "Guifang Kunyi Xianyun kao," p. 382.

[5] See Meng Wentong, "Quanrong dongqin kao," pp. 1–2; Gu Jiegang, "Cong guji zhong tansuo woguo de xibu minzu-qiangzu," p. 126; and most recently, in English, Shaughnessy, "Western Zhou History," p. 350.

[6] For the Forty-Second Year Lai *ding*, see *Wenwu* 2003.6, 6–19.

[7] See *Shijing*, 9.4, pp. 415–16 (Waley, *The Book of Songs*, pp. 141–42).

11	今我來思，	Now that we are on the march again
12	雨雪載塗。	Snow falls upon the mire.
13	王事多難，	The king's service brings many hardships.
14	不遑啟居。	We have no time to rest or bide.
15	豈不懷歸	We do indeed long to return;
16	畏此簡書。	But we fear the writing on the strips.

17	喓喓草蟲，	"Dolefully cry the cicadas,
18	趯趯阜螽。	Hop and skip go the grasshoppers.
19	未見君子，	Before I saw my lord
20	憂心忡忡。	My heart was full of grief.
21	既見君子，	But now that I have seen my lord
22	我心則降。	My heart is still."
23	赫赫南仲，	Terrible is Nanzhong;
24	薄伐西戎。	Lo, he has stricken the Western Rong![8]

25	春日遲遲，	The spring days are drawn out;
26	卉木萋萋。	All plants and trees are in leaf
27	倉庚喈喈，	Tuneful is the oriole's song.
28	采蘩祁祁。	The women gather aster in crowds.
29	執訊獲醜，	We have bound the culprits; we have captured the chieftains,
30	薄言還歸。	And here we are home again!
31	赫赫南仲，	Terrible is Nanzhong;
32	獫狁于夷。	The Xianyun are leveled low.

In this poem, the term *xirong* is used as an alternative name for *xianyun*. After mentioning for the first time that Nanzhong defeated the Xianyun, the poet went on to say that Nanzhong attacked the Western Rong, and concluded by saying that the Xianyun were pacified. The context of this poem suggests that *xirong*, or the "Western Rong," was just another term for the Xianyun; or it is possible that "Xianyun" was a generic term referring to the widely distributed society of the Xianyun sharing the same cultural features and probably also the same ethnic origin, while *xirong* referred in particular to those Xianyun who were located to the west of Zhou. This identification of the Western Rong with the Xianyun is further supported by evidence in the bronze inscriptions: (1) in the Duoyou *ding* (JC: 2835) and the Buqi *gui* (JC: 4328), while the term "Xianyun" appears at the beginning of the two inscriptions, through the rest of the inscriptions the Xianyun are simply referred to as "Rong," the "war-like foreigners"; (2) both inscriptions mention that Zhou troops were sent to the west to attack the Xianyun, or pursued the Xianyun all the way to the west. Therefore, there is no reason to doubt that the Xianyun could have been conventionally called the "Western Rong" during the Western Zhou dynasty.

---

[8] Waley has "Warriors of the West" for *xirong* 西戎.

The second piece of evidence concerns the geographical location of the two. Both the *Guoyu* and the *Bamboo Annals* mention King Mu's campaign against the Quanrong. The *Ancient Bamboo Annals* then mentions that after the campaign King Mu brought the five kings of Quanrong back to the east and relocated them at Taiyuan 太原. It is clear from the discussion of the history of the Zhou–Xianyun war in chapter 3 that Taiyuan was an important base of Xianyun power. During the battle of 823 BC, according to the poem "Liuyue" and the *Current Bamboo Annals*, the royal army led by Jifu chased the Xianyun all the way back to Taiyuan.[9] This suggests a direct link between the Quanrong and the Xianyun in their geographical locations.

The third piece of evidence indicates that "Xianyun" and "Quanrong" are closely related in meaning. The character *xian* 獫 appears in the poem "Sitie" 駟驖 (Mao 127) of the *Book of Poetry*, and refers to a certain kind of hunting dog.[10] Two texts give exegeses for the word *xian*: the *Erya* says that it is a kind of dog with a long snout,[11] while the *Shuowen jiezi*, adding to the same explanation, says that it also refers to a black dog with a yellow face.[12] It is very probable that when the term Xianyun came to be written with the two characters *xianyun* 獫狁, the notion of "dog" associated with the character *xian* thus gave rise to the term Quanrong 犬戎, or the "Dog Barbarians."

Here I believe that we have an interesting case where the Chinese characters that were used to transcribe the sound of a foreign name gave new meaning to it, and this new meaning then became the basis for the creation of new terms that are totally detached from the original sound of the foreign name. In conclusion, the term *quanrong* in the later texts refers to the same people who are referred to as Xianyun in the Western Zhou sources. In these sources, the Xianyun are also simply called "Rong" or the "Western Rong" because they were located to the northwest of Zhou. But the term "Rong" had a much broader meaning. It certainly was not restricted to the Xianyun or the Quanrong, but could be used for other hostile societies beyond the frontiers of the Western Zhou state.

---

[9] See *Zhushu jinian*, 2, p. 14 (Legge, *The Shoo King*, Prolegomena, p. 155).
[10] See Zhu Xi, *Shi ji zhuan*, p. 75.   [11] See *Erya*, 10, p. 2653.   [12] See *Shuowen jiezi*, p. 204.

APPENDIX 3

The Bamboo Annals *and issues of the chronology of King You's reign*

In order to understand the fall of the Western Zhou, it is important first to establish a reliable chronology of events that happened in the eleven years of the reign of King You. This chronology will help us not only to understand the political changes at the Zhou court, but also to correlate them with the historical happenings in some of the regional polities. The most important chronological account of King You's reign is found in the *Current Bamboo Annals*. As already said in the introduction, after the text on the bamboo strips was excavated in AD 281 in northern Henan, its entries were quoted extensively by the medieval writers in their works, especially their commentaries on the transmitted texts. Since the *Current Bamboo Annals* was declared a fake by most Qing authorities, starting with Zhu Youzeng in late Qing, the fragmentary quotations were retrieved from the various texts and their commentaries to reconstruct what is supposed to be the "original text," the *Ancient Bamboo Annals*.[1] As far as the eleven years of King You's reign are concerned, there are a number of discrepancies between the *Current* and *Ancient* versions, discrepancies that have contributed in part to the reasoning accusing the *Current Bamboo Annals* of being a later forgery. The issue certainly concerns not only the political history of the last Western Zhou reign, but also the authenticity and historical reliability of this critical ancient text; therefore, a separate analysis is necessary here. However, it is impossible to explore the issue of authenticity of the *Current Bamboo Annals* here fully. For this the reader is advised to review the respected works by Nivison, Shaughnessy, and Pankenier, already noted in the introduction. While the purpose here is to clarify the chronological issues concerning the political history of the late Western Zhou, I hope nevertheless that the analysis may add in some way to the weight of our evidence for the authenticity of the *Current Bamboo Annals*.

The main historical events of the eleven years, as shown in Table 2, largely follow the sequence given in the *Current Bamboo Annals* entries for King You. Wherever the *Current Bamboo Annals* differs from the *Ancient Bamboo Annals* or from other sources, the difference is marked with a question mark. There are three major discrepancies in this chronological

[1] For a textual history of the *Bamboo Annals*, see Loewe, *Early Chinese Texts*, pp. 39–47.

Table 2 *Chronology of the reign of King You*

BC	Year of King You	Zhou court	Regional states or lineages
781	1	Spring, King You established; Minister Huangfu invested	(Jin) Prince Chou killed Shangshu
780	2	Three Rivers dry up; earthquake in Qishan; increased tax	(Jin) 1st year of Ruler Wen; (Jin) Ruler Wen and (Zheng) Duofu jointly attack Zeng; Duofu settles at the Hill of Zhengfu (?)
779	3	King You infatuated with Bao Si; winter, great lightning	Qin attack Western Rong; (Chen) Duke Yi dies
778	4	Summer, 6th month, fog	
777	5	Huangfu leaves the capital for Xiang; Prince Yijiu goes into exile at Western Shen (?)	(Qin) Duke Xiang marries sister of the King of Feng
776	6	Winter, 10th month, solar eclipse; Bo Shi attacks Rong of Liuji, defeated and killed (?)	Western Rong exterminate Gai; Rong surround Quanqiu, capture (Qin) Shifu
775	7		Guo exterminate Jiao
774	8	Bo Fu established as royal heir; Duke Huan of Zheng becomes Minister of the Multitudes	(Zheng) Duke Huan consults Shi Bo
773	9	Turmoil begins in Zhou court	Ruler of Shen sends envoys to Western Rong and Zeng; (Zheng) Duke Huan sends treasury to Guo and Kuai (?)
772	10	Spring, oath of alliance with regional rulers on Taishi Mountain; autumn, 9th month, peaches and apricots mature; royal army attacks Shen	
771	11	Spring, 1st month, corona on sun; Shen, Zeng, and Quanrong sack Zhou capital, kill King You, Duke Huan of Zheng, and Bo Fu, and capture Bao Si; Prince Yuchen established king at Xie	Prince Yijiu established king at Shen

table: (1) the date of Prince Yijiu's exile; (2) the date of the campaign led by Bo Shi against the Rong of Liuji 六濟; and (3) the date of the eastward migration of the state of Zheng.

Regarding the first question, the *Current Bamboo Annals* dates the exile of Prince Yijiu to the fifth year of King You (777 BC), two years after Bao Si came into favor with King You, and three years before Bo Fu was established as the royal heir.[2] However, in all three reconstructions of the *Ancient Bamboo Annals*, the exile of Prince Yijiu is placed under the seventh year of King You (774 BC), in the same year as the establishment of Bo Fu.[3] This later date is entirely based on a quote from the *Bamboo Annals* in Kong Yingda's commentary to the *Zuozhuan* (twenty-sixth year of Duke Zhao), which, the editors of the reconstructions think, suggests that the exile of Prince Yijiu and the establishment of Bo Fu were in the same year:[4]

汲冢書《紀年》云：平王奔西申，而立伯盤以爲太子，與幽王俱死于戲。先是，申侯、魯侯及許文公立平王于申。以本太子，故稱天王。幽王既死，而虢公翰又立王子余臣于攜，周二王並立。二十一年，攜王爲晉文公所殺。以本非適，故稱攜王。

The *Annals* among the books from the Ji tomb says: King Ping fled to Western Shen, then [the king] established Bo Pan (= Bo Fu) as the heir, who died together with King You at Xi. Before this, the Ruler of Shen, Ruler of Lu, and Duke Wen of Xu established King Ping at Shen. In accord with the fact that he was the legitimate heir, therefore [the text] calls [him] the Heavenly King. After King You died, then the Duke of Guo, Han, established Prince Yuchen at Xie, (so) Zhou had two kings reigning at the same time. Twenty-first year, the King of Xie was killed by Duke Wen of Jin. In accord with the fact that [he] was not the legitimate successor, therefore [the text] calls [him] King of Xie.

We are not here immediately concerned with the authenticity of the original *Bamboo Annals* that was excavated from the tomb, but with the way the text was quoted in ancient times and with how those quotations were then used to reconstruct what have been regarded as the authentic entries of the ancient text from the tomb. In other words, we are concerned with the current appearance of the *Ancient Bamboo Annals* as it has been reconstructed by the late Qing and modern scholars. What is generally problematic is that, owing to the lack of punctuation in ancient Chinese texts, it is not always clear whether the author was making a direct quotation (copying the original sentence word by word) of the text or an indirect quotation paraphrasing the original sentence in the text that he says he quotes from. Without deciding on this basic point, the accuracy of any reconstruction of ancient texts from quotations can be questionable. In this particular case regarding Prince Yijiu's exile, it is clear that Kong Yingda was not making

---

[2] See *Zhushu jinian*, 2, pp. 16–17 (Legge, *The Shoo King*, Prolegomena, p. 157).
[3] See Zhu Youzeng, *Jizhong jinian cunzhen* (Guiyanzhai, 1846), 2, p. 2; Wang Guowei, *Guben zhushu jinian jijiao*, in *Haining Wang Jing'an xiansheng yishu* (1936), p. 10; Fan Xiangyong, *Guben zhushu jinian*, p. 34.
[4] See *Zuozhuan*, 52, p. 2,114.

a direct quotation, and apparently he was quoting from entries that had to be located under different years. As has already been noted by Fan Xiangyong in his reconstruction of the text, it is highly probable that the "In accord with the fact that [he] was not the legitimate successor" (*yi ben fei shi* 以本非適) and "In accord with the fact that he was the legitimate heir" (*yi ben taizi* 以本太子) are the commentator's own words added to the quotations from the original text to explain the term "King of Xie" (*xie wang* 攜王) in the *Zuozhuan* text for which Kong's commentary was written.[5] Evidently, the context of this quotation does not firmly suggest that Prince Yijiu's exile and Bo Fu's establishment must have taken place in the same year. If, as the editors of the reconstructions of the *Ancient Bamboo Annals* think, the first sentence in the above paragraph written by Kong Yingda indicates that the two events happened in the same year, then by the same logic of reasoning it would also suggest that Bo Fu was established in the same year that he died together with his father King You at Xi, but this is clearly not the case. In short, there is really no ground to date the exile of Prince Yijiu to 774 BC; therefore, in the table I maintain the *Current* version's date of 777 BC for Prince Yijiu's exile.

The second question is the date of the campaign against the Rong of Liuji.[6] While the *Current Bamboo Annals* dates it to the sixth year of King You (776 BC), the producers of the reconstructions of the *Ancient* version place the event under the first or second year of Ruler Wen of Jin, which is the second or third year of King You (780/779 BC).[7] These dates are based on the following record in the *Houhan shu*:[8]

明年，（宣）王征申戎，破之。後十年，幽王命伯士伐六濟之戎，軍敗，伯士死焉。其年，戎圍犬丘，虜秦襄公之兄伯父。

Next year, King [Xuan] attacked the Shen Rong, and defeated them. Ten years later, King You commanded Bo Shi to attack the Rong of Liuji; the army was defeated and Bo Shi died there. In that year, the Rong surrounded Quanqiu and captured Bofu, the elder brother of Duke Xiang of Qin.

Since Li Xian's 李賢 commentary following the words *Boshi siyan* 伯士死焉 says that these events are all seen in the *Bamboo Annals*, the preceding phrases were retrieved as the original entries of the *Ancient Bamboo Annals*. The *Houhan shu* chronology was therefore taken as the original chronology of the *Ancient Bamboo Annals*, resulting in a systematic discrepancy of two years between the *Ancient* and the *Current* with regard to a number of events in the reign of King Xuan. According to this chronology, the

5 See Fan Xiangyong, *Guben zhushu jinian*, p. 34.
6 See *Zhushu jinian*, 2, p. 17 (Legge, *The Shoo King*, Prolegomena, p. 157).
7 Both Zhu Youzeng and Wang Guowei list it under the first year of Ruler Wen of Jin; see Zhu Youzeng, *Jizhong jinian*, 2, p. 1; Wang Guowei, *Guben zhushu jinian jijiao*, p. 10. Fan Xiangyong, on the other hand, suggests that a correct calculation of the years given in the *Houhan shu* should date it to the second year of Ruler Wen of Jin; see Fan Xiangyong, *Guben zhushu jinian*, p. 33.
8 See *Houhan shu*, 87, p. 2,872.

campaign took place forty-nine years after King Xuan's establishment, and was therefore dated to the second year of Ruler Wen of Jin (779 BC). I believe that the *Ancient* version (i.e. the *Houhan shu*) chronology is incorrect, while the *Current* chronology is correct for two reasons. First, the *Current* version dating seems to be supported by another independent source. The phrases in the *Houhan shu* reproduced above date the capture of Bofu 伯父 (= Shifu 世父) of Qin to the same year as the campaign against the Rong of Liuji. According to the "Basic Annals of Qin" of the *Shiji*, this happened in the second year of Duke Xiang of Qin (776 BC), consistent with the *Current* version dating of the campaign in question.[9] Second, there is indeed another entry in the *Current* version under the same year as the campaign against the Rong of Liuji, the sixth year of King You: the Western Rong exterminated Gai 蓋. Wang Guowei insightfully suggested that the character *gai* 蓋 is a mistranscription of the two characters *quanqiu* 犬丘 combined.[10] So, this entry actually records the same event – the capture of Bofu; again, the *Shiji* agrees with the *Current* version. I think this demonstrates that Fan Ye, author of the *Houhan shu*, did actually see the tomb version of the *Bamboo Annals*, so he dated the campaign against the Rong of Liuji and the capture of Shifu to the same year; but clearly he miscalculated the number of years.[11] This will cast doubt on the *Ancient* version's chronology for the entire period of King Xuan based on the *Houhan shu*, but this is an important question that should be discussed elsewhere.[12]

The third question is a more difficult one. The entry in the *Ancient Bamboo Annals* that mentions the move of the state of Zheng to the east was retrieved from the *Shuijing zhu*, saying:[13]

晉文侯二年，同惠王子多父伐鄶，克之。乃居鄭父之丘，名之曰鄭，是曰桓公。

In his second year, Ruler Wen of Jin and the son of King Hui (Li), Duofu, attacked Kuai and defeated it. Therefore [he] settled at the Hill of Zhengfu, and named it Zheng, and [he] was called Duke Huan.

The *Current Bamboo Annals* says:[14]

(幽王二年) 晉文侯同王子多父伐鄶，克之。乃居鄭父之丘，是為鄭桓公。

---

[9] See *Shiji*, 5, p. 179 (Nienhauser, *The Grand Scribe's Records*, 1, p. 90).

[10] See Wang Guowei, *Jinben zhushu jinian shuzheng*, in *Haining Wang Jing'an xiansheng yishu* (1936), 2, p. 15.

[11] It should be noted that the year notation "X-years later" for all of these events in the *Houhan shu* is clearly different from the way the events are dated in the original tomb version of the *Bamboo Annals*. There was a transformation from the dating system of the original *Bamboo Annals* to that of the *Houhan shu*, which is likely to have resulted in miscalculations.

[12] More importantly, this demonstrates the validity of the *Current* chronology or of the *Current Bamboo Annals* in general. The character *gai* 蓋 in the *Current* version, though a mistranscription, also shows the reliability of the *Current Bamboo Annals*. Below, with regard to the date of the eastward migration of the state of Zheng, I will demonstrate that while the authentic character *zeng* 鄫 is maintained by the *Current* version, the character is miswritten *kuai* 鄶 in the *Ancient* version.

[13] See *Shuijing zhu*, p. 703; Fan Xiangyong, *Guben zhushi jinian*, p. 33.

[14] See *Zhushu jinian*, 2, p. 16 (Legge, *The Shoo King*, Prolegomena, p. 157).

In the second year of King You, Ruler Wen of Jin and Prince Duofu attacked Zeng and defeated it. Therefore [he] settled at the Hill of Zhengfu, and [he] was called Duke Huan of Zheng.

There are three discrepancies between the two versions of the *Bamboo Annals*. Hui Wang 惠王 in the *Shuijing zhu* quotation of the *Bamboo Annals* is clearly a misquote of Li Wang 厲王. While the state attacked is Kuai 鄶 in the *Shuijing zhu* version, it is Zeng 鄫 in the *Current* version of the *Bamboo Annals*. On this last point, most previous scholars have taken a wrong approach to consider Zeng to be a miswriting of Kuai, since the two characters are very similar. Since Kuai is traditionally known to have been located close to Eastern Guo in the eastern plain and both states were annexed by Zheng to form its new base, the *Shuijing zhu* quote would suggest that an attack on Kuai in the eastern plain was launched by the state of Zheng in 779 BC, eight years before the fall of the Western Zhou. But in the *Current Bamboo Annals*, since the attacked state was Zeng, it does not require such a Zheng campaign to the east. There is also a discrepancy between the second year of Ruler Wen (779 BC) in the *Shuijing zhu* version of the *Bamboo Annals* and the second year of King You (780 BC) in the *Current* version.

However, the date 779 BC as suggested by the *Shuijing zhu* quote for Zheng's attack on the east and the subsequent occupation of the "Hill of Zhengfu," thereby founding the state of Zheng, clearly contradicts a much later date (773/2 BC) for Zheng's eastward migration that is suggested by the "Zhengyu" chapter of the *Guoyu* and the "Genealogical Account of Zheng" in the *Shiji*. The *Guoyu* says:[15]

（鄭）桓公為司徒，甚得周眾及東土之人，問于史伯曰：「王室多故，余懼及焉，其何所以逃死？」史伯對曰 … 公悅，乃寄帑與賄，虢、鄶受之，十邑皆有寄地。

Duke Huan (of Zheng) was the Minister of the Multitudes, greatly winning the support of the people of Zhou and of the eastern lands. [He] asked Shi Bo: "The royal house is having much trouble, and I am afraid of being caught [in the trouble], so what should I do to avoid death?" Shi Bo answered... The duke was thus pleased, and therefore sent [his] treasury and wealth east, and the states of Guo and Kuai received them. In ten settlements there were places entrusted.

Clearly, the migration of Zheng took place after Duke Huan became a minister in the Zhou court, which in fact, I believe, empowered him to impose his personal interests on the two small regional states in the eastern plain. Three sources, the *Guoyu*, the *Current Bamboo Annals*, and the "Genealogical Account of Zheng" in the *Shiji*, unanimously date Duke Huan's appointment as Minister of the Multitudes to the eighth year of King You (774 BC).[16] The "Genealogical Account of Zheng" also mentions that Zheng moved its people to the east of Luoyang, and the states of Guo

[15] See *Guoyu*, 16, pp. 507–23.   [16] See *Guoyu*, 16, p. 524; *Zhushu jinian*, 2, p. 17; *Shiji*, 42, p. 1,757.

and Kuai yielded ten settlements for Zheng to relocate its population in the east.[17] This will certainly date the eastward migration of Zheng sometime after 774 BC and before the fall of the dynasty in 771 BC.

This later date is further supported by another tradition, the commentary on the "Geographical Records" chapter of the *Hanshu* quoting Xue Zan 薛瓚 of the third century:[18]

初，桓公為周司徒，王室將亂，故謀于史伯而寄帑與賄于虢、鄶間。幽王既敗，二年而滅鄶，四年而滅虢，居于鄭父之丘，是以爲鄭桓公。

Earlier, Duke Huan was the Minister of the Multitudes of Zhou; when the royal house was going to be disordered, he consulted with Shi Bo and then sent [his] treasury and wealth to Guo and Kuai. After King You was defeated, in the second year [he] exterminated Kuai, and in the fourth year [he] exterminated Guo, and then settled on the Hill of Zhengfu, and he was called Duke Huan of Zheng.

Since both this passage and the *Current Bamboo Annals* date the extermination of Eastern Guo to the fourth year of King Ping (767 BC), this would date Zheng's attack on Kuai to the second year of King Ping (769 BC). This appears to suggest that we may need to move the entry under the second year of King You in the *Current Bamboo Annals* down to King Ping's second year, but by doing so we would then create a new conflict with other entries in the *Current* version and *Shiji*, because both texts say that Duke Huan was killed together with King You in 771 BC. But I believe that we have a much better solution than this.

Our sources suggest that a campaign carried out by Zheng against another state in the eastern plain could not have taken place before Duke Huan became the Minister of the Multitudes in the Zhou court. And if indeed Kuai was exterminated by Zheng in 769 BC, the ruler of Zheng who achieved this would not be Duke Huan but his son, Duke Wu of Zheng. In this regard, another quotation from Ying Zhao 應昭 also included in the commentary to the "Geographical Records" seems to explain the situation:

國語曰：鄭桓公為司徒，王室將亂，寄帑與賄于虢、鄶間。幽王敗，威公死之。其子武公與平王東遷洛陽，遂伐虢、鄶而並其地，而邑於此。

The *Guoyu* says: Duke Huan of Zheng was the Minister of the Multitudes, and when the royal house was going to be disordered, he sent treasury and wealth to the area between Guo and Kuai. When King You was defeated, Duke Wei (= Huan) died with him. His son Duke Wu together with King Ping moved to Luoyang, and then he attacked Guo and Kuai and annexed their land, on which he settled.

The eastward migration of Zheng has been discussed in chapter 5 (see pp. 248–50); it suffices here to conclude, from the foregoing analysis, that in the ninth or tenth year of King You (773/2 BC), Duke Huan sent the treasury of Zheng east to the states of Eastern Guo and Kuai, and then in the second and fourth years of King Ping (769 and 767 BC), respectively,

---

[17] See *Shiji*, 42, pp. 1,757–58. [18] See *Hanshu*, 28, p. 1,544.

his son Duke Wu attacked the two states and formally reestablished Zheng on the conquered territory.

How do we then explain the record in the *Current Bamboo Annals* that suggests an attack on Zeng by Zheng in 780 BC? I think the explanation is clear: it is that the *Shuijing zhu* misquoted "Zeng" 鄫 in the tomb version of the *Bamboo Annals* as "Kuai" 鄶, not that the *Current* version miswrote "Kuai" as "Zeng." The *Shuijing zhu* also misquoted Li Wang 厲土 as Hui Wang 惠土, indicating the inaccuracy of the *Shuijing zhu* quote in general. There are two pieces of internal evidence from the *Current Bamboo Annals* that suggest that the campaign recorded in the *Current* version under the second year of King You (or under the second year of Ruler Wen of Jin in the *Ancient* version) was a military operation conducted by the royal court *against the state of Zeng but not against Kuai*. First, under the eleventh year of King You, it is said that the state Zeng 鄫, written with the same character in the *Current Bamboo Annals*, joined the alliance of Shen and the Western Rong to attack the Zhou capital, and hence brought the Western Zhou dynasty to an end. This suggests that Zeng was an adversary of the Zhou court. Therefore, the character *zeng* 鄫 makes much better sense than *kuai* 鄶 (as in the *Ancient* version) in the context of the campaign of 780 BC that actually explains the position that Zeng took in the event of 771 BC. Second, if the campaign was one designed to pursue the ambition of Zheng, there would be no reason why Jin should have ever taken part in it. But if the campaign was carried out by the royal court with Prince Duofu 多父 (the later Duke Huan of Zheng) as commander, Jin's involvement is much easier to understand since the Jinhou Su *bianzhong* (JL: 35–50) indicates that a previous Ruler of Jin, Su, had also assisted the Zhou court in a military campaign in the east.

This analysis, I believe, again indicates that the *Current Bamboo Annals* has maintained the genuine features of the original tomb version of the *Bamboo Annals*. At the same time, it also demonstrates that the *Ancient Bamboo Annals*, in the long process of being quoted and then restored, was subject to serious distortions and subjective editing by later authors. Therefore, records in the three reconstructed *Ancient Bamboo Annals* must be used with great caution.

Bibliography

ANCIENT TEXTS

The Analects of Confucius, trans. Arthur Waley, New York: Vintage Books, 1938.

Erya 爾雅, in *Shisanjing zhushu* 十三經註疏, pp. 2,563–2,653, Beijing: Zhonghua, 1979.

Guliangzhuan 穀梁傳, in *Shisanjing zhushu* 十三經註疏, pp. 2,357–2,451, Beijing: Zhonghua, 1979.

Guoyu 國語, 2 vols., Shanghai: Shanghai guji, 1988.

Hanshu 漢書 (by Ban Gu 班固), 12 vols., Beijing: Zhonghua, 1962.

Houhan shu 後漢書 (by Fan Ye 范曄), 11 vols., Beijing: Zhonghua, 1964.

Liji 禮記, in *Shisanjing zhushu* 十三經註疏, pp. 1,221–1,696, Beijing: Zhonghua, 1979.

Lüshi chunqiu 呂氏春秋 (by Lü Buwei 呂不韋), in *Ershier zi* 二十二子, pp. 625–728, Shanghai: Shanghai guji, 1986.

Mencius, trans. David Hinton, Washington, DC: Counterpoint, 1998.

Mu tianzi zhuan 穆天子傳, in *Sibu congkan* 四部叢刊, Shanghai: Shangwu, 1920.

Sanguo zhi 三國志 (by Chen Shou 陳壽), 5 vols., Beijing: Zhonghua, 1959.

Shangshu 尚書, in *Shisanjing zhushu* 十三經註疏, pp. 113–258, Beijing: Zhonghua, 1979.

Shanhai jing 山海經, in *Ershier zi* 二十二子, pp. 1,334–87, Shanghai: Shanghai guji, 1986.

Shiji 史記 (by Sima Qian 司馬遷), 10 vols., Beijing: Zhonghua, 1959.

Shijing 詩經, in *Shisanjing zhushu* 十三經註疏, pp. 259–630, Beijing: Zhonghua, 1979.

Shuijing zhu jiao 水經注校 (by Li Daoyuan 酈道元; collated by Wang Guowei 王國維), Shanghai: Shanghai renmin, 1984.

Shuowen jiezi 說文解字 (by Xu Shen 許慎), Beijing: Zhonghua, 1963.

Taiping huanyu ji 太平寰宇記 (by Le Shi 樂史), Jingling shuju, 1882.

Taiping yulan 太平禦覽, Beijing: Zhonghua, 1963.

Tongdian 通典 (by Du You 杜佑), Beijing: Zhonghua, 1963.

Tongzhi 通志 (by Zheng Qiao 鄭樵), Shanghai: Shangwu, 1935.

Wenxuan 文選 (ed. Xiao Tong 蕭統), Kyoto: Chûbun, 1971.

Xiao erya 小爾雅 (by Kong Fu 孔鮒; commentary by Song Xian 宋咸), Shanghai: Shangwu, 1960.

Yi Zhoushu 逸周書, in *Sibu beiyao* 四部備要, Shanghai: Zhonghua, 1930.

Yuanhe junxian tuzhi 元和郡縣圖志 (by Li Jifu 李吉甫), 2 vols., Beijing: Zhonghua, 1983.

Zhouli 周禮, in *Shisanjing zhushu* 十三經註疏, pp. 631–943, Beijing: Zhonghua, 1979.

Zhouyi 周易, in *Shisanjing zhushu* 十三經註疏, pp. 1–108, Beijing: Zhonghua, 1979.

Zhushu jinian 竹書紀年, in *Sibu congkan* 四部叢刊, Shanghai: Shangwu, 1920.

Zizhi tongjian waiji 資治通鑒外記 (by Liu Shu 劉恕), Shanghai: Shangwu, 1929.

Zuozhuan 左傳, in *Shisanjing zhushu* 十三經註疏, pp. 1,697–2,188, Beijing: Zhonghua, 1979.

STUDIES AND ARCHAEOLOGICAL REPORTS

Ai, Yanding 艾延丁, "Shen guo zhi mi zhi wojian" 申國之謎之我見, *Zhongyuan wenwu* 中原文物 1987.3, 107–11.

Allan, Sarah, "Review: The Cambridge History of Ancient China: From the Origins of Civilization to 221 B.C.," *American Historical Review* 106.1 (2001), 144–45.

An, Weijun 安維峻, *Gansu xin tongzhi* 甘肅新通志, Lanzhou, 1909.

Bagley, Robert, "Shang Archaeology," in *The Cambridge History of Ancient China: From the Origins of Civilization to 221 B.C.*, ed. Michael Loewe and Edward L. Shaughnessy, pp. 124–231, Cambridge: Cambridge University Press, 1999.

Bai, Guangqi 白光琦, "Qingong hu yingwei Dong Zhou chuqi qi" 秦公壺應為東周初期器, *Kaogu yu wenwu* 考古與文物 1995.4, 71.

Baoji Yu guo mudi 寶鷄強國墓地 (Lu Liancheng 盧連成 and Hu Zhisheng 胡智生), Beijing: Wenwu, 1988.

Beijing kaogu sishi nian 北京考古四十年 (Beijing shi wenwu yanjiusuo 北京市文物研究所), Beijing: Yanshan, 1990.

Blakeley, Barry B., "Regional Aspects of Chinese Socio-Political Development in the Spring and Autumn Period (722–464 B.C.): Clan Power in a Segmentary State," unpublished PhD thesis, University of Michigan, 1970.

  "In Search of Danyang I: Historical Geography and Archaeological Site," *Early China* 13 (1988), 116–52.

  "On the Location of the Chu Capital in Early Chunqiu Times in Light of the Handong Incident of 701 B.C.," *Early China* 15 (1990), 49–70.

Brown, Elizabeth A. R., "The Tyranny of a Construct: Feudalism and Historians of Medieval Europe," *American Historical Review* 79.4 (1974), 1,063–88.

Cai, Yunzhang 蔡運章, "Lun Guozhong qiren" 論虢仲其人, *Huaxia kaogu* 華夏考古 1994.2, 86–89.

  "Guo Wengong mu kao" 虢文公墓考, *Huaxia kaogu* 1994.3, 42–45, 94.

Cen, Zhongmian 岑仲勉, *Zhongwai dili kaozheng* 中外地理考證, Hong Kong: Taiping, 1966.

Chai, Xiaoming 柴小明, "Huabei diqu Xi Zhou taoqi chulun" 華北地區西周陶器初論, in *Yan wenhua yanjiu lunwenji* 燕文化研究論文集, ed. Chen Guang 陳光, pp. 105–16, Beijing: Zhongguo shehui kexue, 1995.

Chambers, Mortimer (ed.), *The Fall of Rome: Can It Be Explained?* New York: Holt, Rinehart and Winston, 1970.

Chang, Kwang-chih, *Shang Civilization*, New Haven: Yale University Press, 1980.
  The Archaeology of Ancient China, 4th edition, New Haven: Yale University Press, 1986.

Chang, Kwang-chih, and Zhang Changshou, "Looking for City Shang of the Shang Dynasty in Shangqiu: A Brief Report of a Sino-American Team," *Symbols* (1998, Spring), 5–10.

Chang, Xingzhao 常興照, and Cheng Lei 程磊, "Shilun Laiyang Qian Heqian mudi ji youming taohe" 試論萊陽前河前墓地及有銘陶盉, *Beifang wenwu* 北方文物 1990.1, 20–25.

Chang'an Zhangjiapo Xi Zhou tongqi qun 長安張家坡西周銅器群 (Zhongguo kexueyuan kaogu yanjiusuo 中國科學院考古研究所), Beijing: Wenwu, 1965.

Chao, Fucun 晁福村, "Lun Pingwang dongqian" 論平王東遷, *Lishi yanjiu* 歷史研究
1991.6, 8–23.

Chen, Banghuai 陳邦懷, "Caobo Di gui kaoshi" 曹伯狄簋考釋, *Wenwu* 文物 1980.5,
27, 67.

Chen, Changyuan 陳昌遠, "Gu Xing guo shifeng diwang kaobian" 古邢國始
封地望考辯, *Zhongguo lishi dili luncong* 中國歷史地理論叢 1991.3, 235–42.
 "Xu guo shifeng diwang jiqi qianxi de lishi dili wenti" 許國始封地望及其遷徙的
歷史地理問題, *Zhongguo lishi dili luncong* 1993.4, 41–54.

Chen, Fengheng 陳逢衡, *Zhushu jinian jizhu* 竹書紀年集注, China: Yiluxuan, 1813.

Chen, Gongrou 陳公柔, "Ji Jifu hu Zha zhong jiqi tongchu de tongqi" 記幾
父壺柞鐘及其同出的銅器, *Kaogu* 1962.2, 88–101.
 "Xi Zhou jinwen zhong de Xinyi Chengzhou yu Wangcheng" 西周金文
中的新邑成周與王城, in *Qingzhu Su Binqi xiansheng kaogu wushiwu nian lunwenji* 慶祝蘇秉琦先生考古五十五年論文集, pp. 386–97, Beijing: Wenwu, 1989.

Chen, Huaiquan 陳懷荃, "Daxia yu Dayuan" 大夏與大原, *Zhongguo lishi dili luncong* 1993.1, 95–105.

Chen, Huan 陳奐, *Shi Maoshi zhuan shu* 詩毛氏傳疏, 3 vols., Beijing: Zhongguo
shudian, 1984 (reprint of Shufangzhai, 1851).

Chen, Li 陳力, "Jinben zhushu jinian yanjiu" 今本竹書紀年研究, *Sichuan daxue
xuebao congkan* 四川大學學報叢刊 28 (1985), 4–15.

Chen, Mengjia 陳夢家, *Xi Zhou niandai kao* 西周年代考, Shanghai: Shangwu, 1945.
 "Xi Zhou tongqi duandai I–VI" 西周銅器斷代, *Kaogu xuebao* 考古學報 9 (1955),
137–75; 10 (1955), 69–142; 1956.1, 65–114; 1956.2, 85–94; 1956.3, 105–278; 1956.4,
85–122.
 Yinxu buci zongshu 殷墟卜辭綜述, Beijing: Kexue, 1956.
 "Xi Zhou tongqi duandai" 西周銅器斷代, *Yanjing xuebao* 燕京學報 (new) 1 (1995),
235–89.

Chen, Pan 陳槃, *Chunqiu dashi biao lieguo juexing ji cunmie biao zhuanyi*
春秋大事表列國爵姓及存滅表譔異, Taipei: Academia Sinica, 1969.
 Bujian yu Chunqiu dashi biao zhi Chunqiu fangguo gao 不見於春秋大事表
之春秋方國稿, Taipei: Academia Sinica, 1970.

Chen, Ping 陳平, "Qiantan Lixian Qingong mudi yicun yu xiangguan wenti"
淺談禮縣秦公墓地遺存与相關問題, *Kaogu yu wenwu* 1998.5, 78–87.

Chen, Quanfang 陳全方, *Zhouyuan yu Zhou wenhua* 周原與周文化, Shanghai: Renmin, 1988.

Chen, Shou 陳壽 (Chen Gongrou and Zhang Changshou), "Taibao gui de fuchu
he Taibao zhuqi" 太保簋的復出和太保諸器, *Kaogu yu wenwu* 1980.4, 23–30.

Chen, Zhaorong 陳昭榮, "Tan xinchu Qingong hu de shidai" 談新出秦公壺的時代,
Kaogu yu wenwu 1995.4, 64–70.

Cheng, Faren 程發軔, *Chunqiu Zuoshi zhuan diming tukao* 春秋左氏傳地名圖考,
Taipei: Guangwen, 1967.

"China Unearthed Shang Oracle Bones Again, 104 Years after the First Discovery,"
People's Daily Online (http://english.peopledaily.com.cn), April 9, 2003.

Chinese Archaeology (Beijing) 4 (2004), 29–31, "Inscribed Oracle Bones of the Shang
Period Unearthed from the Daxinzhuang Site in Jinan City."

Cipolla, Carlo M. (ed.), *The Economic Decline of Empires*, London: Methuen, 1970.

Clarke, David, *Analytical Archaeology*, London: Methuen, 1968.

Cohen, David, "The Yueshi Culture, the Dongyi, and the Archaeology of Ethnicity in Early Bronze Age China," unpublished PhD thesis, Harvard University, 2001.

Cook, Constance, "Wealth and the Western Zhou," *Bulletin of the School of Oriental and African Studies* 60.2 (1997), 269–73.

Creel, Herrlee G., "Bronze Inscriptions of the Western Chou Dynasty as Historical Documents," *Journal of the American Oriental Society* 56 (1936), 335–49.

"The Beginnings of Bureaucracy in China: The Origins of the Hsien," *Journal of Asian Studies* 23.2 (1964), 155–83.

The Origins of Statecraft in China, vol. 1: The Western Chou Empire, Chicago: University of Chicago Press, 1970.

Cui, Lequan 崔樂泉, "Shandong diqu Dong Zhou kaoguxue wenhua de xulie" 山東地區東周考古學文化的序列, *Huaxia Kaogu* 華夏考古 1992.4, 73–97.

Cui, Shu 崔述, *Cui Dongbi yishu* 崔東壁遺書, ed. Gu Jiegang 顧頡剛, Shanghai: Shanghai guji, 1983.

Dai, Chunyang 戴春陽, "Gu Guazhou kaobian" 古瓜州考辯, *Xibei shidi* 西北史地 1989.11, 40–51.

Deng, Shoulin 鄧綏林, Liu Wenzhang 劉文彰 et al., *Hebei sheng dili* 河北省地理, Shijiazhuang: Hebei renmin, 1986.

Di Cosmo, Nicola, "Ancient Inner Asian Nomads: Their Economic Basis and Its Significance in Chinese History," *Journal of Asian Studies* 53.4 (1994), 1,092–1,126.

"The Northern Frontier in Pre-Imperial China," in *The Cambridge History of Ancient China: From the Origins of Civilization to 221 B.C.*, ed. Michael Loewe and Edward L. Shaughnessy, pp. 885–966, Cambridge: Cambridge University Press, 1999.

Ancient China and Its Enemies, Cambridge: Cambridge University Press, 2002.

Ding, Shan 丁山, "Shao Mugong zhuan" 召穆公傳, *Zhongyang yanjiuyuan lishi yuyan yanjiusuo jikan* 中央研究院歷史語言研究所集刊 2 (1930), 89–111.

Jiaguwen suojian shizu jiqi zhidu 甲骨文所見氏族及其制度, Beijing: Zhonghua, 1988.

Dong, Zuobin 董作賓, "Jiaguwen duandai yanjiu li" 甲骨文斷代研究例, in *Cai Yuanpei xiansheng liushi wu sui qingzhu lunwenji* 蔡元培先生六十五歲慶祝論文集 (Monograph of *Guoli zhongyang yanjiuyuan lishi yuyan yanjiusuo jikan* 國立中央研究院歷史語言研究所集刊), pp. 323–424, Beiping: Academia Sinica, 1933.

Du, Zhengsheng 杜正勝, "Zhou Qin minzu wenhua Rongdi xing de kaocha: Jianlun Guanzhong chutu de beifangshi qingtongqi" 周秦民族文化戎狄性的考察：簡論關中出土的北方式青銅器, *Dalu zazhi* 大陸雜誌 87.5 (1993), 1–25.

Duan, Lianqin 段連勤, "Guanyu Yizu de xiqian he Qinying de qiyuandi zushu wenti" 關於夷族的西遷和秦嬴的起源地族屬問題, in *Xianqin shi lunji* 先秦史論集 (Monograph of *Renwen zazhi* 人文雜誌), pp. 166–75, Xi'an, 1982.

Duan, Yucai 段玉裁, *Shuowen jiezi zhu* 說文解字注, Shanghai: Shanghai guji, 1981 (punctuated reprint of 1815 edition).

East, W. Gordon, *The Geography behind History*, New York: W. W. Norton, 1965.

Falkenhausen, Lothar von (see also Luo Tai 羅泰), "Issues in Western Zhou Studies: A Review Article," *Early China* 18 (1993), 139–226.

Suspended Music: Chime-Bells in the Culture of Bronze Age China, Berkeley: University of California Press, 1993.

"The Regionalist Paradigm in Chinese Archaeology," in *Nationalism, Politics, and the Practice of Archaeology*, ed. Phillip L. Kohl and Clare Fawcett, pp. 198–217, Cambridge: Cambridge University Press, 1995.

"The Waning of the Bronze Age," in *The Cambridge History of Ancient China: From the Origins of Civilization to 221 B.C.*, ed. Michael Loewe and Edward L. Shaughnessy, pp. 292–351, Cambridge: Cambridge University Press, 1999.

"Late Western Zhou Taste," *Études Chinoises* 18 (1999), 143–78.

"The Chengdu Plain in the Early First Millennium BC: Zhuwajie," in *Ancient Sichuan: Treasures from a Lost Civilization*, ed. Robert Bagley, pp. 177–88, Princeton: Princeton University Press, 2001.

Fan, Shifeng 樊士鋒, and Hong Liangji 洪亮吉, *Changwu xian zhi* 長武縣誌, 1783.

Fan, Xiangyong 范祥雍, *Guben Zhushu jinian jijiao dingbu* 古本竹書紀年輯校訂補, Shanghai: Xinzhishi, 1956.

Fang, Shanzhu 方善柱, "Xi Zhou niandai xue shang de jige wenti" 西周年代學上的幾個問題, *Dalu zazhi* 51.1 (1975), 15–23.

Fengxi fajue baogao 灃西發掘報告 (Zhongguo kexueyuan kaogu yanjiusuo 中國科學院考古研究所), Beijing: Wenwu, 1962.

Ferrill, Arther, *The Fall of the Roman Empire: The Military Explanation*, London: Thames and Hudson, 1986; reprint, 1994.

Finley, M. I., "Archaeology and History," *Daedalus* 100.1 (1971), 168–86.

Fu, Sinian 傅斯年, "Dadong xiaodong shuo" 大束小束說, in *Fu Mengzhen xiansheng ji* 傅孟真先生集, pp. 1–17, Taipei: Taiwan daxue, 1952.

Fufeng Qijiacun qingtongqi qun 扶風齊家村青銅器群 (Shaanxi sheng bowuguan 陝西省博物館), Beijing: Wenwu, 1963.

Gao, Heng 高亨, "Zhou dai dizu zhidu kao" 周代地租制度考, *Wenshizhe* 文史哲 1956.10, 42–57.

Gao, Hongjin 高鴻縉, "Guoji Zibai pan kaoshi" 虢季子白盤考釋, *Dalu zazhi* 2.2 (1951), 7–9.

Gao, Jingming 高景明, "Sichou zhi lu Chang'an – Longzhou dao" 絲綢之路長安 – 隴州道, *Wenbo* 文博 1988.6, 46–50.

Gao, Shiqi 高士奇, *Chunqiu diming kaolue* 春秋地名考略, Qingyingtang, 1688.

Gao, Zhixi 高至喜, "Lun Hunan chutu de Xi Zhou tongqi" 論湖南出土的西周銅器, *Jianghan kaogu* 江漢考古 1984.3, 59–66.

Green, D. Brooks (ed.), *Historical Geography: A Methodological Portrayal*, Savage, MD: Rowman and Littlefield, 1991.

Gu, Jiegang 顧頡剛, *Shilin zashi* 史林雜識, Beijing: Zhonghua, 1963.

"Cong guji zhong tansuo woguo de xibu minzu – qiangzu" 從古籍中探索我國的西北民族 – 羌族, *Shehui kexue zhanxian* 社會科學戰綫 1980.1, 117–52.

Gu, Tiefu 顧鐵符, "Xinyang yihao Chu mu de diwang yu renwu" 信陽一號楚墓的地望与人物, *Gugong bowuyuan yuankan* 故宮博物院院刊 1979.2, 76–84.

Gu, Zuyu 顧祖禹, *Dushi fangyu jiyao* 讀史方輿紀要, Taipei: Letian, 1973 (first complete edition, 1811).

Gugong tongqi tulu 故宮銅器圖錄 2 vols. (Guoli gugong zhongyan bowuyuan lianhe guanlichu 國立故宮中央博物院聯合管理處), Taipei: Palace Museum, 1958.

Guo, Baojun 郭寶鈞, *Shang Zhou tongqiqun zonghe yanjiu* 商周銅器群綜合研究, Beijing: Wenwu, 1981.

Guo, Moruo 郭沫若, "Li qi ming kaoshi" 盠器銘考釋, *Kaogu xuebao* 1957.2, 1–6.

"Sanmenxia chutu tongqi er san shi" 三門峽出土銅器二三事, *Wenwu* 1959.1, 13–15.

Liang Zhou jinwen ci daxi tulu kaoshi 兩周金文辭大係圖錄考釋, 8 vols., Beijing: Kexue, 1958 (1st edition, Tokyo: Bunkyūdō, 1932).

"Shi Ying Jian yan" 釋應監甗, *Kaogu xuebao* 1960.1, 7–8.

(ed.), *Zhongguo shigao* 中國史稿, Beijing: Renmin, 1976.

Haidai kaogu 海岱考古 1 (1989), 292–312, "Shandong Changle xian Shang Zhou wenhua yizhi diaocha" 山東昌樂縣商周文化遺址調查.

1 (1989), 314–19, "Shandong Huangxian Dongying Zhoujiacun Xi Zhou canmu qingli jianbao" 山東黃縣束營周家村西周殘墓清理簡報.

Han, Wei 韓偉, "Guanyu Qinren zushu ji wenhua yuanyuan guanjian" 關於秦人族屬及文化淵源管見, *Wenwu* 1986.4, 23–27.

"Lun Gansu Lixian chutu de Qin jinbo shipian" 論甘肅禮縣出土的秦金箔飾片, *Wenwu* 1995.6, 4–11.

Hao, Tiechuan 郝鉄川, "Xi Zhou de guoren yu Zhi zhi luan" 西周的國人與彘之亂, *Henan shida xuebao* 河南師大學報 1984.1, 39–42.

He, Fan 何凡, "Guoren baodong xingzhi bianxi" 國人暴動性質辨析, *Renwen zazhi* 人文雜誌 1983.5, 76–77.

He, Guangyue 何光岳, "Qun Shu yu Yan xing zhuguo de laiyuan he fenbu" 群舒與偃姓諸國的來源和分佈, *Jiang Huai luntan* 江淮論壇 1982.6, 75–80.

He, Hao 何浩, "Xishen Dongshen he Nanshen" 西申束申和南申, *Shixue yuekan* 史學月刊 1988.5, 5–8.

Heckel, Waldemar, and J. C. Yardley, *Alexander the Great: Historical Texts in Translation*, Malden, MA: Blackwell, 2004.

Henan kaogu sishi nian 河南考古四十年 (Henan sheng wenwu yanjiusuo 河南省文物研究所), Zhengzhou: Henan renmin, 1994.

Henan sheng zhi: Quyu jianzhi zhi, dimao shanhe zhi 河南省志: 區域建置志, 山川地貌志 (Henan sheng difang zhi bianji weiyuanhui 河南省地方誌編輯委員會), Zhengzhou: Henan renmin, 1994.

Henan sheng zhi: wenwu zhi 河南省志: 文物志 (Henan sheng difang zhi bianji weiyuanhui 河南省地方誌編輯委員會), Zhengzhou: Henan renmin, 1994.

Higuchi, Takayasu 樋口隆康, "Kaku koku dōki kō" 虢國銅器考, *Tōhōgaku* 東方學 20 (1960), 1–21.

Hodder, Ian, "Simple Correlation between Material Culture and Society: A Review," in *The Spatial Organization of Culture*, pp. 3–24, Pittsburgh: University of Pittsburgh Press, 1978.

Hsu, Cho-yun, and Katheryn M. Linduff, *Western Chou Civilization*, New Haven: Yale University Press, 1988.

Hsu, Kenneth J. "Did the Xinjiang Indo-Europeans Leave Their Home because of Global Cooling," in *The Bronze Age and Early Iron Age Peoples of Eastern Central Asia*, vol. 2, ed. Victor Mai, pp. 686-90, Washington, DC: The Institute for the Study of Man, 1998.

Hu, Qianying 胡謙盈, "Lun Siwa wenhua" 論寺洼文化, *Wenwu jikan* 文物集刊 2 (1980), 118–24.

"Feng Hao kaogu gongzuo sanshi nian (1951–1981) de huigu" 豐鎬考古工作三十年 (1951–1981) 的回顧, *Wenwu* 1982.10, 57–67.

"Ji Zhou zushu ji wenhua yuanyuan" 姬周族屬及文化淵源, in *Yazhou wenmin luncong* 亞洲文明論叢, pp. 59–72, Chengdu: Sichuan renmin, 1986.

"Shitan Xian Zhou wenhua jiqi xiangguan wenti" 試談先周文化及其相關問題, in *Hu Qianying Zhou wenhua kaogu yanjiu xuanji* 胡謙盈周文化考古研究選集, pp. 124-38, Chengdu: Sichuan daxue, 2000.

"Nanbin Nianzipo xian Zhou wenhua juzhuzhi he muzang fajue de xueshu yiyi" 南關碾子坡先周文化居住址和墓葬發掘的學術意義, in *Zhou Qin wenhua yanjiu* 周秦文化研究, pp. 153–62, Xi'an: Shaanxi renmin, 1998.

Hu, Wei 胡渭, *Yugong zhui zhi* 禹貢錐指, in *Huang Qing jingjie* 皇清經解, vols. 8–15, Guangzhou: Xuehaitang, 1829.

Hu, Zhixiang 胡志祥, "Xi Zhou dui Huaiyi zhengce chutan" 西周對淮夷政策初探, *Huadong shifan daxue xuebao* 華東師範大學學報 1989.1, 84–89.

Huang, Rucheng 黃汝成, *Ri zhi lu jishi* 日知錄集釋, Changsha: Yuelu shushe, 1994.

Huang, Shengzhang 黃盛璋, "Jufu xu gai mingwen yanjiu" 駒父盨蓋銘文研究, *Kaogu yu wenwu* 1983.4, 52–55.

"Tongqi mingwen Yi Yu Ze de diwang jiqi yu Wu guo de guanxi" 銅器銘文宜虞矢的地望與吳國的關係, *Kaogu xuebao* 1983.3, 295–305.

"Duoyou ding de lishi yu dili wenti" 多友鼎的歷史与地理問題, in *Guwenzi lunji* 古文字論集 (*Kaogu yu wenwu congkan* 考古与文物叢刊2), pp. 12–20, Xi'an, 1983.

Huaxia kaogu 華夏考古 1988.1, 30–44, "Pingdingshan shi Beizhicun liang Zhou mudi yihao mu fajue jianbao" 平頂山市北滍村兩周墓地一號墓發掘簡報.

1992.3, 92–103, "Pingdingshan Ying guo mudi jiushiwu hao mu de fajue" 平頂山應國墓地九十五號墓的發掘.

1992.3, 104–13, "Sanmenxia Shangcunling Guo guo mudi M2001 fajue jianbao" 三門峽上村嶺虢國墓地M2001發掘簡報.

Hui, Dong 惠棟, *Chunqiu Zuozhuan buzhu* 春秋左傳補注, in *Huang Qing jingjie* 皇清經解, *juan*: 353–58, Guangzhou: Xuehaitang, 1829.

Iijima, Taketsugu 飯島武次, *Chūgoku Shū bunka kōkogaku kenkyū* 中國周文化考古學研究, Tokyo: Dōseisha, 1998.

Itō, Michiharu 伊藤道治, *Chūgoku kodai ōchō no keisei* 中國古代王朝の形成, Tokyo: Sōbunsha, 1975.

"Kyūei shoki kō – Sei Shū ki tochi shoyū keitai ni kansuru shiken" 裘衛諸器考 – 西周期土地所有形態に關する私見, *Tōyōshi kenkyū* 37.1 (1978), 35–58.

Chūgoku kodai kokka no shihai kōzō 中國古代王朝の支配構造, Tokyo: Chūō kōronsha, 1987.

Jackson, John Brinckerhoff, *Discovering the Vernacular Landscape*, New Haven: Yale University Press, 1984.

Ji, Naijun 姬乃軍, *Yan'an shihua* 延安史話, Beijing: Jiaoyu kexue, 1988.

Jia, Jinbiao 賈金標, Ren Yashan 任亞珊, *et al.*, "Xingtai diqu Xi Zhou taoqi de chubu yanjiu" 邢臺地區西周陶器的初步研究, in *Sandai wenming yanjiu* 三代文明研究, pp. 65–75, Beijing: Kexue, 1999.

Jian, Bozan 翦伯贊, *Qin Han shi* 秦漢史, Beijing: Beijing daxue, 1983.

Jiang, Tao 姜濤, "Guo guo mudi fajue jishi" 虢國墓地發掘紀實, *Wenwu tiandi* 文物天地 1992.1, 9–12.

Jiang, Yong 江永, *Chunqiu dili kaoshi* 春秋地理考實, in *Huang Qing jingjie* 皇清經解, *juan*: 252–55, Guangzhou: Xuehaitang, 1829.

Jianghan kaogu 江漢考古 1982.2, 37–61, "Hubei Huangpi Lutaishan liang Zhou yizhi yu muzang" 湖北黃陂魯臺山兩周遺址與墓葬.

1983.1, 51–53, "Xiangyang Shanwan chutu de Ruo guo he Deng guo tongqi" 襄陽山灣出土的鄀國和鄧國銅器.

1983.1, 80, "Jingshan xian faxian yipi Xi Zhou qingtongqi" 京山縣發現一批西周青銅器.

1984.2, 7–12, "Dangyang Mopanshan Xi Zhou yizhi shijue jianbao" 當陽磨盤山西周遺址試掘簡報.

1990.2, 31–43, "Hubei Dawu Lüwangcheng yizhi" 湖北大悟呂王城遺址.

Jiao, Xun 焦循, *Diaogu ji* 雕菰集, Shanghai: Shangwu, 1936.

Jijin wenlu 吉金文錄 (Wu Kaisheng 吳闓生), 1933.

Jin, Jingfang 金景芳 *Gushi lunji* 古史論集, Jinan: Qilu, 1982.

Jinchu Yin Zhou jinwen jilu 近出殷周金文集錄, 4 vols. (Liu Yu 劉雨 and Lu Yan 盧岩), Beijing: Zhonghua, 2002.

Jing, Zhichun, "Geoarchaeological Reconstruction of the Bronze Age Landscape of the Shangqiu Area, China," unpublished PhD thesis, University of Minnesota, 1994.

Jining zhou jinshi zhi 濟寧州金石誌 (Xu Zonggan 徐宗榦), 1845.

Jinwen fenyu bian 金文分域編 (Ke Changji 柯昌济), 1940.

Jungu lu 攈古錄 (Wu Shifen 吳式芬), Haifeng: Wu shi, 1850.

Jungu lu jinwen 攈古錄金文 (Wu Shifen 吳式芬), Haifeng: Wu shi, 1895.

Kagan, Donald (ed.), *Decline and Fall of the Roman Empire: Why Did It Collapse?* Boston: D.C. Heath, 1962.

Kaizuka, Shigeki 貝塚茂樹, "In matsu Shū sho no tōhō keiryaku ni tsuite" 殷末周初の東方経略について, in *Kaizuka Shigeki chosaku shū* 貝塚茂樹著作集, vol. 2, pp. 105–69, Tokyo: Chūō kōronsha, 1977.

Kane, Virginia C., "The Independent Bronze Industries in the South of China Contemporary with the Shang and Western Chou Dynasty," *Archives of Asian Art* 28 (1974–75), 77–106.

——— "Aspects of Western Chou Appointment Inscriptions: The Charge, the Gifts, and the Response," *Early China* 8 (1982–83), 14–28.

Kaogu 考古 1959.4, 187–88, "Luoyang dongjiao Xi Zhou mu fajue jianbao" 洛陽東郊西周墓發掘簡報.

——— 1959.10, 531–36, "1957 nian Handan fajue jianbao" 1957年邯鄲發掘簡報.

——— 1959.11, 588–91, "Shaanxi Weishui liuyu diaocha jianbao" 陝西渭水流域調查簡報.

——— 1961.6, 289–97, "Shandong Linzi Qi gucheng shijue jianbao" 山東臨淄齊故城試掘簡報.

——— 1962.1, 1–9, "Hubei Qichun Maojiazui Xi Zhou mugou jianzhu" 湖北蘄春毛家嘴西周木構建築.

——— 1962.1, 20–22, "1960 nian qiu Shaanxi Chang'an Zhangjiapo fajue jianbao" 1960年秋陝西長安張家坡發掘簡報.

——— 1963.4, 224–25, "Hubei Jiangling Wancheng chutu Xi Zhou tongqi" 湖北江陵萬城出土西周銅器.

——— 1964.9, 441–47, 474, "Shaanxi Chang'an Fengxi Zhangjiapo Xi Zhou yizhi de fajue" 陝西長安灃西張家坡西周遺址的發掘.

——— 1965.9, 447–50, "Shaanxi Chang'an Zhangjiapo Xi Zhou mu qingli jianbao" 陝西長安張家坡西周墓清理簡報.

——— 1972.2, 35–36, "Luoyang Beiyao Xi Zhou mu qingli ji" 洛陽北窯西周墓清理記.

——— 1973.4, 225–26, "Liaoning Kazuo xian Beidongcun faxian Yin dai qingtongqi" 遼寧喀左縣北洞村發現殷代青銅器.

——— 1974.1, 1–5, "Shaanxi Chang'an Xinwangcun Mawangcun chutu de Xi Zhou tongqi" 陝西長安新旺村馬王村出土的西周銅器.

——— 1974.5, 309–21, "Beijing fujin faxian de Xi Zhou nuli xunzangmu" 北京附近發現的西周奴隸殉葬墓.

——— 1974.6, 356–63, "Cixian Jieduanying fajue jianbao" 磁縣界段營發掘簡報.

——— 1974.6, 364–72, "Liaoning Kazuo xian Beidongcun chutu de Yin Zhou qingtongqi" 遼寧喀左縣北洞村出土的殷周青銅器.

1976.1, 31–38, "Shaanxi Qishan Hejiacun Xi Zhou muzang" 陝西岐山賀家村西周墓葬.

1976.1, 39–48, "Gansu Lingtai xian liang Zhou muzang" 廿肅靈臺縣兩周墓葬.

1976.4, 246–58, 228, "Beijing diqu de youyi zhongyao kaogu shouhuo – Changping Baifu Xi Zhou muguomu de xin qishi" 北京地區的又一重要考古收穫－昌平白浮西周木槨墓的新啓示.

1976.4, 274, "Jiangsu Lishui faxian Xi Zhou mu" 江蘇溧水發現西周墓.

1977.1, 71–72, "Shaanxi Chang'an Fengxi chutu de Pu yu" 陝西長安澧西出土的鋪盂.

1977.5, 292–360, "Jiangsu Gourong xian Fushan guoyuan Xi Zhou mu" 江蘇句容縣浮山果園西周墓.

1978.3, 151–54, "Jiangsu Jintan Biedun Xi Zhou mu" 江蘇金壇鱉墩西周墓.

1979.1, 23–26, "Hebei Yuanshi xian Xizhangcun de Xi Zhou yizhi he muzang" 河北元氏縣西張村的西周遺址和墓葬.

1979.2, 107–18, "Jiangsu Gourong Fushan gouyuan tudun mu" 江蘇句容浮山果園土墩墓.

1980.1, 32–44, "Shandong Tengxian guyizhi diaocha jianbao" 山東滕縣古遺址調査簡報.

1981.1, 13–18, "1976–1978 nian Chang'an Fengxi fajue jianbao" 1976–1978 年長安澧西發掘簡報.

1981.2, 111–18, "Henan Luoshan xian Mangzhang Shang dai mudi di yici fajue jianbao" 河南羅山縣蟒張商代墓地第一次發掘簡報.

1981.2, 128, "Shaanxi Wugong xian chutu Chu gui zhuqi" 陝西武功縣出土楚簋諸器.

1981.4, 314, 370, "Henan Pingdingshan shi faxian Xi Zhou tong gui" 河南平頂山市發現西周銅簋.

1981.6, 496–99, 555, "Sichuan Pengxian Xi Zhou jiaozang tongqi" 四川彭縣西周窖藏銅器.

1981.6, 557–58, "Gansu Lingtai liangzuo Xi Zhou mu" 廿肅靈臺兩座西周墓.

1982.2, 139–41, "Hubei Suixian xin faxian gudai qingtongqi" 湖北隨縣新發現古代青銅器.

1982.6, 584–90, "Gansu Zhuanglang xian Xujianian Siwa wenhua muzang fajue jiyao" 甘肅庄浪縣徐家碾寺窪文化墓葬發掘紀要.

1983.4, 289–92, "Yantai Shangkuangcun chutu Ji guo tongqi" 煙臺上夼村出土曩國銅器.

1983.5, 388, 430–41, "1975–1979 nian Luoyang Beiyao Xi Zhou zhutong yizhi de fajue" 1975–1979 年洛陽北窯西周鑄銅遺址的發掘.

1983.11, 982–84, "Ningxia Guyuan xian Xi Zhou mu qingli jianbao" 寧夏固原縣西周墓清理簡報.

1984.4, 333–37, "Shandong Tengxian faxian Tenghou tongqimu" 山東滕縣發現滕侯銅器墓.

1984.5, 404, 405–16, "1981–1983 nian Liulihe Xi Zhou Yan guo mudi fajue jianbao" 1981–1983 年琉璃河西周燕國墓地發掘簡報.

1984.6, 510–14, "Hubei Suixian faxian Shang Zhou qingtongqi" 湖北隨縣發現商周青銅器.

1984.7, 594–97, "Shandong Rizhao Guheya chutu yipi qingtongqi" 山東日照崮河崖出土一批青銅器.

1984.9, 779–83, "Chang'an Fengxi zao Zhou muzang fajue jilue" 長安澧西早周墓葬發掘紀略.

1985.3, 284–86, "Pindingshan shi chutu Zhoudai qingtongqi" 平頂山市出土周代青銅器.

1985.4, 349–52, "Gansu Ningxian Yucun chutu Xi Zhou qingtongqi" 甘肅寧縣宇村出土西周青銅器.

1986.1, 11, 22–27, "Chang'an Zhangjiapo Xi Zhou Jingshu mu fajue jianbao" 長安張家坡西周井叔墓發掘簡報.

1986.3, 197–209, "1979–1981 nian Chang'an Fengxi Fengdong fajue jianbao" 1979–1981年長安灃西灃東發掘簡報.

1986.11, 977–81, "1984 nian Fengxi Dayuancun Xi Zhou mudi fajue jianbao" 1984年灃西大原村西周墓地發掘簡報.

1987.1, 15–32, "1984–85 nian Fengxi Xi Zhou yizhi muzang fajue baogao" 1984–85年灃西西周遺址墓葬發掘報告.

1987.8, 678–91, "Gansu Xihe Lanqiao Siwa wenhua muzang" 甘肅西和欄橋寺窪文化墓葬.

1987.8, 692–700, "Shaanxi Chang'an Fengxi Keshengzhuang Xi Zhou hangtu jizhi fajue baogao" 陝西長安灃西客省庄西周夯土基址發掘報告.

1987.9, 773–77, 864, "Ningxia Zhongning xian qingtong duanjian mu qingli jianbao" 寧夏中寧縣青銅短劍墓清理簡報.

1988.1, 15–23, "Luoyang laocheng faxian sizuo Xi Zhou chemakeng" 洛陽老城發現四座西周車馬坑.

1988.1, 24–26, "Shandong Linzi Qi guo gucheng Xi Zhou mu" 山東臨淄齊國故城西周墓.

1988.5, 466, "Henan Pingdingshan faxian Xi Zhou yongzhong" 河南平頂山發現西周甬鐘.

1988.7, 601–15, "1982–1983 nian Shaanxi Wugong Huangjiahe yizhi fajue jianbao" 1982–1983年陝西武功黃家河遺址發掘簡報.

1988.9, 769–77, 799, "1984 nian Chang'an Puducun Xi Zhou muzang fajue jianbao" 1984年長安普渡村西周墓葬發掘簡報.

1988.10, 882–93, "Anyang Guojiazhuang xinan de Yindai chemakeng" 安陽郭家庄西南的殷代車馬坑.

1989.1, 10–19, "Henan Xinyang xian Shihegang chutu Xi Zhou zaoqi tongqiqun" 河南信陽縣獅河港出土西周早期銅器群.

1990.1, 20–31, "Beijing Liulihe 1193 hao damu fajue jianbao" 北京琉璃河1193號大墓發掘簡報.

1990.6, 504–10, "Shaanxi Chang'an Zhangjiapo M170 hao Jingshu mu fajue jianbao" 陝西長安張家坡M170號井叔墓發掘簡報.

1991.1, 332–36, "Shandong Rushan xian Nanhuangzhuang Xi Zhou shiban mu fajue jianbao" 山東乳山縣南黃庄西周石板墓發掘簡報.

1991.10, 910–18, "Shandong Huangxian Guicheng yizhi de diaocha yu fajue" 山東黃縣歸城遺址的調查與發掘.

1994.4, 377–78, "Shandong Zhaoyuan chutu Xi Zhou qingtongqi" 山東招遠出土西周青銅器.

1995.9, 788–91, 801, "Luoyang dongjiao C5M906 hao Xi Zhou mu" 洛陽東郊C5M906號西周墓.

1996.5, 93–94, "Shandong Guangrao xian Caoqiao yizhi faxian Xi Zhou taoqi" 山東廣饒縣草橋遺址發現西周陶器.

2000.9, 9–23, "Henan Luyi xian Daqinggong Xi Zhou mu de fajue" 河南鹿邑縣大清宮西周墓的發掘.

Kaogu jinghua 考古精華 (Zhongguo shehui kexueyuan kaogu yanjiusuo 中國社會科學院考古研究所), Beijing: Kexue, 1993.

Kaogu tongxun 考古通訊 1956.1, 27–28, "Luoyang de liangge Xi Zhou mu" 洛陽的兩個西周墓.

Kaogu xuebao 考古學報 9 (1955), 91–116, "1952 nian qiuji Luoyang dongjiao fajue baogao" 1952 年秋季洛陽東郊發掘報告.

　　1957.1, 103–18, "Shanxi Changzhishi Fenshuiling gumu de qingli" 山西長治市分水嶺古墓的清理.

　　1959.2, 15–36, "Luoyang Jianbin Dong Zhou chengzhi fajue baogao" 洛陽澗濱東周城址發掘報告.

　　1959.4, 59–87, "Anhui Tunxi Xi Zhou muzang fajue baogao" 安徽屯溪西周墓葬發掘報告.

　　1973.2, 27–39, "Ningcheng xian Nanshangen de shiguo mu" 寧城縣南山根的石槨墓.

　　1975.1, 73–111, "Cixian Xiapanwang yizhi fajue baogao" 磁縣卞潘旺遺址發掘報告.

　　1977.2, 99–130, "Gansu Lingtai Baicaopo Xi Zhou mu" 甘肅靈臺白草坡西周墓.

　　1979.1, 27–146, "1969–1977 nian Yinxu xiqu muzang fajue baogao" 1969–1977 年殷墟西區墓葬發掘報告.

　　1980.4, 457–502, "1967 nian Chang'an Zhangjiapo Xi Zhou muzang de fajue" 1967 年長安張家坡西周墓葬的發掘.

　　1987.3, 359–95, "Gansu Gangu Maojiaping yizhi fajue baogao" 甘肅甘谷毛家坪遺址發掘報告.

　　1991.4, 449–95, "Xue guo gucheng kancha he muzang fajue baogao" 薛國故城勘查和墓葬發掘報告.

　　1992.3, 365–92, "Tengzhou Qianzhangda Shangdai muzang" 滕州前掌大商代墓葬.

Kaoguxue yanjiu 考古學研究 3 (1997), 300–460, "Gansu Heshui Jiuzhan yizhi fajue baogao" 甘肅合水九站遺址發掘報告.

Kaogu yu wenwu 考古與文物 1980.1, 7–12, "Qishan Hejiacun Zhou mu fajue jianbao" 岐山賀家村周墓發掘簡報.

　　1980.2, 17–20, "Shaanxi Chunhua Shijiayuan chutu Xi Zhou da ding" 陝西淳化史家原出土西周大鼎.

　　1981.1, 8–11, "Xianyang diqu chutu Xi Zhou qingtongqi" 咸陽地區出土西周青銅器.

　　1981.4, 27–28, "Mugong gui gai mingwen jianshi" 穆公簋蓋銘文簡釋.

　　1982.2, 6, "Meixian chutu wang zuo Zhong Jiang bao ding" 眉縣出土王作中姜寶鼎.

　　1982.4, 15–38, "Fengxiang Nanzhihui Xicun Zhou mu de fajue" 鳳翔南指揮西村周墓的發掘.

　　1983.1, 109, "Henan Pingdingshan you chutu yi jian Denggong gui" 河南平頂山又出土一件鄧公簋.

　　1983.3, 8–11, "Gansu Qingyang diqu chutu de Shang Zhou qingtongqi" 甘肅慶陽地區出土的商周青銅器.

　　1984.1, 53–65, "Shaanxi Fengxiang chutu de Xi Zhou qingtongqi" 陝西鳳翔出土的西周青銅器.

　　1985.1, 12–18, "Fufeng Qijiacun qi ba hao Xi Zhou tongqi jiaocang qingli jianbao" 扶風齊家村七八號西周銅器窖藏清理簡報.

　　1986.1, 1–7, "Gansu Chongxin Yujiawan Zhou mu fajue jianbao" 甘肅崇信于家灣周墓發掘簡報.

　　1986.5, 12–22, "Shaanxi Chunhua xian chutu de Shang Zhou qingtongqi" 陝西淳化縣出土的商周青銅器.

　　1986.6, 15–21, "Shaanxi Longxian Bianjiazhuang yihao chunqiu Qin mu" 陝西隴縣邊家庄一號春秋秦墓.

1987.5, 100–1, "Gansu Lingtai xian you faxian yizuo Xi Zhou muzang" 甘肅
靈臺縣又發現一座西周墓葬.

1989.3, 7–9, "Shaanxi Ankang shi chutu Xi Zhou Shimi gui" 陝西安康市
出土西周史密簋.

1989.12, 24–27, "Gansu Ningxian Jiaocun Xigou chutu de yizuo Xi Zhou mu"
甘肅寧縣焦村西溝出土的一座西周墓.

1990.1, 53–57, "Shaanxi Chunhua xian xin faxian de Shang Zhou qingtongqi"
陝西淳化縣新發現的商周青銅器.

1993.5, 8–12, "Shaanxi Yanchang xian chutu yipi Xi Zhou qingtongqi" 陝西延
長縣出土一批西周青銅器.

1997.3, 78–80, "Hu gui gai ming jianshi" 虎簋蓋銘簡釋.

1998.3, 69–71, "Shaanxi Chang'an xian chutu Xi Zhou Wu Hu ding" 陝西長
安縣出土西周吳虎鼎.

2003.3, 3–12, "Shaanxi Meixian Yangjiacun Xi Zhou qingtongqi jiaocang"
陝西眉縣楊家村西周青銅器窖藏

Katz, Solomon, *The Decline of Rome and the Rise of Mediaeval Europe*, Ithaca, NY:
Cornell University Press, 1955.

Keightley, David N., *Sources of Shang History: The Oracle-Bone Inscriptions of Bronze
Age China*, Berkeley: University of California Press, 1978.

"The Late Shang State: When, Where, and What?" in *The Origins of Chinese
Civilization*, ed. David N. Keightley, pp. 523–64, Berkeley: University of
California Press, 1983.

"The Shang: China's First Historical Dynasty," in *The Cambridge History of
Ancient China: From the Origins of Civilization to 221 B.C.*, ed. Michael Loewe
and Edward L. Shaughnessy, pp. 232–91, Cambridge: Cambridge University
Press, 1999.

*The Ancestral Landscape: Time, Space, and Community in Late Shang China (ca.
1200–1045 B.C.)*, Berkeley: Institute of East Asian Studies, 2000.

Kelley, Charles Fabens, and Ch'en Meng-chia (Chen Mengjia), *Chinese Bronzes
from the Buckingham Collection*, Chicago: The Art Institute of Chicago,
1946.

Lally, J. J., *Archaic Chinese Bronzes, Jades and Works of Art*, New York: J. J. Lally
and Co., 1994.

Lattimore, Owen, *Inner Asian Frontiers of China*, New York: American Geographical Society, 1940.

Legge, James, *The Chinese Classics, vol. 3: The Shoo King, or Book of Historical
Documents*, Hong Kong: University of Hong Kong Press, 1960 (reprint of
London: Henry Frowde, 1865).

Lei, Xueqi 雷學淇, *Zhushu jinian yizheng* 竹書紀年義證, 1810.

Li, Boqian 李伯謙, "Tianma–Qucun yizhi fajue yu Jin guo shifengdi de tuiding"
天馬 – 曲村遺址發掘与晉國始封地推定, in *Zhongguo qingtong wenhua jiegou
tixi yanjiu* 中國青銅文化結構體系研究, pp. 114–23, Beijing: Kexue, 1998.

Li, Chaoyuan 李朝遠, "Shanghai bowuguan xinhuo Qingong tongqi yanjiu"
上海博物館新獲秦公銅器研究, *Shanghai bowuguan jikan* 上海博物館集刊 7
(1996), 23–33.

"Meixian xinchu Lai pan yu Da Ke ding de shidai" 眉縣新出逨盤與大克鼎的時代,
in *Disijie guoji Zhongguo guwenzi xue yantaohui lunwen ji* 第四屆國
際中國古文字學研討會論文集, pp. 89–96, Hong Kong: Chinese University of
Hong Kong, 2003.

Li, Feng 李峰, "Shilun Shaanxi chutu Shang dai tongqi de fenqi yu fenqu" 試論陝西出土商代銅器的分期与分區, *Kaogu yu wenwu* 1986.3, 53–63.

"Huanghe liuyu Xi Zhou muzang chutu qingtong liqi de fenqi yu niandai" 黃河流域西周墓葬出土青銅禮器的分期與年代, *Kaogu xuebao* 1988.4, 383–419.

"Guo guo mudi tongqi qun de fenqi jiqi xiangguan wenti" 虢國墓地銅器群的分期及其相關問題, *Kaogu* 1988.11, 1035–43.

"Xian Zhou wenhua de neihan jiqi yuanyuan tantao" 先周文化的內涵及其淵源探討, *Kaogu xuebao* 1991.3, 265–84.

"Ancient Reproductions and Calligraphic Variations: Studies of Western Zhou Bronzes with Identical Inscriptions," *Early China* 22 (1997), 1–41.

"Tayūtei meibun o meguru rekishi chiri teki mondai no kaiketsu – Shū ōchō no seihoku keiryaku o kaimei suru tameni" 多友鼎銘文を巡る歷史地理的問題の解決 – 周王朝の西北経略を解明するために。, in *Chūgoku kodai no moji to bunka* 中國古代の文字と文化, pp. 179–206, Tokyo: Kyūko shoin, 1999.

"The Decline and Fall of the Western Zhou Dynasty: A Historical, Archaeological, and Geographical Study of China from the Tenth to the Eighth Centuries B.C.," unpublished PhD thesis, University of Chicago, 2000.

"'Offices' in Bronze Inscriptions and Western Zhou Government Administration," *Early China* 26–27 (2001–2), 1–72.

"Literacy Crossing Cultural Borders: Evidence from the Bronze Inscriptions of the Western Zhou Period (1045–771 B.C.)," *Bulletin of the Museum of Far Eastern Antiquity* 74 (2002), 210–42.

"'Feudalism' and Western Zhou China: A Criticism," *Harvard Journal of Asiatic Studies* 63.1 (2003), 115–44.

"Textual Criticism and Western Zhou Bronze Inscriptions: The Example of the Mu Gui," in *Essays in Honour of An Zhimin*, ed. Teng Chung and Chen Xingcan, pp. 280–97, Hong Kong: Chinese University of Hong Kong, 2004.

"Succession and Promotion: Elite Mobility during the Western Zhou," *Monumenta Serica* 52 (2004), 1–35.

"Shilun Xi Zhou wangchao xibei bianjiang de wenhua shengtai" 試論西周王朝西北邊疆的文化生態, Academia Sinica, forthcoming.

"Transmitting Antiquity: The Origin and Paradigmization of the 'Five Ranks'," in *Perceptions of Antiquity in China's Civilization*, ed. Dieter Kohn (Monograph of *Monumenta Serica*), forthcoming.

"Ouzhou Feudalism de fansi jiqi dui Zhongguo gushi fenqi de yiyi" 歐洲 Feudalism 的反思及其對中國古史分期的意義, forthcoming.

Li, Junzhi 李俊之, "Zhou dai xifang minzu zhi dongzhi (Ji xing pian)" 周代西方民族之東殖(姬姓篇), *Qinghua zhoukan* 清華周刊 37.9, 10 (1932), 41–60.

Li, Ling 李零, "Shiji zhong suojian Qin zaoqi duyi zangdi" 史記中所見秦早期都邑葬地, *Wenshi* 文史 20 (1983), 15–23.

"Chema yu dache: ba Shitong ding" 車馬與大車: 跋師同鼎, *Kaogu yu wenwu* 1992.2, 72–74.

Li, Xiusong 李修松, "Huaiyi tanlun" 淮夷探論, *Dongnan wenhua* 東南文化 1991.2, 14–21.

Li, Xueqin 李學勤, "Meixian Lijiacun tongqi kao" 眉縣李家村銅器考, *Wenwu* 1957.7, 58.

"Lun Duoyou ding de shidai ji yiyi" 論多友鼎的時代及意義, *Renwen zazhi* 1981.6, 87–92.

Dong Zhou yu Qindai wenming 東周與秦代文明, Beijing: Wenwu, 1984.

"Da Yu ding xinlun" 大盂鼎新論, *Zhengzhou daxue xuebao* 1985.3, 51–65.

Eastern Zhou and Qin Civilizations, trans. K. C. Chang, New Haven: Yale University Press, 1985.

"Lun Xi Zhou jinwen zhong de Liushi Bashi" 論西周金文中的六師八師, *Huaxia kaogu* 1987.2, 207–10.

Xinchu qingtongqi yanjiu 新出青銅器研究, Beijing: Wenwu, 1990.

"Sanmenxia Guo guo mudi xin faxian yu Guo guo shi" 三門峽虢國墓地新發現與虢國史, *Zhongguo wenwu bao* 中國文物報 1991.2.3, 3.

"Shi Guodian jian Zhaigong zhi guming" 釋郭店簡祭公之顧命, *Wenwu* 1998.7, 44–45.

"Lun Suigong xu jiqi zhongyao yiyi" 論遂公盨及其重要意義, *Zhongguo lishi wenwu* 中國歷史文物 2002.6, 4–12.

"Meixian Yangjiacun xinchu qingtongqi yanjiu" 眉縣楊家村新出青銅器研究, *Wenwu* 2003.6, 66–73.

Li, Xueqin 李學勤, and Ai Lan 艾蘭 (Sarah Allan), "Zuixin chuxian de Qingong hu" 最新出現的秦公壺, *Zhongguo wenwu bao* 1994.10, 30.

Li, Zhi 李贄, *Shigang pingyao* 史綱評要, Beijing: Zhonghua, 1974 (1st edition, Nanjing: Wu Congxian, 1613).

Li, Zhongcao 李仲操, "Yeshi Duoyou ding mingwen" 也釋多友鼎銘文, *Renwen zazhi* 1982.6, 95–9.

"Xi Zhou jinwen zhong de funü chengwei" 西周金文中的婦女稱謂, *Baoji wenbo* 寶鷄文博 1991.1, 35–9.

Liang, Xiaojing 梁曉景, "Liu guo shiji kaolue" 劉國史跡考略, *Zhongyuan wenwu* 中原文物 1985.4, 65–72.

"Kuai guo shiji tansuo" 鄶國史跡探索, *Zhongyuan wenwu* 1987.3, 102–6.

Liang, Xiaojing 梁曉景, and Ma Sanhong 馬三鴻, "Lun Yu Ze liangguo de zushu yu Taibo ben Wu" 論彧矢兩國的族屬與太伯奔吳, *Zhongyuan wenwu* 1998.3, 42–47.

Liang, Xingpeng 梁星彭, "Xian Zhou wenhua shangque" 先周文化商榷, *Kaogu yu wenwu* 1982.4, 85–91.

Lin, Jianming 林劍鳴, "Jingtian he yuantian" 井田和援田, *Renwen zazhi* 1979.1, 69–75.

Qin shi 秦史, Taipei: Wunan, 1992.

Lin, Shoujin 林壽晉, "Shangcunling Guo guo mudi buji" 上村嶺虢國墓地記, *Kaogu* 考古 1961.9, 505–7.

Liu, Bida 劉必達, and Shi Bingzhen 史秉珍, *Binzhou xinzhi gao* 邠州新志稿, manuscript, 1929.

Liu, Dunyuan 劉敦愿, "Zhou Muwang zheng Quanrong de si bailang si bailu yigui jie" 周穆王徵犬戎得四白狼四白鹿以歸解, *Renwen zazhi* 1986.4, 110–13.

Liu, Fuliang 劉富良, "Luoyang Xi Zhou taoqi mu yanjiu" 洛陽西周陶器墓研究, *Kaogu yu wenwu* 1998.3, 44–67.

Liu, Junshe 劉軍社, "Bianjiazhuang Qin guo mudi fajue de zhuyao shouhuo jiqi yiyi" 邊家庄秦國墓地發掘的主要收穫及其意義, *Baoji wenbo* 寶鷄文博 1991.1, 12–18.

Xian Zhou wenhua yanjiu 先周文化研究, Xi'an: Shanqin, 2003.

Liu, Li 劉莉, "Tongfu kao" 銅鍑考, *Kaogu yu wenwu* 1987.3, 60–5.

Liu, Li, and Xingcan Chen, *State Formation in Early China*, London: Duckworth, 2003.

Liu, Qingzhu 劉慶柱, "Shilun Qin zhi yuanyuan" 試論秦之淵源, in *Xianqin shi lunwen ji* 先秦史論文集 (Monograph of *Renwen zazhi*), pp. 176–81, Xi'an, 1982.

Liu, Qiyi 劉啓益, "Xi Zhou Ze guo tongqi de xinfaxian yu youguan de lishi dili wenti" 西周夨國銅器的新發現與有關的歷史地理問題, *Kaogu yu wenwu* 1982.2, 42–45.

Liu, Qiyu 劉起釪, "Zhou chu de Sanjian yu Bei Yong Wey sanguo ji Wey Kang-shu fengdi de wenti" 周初的三監與邶鄘衛三國及衛康叔封地的問題, *Lishi dili* 2 (1982), 66–81.

Liu, Xiang 劉翔, "Xi Zhou E guo kao" 西周鄂國考, *Diming zhishi* 地名知識 1982.3, 16–17.

"Zhou Yiwang jingying Nan Huaiyi jiqi yu E zhi guanxi" 周夷王經營南淮夷及其與鄂之關係, *Jianghan kaogu* 1983.3, 40–46.

Liu, Xueyao 劉學銚, *Xiongnu shilun* 匈奴史論, Taipei: Lantian, 1987.

Liu, Yu 劉雨, "Duoyou ding de shidai yu diming kaoding" 多友鼎的時代與地名考訂, *Kaogu* 1983.2, 152–7.

Liu, Zongyuan 柳宗元, *Liu Hedong ji* 柳河東集, vol. 3, Beijing: Zhenghua, 1961.

Liulihe Xi Zhou Yan guo mudi 1973–77 琉璃河西周燕國墓地 1973–77 (Beijing shi wenwu yanjiusuo 北京市文物研究所), Beijing: Wenwu, 1995.

Loewe, Michael (ed.), *Early Chinese Texts: A Bibliographical Guide*, Berkeley: Institute of East Asian Studies, University of California, Berkeley, 1993.

"The Heritage Left to the Empires," in *The Cambridge History of Ancient China: From the Origins of Civilization to 221 B.C.*, ed. Michael Loewe and Edward L. Shaughnessy, pp. 967–1032, Cambridge: Cambridge University Press, 1999.

Loewe, Michael, and Edward L. Shaughnessy (eds.), *The Cambridge History of Ancient China: From the Origins of Civilization to 221 B.C.*, Cambridge: Cambridge University Press, 1999.

Lu, Liancheng 盧連成, "Zhou du Yu Zheng kao" 周都棫鄭考, in *Guwenzi lunji* 古文字論集 (*Kaogu yu wenwu congkan* 考古与文物叢刊 2), pp. 8–11, Xi'an, 1983.

"An di yu Zhaowang shijiu nian nanzheng" 岸地与昭王十九年南征, *Kaogu yu wenwu* 1984.6, 75–79.

"Xi Zhou Ze guo shiji kaolue jiqi xiangguan wenti" 西周夨國史跡考略及其相關問題, in *Xi Zhou shi yanjiu* 西周史研究 (Monograph of *Renwen zazhi* 2), pp. 232–48, Xi'an, 1984.

"Xi Zhou Feng Hao liangjing kao" 西周豐鎬兩京考, paper presented at the conference for the 30th anniversary of the establishment of Shaanxi Provincial Institute of Archaeology and the Banpo Museum, pp. 1–56, Xi'an, 1988.

"Zhangjiapo Xi Zhou Jingshu mudi de zhaomu pailie" 張家坡西周井叔墓地的昭穆排列, *Zhongguo wenwu bao* 1995.3.5, 3.

"Qin guo zaoqi wenwu de xin renshi" 秦國早期文物的新認識, *Zhongguo wenzi* 中國文字 21 (1996), 61–65.

"Tianma – Qucun Jinhou mudi niandai ji muzhu kaoding" 天馬 – 曲村晉侯墓地年代及墓主考定, in *Dingcun wenhua yu Jin wenhua kaogu xueshu yantaohui wenji* 丁村文化與晉文化考古學術研討會文集, pp. 138–51, Taiyuan: Shanxi gaoxiao lianhe, 1996.

Lu, Renyong 魯人勇, Wu Zhongli 吳仲禮 *et al.*, *Ningxia lishi dili kao* 寧夏歷史地理考, Yinchuan: Ningxia renmin, 1993.

Lü, Wenyu 呂文郁, *Zhou dai caiyi zhidu yanjiu* 周代采邑制度研究, Taipei: Wenjin, 1992.

"Zhou dai wangji kaoshu" 周代王畿考述, *Renwen zazhi* 1992.2, 92–101.

Lu, Yun 盧雲, "Zhanguo shiqi zhuyao lulu jiaotong chutan" 戰國時期主要陸路交通初探, in *Lishi dili yanjiu* 歷史地理研究 I, pp. 33–47, Shanghai: Fudan daxue, 1986.

Lü, Zhirong 呂智榮, "Shaanxi Qingjian Lijiaya guchengzhi taowen kaoshi" 陝西清澗李家崖古城址陶文考釋, *Wenbo* 1987.3, 85–86.

"Shilun Shan Jin beibu Huanghe liang'an diqu chutu de Shang dai qingtongqi ji youguan wenti" 試論陝晉北部黃河兩岸地區出土的商代青銅器及有關問題, in *Zhongguo kaoguxue yanjiu lunji – Jinian Xia Nai xiansheng kaogu wushi zhounian* 中國考古學研究論集－紀念夏鼐先生考古五十周年, ed. Shi Xingbang 石興邦, pp. 214–25, Xi'an: Sanqin, 1987.

"Guifang wenhua ji xiangguan wenti chutan" 鬼方文化及相關問題初探, *Wenbo* 1990.1, 32–37.

Luo, Feng 羅豐, "Guyuan qingtong wenhua chulun" 固原青銅文化初論, *Kaogu* 1990.8, 743–50.

Luo, Kun 羅琨, "Gaozong fa Guifang shiji kaobian" 高宗伐鬼方史跡考辨, in *Jiaguwen yu Yinshang shi* 甲骨文与殷商史, ed. Hu Houxuan 胡厚宣, pp. 83–127, Shanghai: Guji, 1983.

Luo, Tai 羅泰 (Lothar von Falkenhausen), "Youguan Xi Zhou wanqi lizhi gaige ji Zhuangbai Weishi qingtongqi niandai de xin jiashe – cong shixi mingwen shuoqi" 有關西周晚期禮制改革及莊白微氏青銅器年代的新假設－從世係銘文說起, in *Zhongguo kaoguxue yu lishixue zhi zhenghe yanjiu* 中國考古學與歷史學之整合研究, pp. 651–75, Taipei: Academia Sinica, 1997.

Luo, Xizhang 羅西章, "Zhouyuan qingtongqi jiaocang jiqi youguan wenti de tantao" 周原青銅器窖藏及其有關問題的探討, *Kaogu yu wenwu* 1988.2, 40–47.

Luoyang Beiyao Xi Zhou mu 洛陽北窯西周墓 (Luoyang shi wenwu gongzuo dui 洛陽市文物工作隊), Beijing: Wenwu, 1999.

Luoyang fajue baogao 洛陽發掘報告 (Zhongguo shehui kexueyuan kaogu yanjiusuo), Beijing: Yanshan, 1989.

Luoyang Zhongzhoulu (Xi gongduan) 洛陽中州路(西工段) (Zhongguo kexueyuan kaogu yanjiusuo 中國科學院考古研究所), Beijing: Kexue, 1959.

Luyi Daqinggong Changzi Kou mu 鹿邑大清宮長子口墓 (Henan sheng wenwu kaogu yanjiusuo 河南省文物考古研究所 and Zhoukou shi wenhuaju 周口市文化局), Zhengzhou: Zhongzhou guji, 2000.

Ma, Chengyuan 馬承源, "Ji Shanghai bowuguan xin shouji de qingtongqi" 記上海博物館新收集的青銅器, *Wenwu* 1964.7, 10–14.

"Guanyu Miaosheng xu he Zhujian zhong de jidian yijian" 關於翏生盨和者減鐘的幾點意見," *Kaogu* 1979.1, 60–62.

Shang Zhou qingtongqi mingwen xuan 商周青銅器銘文選, 4 vols., Beijing: Wenwu, 1986–90.

"Changjiang xiayou tudunmu chutu qingtongqi de yanjiu" 長江下游土墩墓出土青銅器的研究, *Shanghai bowuguan jikan* 上海博物館集刊 4 (1987), 198–220.

"Guo guo damu canguan ji" 虢國大墓參觀記, *Zhongguo wenwu bao* 1991.1, 6.

"Jinhou Su bianzhong" 晉侯蘇編鐘, *Shanghai bowuguan jikan* 7 (1996), 1–17.

(ed.), *Shanghai bowuguan cang Zhanguo Chu zhushu* 上海博物館藏戰國楚竹書, vol. 1, Shanghai: Shanghai guji, 2001.

Ma, Ruichen 馬瑞辰, *Maoshi zhuanjian tongshi* 毛詩傳箋通釋, in *Huang Qing jingjie xubian* 皇清經解續編, *juan*: 94–102, Jiangyin: Nanqing shuyuan, 1888.

Ma, Shizhi 馬世之, "Kuai guo shiji chutan" 鄶國史跡初探, *Shixue yuekan* 1984.5, 30–34.

"Ying guo tongqi jiqi xiangguan wenti" 應國銅器及其相關問題, *Zhongyuan wenwu* 1986.1, 58–62.

"Luelun Luoyang Dong Zhou Wangcheng" 略論洛陽東周王城, in *Luoyang kaogu sishi nian* 洛陽考古四十年, ed. Luoyang shi wenwu gongzuo dui 洛陽市文物工作隊, pp. 230–5, Beijing: Kexue, 1996.

Mackenzie, Colin, "Chu Bronze Work: A Unilinear Tradition, or a Synthesis of Diverse Sources?" in *New Perspectives on Chu Culture*, ed. Thomas Lawton, pp. 107–57, Washington, DC: Arthur M. Sackler Gallery, Smithsonian Institution, 1991.

Maenchen-Helfen, Otto, "Archaistic Names of the Hsiung-nu," *Central Asiatic Journal* 6.4 (1961), 249–61.

Maspero, Henri, "Contribution à l'étude de la société chinoise à la fin des Chang et au début des Tcheou," *Bulletin de l'Ecole française d'Extrême-Orient* 46.2, 335–403.

Matsui, Yoshinori 松井嘉徳, "Sei Shū ki Tei no kōsatsu" 西周期鄭の考察, *Shirin* 史林 69.4 (1986), 1–40.

"Shūō shitei no hōken – Tei no shihō tōsen o megutte" 周王子弟の封建 – 鄭の始封束遷をめぐって, *Shirin* 72.4 (1989), 1–36.

Matsumaru, Michio 松丸道雄, "In Shū kokka no kōzō" 殷周國家の構造, in *Iwanami kōza – Sekai rekishi* 岩波講座 – 世界歴史, pp. 72–79, Tokyo: Iwanami shoten, 1970.

(ed.), *Sei Shū seidōki to sono kokka* 西周青銅器とその國家, Tokyo: Tōkyō daigaku, 1980.

"Sei Shū kōki shakai ni mieru henkaku no hōga – Kotei mei kaishaku mondai no shohoteki kaiketsu" 西周後期社会にみえる変革の萌芽 – 召鼎銘解釈問題初歩的解決, in *Higashi Ajia shi ni okeru kokka to nōmin* 東アジア史における國家と農民, pp. 52–54, Tokyo: Yamakawa, 1984.

"Kanan Rokuyū ken Chōshi Kō bo o meguru sho mondai – kobunken to kōkogaku tono kaikō" 河南鹿邑県長子口墓をめぐる諸問題 –古文献と考古學との邂逅, *Chūgoku kōkogaku* 中國考古学 4 (2004), 219–39.

Mattos, Gilbert, "Eastern Zhou Bronze Inscriptions," in *New Sources of Early Chinese History: An Introduction to the Reading of Inscriptions and Manuscripts*, ed. Edward Shaughnessy, pp. 85–123, Berkeley: Society for the Study of Early China, 1997.

Meng, Wentong 蒙文通, "Quanrong dongqin kao" 犬戎東遷考, *Yugong* 禹貢 6.7 (1936), 3–16.

"Qin wei Rong zu kao" 秦為戎族考, *Yugong* 6.7 (1936), 17–20.

"Chidi Baidi dongqin kao" 赤狄白狄東遷考, *Yugong* 7.1–3 (1937), 67–88.

Zhou Qin shaoshu minzu yanjiu 周秦少數民族研究, Shanghai: Longmen, 1968.

Min, Yuming 閔煜銘, Cao Songtao 曹松濤 *et al., Anhui sheng dili* 安徽省地理, Hefei: Anhui renmin, 1990.

Mochii, Yasutaka 持井康孝, "Sei Shū jidai no Seishū chūdō kōbō ni tsuite" 西周時代の成周鑄銅工房について, in *Sei Shū seidōki to sono kokka* 西周青銅器とその國家, ed. Matsumaru Michio, pp. 185–240, Tokyo: Tōkyō daigaku, 1980.

Musha, Akira 武者章, "Sei Shū satsumei kinbun bunrui no kokoromi" 西周冊命金文分類の試み, in *Sei Shū seidōki to sono kokka* 西周青銅器とその國家, ed. Matsumaru Michio, pp. 241–324, Tokyo: Tōkyō daigaku, 1980.

Nanyang diqu zhi (1986–1994) 南陽地區志 (Nanyang diqu difang shizhi bianzuan weiyuanhui 南陽地區地方史志編纂委員會), Zhengzhou: Zhongzhou guji, 1996.

Nash, Daphne, "Historical Archaeology," in *The Cambridge Encyclopedia of Archaeology*, ed. Andrew Sherratt, pp. 43–45, New York: Crown, 1980.

Needham, Joseph, *Science and Civilisation in China, vol. 3: Mathematics and the Sciences of the Heavens and the Earth*, Cambridge: Cambridge University Press, 1959.

Neimenggu wenwu kaogu 内蒙古文物考古 2 (1982), 5–7, "Zhaomeng faxian de daxing qingtongqi" 昭盟發現的大型青銅器.

Nie, Shuren 聶樹人, *Shaanxi ziran dili* 陝西自然地理, Xi'an: Shaanxi renmin, 1981.

Nie, Xinmin 聶新民, "Qin ba Xirong diyu kao" 秦霸西戎地域考, *Xibei shidi* 西北史地 1986.2, 9–17.

Nienhauser, William H. (ed.), *The Grand Scribe's Records, vol. 1: The Basic Annals of Pre-Han China*, Bloomington: Indiana University Press, 1994.

  The Grand Scribe's Records, vol. 2: The Basic Annals of Han China, Bloomington: Indiana University Press, 2002.

Nishie, Kyotaka 西江清高, "Sei Shū jidai no Kanchū heigen ni okeru Gyo shūdan no ichi" 西周時代の関中平原における強集団の位置, in *Chūgoku kodai no moji to bunka* 中國古代の文字と文化, pp. 207–44, Tokyo: Kyūko shoin, 1999.

Niu, Shishan 牛世山, "Qin wenhua yuanyuan yu Qinren qiyuan tansuo" 秦文化淵源與秦人起源探索, *Kaogu* 1996.3, 41–50.

Nivison, David S., "Western Chou History Reconstructed from Bronze Inscriptions," in *The Great Bronze Age of China: A Symposium*, ed. George Kuwayama, pp. 44–55. Los Angeles: County Museum of Art, 1983.

  "The Dates of Western Chou," *Harvard Journal of Asiatic Studies* 43.2 (1983), 481–580.

  "An Interpretation of the 'Shao Gao'," *Early China* 20 (1995), 177–93.

  "The Key to the Chronology of the Three Dynasties: The 'Modern Text' *Bamboo Annals*," *Sino-Platonic Papers* 93 (1999), 1–24.

Nivison, David, and Edward Shaughnessy, "The Jin Hou Su Bells Inscription and Its Implications for the Chronology of Early China," *Early China* 25 (2000), 29–48.

Nylan, Michael, *The Five Confucian Classics*, New Haven: Yale University Press, 2001.

Ogata, Isamu 尾形勇, and Hirase Takao 平勢隆郎, *Chūka bunmei no tanjō* 中華文明の誕生, Tokyo: Chūō kōron sha, 1998.

Ogawa, Takuji 小川琢治, *Shina rekishi chiri kenkyū (shoshū)* 支那歷史地理研究 (初集), Kyoto: Kobundō, 1928.

  Shina rekishi chiri kenkyū (zokushū) 支那歷史地理研究 (續集), Kyoto: Kobundō, 1929.

Okura, Yoshihiko 小倉芳彦, "I i no toriko – Saden no Ka I kannen" 夷裔の俘－左傳の華裔觀念, *Chūgoku kodaishi kenkyū* 中國古代史研究 2 (1965), 1–35.

Omeljan Pritsak, "Xun: Der Volksname der Hsiung-nu," *Central Asiatic Journal* 5.1 (1959), 27–34.

Pacione, Michael (ed.), *Historical Geography: Progress and Prospect*, London: Croom Helm, 1987.

Pankenier, David W., "Astronomical Dates in Shang and Western Zhou," *Early China* 7 (1981–82), 2–37.

  "The *Bamboo Annals* Revisited: Problems of Method in Using the Chronicles as a Source for the Chronology of Early Zhou, Part 1," *Bulletin of the School of Oriental and African Studies* 55.2 (1992), 272–97; "Part 2: The Congruent

Mandate Chronology in *Yi Zhou shu*," *Bulletin of the School of Oriental and African Studies* 55.3 (1992), 498–510.

Pines, Yuri, "Intellectual Change in the Chunqiu Period: The Reliability of the Speeches in the *Zuo Zhuan* as Sources of Chunqiu Intellectual History," *Early China* 22 (1997), 77–132.

　Foundations of Confucian Thought: Intellectual Life in the Chunqiu Period, 722–453 B.C.E., Honolulu: University of Hawaii Press, 2002.

Průšek, Jaroslav, *Chinese Statelets and the Northern Barbarians in the Period 1400–300 B.C.*, New York: Humanities Press, 1971.

Pulleyblank, E. G. "The Chinese and Their Neighbors in Prehistorical and Early Historical Times," in *The Origins of Chinese Civilization*, ed. David N. Keightley, pp. 411–66, Berkeley: University of California Press, 1983.

Qi, Sihe 齊思和, "Xi Zhou dili kao" 西周地理考, *Yanjing xuebao* 30 (1946), 63–106.

Qian, Mu 錢穆, "Xi Zhou ronghuo kao" 西周戎禍考, in *Gushi dili luncong* 古史地理論叢, pp. 151–70, Taibei: Dongda tushu, 1982.

　"Zhou chu dili kao" 周初地理考, *Yanjing xuebao* 10 (1931), 1955–2008.

Qiang, Zhenzhi 強振志, *(Chongxiu) Baoji xianzhi* (重修) 寶鷄縣志, Baoji, 1922.

Qingtongqi tushi 青銅器圖釋 (Shaanxi sheng bowuguan 陝西省博物館 and Shaanxi sheng wenwu guanli weiyuanhui 陝西省文物管理委員會), Beijing: Wenwu, 1960.

Qingyang diqu bianshiban 慶陽地區編史辦, "Sui Tang Song shiqi Qingyang diqu daolu de fazhan" 隋唐宋時期慶陽地區道路的發展, *Xibei shidi* 1988.4, 83–90.

Qiu, Xigui 裘錫圭, *Gu wenzi lunji* 古文字論集, Beijing: Zhonghua, 1992.

　"Guanyu Kongzi shilun," *International Research on Bamboo and Silk Documents* (Newsletter) 2.3 (2002), 1–2.

　"Du Lai qi mingwen zhaji sanze" 讀逨器銘文札記三則, *Wenwu* 2003.6, 74–77.

Qu, Wanli 屈萬里, *Shijing shiyi* 詩經釋義, 2 vols., Taipei: Zhonghua wenhua, 1953.

　"Shangshu Wenhou zhi ming zhucheng de niandai" 尚書文侯之命著成的年代, *Zhongyang yanjiuyuan lishi yuyan yanjiusuo jikan* 中央研究院歷史語言研究所集刊 29 (1958), 499–511.

　Shijing quanshi 詩經詮釋, Taipei: Lianjing, 1983.

Qufu Lu guo gucheng 曲阜魯國故城 (Shandong sheng wenwu kaogu yanjiusuo 山東省文物考古研究所 *et al.*), Jinan: Qilu, 1982.

Railey, Jim, "Neolithic to Early Bronze Age Sociopolitical Evolution in the Yuanqu Basin, North-Central China," unpublished PhD thesis, Washington University, 1999.

Rawson, Jessica, "Late Western Zhou: A Break in the Shang Bronze Tradition," *Early China* 11–12 (1985–87), 289–96.

　"Statesmen or Barbarians? The Western Zhou as Seen through Their Bronzes," *Proceedings of the British Academy* 75 (1989), 71–95.

　Western Zhou Ritual Bronzes from the Arthur M. Sackler Collections, Washington, DC: Arthur M. Sackler Foundation, 1990.

　"Western Zhou Archaeology," in *The Cambridge History of Ancient China: From the Origins of Civilization to 221 B.C.*, ed. Michael Loewe and Edward Shaughnessy, pp. 352–449, Cambridge: Cambridge University Press, 1999.

Renfrew, Colin, and Paul Bahn, *Archaeology: Theories, Methods, and Practice*, New York: Thames and Hudson, 1991.

Reynolds, Susan, *Fiefs and Vassals: The Medieval Evidence Reinterpreted*, Oxford: Clarendon Press, 1994.

Rong, Geng 容庚, *Shang Zhou yiqi tongkao* 商周彝器通考, Beiping: Yanjing daxue, 1940.

Ruan, Yuan 阮元, *Shanzuo jinshi zhi* 山左吉金志, Yizheng: Xiao langhuan xian guan, 1797.

Sanjin kaogu 三晉考古 1 (1994), 95–122, "Wenxi Shangguocun gumu qun shijue" 聞喜上郭村古墓群試掘.

   1 (1994), 123–38, "1976 nian Wenxi Shangguocun Zhou dai muzang qingli ji" 1976 年聞喜上郭村周代墓葬清理記.

   1 (1994), 139–53, "Wenxi Shangguocun 1989 nian fajue jianbao" 聞喜上郭村1989年發掘簡報.

Sanmenxia Guo guo mu 三門峽虢國菜 (Henan sheng wenwu kaogu yanjiusuo 河南省文物考古研究所), Beijing: Wenwu, 1999.

Schaberg, David, "Texts and Artifacts: A Review of the *Cambridge History of Ancient China*," *Monumenta Serica* 49 (2001), 463–515.

   A Patterned Past: Form and Thought in Early Chinese Historiography, Cambridge, MA: Harvard University Asia Center, 2001.

Schneider, Laurence, *Ku Chieh-kang and China's New History: Nationalism and the Quest for Alternative Traditions*, Berkeley: University of California Press, 1971.

Sekino, Takeshi 関野雄, "Seito Rinji no chōsa: I" 齊都臨淄の調查, *Kokogaku zasshi* 考古学雑誌 32.4 (1942), 173–91.

Sen'oku hakko kan 泉屋博古館 (catalogue), Kyoto: Sen-oku hakko kan (Sumitomo), 1985.

Shaanxi chutu Shang Zhou qingtongqi 陝西出土商周青銅器, 4 vols. (Shaanxi sheng kaogu yanjiusuo 陝西省考古研究所 *et al.*), Beijing: Wenwu, 1979–84.

Shaanxi junshi lishi dili gaishu 陝西軍事歷史地理概述 (Shaanxi junshi lishi dili gaishu bianxiezu 陝西军事历史地理概述编写组), Xi'an: Shaanxi renmin, 1985.

Shaanxi qingtongqi 陝西青銅器 (Li Xixing 李西興), Xi'an: Shaanxi renmin meishu, 1994.

Shandong jinwen jicun 山東金文集存 (Zeng Yigong 曾毅公), 1940.

Shandong sheng wenwu xuanji 山東省文物選集 (Shandong sheng wenwu guanlichu 山東省文物管理處 and Shandong sheng bowuguan 山東省博物館), Beijing: Wenwu, 1959.

Shang, Zhiru 尚志儒, "Xi Zhou jinwen zhong de Feng guo" 西周金文中的豐國, *Wenbo* 1991.4, 28–33.

Shang Zhou jinwen luyi 商周金文錄遺 (Yu Xingwu 于省吾), Beijing: Kexue, 1957.

Shangcunling Guo guo mudi 上村嶺虢國菜地 (Zhongguo kexueyuan kaogu yanjiusuo 中國科學院考古研究所), Beijing: Kexue, 1959.

Shanghai bowuguan cang qingtongqi 上海博物館藏青銅器 (Shanghai bowuguan 上海博物館), Shanghai: Renmin, 1964.

Shanzhai yiqi tulu 善齋彝器圖錄 (Rong Geng 容庚), Beiping: Yanjing daxue, 1936.

Shaughnessy, Edward L. (see also Xia Hanyi 夏含夷), "'New' Evidence on the Zhou Conquest," *Early China* 6 (1981–82), 57–79.

   "The Date of the 'Duo You *Ding*' and Its Significance," *Early China* 9–10 (1983–85), 55–69.

   "The 'Current' *Bamboo Annals* and the Date of the Zhou Conquest of Shang," *Early China* 11–12 (1985–87), 33–60.

   "Zhouyuan Oracle-Bone Inscriptions: Entering the Research Stage?" *Early China* 11–12 (1985–87), 146–63.

"On the Authenticity of the *Bamboo Annals*," *Harvard Journal of Asiatic Studies* 46.1 (1986), 149–80.

"Historical Geography and the Extent of the Earliest Chinese Kingdoms," *Asia Major* 2.2 (1989), 1–22.

Sources of Western Zhou History: Inscribed Bronze Vessels, Berkeley: University of California Press, 1991.

"The Duke of Zhou's Retirement in the East and the Beginnings of the Minister–Monarch Debate in Chinese Political Philosophy," *Early China* 18 (1993), 41–72.

I Ching: The Classic of Changes, New York: Ballantine Books, 1996.

Before Confucius: Studies in the Creation of the Chinese Classics, Albany: State University of New York Press, 1997.

(ed.), *New Sources of Early Chinese History: An Introduction to the Reading of Inscriptions and Manuscripts*, Berkeley: Society for Study of Early China, 1997.

"Western Zhou History," in *The Cambridge History of Ancient China: From the Origins of Civilization to 221 B.C.*, ed. Michael Loewe and Edward L. Shaughnessy, pp. 292–351, Cambridge: Cambridge University Press, 1999.

Shen, Changyun 沈長雲, "Xi Zhou er Hann guo diwang kao" 西周二韓國地望考, *Zhongguo shi yanjiu* 中國史研究 1982.2, 135–38.

Shengshi jijin – Shaanxi Baoji Meixian qingtongqi jiaocang 盛世吉金－陝西寶雞眉縣青銅器窖藏 (Shaanxi sheng wenwuju 陝西省文物局), Beijing: Beijing chuban-she, 2003.

Shi, Congzhi 石從枝, Li Enwei 李恩瑋 *et al.*, "Xingtai diqu taoli chubu yanjiu" 邢臺地區陶器初步研究, in *Sandai wenming yanjiu* 三代文明研究 (Beijing: Kexue, 1999), pp.76–85.

Shi, Nianhai 史念海, *Heshanji* 河山集, vol. 1, Beijing: Sanlian, 1963.

"Zhouyuan de lishi dili yu Zhouyuan kaogu" 周原的歷史地理與周原考古, *Xibei daxue xuebao* 西北大學學報 1978.2, 80–88.

"Lun liang Zhou shiqi Huanghe liuyu de dili tezheng" 論兩周時期黃河流域地理特徵, Part 1, *Shaanxi shida xuebao* 陝西師大學報 1978.3; Part 2, 1978.4.

"Xi Zhou yu Chunqiu shiqi huazu yu fei huazu de zaju jiqi fenbu: 1" 西周與春秋時期華族與非華族的雜居及其分佈, *Zhongguo lishi dili luncong* 中國歷史地理論叢 1990.1, 9–40.

Heshanji 河山集, vol. 4, Xi'an: Shaanxi shifan daxue, 1991.

"Lun Shaanxi sheng de lishi minzu dili" 論陝西省的歷史民族地理, *Zhongguo lishi dili luncong* 1993.1, 1–37.

"Lun xibei diqu zhu changcheng de fenbu jiqi lishi junshi dili" 論西北地區諸長城的分佈及其歷史軍事地理 Part 1, *Zhongguo lishi dili luncong* 1994.2, 1–44.

Shi, Quan 石泉, *Gudai Jing Chu dili xintan* 古代荊楚地理新探, Wuhan: Wuhan daxue, 1988.

Shim, Jae-hoon, "The 'Jinhou Su *Bianzhong*' Inscription and Its Significance," *Early China* 22 (1997), 43–75.

"The Early Development of the State of Jin: From Its Enfeoffment to the Hegemony of Wen Gong (r. 636–628 B.C.)," unpublished PhD thesis, University of Chicago, 1998.

Shima, Kunio 島邦男, *Inkyo bokuji kenkyū* 殷墟卜辭研究, Hirosaki: Hirosaki daigaku Chūgokugaku kenkyūkai, 1958.

Shirakwa, Shizuka 白川静, "Kinbun tsūshaku" 金文通积, *Hakutsuru bijutsukanshi* 白鶴美術館誌, 56 vols., Kobe, 1966–83.

Shiratori, Kurakichi 白鳥庫吉, "Shū dai no Jū Teki ni tsuite" 周代の戎狄について, in *Shiratori Kurakichi zenshū* 白鳥庫吉全集, vol. 5, pp. 183–229, Tokyo: Iwanami, 1970.

Shuangjian chi jijin wenxuan 雙劍誃吉金文選 (Yu Xingwu 于省吾), Beiping, 1933.

Skosey, Laura, "The Legal System and Legal Tradition of the Western Zhou, ca. 1045–771 B.C.E.," unpublished PhD thesis, University of Chicago, 1996.

Small, David B. (ed.), *Methods in the Mediterranean: Historical and Archaeological Views on Texts and Archaeology*, Leiden: E. J. Brill, 1995.

So, Jenny, and Emma Bunker, *Traders and Raiders on China's Northern Frontier*, Washington, DC: Smithsonian Institution, 1995.

Song, Xinchao 宋新潮, "Lishan zhi yi ji Pingwang dongqian lishi kaoshu" 驪山之役及平王東遷歷史考述, *Renwen zazhi* 1989.4, 75–79.

Stephenson, F. R., and M. A. Houlden, *Atlas of Historical Eclipse Maps: East Asia 1500 BC–AD 1900*, Cambridge: Cambridge University Press, 1986.

Su, Bingqi 蘇秉琦, *Doujitai goudongqu muzang* 鬥雞台溝東區墓葬, Beiping: Beiping yanjiuyuan, 1938.

Sun, Qingji 孫慶基, and Lin Yuzhen 林育貞, *Shandong sheng dili* 山東省地理, Jinan: Shandong jiaoyu, 1987.

Sun, Xingyan 孫星衍, *Shangshu jinguwen zhushu* 尚書今古文註疏, 2 vols., Beijing: Zhonghua, 1986 (1st edition, Yecheng shanguan, 1815).

Sun, Yan, "Negotiating Cultural and Political Control in North China: Art and Mortuary Ritual and Practice of the Yan at Liulihe during the Early Western Zhou Period," unpublished PhD thesis, University of Pittsburgh, 2001.

Sun, Yongqing 孫永清, and Zheng Baoxi 鄭寶喜, *Gansu sheng dili* 甘肅省地理, Lanzhou: Gansu jiaoyu, 1990.

Sun, Zuoyun 孫作雲, *Shijing yu Zhou dai shehui yanjiu* 詩經与周代社會研究, Beijing: Zhonghua, 1966.

Tainter, Joseph A., *The Collapse of Complex Societies*, Cambridge: Cambridge University Press, 1988.

Takeuchi, Yasuhiro 竹内康浩, "Shunjū kara mita gotōshakusei – Shū sho ni okeru hōken no mondai" 春秋から見た五等爵制 – 周初に於ける封建の問題, *Shigaku zasshi* 100.2 (1991), 40–144.

Takigawa, Kametar 瀧川亀太郎, *Shiki kaichū kōshō* 史記會注考證, Tokyo: Shiki kaichū kōshō kōho kankōkai, 1956.

Tan, Qixiang 譚其驤, "Xi Han yiqian de Huanghe xiayou hedao" 西漢以前的黃河下游河道, *Lishi dili* 歷史地理 1 (1981), 49–64.

Zhongguo lishi dituji 中國歷史地圖集, 8 vols., Beijing: Zhongguo ditu, 1982.

Tan, Zongyi 譚宗義, *Han dai guonei lulu jiaotong kao* 漢代國內陸路交通考, Hong Kong: Xinya yanjiusuo, 1967.

Tang, Lan 唐蘭, "He zun mingwen jieshi" 何尊銘文解釋, *Wenwu* 1976.1, 60–63.

Tang Lan xiansheng jinwen lunji 唐蘭先生金文論集, ed. The Palace Museum in Beijing, Beijing: Zijincheng, 1995.

Taniguchi, Yoshisuke 谷口義介, "Sei Shū metsubō no ichi sokumen" 西周滅亡の一側面, *Gakurin* 学林 8 (1986), 1–16.

Tengxian jinshi zhi 騰縣金石誌 (Sheng Kezhao 生克昭), Beijing: Fayuansi, 1944.

Thatcher, Melvin, "A Structural Comparison of the Central Government of Ch'u, Ch'i, and Chin," *Monumenta Serica* 33 (1977–78), 140–61.

Tian, Guangjin 田廣金, "Jinnian lai Neimenggu diqu de Xiongnu kaogu" 近年來內蒙古地區的匈奴考古, *Kaogu xuebao* 1983.1, 7–24.

Tian, Guangjin, and Guo Suxin 郭素新, *E'erduosi shi qingtongqi* 鄂爾多斯式青銅器, Beijing: Wenwu, 1986.

Tian, Xingnong 田醒農, and Luo Zhongru 雒忠如, "Duoyou ding de faxian jiqi mingwen shishi" 多友鼎的發現及其銘文試釋, *Renwen zazhi* 1981.4, 115–18.

Tian, Xudong 田旭東, *Ershi shiji Zhongguo gushi yanjiu zhuyao sichao gailun* 二十世紀中國古史研究主要思潮概論, Beijing: Zhonghua, 2003.

Tong, Shuye 童書業, *Chunqiu shi* 春秋史, Hong Kong: Taiping, 1962.

Tong, Weihua 佟偉華, "Shanxi Yuanqu gucheng wenhua yizhi de fajue" 山西垣曲古城文化遺址的發掘, in *Jin wenhua yanjiu zuotanhui jiyao* 晉文化研究座談會紀要, Houma, Shanxi: Shanxi sheng kaogu yanjiusuo, 1985.

Tonglushan gu kuangye yizhi 銅綠山古礦業遺址 (Huangshi shi bowuguan 黃石市博物館), Beijing: Wenwu, 1999.

Uehara, Tadamichi 上原淳道, "Kaku no rekishi oyobi Tei to Tō Kaku to no kankei" 號の歷史および鄭と東號との関係, *Kodaigaku* 古代学 6.2 (1957), 124–43.

"Keishi o meguru arasoi oyobi Teihaku shōōsetsu no kentō" 卿士をめぐる争い及び鄭伯称王説の検討, *Tōkyō daigaku kyōyōbu jinbun kagaku kiyō* 東京大学教養部人文科学紀要 14 (1958), 1–30.

"Kaku koku iseki shutsudo no seidōki meibun ni tsuite" 號國遺跡出土の青銅器銘文について, *Kōkotsugaku* 甲骨學 8 (1960), 638–45.

Waley, Arthur (trans.), *The Book of Songs: The Ancient Chinese Classics of Poetry*, ed. Joseph R. Allen, New York: Grove Press, 1996.

Wang, Aihe, *Cosmology and Political Culture in Early China*, Cambridge: Cambridge University Press, 2000.

Wang, Chengzu 王成祖, *Zhongguo dilixue shi* 中國地理學史, Beijing: Shangwu, 1982.

Wang, Entian 王恩田, "Qufu Lu guo gucheng de niandai jiqi xiangguan wenti" 曲阜魯國故城的年代及其相關問題, *Kaogu yu wenwu* 1988.2, 48–55.

"Luyi Daqinggong Xi Zhou damu yu Weizi feng Song" 鹿邑大清宮西周大墓與微子封宋, *Zhongyuan wenwu* 2002.4, 41–45.

Wang, Guanggao 王光鎬, "Huangpi Lutaishan Xi Zhou yicun guoshu chulun" 黃陂魯臺山西周遺存國屬初論, *Jianghan kaogu* 1983.4, 58–68.

Wang, Guangyong 王光永, "Jieshao xin chutu de liangjian Guo qi" 介紹新出土的兩件號器, *Guwenzi yanjiu* 古文字研究 7 (1982), 185–86.

Wang, Guowei 王國維, *Guben zhushu jinian jijiao* 古本竹書紀年輯校, in *Haining Wang Jing'an xiansheng yishu* 海寧王靜安先生遺書, 1936.

Jinben zhushu jinian shuzheng 今本竹書紀年疏證, in *Haining Wang Jing'an xiansheng yishu* 海寧王靜安先生遺書, 1936.

"Gu zhuhou chengwang shuo" 古諸侯稱王說, in *Guantang jilin* 觀堂集林, p. 779, Shijiazhuang: Hebei jiaoyu, 2001.

"Guifang Kunyi Xianyun kao" 鬼方昆夷獫狁考, in *Guantang jilin* 觀堂集林, pp. 369–83, Shijiazhuang: Hebei jiaoyu, 2001.

"Qin duyi kao" 秦都邑考, in *Guantang jilin* 觀堂集林, pp. 335–37, Shijiazhuang: Hebei jiaoyu, 2001.

Wang, Hui 王輝, "Jufu xu gai mingwen shishi" 駒父盨蓋銘文試釋, *Kaogu yu wenwu* 1982.5, 7–59.

"Sishi'er nian Lai ding jianshi" 四十二年逨鼎簡釋, in *Disijie guoji Zhongguo guwenzi xue yantaohui lunwen ji* 第四屆國際中國古文字學研討會論文集, pp. 73–87, Hong Kong: Chinese University of Hong Kong, 2003.

"Zhou jinei diming xiaoji" 周畿內地名小記, *Kaogu yu wenwu* 1985.3, 26–31.

Qin tongqi mingwen biannian jishi 秦銅器銘文編年集釋, Xi'an: Sanqin, 1990.

"Yetan Lixian Dabuzishan Qingong mudi jiqi tongqi" 也談禮縣大堡子山秦公墓地 及其銅器, *Kaogu yu wenwu* 1998.5, 88–93.

Wang, Jin 王勁, "Dui Jianghan diqu Shang Zhou shiqi wenhua de jidian renshi" 對江漢地區商周時期文化的幾點認識, *Jianghan kaogu* 1983.4, 47–51.

Wang, Kelin 王克林, "Shilun Qijia wenhua yu Jinnan Longshan wenhua de guanxi – jianlun Xian Zhou wenhua de yuanyuan" 試論齊家文化與晉南龍山文化的關係 – 兼論先周文化的淵源, *Shiqian yanjiu* 史前研究 1983.2, 70–80.

Wang, Rencong 王人聰, "Yang Ji hu ming shidu yu Beizhao 63 hao mu muzhu wenti" 楊姞壺銘釋讀與北趙63號墓墓主問題, *Wenwu* 1996.5, 31, 32.

Wang, Shimin 王世民, "Zhou du Feng Hao weizhi shangque" 周都豐鎬位置商榷, *Lishi Yanjiu* 歷史研究 1958.2, 63–70.

Wang, Wenchu 王文楚, "Xi'an Luoyang jian lulu jiaotong de lishi fazhan" 西安洛陽閒陸路交通的歷史發展, in *Lishi dili yanjiu* 歷史地理研究 1, pp. 12–32, Shanghai: Fudan daxue, 1986.

Wang, Xiantang 王獻唐, *Shandong guguo kao* 山東古國考, Jinan: Qilu shushe, 1983.

Wang, Xiping 王錫平, "Jiaodong bandao Xia Shang Zhou shiqi de Yiren wenhua" 膠東半島夏商周時期的夷人文化, *Beifang wenwu* 北方文物 1987.2, 19–23, 60.

Wang, Yinglin 王應麟, *Shi dili kao* 詩地理考, in *Qingzhaotang congshu* 青照堂叢書, vol. 41–42, Chaoyi: Liu shi, 1835.

Kunxue jiwen 困學記聞, vol. 1, Shanghai: Shangwu, 1935.

Wang, Yuzhe 王玉哲, "Zhou Pingwang dongqian nai bi Qin fei bi Quanrong shuo" 周平王東遷乃避秦非避犬戎說, *Tianjin shehui kexue* 天津社會科學 1986.3, 49–52.

"Qinren de zuyuan jiqi qianxi luxian" 秦人的族源及其遷徙路綫, *Lishi yanjiu* 1991.3, 32–39.

Wang, Zhankui 王佔奎, "Zhou Xuanwang jinian yu Jin Xianhou mu kaobian" 周宣王紀年與晉獻侯墓考辨, *Zhongguo wenwu bao* 1996. 7, 7.

Wang, Zhaojun 王朝俊, *Chongxiu Lingtaixian zhi* 重修靈臺縣誌, manuscript, 1935.

Watson, William, *Inner Asia and China in the Pre-Han Period*, London: University of London Press, 1969.

Wei, Juxian 衛聚賢, *Gushi yanjiu* 古史研究, vol. 1, Shanghai: Shangwu, 1934.

Wei, Tingsheng 衛挺生, *Shanhaijing dili tukao* 山海經地理圖考, Taipei: Zhonghua xueshuyuan, 1974.

Wenbo 文博 1987.2, 17–25, "Meixian chutu yipi Xi Zhou jiaocang qingtong yueqi" 眉縣出土一批西周窖藏青銅樂器.

1987.4, 5–20, "Shaanxi Fufeng Qiangjia yihao Xi Zhou mu" 陝西扶風強家一號西周墓.

1992.4, 76–80, "Haojing Xi Zhou wuhao daxing gongdian jianzhu jizhi fajue jianbao" 鎬京西周五號大型宮殿建築基址發掘簡報.

Wenwu 文物 1955.5, 58–69, "Jiangsu Dantu xian Yandunshan chutu de gudai qingtongqi" 江蘇丹徒縣煙墩山出土的古代青銅器.

1960.2, 9–10, "Shaanxi Lantian xian chutu Mishu deng yiqi jianjie" 陝西藍田縣出土 弭叔等彝器簡介.

1960.7, 69–70, "Xingtai Xiguanwai yizhi shijue" 邢臺西關外遺址試掘.

1961.11, 28–30, "Ji Sichuan Pengxian Zhuwajie chutu de tongqi" 記四川彭縣竹瓦街出土的銅器.

1963.2, 53–55, "Jiangling faxian Xi Zhou tongqi" 江陵發現西周銅器.

1963.5, 69–70, "Fengxiang xian faxian Niangong yu Yu zi de wadang"鳳翔縣發現年宮與棫字的瓦當.

1964.7, 10–14, "Ji Shanghai bowuguan xin shouji de qingtongqi" 記上海博物館新鳳翔集的青銅器.

1964.7, 20–25, "Shaanxi sheng Yongshou xian Wugong xian chutu Xi Zhou tongqi" 陝西省永壽縣武功縣出土西周銅器.

1966.1, 4–6, "Ji Shaanxi Lantian xian chutu de Xi Zhou tong gui" 記陝西藍田縣出土的西周銅簋.

1972.1, 58–62, "Yong yu mingwen jieshi" 永盂銘文解釋.

1972.2, 47–50, "Hubei Jingshan faxian Zeng guo tongqi" 湖北荊山發現曾國銅器.

1972.5, 3–16, "Gaishu jinnian lai Shandong chutu de Shang Zhou qingtongqi" 概述近年來山東出土的商周青銅器.

1972.5, 45–54, "Linzi Qi guo gucheng kantan jiyao" 臨淄齊國故城勘探紀要.

1972.7, 3–4, "Meixian Yangjiacun da ding" 眉縣楊家村大鼎.

1972.8, 17–30, "Shandong Yidu Subutun di yihao nuli xunzangmu" 山東益都蘇阜屯第一號奴隸殉葬墓.

1972.10, 20–37, "Luoyang Pangjiagou wuzuo Xi Zhou mu de qingli" 洛陽龐家溝五座西周墓的清理.

1972.10, 66, "Xinzheng chutu Xi Zhou tong fanghu" 新鄭出土西周銅方壺.

1973.5, 14–16, "Henan Xinye faxian de Zeng guo tongqi" 河南新野發現的曾國銅器.

1975.5, 89–90, "Shaanxi Changwu xian wenhua dageming yilai chutu de jijian Xi Zhou tongqi" 陝西長武縣文化大革命以來出土的幾件西周銅器.

1975.8, 57–62, "Shaanxi sheng Fufeng xian Qiangjiacun chutu de Xi Zhou tongqi" 陝西省扶風縣強家村出土的西周銅器.

1975.10, 55–67, "Shaanxi Huxian Songcun chunqiu Qin mu fajue jianbao" 陝西戶縣宋村春秋秦墓發掘簡報.

1975.10, 68–69, "Ji Shaanxi Lantian xin chutu de Yinghou zhong" 記陝西藍田新出土的應侯鐘.

1976.4, 34–56, "Shaanxi sheng Baoji shi Rujiazhuang Xi Zhou mu fajue jianbao" 陝西省寶雞市茹家莊西周墓發掘簡報.

1976.5, 26–44, "Shaanxi sheng Qishan xian Dongjiacun Xi Zhou tongqi jiao xue fajue jianbao" 陝西省岐山縣董家村西周銅器窖穴發掘簡報.

1977.4, 63–70, "Jiao xian Xi'an yizhi diaocha shijue jianbao" 膠縣西庵遺址調查試掘簡報.

1977.8, 1–9, "Shaanxi Lintong faxian Wuwang zheng Shang gui" 陝西臨潼發現武王征商簋.

1977.8, 13–16, "Henan sheng Xiang xian Xi Zhou mu fajue jianbao" 河南省襄縣西周墓發掘簡報.

1977.9, 92, "Gansu Jingchuan faxian zao Zhou tongli" 甘肅涇川發現早周銅鬲.

1977.12, 23–33, "Liaoning Kazuo xian Shanwanzi chutu Yin Zhou qingtongqi" 遼寧喀左縣山灣子出土殷周青銅器.

1978.3, 1–18, "Shaanxi Fufeng Zhuangbai yihao Xi Zhou qingtongqi jiaocang fajue jianbao" 陝西扶風莊白一號西周青銅器窖藏發掘簡報.

1978.4, 94–96, "Shandong Tengxian chutu Qi Xue tongqi" 山東滕縣出土齊薛銅器.

1979.4, 88, "Shandong Tengxian chutu Xi Zhou Teng guo tongqi" 山東滕縣出土西周滕國銅器.

1979.4, 89–91, "Shaanxi Fufeng faxian Xi Zhou Liwang Hu gui" 陝西扶風發現西周厲王㝬簋.

1979.10, 27–34, "Shaanxi Qishan Fengchucun Xi Zhou jianzhu jizhi fajue jian-bao" 陝西岐山鳳雛村西周建築基址發掘簡報.

1979.11, 1–11, "Shaanxi Fufeng Qijia shijiu hao Xi Zhou mu" 陝西扶風齊家十九號西周墓.

1980.1, 51–53, "Henan Luoshan xian faxian Chunqiu zaoqi tongqi" 河南羅山縣發現春秋早期銅器.

1980.4, 27–38, "Fufeng Yuntang Xi Zhou guqi zhizao zuofang yizhi shijue jian-bao" 扶風雲塘西周骨器製造作坊遺址試掘簡報.

1980.4, 39–55, "Fufeng Yuntang Xi Zhou mu" 扶風雲塘西周墓.

1980.8, 7, "Jiangsu Danyang chutu de Xi Zhou qingtongqi" 江蘇丹陽出土的西周青銅器.

1980.8, 10–12, "Nanjing Pukou chutu yipi qingtongqi" 南京浦口出土一批青銅器.

1980.9, 1–9, "Baoji xian Xigaoquancun Chunqiu Qin mu fajue ji" 寶雞縣西高泉村春秋秦墓發掘記.

1980.12, 38–40, "Sichuan Pengxian chutu de tongqi" 四川彭縣出土的銅器.

1981.3, 10–22, "Fufeng Shaochen Xi Zhou jianzhu qun jizhi fajue jianbao" 扶風召陳西周建築群基址發掘簡報.

1981.7, 52–64, "Luoyang Beiyaocun Xi Zhou yizhi 1974 nian du fajue jianbao" 洛陽北窯村西周遺址 1974 年度發掘簡報.

1981.9, 18–24, "Shandong Jiyang Liutaizi Xi Zhou zaoqi mu fajue jianbao" 山東濟陽劉臺子西周早期墓發掘簡報.

1981.9, 25–29, "Tengxian Houjinggou chutu Buqi gui deng qingtongqi qun" 滕縣后荊溝出土不嬰簋等青銅器群.

1982.1, 87–89, "Lintong Nanluo Xi Zhou mu chutu qingtongqi" 臨潼南羅西周墓出土青銅器.

1982.2, 48–57, "Gu Ze guo yizhi mudi diaocha ji" 古夨國遺址墓地調查記.

1982.7, 1–16, "Jin Yu E sansheng kaogu diaocha jianbao" 晉豫鄂三省考古調査簡報.

1982.10, 43, "Lüji Jiang li hu" 呂季姜醴壺.

1982.12, 43–45, "Zhouyuan faxian Shitong ding" 周原發現師同鼎.

1982.12, 51–55, "Hubei Suixian Anju chutu qingtongqi" 湖北隨縣安居出土青銅器.

1983.7, 93, "Shaanxi sheng Zhouzhi xian jinnian zhengji de jijian Xi Zhou qingtongqi" 陝西省周至縣近年徵集的幾件西周青銅器.

1983.11, 64–67, "Beijing Shunyi xian Niulanshan chutu yizu Zhou chu daiming qingtongqi" 北京順義縣牛欄山出土一組周初帶銘青銅器.

1983.12, 1–6, "Shandong Linqu faxian Qi Xun Zeng zhu guo tongqi" 山東臨朐發現齊郯曾諸國銅器.

1983.12, 7–8, "Shandong Laiyang xian chutu Ji guo tongqi" 山東萊陽縣出土己國銅器.

1984.5, 1–10, "Jiangsu Dantu Dagang Muzidun Xi Zhou tongqi mu fajue jian-bao" 江蘇丹徒大港母子墩西周銅器墓發掘簡報.

1984.7, 16–29, "Fufeng Liujia Jiangrong muzang fajue jianbao" 扶風劉家姜戎墓葬發掘簡報.

1984.12, 29–31, "Henan Pingdingshan shi chutu Xi Zhou Ying guo qingtongqi" 河南平頂山市出土西周應國青銅器.

1985.3, 1–11, "Shandong Shouguang xian xin faxian yipi Ji guo tongqi" 山東壽光縣新發現一批紀國銅器.

1985.12, 15–20, "Shandong Jiyang Liutaizi Xi Zhou mudi dierci fajue" 山東濟陽劉臺子西周墓地第二次發掘.

1986.1, 1–31, "Xi Zhou Haojing fujin bufen muzang fajue jianbao" 西周鎬京附近部分墓葬發掘簡報.

1986.2, 40–43, "Qin'an xian linian chutu de beifang xi qingtongqi" 秦安縣歷年出土的北方係青銅器.

1986.4, 1–7, "Lü Fuyu pan ming kaoshi jiqi xiangguan wenti" 呂服余盤銘考釋及其相關問題.

1986.4, 15–20, "Xiangfan shi Gucheng xian guancang qingtongqi" 襄樊市谷城縣舘藏青銅器.

1986.8, 69–72, "Shandong Huangxian Zhuangtou Xi Zhou mu qingli jianbao" 山東黃縣莊頭西周墓清理簡報.

1987.2, 1–16, "Shanxi Hongdong Yongningbu Xi Zhou muzang" 山西洪洞永凝堡西周墓葬.

1988.11, 14–23, "Shaanxi Longxian Bianjiazhuang wuhao Chunqiu mu fajue jianbao" 陝西隴縣邊家莊五號春秋墓發掘簡報.

1991.5, 84–85, "Shandong sheng Longkou shi chutu Xi Zhou tong ding" 山東省龍口市出土西周銅鼎.

1993.3, 11–30, "1992 nian chun Tianma – Qucun yizhi muzang fajue baogao" 1992 年春天馬 – 曲村遺址墓葬發掘報告.

1994.1, 4–28, "Tianma – Qucun yizhi Beizhao Jinhou mudi dierci fajue" 天馬 – 曲村遺址北趙晉侯墓地第二次發掘.

1994.3, 42–43, "Shandong Jining shi chutu yipi Xi Zhou qingtongqi" 山東濟寧市出土一批西周青銅器.

1994.8, 1–21, "Tianma – Qucun yizhi Beizhao Jinhou mudi disici fajue" 天馬 – 曲村遺址北趙晉侯墓地第四次發掘.

1994.8, 22–33, 68, "Tianma – Qucun yizhi Beizhao Jinhou mudi disanci fajue" 天馬 – 曲村遺址北趙晉侯墓地第三次發掘.

1995.1, 4–31, "Shangcunling Guo guo mudi M2006 de qingli" 上村嶺虢國墓地 M2006 的清理.

1995.7, 4–39, "Tianma – Qucun yizhi Beizhao Jinhou mudi diwuci fajue" 天馬 – 曲村遺址北趙晉侯墓地第五次發掘.

1996.6, 4–27, "1995 Liulihe Zhou dai juzhi fajue jianbao" 1995 年琉璃河周代居址發掘簡報.

1996.12, 4–25, "Shandong Jiyang Liutaizi Xi Zhou liuhao mu qingli baogao" 山東濟陽劉臺子西周六號墓清理報告.

1997.12, 4–15, "1991–1992 nian Shanxi Yuanqu Shang cheng fajue jianbao" 1991–1992 年山西垣曲商城發掘簡報.

1998.9, 4–17, "Pingdingshan Ying guo mudi bashisi hao mu" 平頂山應國墓地八十四號墓.

2001.8, 4–21, "Tianma-Qucun yizhi Beizhao Jinhou mudi diliuci fajue" 天馬 – 曲村遺址北趙晉侯墓地第六次發掘.

2003.6, 4–42, "Shaanxi Meixian Yangjiacun Xi Zhou qingtongqi jiaocang fajue jianbao" 陝西眉縣楊家村西周青銅器窖藏發掘簡報.

2003.6, 43–65, "Shaanxi Meixian chutu jiaocang qingtongqi bitan" 陝西眉縣出土窖藏青銅器筆談.

2005.2, 4–27, "Gansu Lixian Yuandingshan 98LDM2, 2000LDM4 Chunqiu Qin mu" 甘肅禮縣圓頂山 98LDM2, 2000LDM4 春秋秦墓.

Wenwu cankao ziliao 文物參考資料 1955.5, 58–62, "Jiangsu Dantu xian Yandunshan chutu de gudai qingtongqi" 江蘇丹徒縣煙墩山出土的古代青銅器.

1955.6, 117–18, "Gansu Tianshui xian jumin juanzeng zhengui tongqi" 甘肅天水縣居民捐贈珍貴銅器.

1957.4, 5–10, "Zuguo lishi wenwu de you yici zhongyao faxian – Shaanxi Meixian fajue chu sijian Xi Zhou tongqi" 祖國歷史文物的又一次重要發現 — 陝西眉縣發掘出四件西周銅器.

1957.8, 42–44, "Shanxi Hongzhao xian Yongning Dongbu chutu de tongqi" 山西洪趙縣永凝東堡出土的銅器.

1957.11, 66–69, "Henan Shangcai chutu de yipi tongqi" 河南上蔡出土的一批銅器.

1958.5, 73, "Lushan xian faxian yipi zhongyao tongqi" 魯山縣發現一批重要銅器.

Wenwu kaogu gongzuo sanshi nian 文物考古工作三十年 (Wenwu bianji weiyuanhui 文物編輯委員會), Beijing: Wenwu, 1979.

Wenwu kaogu gongzuo shi nian 文物考古工作十年 (Wenwu bianji weiyuanhui), Beijing: Wenwu, 1990,

Wenwu ziliao congkan 文物資料叢刊 2 (1978), 45–68, "Henan sheng Xinzheng xian Tanghu liang Zhou muzang fajue jianbao" 河南省新鄭縣唐戶兩周墓葬發掘簡報.

2 (1978), 70–74, "Henan Xinye gu muzang qingli jianbao" 河南新野古墓葬清理簡報.

3 (1980), 35–38, "Henan Hebi Pangcun chutu de qingtongqi" 河南鶴壁龐村出土的青銅器.

3 (1980), 44, "Luoyang bowuguan de jijian qingtongqi" 洛陽博物館的幾件青銅器.

8 (1983), 77–94, "Shaanxi Qishan Hejiacun Xi Zhou mu fajue baogao" 陝西岐山賀家村西周墓發掘報告.

Whittaker, C. R., *Frontiers of the Roman Empire: A Social and Economic Study*, Baltimore: Johns Hopkins University Press, 1994.

Wu, Chen 吳忱, and He Naihua 何乃華, "2 wan nian lai Huabei pingyuan zhuyao heliu de hedao bianqian" 2 萬年來華北平原主要河流的河道變遷, in *Huabei pingyuan gu hedao yanjiu lunwenji* 華北平原古河道研究論文集, ed. Wu Chen, pp. 132–48, Beijing: Zhongguo kexue jishu, 1991.

Wu, Chengzhi 吳承志, *Shanhai jing dili jinshi* 山海經地理今釋, in *Qiushuzhai congshu* 求恕齋叢書, Liu Chenggan, 1929.

Wu, En 烏恩, "Yinmo Zhouchu de beifang qingtongqi" 殷末周初的北方青銅器, *Kaogu xuebao* 1985.2, 135–55.

"Lun Xiongnu kaogu yanjiu zhong de jige wenti" 論匈奴考古研究中的幾個問題, *Kaogu xuebao* 1990.4, 409–37.

Wu, Hung, *Monumentality in Early Chinese Art and Architecture*, Stanford, CA: Stanford University Press, 1995.

Wu, Xifei 鄔錫非, "Yetan Xi Zhou Shen guo de youguan wenti" 也談西周申國的有關問題, *Hangzhou daxue xuebao* 杭州大學學報 1992.1, 127–31.

Wugong fajue baogao 武功發掘報告 (Zhongguo shehui kexueyuan kaogu yanjiusuo), Beijing: Wenwu, 1988.

Xia, Hanyi 夏含夷 (Edward Shaughnessy), "Zaoqi Shang Zhou guanxi jiqi dui Wu Ding yihou Yin Shang wangshi shili fanwei de yiyi" 早期商周關係及其對武丁以後殷商王室勢力範圍的意義, *Jiuzhou xuekan* 九州學刊 2.1 (1987), 20–32.

"Xi Zhou zhi shuaiwei" 西周之衰微, in *Jinxinji – Zhang Zhenglang xiansheng bashi qingshou lunwenji* 盡心集－張政烺先生八十慶壽論文集, ed. Wu Zengrong 吳曾榮, pp. 120–27, Beijing: Zhongguo shehui kexue, 1996.

"Cong Xi Zhou lizhi gaige kan Shijing Zhousong de yanbian" 從西周禮制改革看詩經周頌的演變, *Hebei shiyuan xuebao* 河北師院學報 1996.3, 26–33.

Wengu zhixin lu – Shang Zhou wenhua shi guanjian 溫故知新錄 – 商周文化史管見, Taibei: Daohuo, 1997.

Xia Shang Zhou duandai gongcheng – 1996–2000 nian jieduan chengguo baogao 夏商周斷代工程 – 1996–2000 年階段成果報告 (Xia Shang Zhou duandai gongcheng zhuanjiazu 夏商周斷代工程專家組), Beijing: Shijie tushu, 2000.

Xiao, Menglong 蕭夢龍, "Muzidun mu qingtongqi ji youguan wenti tansuo" 母子墩墓青銅器及有關問題探索, *Wenwu* 1984.5, 11–15.

Xin Zhongguo de kaogu faxian he yanjiu 新中國的考古發現和研究 (Zhongguo shehui kexueyuan kaogu yanjiusuo 中國社會科學院考古研究所), Beijing: Wenwu, 1984.

Xing, Wen (ed.), "The X Gong *xu*: A Report and Papers from the Dartmouth Workshop," in *International Research on Bamboo and Silk Documents* (Newsletter special issue), pp. 3–48, Hanover, NH: Dartmouth College, 2003.

Xu, Cheng 許成, and Li Jinzeng 李進增, "Dong Zhou shiqi de Rong Di wenhua" 東周時期的戎狄文化, *Kaogu xuebao* 1993.1, 1–12.

Xu, Zhuoyun 許倬雲 (Cho-yun Hsu), "Zhou dongqian shimo" 周東遷始末, in *Qiugu bian* 求古編, Taipei: Lianjing, 1982.

Xu, Hongpan 許鴻磐, *Fangyu kaozheng* 方域考證, Jining: Huajiange, 1932.

Xu, Shaohua 徐少華, "Zeng ji Sui jiqi lishi yuanyuan" 曾即隨及其歷史淵源, *Jianghan luntan* 1986.4, 71–75.

　　Zhou dai nantu lishi dili yu wenhua 周代南土歷史地理與文化, Wuhan: Wuhan daxue, 1994.

Xu, Xitai 徐錫台, *Zhouyuan jiaguwen zongshu* 周原甲骨文綜述, Xi'an: Sanqin, 1987.

Xu, Xusheng 徐旭生, *Zhongguo gushi de chuanshuo shidai* 中國古史的傳說時代, Beijing: Wenwu, 1985.

Xu, Yongsheng 許永生, "Cong Guo guo mudi kaogu xin faxian tan Guo guo lishi gaikuang" 從虢國墓地新發現談虢國歷史概況, *Huaxia kaogu* 1993.4, 92–95.

Xu, Zhongshu 徐仲舒, "Yu ding de niandai jiqi xiangguan wenti" 禹鼎的年代及其相關問題, *Kaogu xuebao* 1959.3, 53–67.

Xunxian Xincun 濬縣辛村 (Guo Baojun 郭寶鈞), Beijing: Kexue, 1964.

Xunxian yiqi 濬縣彝器 (Sun Haibo 孫海波), Henan tongzhi guan, 1937.

Yan, Zi 晏子, "Cai guo shifeng diwang kaobian" 蔡國始封地望考辨, *Zhongguo lishi dili luncong* 1991.3, 42.

Yang, Bojun 楊伯峻, *Chunqiu Zuozhuan zhu* 春秋左傳注, 4 vols., Beijing: Zhonghua, 1990.

Yang, Jialuo 楊家駱 (ed.), *Xiao erya xunzuan deng liuzhong* 小爾雅訓纂等六種, Taipei: Dingwen, 1972.

Yang, Kuan 楊寬, *Gu shi xin tan* 古史新探, Beijing: Zhonghua, 1965.

　　"Xi Zhou shidai de Chu guo" 西周時代的楚國, *Jianghan luntan* 1981.5, 101–8.

　　"Xi Zhou Chunqiu shidai dui dongfang beifang de kaifa" 西周春秋時代對東方北方的開發, *Zhonghua wenshi luncong* 1982.4, 109–32.

Yang, Shanqun 楊善群, "Xi Zhou Yi guo shi kaojiu" 西周宜國史考究, *Shilin* 史林 1989.4, 1–5.

Yang, Shuda 楊樹達, *Jiweiju jinwen shuo* 積微居金文說 (supplemented), Beijing: Zhonghua, 1997 (1st edition, Beijing: Kexue, 1952).

Yao, Jiheng 姚際恒, *Shijing tonglun* 詩經通論, Beijing: Zhonghua, 1958 (1st edition, Wang Nu, 1837).

Ye, Wansong 葉万松, and Yu Fuwei 余扶危, "Guanyu Xi Zhou Luoyi chengzhi de tansuo" 關於西周洛邑城址的探索, in *Xi Zhou shi yanjiu* 西周史研究 (monograph of *Renwen zazhi* 2), pp. 317–24, Xi'an, 1984.

"Luoyang Beiyao Xi Zhou yizhi taoqi de fenqi yanjiu" 洛陽北窰西周遺址陶器的分期研究, *Kaogu* 1985.9, 834–42.

"Zhongyuan diqu Xi Zhou taoqi de chubu yanjiu" 中原地區西周陶器的初步研究 *Kaogu* 1986.12, 1104–11, 1120.

Ye, Xueqi 葉學齊, Liu Shengjia 劉盛佳 *et al.*, *Hubei sheng dili* 湖北省地理, Wuhan: Hubei jiaoyu, 1987.

Yin, Zhiyi 殷之彝 (Zhang Changshou), "Shandong Yidu Subutun mudi he Yachou tongqi" 山東益都蘇阜屯墓地和亞醜銅器, *Kaogu xuebao* 1977.8, 23–34.

Yin Zhou jinwen jicheng 殷周金文集成, 18 vols. (Zhongguo shehui kexueyuan kaogu yanjiusuo 中國社會科學院考古研究所), Beijing: Zhonghua, 1984–94.

Yin Zhou jinwen jicheng shiwen 殷周金文集成釋文, 6 vols. (Zhongguo shehui kexueyuan kaogu yanjiusuo), Hong Kong: Chinese University of Hong Kong Press, 2001.

Yoshimoto, Michimasa 吉本道雅, "Shiki genshi – Sei Shū ki tōsen ki" 史記原始 – 西周期東遷期, *Koshi shunjū* 古史春秋 4 (1987), 59–82.

"Shūshitsu tōsen kō" 周室東遷考, *Tōyō gakuhō* 東洋學報 71.3, 4 (1990), 33–56.

Yu, Fengchun 于逢春, "Zhou Pingwang dongqian fei bi Rong nai tou Rong bian" 周平王東遷非避戎乃投戎辯, *Xibei shidi* 1983.4, 54–60.

Yu, Haoliang 于豪亮, *Yu Haoliang xueshu wencun* 于豪亮學術文存, Beijing: Zhonghua, 1985.

Yu, Weichao 余偉超, *Xianqin Lianghan kaoguxue lunji* 先秦兩漢考古學論集, Beijing: Wenwu, 1985.

Yu, Weichao 俞偉超, and Gao Ming 高明, "Zhou dai yong ding zhidu yanjiu," 周代用鼎制度研究 (part I), *Beijing daxue xuebao* 北京大學學報 1978.1, 84–89; (part II), 1978.2, 84–97; (part III), 1979.1, 83–96.

Yuan, Junjie 袁俊傑, Jiang Tao 江濤 *et al.*, "Xin faxian de Zhabo gui jiqi mingwen kaoshi" 新發現的柞伯簋及其銘文考釋, *Wenwu* 1998.9, 53–61.

Yudong Qixian fajue baogao 豫東杞縣發掘報告 (Zhengzhou daxue wenbo xueyuan 鄭州大學文博學院 and Kaifeng shi wenwu gongzuo dui 開封市文物工作隊), Beijing: Kexue, 2000.

Zeng, Zhaoxuan 曾昭璇, *Zhongguo de dixing* 中國的地形, Taibei: Shuqing, 1995.

Zeng, Zhaoyu 曾昭燏, and Yin Huanzhang 尹煥章, "Gudai Jiangsu lishi shang de liangge wenti" 古代江蘇歷史上的兩個問題, in *Jiangsu sheng chutu wenwu xuanji* 江蘇省出土文物選集, ed. Nanjing bowuyuan 南京博物院官 *et al.*, pp. 1–36. Beijing: Wenwu, 1963.

Zhang, Changshou 張長壽, "Yin Shang shidai de qingtong rongqi" 殷商時代的青銅容器, *Kaogu xuebao* 1979.3, 271–300.

"Lun Baoji Rujiazhuang faxian de Xi Zhou tongqi" 論寶鶏茹家庄發現的西周銅器, *Kaogu* 1980.6, 526–29.

"Lun Jingshu tongqi – 1983–86 nian Fengxi fajue ziliao zhi er" 論井叔銅器 – 1983–86 年灃西發掘資料之二, *Wenwu* 1990.7, 32–35.

"Guo guo mudi de xin faxian" 虢國墓地的新發現, *Zhongguo wenwu bao* 1991.3.17, 3.

"Guanyu Jingshu jiazu mudi – 1983–86 nian Fengxi fajue ziliao zhi yi" 關於井叔家族墓地 – 1983–86 年灃西發掘資料之一, in *Kaoguxue yanjiu: jinian Shaanxi sheng kaogu yanjiusuo chengli sanshi zhounian* 考古學研究: 紀念陝西省考古研究所成立三十周年, ed. Shi Xingbang 石興邦 *et al.*, pp. 398–401, Xi'an: Sanqin, 1993.

"Da xu gai ming – 1983–86 nian Fengxi fajue ziliao zhi san" 達盨蓋銘 – 1983–86 年澧西發掘資料之三, *Yanjing xuebao* 燕京學報 (New) 2 (1996), 163–70.

"Guanyu Jinhou mudi de jige wenti" 關於晉侯墓地的幾個問題, *Wenwu* 1998.1, 41–44.

Zhang, Maorong 張懋鎔, "Xi Zhou Nan Huaiyi chengming yu junshi kao" 西周南淮夷稱名与軍事考, *Renwen zazhi* 1990.4, 81–86.

Guwenzi yu qingtongqi lunji 古文字與青銅器論集, Beijing: Kexue, 2002.

Zhang, Pingzhe 張平轍, "Xi Zhou Gonghe xingzheng zhenxiang jiemi" 西周共和行政眞相揭祕, *Xibei shida xuebao* 西北師大學報 1992.4, 51–54.

Zhang, Tian'en 張大恩, "Bianjiazhuang Chunqiu mudi yu Qianyi diwang" 邊家庄春秋墓地与汧邑地望, *Wenbo* 1990.5, 227–31.

Zhang, Yachu 張亞初, "Tan Duoyou ding mingwen de jige wenti" 談多友鼎銘文的幾個問題, *Kaogu yu wenwu* 1982.3, 64–68.

"Lun Lutaishan Xi Zhou mu de niandai he zushu" 論魯臺山西周墓的年代和族屬, *Jianghan kaogu* 1984.2, 23–28.

Zhang, Yachu 張亞初, and Liu Yu 劉雨, *Xi Zhou jinwen guanzhi yanjiu* 西周金文官制研究, Beijing: Zhonghua, 1986.

Zhang, Yanfu 張延福, *Jingzhou zhi* 涇州誌, manuscript, 1753.

Zhang, Yiren 張以仁, "Zheng guo mie Kuai ziliao de jiantao" 鄭國滅鄶資料的檢討, *Zhongyang yanjiuyuan lishi yuyan yanjiusuo jikan* 50.4 (1979), 615–43.

Zhangjiapo Xi Zhou mudi 張家坡西周墓地 (Zhongguo shehui kexueyuan kaogu yanjiusuo), Beijing: Zhongguo da baike quanshu, 1999.

Zhao, Guangxian 趙光賢, *Zhou dai shehui bianxi* 周代社會辨析, Beijing: Renmin, 1982.

Zhao, Huacheng 趙化成, "Xunzhao Qin wenhua yuanyuan de xin xiansuo" 尋找秦文化淵源的新綫索, *Wenbo* 1987.1, 1–7.

"Gansu dongbu Qin he Qiangrong wenhua de kaoguxue tansuo" 甘肅東部秦和羌戎文化的考古學探索, in *Kaogu leixingxue de lilun yu shijian* 考古類型學的理論與實踐, ed. Yu Weichao 余偉超, pp. 145–76, Beijing: Wenwu, 1989.

Zhao, Songqiao, *Physical Geography of China*, Beijing: Science Press, 1986.

Geography of China: Environment, Resources, Population and Development, New York: John Wiley and Sons, 1994.

Zhao, Tiehan 趙鐵寒, "Chunqiu shiqi de Rong Di dili fenbu jiqi yuanliu (I, II)" 春秋時期的戎狄地理分佈源流, *Dalu zazhi* 大陸雜誌 11.2 (1955), 38–45; 11.3 (1955), 85–98.

Zhensong tang jigu yiwen 貞松堂集古遺文 (Luo Zhenyu 羅振玉), 1931.

Zhongguo kaoguxue zhong tan shisi niandai shujuji 中國考古學中碳十四年代數據集 (Zhongguo shehui kexueyuan kaogu yanjiusuo 中國社會科學院考古研究所), Beijing: Wenwu, 1983.

Zhongguo qingtongqi quanji 中國青銅器全集 (Zhongguo qingtongqi quanji bianji weiyuanhui 中國青銅器全集編輯委員會), Beijing: Wenwu, 1993–99.

Zhongguo wenwubao 中國文物報 2003.1.29, 2, "Shaanxi Meixian Xi Zhou qingtongqi jiaocang jingshi" 陝西眉縣西周青銅器窖藏驚世.

Zhongguo ziran dili 中國自然地理 (Zhongguo kexueyuan Zhongguo ziran dili bianji weiyuanhui 中國科學院中國自然地理編輯委員會), 12 vols., Beijing: Kexue, 1979–85.

Zhongyuan wenwu 中原文物 1981.2, 59, "Huaiyang xian faxian liangjian Xi Zhou tongqi" 淮陽縣發現兩件西周銅器..

1988.1, 21–22, "Pingdingshan shi xin chutu Xi Zhou qingtongqi" 平頂山市新出土
西周青銅器.

1984.4, 13–16, "Nanyang shi beijiao chutu yipi Shen guo qingtongqi" 南陽市
北郊出土一批申國青銅器.

Zhou, Houqiang 周厚強, "Xiaogan diqu Xi Zhou shiqi wenhua chuxi" 孝感地區
西周時期文化初析, *Jianghan kaogu* 1985.4, 65–74.

"Hubei Xi Zhou taoqi de fenqi" 湖北西周陶器的分期, *Kaogu* 1992.3, 236–44.

Zhou, Yongzhen 周永珍, "Xi Zhuo shiqi de Ying guo Deng guo tongqi jiqi dili
weizhi" 西周時期的應國鄧國銅器及其地理位置, *Kaogu* 1982.1, 48–53.

"Guanyu Luoyang Zhou cheng" 關於洛陽周城, in *Luoyang kaogu sishi nian*
洛陽考古四十年, ed. Ye Wansong, pp. 227–29, Beijing: Kexue, 1996.

Zhou jinwen cun 周金文存 (Zou An 鄒安), Shanghai: Cangsheng mingzhi daxue,
1916.

"Zhougongmiao yizhi kaogu fajue zhunbei gongzuo jiben jiuxu" 周公廟遺址
考古發掘準備工作基本就緒, *Cultural Relics of China Information Online*
(http://www.ccrnews.com.cn), accessed on September 23, 2004.

Zhu, Fenghan 朱鳳翰, *Shang Zhou jiazu xingtai yanjiu* 商周家族形態研究, Tianjin:
Tianjin guji, 1990.

Zhu, Kezhen 竺可楨, "Zhongguo jin wuqian nian lai qihou bianqian de chubu
yanjiu" 中國近五千年來氣候變遷的初步研究, *Kaogu xuebao* 1972.1, 15–38.

Zhu, Shilin 祝世林, "Pingliang zhuyao gudao kaolue" 平涼主要古道考略, *Xibei
shidi* 1989.1, 92–93.

Zhu, Xi 朱熹, *Shi ji zhuan* 詩集傳, Shanghai: Guji, 1980 (compiled 1177; reprint of
Shanghai: Zhonghua, 1962).

Sishu zhangju jizhu 四書章句集注, Beijing: Zhonghua, 1983 (1st edition, 1190).

Zhu, Youzeng 朱右曾, *Shi dili zheng* 詩地理徵, in *Huang Qing jingjie* 皇清經解,
juan: 1,039–45, Guangzhou: Xuehaitang, 1829.

Jizhong jinian cunzhen 汲冢紀年存眞, Guiyanzhai, 1846.

Zhoushu jixun jiaoshi 周書集訓校釋, 2 vols., Guiyanzhai, 1846.

Zong, Li 宗禮, and Liu Dong 劉棟, "Xian Zhou wenhua yanjiu liushi nian"
先周文化研究六十年, in *Zhou Qin wenhua yanjiu* 周秦文化研究, pp. 268–85,
Xi'an: Shaanxi renmin, 1998.

Zou, Heng 鄒衡, "Lun Xian Zhou wenhua" 論先周文化, in *Xia Shang Zhou kaoguxue
lunwen ji* 夏商周考古學論文集, pp. 295–355, Beijing: Wenwu, 1980.

Zou, Yilin 鄒逸麟, "Lishi shiqi Huabei dapingyuan huzhao bianqian shulue"
歷史時期華北大平原湖沼變遷述略, *Lishi dili* 歷史地理 5 (1987), 25–39.

Index of inscribed bronzes

General index

LaVergne, TN USA
22 September 2010
197932LV00001B/1/P